Herstellung und Verlag:
BoD - Books on Demand, Norderstedt
ISBN: 978-3-7347-6096-9

Roman Egger,
Christian Maurer (Eds.)

ISCONTOUR 2015
Tourism Research Perspectives

Proceedings of the International Student Conference in Tourism Research 2015

Preface & Acknowledgements

The 3rd International Student Conference in Tourism Research (ISCONTOUR) was held at the campus of the Salzburg University of Applied Sciences, Austria, on May 18-19, 2015. The annual ISCONTOUR was collaboratively founded by Christian Maurer, Professor at IMC University of Applied Sciences Krems, Austria, and Roman Egger, Professor at Salzburg University of Applied Sciences, Austria. Therefore, the conference is alternately held at both venues.

The aim of ISCONTOUR is to provide international students and graduates of Bachelor and Master programmes with a platform where they can submit and present tourism related research papers based on their approved Bachelor- and Master-theses. In particular, ISCONTOUR strives to encourage students and graduates to engage in academic research and foster the knowledge transfer between academic education institutions and the tourism industry. The first day of ISCONTOUR starts with a half-day Research Methodology Workshop, the submitted research papers will be presented on the second conference day.

In total 40 full research papers by 61 authors from 17 different countries were submitted to ISCONTOUR 2015. Each submission went through a thorough double blind review process with at least three members of the ISCONTOUR 2015 Research Programme Committee assigned as reviewers. The authors then received the comments of the reviewers and had to mend the papers accordingly. Only papers of authors who adhered to this process were accepted for the conference. As a result, 25 full research papers were accepted for presentation at the conference and are included in this proceedings. The conference covered a wide variety of topics, ranging from smart tourism, customer loyalty, sustainable tourism, information and communication technologies, destination management and marketing. This does not only indicate the complexity of the tourism system, but also how relevant and impactful applied research projects conducted by students and graduates can be for the further developments in tourism in particular and the society in general. We hope this proceedings will serve as a valuable source of information on applied tourism research for students, scholars and practitioners.

Above all, we want to thank all authors who submitted their papers for the conference. We further appreciate the considerable time put in by all members of the ISCONTOUR 2015 Research Programme Committee who helped us to ensure that the content of the research papers was of high quality. We are also grateful for the support we receive from the management board, rectorate and staff of both the IMC University of Applied Sciences Krems as well as the Salzburg University of Applied Sciences. We are also indebted to the conference keynote speaker, Professor Iis Tussyadiah, and to the research workshop presenters Po-Ju Chen, Sofia Reino, Nicole Wiggert, and Iis Tussyadiah. Last but not least, we want to express our gratitude to the sponsors and supporters of ISCONTOUR 2015, namely *Wirtschaftskammer Salzburg, Salzburg Convention Bureau, Tourismus Salzburg GmbH, Stiegl, TUI Austria, Prodinger / GFB Tourismusmarketing, SalzburgerLand Tourismus, Springer, Red Bull, European Travel Commission, IFITT and our universities.*

We hope that ISCONTOUR will continue to establish an international community that motivates more students and graduates to engage in applied research and submit papers to ISCONTOUR 2016.

Roman Egger & Christian Maurer
ISCONTOUR 2015 Conference Chairs
Salzburg / Krems, May 2015

TABLE OF CONTENTS

Personal Technology and Tourism Experiences

Iis. P. Tussyadiah, Washington State University, USA 1

Innovative City Map

Emre Ronay, Salzburg University of Applied Sciences, Austria 11

The Use of Smart Technology in Tourism: Evidence from Wearable Devices

Roland Atembe, and Feisal Abdalla, Salzburg University of Applied Sciences, Austria 23

A Scenario Technique Application

to Implement Smart City Concepts in Tourism Destinations

Emre Ronay, Salzburg University of Applied Sciences, Austria 33

Social E-couponing and Customer Loyalty in the Tourism Industry

Stefanie Bohacek, Vienna University of Economics and Business, Austria 45

Value Formation of Loyalty Programs in the Hotel Industry:

Starwood Preferred Guest, Marriott Rewards, Hyatt Gold Passport

Ksenia Lakhtina, Modul University Vienna, Austria 59

Tourism Products in Deal of the Day Platforms:

Key Drivers to Repurchase and E-Loyalty

Dorothy Alinda, Raquel Daneluz, Paula Harasymowicz, and Tatiana Yano

Salzburg University of Applied Sciences, Austria 73

An Analysis of the Voluntary Carbon-Offsetting of German Tourists

Isabell Wulfsberg, and Dirk Reiser, Cologne Business School, Germany 83

Outernet Technologies in Tourism:

A Conceptual Framework and Applications for the Travel Industry

Paula Monteiro Harasymowicz, Salzburg University of Applied Sciences, Austria 97

The Evaluation of Augmented Reality in Practice:

Enriching Tourists' Experience through Offline Media

Meng Zhang, Wandi Zhang, Yefei Liu, and Yichen Zhao, University of Surrey, UK 111

The Acceptance of LBS in Tourism Destinations - Case Study: Wörthersee
Maximiliane Frey, Bianca Hinterdorfer, Julia Krippel, and Anton Wrann
Salzburg University of Applied Sciences, Austria.. **123**

The Digital Divide and User Experience of Blind and Visually Impaired Tourists
Zsofia Horvath, Agnes Kraushofer, Ekaterina Pok, and Sina Wedl
Salzburg University of Applied Sciences, Austria **137**

The Advantages of the "Great Place to Work" Award for Companies
in the Tourism Industryand its' Role in Job Application and Job Choice Decisions
of Applicants in the German-Speaking Countries
Ekaterina Pok, Salzburg University of Applied Sciences, Austria **151**

The Glass Ceiling in the Hotel Industry
Marta Ortega Martínez, Universidad Rey Juan Carlos Madrid, Spain **163**

Online Hotel Reviews: Rating Symbols or Text... Text or Rating Symbols?
That is the Question!
Johanna Aicher, Flavia Asiimwe, Bujinlkham Batchuluun,
Miriam Hausschild, and Martina Zöhrer
Salzburg University of Applied Sciences, Austria **175**

A Study of Web 2.0 Applications Usage
in the Lake Constance Area Conference Venues' Marketing Strategies
Anja Gunz, SKEMA Business School, Austria **189**

Small Medium Sized Hotels and Use of Social Media, the Case of Austria
Ali Gouhar, Salzburg University of Applied Sciences, Austria **205**

The Impact of Longer Visits on Destination Image Perception:
The Case of Exchange Students in University of Ljubljana
Konstantinos Vitoratos, University of Ljubljana, Slovenia **217**

Seeing, Feeling, Smelling, Hearing, and Tasting Austria:
A Qualitative Study of Austria's Destination Image
Andrea Ettinger, Vienna University of Economics and Business, Austria **229**

Film-Induced Tourism: The Use of Film as a Marketing Tool and its Impact on the Austrian Tourism Industry

Florentine Ramböck, Salzburg University of Applied Sciences, Austria 243

A Critical Analysis on the Implementation, Activeness and Level of Engagement of Destination Marketing Organisations across Social Media Platforms of YouTube & Google+

Sarah Nelum Rajika Wijesinghe, and Magdalena Pozgaj, University of Surrey, UK 255

Competitiveness of a Travel Destination – A Case Study of Montenegro in Relation to Relevant Models of Competitiveness

Marija Cimbaljević, and Andela Bučić, University of Novi Sad, Serbia 271

Service Design for Product Development in Tourist Destinations

Janosch Untersteiner, Management Center Innsbruck, Austria 285

Local Entrepreneurs' Perceptions of Cruise Tourism's Economic Impacts: The Case of Kavala (Greece)

Nikolaos Chrysanidis, University of Surrey, UK.. 297

Luxuy Tourism and Destination Branding: A Case Study of the Tourism Destination Vienna

Catherine S. Latzenhofer, Modul University Vienna, Austria 311

Paris Destination Image from the Point of View of Asian Students

Claire Dupain, Olga Novitskaya, Glion Institute of Higher Education, Switzerland 325

Research Programme Review Committee

ARIKAN Irfan, IMC University of Applied Sciences Krems, Austria

AUBKE Florian, Modul University Vienna, Austria

BAGGIO Rodolfo, Bocconi University Milan, Italy

BAUER-KRÖSBACHER Claudia, IMC University of Applied Sciences Krems, Austria

BRUCKER Eva, University of Applied Sciences Salzburg, Austria

BUHALIS Dimitrios, University of Bournemouth, UK

BUSBY Graham, Plymouth University, UK

CANTONI Lorenzo, Universitá dell Svizzera italiana Lugano, Switzerland

EBSTER Claus, University of Vienna, Austria

EGGER Roman, University of Applied Sciences Salzburg, Austria

FENSEL Dieter, University of Innsbruck, Austria

FESENMAIER Daniel, Temple University, USA

FUCHS Matthias, Mid-Sweden University, Sweden

FURTMÜLLER Elfi, University of Innsbruck, Austria

GRETZEL Ulrike, University of Wollongong, Australia

HATAK Isabella, Vienna University of Economics and Business, Austria

HERMANN Inge, Saxion University of Applied Sciences, Netherlands

JOOSS Mario, University of Applied Sciences Salzburg, Austria

KAGERMEIER Andreas, University of Trier, Germany

KASTNER Margit, Vienna University of Economics and Business, Austria

KOTEK Klaus, IMC University of Applied Sciences Krems, Austria

LASSNIG Markus, Salzburg Research, Austria

LIEBRICH Andreas, Lucerne University of Applied Sciences and Arts, Switzerland

MAURER Christian, IMC University of Applied Sciences Krems, Austria

MURPHY Jamie, Murdoch Business School, Australia

NEUHOFER Barbara, Bournemouth University, UK

PETERS Mike, MCI Management Center Innsbruck, Austria

PIKKEMAAT Birgit, Institute for Innovative Tourism, Austria

PRISKIN Julianna, Lucerne University of Applied Sciences and Arts, Switzerland

PÜHRETMAIR Franz, Kompetenznetzwerk IT zur Förderung der Integration von Menschen mit Behinderungen, Austria

REINO Sofia, Cooperative Research Center in Tourism, Spain

ROMERO Alberto, Rey Juan Carlos University, Spain

SCHACHNER Max, IMC University of Applied Sciences, Austria

SCHEGG Roland, HES-SO Valais, Switzerland

SOMMER Guido, Cologne Business School (CBS), Germany

STANGL Brigitte, University of Surrey, UK

STECKENBAUER Georg Christian, IMC University of Applied Sciences Krems, Austria

TEICHMANN Karin, University of Innsbruck, Austria

TISCHLER Stephanie, IMC University of Applied Sciences Krems, Austria

TUSSYADIAH Iis, Washingten State University, USA

VOLO Serena, Free University of Bolzano, Italy

ZEHRER Anita, MCI Management Center Innsbruck,

Personal Technology and Tourism Experiences

Iis P. Tussyadiah

Washington State University Vancouver, USA
iis.tussyadiah@wsu.edu

Abstract

Personal technologies have become an integral part of and caused dramatic impacts on human experiences. As people increasingly use personal devices to plan, organize, and reflect on a trip, the roles of personal technologies in travel and tourism become more and more prominent. These roles are typically associated with enablement (i.e., making certain experiences possible) and facilitation (i.e., assistive technology to enhance experiences), which often result in transformation of the various aspects of travel experiences. Recent development indicates that personal technologies evolve from being portable to wearable, implying the potential changes in the ways users interact with technology and, consequently, the ways they use it during traveling. This article addresses the potential implications of the development in personal technology, including wearables, on the transformation of travelers' behavior and overall travel patterns.

Keywords: Personal Technology; Mobile; Wearable; Travel

1 PERSONAL TECHNOLOGIES

The modern life is characterized with the widespread use of information and communication technologies (ICTs), where people increasingly live with and rely on electronic devices to search, record, and distribute information. Importantly, personal technology now pervades our lives and become the primary means by which people interact with each other. In a broader context, the term personal technology is used to explain electronic devices that are relatively small and easy to carry (i.e., portable machines), which typically refers to ubiquitous, pervasive, and mobile computing. Personal technology can also refer to approaches to computing that demonstrate how advanced technologies can be personalized to meet the unique informational needs of their users (e.g., Weiss, Whiteley, Treviranus, & Fels, 2001), allowing for electronic devices to serve for an individual's personal (e.g., educational, social, entertainment, and emotional) use. For example, the term personal computer (PC) was introduced to describe a general-purpose computer (also called a microcomputer) that is intended to be operated by an end-user (i.e., single-person use) without an intervening computer operator. Today, personal technology has moved beyond PC and is generally associated with "consumer tech," referring to smart mobile devices that are designed (i.e., in terms of their size, capabilities, and price) for general and/or specialized personal use (e.g., smartphones, tablets, e-readers, etc.).

To illustrate the pervasive nature of personal technology, Nielsen (2014a) reported that smartphones are adopted at a phenomenal pace, with 71% overall penetration rate in the US in 2014. Indeed, PC has been dethroned by smartphones as primary computing devices since people are increasingly performing digital tasks from reading news articles to editing a spreadsheet using smartphone apps (Mossberg, 2014). Smart mobile devices are characterized with constant connectivity (i.e., ubiquitous access to information and social connections; always on and always accessible) supported by intelligent systems and robust, rapid networks. These provide smartphone users with world's information and entertainment at their disposal and "on demand", enabling the performance of many aspects of life anytime anywhere. Consequently, the use of smartphones causes changes in the ways in which people socialize, do tasks, find, gather and share information, have fun, and manage their lives (Oulasvirta, Rattenbury, Ma, & Raita, 2012; Nielsen, 2014b). Many have demonstrated the impacts of smartphones on their users (e.g., Darrell, 2014; Derks et al., 2014), which include such aspects as consumer behavior (e.g., mobile banking, mobile payment systems), social interaction (e.g., relationships with circles of friends and families, online social networking), and general work-life balance (i.e., less separation of work and personal life), as well as the society in general (e.g., Laird, 2012; Penn, 2015; Sarwar & Somro, 2013), which include impacts on business (e.g., increase in productivity), education (e.g., distraction in the classrooms, bullying and hazing in schools), and health (e.g., access to healthcare facilities, ease of health monitoring), among others.

The latest development in personal technology is the introduction of wearable computing devices, the next generation of portable machines. Today, the array of wearable computers ranges from wristbands and smart watches that intelligently monitor users' fitness (e.g., heart rate, blood pressure), activities (e.g., movement, sleep) and communication, to smart eyewear that run apps (e.g., Google Glass), to wearable fashion technology making use of wearable sensors and smart textiles (e.g., performance enhancing footwear). As they are worn on the body (i.e., head-mounted, on the wrist, etc.), wearable computing devices are subsumed into the personal space of the users and, at the same time, controlled by the users. These devices also provide both operational and interactional constancy, making it possible for the users to obtain real-time feedback on their experiences and dramatically improve their performance. Consequently, they have tremendous potentials in shaping user behavior on a moment-to-moment basis (e.g., through regular prompts), motivating habit forming positive behavior for healthy lifestyle, smart consumption, etc. (Patel, Asch, & Volpp, 2015). Therefore, wearable computers promise to let technology impact users on a more personal, intimate level. According to Ledger and McCaffrey (2014), wearable devices are achieving mass market penetration in the US with one in 10 Americans 18 years and older owns an activity tracker. Statista (2015) shows that the market for wearables was US$5 billion in 2014 and is expected to rise to US$12 billion by 2018. These demonstrate the potentials of wearable computing devices to start dominating the landscape of personal technology in the near future.

The development in personal technology has a remarkable impact on travel and, consequently, studies on the impacts of personal technology on tourism experiences have emerged. In general, the literature on travel and tourism associate the roles of ICT with facilitation and enhancement of tourism experiences (Neuhofer, Buhalis & Ladkin, 2012; Tussyadiah & Fesenmaier, 2009; Wang, Park & Fesenmaier, 2012). Smartphones support travelers with convenience in travel planning and enhancement in the overall tourism experience by providing access to information and interpretation, direction and navigation, social networks, and entertainment (Wang, Park, & Fesenmaier, 2012; Wang, Xiang, & Fesenmaier, 2014a; 2014b). Smart mobile devices allow tourists to stay connected, well-informed and fully equipped for travel-related performances such as information search, navigation, social networking, and travel reporting (Tussyadiah, 2014a). Most recently, Tussyadiah (2014a) propose that almost hands-free wearable devices such as Google Glass are expected to enable these processes to be even more immediate, less cumbersome (e.g., allowing people to look ahead instead of down on a mobile phone screen), and rather surreptitious. Additionally, using the context of use of wearable videos for travel, Dinhopl and Gretzel (2015) demonstrate that hands-free videography impacts the structure of tourism experience. Furthermore, many have speculated how wearable computing devices will revolutionize tourists' behavior and the tourism industries (Dickey, 2013; Prabu, 2012), specifically in the areas of guiding with augmented reality and information overlay, travel reporting with first-person view (FPV), and instant navigation. The recent introduction of Apple Watch also encourages expectation for a new level of convenience in travel experiences, from getting direction and unlocking your hotel room to e-hailing your Uber car (Clampet, 2015).

2 THE SMART TRAVELERS

The pervasive use of personal technology for travel is directly impacting travelers' performance (i.e., in terms of effectiveness and efficiency of task completion) and overall tourism experiences. Thanks to the operational and interactional constancy as well as a higher extent of sensitivity (i.e., always aware) and intelligence, travelers are able to receive constant feedback on their experiences and continuously improve their performance. Therefore, it can be suggested that travelers equipped with smart personal technology can become smarter in various aspects of travel, because of the facilitation in various travel-related decision making and performances. Indeed, research shows that travelers use smartphones for various travel-related experiences including such activities as navigation and information search, itinerary management/facilitation, sharing and communication, as well as entertainment (Modschein, 2011; Tussyadiah, Fesenmaier, & Yoo, 2008; Verkasalo et al., 2010; Wang, Xiang, & Fesenmaier, 2014a; 2014b). Wang, Xiang and Fesenmaier (2014b) summarize these use types into two broad categories: en-route planning and en-route sharing. Importantly, with these categories, they emphasize the shift in travelers' behavior as they rely more and more on technology where activities typically associated with pre-trip and post-trip experience are enacted on-site (Tussyadiah and Wang, 2014). For example, with the help of context-aware applications, travelers are able to screen and evaluate alternatives and make informed decisions on-site (Tussyadiah, 2012; Tussyadiah & Zach, 2012). They are also able to post immediate reflection on trip experiences to gauge real-time feedback from social networks (Wang, Xiang and Fesenmaier, 2014b). In summary, as technology takes the burden of carrying out actions to assist travelers (e.g., sensing the environment, monitoring user actions and providing feedback, etc.), travelers are becoming more well informed and "literate" in various aspects of tourism destinations. It is worth noting that a recent research on the roles of intelligent agents among tourists, Tussyadiah and Wang (2014) found the paradox resulting from the use of smartphones for on-site experiences. That is, the use of intelligent agents may result in amplification of certain aspects of travel (e.g., better, more relevant information for cognitive experiences), but reduction in opportunities to learn from making mistakes or exercising own trial and error decisions.

Further, the use of personal technology is also associated with enhancement in travel experiences due to the augmentation in travelers' cognitive abilities. For example, facilitated by augmented reality and information layering, travelers can learn more about tourism attractions. Recent studies on wearable augmented reality applications (Leue, Han, & Jung, 2014; Leue, Jung, & Dieck, 2015) found that visitors who received augmented information in an art gallery indicated that they had an enhanced learning experience. They further argue that in addition to providing additional information, enjoyment and flow (i.e., via interactivity, vividness, etc.) also contributed to the enhancement of travelers' cognitive experiences. In terms of social connections, with smartphones or wearable devices, everyone in the travelers' social networks is only a swipe (or touch) away. Tussyadiah (2014a) points out that the use of Google Glass allows travelers to maintain real-time connectivity with family and friends (e.g., by using Google+ Hangout app simultaneously while experiencing tourism destinations), which can be helpful to provide necessary social support for travelers on the move (Kim & Tussyadiah, 2013). Additionally, the use of Google Translate app assists travelers in eliminating language barriers between them and local residents real-time, which can be conducive in facilitating social interactions. Moreover, personal technology is increasingly designed with anthropomorphism in mind (Guthrie, 1993; Marakas, Johnson, & Palmer, 2000), enabling technology to serve its users as social actors in addition to its roles as tools and media. Fogg (2003) calls these roles the "functional triad" of technology. As a result, travelers regard the social role of smartphones as travel buddies or companions (Tussyadiah, 2014b; Tussyadiah & Wang, 2014).

In summary, the use of personal technology eases decision making and provides travelers with necessary support, resulting in an increase in travelers' confidence while experiencing tourism destinations. As a consequence, Tussyadiah (2014a) suggests that the use of wearable technology encourages the transformation from "tourists" to "explorers" (i.e., or simply from "travelers" to "smart travelers"), where well-informed travelers (with extended cognitive abilities) are able to roam around the destinations independently, enjoy en-route experiences, and explore unfamiliar places with a higher degree of confidence. This transformation in travel behavior will surely impact not only the management of tourism destinations and the design approach to create personalized tourism experiences, but also the strategic use of data (i.e., digital traces left by travelers) to better capture relevant tourism market and shape traveler behavior.

3   THE SMART DESTINATIONS

Tourism destinations realizing the potentials of ICT in enhancing their offerings and attracting a wider market often invest in developing specialized devices to assist travelers, such as hand-held audio guides or destination-specific recommender systems. With tremendous computing power and greater personalization capability (and the abundance of apps), travelers now use their own devices for various travel-related activities (from booking to navigation to mobile payment) and to experience different destinations. Moreover, as technology enters the personal (and intimate) space of its users (worn as part of human bodies), it gives users a greater control over what, where, when, and to what extent certain functions should be performed. This leads to the prevalence of silent travelers, those who turn to their own devices first to search for information and make decisions instead of contacting tourism offices. Therefore, the pervasive use of personal technologies present strategic challenges for tourism destinations in terms of communicating with and tapping into consumer technologies for various marketing and management decisions.

The concept of "smart destination" is suggested as an umbrella term describing tourism destinations where technology infrastructures are embedded within them allowing the synergy among various entities (i.e., stakeholders) for better coordination and management of visitor experiences as well as improvement of residents' quality of life (Buhalis & Amaranggana, 2014; 2015). Drawing from a smart tourism destination project in China, Wang, Li and Li (2013) describe smart destinations as platforms where information on tourist behavior, tourism consumption, and resources are integrated and then fed back to the various stakeholders (i.e., tourists, enterprises, tourism organizations, government) through a variety of end-user devices. They further suggest that the components of technology infrastructure necessary to create such smart platforms include cloud services, the internet-of-things, and end-user internet service systems, highlighting the importance of machine-to-machine interactions to synergize the inter-connected processes involving the different components of tourism destinations. At the core of this technology infrastructure, the internet-of-things (i.e., a system that allows a variety of things or objects to interact and cooperate with each other to reach common goals [Atzori, Iera & Morabito, 2010]) plays a prominent role in the ways destination can communicate with travelers' personal technology.

As travelers use their personal technologies to interact with their surroundings (e.g., making reservation, retrieving recommendations, searching for information, taking pictures), they leave traces of digital information related to the users, such as preferences, relative positions, activities, etc. Therefore, smart destination platform is also characterized with the capability of technological infrastructure to capture and process large scale data (i.e., big data), often in real-time, and to recognize, extract, and analyze patterns in order to generate feedback and suggest relevant recommendations for travelers as well as other entities. While a solid infrastructure facilitating communication and dissemination of information is a backbone of smart destinations, data management is an important process that fuels the dynamics of smart destinations. In practice, wearable computers provide tremendous opportunities for tourism destinations in management and marketing. For example, embedding sensors and objects that ping travelers' wearable devices (Investopedia, n.d.) can assist tourism destinations in determining areas visited by travelers in a point in time as well as travelers' flow based on changes in their positions. Tourism enterprises can leverage consumer technologies by targeting the users based on their preference, physical and emotional states (e.g., location, fitness) as well as activities performed before to push relevant recommendations and notifications. Finally, the development in cloud services should be able to capture, store and process information specific to individual users that can be useful for market targeting.

4 IMPLICATIONS FOR TRAVEL AND TOURISM RESEARCH

The development in personal technology and the transformation it causes on user behavior as well as management practices call for tourism research that not only explains the phenomenon and prescribe future states, but also shed a new light in understanding the phenomenon from various theoretical lenses. For example, Tussyadiah (2014a) suggests a second look into the concept of mediation, which is prevalently used to explain the roles of technology in tourism experience. She exercises the concept of embodiment to explain user experiences with wearable computing, describing its use on the contexts of travelers' interaction with physical objects and near surroundings. According to Ihde (1990), technology-mediated experiences are non-neutral. That is, technologies appear in between humans and the world (i.e., mediation) and change human experiences (i.e., transformation), enhancing some aspects while reducing others. He further explains that embodiment of technology results in a symbiosis of technology and user within human actions. In an example of seeing experience that is mediated by optical technologies, he suggests that user is experiencing "seeing through glasses" experience, which, in itself, is a transformed experience. Similarly, seeing a painting with augmented information through Google Glass in an art gallery (as in the study of Leue, Han, and Jung, 2014) can be interpreted as a transformed experience, where technology is embodied and becomes inseparable from the action of seeing a painting.

To explain embodied interactions, it is important to think of the integration of technological capacity into human actions and its role in extending the perceptual bodily (as well as cognitive) sense of its users (Ihde, 1990). That is, technology plays an important role in the performance of human actions relative to their contexts and near environments. In other words, the use of personal technology means enriching user skills with the technological capabilities. Previous studies confirmed that travelers expected the use of Google Glass to extend their perceptual sense (the body and the mind), such as in the example of "seeing through Glass eyes" for hypothetical travels (Tussyadiah, 2014a) as well as actual visitor experiences in an art gallery (Leue, Han & Jung, 2014). From the viewpoint of Human-Computer Interaction (HCI), the use of wearable personal technology stimulates a phenomenon called "a technology withdraw", where technology "disappears" (or perceived to be) as they become an integral part of the users' actions. Indeed, it is suggested that the biggest challenge for wearable technology to penetrate a wider market is for it to disappear, to be naturally embedded with the wearer, and not to attract too much attention (Porges, 2015) that might disrupt users' daily activities and social interactions.

As wearable technology penetrates deeper into users' personal space, the dynamics that explain man-machine interactions are increasingly complex. On one hand, personal technology is there to take tasks away from its users, it also impinges behavior back to its users, influencing and shaping their experiences. In their study on how tourists perceive proactive smartphones as intelligent agents, Tussyadiah and Wang (2014) refer to this issue as the inter-related processes of social and technological determinisms (Latour, 1988; 1993), demonstrating the complicated role of technology in the society. Therefore, researching the behavioral and experiential impacts of the use of personal technology requires different ways of gathering, processing, and analyzing information from travelers. Importantly, it requires different ways of asking questions to capture the richness of qualitative data to support conventional usability testing methods.

Additionally, the use of wearable technology allows users to leave a large amount of information that are not easily captured and interpreted in such ways that make them useful for the various entities in the tourism ecosystem. The availability of big data consisting of information atypical for conventional marketing and management research (e.g., fitness data, sentiments revealed in geotagged microblog posts, phone calls, reservation, etc.) requires travel and tourism researchers to apply alternative methodologies to "listen" to the data and extract unexpected patterns that can be useful to explain and predict trends. In other words, tourism researchers should equip themselves with various tools and interdisciplinary approaches to make sense of big data and produce actionable insights for more impactful research.

5   THE PET PEEVES, OR REALLY BIG PROBLEMS

One of the promises of personal technology is the ability to monitor, record, and share a large amount of information (often sensitive personal information) with minimal efforts. This creates a big challenge for users as they face a heightened sense of trade-off between personalization and privacy (and, to some extent, security). Indeed, the study conducted by Microsoft (Penn, 2015) revealed that internet users from around the globe think that personal technology is bad for privacy, with the majority indicating that they are not fully aware of what types of data are being collected and stored about them and who might have access to those data (i.e., third-party issues). Moreover, they perceive the lack of legal protection for users and insufficient regulation on who should be able to obtain user data and for which purposes. Porter (2014) also suggests that in the era of big data, personal data is routinely collected and traded and there are few effective controls over how they are used or secured. For example, heightened by the negative sentiments over government surveillance, the introduction of Google Glass (with the capacity to take images surreptitiously and, potentially, apply facial recognition features) was welcomed by fear of ubiquitous mass online surveillance (i.e., personal privacy in proximity). Furthermore, as many companies (including hotels) have experienced data breach problems (i.e., where third parties illegally obtained customer information), data security is an important issue facing travelers from the use of personal technology. Governments are realizing the privacy issues in the era of big data and starting to think strategically to solve these issues. For example, the President's Council of Advisors on Science and Technology (PCAST) in the US recognizes the importance of emphasizing regulation on the use of big data more than the collection and analysis (2014).

For travelers, having smart devices that are always on and always aware can negatively impact tourism from receiving constant notifications that might distract them from immersing themselves with the physical and social surroundings. As illustrated in Tussyadiah and Wang (2014), travelers are also concerned about the sense of control over their tourism experiences and over-dependency on technology when making decisions (i.e., they do not want their tourism experience and decisions to be dictated by the technology). That is, while personal technology can enhance their experience by helping solve their problems at the destination (e.g., navigation to avoid getting lost at the destination), some travelers think that facing and solving problems is an experience in itself that every traveler needs to go through.

Making sure that personal technology is monitoring users' states and behaviors accurately is another challenge (Patel, Asch, & Volpp, 2015). It is suggested that some wearables record and present data on physical activities, such as sleep patterns, based on 'guestimation' instead of accurate measurements (Fowler & Stern, 2015), which can be an issue for both the users and service providers because it has a direct impact on the quality of feedback generated for users. Service providers also face several challenges from lack of consistency in the use of wearables (e.g., users might forget to recharge the battery, resulting in loss of data points). In order to be able to track patterns and insights from user data, it is necessary to have consumers consistently use their devices, providing a constant stream of information for service providers to get the 'full picture' of user performance. Therefore, making sure that personal technology is more user friendly and does not require complex behavior to actively update the data is important. Finally, Patel, Asch and Volpp (2015) suggest that presenting information back to users in an easy to understand and motivating manner is another challenge for anyone attempting to influence behavior changes. For example, some providers may introduce social feedback (e.g., sharing data to social network) and social gaming (i.e., leaderboard) to encourage target behavior.

REFERENCES

Atzori, L., Iera, A., & Morabito, G. (2010). The internet-of-things: A survey. *Computer Networks*, 54, 2787-2803.

Buhalis, D. & Amaranggana, A. (2014). Smart tourism destinations. *In* Xiang, Z. & Tussyadiah, I. (Eds.), Information and Communication Technologies in Tourism 2014. Switzerland: Springer International Publishing.

Buhalis, D. & Amaranggana, A. (2015). Smart tourism destinations enhancing tourism experience through personalisation of services. *In* Tussyadiah, I. & Inversini, A. (Eds.), Information and Communication Technologies in Tourism 2015. Switzerland: Springer International Publishing.

Clampet, J. (2015). All the Apple Watch travel apps ready for launch. *Skift*. Available at http://skift.com/2015/03/09/all-the-apple-watch-travel-apps-ready-for-launch/

Darrell, R. (2014). The impressive effects of smartphones on society (infographic). *Bit Rebels*. Retrieved from http://www.bitrebels.com/technology/the-effects-of-smartphones-on-society/

Derks, D., ten Brummelhuis, L. L., Zecic, D. & Bakker, A. B. (2014). Switching on and off...: Does smartphone use obstruct the possibility to engage in recovery activities? *European Journal of Work and Organizational Psychology*, 23(1), 80 – 90.

Dickey, M. R. (2013). How Google Glass will Revolutionize 9 Industries. Retrieved from http://www.businessinsider.com/google-glass-will-totally-disrupt-these-tktk-industries-2013-3?op=1

Dinhopl, A., & Gretzel, U. (2015). Changing practices/new technologies: Photos and videos on vacation. *In* Tussyadiah, I. & Inversini, A. (Eds.), Information and Communication Technologies in Tourism 2015. Switzerland: Springer International Publishing.

Ledger, D. & McCaffrey, D. (2014). Inside wearables: How the science of human behavior change offers the secret to long-term engagement. *Endeavour Partners*. Retrieved from http://endeavourpartners.net/assets/Endeavour-Partners-Wearables-White-Paper-20141.pdf

Fogg, B. J. (2003). *Persuasive Technology: Using Computers to Change What We Think and Do*. San Francisco, CA: Morgan Kaufmann Publishers.

Fowler, G. A. & Stern, J. (2015). The 12 tech nuisances that annoy us the most. The Wall Street Journal. Retrieved from http://www.wsj.com/articles/the-12-tech-nuisances-that-annoy-us-most-1426009886

Guthrie, S. E. (1993). *Faces in the Clouds: A New Theory of Religion*. New York: Oxford University Press.

Ihde, D. (1990). *Technology and the Lifeworld: From Garden to Earth*. Bloomington, IN: Indiana University Press.

Investopedia (n.d.). Wearable technology. Retrieved from http://www.investopedia.com/terms/w/wearable-technology.asp

Kim, J. Tussyadiah, I.P. (2013). Social networking and social support in tourism experience: The moderating role of online self-presentation strategies. *Journal of Travel & Tourism Marketing* 30 (1), 78-92.

Laird, S. (2012). How smartphones are changing healthcare (Infographic). *Mashable*. Retrieved from http://mashable.com/2012/09/26/smartphones-health-care-infographic/

Latour, B. (1988). Mixing humans and nonhumans together: The sociology of a door closer. *Social Problems, 35*, 298–310.

Latour, B. (1993). *We Have Never Been Modern* (Translated by C. Porter). Cambridge, MA: Harvard University Press.

Leue, M.C., Han, D. & Jung, T. (2014). *Google Glass Creative Tourism Experience: A Case Study of Manchester Art Gallery*. Paper presented at WHTF, Seoul, 26-29 June 2014.

Leue, M. C., Jung, T., & Dieck, D. (2015). Google Glass augmented reality: Generic learning outcomes for art galleries. *In* Tussyadiah, I. & Inversini, A. (Eds.), Information and Communication Technologies in Tourism 2015. Switzerland: Springer International Publishing.

Marakas, G. M., Johnson, R. D., & Palmer, J. W. (2000). A theoretical model of differential social attributions toward computing technology: When metaphor become the model. *International Journal of Human-Computer Studies*, 52, 719-750.

Modschein, A. (2011). Passeggiata Nuova: Social Travel in the Era of the Smartphone (Working Paper). Center for Transportation Policy & Management, New York University. Retrieved from http://wagner.nyu.edu/files/rudincenter/mondschein_passeggiata_it_social_travel.pdf.

Mossberg, W. (2014). 25 years of personal technology. *re/code*. Available at http://recode.net/2014/04/29/25-years-of-personal-technology/

Neuhofer, B., Buhalis, D., & Ladkin, A. (2012). Conceptualising technology enhanced destination experiences. *Journal of Destination Marketing & Management*, 1, 36-46.

Nielsen (2014a). Mobile Millenials: Over 85% of Generation Y Owns Smartphones. Retrieved from http://www.nielsen.com/us/en/insights/news/2014/mobile-millennials-over-85-percent-of-generation-y-owns-smartphones.html

Nielsen (2014b). How Smartphones are Changing Consumers' Daily Routines around the Globe. Retrieved from http://www.nielsen.com/content/corporate/us/en/insights/news/2014/how-smartphones-are-changing-consumers-daily-routines-around-the-globe.html

Oulasvirta, A., Rattenbury, T., Ma, L., & Raita, E. (2012). Habits make smartphone use more pervasive. *Personal and Ubiquitous Computing*, 16(1), 105-114.

Patel, M. S., Asch, D. S., & Volpp, K. G. (2015). Wearable Devices as Facilitators, Not Drivers, of Health Behavior Change. *The Journal of the American Medical Association*, 313(5), 459-460.

Penn, M. (2015). Views from around the globe: 2nd annual poll on how personal technology is changing our lives. *Mircrosoft*. Retrieved from http://mscorp.blob.core.windows.net/mscorpmedia/2015/01/2015DavosPollFINAL.pdf

Porges, S. (2015). The smartest thing a smart watch can do: Disappear. *Forbes*. Retrieved from http://www.forbes.com/sites/sethporges/2015/03/17/the-smartest-thing-a-smartwatch-can-do-disappear/

Porter, C. (2014). Little privacy in the age of big data. *The Guardian*. Retrieved from http://www.theguardian.com/technology/2014/jun/20/little-privacy-in-the-age-of-big-data

Prabu, K. (2012). How Google's Project Glass is Going to Revolutionize Travellers and Travel Companies. Retrieved from http://www.travopia.com/2012/04/how-googles-project-glass-is-going-to.html

President's Council of Advisors on Science and Technology, The (2014). Big Data and Privacy: A technological perspective. *The White House*. Retrieved from https://www.whitehouse.gov/sites/default/files/microsites/ostp/PCAST/pcast_big_data_and_privacy_-_may_2014.pdf

Sarwar, M., & Soomro, R. T. (2013). Impact of smartphone's on society. *European Journal of Scientific Research*, 98(21), 216-226.

Statista (2015). Wearable device market value from 2010 to 2018 (in million U.S. dollars). Retrieved from http://www.statista.com/statistics/259372/wearable-device-market-value/

Tussyadiah, I.P. (2012). A concept of location-based social network marketing. *Journal of Travel and Tourism Marketing*, 29(3), 205-220.

Tussyadiah, I. (2014a). Expectation of travel experiences with wearable computing devices. In Xiang, Z., Tussyadiah, I. (Eds.), Information and Communication Technologies in Tourism 2014 (pp. 539-552). Switzerland: Springer International Publishing.

Tussyadiah, I.P. (2014b). Social actor attribution to mobile phones - The case of tourists. *Information Technology & Tourism*, 14, 21-47.

Tussyadiah, I.P. & Fesenmaier, D. R. (2009). Mediating tourist experiences - Access to places via shared videos. *Annals of Tourism Research*, 36(1), 24-40

Tussyadiah, I.P., Fesenmaier, D. R., & Yoo, Y. (2008). Designing interactions in tourism mediascape: Identification of patterns for mobile 2.0 platform. In O'Connor, P., Hopken, W. Gretzel, U. (Eds.), Information and Communication Technologies in Tourism 2008. Vienna - New York: Springer.

Tussyadiah, I.P., & Wang, D. (2014, OnlineFirst). Tourists' attitudes toward proactive smartphone systems. *Journal of Travel Research*. DOI: 10.1177/004728751456316.

Tussyadiah, I.P., Zach, F. (2012). The role of geo-based technology in place experiences. *Annals of Tourism Research* 39 (2), 780-800.

Verkasalo, H., Lopez-Nicolas, C., Molina-Castillo, F. J., & Bouwman, H. (2010). Analysis of users and non-users of smartphone applications. *Telematics and Informatics*, 27, 242-255.

Wang, D., Li, X., & Li, Y. (2013). China's "smart tourism destination" initiative: A taste of the service-dominant logic. *Journal of Destination Marketing & Management*, 2(2), 59-61.

Wang, D., Park, S., & Fesenmaier, D. R. (2012). The role of smartphones in mediating the touristic experience. *Journal of Travel Research*, 51(4), 371-387.

Wang, D., Xiang, Z., & Fesenmaier, D. R. (2014a). Adapting to the mobile world: A model of smartphone use. *Annals of Tourism Research*, 48, 11-26

Wang, D., Xiang, Z., & Fesenmaier, D. R. (2014b). Smartphone use in everyday life and travel. *Journal of Travel Research*. doi:10.1177/0047287514535847

Weiss, T., Whiteley, C., Treviranus, J., & Fels, D.I. (2001). PEBBLES: A personal technology for meeting educational, social and emotional needs of hospitalized children. *Personal and Ubiquitous Computing*, 5, 157-168.

Innovative City Map

Emre Ronay

Salzburg University of Applied Sciences, Austria
eronay.imte-m2011@fh-salzburg.ac.at

Abstract

One of the most promising technologies for the future and currently much discussed is the Near Field Communication (NFC), which will most likely become the standard in mobile devices in the years to come. The usage of NFC in tourism is a new dimension which has been examined only by a few scholars so far. This paper presents an innovative form of NFC usage in the Tourism field: NFC enabled travel maps. A prototype of such a map was developed and tested by the author with the aim of measuring their perceived value. Therefore a multidimensional model was implemented and tested. In addition, the customer satisfaction dimension was investigated, to comprehend its relationship with the perceived value. The results indicated that the perceived value of the map was high and that it positively influenced customer satisfaction. In addition, the map preference of tourists was clarified, as paper maps are still preferred over map applications.

Keywords: NFC; ICT; Smart Map; Perceived Value; PERVAL

1 INTRODUCTION

Recently, technological progress, the increase of income and mobility as well as new norms and values in our society led to a rapid change concerning products and services. Additionally, this progress also initiated a fast and tremendous change within the tourism industry (Sawng et al., 2011). After the year 2000, a profound transformation of communication technologies can be observed. New developments of innovative products and services can be noticed. Furthermore, the interaction between technology and tourism led to elementary changes in the tourism industry (Buhalis and Egger, 2006). For instance, the engagement of Information and Communication Technologies (ICT) into the tourism industry altered the structure of the whole sector. ICTs provided new opportunities and threats and started to be a competition factor for organizations in tourism (Egger and Buhalis, 2008). New technological advancements such as innovative ICT cases are inevitable for the future (Ronay and Egger, 2014). Recently, modern society is inconceivable without mobile devices and the consequent use of mobile services. The multitude of technologies incorporated in the tiniest space has turned mobile phones, and smart phones in particular, into the Swiss knives of our times (Egger, 2013). Recently, the potential of these mobile services forced companies to invest in this segment (Wang et al., 2006). Mobile services are finding increased acceptance and deliver unique opportunities and challenges for tourism companies (Bortenschlager, 2010; Kim, Park and Morrison, 2008). These technologies can serve as a critical point for organizations as they force companies to keep track and deliver innovative solutions in order to survive in a very competitive market. As a result, this can lead to an increased efficiency improving the communication with customers and partners as well as improving profitability (Egger and Buhalis, 2008). A very promising technology that will most probably be integrated in our smartphones, offering a variety of new applications for the tourism industry, is the wireless connectivity technology Near Field Communication (NFC) (Egger, 2013; Pesonen and Horster, 2012). For the future, Ryan and Rao (2008) predicted that the usage of mobile phones while travelling will become inevitable for travelers and will render other technologies obsolete. Furthermore, mobile phones will become a cornerstone in multi-channel distribution and service strategies (Egger and Jooss, 2010).

This paper introduces a prototype of a new map with a distinctive design and divergent navigation opportunity for tourists; a regular travel map with embedded NFC tags. The map was developed by the author and is called "Smart Map". This paper investigates the perceived value of such a Smart Map by adopting the PERVAL model from Sweeney and Soutar (2001). Moreover, the study aims to understand whether the perceived value can be considered as a determinant that influences customer satisfaction.

2 LITERATURE VIEW

2.1 NFC-Technology

Innovative developments of technologies are emerging rapidly, such as the spread of mobile devices (Canadi et al., 2010). The penetration of new mobile devices and the increasing need to establish communication between them with a simple and secure technology displays the present situation of mobile communication (Pesonen and Horster, 2012). NFC technology is a short-range wireless communication technology based on Radio Frequency Identification (RFID) technology (Ozdenizci et al., 2010). The technology creates a linkage between interoperable systems that provide a wireless short range communication between mobile phones, computers or intelligent objects. Hence, NFC which is based on a touching paradigm facilitates information exchange to reach content and services in a heuristic approach (Jaraba et al., 2010). The transaction of data starts when one device is getting close to another device (Ok et al., 2011). Three modes in which NFC operates have been identified. In the Reader/Writer Mode, NFC enabled devices can read and write data which are stored on tags or Smart Cards. According to the data loaded on the tag, the device takes action without any other user interaction. For example, a URI (Uniform Resource Identifier) can be stored on a tag with the help of one of the many free available NFC-Apps. As soon as the NFC device reads the tag, a web browser opens with the website (Miraz et al., 2009). The Card Emulation mode enables the NFC device to act as a Smart Card. This allows the device to function as a contactless credit, debit or loyalty card. This mode is important as it enables contactless payment and ticketing possibilities (Madlmayr and Scharinger 2010). The Peer-to-Peer mode allows interaction and creation of a bilateral interaction between two NFC devices (Ok et al., 2011). More than one NFC tag can be attached to any physical object which is desired to augment. This act generates a liaison between the physical object and the virtual world. The virtual liaison can be united with any object and could contain not only text data but visual media information as well (Want et al., 1999).

In the case of the Smart Map, NFC tags are attached to a city map and information about selected points of interests is stored on them. This article is therefore closely related to the topic of Location Based Service (LBS) and TeleCartography. The increased possibilities of satellite positioning, telecommunication and the increasing number of mobile devices, currently drive the market towards LBS's, which are defined as services that reveal the location of specific mobile devices via wireless data transfer (Gartner, 2004). The new advancements sound alluring at first but these mobile maps bring along their problems. A number of mobile applications with cartographic interfaces and maps are already available. However, most frequently they are devoted to navigation by car and are not convenient for pedestrian usage (Delikostidis and Elzakker, 2009).

Panorama Tours is a tour operator located in Salzburg which also operates in Vienna and Budapest. They provide tours such the Sound of Music tour to their customers by travelling to all the movie-related locations. However, buses are not allowed to enter the old city of Salzburg. Therefore, tourists receive a map and have to visit the places within the old city by themselves. This solution lacks the variety of information offered by the guided tour. Thus the idea was to attach NFC tags to a city map in order to provide additional information about the most important points of interest (POIs) in an innovative and convenient way. Due to restricted time resources the author concentrated on the function of providing information. In addition to routing and navigation, the possibility to buy entrance tickets and many other functionalities could be implemented on a NFC enabled city map as well.

2.2 Measuring the perceived value

The literature offers several definitions of perceived value. Zeithaml (1988) defined it as "The consumer's overall assessment of the utility of a product based on perceptions of what is received and what is given". Woodruff (1997) defined it as "Customer's perceived preference for and evaluation of those product attributes, attribute performances, consequences arising from use that facilitate (or block) achieving the customer's goals and purposes in use situations". The concept of perceived value can have a direct influence on the attitude of consumers, where attitude in this context is associated with the positive or negative tendency the costumer has towards a product linked to past experiences (Ruiz-Molina and Gil-Saura, 2008). Perceived value is a continuous measurement for building a close relationship with customers (Sweeney and Soutar, 2001). Furthermore, companies seeking the maintenance of relationship marketing have to focus on two directions when considering the perceived value of a product: the company can try to either decrease the sacrifices faced by the consumer, or to create more benefits. To reduce the sacrifices, the company needs to investigate the value chain as a whole in order to understand the wants and needs of a customer. This helps to define a convenient strategy to pursue and thus increase the perceived value. In order to increase the benefits of the product, a determinant has to be added to the core of the product which the consumer could perceive as beneficial, advantageous or prestigious (Ravald and Grönroos, 1996).

3 METHODOLOGY

In the case of the Smart Map, embedding NFC tags to a regular paper map is an attempt to enhance the perceived value with an innovative idea, simply by adding the NFC feature to the core of the product. Small Midas NFC tags (NTAG203) with 12x19mm and 168bytes memory were used and stuck on the back of the map. Each tag was placed behind the most important POIs. A website was developed with Wordpress where the information was stored. A Samsung Nexus S was used as NFC enabled Smartphone to retrieve the relevant information as soon as the mobile was held close to one of the POIs of the map. In total of 22 POIs were NFC enabled. There were hardly any misunderstandings when it came to accessing the different information, since the tags were situated next to each other.

Fig. 1. and 2. Smart Map – NFC enabled City Map of Salzburg; Midas NFC tag

In this paper, the investigation on perceived value is conducted on the multi-dimensional model of Sweeney and Soutar (2001), called PERVAL. They stated that including various value dimensions is important, depending on the product type or service, as well as on the selection level (whether to buy/not buy, or which brand to buy). This model was chosen because it covers all the values which are essential in order to understand the perceived value of the Smart Map. The investigations focus on the functional (price and quality), social and emotional dimensions.

Emotional value is described as the customer's emotional evaluation of a certain product (Cengiz and Kirkbir, 2007). Social value is defined as the pressure from society to adopt a new technology. It contains aspects like the image in society, self-conceptualization, indication of personality and social acceptance (Pihlström, 2008). Seth et al. (1991) stated that functional value is "The primary driver for consumer choice". The values can be associated with the product's reliability, quality or price. In their research, Dodds et al. (1991) identified that the quality of a product is interrelated with its price, meaning that consumers measure quality according to its price and reconcile it with the given price. Oliver (1999) defined customer satisfaction as a "Pleasurable fulfillment. That is, the consumer senses that consumption fulfills some need, desire, goal, or so forth and that this fulfillment is pleasurable. Thus, satisfaction is the consumer's sense that consumption provides outcomes against a standard of pleasure versus displeasure". Customer satisfaction/dissatisfaction arises from the mismatch between the expectations beforehand and the actual performance. Thus, the expectations and perceptions of the performance level of a product affect customer satisfaction and dissatisfaction directly (Bolton and Drew, 1991). Williams and Soutar (2009) indicated that satisfaction is the emotional state of mind of tourists after a specific experience.

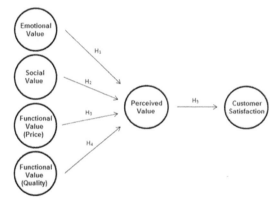

Fig. 3. The Dimensions of the Model and the 5 Hypotheses
Source: Adapted from Sweeney and Soutar (2001)

Customer Satisfaction consists of dimensions such as expectations, performance assessment and disconfirmation. However, they might differ for certain products or services (Bolton and Drew, 1991). The customer satisfaction dimension was added in order to understand whether perceived value has a positive influence on customer satisfaction. The correlation between the dimensions and the perceived value for the usage of the new NFC map were hypothesized and can be observed below.

H1: Emotional value of the Smart Map has a significant positive effect on perceived value.

H2: Social value of the Smart Map has a significant positive effect on perceived value.

H3: Functional value in terms of the price of the Smart Map has a positive effect on perceived value.

H4: Functional value in terms of the quality of the Smart Map has a significant effect on perceived value.

H5: Perceived value has a positive influence on customer satisfaction.

The research was conducted with the customers of Panorama Tours in Salzburg, Austria. The tourists were asked to take part in the research after they came back from their bus trips. The NFC enabled device was used to show the corresponding participants how the Smart Map functions. A sample of 100 people was asked in total for the purpose of this research.

4 STUDY RESULTS

Most of the participants, namely 76%, were not familiar with the NFC technology. Mostly they had even never heard about it. Half of the probands (54%) were between 20-29 years, 24% between 30-39, the rest was split up quite equally between the ages 40-49 and 50+. As the participants were tourists who booked the Sound of Music Tour, this naturally represents the quota allocation of Panorama Tours' target group.

In a first stage, the author tried to investigate on some general information which seemed to be interesting about the Smartphone usage and the Smart Map, in order to get a better feeling on the topic. The tourists had different Smartphone brands, while some of them (7%) did not have a Smartphone. Apple phone users were the majority, with 31%. As expected, Samsung (Android) phone users were second with 17%. The third brand is HTC (Android) with 4%, followed by Sony with 2%, Nokia with only 1%, and 5% owned other Smartphone brands. Another part of the research was the price of the map. The aim was to see how much people are willing to pay (in Euros) for the Smart Map in different cities. The cities have been chosen according to their prosperities in terms of population and places of interest. The list started from cities with smaller number of visitor attractions where a Smart Map might not be necessary, to big cities where it would be essential for keeping a better overview of the place. The average price the respondents were willing to pay for the Smart Map amounts to 7,22 Euros.

Table 1. Willingness to pay for a Smart Map (N=100)

	Salzburg	Zurich	London	Paris	Beijing	New York
Mean	6,75 €	6,74 €	7,59 €	7,50 €	7,31 €	7,48 €

91% of the respondents said that they were interested in further examples of NFC use, which is an important information concerning future research implications. Interesting at this point was also to investigate how the Smart Map experience changed the preference for using other types of maps when travelling. Therefore a comparison was made among the Smart Map, regular paper maps and map applications on smartphones. The results indicated a higher preference with a mean of 4,23 (on a five-point Likert scale) for the Smart Map over the paper map with 3,52. Mobile map applications with a mean of 3,19 had the lowest preference. It needs to be indicated that the regular paper map has still a higher preference than the mobile map applications, even though the highest proportion of the age ranges were young people between 20 and 29 years.

The next step was to analyse the model for perceived value. IBM SPSS AMOS 21 has been used for measuring the multidimensional structured equation model. The proposed model was applied by taking the four dimensions – quality, social, emotional, and price value – as a basis for a Confirmatory Factor Analysis (CFA). The variances and covariances have been estimated successfully. However, the index for model fit indicated that no proper fit was obtained. The smaller the RMR (Root mean square residual) is, the better fit the model indicates (Tabachnik and Fidell, 2007). The CFA value estimated for 0,044. Therefore, the value has still potential to decrease in order to show a better fit. The same situation was observed with the goodness-of-fit (GFI) index which only gives a value of 0,808. However, the mutual accepted value for GFI 0.90 or greater shows a good fitting model (Hooper et al., 2008).

Table 2. Dimensions for Perceived Value

Sweeney and Soutar, 2001	Dimensions	Evaluation Components
Dimension 1 - Quality	Quality Value	
		Map has good good quality
		Map is constructed well
		Map has an acceptable standard
		Map shows a good performance
Dimension 2 - Price	Price Value	
		Is a good return for money
		Offers good value
		Is good for the price
		Has a reasonable price
Dimension 3 - Emotional	Emotional Value	
		I enjoyed using the map
		I was excited while using the map
		I was feeling good while using the map
		I had pleasure using the map
Dimension 4 - Social	Social Value	
		Made me more acceptable by others
		Improve how perceived by others
		I made a good impression on others
		I was socially approved
	Satisfaction	
		The overall value satisfies me

Source: Adapted from Sweeney and Soutar (2001)

Hu and Bentler (1999) suggested that a value higher than 0,95 shows good fit for NFI (Normed-fit index) and CFI (Comparative Fit Index), which are the thresholds. Hence, the model shows a poor fit in regard to NFI as well, as the value is 0,833. The CFI had a value of 0,912 and is close to the threshold. However, a better fit is sought for the model. The common threshold for RMSEA for a well-fitting model is 0 for the lower level (Hooper et al., 2008) but should be less than 0.08 according to MacCallum et al. (1996). 0,7 is the threshold defined by Steiger (2007), for Hu and Bentler (1999) it is 0,6. The value 0,5 is taken as a threshold for this paper, since the model shows a better fit the closer it is to zero, and so the CFA shows an inadequate fit. The chi-square (CMIN) resulted as x^2: 219,319 and the degree of freedom (df) is 116. The division CMIN/DF, namely the chi-square divided by degree of freedom resulted with 1,891. This shows a good fit for the model due to it being lower than 2. An exploratory factor analysis (EFA) is proposed in order to meet the desired fit indexes according to the indicators. Several changes have been made on the model. A closer investigation of the standardized residual covariance's had to be made on the estimations. For achieving a perfect fit, the standardized residuals essentially require a value of less than 2 (Jöreskog and Sörbom, 1984). In this regard, the highest values of the dimensions were listed. The "enjoyment" value shows a high rate with 2,760, and also the "good impression" is over 2 with a rate of 2,214. These two factors were dropped in order to get a better model fit. However, the results indicated that the model still did not meet the required fit indexes. Moreover, the determinant "offers good value" had too low rates in many comparisons like -

1,582, -1,419, -1,931, -1,309 or -2,484, and the "constructed well" was the last determinant with too low rates. These two have been eliminated from the model. Model 1 shows the first model; model 2 shows the fit indexes after the elimination of "enjoyment" and "good impression"; and model 3 shows us the final fit indexes after dropping two more determinants. The model fit indexes show a very good fit, even though GFI is right at the border and NFI is still under the threshold. The chi-square/df and the RMR were lowered. TLI and CFI show a very good rate and the most important, RMSEA, was lowered to a perfect level for a good fit index. Now that the model shows a good fit, further data was analysed in order to measure the perceived value. Four evaluation dimensions have been taken out of the main perceived value model of Sweeney and Soutar (2001).

Table 3. and 4. Correlation Analysis

		Good Quality	Acceptable Standard	Good Performance
Good Quality	Pearson Correlation	1	,626"	,503"
	Sig. (2-tailed)		0	0
Acceptable Standard	Pearson Correlation	,626"	1	,656"
	Sig. (2-tailed)	0		0
Good Performance	Pearson Correlation	,503"	,656"	1
	Sig. (2-tailed)	0	0	

		Good Return Money	Good For Price	Reasonable Price
Good Return Money	Pearson Correlation	1	,719"	,603"
	Sig. (2-tailed)		0	0
Good For Price	Pearson Correlation	,719"	1	,795"
	Sig. (2-tailed)	0		0
Reasonable Price	Pearson Correlation	,603"	,795"	1
	Sig. (2-tailed)	0	0	

		Excited	Feel Good	Pleasure
Excited	Pearson Correlation	1	,769"	,735"
	Sig. (2-tailed)		,000	,000
Feel Good	Pearson Correlation	,769"	1	,836"
	Sig. (2-tailed)	,000		,000
Pleasure	Pearson Correlation	,735"	,836"	1
	Sig. (2-tailed)	,000	,000	

		Made Acceptable	Improve How Perceived	Socially Approved
Made Acceptable	Pearson Correlation	1	,784"	,630"
	Sig. (2-tailed)		,000	,000
Improve How Perceived	Pearson Correlation	,784"	1	,744"
	Sig. (2-tailed)	,000		,000
Socially Approved	Pearson Correlation	,630"	,744"	1
	Sig. (2-tailed)	,000	,000	

**. Correlation is significant at the 0.01 level (2-tailed). N = 100

Additionally, the overall value of the map, namely the customer satisfaction, was added to the model. After the exploratory factor analysis, the model with the four values and three evaluated dimensions each it was possible to obtain the weighted mean values, namely the factor loadings. With this model, which was obtained after the exploratory factor analysis, the hypotheses will be tested (Moliner et al., 2006). A correlation analysis was conducted via SPSS between the evaluated dimensions within each value in order to identify any negative or positive correlation among the dimensions, which would result in a significant effect on perceived value, so basically every dimension was correlated with the other dimensions in the same value determinant of the model. All dimensions correlated positively with each other on a 0,01 significance level.

Table 5 displays the means of each dimension as well as the factor loadings and the standard deviations. The means resulted very high considering the scale from 1 to 5, and the standard deviations are very low. The quality and emotional value display a higher value than the price and social value. The "good quality" and the "good performance" dimensions rank highest with a mean of 4,41 whereas the "improved how perceived" shows the lowest rate with a mean of 3,27.

Table 5. Factor Loadings and Standard Deviations

Evaluated Dimension	Mean	Factor Loadings	Standard Deviation
Quality Value		0,756	
Good Quality	4,41	0,726	0,534
Acceptable Standard	4,28	0,852	0,621
Good Performance	4,41	0,787	0,534
Price Value		0,627	
Good Return on Money	4,02	0,742	0,681
Good for Price	3,96	0,97	0,724
Reasonable Price	3,95	0,819	0,716
Emotional Value		0,733	
Excited	4,32	0,815	0,737
Feeling Good	4,12	0,948	0,769
Pleasure	4,1	0,884	0,798
Social Value		0,557	
Made Acceptable	3,31	0,835	0,971
Improved how Perceived	3,27	0,935	0,897
Socially Approved	3,48	0,789	0,893
Overall Value	4,26	0,561	0,613

The last step for testing the hypotheses was examining the beta values. In order to retrieve the beta and t values (t values acceptable when greater than 2 or less than -2), a regression analysis was conducted by taking the three dimensions of each value as independent variables and the mean of the value of the three dimensions as the dependent variable. The results can be observed on table 6. Important here are the Beta values of each dimension. When the dimension increases by one, the value will increase by the amount of the Beta Ceteris Paribus.

By extracting the Beta values for each dimension, the significant effects on the values can be observed. "Good quality" (ß=0,27, t=5,96), "acceptable standard" (ß=0,48, t=9,09) and the "good performance" (ß=0,31, t=6,60) dimensions have a positive effect on quality value. "Good return money" (ß=0,15, t=3,97) has a rather low but still positive effect on price value, whereas "good for price" (ß=0,53, t=10,27) and "reasonable price" (ß=0,36, t=8,08) have a positive effect as well. "Excited" (ß=0,32, t=7,54), "feel good" (ß=0,35, t=6,80) and "pleasure" (ß=0.36, t=7,30) have a positive effect on the emotional value. The dimensions "Made acceptable" (ß=037, t=8,24), "improve how perceived" (ß=0,39, t=7,35) and the "socially approved" (ß=0,29, t=6,92) have a positive effect on the social value.

Table 6. Factor Loadings and Standard Deviations

Value	Dimension	Standardized Coefficients Beta	t	Sig.*
Quality		0,21	3,472	0,001
	Good quality	0,27	5,962	0,00
	Acceptable standard	0,48	9,095	0,00
	Good performance	0,31	6,609	0,00
Price		0,31	5,295	0,00
	Good return money	0,15	3,973	0,00
	Good for price	0,53	10,272	0,00
	Reasonable price	0,36	8,081	0,00
Emotional		0,31	5,252	0,00
	Excited	0,32	7,548	0,00
	Feel good	0,35	6,801	0,00
	Pleasure	0,36	7,306	0,00
Social		0,36	6,351	0,00
	Made acceptable	0,37	8,242	0,00
	Improve how perceive	0,39	7,357	0,00
	Socially approved	0,29	6,926	0,00

*Correlation is significant at the 0.01 level (2-tailed) N=100

The next step was to analyse the standardized coefficients for each value by conducting the regression analysis, where the perceived value was taken as a dependent variable. The results can be investigated on table 6 again. If we take a look at the results, quality (ß=0,21, t=3,47, H4), price (ß=0,31, t=5,29, H3), emotional (ß=0,31, t=5,25, H1) and social (ß=0,36, t=6,35, H2) value have all a positive significant effect on perceived value. The first four hypotheses were herewith supported.

Hypothesis1: Emotional Value   →   Perceived Value (Supported)

Hypothesis2: Social Value   →   Perceived Value (Supported)

Hypothesis3: Price Value   →   Perceived Value (Supported)

Hypothesis4: Quality Value   →   Perceived Value (Supported)

The same regression analysis was conducted with perceived value and customer satisfaction where customer satisfaction was set as the dependent variable. The results indicated a beta value of 0,525 (t=6,10, Sig.: 0,00) with a correlation significant at the 0,01 level and a positive significant influence of the perceived value on customer satisfaction, namely the "overall value". The last hypothesis was supported as well.

Hypothesis5: Perceived Value   →   Customer Satisfaction (Supported)

5 CONCLUSION

This study provides a deeper insight into a new NFC technology use case in the tourism industry and its perceived value by the customers. The Smart Map is a good example of an innovative idea, connecting ubiquitous ICT and tourism. The results of the measured perceived value demonstrate its salient potential. For most of the respondents, NFC technology was a very new experience. The first experience with NFC was quite fascinating for them and so the Smart Map was perceived with a very high value. The value was even high enough to change their perception and influence their future choice of mobile phones. Also the price people would be willing to pay for the Smart Map has a surprisingly high mean, with around six to seven Euros. The results showed that the quality and emotional value are higher than the price and social value. Since no price range was given to the tourists, the price value was rather low and the social value was rather low due to other people not seeing the product, which would make them look better or create a better reputation or social approval for them. The quality value was high because of the good construction and the fact that it still looks like a regular paper map despite its NFC features. This also influenced the emotional value, because the technological features added a great value to the map. The value concepts provide the opportunity for retail strategists to investigate all necessary dimensions, initially approaching an appropriate market (Sweeney and Soutar, 2001). Lateral analysis between perceived value and customer satisfaction displayed a positive influence. Henceforward the configured model can be implemented for investigations on customer satisfaction after measuring the perceived value of a certain product. The Smart Map, which was developed by the author, resulted in a high customer satisfaction and has the potential to spread within the current tourism market by creating high value in terms of quality, price, emotional and social values.

Unreliable responses concerning the questionnaire could have been made. In particular, this is relevant in the context of tourism, where the respondents are on vacation and do not want to be disturbed in their experience by filling out a questionnaire. That is why some responses might deviate from the perceptions of the tourists (Williams and Soutar, 2009) and provide misleading results. The tourists had only a rather short time at their disposal to experience the Smart Map and could not move around with it. Prolonged testing time could have led to deeper insight into the subject and the experience would have been more intense. Moreover, the Smart Map needs to be tested in different cities in order to understand the necessity of such a map in other places as well. In addition, almost every participant was interested in further instances of NFC use, which indicates the importance of future research in this field.

REFERENCES

Bolton, R., N. and Drew, J., H., 1991. "A Multi-Stage Model of Customers' Assessments of Service Quality and Value". Journal of Consumer Research, 17 (4), pp. 375-384.

Bortenschlager, M., Häusler, E., Schwaiger, W., Egger, R., and Jooss, M., 2010. Evaluation of the concept of early acceptance tests for touristic mobile applications. Information and Communication Technologies in Tourism 2010, pp. 149-158.

Buhalis, D. and Egger, R., 2006. Informations-und Kommunikationstechnologien als Mittel zur Prozess-und Produktinnovation für den Unternehmer. In: Pikkemaat, B. and Peters, M. (Eds.) Innovationen im Tourismus. ESV-Verlag, pp. 163-176.

Buhalis, D. and Law, R., 2008. Progress in information technology and tourism management: 20 years on and 10 years after the Internet — The state of eTourism research. Journal of Tourism Management, 29 (4), pp. 609–623.

Canadi, M., Höpken, W. and Fuchs, M., 2010. Application of QR Codes in Online Travel Distribution. In: Proceedings of the International Conference on Information and Communication Technologies in Tourism, Lugano, Switzerland, February 10-12, pp. 137-148.

Cengiz, E. and Kirkbir, F., 2007. Customer perceived value: The development of a multiple item scale in hospitals. Problems and Perspectives in Management, 5 (3), pp. 252-267.

Coskun, V., Ok, K. and Ozdenizci, B., 2012. Near Field Communication – From Theory to Practice. 1st ed. West Sussex, UK: John Wiley & Sons Ltd.

Delikostidis, I. and Elzakker, C., P., J., M., 2009. Geo - identification and pedestrian navigation with geo - mobile applications : how do users proceed?. In: Location based services and Telecartography II: From sensor fusion to context models: 5th International Conference on Location Based Services and TeleCartography, 2008, Salzburg, pp. 185-206.

Dodds,W., B., Monroe, K., B. and Grewal, D., 1991. Effects of Price, Brand, and Store Information on Buyers' Product Evaluations. Journal of Marketing Research 28 (3), pp. 307-319.

Egger, R. and Buhalis, D., 2008. eTourism Case Studies: Management and Marketing issues in eTourism. Butterworth Heinemann.

Egger, R. and Jooss, M., 2010. Die Zukunft im mTourism–Ausblick auf Technologie-und Dienstentwicklung. In: mTourism – mobile Dienste im Tourismus. Gabler, pp. 11-25.

Egger, R., 2013. The impact of Near Field Communication on Tourism. Journal of Hospitality and Tourism Technology, 4(2), 119-133.

Gartner, G., 2009. Location Based Services and TeleCartography II – From Sensor Fusion to Context Models. Berlin: Springer-Verlag.

Hooper, D., Coughlan, J. and Mullen, M. R., 2008. Structural Equation Modelling: Guidelines for Determining Model Fit. Electronic Journal of Business Research Methods, 6 (1), pp. 53-60.

Hu, L.T. and Bentler, P.M., 1999. Cutoff Criteria for Fit Indexes in Covariance Structure Analysis: Conventional Criteria Versus New Alternatives. Structural Equation Modeling, 6 (1), pp. 1-55.

Jaraba, F., B., Ruiz, I., L. and Nieto, M., A., G., 2010. A NFC-based pervasive solution for city touristic surfing. Journal of Personal and Ubiquitous Computing, 15 (7), pp. 731-742.

Jöreskog, K. and Sörbom, D., 1984. Lisrel – 6 User's guide, 3th Edition, Mooresville.

Kim, D., Park, J., Morrison, A., M., 2008. A Model of Traveller Acceptance of Mobile Technology. International Journal of Tourism Research, 10 (5), pp. 393-407.

Langelund, S., 2007. Mobile Travel. Journal of Tourism and Hospitality Research, 7 (3/4), pp. 284-286.

MacCallum, R.C., Browne, M.W., and Sugawara, H., M., 1996. Power Analysis and Determination of Sample Size for Covariance Structure Modeling. Psychological Methods, 1 (2), pp. 130-49.

Madlmayr, G. and Scharinger, J., 2010, Neue Dimensionen von mobile Tourismusanwendungen durch Near Field Communication Technologie. In Egger, R. and Jooss, M. (Eds) mTourism – mobile Dienste im Tourismus, Gabler, pp. 75-88.

Miraz, M., G., Ruiz, I., R. and Nieto, M., A., G., 2009. University of Things: Application of Near Field Communication Technology in University Environments. Journal of E-working, 3 (1), pp. 52-64.

Moliner, M., A., Sanchez, J., Rodriguez, R., M. and Callarisa, L., 2006. Relationship quality with a travel agency: The influence of the postpurchase perceived value of a tourism package. Journal of Tourism and Hospitality Research, 7(3/4), pp. 194–211.

Ok, K., Aydin, M., N., Coskun, V. and Ozdenizci, B., 2011. Exploring Underlying Values of NFC Applications. In: Proceedings of the 3rd International Conference on Information and Financial Engineering, ICMTA 2010, Singapore, Singapore, pp. 10-12.

Oliver, R. L., 1999. Whence consumer loyalty? Journal of Marketing, 63, pp. 33-44.

Ozdenizci, B., Aydin, M.N., Coskun, V. And Ok, K., 2010. NFC Research Framework: A Literature Review and Future Research Directions. In: Proceedings of the 14th IBIMA Conference on Global Business Transformation through Innovation and Knowledge Management, Istanbul, Turkey, 23-24 June, pp. pp. 2672-2685.

Pesonen, J. and Horster, E., 2012. Near Field Communication technology in Tourism. Tourism Management Perspectives, 4, pp. 11-18.

Pihlström, M., 2008. Perceived value of mobile service use and its consequences. Helsinki: Edita Prima Ltd.

Ravald, A. and Grönroos, C., 1996. The Value Concept and Relationship Marketing. European Journal of Marketing, 30 (2), pp. 19-30.

Ronay, E. and Egger, R., 2014. NFC Smart City: Cities of the Future—A Scenario Technique Application. In: Xiang, Z., and Tussyadiah, I. (Eds.), 2014. Information and Communication Technologies in Tourism Dublin, Ireland, January 21-24, 2014, pp. 565-577, Springer International Publishing.

Ruiz-Molina, M. and Gil-Saura, I., 2008. Perceived value, customer attitude and loyalty in retailing. Journal of Retail and Leisure Property, 7 (4), pp. 305-314.

Ryan, C., and Rao, U., 2008. Holiday users of the Internet—ease of use, functionality and novelty. International Journal of Tourism Research, 10(4), pp. 329-339.

Sawng, Y.-W., Kim, S.-H., Lee, J. and Oh, Y. S., 2011. Mobile service usage behavior in Korea: an empirical study on consumer acceptance of innovative technologies. Journal of Technological and Economic Development of Economy, 17 (1), pp. 151–173.

Sheth, J., N., Newman, B., I. and Gross, B., L., 1991. Why We Buy What We Buy: A Theory of Consumption Values. Journal of Business Research, 22 (2), pp. 159-170.

Steiger, J.H., 2007. Understanding the limitations of global fit assessment in structural equation modeling. Personality and Individual Differences, 42 (5), pp. 893-988.

Sweeney, J., C. and Soutar, G., N., 2001. Consumer perceived value: The development of a multiple item scale. Journal of Retailing, 77 (2), pp. 203–220

Tabachnick, B., G. and Fidell, L., S., 2007. Using Multivariate Statistics. 5th edition, New York, Allyn and Bacon.

Wang, Y., S., Lin, H., H., Luarn, P., 2006. Predicting consumer intention to use mobile service. Journal of Info Systems, 16 (2), pp. 157-179.

Want, R., Fishkin, K., P., Gujar, A. and Harrison, B., L., 1999. Bridging Physical and Virtual Worlds with Electronic Tags. In: CHI '99 Proceedings of the SIGCHI conference on Human factors in computing systems: the CHI is the limit, New York, pp. 370-377.

Williams, P. and Soutar, G., N., 2009. Value Satisfaction and Behavioral Intentions in an Adventure Tourism Context. Annals of Tourism Research, 36 (3), pp. 413-438.

Woodruff, R., B., 1997. Customer Value: The next source for competitive advantage. Journal of the academy of marketing science, 25(2), pp. 139-153

Zeithaml, V., A., 1988. Consumer Perceptions of Price, Quality, and Value: A Means-End Model and Synthesis of Evidence. Journal of Marketing, 52 (3), pp. 2-22.

The Use of Smart Technology in Tourism: Evidence from Wearable Devices

Roland Atembe, and

Feisal Abdalla

Salzburg University of Applied Science, Austria
ratembe.imte-m2012@fh-salzburg.ac.at

Abstract

The development of wearable personal technology *"Google Glass"* has triggered several speculations about its impact on tourism. Thus, exploring its usage in the tourism industry is of paramount importance. The objectives of this research are to understand the valued wearable device has created, and to conceptualize a framework for using *Google Glass* as smart technology. The essay aims at providing an insight of the influence of *google glass* on tourists' behavior. It also seeks to contribute to the literature of wearable devices and tourism. The study employs qualitative approach with data triangulation which includes a text content analysis and a focus group interview.

Keywords: Wearable Device; Google Glass; Tourism; Technology

1 INTRODUCTION

Information and communication technologies (ICTs) have substantially influenced the tourism industry, and they continue to serve as the main driver for tourism innovations. We see evidence in literature that ICTs have drastically transformed the way tourism products are developed, presented and offered (Buhalis, 2003; Buhalis and Law, 2008). The technological influence in the tourism industry does not only impact the suppliers, but also the consumers. Central to the entire discipline of ICTs usage in tourism is that the furtherance of ICTs has specifically denoted changes in tourists' behavior. The great success of ICTs is influencing tourists' attitude towards mobile applications thereby increasing users experience (Compuware, 2012). Indeed, the wide scope involvement of ICTs in tourism has triggered significant discussions between scholars. It is believed that the transformation of best operations and strategic practices in the tourism industry emerges as a result of internet (Buhalis and Law, 2008). Perhaps, this is because internet facilitates access of information to every corner of the globe. It is inevitable to admit that the use of ICTs in tourism is an important component in the supply chain (Tourism Embassy, 2013).

Evidence points out that, ICTs create more accessibility and enjoyment for both residents and tourists through interactive service and interconnectivity (Buhalis and Amaranggana, 2014). One other view is that we live in a *"smart world"* in which its landscape works in a permanent process of evolution and getting friendly (Blanco, 2011). The employment of ICTs is providing clearer solutions which are serving towards reduction of spending time and money; on the other hand triggers new tourists' reactions (Tourism Embassy, 2013; Apichai, 2011).

The world continues to go digital with numerous forms of ICTs, which are being developed on the daily basis. These ICTs have powerful operating systems such as iOS5, Android and many more, which are standard features of modern mobile phones. Indeed, with access to mobile web or "apps" multitudes of new circumstances will probably be created (Egger, 2012). For instance, wireless and mobile technologies such as smart phones, notebooks and tablets have had a large influence on tourists' behavior in the recent years. These technologies allow tourists to perform mobile social web activities hence creating a new way of life (Fesenmaier et al., 2000; Ye, and Tussyadiah, 2011; Kook Lee and Mills, 2010; Luz, Anacleto, and Almeida, 2010; Tourism Review, 2014; (Tussyadiah and Fesenmaier, 2009; Wang et al, 2012); and also smoothen the creation of significant personalized experiences (Neuhofer, Buhalis, and Ladkin, 2015).

2 BACKGROUND

The developments in the field of ICTs have led to an increased interest in its application and impact on tourism. The changes experienced in the tourism industry over the past decade remain unprecedented. This is because new era of ICTs has uncovered a wealth of new tools for the tourism sector. Other observers have already drawn attention to the impacts of ICTs on tourists' behavior. In fact, ICTs development has influence and leads to a greater personalization, adjustments and interaction between tourists and entities in tourism (Mihajlovic, 2014). At the present time, tourism industry is confronted with a set of new challenges resulting from changes in consumers' attitudes and the environment which is influenced by the emerging technologies (Buhalis and Amaranggana, 2014). Tourists make choices from the variety of available options empowered by ICTs. Moreover, it is believed that ICTs serves tourists conveniently during pre-trip as well as on the trip (Mihajlovic, 2014). Indeed, technology devices are getting smaller and they come inform of smartphone, notebooks, tablets computers, and also inform of wearable devices such as smart glasses, smart watches, and smart clothing. These devices are online web accessible, and increasingly interconnected (Wang, Park and Fesenmaier, 2012; Tussyadiah, 2013; Tussyadiah and Wang, 2014; Tussyadiah, 2014). As with many technologies that have come before, wearable devices present incredible opportunities for improving accessibility for tourists.

The wearable devices are anticipated to have a significant effect on people's interaction with surroundings (Tate, 2012). Furthermore, there is an increasing concern that this new technologies have the potentials to drastically transform tourists' behavior due to the perceived new ways of interaction with the technologies (Cortland, 2013; Steele, 2014; Tussyadiah, 2014).

Nevertheless, Tussyadiah (2014) explored the potential use of wearable computing devices for travel and tourism; and identified five patterns which include exploration, adventure tourism, travel documentation, travel reporting, and positive transformation. However, there is a need for more studies to apprehend the findings. Indeed, no research has been found that explore the actual usages wearable devices in tourism. This paper attempt to explore the usage of *Google Glass* in Tourism, it value created, as well as conceptualizing a framework for using *Google Glass* as smart technology.

3 RESEARCH PURPOSE

This essay critically examines how wearable devices will change the tourists' behavior. The specific objective of the paper is: a) to understand the use of *Google Glass* for travel purposes; b) to conceptualize a framework for using *Google Glass* as smart technology; c) to evaluate and validate the value that can be created by using *Google Glass* for tourism purposes.

4 LITERATURE REVIEW

4.1 Google Glass

According to Egger (2012) infrared, Bluetooth, or WLAN transmission technologies are the main catalysts for mobile interaction with the environment. The portable hand free wearable device *"Google Glass"* imbues augmented reality features. The glass is designed in the form of spectacles and it has a tiny computer screen and camera build into one corner of the frames (Casey, 2013; Google Inc., 2014). The smart glass illustration in fig 1 depicts that the glass has four main categories to control input and output of human –computer interaction. These include the visual based, audio based, sensor based and the touch based (Dodge, and Kitchin, 2011).

The device is compatible to a smart phone that has Android version 4.3.0 (ice cream sandwich) or with an apple phones with 'IOS7' software (Lendino, 2014). With the aid of this software an application called "my glass" can be installed. This app set-up facilitated by internet and blue tooth connection enables the running and functionality of Google Glass.

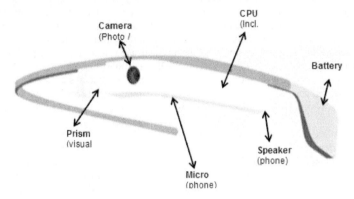

Fig. 1. Features of Google glass
Source: Authors, (2015).

Google Glass has a processor of TI OMAP 4430 1GB RAM, 802.11 b/g WIFI, GPS, and a capacity of 16 GB of internal storage as well as 12.5GB free for the user (Lendino, 2014; Google Inc., 2014). The usage of *Google Glass* is done by voice commands, head tilts, taping the touch pad on the side or head lifts. When this is done the glass activates its different functionalities such as pictures shooting, video streaming, message sending, getting directions, sharing pictures etc (Lendino, 2014). The first version of the device was manufactured in the summer of 2011 and subsequently, it was presented to the public for the first time on 5th April 2012. Since then, the device is undergoing software updates. The most current version of the Glass is the XE-C with double amount of RAM and other upgrades. Since then, Google Inc. continues to add more applications to the glassware (Widmer and Muller, 2014).

The Google Glass has several distinct applications which have different input methods such as voice commands, touchpad, taking pictures, recording videos (Almanac, 2013). The notion is that Google Glass assist people to experience technology without it interference on their beloved activities (Jordan, 2013). The Glass provides the possibility to capture extreme moments of adventure that would normally not be easy to capture using different devices like cameras or smart phones (Steve, 2012). In addition, Google Glass gives users the possibility to post status updates, share images, videos on social media such as Google plus, Face book and Twitter. In addition, Glass users obtain timely notifications as well as direct messages (Widmer and Muller, 2014). It is considered to be significant for the dissemination of helpful information to users about their surroundings). However, this functionality of *Google Glass* is closely related to location based services (Almanac, 2013).

4.2 Application of Google Glass in Tourism

As the demands of consumers are currently increasing, many companies are constantly striving for new strategies to satisfy their customers. Perhaps this is because customer satisfaction is the core determinant for the success of every business. The tourism industry is a service intense sector thus; tourism related companies are always employing new strategies to meet the needs and demands of the tourists (Safak et al., 2003). The convergence of personal technologies and internet connectivity enables tourists to consume media content universally at whatever chosen times (Schanke Sundet, 2012). In this light, tourism practitioners are constantly employing the use of ICT's to their advantage. Indeed, evidence can be seen from the use cases of wearable technology "*Google Glass*" being applied in travel and tourism.

Use Case - Air Travel: The nature of air travel industry is associated with high level of processes between passengers and the airlines (Egger, 2012). In order to cope with these challenges the airlines companies are required to adopt alternative approaches to manage the traffic flow of their customers. Several use cases of *Google Glass* in the aviation sector has been noticed within it explorer programme. The Virgin Atlantic airlines staff at Heathrow Airport, London, has used the Google Glass to provide the best of service to their customers in early 2014. The Glass enables Virgin Atlantic Airlines to offer timely information regarding local weather and language translations to their customers (Suleman, 2014; Clark, 2014).

Similarly, Copenhagen Airport has also adopted the use of *Google Glass* for it operations. The wearable device helps passengers' questions relating to their airport journey, reducing passenger queue up at the customer service desk. Indeed, the smart glass also enables the reporting of common use of the airport facilities. For instance the glass is used to document the state of the departure gate area via photos and videos after the use of every airline's staff. Thus it facilitates accountability of untidy work stations at the airport (Ghee, 2015). Furthermore the Copenhagen airport staffs' reports that use of *Google Glass* enabled them to reduce paper work, increase efficiency in language translations. It also provides availing information such as gates, baggage and flight to customers. The use of *Google Glass* at airports eases stress of travelers, provides information about flight running late, traffic delays on the way to the airport, location of luggages and check-in gates (Travel Mail Reporter, 2014).

Another use case of *Google Glass* within the aviation sector can be exemplified in Spring Airline. A Chinese based low cost carrier (Spring Airline) is the first to use glass onboard to improve customer services. The airlines flights attendants are empowered with *Google Glass* to help them identify specific passengers who had placed orders for food and beverages. Furthermore, the Edinburgh Airport is reported to be the second UK airport to embrace wearable technology. The Glass facilitates and provides passengers with real time flight information, translate foreign language documents and to response to general questions about the airport (Future Travel Experience, 2014). Several great benefits offered by *Google Glass* have been identified by the airlines and airports and there is more potential usage in other areas such as operations, customer services, security and immigration in the air transport industry (Ghee, 2015).

Use Case - Lodging Services: The hospitality industry is another sector adopting and making use of the *Google Glass*. The Starwood hotel chain pilot programme that was initially introduced to allow guest to swap physical key for virtual keys facilitating guest to use their smartphones has been flash forward. Starwood hotels have implemented the Starwood Preferred Guest (SPG) app for Google Glass (Nelson, 2014). Starwood hotel's SPG app empowers guest to get directions to the hotel, explore and share image of the hotel with friends. In addition, guests are able to access their room reservations, star point balances, and upcoming events (Moscaritolo, 2014).

Other examples of use case of *Google Glass* in the hospitality industry can be seen in ACME Hotel. Travelers who are curious about *Google Glass* have the possibility to experiment it at the hotel. The guests are given the opportunity to rent *Google Glass* complementarily for duration of three (3) hours to explore their surroundings (Coyle, 2014).

Potential Use of Google Glass – Consumers

As with other portable devices, Google Glass can elucidate tourist experiences. It can enable tourists through the provision and limitation of access to experiences. In fact, as Fowler (2015) noted, personal technologies are intermediaries between the users and artefacts. Technologies appear in humans and the world and it changes human experiences (Ihde, 1990). Based on the multiplicity of apps and features in *Google Glass* that allows the possibility for tourists to experience technology without its interference on their beloved activities (Jordan, 2013), it is reasonable enough to consider that the Glass can be used for tourism experiences. These includes cognitive activities such exploring environments, retrieve information, take pictures and videos and share their overall experiences at a destination.

5 CONCEPTUAL DEVELOPMENT

Previous researchers have found that personal technologies such as notebook, tablets and smartphones plays a significant role in tourists experiences (Tussyadiah and Fesenmaier, 2007; Wang, Park and Fesenmaier, 2012; Tussyadiah, 2013; Tussyadiah and Wang, 2014). This is conceivable because currently, personal technologies are associated with one's everyday life (Gretzel and Jamal, 2009; Wang, Xiang and Fesenmaier, 2014).

This essay is set into the context of wearable device. It seeks to understand the specific activities performed by tourist using the *Google Glass*. The paper strives to conceptualize a framework for using *Google Glass* as smart technology, and to understand how wearable devices will change the tourists' behavior. Nevertheless, Tussyadiah (2014) study concluded that the distinct features and functionalities on wearable technology triggers the shift from tourists to explorers, an explosion of first person visual travel narratives, and more social travel supported by real time connectivity. This provides the underlying rationale for this study to advance the theoretical framework of the usage of *Google glass* for tourism related purposes. Building on this rationale, this study aims at contributing to literature of wearable devices and tourism.

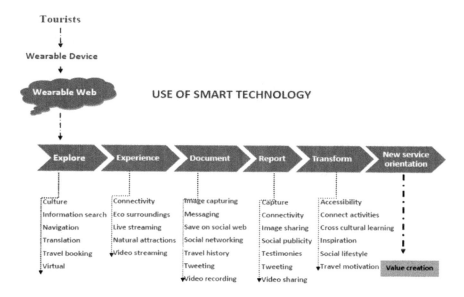

Fig. 2. Conceptualizing the Use Google Glass in Tourism
Source: Adapted and modified from Tussyadiah (2014).

6 PROPOSED METHOD

This is an ongoing research with two phases of data collection planned. In order to explore the usage of smart technology in tourism, qualitative approach is adopted using internet research strategy. Internet research involves how people use and access the internet through the collection of data, observations of activities, participation on social networks sites, websites, blogs, games, virtual worlds as well as other online environments and contexts (Bryman and Bell, 2011; Markham and Buchana, 2012). As such, in order to enhance confidence in the findings data triangulation is employed. Triangulation is the use of more than one approach to the investigation of a research question (Bryman, n.d).

A text based content analysis will be conducted on *Google Glass* explorers' blogs, group of Google Project Glass, Tnooz and Google Almanac. The blogs will be selected by tracking travel blogs where users share their experience of Google Glass. Based on the results of the content analysis various themes will be developed. After that, a snow ball sampling technique will be used to trace and contact users to conduct a focus group interview to gather data from those explorers who have actually used *Google Glass*. The purpose of the interview is to validate the findings.

A significant consideration in every research is selection bias. In research projects, selection bias occurs at the stage of recruitment of participants or during the process of retaining them in a research (Herna, Ndez-Diz and Robins, 2004). Thus, in order to avoid selection bias some screening question will be adopted to ensure the eligibility of the respondents: Have you ever used *Google Glass*? This will assist in making sure that only those participants that have actually used the *Google Glass* are included in the interview. Thus eliminating those that are not qualified for the study

The expected outcome of this research is that the use of smart technology specifically *Google Glass,* for travel purposes will be confirmed. In addition, the specific activities that tourists perform with *Google Glass* during travel and how valuable these activities are to the tourists will also be outlined. The results of the study should inform tourism practitioners about any changes in the tourists' behavior. Hence, they should adopt new strategies to cope with the demand.

Furthermore, it is expected that the outcome of this study will also contribute to the literature on tourists and smart technology. Based on that, tourism practitioners and academics could adopt the recommendations as basis to understand the implications of wearable technologies in the tourism industry.

REFERENCES

Apichai, S. (2011). How technology is changing global tourism. In World Tourism Organization Affiliate Members AM-reports – Technology in Tourism Vol. 1, (2011)

Bryman, A. (n.d). Triangulation. Department of social sciences Loughborough University Leicestershire

Blanco, J. (2011).Understanding and managing innovation and technological change: a major opportunity for tourism organizations. In World Tourism Organization Affiliate Members AM-reports – Technology in Tourism (Vol. 1, 2011)

Buhalis, D. & Law, R. (2008). Progress in information technology and tourism management: 20 years on and 10 years after the Internet The state of eTourism research. Tourism Management, 29(4), 609– 623.

Bryman, A. & Bell, E. (2011). Business Research Methods. 3rd ed. California: UK.Oxford University Press.

Buhalis, D. (2003). eTourism: Information technology for strategic tourism management. Pearson Time / Prentice-Hall

Buhalis, D. & Amaranggana, A. (2014). Smart Tourism Destination. In Z. Xiang and I. Tussyadiah (eds.), Information and Communication Technologies in Tourism 2014. Springer International Publishing Switzerland

Compuware (2012) Mobile Apps. What Consumers Really Need and Want. A Global Study of Consumer's Expectations and Experiences of Mobile Applications.

Clark, N. (2014). Airlines Use Digital Technology to Get Even More Personal. Available from: http://www.nytimes.com . [Accessed 11th January, 2015]

Coyle, P. (2014). Cities, Hotels, Destinations Eye Google Glass to Promote Tourism. Available from:http://livability.com/cities-hotels-destinations-eye-google-glass-promote-tourism. [Accessed 18th, 2014]

Cortland .S. (2013). Google Glasses. Available from: https://sites.google.com/a/cortland.edu/google-glasses/disadvantages. [Accessed 3rd February, 2015]

Dodge, M. & Kitchin, R. (2011). Code and space: Software and Everyday Life. MIT Press. Cambridge MA

Egger, R. (2012). The Impact of Near Field Communication on Tourism. Journal of Hospitality and Tourism Technology Vol. 4 No. 2, 2013 pp. 119-133

Fesenmaier, D., et al., Eds. (2000): Information and communication technologies in tourism, Springer.

Gretzel, U. & Jamal, T. (2009). Conceptualizing the Creative Tourist Class: Technology, Mobility, and Tourism Experiences, Tourism Analysis, 14 (4) 471 - 481

Ghee, R. (2015). Google Glass still has huge potential for Airlines and Airports Despite Google Ending sales of the product. - See – report Future Travel Experience

Green, N. (2002). On the Move: Technology, Mobility, and the Mediation of Social Time and Space. The Information Society, 18(4), 281–292

Glass Almanac. (2013). The History of Google Glass. Available from: http://glassalmanac.com/history-google-glass/5/. [Accessed 1st February, 2015]

Fowler, A. G. (2015). Sling TV: A Giant Step from Cable. The Wall Street Journal

Herna, A. M., Herna Ndez-Diz, S. & Robins, M. J. (2004). A Structural Approach to Selection Bias.Epidemiology. Vol 15, no 5

Ihde, D. (1990). Technology and the Lifeworld: from Garden to Earth. Bloomington, In: Indiana University press

Jordan, T. (2013).Google I/O 2013: Developing for Glass. Available from: https://www.youtube.com/watch?v=UK8Ho4p3bZc . [Accessed 19th January, 2015]

Kook Lee, J. Mills, E. J. (2010). Exploring Tourist Satisfaction with Mobile Experience Technology. International Management Review, Vol. 6 No. 1 2010

Lis, P.T. (2008). Destination Visual Image and Expectation of Experiences. Journal of Travel & Tourism Marketing 02/2011; 28:129-144

Luz, N. Anacleto, R., & Almeida, A. (2010). Tourism Mobile and Recommendation Systems - A State of the Art. International Conference on E-Learning, E-Business, Enterprise Information Systems, & E-Government. Las Vegas Nevada.

Lendino, J. (2013). Google Glass: Everything You need to Know. Available from: http://www.pcmag.com/article2/0,2817,2416488,00.asp. [Accessed 18th, 2014]

Markham, A. & Buchana, E. (2012). Ethical Decision-Making and Internet Research. See - Association of Internet Researchers

Mihajlovic, I. (2014). ICT and New Trends in Consumer behavior – new experiential Knowledge, Opportunities or challenges for Intermediaries. Journal of marketing management march 2014, Vol. 2, No. 1, pp. 43-64

Moscaritolo, A. (2014). Use Google Glass App to Book Starwood Hotel Rooms. Available from: http://www.pcmag.com. [Accessed 23th November, 2014]

Nelson, R. (2014). Starwood hotels Welcomes Google Glass with SPG Glassware. Available from: http://androidcommunity.com/starwood-hotels-welcome-google-glass-with-spg-glassware-20140416. [Accessed 29 January, 2015]

Neuhofer,B., Buhalis, D., and Ladkin, A. (2015). Smart Technologies for personalized experience: a case study in the hospitality domain. Electron Markets

Suleman, K. (2014).Virgin Atlantic Hails Google Glass Trial a Success. Available from: http://www.itpro.co.uk/mobile/22098/virgin-atlantic-hails-google-glass-trial-a-success. [Accessed October, 14th 2014]

Safak, I. Allison, M.A. Sheremet, A. (2013). Floc Variability under changing Turbulent Stresses and Sediment Availability on a Wave Energetic Muddy Shelf. Continent Shelf Research 53, 1-10

Schanke Sundet, V. (2012). Making Sense of Mobile Media: Institutional Working Notions, Strategies and Actions in convergent Media markets. PHD. University of Oslo

Steve, M. (2012). Eye am a camera: Surveillance and sousveillance in the glassage. Time Magazine 2

Steele. C. (2014). Should You Buy Google Glass. Available from: http://www.pcmag.com/article2/0,2817,2456442,00.asp [Accessed November, 26th 2014]

Travel Mail Reporter (2014). Flying into the future: Copenhagen becomes first airport to trail staff use of Google Glass. Available from: http://www.dailymail.co.uk

Tussyadiah, I. (2014). Expectation of Travel Experiences with Wearable Computing Devices. In Xiang, Z., Tussyadiah, I. (Eds.), Information and Communication Technologies in Tourism 2014 (pp. 539-552). Switzerland: Springer International Publishing

Tussyadiah, I.P. (2014). Toward a Theoretical Foundation for Experience Design in Tourism. Journal of Travel Research, 53 (5), 543-564

Tussyadiah, I. P., Wang, D. (2014). Tourists Attitudes towards proactive Smartphone Systems. Journal of Travel Research

Tussyadiah, I. (2013). When Cell Phones Become Travel Buddies: Social Attribution to Mobile Phones in Travel. In Cantoni, L., Xiang, Z. (Eds.), Information and Communication Technologies in Tourism 2013. Berlin- Heidelberg: Springer – Verlag

Tourism-Review. (2014). Mobile Travel Consumers' Trends. Available from: http://www.tourism-review.com/mobile-travel-consumers-trends-news4124. [Accessed 16th December, 2014]

Tourism Embassy. (2013).The Use of New technologies in the tourism industry. Available from http://tourismembassy.com/en/blog/tourism-trends/the-use-of-new-technologies-in-the-tourism-industry. [Accessed 10th, October, 2014]

Tate. (2012). Google Glasses - Project Glass: The Future of Human – Computer Interactions? Available from: http://usabilitygeek.com/google-glasses-project-glass-thefuture-of-human-computer-interaction. [Accessed 5th January 2015]

Wang, D., Park, S. & Fesenmaier, D. R. (2012). The Role of Smartphones in Mediating the Touristic experience. Journal of Travel Research, 51 (4), 371-387

Widmer, A & Muller, H. (2014) Using Google to enhance pre-hospital Care. BA. University of Applied Sciences Western Switzerland (HES-SO)

Ye, H., & Tussyadiah, I.P. (2011). Destination Visual Image and Expectation of Experiences. Journal of Travel & Tourism Marketing 28(2), 129-144

A Scenario Technique Application to Implement Smart City Concepts in Tourism Destinations

Emre Ronay

Salzburg University of Applied Sciences
eronay.imte-m2011@fh-salzburg.ac.at

Abstract

Our world is facing dramatic changes. In 2050 nine billion people will live on our earth, 70 percent of them in cities. It is therefore crucial for cities to think in a future orientated way. To be prepared for challenges caused by globalization, urbanization, climate change, socio-demographic changes, new values and norms in societies, so-called Smart City concepts have been developed. These cities implement Information and Communication Technologies (ICT) to enhance life quality, efficiency of mobility, economy and sustainability. The short range wireless communication technology, Near Field Communication (NFC), is named to be the key technology for developing Smart Cities. This article intends to comprehend the symptoms which indicate the future implication of NFC technology in its role within Smart City concepts. Furthermore, scenarios for stakeholders in tourism destinations are illuminated by applying a scenario technique. This study explores the role of system theory in scenario processes to understand whether scenarios can be regarded as systems. Results of the study clarify the factors that influence the implementation of the concept. Moreover, they implicate that a secret leader in the ecosystem is crucial for the concept's success. This study contributes to the strategic orientation for future directions of tourism destinations.

Keywords: NFC; Smart City; Scenario Technique; System Theory; Complex System Framework

1 INTRODUCTION

Approximately half of the world's population currently resides in cities, while urbanization shows constant growth (Krawczyk and Ratcliffe, 2005). Cities are confronted with some obstacles such as economical or environmental issues. Implementing ICTs can provide solutions, while they enhance the efficiency of services and life quality as well as reducing costs (Falconer and Mitchell, 2012). The increase of mobile technologies and wireless connection withstands time and distance limitation which leads to positive communication and relationships between tourists and stakeholders of a destination. From the stakeholders' point of view, these increases support the provision of constant experience to tourists. On the other hand, it enables tourist the exchange of information and creates new possibilities to enhance the real life experience (Racherla, et al., 2008). A city that adopts ICT solutions in order to cope with certain challenges is referred to as Smart City (Hodgkinson, 2011; Falconer and Mitchell, 2012; Cosgrave et al., 2013; GSMA, 2013). Smart Cities have the potential to become a standard living concept in the future (Hodgkinson, 2011). For developing a Smart City concept, the city has to address and use numerous technologies, including short range wireless technologies (Haubensack, 2011). For instance, some services will require NFC (Near Field Communication) technology and its close range transmission ability (GSMA, 2013).

The major challenges of cities and communities that are recently encountered are demographic change resulting in a population increase, polarized growth of economy, increasing greenhouse-gas emissions and a decrease of available budgets (Falconer and Mitchell, 2012). Furthermore, Dwyer and Edwards (2009) identified economic, political, environmental, technological, demographic and social trends as global trends affecting the tourism industry. In regard to this, the challenges cities and the tourism industry are facing are identical. Haubensack (2001) mentions, that attracting tourism is a smart-cities success criterion besides attracting business, creating jobs and offering a rich culture. A major problem is that governments neglect the basic understanding that even though tourism generates revenue and increases income and taxation, it is essential to reinvest in order to stay competitive (Page et al., 2010). This study focuses on Smart City concepts and investigates the roles of the stakeholders and the NFC technology within the concepts. In order to illuminate the uncertain future, a scenario technique approach is applied. The author refers to the concept as NFC Smart City and takes the phenomenon to a new level by focusing on the tourism industry.

2 LITERATURE REVIEW

2.1 NFC and Smart Cities

ICTs play an important role for the strategic positioning of the organisation (Werthner and Klein, 1999). Therefore, ICTs can produce competitive advantages for organisations (Buhalis and Egger, 2006; Dwyer and Edwards, 2009) in terms of cost effectiveness or differentiation strategies (Porter, 1985). A broad range of technological developments shows that ICTs became a key factor in terms of competitive advantages (Buhalis and O'Connor, 2005). In terms of technological developments, tourism has always been an initial implementation field (Öztaysi et al., 2009). In the communication trend, travelling with the mobile phone has changed from being comfortable to being obligatory. Mobile services offer many benefits to travelers. Accessibility is fast and services are easy to use, they are optimal for travelers (Egger and Buhalis, 2009). Travelling with a mobile phone is easier and decreases the stress of customers during a trip. Therefore, they will become an obligation for travelers and play a huge role in service strategies of companies (Langelund, 2007). People are in constant search of new methods to observe their surroundings and connect their activities to digital interfaces. NFC technology is gaining huge attention while it enables such connection (Chatzigiannakis et al., 2011). A specific example for this could be the NFC enabled "Smart Map" that allows to retrieve information with an NFC enabled mobile phone from a paper map via NFC-tags (Ronay and Egger, 2014). NFC has a significant positive impact on the tourism industry (Egger and Jooss 2010; Pesonen and Horster, 2012). Egger (2013) states that NFC offers a range of possible functions for the tourism industry like mobile payment, information supply, access authorization, object identification, workforce management, location based services etc. Smart cities have the potential to attract investors and create significant economic benefits through developing strong infrastructure (GSMA, 2013). At the moment, models for developing Smart Cities and general information on the concept are in the beginning phase (Cosgrave et al., 2013). It is important to identify companies with common aims and objectives as this will have a positive influence on the whole ecosystem. Each party within the ecosystem should provide vigorous products and services which otherwise would lead to a decrease of the overall performance (Iansiti and Levien, 2004). Two versatile Smart City projects have been analysed, in order to gain a profound knowledge of the concept and to extract the relevant NFC services for a tourism industry based Smart City. The first project was Europe's first NFC pilot project launched in Nice. Several NFC trials have been launched and promoted in June 2010, under the brand name Cityzi (Balaban, 2010). The second NFC project under investigation was the SmartTouch in Oulu that revealed several innovative mobile services which were made available via NFC enabled (ITEA and Tekes, 2008). In order to comprehend the feasibility of NFC applications, 33 trials and 44 technology presentations have been launched by the SmartTouch project (Tuikka, 2009). A comparison was made of all NFC use cases and the services relevant for the tourism industry have been identified. These four NFC services are payment, navigation, information provision and couponing.

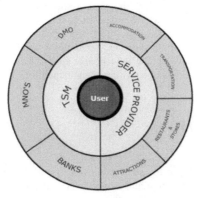

Fig. 1. Diagram of the proposed NFC Smart City Ecosystem

In order to become competitive and survive in today's fierce business environment, companies ought to adapt themselves to a certain ecosystem (Basole, 2009). According to Coskun et al. (2012) the first step to adopt a NFC Smart City concept is to create a corresponding ecosystem. Therefore, the author proposes an ecosystem for NFC Smart City concepts. Through a literature review and the adaption of two ecosystems developed by GMSA (2013) and the NFC-Forum (2008), the possible stakeholders (Destination Management Organisations (DMOs), Mobile Network Operators (MNOs), Trusted Service Managers (TSMs), Banks, Attractions, Restaurants and Stores, Transportation, Accommodation, Service Providers and Users)) of a NFC Smart City with tourism focus were identified (see figure 1).

2.1 Scenario Technique and System Theory

A scenario method can be used for any situation in which a thinker envisions how the future might look (Schoemaker, 1995). Therefore, scenario technique is a valuable method when planning for the future (Shumadine, 2005). Future research and the scenario technique as one of its methods are critical issues in terms of strategic planning of destinations. They contribute to the research conducted in the destination in order to develop new concepts. Therefore, the destination is prepared to address future events which might occur, thus enhancing their competitiveness. The scenario technique is essential for the tourism industry to get insights into the way the future might develop (Page et al., 2010). When studying the future, the future view must illuminate the present which is the fundamental requirement for future thinking. Future thinking is also called "la prospective" (Godet, 1987). This study adopts the scenario philosophy of Michel Godet. As foresight and prediction of the future, organisations must learn to consider multiple future alternatives rather than seeing only a single future (Popp and Schüll 2008; Fink and Schlake, 2000; Chermack, 2004). The reason for this is that multiple futures enable diverse thinking of what may probably happen in the future (Chermack, 2004). Implying and clarifying theories in scenario technique processes are not common (Wilkinson, 2009). However, the system theory aims to create and provide a strong framework, in order to support integration of elements (Chen and Stroup, 1993). Skyttner (1996) defines a system as a group of interacting components or elements which can form a compound that aims to perform certain functions. Science investigated systems that are simple or can be separated and analysed as simple compounds. Complex systems, on the other hand, are quite dynamic and interrelated. When change occurs in one factor, it directly initiates an effect on other determinants (Ashby, 1956). The interactions among the determinants are nonlinear (Cilliers, 2004; Baggio, 2008), which is stated as a precondition for complex systems. Otherwise, it would be impossible to keep track of all the relationships between the variables (Cilliers, 2004). Furthermore, certain loops are present in a system (van der Heijden, 1997; Cilliers, 2004). Each activity feeds back of its effect which it caused (Cilliers, 2004).

3 METHODOLOGY

3.1 Influence Analysis

Through the analysis of the various influence factors within the sphere of influence, the key factors which are later needed for the influence matrix are determined (Gausemeier et al., 1996). Expert interviews are essential at this stage in order to reduce uncertainties (Godet, 1987; van der Heijden, 1996). Therefore, semi-structured interviews with one open-ended question were conducted with six experts, each of them representing a stakeholder of the ecosystem. The experts work for Türkcell and AVEA representing the MNO's, ABank the banks, Mezzaluna the restaurants and at a 5-star Hotel in Salzburg which wishes not to be mentioned. In addition, Nikolas Psaroudakis, an ICT expert was interviewed. Four interviews were conducted via Skype, the others face-to-face. The influence factors given by the experts were analysed and those that are similar have been clustered and the key influence factors were identified. These are security, user acceptance, infrastructure, partnerships, privacy, investments, stakeholders, marketing and consumer experience.

3.2 Influence Matrix

The next step was to investigate the direct influence of each factor on one another. The intensity of influence among the factors is then rated according to a scale (von Reibnitz, 1987; Gausemeier et al., 1996). The influence rates have been identified through an online focus group via Skype 6.6.0.106. The participants were Hasan H. Erdogan (University of Dokuz Eylül), Mahmut Firat (Sworn Bank Auditor) from the Banking Regulation and Supervision Agency (BRSA) in Turkey, Cem Ferdi Ordu (Commercial Marketing Manager) from ABank Turkey, and Nijat Baghirov (Intern – Marketing Department) at the Liberty International Tourism Group Salzburg.

Figure 2 shows the influence matrix with the weighting determined by the online focus group. The addition of the rows gives us the active sum for each factor. Active sum shows how strong the influence of one factor is on the whole system. On the other hand, the addition of the columns gives us the passive sum for each factor. Passive sum shows how strong one factor is influenced by all the other factors (Herdin, 2007; von Reibnitz, 1987; Gausemeier et al., 1996).

System Element Influence → On / Of	Security	User Acceptance	Infrastructure	Partnerships	Privacy	Investments	Stakeholders	Marketing	Consumer Experience	Active Sum
Security		3	0	0	3	3	2	0	1	12
User Acceptance	0		0	0	1	0	2	0	0	3
Infrastructure	2	1		1	3	3	3	1	3	15
Partnerships	2	3	3		2	3	1	1	1	14
Privacy	3	3	0	0		0	0	1	2	6
Investments	1	0	2	1	3		3	3	2	14
Stakeholders	0	2	0	2	1	3		2	1	11
Marketing	0	3	0	0	3	1	3		3	13
Consumer Experience	0	3	0	0	0	0	2	3		8
Passive Sum	8	15	5	4	13	10	14	11	12	

Fig. 2. Influence Matrix

3.3 System-Grid

In this step, the results of the direct influence analysis are transmitted into a so called System-Grid. The System-Grid provides a more convenient illustration of the influence matrix (von Reibnitz, 1987; Gausemeier et al., 1996).

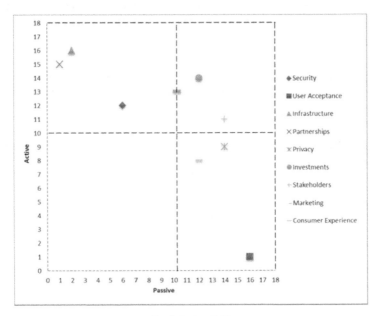

Fig. 3. System-Grid

The System-Grid can be seen on figure 3. Area I is the field where the active system elements are positioned. Area II is the field for the so-called ambivalent system elements (high activity and passivity). The elements falling onto Area III are the so-called buffering or low ambivalent system elements that have a low influence on other elements and are weakly influenced by them. The Area IV is the field of passive system elements. They are influenced strongly by all other system elements but have rather a weak influence on them (von Reibnitz, 1987).

The influence factors privacy, consumer experience and user acceptance are all situated in area IV. These three influence factors have been excluded from further discussions for the scenario method. The influence factors infrastructure, partnerships and security have a very high influence on the system, as they are located in area I. Marketing is between the areas I and II, and has therefore a high influence as well. Investment and stakeholders are located on area II. Hence, they have a high influence on the system and are highly influenced by other elements. These elements were considered for further discussion in the scenario method.

3.4 Complex System Framework

After eliminating the factors without a significant influence on the system and the similarity analysis, the complex system framework can be constructed. The remaining factors which have an influence on the system are infrastructure, partnerships, security, investments, marketing and stakeholders. According to the weight of their influence identified on the influence matrix, the feedback vectors are dragged. The complex system framework is shown on figure 4. For drawing vectors among the influence factors, only the influences with a weight of 3 have been considered. However, as the author sees some influences as important for the framework, two influences weighing 2 have been added to the framework as well. The first one is the influence of investment on infrastructure, the second the influence of infrastructure on security. Moreover, no negative values are included, because there are no factors which influence each other negatively.

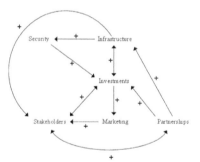

Fig. 4. Complex System Framework

3.5 Projection of Alternative Future States and Consistency Analysis

The next step in the scenario method is the future projection of the influence factors. This means to identify the alternative situations or states of the influence factors in the future. Hereby, it is important to describe the future states very transparent in order to avoid biases (von Reibnitz, 1987). After identifying the alternative future states for each influence factor, the list was entered into the option development box on Parmenides EIDOS 7.6. The alternative future states for each influence factor can be observed on the consistency analysis on figure 5. The final step of the scenario method is the consistent analysis. The aim of this step is to prove the consistency between all the future alternatives. Therefore, the logic or compatibility of the alternatives (Mietzner and Reger, 2005; Gausemeier et al. 1998) identified can be tested. For the analysis, the Parmenides EIDOS 7.6 software was used. After entering the future alternatives to the option development box, the software automatically created the consistence matrix. Thereafter, the consistency for all alternatives was weighted pairwise, on a scale from -3 to 3. The rating was performed via an online focus group by using Skype 6.6.0.106. The participants were the same as those for the influence matrix. After the ratings were entered, the software calculated the consistency of all the compared pairs (see figure 5).

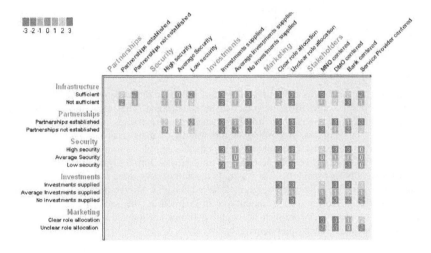

Fig. 5. Consistency Matrix Source: Snapshot – Parmenides EIDOS 7.6

100 scenarios were created and listed according to their consistence. The consistence rate indicates the stability of the scenarios and shows which have a higher validity in the long term. Therefore, the high consistency rates are an indicator for the selection of scenarios (von Reibnitz, 1987). Furthermore, it is important to choose scenarios which are stable and rather different from each other (von Reibnitz, 1987; Gausemeier et al., 1996).

4 STUDY FINDINGS

It is important to notice that the more scenarios are drawn out, the more uncertainties occur (Godet, 2000). The author decided for three scenarios, due to the three main stakeholders in the concept. Godet (2006) argues that in some industries such as electronics, a range of two to four years is already considered to be long term scenarios. However, the scenarios are investigated on a 5-year time horizon. Furthermore, the influences shown on the complex system framework are analysed within the scenarios.

Scenario 1 – The Vital Veins
In this scenario, the MNOs adopt the position of the secret leader in the ecosystem. The usage of NFC technology is considered to be accepted by the users. As NFC services are mainly based on mobile phones, the MNOs and banks have already the essential infrastructure to provide NFC services. Furthermore, MNOs deliver internet connection for locals as well as tourists. This increases the efficiency of retrieving relevant tourist and navigation information. In addition, they offer mobile couponing solutions to the society. On the other hand, banks are able to offer contactless mobile payments for local inhabitants. By providing interbank services, tourists are able to pay via NFC enabled mobile phones. Partnerships are

established among the TSMs and the service providers which affect the infrastructure, investments and the stakeholders according to the complex system framework. The transportation, hotel-motels, restaurants, stores and attractions are all part of the concept, by delivering NFC services. Payment services are facilitated through the partnership with banks. Therefore, people are able to pay in stores, restaurants, etc. Retrieving information services via NFC are supplied through the partnership with MNOs. While MNOs own the secure element, security has been fully supplied for users which influence investments. Banks provide additional security for contactless payment. Due to the unique identification of the NFC devices, the security concerns do not show any flaws. Investments are sufficient for the concept realization. Investments have been supplied by the state through the Destination Management Organisations (DMO) as well. The marketing roles have been allocated and each stakeholder within the ecosystem appears to know their responsibilities. As the DMO is in the ecosystem, the marketing role for promoting the destination is emphasized. In this scenario, the future indicates the implementation of the NFC Smart City concept without any significant problems.

Scenario 2 – DMOs with flaws

The DMO takes the lead on the concept. They accomplished all the crucial steps for realizing the concept. However, some flaws are detected during their leadership. For this scenario NFC is considered to be adopted by the users. First of all, the DMO could not provide the necessary infrastructure for all NFC services. This seems to be the major problem which they are confronted with, as it has a direct influence on stakeholders, security and investments. Even though the partnerships are established among all stakeholders, the infrastructure appears to be insufficient. More investments have to be supplied in order to enhance the quality and quantity of NFC services in the destination. Furthermore, the established partnerships might fluctuate due to the inexistence of adequate infrastructure. Moreover, the service providers supply investments merely to provide NFC services within their means and not to support others. Another flaw appears to be the average security issue. When security shows to be lacking, the users might be unwilling to utilize the services. Concerning the required investments, the DMO was capable to supply the required amount. Moreover, investments have been supplied by the other stakeholders in the ecosystem. This can also be observed on the complex system framework, as investments are influenced by partnerships and stakeholders. The DMO is capable of allocating the marketing activity roles. In fact, the major marketing role is played by the DMO. In this scenario, DMO is the main actor of the concept. They seem to be capable of providing enough investments and establish the necessary partnerships. Furthermore, the marketing activities are clarified under their lead. Nevertheless, the DMO offers insufficient security as well as deficient infrastructure.

Worst Case Scenario – Alone in the Dark

The worst case scenario is described in the aspect of the service providers. Even though the consistency rate for this scenario is rather low compared to the others, the scenario has been described due to its plausibility in an uncertain future. In this scenario, the service providers are left alone completely. No partnerships were established, each company following its own lead. The infrastructure is insufficient as each stakeholder is not capable of providing it separately. Security cannot be provided adequately as banks and MNOs do not cooperate with the other stakeholders. The concept is neglected by the TSMs, which diminishes the unique value of the concept. As the service providers consist of several stakeholders, an impressive amount of investment has been supplied. Each stakeholder invested enough amounts to develop the concept. However, the supplied investment of each stakeholder is merely used for themselves, instead of investing into the concept as a whole. Each stakeholder is responsible to conduct its' own marketing activities in this scenario. The stakeholders in this scenario seem to be quite isolated from each other. Managing the NFC Smart City has become a major challenge. The problems may cause a chaos situation, as they influence many of the key factors on the complex system framework. Therefore, the system of the concept might collapse, if the service providers are not supported by the TSMs.

5 DISCUSSION

In the first scenario, the ecosystem was managed by the MNOs and the banks. It has the highest consistency rate and is therefore the most plausible and stable description of the future situation. Gaur and Ondrus (2012) stated that the implementation phase for banks might be difficult due to the complexity of mobile payments. Furthermore, they stressed that their implementation strategy will depend on other actors of the ecosystem, such as the MNOs. Therefore, the results of the first scenario match with the statement in the literature. The second secret leader, and according to the consistency rate, the main leader of the ecosystem, are the MNOs. Accenture et al. (2011) stated that MNOs are essential for the leadership of Smart City concepts. They are currently the only providers of mobile services. Therefore, they have an important place in the NFC ecosystem (Coskun et al., 2012). These arguments were verified by their significance in the ecosystem as described in the scenario. The second scenario depicts the future by placing the DMO as the secret leader. This scenario has certain commonalities with scenario 1. However, the concept is confronted with certain problems, which affect the concept negatively. DMOs can include local, regional and national governments. Therefore, they possess a certain political significance which provides them with the necessary infrastructure and financial assets (Buhalis, 2000). In regard with this argument, the DMO was not able to deliver the necessary infrastructure but capable of providing the required investments for the concept. The DMO was neglected in the Smart City literature. Nevertheless, the results indicate that DMOs can act as a secret leader. Considering the disaster in the worst case scenario, it is elucidated that service providers are not capable of implementing the concept solely on their own. Compared to scenario 1 and 2, it becomes clear that at least one major stakeholder is vital for the concept. The NFC Forum (2008) claims that service providers are a potential TSM in the ecosystem. However, the worst case scenario points out disapproval regarding this argument. Coskun et al. (2012) stress that TSMs are a necessary branch for managing a trusted environment, whereas the NFC Forum (2008) claims that TSMs act as a linkage among the stakeholders in the ecosystem. As the service providers did not provide the expected security and are not capable of establishing the requisite partnerships according to the scenario, the author can eliminate the service providers from the role as a TSM and justify the proposed ecosystem. Chermack (2004) claims that system theory informs the scenario process, as scenarios can be regarded as systems. The complex system framework proposed in this study was created according to the results of the influence analysis and the System-Grid. The positive vectors were added by linking each of the influence factors that have a strong effect on another. This indicates that scenarios can be regarded as systems. In addition, the framework was shown to the online focus group participants. Therefore, the framework had a significant contribution to the consistency matrix and the outcomes which were the fundaments of the described scenarios. In regard to this, the system theory informed the scenario process in this study. As a result, the hypothesis defined by Chermack (2004) can be verified through this contribution.

6 CONCLUSION

Smart Cities are truly the vision of cities for the future. Tourism destinations can attain uniqueness and a niche through the realization of the concept. The implementation of ICTs in cities is the key success factor to encounter global problems. Technological developments, especially emerging innovative ICTs, are inevitable. The short range communication technology NFC was identified as one of these ICT technologies which will shape our lives and movements in cities. This article investigated the NFC Smart City concept, and how plausible future scenarios for implementing such a concept in tourism destinations might look. The described scenarios have illuminated the future of NFC Smart City concepts. Only a small amount of journal articles and proceedings papers concerning NFC technology and Smart City concepts was found. Furthermore, scenario techniques are not common in tourism research. An additional omission was detected while searching for papers investigating scenario methods built on theoretical foundations. Certain influence factors have not been considered for the scenarios, as they seemed not to have any significant effect on the system. The scenarios created were industry-oriented while isolating the consumer side of the concept. Further research can be conducted with different technologies such as Location-Based services. Additionally investigations can be made on focusing mainly on the consumer side of the ecosystem. Finally, risk evaluations can be investigated for the created scenarios and probability tests with experts can be conducted in order to predict the probability of the hypothetical alternative future states.

REFERENCES

Accenture, Cisco and GSMA, 2011. Smart Mobile Cities: Opportunities for Mobile Operators to Deliver Intelligent Cities. April 2011. London: Associated Report by GSMA, Accenture and Cisco.

Ashby, W.R., 1956. An Introduction to Cybernetics. 2nd ed. London: William Clowes and Sons.

Baggio, R., 2008. Symptoms of Complexity in a Tourism System. Journal of Tourism Analysis, 13 (1), pp. 1-20.

Balaban, D., 2012. French Make it Official With Nice NFC Launch [WWW]. Available from: http://nfctimes.com/news/french-make-it-official-nice-nfc-launch [Accessed 21.04.2013].

Basole, R.C., 2009. Visualization of interfirm relations in a converging mobile ecosystem. Journal of Information Technology, 24 (2), pp. 1-16.

Buhalis, D. and Egger, R., 2006. Informations-und Kommunikationstechnologien als Mittel zur Prozess-und Produktinnovation für den Unternehmer. In: Pikkemaat, B. and Peters, M. (Eds.) Innovationen im Tourismus. ESV-Verlag, pp. 163-176.

Buhalis, D. and O'Connor, P., 2005. Information Communication Technology: Revolutionizing Tourism. Journal of Tourism Recreation Research, 30 (3), pp. 7–16.

Buhalis, D., 2000. Marketing the competitive destination of the future. Journal of Tourism Management, 21, pp. 97-116.

Buhalis, D., 2003. eTourism – Information technology for strategic tourism management. 1st ed. Essex, England: Prentice Hall.

Chen, D. and Stroup, W., 1993. General System Theory: Toward a Conceptual Framework for Science and Technology Education for All. Journal of Science Education and Technology, 2 (7), pp. 447-459.

Chermack, T.J., 2004. The Role of System Theory in Scenario Planning. Journal of Futures Studies, 8 (4), pp. 15-30.

Cilliers, P., 2004. A Framework for Understanding Complex Systems. In: Andriani, P. and Passiante, G. (Eds.) Complexity Theory and The Management Of Networks: Proceedings Of The Workshop On Organizational Networks as Distributed Systems of Knowledge, Lecce, Italy, 2001, World Scientific Publishing Company.

Cosgrave, E., Arbuthnot, K. and Tryfonas, T., 2013. Living Labs, Innovation Districts and Information Marketplaces: A Systems Approach for Smart Cities. Journal of Procedia Computer Science, 16, pp. 668–677.

Coskun, V., Ok, K. and Ozdenizci, B., 2012. Near Field Communication – From Theory to Practice. 1st ed. West Sussex, UK: John Wiley & Sons Ltd.

Dwyer, L. and Edwards, D., 2009. Tourism Product and Service Innovation to Avoid 'Strategic Drift'. International Journal of Tourism Research, 11 (4), pp. 321-335.

Egger, R. and Buhalis, D., 2008. Mobile Systems. In: Egger, R. and Buhalis, D. (Eds.) eTourism Case Studies: Management and Marketing issues in eTourism. Butterworth Heinemann, pp. 417-425.

Egger, R. and Jooss, M., 2010. Die Zukunft im mTourism – Ausblick auf Technologie- und Dienstentwicklung. In: Egger, R. and Jooss, M. (eds). mTourism – Mobile Dienste im Tourismus. Wiesbaden, Germany, Gabler Verlag, pp. 11-25.

Egger, R., 2013. The impact of Near Field Communication on Tourism. Journal of Hospitality and Tourism Technology, 4(2), pp. 119-133.

Egger, R., and Jooss, M., 2010. Evaluation of the concept of early acceptance tests for touristic mobile applications. Information and Communication Technologies in Tourism 2010, pp. 149-158.

Falconer, G. and Mitchell, S. (2012). Smart City Framework: A Systematic Process for Enabling Smart + Connected Communities. September 2012. San Jose: Cisco Internet Business Solutions Group.

Fink, A. and Schlake, O., 2000. Scenario Management - An Approach for Strategic. Foresight. Competitive Intelligence Review, 11 (1), pp. 37–45.

Gaur, A. and Ondrus, J., 2012. The Role of Banks in the Mobile Payment Ecosystem: A Strategic Asset Perspective. In: Proceedings of the International Conference on Electronic Commerce, Singapore Management University, Singapore, August 7-8, 2012, pp. 171-177.

Gausemeier, J., Fink, A. and Schlake, O., 1996. Szenario-Management: Planen und Führen mit Szenarien. 2nd ed. München; Wien: Carl Hanser Verlag.

Gausemeier, J., Fink, A., and Schlake, O., 1998. Scenario management: An approach to develop future potentials. Technological Forecasting and Social Change, 59(2), pp. 111-130.

Godet, M., 1987. Scenarios and Strategic Management (Translation of: Prospective et Planification Strategique). 1st ed. Bodmin: Butterworth Scientific. Godet, M. (2000a). The Art of Scenarios and Strategic Planning: Tools and Pitfalls. Journal of Technological Forecasting and Social Change, 65 (1), pp. 3–22.

Godet, M., 2006. Creating Futures - Scenario Planning as a Strategic Management Tool. 2nd ed. France: Economica. GSMA (2013). Guide to Smart Cities - The Opportunity for Mobile Operators. February 2013. 1st Edition. London: GSMA Head Office.

Haubensak, O., 2011. Smart cities and internet of things. In Business Aspects of the Internet of Things, Seminar of Advanced Topics, ETH Zurich (pp. 33-39).

Herdin, T., 2007. Die Zukunft im Blick. Szenario-Coaching als Katalysator touristischer Entwicklungen. Egger, R./Herdin, T.(Hg.): Tourismus: Herausforderung: Zukunft. Wien: Lit Verlag, pp. 641-656.

Hodgkinson, S., 2011. Is Your City Smart Enough? Digitally enabled cities and societies will enhance economic, social, and environmental sustainability in the urban century. March 2011. Report by OVUM.

Iansiti, M. and Levien, R., 2004. Strategy as Ecology. Harvard Business Review, 82 (3), pp. 1-10. ITEA and TEKES (2008). SmartTouch City of Oulu - Services through NFC Technology [WWW]. Available from:http://ttuki.vtt.fi/smarttouch/www/kuvat/December08_Newsletter.pdf [Accessed 18.04.2013].

Krawczyk, E. And Ratcliffe, J., 2005. Imagine ahead, plan backwards: prospective methodology in urban and regional planning. Futures Academy, Dublin Institute of Technology.

Langelund, S., 2007. Mobile Travel. Journal of Tourism and Hospitality Research, 7 (3/4), pp. 284-286.

Mietzner, D., and Reger, G., 2005. Advantages and disadvantages of scenario approaches for strategic foresight. International Journal of Technology Intelligence and Planning, 1(2), pp. 220-239. NFC Forum (2008). Essentials for Successful NFC Mobile Ecosystems. October 2008. Wakefield, MA: NFC Forum.

Oztaysi, B., Baysan, S. and Akpinar, F., 2009, Radio Frequency Identification (RFID) in Hospitality. Technovation, 29 (9), pp. 618–624.

Page, S.J., Yeoman, I., Connell, J. and Greenwood, C., 2010. Scenario planning as a tool to understand uncertainty in tourism: the example of transport and tourism in Scotland in 2025. Journal of Current Issues in Tourism, 13 (2), pp. 99-137.

Pesonen, J. and Horster, E., 2012. Near Field Communication Technology in Tourism. Tourism Management Perspectives, 4, pp. 11-18.

Popp, R., and Schüll, E. (Eds.)., 2008. Zukunftsforschung und Zukunftsgestaltung: Beiträge aus Wissenschaft und Praxis (Vol. 1). Springer.

Racherla, P., Hu, C. and Hyun, M.Y., 2008. Exploring the Role of Innovative Technologies in Building a Knowledge-Based Destination. Journal of Current Issues in Tourism, 11 (5), pp. 407-428.

Ronay, E. and Egger, R., 2014. NFC-enabled City Maps Measuring their Perceived Value. E-Review of Tourism Research (eRTR), 5.

Schoemaker, P.J.H., 1995. Scenario Planning: A Tool for Strategic Thinking. Sloan Management Review, 36 (2), pp. 25-40.

Shumadine, A., 2005. Anticipating the Future: Scenario Planning as an Investment Tool. Journal of Wealth Management, 8 (3), pp. 77-80.

Skyttner, L., 1996. General systems theory: origin and hallmarks. Journal of Kybernetes, 25 (6), pp. 16-22.

Tuikka, T., 2009. SmartTouch project. In: Tuikka, T. and Isomursu, M. (eds). Touch the Future with a Smart Touch. VTT Tiedotteita - Research Notes 2492, Helsinki, Finland, Edita Prima Oy, pp. 24-30.

Van der Heijden, K., 1996. Scenarios – The Art of Strategic Conversation.1st ed. West Sussex: John Wiley & Sons.

Van der Heijden, K., 1997. Scenarios, Strategy, and the Strategy Process. Presearch: Provoking Strategic Conversation (GBN), 1 (1), pp. 1-32.

Von Reibnitz, U., 1987. Szenarien Optionen für die Zukunft. 1st ed. Hamburg: McGraw-Hill.

Werthner, H. and Klein, S., 1999. Information Technology and Tourism - A Challenging Relationship. 1st ed. Wien, Austria: Springer Verlag.

Wilkinson, A., 2009. Scenarios Practices: In Search of Theory. Journal of Futures Studies, 13 (3), pp. 107 – 114.

Social E-couponing and Customer Loyalty in the Tourism Industry

Stefanie Bohacek

Vienna University of Economics and Business, Austria
Stefanie.Bohacek@gmail.com

Abstract

Service providers in the tourism industry make increasingly use of the option to post an offer with a steep discount on a daily deal website. They are expecting to boost their degree of fame and gain a large group of new customers. But what are the consequences of the recently pursued promotional strategy? Are those new customers loyal customers to the brand or are they going to switch as soon as the next coupon of the competitor appears on the website? This study investigates the effect of the trend of social e-couponing on the concept of customer loyalty. The results of a survey among Austrian e-coupon users reveal that deal proneness and variety-seeking change the purchasing pattern of the consumers in a positive way with respect to loyalty. The findings also suggest that loyalty programs should take the influences of value- and price-conscious consumer behaviour on loyalty objectives into consideration. Important adaptions in customer retention initiatives are inevitable to address upcoming tendencies resulting from the concept of social e-couponing.

Keywords: e-coupon; e-tourism; customer loyalty; consumer-behaviour

1 INTRODUCTION

"Two Nights in Madrid", a "Weekend at a Spa Hotel in Paris", or a "Ski Trip to the Alps" – only a few examples of eye-catching headlines for tourism advertisements, which enter the world of electronic couponing, designed by powerful daily deal websites[1] like Groupon, Daily Deal, and Living Social. This way, e-tourism, as a form of web marketing for tourism businesses (Liu, et al., 2014), gained a new promotional tool. Recent developments and technical advancements over the past years, following the emergence of the Internet in 1994, gave access to a fast and convenient distribution network of online deals (Hughes and Beukes, 2012). Entering a so-called daily deal website enables the Internet user to select a geographic place of choice and choose from a wide range of different offers with considerably high discount rates, often between 50-70% (Boon, et al., 2012). The consumer can buy the coupon online and redeem it afterwards from the tourism business, which contracted the deal provider to offer the coupon. Statistics confirm the success of this model: within only one year, from 2009 to 2010, daily deal websites noticed a growth of 162% regarding the number of unique visitors. Furthermore, in accordance with this tendency, it was found that the number of active Groupon customers increased from 0.04 to 42.60 million between the second quarter of 2009 and the same quarter in 2013 (Statista, 2013). An explanation for the remarkable boom in the usage of discounts as a sales promotion measure is offered by Grewal, et al. (2003), who state that the increasing pressure exerted by competition, along with the related tendency for securing competitive advantages through falling prices, is recently influencing the nature of conducting business. The rapid development of the Internet and related technologies also contributed to the establishment of the market for e-couponing. These developments resulted in several attempts for research in

---

[1] In this study the term "daily deal website" will be used to describe the Internet portal that establishes the playground for the interactions between different players participating in a coupon trade. Synonyms to be found frequently in literature are "coupon-", "e-coupon-", "Deal of the Day-", or "group buying deal-website".

this area and the adaption of already existing sales and marketing models to the new trends in e-commerce. This affects interpretations in the context of consumer behaviour including the concept of customer loyalty, or in this case referred to by the widely used term "e-customer loyalty". Therefore, the fact that a lot of tourism service providers adapted their business strategy to this new model raises the question of whether the concept is also successful in securing a loyal customer base for the business, which is able to guarantee a long-term profitability of the pursued commercial policy (e.g. Boon, et al., 2012, Hughes and Beukes, 2012). In particular, this study aims to address the following research question: *Are customers, who are buying coupons on online daily deal platforms, loyal to the businesses that offer these deals?*

In order to find an answer to the research question, the focus of the study is directed to an increasing extent on the consumer perspective. The relationship between selected customer characteristics, which are especially relevant in the context of daily deals and customer loyalty, should provide meaningful indications: value-consciousness, price-consciousness, variety-seeking and deal proneness.

2 THEORETICAL BACKGROUND

2.1 E-couponing and Group Buying Schemes

"Coupons are a popular sales promotion device that offer a discount to consumers who purchase a product or service" (Kang, et al., 2006, p.859). Traditional coupons are distributed through advertising channels like newspapers, e-mails, and leaflets. Consumers need to collect the coupons and wait passively for them to show up. However, with recent technological advances and the emergence of the Internet, this marketing tool experienced considerable changes and a new form, e-coupons, emerged. E-coupons are an electronic, paperless version of the traditional coupons that are distributed over the Internet. Important changes are reflected in the advanced ease and scope of distribution for the marketers, as well as the reduced costs of searching and obtaining on the consumer side. A considerable amount of literature (e.g. Köpp, et al., 2013, Boon, et al., 2012, Tuten and Ashley, 2011) attempts to explain the business model behind the transactions on these specified websites such as Groupon and DailyDeal, here referred to as group buying scheme. The rationale behind group buying is that people are brought together through offering a system of coupons. This way, they can enjoy the bargaining power of a large group, while businesses can attract new customers and expand their customer bases (Köpp, et al., 2013). The authors identify a traditional business model as one within which the merchant offers the customer a product or service in exchange for the respective price of the good. The group buying scheme, however, includes additional characteristics: the starting point is where the operator of the daily deal website finalises a contract with a local business merchant to sell his product or service with a discount. The consumer enters into the sales transaction when receiving a coupon from the intermediary website operator and paying the discounted price. Next, the operator of the daily deal website transfers the payment to the merchant, deducting an additional fee for the service. A further difference to traditional business models are the constraints regarding time and quantity: on the daily deal website, each deal comes with a minimum number of buyers, which must be reached in a certain period of time. In the case that this number is not reached before the deal expires, the distributed coupons become useless and the consumers get their money back at the same time. The success of group buying schemes "is based upon several influential promotional strategies including couponing, the presence of social proof, and offer scarcity" (Tuten and Ashley, 2011, p.17). However, other scholars have discovered potential weaknesses in this model. Boon, et al. (2012) suggest that the steep discount as well as the fee for the operator of the daily deal website can present restraints for some companies. Overall, by accepting these financial concessions the company hopes to be able to stimulate purchases among new customers and in the following keep them as loyal customers. Hence, the customer lifetime value (CLV) plays an integral role for the company (Kumar, 2008). The author describes the CLV "as the total financial contribution from the current period into the future – that is, revenues minus costs – of a customer over his/her future lifetime with the company and therefore reflects the future profitability of the customer." With the calculation of the CLV, the company is able to assess how much it can invest into the retention of a customer, while securing a positive ROI. Accordingly, if the company is not able to gain the coupon-buyers as loyal customers, it will make a loss, especially if it has sold beyond production costs.

2.2 Customer Loyalty

Hellier, et al. (2003, p.1756) describe customer loyalty as "the degree to which the customer has exhibited, over recent years, repeat purchase behaviour of a particular company service; and the significance of expenditure in terms of the customer's total outlay on that particular type of service". Within a large and growing body of literature covering various aspects of customer loyalty, studies like those of Mei-Lien, et al. (2012), Reichheld and Markey Jr (2000) or Srinivasan, et al. (2002) focused on arguments that emphasise the importance of customer loyalty. Reichheld and Markey Jr (2000, p.173) formulated their findings as the following: "High rates of customer retention and increasing profitability from long-time committed customers reduce the drain on margin caused by expensive new customer acquisition". The authors support the idea that the costs of acquiring customers are increasing, since entry barriers are low for new e-retailers and the choices that customers make are no longer restricted by the access to information or geographic constraints. Moreover, customer loyalty can be portrayed under the concept of social exchange theory (SET). SET explains the relationship between individuals with an exchange process, which is evaluated according to the costs and benefits involved (Priluck Grossmann, 1998). In this context, consumers are motivated to enter voluntarily into a relationship with a marketer, if they perceive that the costs are outweighed by the benefits. Belk and Coon (1993) explain under this perspective that someone giving a gift is aiming to forge an emotional bond with the receiver. Under this rationale, firms often use promotions like the here-analysed discounts to develop a relationship with the customers. These can have different effects on the desired outcome, depending, among other influences, on the consumer's characteristics.

According to the behavioural perspective, a way to distinguish loyal consumers from one's customer base is to assess their *repurchase intention*. Study results indicate a significant and positive relationship between repurchase intention and customer loyalty (Bojei and Wong Chee, 2012). They draw their conclusions with a reference to the distinction between intentions and attitudes. While an attitude is adopted when summing up evaluations, an intention is based on the person's motivation to consciously take out certain behaviour. The authors remark that "repurchase intention is similar with purchase intention except with the element of experience" and define repurchase intention as "the likelihood the user will purchase again […] in the future" (p.39). In this context, the concept of repurchase intention is of great importance, because it offers long-term implications. For instance Srinivasan, et al. (2002, p.45) summed up that loyal customers "forge bond to the company [and reduce their] consideration set size and amount of effort expended in searching for alternatives". In addition, Mei-Lien, et al. (2012) suggest measuring customer loyalty by positive *word-of-mouth*. In general, literature defines word-of-mouth as an informal type of communication in terms of a purchase evaluation. In these situations the consumer tends to accept recommendations, because the communication partner seems unbiased and trustworthy

(Dichter, 1966). Srinivasan, et al. (2002) differentiate positive word-of-mouth from this general concept and describe it as the positive things and favourable recommendations that an individual shares with others about the product or the brand.

2.3 Value-Consciousness

Value-consciousness is described as the "concern for paying low prices subject to some quality constraint" (Lichtenstein, et al., 1990, p.56). With the argument that value is the ratio of quality to price, it can be explained that within this value-conscious consumer segment the incentive for redeeming coupons results from the increase in value. Rao (2009) builds on these arguments and concluded that the driving force behind the purchase decision of a value-conscious consumer is the perception of a "good deal". However, he also acknowledged that if prices are too low they could be interpreted as a signal for a lower value. Previous research in that field has found a positive relationship between value-consciousness and customer loyalty (e.g. Gómez and Rubio, 2010). It has been argued that a positive attitude is shown towards brands if consumers are aware of the value and if the price-quality-relationship is taken into account. On the basis of the above literature, the following hypothesis is concluded:

H_1: The higher the value-consciousness, the more loyalty is shown to the brand.

2.4 Price-Consciousness

Hur, et al. (2013, p.149) state that "more price-conscious consumers find relatively low-priced products more desirable" which leads to the conclusion that a price-conscious behaviour reflects a negative role of cost when it comes to consumer decision-making. Gázquez-Abad and Sánchez-Pérez (2009) refer to the idea that the concept of price sensitivity is used to describe how the customer responds to changes in the price and that price-conscious customers accept a higher effort in order to look for a promotion. Focusing on a similar context, Lichtenstein, et al. (1988, p.245) found that "price conscious consumers may not necessarily pay the lowest price available but tend to pay a lower price when the distinguishing features of more expensive alternatives cannot be justified". Throughout existing literature, researchers, such as Gázquez-Abad and Sánchez-Pérez (2009) and Hur, et al. (2013), found evidence for a negative relationship between price and loyalty. As a conclusion, the following hypothesis is defined:

H_2: The higher the price-consciousness, the less loyalty is shown to the brand.

2.5 Variety-Seeking

Along with the examination of the functions of couponing, Bhasin and Dickinson (1987) suggest that coupons can stimulate the trial of new brands and can support brand switching. In this context, Gázquez-Abad and Sánchez-Pérez (2009) note that brand switching is the predominant effect of a promotion. Gómez and Rubio (2010) explain that a variety-seeking behaviour reflects "the consumer's intention to experiment with different brands as a way of satisfying his or her purchasing needs". Other findings include the categorisation of variety-seeking as one aspect of exploratory behaviour (Van Trijp, et al., 1996). This consumer segment is driven by experiential motives or motives of pleasure, rather than by the utilitarian aspects of consumption. Berné, et al. (2001) argued that customer retention depends on the presence and intensity of variety-seeking among the customers. The study focused on the customer service sector and results showed that "variety-seeking negatively affects customer retention and lessens the impact of the management efforts to improve service quality and customer satisfaction" (p.335). Van Trijp, et al. (1996) define the brand-loyal behaviour as a choice pattern that is opposite to variety-seeking behaviour and state the argument that repeat purchasing is a reflection of brand-loyal behaviour that makes choice-seeking behaviour less likely. Considering the above arguments the following hypothesis is derived:

H₃: The stronger the desire for variety, the less loyalty is shown to the brand.

2.6 Deal Proneness

Literature defines deal proneness as "an increased propensity to respond to a purchase offer because the form of the purchase offer positively affects purchase evaluations" (Lichtenstein, et al., 1990, p.56). This suggests that individuals, who show a strong appliance of this dimension, respond to this type of promotion, because they are in deal form. Gázquez-Abad and Sánchez-Pérez (2009) report that deal-prone consumers are more likely to respond to deals rather than brands. The scholars state that customers who are loyal to certain brands are less prone to sales promotions because the product is more important to them than the price. Moreover, loyal consumers are presumably satisfied with their brand of choice and subsequently, they do not need an incentive to buy that brand again. Also, brands that these customers do not usually buy are unlikely to influence and change their choice. Based on these findings the hypothesis is formulated as following:

H₄: The higher the proneness to deals, the less loyalty is shown to the brand.
In order to measure loyalty this study includes the behavioural component of the concept in the form of repurchase intentions of the customers, as well as the aspect of attitude with the indicator being positive word-of-mouth. For the empirical analysis of the derived hypotheses, a correlation was modelled between the two measures to describe their relationship. To sum up this chapter, all hypotheses are visualized in Figure 1, the suggested research model.

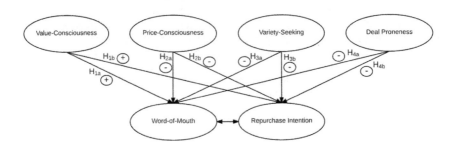

Fig. 1. Research model.

3   RESEARCH DESIGN AND METHODOLOGY

3.1 Empirical Research Design

To test the hypotheses, an online questionnaire was developed that included several constructs arising from the hypotheses. The selection process of the items of the questionnaire was based on an extensive literature review, considering previously developed and tested scales. For the reliabilities of the included scales alphas ranging from 0.75 to 0.95 were measured. Items of value-consciousness and deal proneness are borrowed from Lichtenstein, et al. (1990), items of price-consciousness from Wells and Tigert (1971), items of variety-seeking from Feick, et al. (2003) and Van Trijp, et al.(1996), items of word-of-mouth and repurchase intention from Tuten and Ashley (2011) and Zeithaml (1988), as well as Algesheimer, et al. (2005) and Hess Jr, et al. (2003) respectively. Furthermore, the questionnaire contained general items about participants' demographics and their usage of daily deal websites. Starting with a pre-test that was followed by several adjustments to secure readability and consistency, the questionnaire was distributed via email and social media. In addition, students of an economics and business university located in Austria formed part of the sample. After the time frame from May 2013 to August 2013 the final sample size reached a number of 330 Austrians questioned.

3.2 Analysis

The present study is based on a structural equation modelling approach, applying the software package 'lavaan' in R (Rosseel, 2012). First, the measurement model is calculated to assess the convergent and discriminant validity as well as the reliability of the model (Fornell and Larcker, 1981). In a second step the structural equation model is evaluated, using a combination of absolute and incremental fit indices (Hu and Bentler, 1995). On the one hand the Chi-square, the root mean squared error of approximation (RMSEA), and the standardized root mean square residual (SRMR) serve as absolute fit indices and on the other hand the Tucker-Lewis index (TLI) and the comparative fit index (CFI) are used as incremental fit indices. The threshold levels that indicate a good fit are provided in Table 1.

Table 1. Fit indices and threshold levels.

Fit indices	Threshold levels indicating good fit
Chi-square test	Insignificant result at a 0.05 threshold (Barrett, 2007)
RMSEA	Value close to 0.06 (Hu and Bentler, 1999) or upper limit of 0.07 (Steiger, 2007)
SRMR	Value less than 0.05 good fit (Diamantopoulos and Siguaw, 2000)
TLI	Value greater than 0.95 (Hu and Bentler, 1999)
CFI	Value greater than 0.95 (Hu and Bentler, 1999)

Pertaining the effect size between the latent variables, path coefficients above 0.10, 0.30, and 0.50 are considered small, medium, and large, respectively (Kline, 2011).

4 EMPIRICAL RESULTS

4.1 Description of the Sample

Since one constraint in the applied model is that the persons have already used a deal of the day website, the original sample of 330 respondents has been reduced to 97 persons fulfilling the criteria. This final sample consists of 67.0% female and 33.0% male daily deal users with an average age of 26.8 years. With respect to their education status 26.8% of the respondents obtained a university degree, 64.9% a high-school diploma, 6.2% finished their education with an apprenticeship or a technical college and 2.1% with a compulsory school. Furthermore, the financial situation of the respondents is rather equally distributed with 42.3% considering themselves in a completely or rather good healthy financial situation, while 36.5% of the respondents agreed fully or partially that an unexpected expense of 1000 € would result in a financial burden for them. Concerning the daily deal websites the results reveal that the users acquired an average number of three deals in the past.

4.2 Measurement Model

Following the procedure recommended by Anderson and Gerbing (1988), the constructs of the study were first examined for reliability and validity. Through a stepwise approach items with factor loadings lower than 0.5 were removed. Then, the measurement model was adjusted according to the modification indices provided by the respective R function. The remaining items show factor loadings between 0.530 and 0.914. Hence, they are well above the cut-off of 0.4 suggested by Schmitt and Sass (2011). Next, the convergent as well as the discriminant validity are assessed. For the present research study, three measures were considered that allow the assessment of the convergent validity of the measurement model. First, the factor loadings were analysed and Schmitt and Sass (2011) suggest using the common rule-of-thumb cut-offs for standardised factor estimates at 0.4 which is fulfilled. In a second step for the assessment of the convergent validity, the average variance extracted (AVE) and the reliability were calculated. Fornell and Larcker (1981) recommend cut-off values of 0.5 for the AVE and 0.7 for the reliability. Concerning the AVE (see Table 2) the results of the study show that most values meet the recommended thresholds. The AVE of the construct of "price-consciousness" is only slightly below the benchmark of 0.5. All the other constructs show results between 0.550 and 0.745. For the reliability requirements, all the constructs show values significantly above the cut-off, ranging between 0.792 and 0.964. Summarising the previous results, the level of convergent validity of the measurement model is regarded as sufficient, in order to provide meaningful interpretations from the results.

Table 2. Convergent and discriminant validity.

		CR	VC	PC	VS	PR	WOM	RP
VC	Value Consciousness	0.894	**0.550**					
PC	Price Consciousness	0.792	0.506	**0.441**				
VS	Variety Seeking	0.839	0.033	0.272	**0.504**			
PR	Deal Proneness	0.914	0.025	0.071	0.007	**0.670**		
WOM	Word-of-Mouth	0.964	0.010	0.000	0.023	0.004	**0.745**	
RP	Repurchase Intention	0.946	0.002	0.007	0.001	0.001	0.817	**0.663**

Note: AVE is reported on the diagonal

What can further be seen from Table 2 is that all constructs except for positive word-of-mouth and repurchase intention meet the criterion for discriminant validity. The AVE of positive word-of-mouth is significantly smaller than the correlation between positive word-of-mouth and repurchase intention. The same is true for the AVE of repurchase intention. According to the before mentioned criterion, this would indicate that these two constructs are not sufficiently different from each other. However, when assessing the constructs regarding their function in the model, one can argue that from a substantive point of view, the discriminant validity is satisfied. Positive word-of-mouth as well as repurchase intention are specified as the measures implemented for the loyalty concept. Therefore, both constructs are required to be correlated and the result of a small discrimination between each other is not surprising and will not cause discrepancies in the validity of the test results.

4.3 Structural Model

For the absolute fit indices a Chi-Square value of 0.495 was observed, which is significantly higher than the specified cut-off of 0.05. Furthermore, the RMSEA shows a value of 0.000 and the SRMR a value of 0.061. Overall, the three indices are all indicating a relatively good fit between the model, which was hypothesised, and the data, which was observed. Regarding the CFI and the TLI, both of the consulted indices report a value of 1.000 (> 0.95) and can be interpreted as a good fit. In conclusion, what can be seen from the results is that the absolute as well as the incremental indices are indicating a well-fitting model. Given the fact, that there were no further modification indices, the specified SEM was considered the most appropriate model. A more detailed examination of the research model reveals that the proposed hypotheses are supported only to a limited extent. The obtained results illustrate that the value-conscious behaviour is positively regressed on the positive word-of-mouth communication with a beta-coefficient of $\beta=0.330$ as well as on the intention to repurchase with $\beta=0.320$. Both paths show a significant relationship with $p<0.1$ for word-of-mouth and for repurchase intention and support the idea that value-consciousness has a positive effect on customer loyalty (H_1). Furthermore, as expected, price-consciousness is negatively related with positive word-of-mouth ($\beta=-0.634$; $p<0.05$) and repurchase intention ($\beta=-0.531$; $p<0.05$) and has, therefore, a strong and significant negative effect on customer loyalty. This supports H_2 and with a β-coefficient of -0.634, the effect of price-consciousness on word-of-mouth is the strongest effect observed. On the contrary, H_3 und H_4 are partly rejected by the results. What is interesting in these results is that the p-value for the regression of variety-seeking on repurchase intention has a not significant level to be able to give a meaningful statement about its effect, while on the other hand the p-value ($p<0.01$) for the regression of variety-seeking on positive word-of-mouth indicates a highly significant relationship and also the effect is comparatively strong and positive with $\beta=0.493$, a fact that stands in contrast to the hypothesised negative relationship between variety-seeking and customer loyalty (H_3). Similarly contrasting results could be obtained for the effect of deal proneness on customer loyalty. In this case no significant effect of deal proneness on positive word-of-mouth could be observed, but a positive effect of deal proneness on repurchase intention ($\beta=0.313$; $p<0.05$), with a weaker but still significant p-value. Thus, there is also an evidence for a positive effect of deal proneness on customer loyalty. H_4 is so far partly rejected and like in the case of the previously analysed hypothesis an effect could be observed for only one of the two measures of customer loyalty, but likewise an effect that stands in contrast to the one proposed. The results are summarised in Table 3.

Table 3. Results of the model test.

Hypotheses	Independent variable		Dependent variable	β-coefficient	p-value
H_{1a}	Value-Consciousness	⇨	Word-of-Mouth	0.327	0.065
H_{1b}	Value-Consciousness	⇨	Repurchase Intention	0.317	0.072
H_{2a}	Price-Consciousness	⇨	Word-of-Mouth	-0.643	0.013
H_{2b}	Price-Consciousness	⇨	Repurchase Intention	-0.531	0.032
H_{3a}	Variety-Seeking	⇨	Word-of-Mouth	0.493	0.007
H_{3b}	Variety-Seeking	⇨	Repurchase Intention	0.253	N.S.
H_{4a}	Deal Proneness	⇨	Word-of-Mouth	0.219	N.S.
H_{4b}	Deal Proneness	⇨	Repurchase Intention	0.313	0.030

N.S. (not significant): the p-value is above the significance level of 0.1.

5   DISCUSSION AND IMPLICATIONS

5.1 Discussion of the Results

With the research focus on customer loyalty in the tourism industry the current study contributes to existing research on e-couponing, especially on the recently emerging trend of social group buying. The aim of the study was to find an answer to the question whether the customers, who are buying coupons on online daily deal platforms, tend to be loyal to the tourism service providers, who offer the deals. The obtained results reveal that the most significant relationship that could be confirmed is between customer loyalty and price-consciousness. The second clearly identified relationship is the one between customer loyalty and value-consciousness. This is perhaps not really surprising as literature acknowledges that "price and quality are among the most persuasive evaluative criteria used by purchasers" (Hur, et al., 2013, p.149). The present results illustrate that this is also true in the context of social e-couponing. In the case of price-consciousness a negative relationship was observed with positive word-of-mouth as well as repurchase intention. The conclusion that can be drawn from this result is that those customers, who buy an e-coupon on a daily deal website, because they are seeking for lower prices and because their buying decision is driven by the offered discount, tend to be less loyal to the provider of the purchased service. An effect of value-conscious consumer behaviour was confirmed for communication in the form of positive word-of-mouth and the intention to repurchase. However, in contrast to price-consciousness the effect is positive. This indicates that consumers, who are concerned about product quality and decide for a certain product or service under the premise to get the best value for the money they spend, are predisposed to become a loyal customer of the business once their quality constraint is fulfilled. Therefore, they become an interesting customer segment for the tourism industry. With regard to variety-seeking consumer behaviour, the results turned out to be different from what was expected, because there were no indicators for a negative relationship between variety-seeking and customer loyalty. Only on word-of-mouth could a significant effect be observed and surprisingly, this effect was positive. Therefore, the assumption can be made that the satisfied consumers of this segment of e-coupon buyers, will engage in positive word-of-mouth and recommend the service, but still do not intend to repurchase it, because of their desire for variety. The fact that there was no direct link from variety-seeking to repurchase intention, could reflect that these e-coupon users are loyal to the deals, but not to brand. Further explanations could build on the supposition that in the case of the exploration value, the similarities between purchase decisions in general and e-couponing are too small. Coupons are offered from different destinations and players in the tourism industry and are only available for a limited period of time, a framework that is not built for a continuing repurchase of the same service. Moreover, this changed setting could also deliver other possible explanations for the positive implications on word-of mouth. Tsai, et al. (2011, p.1101) examined the impact of social factors on online group buying and reported that the sense of a virtual community (VC) "appears to lead to positive outcomes such as increased satisfaction and communication with the VC as well as to greater trust and social interaction". Generally speaking, this reversed effect of variety-seeking would be subject for a more profound analysis in the context of social e-couponing. Together with the previously mentioned suspected relationship between variety-seeking and customer loyalty to deals, these considerations can be included into future research models. The study further reveals that there is also room for discussion with respect to the relationship between a deal proneness and customer loyalty. The results report that deal proneness has no significant effect on word-of-mouth, but a significant positive effect on the repurchase intention of customers. These findings do not support previous research. Where literature explains that loyal customers are not deal prone, because they are satisfied with the product or service and do not respond to promotional offers (Gázquez-Abad and Sánchez-Pérez, 2009), e-coupons found on daily deal websites seem to have a different effect. The similarities between e-coupons and more traditional formats of price reductions might be as well too small in order to apply the same assumptions in that context. Traditional deal hunters might enjoy the process of searching for promotions in newsletters, advertisements, or the stores itself and this process might be the reason that provokes their good feeling. In contrast, entering the daily deal website eliminates this process. Therefore, e-coupon buyers might prefer to invest less time and resources to obtain the deals and this could explain the fact, that they tend to repurchase products or services they discovered and are satisfied with. From the fact that the hypothesised effects are only supported to a limited extent, it becomes clear that the impact of the different forms of consumer behaviour in social e-couponing changes the consumer structure with regards to loyalty. In order to implement successful loyalty program measures tourism service providers should consider managerial implications for this special customer environment to address the right problem-solution-path.

5.2 Managerial Implications

The research reveals that the distinct consumer characteristics (i.e. value-consciousness, price-consciousness, variety-seeking and deal proneness) have different effects on customer loyalty and it can vary from a positive over a negative effect, to no effect at all. Tourism service providers should profile their customers and try to find out information about their purchasing pattern, strengths, and weaknesses. The present study discovered that price-conscious consumers are not predisposed to be loyal to the brand. It is an imperative today that businesses face a serious challenge to turn the negative effect of price-consciousness on customer loyalty around. While companies cannot decrease prices indefinitely and without a time constraint, they could offer rewards for loyal customers for example in the form of recurring price reductions. Since research found that price-conscious consumer are willing to make an extra effort to look for promotions (Gázquez-Abad and Sánchez-Pérez, 2009), they are probably more prone to show attention to these kind of initiatives and the tourism industry could make use of that advantage. At the same time the study was able to discover that value-conscious customers are an attractive consumer segment. In the case that customers, who acquired an e-coupon on a daily deal website, are satisfied with the obtained value for the money, they show a tendency to become loyal to the brand. However, there are some issues that tourism businesses should consider when they are targeting this segment. It is important to provide the consumers with sufficient background information about their services. Such information can help them to understand what they can derive from the coupon and will influence their purchase decision. Dickinger and Kleijnen (2008) suggest to target specific direct marketing campaigns to value seekers with the argument that they are positively disposed to the extra information and can become better informed than the other customers. For the variety-seeking customer segment it is important to take into consideration and try to manage the differentiating effects on positive word-of-mouth and repurchase intention. An understanding of these two dimensions is essential if the enterprises want to make efficient use of their promotional budgets. Even if variety-seekers do not show a tendency to repurchase the same products or services, companies should not neglect them while designing their loyalty programs. The positive effect on word-of-mouth indicates that variety-seeking customers have the power to bring new customers to the destination. The players in the tourism industry are recommended to devote an extra attention to convince those existing customers that it is worth trying their services. Managerial implications for deal prone customers take hold from a different angle. While coupon providers might expect deal prone customers to be loyal rather towards the deals than towards the brand, the results of the present study indicate the opposite. The group of customers, responding to deals and promotional offers, show a clear intention to repurchase. Service providers in the tourism industry are advised to strengthen this tendency and try to evoke also effects on positive word-of-mouth by building on the synergies between the two dimensions of customer loyalty. Even though, the purchase decision of the e-coupon was driven by the consumers' proneness to deals, enterprises could reinforce their intention to repurchase by using promotional tools in deal form at times. With an accompanying positive attitude towards the brand, the basis for positive word-of-mouth can be established (Mei-Lien, et al., 2012). By leveraging on these subsequent effects the company would be able to obtain additional benefits from their decision to offer e-coupons. Connecting the link to the rationale behind the customer lifetime value, it can be highlighted, that by providing these coupons, companies are able to quantify the acquisition costs of their consumers and also to direct business to times where they have excess capacity. Part of their fixed costs can possibly be covered and profitability secured. In case that positive word-of-mouth and recommendations can be enhanced additionally, the deal-provider has the chance to acquire new customers initiated by this positive interplay.

In a conclusion it can be summarized that merchants could increase the effectiveness of loyalty programs by targeting each customer segment with a corresponding, appropriate approach, since not all the consumers respond in the same way to the practices that intend to strengthen their loyalty towards the brand. Building on that assumption the fulfilment of customer retention objectives can be improved and contrasting effects to the one desired can be avoided.

5.3 Limitations and further research implications

The present research study contributes to existing literature about the fairly new trend of social e-couponing. Nevertheless, the study suffers from various limitations and leaves several research avenues in this area to pursue. First, there is to mention the small sample size, which is a main concern. From the 330 people questioned, only 97 formed part of the final sample. The study should be repeated with a larger sample size, which could deliver more significant results and reduce some doubt about the investigated relationships. Moreover, the enriched sample size would give room for more in-depth analysis. Especially relevant in this context would be a multi-group analysis, in order to identify possible differences within the groups of the sample, such as gender or financial situation. Another weakness of the sample is that it consists to a rather large extent of students and far more women than men. Therefore, the study provides only first indications, but no generalised assumptions for the e-coupon using society. Further limitations lie within the established underlying research model, which builds the essential basis for building the connection to the concept of customer loyalty. Extending discussions and research should include further measures for customer loyalty. In the current study positive word-of-mouth and repurchase intention are regarded to measure customer loyalty. However, the measurement should be enriched by another dimension, namely pricing insensitivity, as suggested by Mei- Lien, et al. (2012). Another limiting aspect in the measurement part is that the items, which determine the construct of deal proneness, focus on deals in general and not specifically on e-coupons to be found on daily deal websites. This differentiation might affect significantly the research findings and overcoming this restriction raises the need for further investigation. Overall, it is essential to keep the research models up-to-date with current developments in the coupon business.

REFERENCES

Algesheimer, R., Dholakia, U. M. & Herrmann, A. 2005. The Social Influence of Brand Community: Evidence from European Car Clubs. *Journal of Marketing,* 69 (3), pp.19-34.

Anderson, J. C. & Gerbing, D. W. 1988. Structural Equation Modeling in Practice: A Review and Recommended Two-Step Approach. *Psychological Bulletin,* 103 (3), pp.411-423.

Barrett, P. 2007. Structural Equation Modelling: Adjudging Model Fit. *Personality and Individual Differences,* 42 (5), pp.815-824.

Berné, C., Múgica, J. M. & Jesus, Y. M. 2001. The Effect of Variety-Seeking on Customer Retention in Services. *Journal of Retailing and Consumer Services,* 8 (6), pp.335–345.

Belk, R. W. & Coon, G. S. 1993. Gift Giving as Agapic Love: An Alternative to the Exchange Paradigm Based on Dating Experiences. *Journal of Consumer Research*, 20 (3), pp.*393-417*.

Bhasin, A. & Dickinson, R. 1987. Extra Value Couponing: Strategic Implications for Supermarkets. *Agribusiness*, 3 (3), pp.293-306.

Bojei, J. & Wong Chee, H. 2012. Brand Equity and Current Use as the New Horizon for Repurchase Intention of Smartphone. *International Journal of Business & Society*, 13 (1), pp.36-48.

Boon, E., Wiid, R. & Desautels, P. 2012. Teeth Whitening, Boot Camp, And a Brewery Tour: A Practical Analysis of 'Deal of the Day'. *Journal of Public Affairs*, 12 (2), pp.137-144.

Diamantopoulos, A. & Siguaw, J. A. 2000. *Introducing Lisrel*, London, Sage Publications.

Dichter, E. 1966. How Word-of-Mouth Advertising Works. *Harvard Business Review*, 44 (6), pp.147-166.

Dickinger, A. & Kleijnen, M. 2008. Coupons Going Wireless: Determinants of Consumer Intentions to Redeem Mobile Coupons. *Journal of Interactive Marketing*, 22 (3), pp.23-39.

Feick, L., Coulter, R. A. & Price, L. L. 2003. Rethinking the Origins of Involvement and Brand Commitment: Insights from Postsocialist Central Europe. *Journal of Consumer Research*, 30 (2), pp.51-169.

Fornell, C. & Larcker, D. F. 1981. Evaluating Structural Equation Models with Unobservable Variables and Measurement Error. *Journal of Marketing Research*, 18 (1), pp.39-50.

Grewal, D., Iyer, G. R., Krishnan, R. & Sharma, A. 2003. The Internet and the Price–Value–Loyalty Chain. *Journal of Business Research*, 56 (5), pp.391-398.

Gázquez-Abad, J. C. & Sánchez-Pérez, M. 2009. Characterising the Deal-Proneness of Consumers by Analysis of Price Sensitivity and Brand Loyalty: An Analysis in the Retail Environment. *International Review of Retail, Distribution & Consumer Research*, 19 (1), pp.1-28.

Gómez, M. & Rubio, N. 2010. Re-Thinking the Relationship between Store Brand Attitude and Store Brand Loyalty: A Simultaneous Approach. *International Review of Retail, Distribution & Consumer Research*, 20 (5), pp. 515-534.

Hellier, P. K., Geursen, G. M., Carr, R. A. & Rickard, J. A. 2003. Customer Repurchase Intention: A General Structural Equation Model. *European Journal of Marketing*, 37 (11/12), pp.1762-1800.

Hess Jr, R. L., Ganesan, S. & Klein, N. M. 2003. Service Failure and Recovery: The Impact of Relationship Factors on Customer Satisfaction. *Journal of the Academy of Marketing Science*, 31 (2), pp.127-145.

Hu, L. T. & Bentler, P. M. 1995. Evaluating Model Fit. *Structural Equation Modeling: Concepts, Issues, and Applications*. Thousand Oaks, Ca, Us: Sage Publications, Inc., pp.76-99.

Hu, L. T. & Bentler, P. M. 1999. Cutoff Criteria for Fit Indexes in Covariance Structure Analysis: Conventional Criteria versus New Alternatives. *Structural Equation Modeling: A Multidisciplinary Journal*, 6 (1), pp.1-55.

Hughes, S. & Beukes, C. 2012. Growth and Implications of Social E-Commerce and Group Buying Daily Deal Sites: The Case of Groupon and Livingsocial. *International Business & Economics Research Journal*, 11 (8), pp.921-934.

Hur, W.-M., Kim, Y. & Park, K. 2013. Assessing the Effects of Perceived Value and Satisfaction on Customer Loyalty: A 'Green' Perspective. *Corporate Social Responsibility & Environmental Management*, 20 (3), pp.146-156.

Kang, H., Hahn, M., Fortin, D. R., Hyun, Y. J. & Eom, Y. 2006. Effects of Perceived Behavioral Control on the Consumer Usage Intention of E-Coupons. *Psychology & Marketing*, 23 (10), pp.841-864.

Kline, R. B. 2011. *Principles and Practice of Structural Equation Modeling,* New York, Guilford Press.

Kumar, V. 2008. *Customer Lifetime Value: The Path to Profitability.* Now Publishers Inc.

Köpp, S., Mukhachou, A. & Schwaninger, M. 2013. Group Buying Schemes: A Sustainable Business Model? *University of St. Gallen - Discussion Paper,* St.Gallen: Institute of Management, 58 (1), pp.1-53.

Lichtenstein, D. R., Bloch, P. H. & Black, W. C. 1988. Correlates of Price Acceptability. *Journal of Consumer Research,* 15 (2), pp.243-252.

Lichtenstein, D. R., Netemeyer, R. G. & Burton, S. 1990. Distinguishing Coupon Proneness from Value Consciousness: An Acquisition-Transaction Utility. *Journal of Marketing,* 54 (3), pp.54-67.

Liu, C., Ouzrout, Y., Nongaillard, A., Bouras, A. & Zhou, J. 2014. Evaluation Model for E-Tourism Product: A Hidden Markov Model-Based Algorithm. *International Journal of Technology Management,* 64 (1), pp.45-63.

Mei-Lien, L., Green, R. D., Farazmand, F. A. & Grodzki, E. 2012. Customer Loyalty: Influences on Three Types of Retail Stores' Shoppers. *International Journal of Management & Marketing Research,* 5 (1), pp.1-19.

Priluck Grossmann, R. 1998. Developing and Managing Effective Consumer Relationships. *Journal of Product & Brand Management,* 7 (1), pp.27-40.

Rao, V. G. 2009. Effect of Sales Promotions on Consumer Preferences - The Moderating Role of Price Perceptions and Deal Proneness (A Study of FMCG Products). *The Ximb Journal of Management,* 6 (1), pp.1-18.

Reichheld, F. F. & Markey Jr, R. G. 2000. E-Customer Loyalty-Applying the Traditional Rules of Business for Online Success. *European Business Journal,* 12 (4), pp.173-179.

Rosseel, Y. 2012. An R Package for Structural Equation Modeling. *Journal of Statistical Software,* 48 (2), pp.1-36.

Schmitt, T. A. & Sass, D. A. 2011. Rotation Criteria and Hypothesis Testing for Exploratory Factor Analysis: Implications for Factor Pattern Loadings and Interfactor Correlations. *Educational & Psychological Measurement,* 71 (1), pp.95-113.

Srinivasan, S. S., Anderson, R. & Ponnavolu, K. 2002. Customer Loyalty in E-Commerce: An Exploration of its Antecedents and Consequences. *Journal of Retailing,* 78 (1), pp.41-50.

Statista.Com. 2013. *Groupon - Statista Dossier 2013* [Online]. Statista-Das Statistikportal. Available at: <http://de.statista.com/themen/699/Groupon/> [Accessed 04 October 2013].

Steiger, J. H. 2007. Understanding the Limitations of Global Fit Assessment in Structural Equation Modeling. *Personality and Individual Differences,* 42 (5), pp.893-898.

Tsai, M.-T., Cheng, N.-C. & Chen, K.-S. 2011. Understanding Online Group Buying Intention: The Roles of Sense of Virtual Community and Technology Acceptance Factors. *Total Quality Management & Business Excellence,* 22 (10), pp.1091-1104.

Tuten, T. L. & Ashley, C. 2011. Promotional Strategies for Small Businesses: Group Buying Deals. *Small Business Institute Journal,* 7 (2), pp.15-29.

Van Trijp, H. C. M., Hoyer, W. D. & Inman, J. J. 1996. Why Switch? Product Category-Level Explanations for True Variety-Seeking Behavior. *Journal of Marketing Research,* 33 (3), pp.281-292.

Wells, W. D. & Tigert, D. J. 1971. Activities, Interests and Opinions. *Journal of Advertising Research,* 11 (4), 27-35.

Zeithaml, V. A. 1988. Consumer Perceptions of Price, Quality, and Value: A Means-End Model and Synthesis of Evidence. *Journal of Marketing,* 52 (3), pp.2-22.

Value Formation of Loyalty Programs in the Hotel Industry: Starwood Preferred Guest, Marriott Rewards, Hyatt Gold Passport

Ksenia Lakhtina,

Modul University Vienna, Austria
lakhtina.ksenia@gmail.com

Abstract

This research investigates the commonly significant variables that describe and characterise loyalty programs of the hotel industry. The three loyalty programs of worldwide-known hotel companies were selected, namely, Starwood Preferred Guest, Marriott Rewards, and Hyatt Gold Passport. Three case studies were compared and contrasted according to the variables indicated in article by Kim et al. (2003), such as enrolment fee, enrolment bonus, expiration, points pooling policy, points purchase, offering other products for award, award transfer, award threshold, affinity card, and elite level qualification. The findings of the study are as follows. First, the hotel companies need to be very careful about setting sensible thresholds and limits to their programs. Consumers tend to turn away from high barriers and choose the path where they find less resistance. Moreover, it is essential that all of the benefits provided to the consumers by the loyalty program are available in all parts of the world where the program exists. In the end, cooperation and partnership with other industries are not less essential than other indicated factors. The hotel firms should reinforce their relationships with companies to provide customers with the greater choice of rewards of their taste and therefore increase the value proposition of the loyalty program itself.

Keywords: customer relationship management; loyalty program; value formation; customer loyalty; hotel industry

1 INTRODUCTION

In the 21st century, the age of double digit growth and severe competitiveness, companies are getting into fierce battles for consumers. Moreover, they attempt to approach not plainly any consumer but rather strive to attract 'best' customers for their businesses. It is strongly believed that the ability not merely to attract wanted customers but also to keep them and to increase their repeating patronage will positively affect the firms' performance (Bowen and Shoemaker, 1998). In order to achieve this goal and deliver desired experience for customers, managers and marketers introduce various customer relationships and marketing techniques (Bowen and Shoemaker, 1998). Customer relationship management (CRM) and loyalty programs are one of those techniques that are pursued by number of companies through various industries to increase yield through interactive and value-added relationship with the best customers (Capizzi and Ferguson, 2005). Nonetheless, not all of the developed CRM techniques reach its initial aim. Researchers argue that this is a consequence of flawed design of loyalty programs with a weak value proposition (Capizza and Ferguson, 2005). What is the value for the customer then? How to create it? What are the aspects of loyalty program that deserve attention to reinforce the value proposition?

This paper attempts to discuss all these vital questions by analysing three examples in the hotel industry. It will aid to understand how companies develop their customer relationship strategy on a real-life example. Moreover, it will provide hints on value creation process for their new and already existing customers. This paper is organised in three main parts. First, the existing literature on CRM and loyalty programs will be reviewed to determine the value of loyalty programs in the hotel industry. Second, the value created by the loyalty programs of three international corporations will be presented. Their main policies and conditions will be distributed according to nine variables which have been proved to be significant in the process of value formation for loyalty programs (Kim et al., 2003). Finally, the recommendations and conclusions will be provided for the adjustments and alterations of the loyalty programs at place.

1.1 Loyalty programs in the hotel industry

In the hotel industry, reward programs that encourage guests to earn points during every stay dominate. The amount of earned points depends on the amount spent for the purchase. The accumulated points can be redeemed for other services at any hotel-participant of the program. For instance, it could be any discounts (spa, F&B), future nights, up-grades, and other rewards. Additionally, programs may involve partnership with other complimentary marketers (such as an airline or car rental firm) to facilitate accumulating points and to increase variety of rewards (Berman, 2006). Most of the major hotel brands have their loyalty programs that slightly differ in some aspects, but the principle is the same (Hilton Honors, Marriott Rewards, Hyatt Gold Passport, Starwood Preferred Guest, InterContinental and others). Such programs strengthen customer relationship and encourag repeating patronage by rewarding guests for each repeated action (Sharp and Sharp, 1997).

1.2 Problem discussion

The main purpose of the loyalty programs in hotels as a part of CRM is to retain existing customers and create an efficient emotional bond with the brand 'in order to increase profitability of stable customer relationships' (Sharp and Sharp, 1997:474). Retaining existing customers takes fewer efforts, time, and financial resources in comparison to attracting new clients (Reichheld, 1993). Although studies have proven that implementing loyalty programs has a remarkable effect on customer satisfaction and retention (Stauss et al., 2001 cited in Stauss et al., 2005), there is a debate in the field doubting the effectiveness and efficiency of the programs.

Some authors (Stauss et al., 2005; Dowling and Uncles, 1997; Hu et al, 2010; Leenheer et al., 2007; O'Malley, 1998; Keh, 2006; O'Brien and Jones, 1995; Shugan, 2005) question the ability of loyalty programs to satisfy customers and thus to outperform the financial advantage of searching for new ones. Nevertheless, it has been claimed that it is expensive to attract new customers to the business, the implementation and realisation of loyalty program could be pricey as well (Butcher, 2002). Having such program in place means that potential participants have to be captivated first to sign up, and then they need to be engaged enough and feel benefits program provides to build an effective relationship with the brand. Moreover, it has argued that value perception of the loyalty program does not automatically lead to brand loyalty (Dowling and Uncles, 1997). This happens because customers are more likely to derive satisfaction from a program but not from the brand itself (Dowling and Uncles, 1997). If customers do not feel any connection to the brand, they will switch to another rival hotel that provides lower price despite all the incentives available in a more expensive option (Hu, 2010). An effective loyalty program is built on a thorough strategy that is able to be competitive in the external environment within rival companies, and also be able to keep up with new emergent trends (Mintzberg, 1987).

1.3 Research aims

The purpose of the research is to contrast the value formation factors underlying chosen loyalty programs as stipulated by Kiem et al. (2003). These authors suggested ten values that should be incorporated in hotel loyalty programs to be beneficial: enrolment bonuses, enrolment fees, expiration policy, miles or points pooling policy, miles or points purchase policy, offers of products produced by other industry categories as awards, award transfer policy, award threshold, affinity card, and elite level qualification.. A comparison on that basis allows for a better understanding of how the value of a particular program is formed.

2 LITERATURE REVIEW

2.1 CRM and purpose of loyalty programs

'CRM is a strategic approach that is concerned with creating improved shareholder value through the development of appropriate relationship with key customers and customer segments' (Payne and Frow, 2005:168). It has been argued that implementation of CRM is a crucial part of a business strategy (Reinartz and Kumar, 1997). Intending to outperform competitors and ensure stable profit gaining businesses face the challenge of retaining the key customers to create and maintain customer database (Tideswell and Fredline, 2004). The complexity of this task is to identify valuable clients that are worthy of the necessary investments. Dowling and Uncles (1997) argue that not all customers are important, and only specific customers should be catered rather than all of them. According to Reinanrtz and Kumar (2003) the value of customer is determined by its lifetime value to the firm. Short-term and long-term oriented customers differ in factors that determine their future exchange (Garbarion and Johnson, 1999). Garbarion and Johnson (1999) state that focus on customer satisfaction is likely to be more effective on weak-relationship customers, whilst brand commitment and loyalty affect long-term oriented clients in a greater way.

Organizations that develop and implement loyalty programs follow the common belief that the costs for attracting new customers exceed the ones necessary to keep an existing one and enhance the frequency of his/her purchase behaviour (Wansink, 2003). However, many executives discover little differences between continued patronage of existing customers and increased costs tied to managing and maintaining a loyalty program (Wansink, 2003). Critics argue that the programs' designs are flawed, thus, lacking some of the five key cross-functional stages: strategy development process, value creation process, multichannel integration process, information management process, and performance assessment process (Payne and Frow, 2005). The central point that matters most in the whole process is creating a favourable attitude toward an entity by providing value that therefore leads to repeated patronage (Dick and Basu, 1994).

2.2 Goals of loyalty programs

One of the fundamental goals of loyalty schemes is to manipulate people's behaviour in a sophisticated system (O'Malley, 1998). The use of rewards and incentives, which are individually targeted, is aimed to encourage customers to try a new product, pay premium prices or try additional services. They are also used to reward repeat purchasing. Customers are willing to engage in such schemes because people like to get something for nothing (Dowling and Uncle, 1997).

Also, loyalty programs are perfectly accurate tools to collect detailed and correct information on the customers. It has been indicated that loyalty program (LP) can help firms to implement database marketing (Xie and Chen, 2013), become more competitive (Butscher, 2002).and provides insights on customers` desires (Bayraktar et al., 2010). A robust database has a potential to bring a company closer to one-on-one marketing (Butscher, 2002). Companies implement LP to reach competitive advantage and a unique position in the market (Porter, 1979), mainly by providing added-value. Dowling and Jones (1997:73) state that the decision to introduce a loyalty scheme is often motivated 'by fears of competitive parity'. The biggest problem with LPs is that companies are often uncertain about what exactly the program is targeted to achieve (O'Malley, 1998). As a result programs are widely misunderstood and misapplied (O'Brien and Jones, 1995).

Loyalty programs are designed to deter acquisition expenses.. On this matter, Butscher (2002) argues that expenses for LPs should not be considered operational costs but rather as investments in a marketing tool that is strategically necessary to survive in a severe business world. A smartly developed reward program can accelerate the loyalty cycle by encouraging second- or even first- year customers to behave like tenth-year ones (O'Brien and Jones, 1995). Moreover, JiungYee Lee et al. (2014) found out that LPs help not merely decrease costs, but also to increase occupancy and profitability. Although the results show modest impact on revenue, the change in other figures is still applicable in managerial purposes in the hospitality industry (JiungYee Lee et al., 2014).

2.3 Flaws of loyalty programs

O'Brien and Jones (1995) argue that the root of all problems and failures lays in an inability of management to develop a strategic CRM program. When planning is wrong and inadequate, the achievement of financial objectives is hindered. The value created by means of the program must exceed the cost of value delivered (O'Brien and Jones, 1995). Moreover, Banasicwicz (2005) claims that insufficient customer insight is another source of underperformance. The issue here is that consumers merely register for any program, and in the end they become more often loyal not to the brand but to incentives of the reward program.

Conducting research on profitable lifetime duration, Reinartz and Kumar (2003) have concluded that the main managerial challenge is to satisfy important clients whilst containing operational cost. O'Brien and Jones (1995) explain the exacerbation of the problem of falling ability to detect the most valuable customers by growth in size and complexity of the firms..

2.4 Success Measurement

The metrics chosen for the evaluation of the performance must clearly differentiate level of success, average performance and failure (Butscher, 2002). Those metrics should combine as quantitative factors, such as response rate, as well as qualitative factors, such as brand loyalty (Butscher, 2002). The crucial thing is to utilise proper indices. Many companies are not able to realise the actual effect that LP has on their success as the result of a wrong choice of success factors. For instance, choosing registration rate as a performance metrics will lead to erroneous conclusions (Banasiewicz, 2005). This metric is just an indicator of number of customers without purchase intention. Satisfaction is also not a reliable measurement. Especially in tourism, customers express high satisfaction even without intention of returning (McKercher, 2012). Berman (2006) and Butscher (2002) argue that the performance of any loyalty program needs to be compared to results of non-member control group of customers. It aids to track differences in sales, loyalty, profitability behaviour of different groups (Berman, 2006). Moreover, it isolates influence of loyalty program's marketing from other activities. Such initiative to compare non-member group customers and members of LP has been attempted by Vorhees et al. (2014). By analysing return on investment (ROI), the researchers concluded that hotels to have a significant revenue rise when their guests enrol to a LP (Vorhees et al., 2014).

According to Berman (2006) the success of the loyalty program can vary significantly depending on the market segment (customers close to leaving, customer whose volume of purchase cannot be increased, etc.), time horizon chosen to measure the effectiveness, ROI compared to the alternatives. All of these performance measurements are worth being considered only according to the defined goals of the loyalty program (Butscher, 2002).

3 METHODOLOGY

To provide a better insight into chosen phenomenon, such as value formation of loyalty programmes, the comparative research is conducted among three case studies: Starwood Preferred Guest (SPG), Marriott Rewards (MR), and Hyatt Gold Passport (HGP). Comparative research has been chosen to uncover differences and reveal unique aspects of a particular program (Atkinson and Delamont, 2010), so to make emphasis on context to understand specificities. Moreover, the examination of brand in the nature of relative attitudes is more likely to indicate the background of repeat patronage than relationships with the brand determined in isolation (Dick and Basu, 1994).

The hotel chains were chosen on the basis of similarity, and thus comparability in terms of size and geographical spread. All three brands are leading players in the hotel market with a variety of brands ranging from budget to luxury scale targeting different market segments .

Comparison and analysis of the three reward programs was be performed according to the value formation factors proposed by Kim et al. (2003). In the article the information on data set of all variables was collected through various sources, such as websites, Frequently Asked Questions from customers, books and articles on the related subjects, and interviews with field experts. Further, a multiple regression analysis was conducted in order to examine whether return on equity (ROE) is affected by the presence or absence of the policy according to each of ten variables. These ten variables are as follows: *enrolment fee, enrolment bonus, expiration policy, points pooling policy, points purchase policy, offering other products for award, award transfer policy, award threshold, affinity card, elite level qualification.* First, during the study it was revealed that variables, such as elite level qualification, affinity credit card and award threshold were statistically significant. Second, the three variables: purchasing points, enrolment bonus, and award threshold had a significant impact on firms` ROE. The first two, purchasing points and enrolment bonus, contributed positively while the award threshold had a negative impact on firms` earned ROE.

The results of the study prove that some factors are more significant and affect firms` success in either positive or negative way. Further, this paper compares three hotel reward programs according to the ten identified variables and analyses which value the suggested variables offer for customers, which affect it may have on them, and consequently on the firms` performance.

4   DATA PRESENTATION AND ANALYSIS

4.1 Comparison and analysis

To compare and contrast the core dimensions of the three loyalty programs - Starwood Preferred Guest, Marriott Rewards, and Hyatt Gold Passport - all the data on comparing variables was retrieved from companies' websites and organised into Table1. In the next paragraphs every single variable will be described and analysed based on this information and core findings by Kim et al. (2003).

The first two factors of all three loyalty programs that were assumed to deliver value for consumers are identical and can be eliminated as variables for competition basis. However, they are still worthy of a discussion. To become a member of any of three programs no enrolment fees are required, although there are also no entry bonuses. Correspondingly, the hotel companies assume their programs already benefit without enrolment fees and seek to evolve other aspects of the LPs. Nonetheless, 'enrolment bonuses' variable was still proved by Kim et al. (2003) to have a positive effect on firm's ROE.

The next factor is an expiration policy for accumulated points. According to the main terms and conditions of all three programs, all points that a member has earned will forfeit in case the customer turns inactive. SPG cuts down this time up to 12 months. It deliberately diminishes the time restrictions to foster the purchases and encourage its members to be active all the time in order not to lose their points and therefore spend more money.

The next variable shows if the loyalty program provides an opportunity to combine points from various programs. The pooling policy is mostly represented by cooperation with other loyalty programs within the travel industry. The most consideration this value received from SPG and MR programs. SPG has established the affiliations with Amtrak Guest Rewards (The National Railroad Passenger Corporation) and with more than 150 airlines as for train and airline industry respectively. MR provides an opportunity to redeem points on travelling with Venice Simplon-Orient-Express trains that belong to the Belmond group. As for the airline industry, the points can be converted to United Mileage Plus miles and redeemed afterwards. Comparing with these two programs, HGP is considerably loosing with its solely 27 participating airlines and one Amtrak railroad company.

Points purchasing policy was also identified as a statistically significant variable that influences a firms' performance. In all three loyalty programs the policies differ with respect to the prices per point and purchase threshold. The highest price per point is indicated by SPG, which is \$0.035. The lowest price one would have to pay for MR point - \$0.0125, and HGP value of one point lays somewhere in the middle with \$0.024. There is also a threshold amount of min and max number of points that can be purchased. Therefore, to make one purchase member of SPG would spend \$17.5, member of MR – \$12.5, and member of HGP - \$24.

'Awards offered from other industries' dimension is not proved to be a significant variable for the firms' performance, although there are considerable discrepancies in redeem options varying from on program to another. SPG and MR provide a wide variety of shopping, transportation and other options to acquire the rewards. Moreover, SPG enhanced its program by providing an opportunity to redeem accumulated points in an online auction to bid on 'no-money-can't-buy experiences' and events. After this extended list of options, the redeem options of HPG appear to be fairly scanty. On its website only one option with Avis cars is indicated.

The conditions for the seventh variable – 'award transfer policy' – do not differ in all three sample LPs to the great extent. All three state that points can be transferred exclusively to member of the respective loyalty program, points can be transferred to the family members with the same address, and points can be gifted to other members to help them reach amount needed to complete an eligible stay or upgrade for the better room. However, only SPG and MR provide an option to transfer the points to charity organisations. SPG has affiliations with The American Red Cross and UNICEF while MR gives an opportunity to choose from over one million charity organisations. HGP does not mention any donation to charity organisation as a transfer option.

Award threshold is one of the most significant dimensions that influence companies' ROE (Kim et al., 2003) but in a reverse way. The higher the threshold, the lower the firms' earned ROE. The highest threshold for the cheapest category of hotels from the sample is established by MR – 7,500 points, followed by HGP – 5,000 points and SPG – 2,000 points. At the glance it seems that it is easier to get points for one night with SPG, however, it is worth mentioning the sum of money that members will need to spend to accumulate the appropriate amount of points. To reach 2,000 Starpoints SPG member will need to spend \$1,000 (2 points for \$1 spent); to reach 7,500 point MR points - spend just \$750 (10 points for \$1 spent); to reach 5,000 HGP points - spend \$1,000 (5 points for \$1). Therefore, although MR has the highest award threshold, it will take less effort to achieve required boundary than by other two programs even though they have lower thresholds.

Another statistically significant variable is 'affinity card'. Possession of one of these credit cards opens one extra channel to earn points. Active users of credit cards would earn points merely by conducting their routine transactions. All sample LPs already have established such affiliations, albeit with varying partners. Both HGP and MR are affiliated with Visa and SPG accordingly has established a partnership with American Express. The affiliation of MR with Visa has the most expanded list of benefits. Moreover, the program differentiates two types of credit card with distinct benefits. The ordinary MR Credit Card has the cheapest annual fee of $45 with no introductory fee. HGP adheres to the same policy, although the annual fee rises until $75. SPG requires the same amount of $75. However, it does not offer a first year free of charge. Moreover, the SPG credit card lacks a number of benefits compared to other two LPs. For instance, higher number of points earned for each dollar spent, different amount of points earned depending on the type of purchase, annual free night stay. Despite the narrowness of the conditions of the SPG credit card, it is available not only to the US residents (like with MR and HGP) but also to the residents of the UK, Canada, and Japan.

Last but not least variable is 'elite level qualification'. That is another statistically significant dimension. Elite status means that a specific threshold has been reached that is required to get additional benefits to the standard membership. SPG an HGP have two elite level qualification which are Gold/Platinum and Platinum/Diamond respectively. MR's elite statuses are broken down into three levels: Silver/Gold/Platinum. The fastest level that can be achieved is a Silver status with MR. The member will need to complete only 10 personal nights. The other LPs require more than 15 eligible nights or more than 5 eligible stays. The main benefits received by holders of the elite statuses are various discounts, complimentary gifts, late check-out, no blackout dates for reservations, upgrades, and faster accumulation of reward points. Although MR and HGP have a greater variety of tiny bonuses, SPG has more advantages already with the first level of elite status. For instance, besides the late check-out until 4 p.m., the Gold SPG member receives a welcome gift in form of complimentary in-room internet or complimentary beverage.

Table 1. Value Formation Factors of SPG, MR and HGP

Factors	SPG	MR	HGP
Enrolment bonuses	Not identified	Not identified	Not identified
Enrolment fees	No	No	No
Expiration policy	Starpoints earned or otherwise obtained by an SPG Member will forfeit without notice if the SPG Member becomes inactive, even if the SPG Member has achieved SPG Lifetime Gold or SPG Lifetime Platinum status.	A Membership Account may be closed at the Company's discretion if no Points or Miles are accrued during a 24-month period. All Points in the Membership Account will be forfeited at that time.	Hyatt Gold Passport accounts that accrue 24 consecutive months of inactivity will be closed and all Hyatt Gold passport points in that account will be forfeited at that time.
Miles or points pooling policy	**Train trips:** Starwood Preferred Guest members can transfer Starpoints to Amtrak Guest Rewards at a 1:1 ratio Transfers must be made in 5,000 Starpoints increments. **Airlines:** Starpoints can be transfer to miles to be redeemed on more than 150 airlines. 5,000-mile bonus when you transfer 20,000 Starpoints to miles (must be transferred as part of the same transaction to receive the bonus miles).	**Train trips:** point accrued with MR can be redeemed for travelling with Venice Simplon-Orient-Express. **Airlines:** points can be converted to United Mileage Plus miles. 20% when points are converted with RewardsPlus.	**Train trips:** Hyatt Gold Passport members can earn 500 miles per stay with Amtrak. **Airlines:** Hyatt Gold Passport members can earn 500 miles per stay with 28 participating travel partners.
Miles or points purchase policy	Starpoints can be purchased for $0.035 per Starpoint. Minimum purchase amount is 500 Starpoints; maximum purchase is up to 20,000 per account per calendar year. Points are applicable toward all Starpoint awards but do not count toward elite (Gold or Platinum) status.	Points can be purchased for $0.0125 per point. Minimum purchase amount is 1000 points; maximum member may purchase or receive as a gift a combined maximum of 50,000 points per calendar year.	Points can be purchased for $0.024 per point. Minimum purchase amount is 1,000 points; maximum purchase is up to 40,000 per account per calendar year. Bonus points purchased do not count toward qualification for Elite membership tier status, such as Platinum or Diamond tier status.
Offers of products produced by other industry categories as awards	**Merchandise:** Amazon, Banana Republic, Bliscertificates, Chateau Ste. Michelle, Conde Nast publications, GAP, MPI, Nordstrom, PCMA, Pottery Barn, Starbucks Card, Williams-Sonoma, ITunes	**Shopping:** Shopmyway (online shopping), Energy Plus (electricity), Exclusive Gifts & Flowers, UR*Tix (event tickets) **Transportation:** Hertz, Cruises Only, Avios, CTRIP, Travelling Connect	**Transportation:** Avis cars

	Partners: Audience Rewards, Live Nation, PGA Tour **Transportation:** Avia, SIXT **Moments:** redeem accumulated Starpoints on online auction to bid on no-money-can't-buy experiences and events	**Financial:** Diners club	
Award transfer policy	SVO (Starwood Vacation Ownership) owners may transfer to other SVO Owners even if not at the same address. Also Starpoints can be sent to family members and friends. Another option to transfer collected points is to donate them one of the Starwood's charity partners (two options: The American Red Cross or UNICEF).	Points can be transferred to a legal spouse or domestic partner at time of reward redemption provided he or she is also a MR member. Also a member of MR can buy up to 50,000 points as a gift for another member. Another option is to donate them to the charity of your choice by searching a database of more than 1 million organizations or by selecting one of Marriott's featured causes.	HGP points are for member's benefit only and are not transferable to another person for any reason including divorce or inheritance. Points can only be combined with any HGP member to redeem an award. Members can also request to issue the award to other individual. Another option is to purchase points for friends or family.
Award threshold	Minimum of 2,000 Starpoints needed to redeem for a free weekend night at a Category 1 hotel (7 Category options). Number of Starpoints needed for a Free Night Award varies by hotel category.	Minimum of 7,500 points needed to redeem for a free night at a Category 1 (9 Category options). Number of points needed for a Free Night Award varies by hotel category.	Minimum of 5,000 points needed to redeem for a free night at a Category 1 hotel (7 Category options). Number of points needed for a Free Night Award varies by hotel category.
Affinity card	Affiliation with American Express (only for US, UK, Canada, and Japan residents) - Welcome bonus of 10,000 Starpoints (3 complimentary nights), when $1,000 spent during the first 3 months of Card membership - 1 Starpoint for every $1 spent from the card - Automatic upgrade to SPG Gold Preferred status when $15,000 spent from the card during the year - Free Weekend Night Award for each year $25,000 spent on the Card - Annual fee $75	Affiliation with Visa (only for US residents) **Marriott Rewards Credit Card and Business Card (extended terms apply to Marriott Rewards Premier Card)** - 30,000 bonus points after $1,000 spent in first 3 months from account opening - 2 free nights after account approval (Category 1-4) - 3 points for every $1 spent at over 3,600 Marriott locations - 1 point for every $1 spent on purchases anywhere else - 10 Nights Credit toward next Elite membership level every year after account anniversary	Affiliation with Visa (only for US residents). - Welcome bonus of 2 free nights, when $1,000 spent within the first 3 months of card membership - 3 points for every $1 spent at all Hyatt properties with the Card. - 2 points for every $1 spent at restaurants, on airline tickets purchased directly from the airline and at car rental agencies. - 1 point for every $1 spent anywhere else the Card is used. - No foreign transaction fees - Upgrade to Elite member status - Every year on card member anniversary

Elite level qualification	- 1 Elite Night for every $3,000 spent - Introductory Annual fee of $0 the first year, then $45 - Introductory Annual Fee of $0 the first year, then $85	one free night at any category 1-4 property - Introductory Annual fee of $0 the first year, then $75

	Gold: achieved by completing 10 eligible stays or 25 nights in a calendar year. Benefits:
	- Three Starpoints for every eligible USD spent
	- 4 p.m. check-out
	- Special elite customer telephone line
	- Welcome gift (complimentary in-room internet or complementary beverage)
	
	Extended benefits for the next elite level: Platinum.
		Silver: achieved by completing 10 personal nights. Benefits:
		- 20% bonuses on reward program points
		- Weekend Rate Discount: 10% discount on the regular room rate for Friday and Saturday night stays at participating Courtyard and SpringHill Suites
		- 10% discount at Marriott Gift Shop
		- 10% discount for The Ritz-Carlton branded merchandise, excluding sundries
		- Priority Late Checkout (on availability)
		- The Ultimate Reservation Guarantee.
		
		  Extended benefits for the
		
		  next elite levels: Gold and
		
		  Platinum.
			Platinum: achieved by completing 5 eligible stays or 15 eligible nights in a calendar year. Benefits:
			- 20% off the daily rate with My Elite Rate
			- Achievement of rewards faster with a 15% point bonus when choosing points
			- Preferred room including rooms on higher floors or larger rooms (on availability upon arrival)
			- Complimentary in-room Internet access
			- Expedite check-in at a dedicated area for elite members
			- Room is always available with 72-hour guarantee
			- Late check out until 2:00 p.m. (on availability)
			- Exclusive Platinum line for reservations
			
			Extended benefits for the next elite level: Diamond.

5 CONCLUSIONS AND RECOMMENDATIONS

The review of literature on customer relationship management showed that there is a general consensus on the positive effects of loyalty programs on the firm's performance. Through the comparison and analysis of the case studies suggested above the following conclusions can be made.

One of the essential variables for the firms' earned ROE is 'enrolment bonuses'. This part in all three programs is not developed at all. It is advised that management will take this issue into consideration and will try to introduce compliments to new members. It will aid to attract new subscribers, and even entice potential members from other programs.

The purchasing policy for points is also indicated as an important variable. Although from the first sight it may seem that the most expensive points are introduced by Starwood Preferred Guest, the greatest value is put into Hyatt Gold Passport points. It is worth admitting that this is an effective marketing trick. As argued by Dick and Basu (1994) loyalty and people's behaviour can be influenced by various descendants: cognitive, affective, and conative. The price can be seen as one of the cognitive descendants. Physiologically people will consider and feel more attracted to lower prices.

As for the threshold levels, hotel companies should be careful and sensitive when establishing high threshold levels. Customers tend to turn away from high barriers and follow the path of least resistance. Therefore, the threshold level should be reasonable and attainable for the customers (Kim et al. 2003). Marriott Rewards has the highest threshold. However, it takes less effort to reach demanded amount of points to redeem them for the cheapest room category. For the Marriott Rewards, it is recommended to pay a greater attention to this issue, and make their conditions more explicit for the consumers.

The biggest issue all the programs encounter with the affinity card policies. The existence of affiliation with the credit card provider was also found to positively impact the firms' performance. Nonetheless, this opportunity is mainly available only for the US residents. However, according to conditions of SPG program these boundaries are spread further to the UK, Canada, and Japan. This defect needs to be fixed. The companies should attempt to evaluate the feasibility of the introduction of affinity cards within other parts of the world. Besides the enrolment percentage, such initiative may increase the loyalty affiliation level what will make the firms' performance improve.

Concerning the further research on loyalty programs in the hotel industry and its value formation, testing of other variables is suggested. For instance, on basis of availability of raw data, more financial variables can be analysed. The future research can also go into path of justifying relationship of guest satisfaction with membership ratio of consumers enrolled in a particular loyalty program. Consequently, the enrolment activity can be linked to the indicators of companies' performance.

6 LIMITATIONS

The major problem in comparative research is that the perfect comparative set is difficult to determine (Atkinson and Delamont, 2010). Moreover, there are possibly hotel companies with suitable profiles, which would warrant their inclusion. This small sample cannot represent all of the companies out at the market. Hence, generalisations cannot be assumed (Yin, 1994). Secondly, the article by Kim et al. (2003) that has been used as a base for the analysis of the case studies is dated back to year 2003. This means that assumptions and results of the article by Kim et al. (2003) are more than ten years old. Therefore, it is important to consider that results of this paper can be distorted by the outdated information, in case if conditions and trends in the market have changed over the past ten years. Lastly, the interpretations and content analysis is based on researcher's opinion. Thus, the findings can be found to have other conclusions. Moreover, the case studies solely describe the phenomenon but do not provide an insight and reasons why the things are done in a certain way (Yin, 1994).

REFFERENCES

Atkinson, P. and Delamont, S. (2010) SAGE qualitative research methods. London: SAGE.

Banasiewicz, A. (2005) 'Loyalty program planning and analytics.' Journal of Consumer Marketing, 22(6), pp. 332–339.

Bayraktar, A., Yilmaz, E. and Yamak, O. (2010) 'Implementation of RFID technology for the differentiation of loyalty programs.' Journal of Relationship Marketing, 9(1), pp. 30-42.

Berman, B. (2006) 'Developing an effective customer loyalty program.' California Management Review, 49(1), pp. 123-148.

Bowen, J. and Shoemaker, S. (1998) 'Loyalty: A strategic commitment.' Cornell and Restaurant and Administration Quarterly, 39, pp. 12–25.

Butscher, S. A. (2002) Customer Loyalty Programmes and Clubs. 2edn. Hants: Gower Publishing Limited.

Capizzi, M. T. and Ferguson, R. (2005) 'Loyalty trends for the twenty-first century.' Journal of Consumer Marketing, 22(2), pp. 72–80.

Dick, A. S. and Basu, K. (1994) 'Customer loyalty: Toward an integrated conceptual framework.' Journal of the Academy of Marketing Science, 22(2), pp. 99–113.

Dowling, G. R. and Uncles, M. (1997) 'Do customer loyalty programs really work?' Sloan Management Review, 38(4), pp. 71–82.

Hu, H. H., Huang, C. T. and Chen, P. T. (2010) 'Do reward programs truly build loyalty for lodging industry?' International Journal of Hospitality Management, 29(1), pp. 128–135.

Hyatt Hotels Corporation (2014) About Hyatt. Available at: http://www.hyatt.com/ (Accessed: 25 April 2014)

JuingYee Lee, J., Capella, L.M., Taylor, R.C., Luo, M.M. and Gabler, C.B. (2014) 'The financial impact of loyalty programs in the hotel industry: A social challenge theory perspective.' Journal of Business Research, 67(10), pp. 2139-2146.

Keh, H. T. and Lee, Y. H. (2006) 'Do reward programs build loyalty for services? The moderating effect of satisfaction on type and timing of rewards.' Journal ofRetailing, 82(2), pp. 127–136.

Kim, W.G., Kim, S.Y. and Leong, J. K. (2003) 'Impact of Guest Reward Programs on the Firms' Performance.' Journal of Quality Assurance in Hospitality and Tourism, 4(1-2), pp. 87-109.

Leenheer, J., van Heerde, H. J., Bijmolt, T. H. A. and Smidts, A. (2007) 'Do loyalty programs really enhance behavioral loyalty? An empirical analysis accounting for self-selecting members.' International Journal of Research in Marketing, 24(1), pp. 31–47.

Marriott International, Inc. (2014) Marriott Brands. Available at: http://www.marriott.com/ (Accessed 25 April 2014)

McCall, M. and Voorhees, C. (2010) 'The drivers of loyalty program success.' Cornell Hospitality Quarterly, 51(1), pp. 35–52.

McKercher, B., Denizci-Guillet, B. and Ng, E. (2012) 'Rethinking Loyalty' Annals of Tourism Research, 39(2), pp. 708-734.

Mintzberg, H. (1987) 'Crafting Strategy'. Harvard Business Review, 65(4), pp. 66-75.

Mittal, B. and Lassar, W. M. (1998) 'Why do customers switch? The dynamics of satisfaction versus loyalty.' Journal of Services Marketing, 12(3), pp. 177–194.

O'Brien, L. and Jones, C. (1995) 'Do rewards really create loyalty?'Long Range Planning, 28(4), pp. 130.

O'Malley, L. (1998) 'Can loyalty schemes really build loyalty?' Marketing Intelligence & Planning, 16(1), pp. 47–55.

Payne, A. and Frow, P. (2005) 'A strategic framework for customer relationship management.' Journal of Marketing, 69(4), pp. 167–176.

Porter, M. E. (1979) 'How Competitive Forces Shape Strategy'. Harvard Business Review, 57(2), pp. 137-145.

Reinartz, W. J. and Kumar, V. (2003) 'The impact of customer relationship characteristics on profitable lifetime duration.' Journal of Marketing, 67(1), pp. 77–99.

Reichheld, F. F. (1993) 'Loyalty-based management.' Harvard Business Review, 71(2), pp. 64-73.

Rowley, J. (2004) 'Loyalty and reward schemes: How much is your loyalty worth?' The Marketing Review, 4(2), pp. 121–138.

Sharp, B. and Sharp, A. (1997) 'Loyalty programs and their impact on repeat-purchase loyalty patterns.' International Journal of Research in Marketing, 14(5), pp. 473–486.

Shoemaker, S. and Lewis, R. C. (1999) 'Customer loyalty: The future of hospitality marketing.' International Journal of Hospitality Management, 18(4), pp. 345–370.

Shugan, S. M. (2005) 'Brand loyalty programs: Are they shams?' Marketing Science, 24(2), pp. 185–193.

Starwood Hotels & Resorts Worldwide, Inc. (2014) Starwood Brands. Available at: https://www.starwoodhotels.com/ (Accessed: 25 April 2014)

Stauss, B., Schmidt, M. and Schoeler, A. (2005) 'Customer frustration in loyalty programs.' International Journal of Service Industry Management, 16(3), pp. 229–252.

Tideswell, C. and Fredline, E. (2004) 'Developing and rewarding loyalty to hotels: The guest's perspective.' Journal of Hospitality & Tourism Research, 28(2), pp. 186–208.

Vorhees, M.C., McCall, M. and Carrol, B. (2014) 'Assessing Benefits of Reward Programs.' Cornell Hospitality Report, 1(1), pp. 1-14.

Wansink, B. (2003) 'Developing a cost-effective brand loyalty program.' Journal of Advertising Research, 43(3), pp. 301–309.

Xie, K.L. and Chen, C.C. (2013) 'Progress in Loyalty Program Research: Facts, Debates, and Future Research.' Journal of Hospitality Marketing and Management, 22(5), pp. 463-489.

Yin, R.K. (1994) Case study research: design and methods. 2edn. London: SAGE.

Tourism Products in Deal of the Day Platforms:
Key Drivers to Repurchase and E-Loyalty

Dorothy Alinda,

Raquel Daneluz,

Paula Harasymowicz, and

Tatiana Yano

Salzburg University of Applied Sciences, Austria
paulakkorny@gmail.com

Abstract

Social commerce platforms, such as Deal of the Day (DoD), have become significant channels for the distribution of tourism products and services online. The repeated customer purchasing pattern in DoD sites raised businesses and academic's interest to investigate what make these platforms successful for online distribution. Recent study of Krasnova et al, "Deal of the Day" Platforms: What Drives Costumer Loyalty" (2013), investigated key factors which drive customers to repurchase and develop e-loyalty towards these platforms. This study, however, lacked focus in investigating intangible and high risk perceived products such as tourism ones. In this sense, this paper is a replication of Krasnova et al's paper and aims building up knowledge by investigating key e-loyalty and repurchase factors for the tourism in DoD platforms. Perceived value for money, saving benefits, quality benefits, exploration benefits, service friendliness, convenience benefits and price consciousness are perceived as key drivers of loyalty on DoD web sites focusing on tourism products.

Keywords: Deal of the day; Groupon; e-loyalty; tourism product

1 INTRODUCTION

With increased number of online platforms appearing each year, placing tourism products and service on the Internet may challenge service providers to select the most appropriate and relevant websites to reach customers and remain competitive. Deal of the Day (DoD) platforms such as Groupon and LivingSocial, have increased significantly their market share in online sales offering a range of products (Krasnova et al, 2013). These platforms characterize the collective power that individuals obtain when bargaining products, services and experiences together online (Hughes & Beukes, 2012). According to Ioncică and Dumitru-Manoliu (2011), more and more tourism products and services are placed in DoD platforms. Krasnova et al (2013) argue that customers are attracted to DoDs not only due to the significant price discount of products, but also by "the opportunity to explore new services, activities, and locations."

Recent studies (Krasnova et al, 2013; Tuten and Ashley, 2011) have generally investigated e-loyalty in daily deal websites, without focusing on complex and high risk perceived products, such as the ones sold in the travel industry. This paper aims building up on the existing knowledge of e-loyalty in DoDs by placing Krasnova et al's 2013 study it in the context of tourism. The research model developed by Krasnova et al (2013), served as base for testing the hypotheses raised in section 3 of this paper. A survey was carried in order to find whether key drivers to e-loyalty and repurchase intention of tourism products in DoD differ to non-tourism products.

2 THEORETICAL BACKGROUND

With private Internet use reaching over one billion users (Egger & Buhalis, 2008) and information technologies becoming an essential support for service providers, the focus towards keeping customers loyal in the e-space has increased significantly. Increased e-commerce transactions and exacerbated competition online made tourism businesses reconsider their selling strategies, which now aim strong online positioning and development of lasting customer relationship. Even though e-loyalty is a relatively new phenomenon, it is strongly based on traditional loyalty theory, for instance also measuring attitudinal and behavioural dimensions; however some factors are particular to the e-space and online customer behaviour (Dunn, et al, 2009; Gommans et al, 2001). According to Smith (2000), offline loyalty is limited to the act of repurchase of a product and\or service whilst online loyalty may include actual purchasing however other aspects such as repeated website visits to without purchase as well as time spent browsing must be considered. Aspects such as trust, website features, pricing and quality perceived are fundamental factors for determining customer returning habits to the website (Gommans et al, 2001).

Additionally, other elements which did not play a role in traditional loyalty, such as perceived purchase risk and product tangibility will also have great impact on repeated customer behaviour. In this sense, service providers of intangible products, such as the ones offered by tourism service providers, will face more challenges to create e-loyalty than tangible products (Gommans et al, 2001; Lin et al, 2009; Kim et al, 2005).

E-loyalty is defined as the "intention to revisit a website or to make a transaction from it in the future" (Cyr et al, 2007). Reichheld and Schefter (2000) affirm that e-loyalty is strongly related to trust in the online sphere, as well as the ease to navigate and product display, quality of customer assistance, pricing and shipping costs. Different to traditional loyalty, aspects such as repeated visits to the website without purchase and time spent browsing must be consider in order to identify whether a customer is or not loyal to the website (Smith, 2000).

When comparing to traditional loyalty, some aspects augment complexity of e-loyalty nature such as exacerbated online competition, abundant information, quality of e-service, lack of time from consumers' side and reduced purchasing cycle, which means that businesses have more difficulties in achieving behavioural loyalty on the e-space (Gommans et al, 2001). This great amount of service providers are in one hand beneficial for customers, who have a great spectrum of option, but in the other hand may generate certain level of insecurity in terms of service quality and online security.

The concepts of trust and loyalty go hand in hand due to the reduced (or often non-existent) personal contact between service providers and consumers online. According to Reichheld and Schefter (2000), e-trust is "the degree of confidence customers have in online exchanges, or in the online exchange channel". Therefore trust plays a key role to develop e-loyalty. According to Gommans et al (2001) there are several tools which can enhance customer security and decrease perceived risk, such as "third party approvals, encryption, authentication, and non-repudiation". In this sense, the higher the customer's perceived risk to buy products online the lower the purchase intentions, therefore, fewer the chances to build e-loyalty.

According to Kim et al (2005) financial risk is one of the main reasons why customers hesitate in buying products online. It is likely that a purchase of an inexpensive item will have a lower perceived risk as for a more complex and costly product, which are often the case for holiday packages, car rentals, airline tickets, among others.

2.1 Tourism products, e-loyalty and daily deal platforms

When looking at the tourism industry, Kim et al (2005) affirm that "travel products are associated with higher risk not only because of their tangibility, but also because they typically involve higher cost and complex choices". As a highly competitive industry, efforts to develop loyalty of customers towards destinations and other tourism products and services are crucial to remain competitive in the market. Although several tourism business are aware of perceived risk of offering products online, more and more these retailers seek for customer attention on the e-space (Kim et al, 2005). It is important to mention that e-loyalty to websites and loyalty to tourism products are differentiated in nature. E-loyalty towards platforms depends in factors such as e-trust, usability of the website, perception of security for online shopping, among other factors described in figure 1 in the third section of this paper. Loyalty towards tourism products is highly dependent on the quality of the service on site, but the desire for exploring new service and destinations may always play a role in the travellers' decision to be a returning guest (Campon et al., 2013).

When it comes to selecting platforms to offer tourism products, businesses must consider several factors such as usability, popularity and security of the website in order to succeed on the e-market. It took time for tourism businesses start to understand the dynamics of e-commerce and the new role taken by users on the web. According to Lee (2001) e-commerce shits paradigms for being "a 'disruptive' innovation that is radically changing the traditional way of doing business".

Another phenomenon discussed by Stephen and Toubia (2009) is social commerce and social shopping, which they define as "forms of Internet-based "social media" that allows people to actively participate in the marketing and selling of products and services in online marketplaces and communities". With the development of Web 2.0 and Tourism 2.0, more and more tourists wish to share their experiences online, making social commerce an important aspect for tourism, especially on the pre and post phases of a trip (Neuhofer et al, 2013).

Dholakia (2010) assumes that a remarkable part of social commerce concerns customers' group-buying in daily deal websites, such as Groupon, Living social, Daily Deal, among others. Daily deals websites, also known as group buying deals or couponing deal of the day are, according to Tuten and Ashley (2011), "a sales promotion tactic designed to generate incremental sales in a set period of time with price-off offer". Literature identifies two main similarities among the various couponing websites: the necessity to pre-purchase the offer and that promotions are valid only when a predetermined number of consumers purchase the deal (Edelman et al, 2011; Tuten & Ashley, 2011; Krasnova et al, 2013).

Placement of tourism products in deal of the day websites has gain significant popularity in the past few year, very likely due to the success of this business scheme (DoD offers) for general products and services. A number of DoD platforms specialized in selling tourism products such as Groupon Getaways and Deal of the Day Holidays. Despite the young nature of deal of the day websites, recent studies of Zhang et al (2013) have demonstrated that Groupon has already achieved trust from both businesses' and customers' perspectives, a crucial element that influence repurchase and loyalty as previously discussed.

Laroche et al (2004) affirm that trusted websites which provide specific and detailed information of the service or product bought online diminish the risk perceived by customers. When looking at Groupon Getaways, for example, the website provides detailed description of touristic offers on their platform including the discount given, possible dates for booking, amount of sold deals, fees and policies, contact of merchant, among other information, providing specific and detailed information for online customers to feel secure when buying with them.

Further important factors which also influence the repurchase and loyalty of tourism products in DoDs, are the user's familiarity with online shopping (Jun et al, 2007), which will be nominated in this research as 'media competence', and users' travel career ladder according to Pearce book published 1988 'The Ulysses Factor'. Jun et al (2007) affirm that "(...) travel experiences influence travel information search and product purchase for certain travel products (...)". This way, it could be inferred that high media competence and an advanced customer travel career might have impact on repurchase and e-loyalty of user when buying online.

Previous studies by Krasnova et al (2013) have tested key drivers for creating loyalty towards deal of the day websites, investigating factors such as perceived benefits, perceived costs and encounter with the merchant. Their study has focused on the purchase of regular products, without specifications. Key drivers to loyalty was also measured by willingness to repurchase, keep track on promotions and involve others in the act of group buying, a parameter which has also been adopted by this study.

As previously stated, this research aims investigating loyalty towards DoD platforms when customers purchase tourism products. Literature review demonstrated the difference between tourism products from others types, where Kim et al (2005) affirm that they are perceived as high risk due to its complexity and intangibility. The higher the perceived risk, the more trust needed to purchase tourism products online, especially when it comes to a rather new concept of social buying.

Krasnova et al (2013) analysed perceived benefits by asking respondents on about savings, quality, exploration and convenience when shopping in DoDs, while perceived costs were tested with signal-to-noise ratio and perceived risk. Additionally, the authors also considered relevant to measure service friendliness and perceived money for value when customer finally encountered the merchant, assuming this encounter would impact on loyalty development do deal of the day websites. As for the control variables, age, gender and country were used as demographic characteristics and number of deals bought as well as discount were considered for DoD-related characteristics (Krasnova et al, 2013). The following section will present detailed description of the framework and methodology used in this research.

3 FRAMEWORKS AND METHODOLOGY

The paper hereby presented differs from previous researches on e-loyalty by focusing on purchasing of tourism products on daily deals websites from the consumers' perspective. Hence, the research model will be based on the model developed by Krasnova et al (2013), adapting to tourism products and e-loyalty. In order to test if travel experience and media competence play a role for creating loyalty and repurchase intention of tourism products on DoD websites both variables were included in the research.

Figure 1 demonstrates the model developed by Krasnova et al (2013), in which relations between deal of the day (DoD) operators' loyalty and variables below presented are established. On the left and down sides are the independent variables: perceived benefits of DoD websites, as savings, quality, exploration of new products and convenience; perceived costs of DoD, as signal-to-noise ratio and perceived risk (the only one that might have a negative relation with DoD operator loyalty); characteristics of the last dealer, as service and price performance ratio; and price awareness. On the right side are the control variables: demographic features, as age, gender and place of residence; and DoD related characteristics, as number of purchased deals and discount (Krasnova et al, 2013).

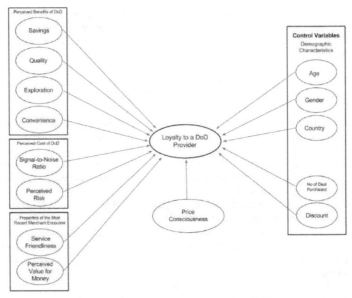

Fig. 1. Research model of loyalty on "Deal of the Day" platforms by Krasnova et al (2013)

3.1 Hypotheses

In order to measure the key factors that influence loyalty on DoD websites when it comes to Tourism products, nine hypotheses used by Krasnova et al (2013) were applied in this study (H1 to H9) and two other hypotheses concerning media competence (H10) and travel experience (H11) complemented this research. The hypotheses described below compose the basis of this paper:

H1: Users' perceptions regarding saving benefits have a positive impact on loyalty to a DoD provider,

H2: Users' perceptions regarding quality have a positive impact on loyalty to a DoD provider,

H3: Users' perceptions regarding exploration have a positive impact on loyalty to a DoD provider,

H4: Users' perceptions regarding convenience have a positive impact on loyalty to a DoD provider.

H5: Users' perceptions regarding favorable signal-to-noise ratio of DoD offerings have a positive impact on loyalty to a DoD provider,

H6: Users' perceived risk associated with deal purchases has a negative impact on loyalty to a DoD provider.

H7: Users perceptions regarding service friendliness when redeeming the most recent deal have a positive impact on loyalty to a DoD provider

H8: Users' perceptions regarding value for money of the most recent redeemed deal have a positive impact on loyalty to a DoD provider

H9: Users' price consciousness has a positive impact on loyalty to a DoD provider

H 10: Users' media competence has a negative impact on loyalty to a DoD provider

H 11: Users' travel experience has a positive impact on loyalty to a DoD provider)

3.2 Survey Design and sample description

The questionnaire used for this study was based on Krasnova et al (2013) research paper and used 7 point Likert scale for every construct. The survey was originally developed in English and then translated carefully into German and Portuguese because the researchers intended to carry out their study in English, German and Portuguese speaking countries. Two different questions were added to the survey in order to be more specifically focused on tourism products. The questionnaire was available online for ten consecutive days, from November 14th to November 24th, 2013, it was shared through social media and students network of Salzburg University of Applied Sciences. The total number of people that attempted to carry out the survey was 221. Due to the fact that this research was to be carried with a population who has purchased tourism products in order to test loyalty towards deal of the day websites, every respondent who answered "No" on the first question of the survey (have you ever purchased a tourism product such as travel packages, hotels, spa, restaurants, flight ticket, tours, museum, ... on a daily deal website?) was automatically re-directed to the last page, concluding the survey. Therefore, the number of valid results for the study was from 81 respondents.

Most of the respondents of this survey were female and made up to 69% of the population. And 52% of the respondents were Brazilian by nationality and also 48% of the respondents currently live in Brazil. It was also interesting that most of the population had an income from $/€ 1000-3000 (52%) and that the most popular DoD platform that was used by this population was Groupon (55% of the population). Another interesting phenomenon is that there was no one in the valid population who purchased from another DoD platform except for the ones that were listed by the researchers (Groupon, livingsocial and travelzoo). The table below summarizes the demographic characteristics of the valid sample of the study.

Table 1:Demographic characteristics of the valid sample

Gender	Female	Male		
	69%	31%		
Age group	20-29	30-39	40-49	50-59
	56%	16%	9%	1%
Occupation	Occupied	Student		
	70%	30%		
Income level	Below EUR 500	EUR 500-1000	EUR 1000-3000	Over EUR 3000
	15%	18%	52%	15%
Country of origin	Brazil	Austria	Germany	Others
	52%	9%	6%	33%
Platform of purchase	Groupon	LivingSocial	TravelZoo	Others
	55%	28%	17%	0%

3.3 Empirical Results

The statistical package software SPSS was used and this research paper as a tool to analyze the collected data. To evaluate and understand the information of the samples descriptive statistics were applied. Furthermore, the reliability was tested, using Cronbach's Alpha value as a tool. The internal consistency was higher than a required reliability of 0.7 (Gilford, 1965) for all variables except price consciousness, as indicated in Table 2. Overall, validity of the variables was confirmed.

Table 2: Cronbach's alpha

	Cronbach's Alpha	Number of Items
Loyalty	.893	4
Signal-to-Noise Ratio	.836	4
Perceived Risk	.842	5
Saving Benefits	.856	3
Quality Benefits	.803	3
Exploration Benefits	.757	3
Convenience Benefits	.794	5
Service Friendliness	.899	4
Perceived Value for Money	.864	3
Price Consciousness	.683	3

In order to analyze the reliability of H10 (media competence) and H11 (travel experience), Spearman's Rho coefficient was applied. The relationship between booking trips online and loyalty was measured by Spearman's Rho coefficient (ρ). The result of -.168 indicates that there is no significant tendency for booking trips online to decrease loyalty when purchasing tourism products on DoD platforms. Additionally, Pearson Correlation (r) equals to -.166 demonstrates a small negative correlation between both variables. Therefore, this variable is not significant to influence loyalty when purchasing tourism products on DoD platforms.

Moreover, the relationship between yearly travel frequency and loyalty was measured by Spearman's Rho coefficient (ρ). The result of .133 indicates that there is no significant dependence between frequency of travels per year and loyalty when purchasing tourism products on DoD platforms. Additionally, Pearson Correlation (r) equals to .101 demonstrates that there is no correlation between both variables. Therefore, this variable is not significant to influence loyalty when purchasing tourism products on DoD platforms.

Next, to analyze the correlation between the dependent variable (loyalty) and independent variables (Signal to Noise Ratio, Perceived Risk, Saving Benefits, Quality Benefits, Exploration Benefits, Convenience Benefits, Service Friendliness, Perceived Value for Money, Price Consciousness) Pearson correlation analysis was applied. The Sig.2-tailed level indicates that all independent variables, except for perceived risk are significant at the level 0.01.

When it comes to loyalty when purchasing tourism products on DoD platforms, the strongest correlation is between loyalty and perceived value for money (r=.664), followed by saving benefits (r=.594), quality benefits (r=.522), exploration benefits (r=.515) and service friendliness (r=.503). Nonetheless, all independent variables cited above represent a significant positive correlation with loyalty. Interestingly, comparing this study to the Krasnova et. al (2013) paper, the three main key drivers to loyalty are the same.

Table 3: Validity of the hypotheses

		Pearson Correlation	Spearman's Rho	Results
H1	Saving Benefits	.594[**]	---	Supported
H2	Quality Benefits	.522[**]	---	Supported
H3	Exploration Benefits	.515[**]	---	Supported

H4	Convenience Benefits	.438**	---	Supported
H5	Signal-to-Noise Ratio	-.343**	---	Rejected
H6	Perceived Risk	-.099	---	Rejected
H7	Service Friendliness	.503**	---	Supported
H8	Perceived Value for Money	.664**	---	Supported
H9	Price Consciousness	.368**	---	Supported
H11	Media Competence	-.166	-.168	Rejected
H12	Travel experience	.101	.133	Rejected

For this research, in order to test the hypothesis, the coefficient of determination (R^2) was applied. Together, all variables on the applied model explain 61.7% of variance to DoD platforms; meaning a substantial level of explanatory power (Fox, 1997).

Table 4: Coefficient of determination

Model	R	R Square	Adjusted R Square	Std. Error of the Estimate
1	,785	,617	,568	,56375

4 CONCLUSION

Innovations in information technologies are changing social lives and attitudes (Nie & Erbring, 2002). When it comes to online purchasing behaviours it has been possible to observe shifts in loyalty and also on how commerce is conducted, going from offline-traditional to online and social Especially in the tourism industry, avant-garde in terms of information and communication technologies (Buhalis, 2003), social commerce plays a key role: it empowers customers, includes new players in the distribution chain and adds new ways of offering tourism products and services online. The literature reviewed showed key drivers from offline to e-loyalty, reviewed concepts around e-commerce focusing on daily deals platform and defined a framework for the research. Through literature review it was also possible to see the relationship between e-loyalty and daily deals website, however, these studies focused on general products and services, with no specific focus.

This research therefore, analysed key drivers of e-loyalty to deal of the day website focusing on tourism products. The study concludes that the main key drivers of loyalty on DoD web sites when it comes to tourism products are: Perceived value for money, saving benefits and quality benefits.

Limitations of the study

- Even though the survey was an online survey, there was a small range of countries covered and most of the respondents were from Brazil.

- The study was on a wide range of tourism products yet tourism products are quite different. A recommendation for further study could be on a particular touristic product. So it can be looked at as a case for example on luxury tourism product.

- Time was also a constraint as the study was online only for a few days.

Despite the limitations of this study, the authors believe it demonstrates the importance considering DoD platforms for the distribution of tourism products online. Future research is recommended to further explore the relationship of travel career and e-loyalty towards DoD sites.

REFERENCES

Austin, N. K., Ibeh, K. N., and Chow Choy Yee, J., 2006. Consumer Trust in the Online Travel Marketplace. *Journal of Internet Commerce*, 5(2), pp.21-39.

Byers, J. W., Mitzenmacher, M., Potamias, M., and Zervas, G., 2011. A Month in the Life of Groupon. [Online] Available at: <http://arxiv.org/abs/1105.0903> [Accessed 17 November 2013].

Byers, J. W., Mitzenmacher, M., and Zervas, G., 2012. Daily deals: Prediction, social diffusion, and reputational ramifications. In Proceedings of the fifth ACM international conference on Web search and data mining. ACM, pp.543-552.

Buhalis, D., 2003. eTourism: Information technology for strategic tourism management. Prentice Hall.

Campon, A.M., Alves, H. and Hernandez, J.M., 2013. Loyalty Measurement in Tourism: Theoretical Reflection. Springer. [Online]. Available at: <http://tinyurl.com/mz2cff2> [Accessed 12 March 2015].

Cyr, D. et al., 2007. The role of social presence in establishing loyalty in e-service environments. *Interacting with Computers*, 19 (1), pp.43-56

Dholakia, U.M., 2010. How Effective are Groupon Promotions for Businesses? Rice University. [Online] Available at: <http://papers.ssrn.com/sol3/papers.cfm?abstract_id=1696327> [Accessed 19 November 2013].

Dholakia, U., 2011. What Makes Groupon Promotions Profitable for Businesses? Harvard Business School. [Online] Available at: <http://www.hbs.edu/faculty/Publication%20Files/11-063_0f0b83d0-807f-4e29-91e6-1fe5a01b71d5.pdf> [Accessed 2 December 2013].

Dunn, G., Baloglu, S., Brewer, P., and Qu, H., 2009. Consumer E-Loyalty to Online Travel Intermediaries. *Journal of Quality Assurance in Hospitality and Tourism*, 10(1), pp.1-22.

Echtner, C. M., and Ritchie, J. B., 2003. The meaning and measurement of destination image. Journal of Tourism Studies, 14(1), pp.37-48. [Online] Available at: <http://www.jcu.com.au/business/public/groups/everyone/documents/journal_article/jcudev_01 2855.pdf> [Accessed 19 November 2013].

Edelman, B., Jaffe, S., and Kominers, S., 2011. To groupon or not to groupon: The profitability of deep discounts. Harvard Business School NOM Unit Working Paper, pp.11-063.

Fox, J., 1997. *Applied Regression Analysis, Linear Models, and Related Methods*. Newbury Park, CA.: Sage

Gilford, J.P., 1965. *Fundamental statistics in psychology and education*. McGraw-Hill, New York, NY.

Gommans, M., Krishnan, K. S., and Scheffold, K. B., 2001. From brand loyalty to e-loyalty: A conceptual framework. *Journal of Economic and Social research*, 3(1), pp.43-58.

Groupon, 2013. About us. [Online] Available at: <http://www.groupon.com/about> [Accessed 2 December 2013].

Hughes, S., and Beukes, C., 2012. Growth and Implications of Social E-Commerce and Group Buying Daily Deal Sites: The Case of Groupon and Livingsocial *International Business and Economics Research Journal (IBER)*, 11(8), pp.921-934. [Online] Available at: <http://journals.cluteonline.com/index.php/IBER/article/view/7169> [Accessed 2 December 2013].

Ioncică, M., and Dumitru-Manoliu, A., 2011. *Modern techniques of tourism products distribution and their impact on the efficiency of the tourism market in Romania Labour.* In Forum Ware International, Special Issue (1), pp.65-69.

Jun, S. H., Vogt, C. A., and MacKay, K. J., 2007. Relationships between travel information search and travel product purchase in pretrip contexts. *Journal of Travel Research,* 45(3), pp.266-274.

Kim, B. C., Lee, J., and Park, H., 2012. Two-Sided Platform Competition in the Online Daily Deals Promotion Market. [Online] Available at: <http://papers.ssrn.com/sol3/papers.cfm?abstract_id=2117790> [Accessed 12 November 2013].

Kim, L. H., Kim, D. J., and Leong, J. K., 2005. The effect of perceived risk on purchase intention in purchasing airline tickets online. *Journal of Hospitality and Leisure Marketing,* 13(2), pp.33-53.

Krasnova, H., Veltri, N. F., Spengler, K., and Günther, O., 2013. *"Deal of the Day" Platforms: What Drives Consumer Loyalty?.* Business and Information Systems Engineering, 5(3), pp.165-177.

Laroche, M., McDougall, G. H., Bergeron, J., and Yang, Z., 2004. Exploring how intangibility affects perceived risk. *Journal of Service Research,* 6(4), pp.373-389.

Lee, C. S., 2001. An analytical framework for evaluating e-commerce business models and strategies. *Internet Research,* 11(4), pp.349-359.

Lin, P., Jones, E., and Westwood, S., 2009. Perceived Risk and Risk-Relievers in Online Travel Purchase Intentions. *Journal of Hospitality Marketing and Management,* 18(8), pp.782-810.

Neuhofer, B., Buhalis, D., and Ladkin, A., 2013. *Experiences, co-creation and technology: A conceptual approach to enhance tourism experiences.* In: CAUTHE 2013 Conference Proceedings. Tourism and Global Change: On the Edge of Something Big, pp.546-555.

Nie, N. H., and Erbring, L., 2002. Internet and Society: A Preliminary Report. *IT and Society,* 1(1), pp. 275-283. [Online] Available at: <http://www.nomads.usp.br/documentos/textos/cultura_digital/tics_arq_urb/internet_society%2 0report.pdf> [Accessed 12 November 2013].

Pearce, P. L., and Lee, U. I., 2005. Developing the travel career approach to tourist motivation. *Journal of Travel Research,* 43(3), pp.226-237.

Reichheld, F. F., and Schefter, P., 2000. *E-loyalty.* Harvard business review, 78(4), pp.105-113.

Seaton, A. V., and Bennett, M. M., 1996. *The marketing of tourism products: Concepts, issues and cases.* Cengage Learning.

Smith, E. R., 2000. *E-loyalty.* HarperCollins World.

Stephen, A.T. and Toubia, O., 2010. Deriving Value from Social Commerce Networks. *Journal of Marketing Research,* 47(2), pp.215-228.

Tiedemann, N., Van Birgele, M., and Semeijn, J., 2009. Increasing hotel responsiveness to customers through information sharing. *Tourism Review,* 64(4), pp.12-26.

Tuten, T. L., and Ashley, C., 2011. Promotional strategies for small businesses: group buying deals. *Small Business Institute Journal,* 7(2), pp.15-29.

Weiermair, K., 2004. *Product improvement or innovation: what is the key to success in tourism.* Innovations in tourism UNWTO conference. [Online] Available at: <https://www1.oecd.org/cfe/tourism/34267947.pdf> [Accessed 17 November 2013].

Werthner, H., and Ricci, F., 2004. E-commerce and tourism. *Communications of the ACM,* 47(12), pp.101-105.

Zhang, Y., Zhu, H., Liu, H., and Mo, Z., 2013. User Acceptance of Groupon Information Technology: An Empirical Analysis. *Journal of Network and Information Security,* 4(4), pp.265-273

An Analysis of the Voluntary Carbon-Offsetting of German Tourists

Isabell Wulfsberg, and

Dirk Reiser

Cologne Business School, Germany
isabell.wulfsberg@googlemail.com

Abstract

This study investigates environmental attitudes and concerns of Germans tourists towards climate change and furthermore analyses their attempt to neutralise air travel emissions by means of voluntary carbon-offsetting. Past research has indicated inconsistencies between tourists' attitudes towards global warming and a missing translation of those into corresponding travel behaviour. In particular the willingness to compensate travel emissions has not obtained much attention in the past. Since previous studies focused on countries like Great Britain, New Zealand, Australia and Hong Kong, there remains a need to analyse whether the attitude-behaviour gap also accounts for German air travellers. Quantitative data was collected by conducting structured face-to-face interviews at the airport of Hamburg. The findings indicate that purchasers of voluntary carbon-offsets are almost non-existent among German air travellers, although they show a reasonable level of concern when it comes to climate change. However, this is rather a consequence of missing consumer awareness since less than half of the respondents are familiar with the opportunity to compensate travel emissions. Yet, the majority of the respondents show a willingness to purchase carbon-offsets in future. The study concludes that behavioural change can only be realised if profound improvements are made in consumer education and communication.

Keywords: carbon offsetting; CO2 compensation; mitigation; tourist behaviour; climate change

1 INTRODUCTION

Tourism is a highly energy-intensive sector and a major anthropogenic source of greenhouse gases, which generate profound changes in the global climate (Becken & Hay, 2007). As reported by the Intergovernmental Panel on Climate Change (IPCC), substantial consequences of climate change entail the increase in median temperatures, rising sea levels and the melting of glaciers and polar icecaps, all of which will have considerable impacts on flora and fauna (IPCC, 2013). Especially air travel was subject to criticism in the past due to its enormous discharge of greenhouse gases (Jenkins, 2013). According to the International Air Transport Association (IATA, 2013), the aviation sector is accountable for 2% of the total anthropogenic carbon output. It carries the greatest share of CO2 emissions in tourism (40%), followed by car usage (32%) and accommodations (21%) (UNWTO & UNEP, 2008). Thus, the reduction of transport emissions is a challenging area of responsibility in tourism management.

Next to mandatory laws and regulations, voluntary behavioural change of consumers display an important mitigation strategy, given that consumer demand implies strong power when it comes to making tourism products more sustainable. Tourists are confronted with a range of possibilities to reduce individual travel emissions, such as the choice of more energy efficient transportation facilities or the denial of long-distance holidays. Another prevailing tool is seen in voluntary carbon-offsetting programmes, which offer to neutralise individual air travel emissions in exchange of a compensatory payment (Broderick, 2009). Each compensation supplier invests in projects with the focus on renewable energy, energy efficiency, industry gases, carbon sequestration or the avoidance of deforestation (Strasdas, Gössling & Dickhut,

2010; UNWTO & UNEP, 2008). When it comes to Germany, Kind et al. (2010) detected that renewable energy projects hold the biggest share in the market.

However, the concept of compensating emissions also faces a lot of criticism, for example the inaccurate calculation of discharges by airplanes. For more precise calculations, the airplane type, capacity and load factors, fuel use and several other factors have to be considered (Gössling et al., 2007). Further criticism by the International Ecotourism Society (2012) comprises the misuse of compensation tools by airline providers in order to improve their company image and attract more customers. In addition, technological and structural changes might be minimised if the responsibility of compensating air travel emissions is passed from the airline to the consumer (UNWTO & UNEP, 2008). Hence, improvements of compensation programmes are obviously needed and definite standards should be implemented to ensure their quality and effectiveness. Nevertheless, it represents a first step into changing the environmental awareness and behaviour of air travellers. As DiPeso (2007) stated, voluntary carbon-offsetting is a reasonable measurement for reducing emissions in air travel, under the conditions that reductions are measurable, additional and verified.

Although the concept of compensating anthropogenic greenhouse gases provides an easy tool for consumers to take charge of their environmental impacts, present purchases of flight offsets only cover about 1% of total air travel (Eijgelaar, 2011). Reasons include deficiencies in educating and raising awareness about the need of compensating travel emissions (McKercher et al., 2010). Generally, communication deficits appear among all stakeholders, including tourism companies, compensation providers, airlines and public authorities. Another explanation for the low participation rate in compensation schemes is given by the attitude-behaviour gap, which will provide the theoretical foundation of this investigation. Past research indicated a discrepancy between pro-environmental attitudes and the transformation of those into corresponding behaviour (Kollmuss & Agyeman, 2002). It can also be defined as the *"discrepancy between verbal and other behavioural expressions of attitude"* (Schuman, 1972, p. 347). In other words, consumers may have pro-environmental values but for some reason these are not automatically translated into appropriate actions.

When looking at the decision-making process of tourists, the gap describes inconsistencies *"between positive opinions of sustainable travel and behavioural commitment"* (Barr & Prillwitz, 2011, p. 163). Several reasons have been outlined in past literature with regards to the attitude-behaviour gap in tourism. Probably the most common explanation when conducting interviews or questionnaires are social desirable responses (Colton & Covert, 2007). Respondents tend to answer in a way that satisfies the interviewers' expectations and viewpoints about a specific topic (Schuman, 1972). Further research rather focused on behavioural reasons that hinder pro-environmental attitudes from being translated into action. Findings by Wherli et al. (2011) and Kennedy et al. (2009) revealed that sustainability is not as important in the decision-making process of tourists as costs. When it comes to purchase decisions, literature indicated that financial constraints play a major role for 45% of the respondents (Kennedy et al., 2009). Thus, unlike environmental concerns, price is an important factor in tourists' purchase decisions (Becken, 2007).

Another reason for the attitude-behaviour gap of travellers may be lower accessibility and convenience when deciding for the sustainable product or service (Hergesell & Dickinger, 2013). In addition, Kennedy et al. (2009) explored that about 60% of the Canadian respondents reported perceived lack of knowledge and information as a constraint for environmentally friendly behaviour. Tourists need clear information on why and how they can make a difference in order to change their decision making behaviour when choosing a holiday (Budeanu, 2007). Confusion about the term 'sustainability' may entail that tourists cannot get sufficient access to information about sustainable alternatives (Bowen & Clarke, 2009). In addition, lack of time to engage in information seeking and lack of support from other household members can also restrain pro-environmental behaviour (Kennedy et al., 2009). Likewise, personal identity may have a strong influence on the mobility decisions since people see a certain role of self in this behaviour (Hibbert et al., 2013). People identify themselves by undertaking a certain holiday, or at least try to reach their desired future self. According to Hibbert et al. (2013), this influence is able to dominate environmental concerns.

Several studies have also supported the existence of the gap when looking at tourist's attitudes and reactions towards climate change and voluntary carbon-offsetting (Mair, 2011; McKercher et al., 2010; Prideaux, Coghlan & McKercher, 2011). Although respondents indicate a certain level of awareness and concern, it is not translated into appropriate behaviour. In this respect, Ajzen and Fishbein (2005) distinguish between two types of attitudes: general attitudes towards people, objects, policies or other targets and the attitude towards performing certain behaviour. Based on this assumption, tourists might have positive attitudes towards climate protection but are not prepared to personally change their behaviour, for instance by switching to alternative transport or neutralising their flight emissions.

Research by Gössling et al. (2006) showed that many travellers see tourism as a critical contributor to environmental problems. However, the majority of them are unaware of their own environmental impact and often choose the airplane to get to a destination. In comparison to pro-environmental behaviour at home, a reduction, abandonment or suppression of climate concerns often occurs with regards to travel activities (Cohen, Higham & Reis, 2013). A study among tourists of New Zealand has indicated a lack of specific knowledge and information about air travel and its consequences (Becken, 2007). It was shown that the majority of participants could not name any mitigation measure when it comes to global warming and just a few knew the concept of voluntary carbon-offsetting. For those who are aware of the connection between air travel and climate change, the responsibility of mitigating these impacts was often seen with the airline (Becken, 2007). McKercher et al. (2010) also detected a low awareness of compensation programmes among Hong Kong residents. Respondents who already compensated CO_2 emissions were almost non-existent. Only 20% have changed their travel patterns due to their environmental concerns although it was widely believed that climate change is a serious environmental issue we face.

Research about the voluntary carbon-offsetting behaviour of Australian and British tourists was carried out by Mair (2011). She found that only 10% of 470 respondents had purchased a voluntary carbon-offset before. Mentioned reasons, such as ease and convenience of offsetting, suggest that these are important factors for voluntary CO_2 compensation. When it comes to German tourists, Wehrli et al. (2011) identified them as being one of the most critical groups, given that 65% do not consider carbon-offsetting as a part of sustainable tourism. The willingness to pay an extra amount for compensating greenhouse gas emissions is among the lowest when considering sustainable attributes.

Next to country-specific differences, several demographic impacts seem to have an influence on the voluntary carbon-offsetting behaviour of air travellers (Mair, 2011): people who compensate their greenhouse gas emissions are prone to be male, younger and better educated whereas non-purchasers are likely to be older with a lower education level. This contradicts findings by Wells, Ponting and Peattie (2011) who discovered that the general environmental responsiveness increases with age. In addition, evidence suggests that tourists who have a high travel frequency and distance tend to be rather unwilling to change their air travel behaviour (McKercher et al., 2010).

Obviously, several researchers have addressed the grounds for the missing participation in carbon compensation schemes. Since these studies were conducted in countries like Hong Kong, Australia, Great Britain and New Zealand, there remains a need to analyse whether the attitude-behaviour gap also accounts for German air travellers. Based on previous findings, this paper will analyse whether there is a gap between pro-environmental attitudes towards climate change and the voluntary carbon-offsetting behaviour of German air travellers. The methodological procedure involves the collection of quantitative data by conducting a survey investigation at the airport of Hamburg. Based on the literature review above, several hypotheses were formulated that will be outlined in the following section.

2 METHODOLOGY

2.1 Aim of Research

Past research has proven an attitude-behaviour gap with regards to the voluntary carbon-offsetting behaviour among Australian (Mair, 2011; Prideaux, Coghlan & McKercher, 2011), British (Mair, 2011) and Hong Kong tourists (McKercher et al., 2010). The question is whether the attitude-behaviour gap also accounts for the compensation behaviour of German tourists. For this reason, the main hypothesis of this study is the following:

H.1: There is a gap between pro-environmental attitudes towards climate change and the voluntary carbon-offsetting behaviour of German air travellers.

Furthermore, Becken (2007) discovered that tourists in New Zealand are significantly unfamiliar with the concept of voluntary carbon-offsetting. McKercher et al. (2010) also detected a low awareness of compensation programmes among Hong Kong residents. Therefore, assumptions are made about a lack of knowledge regarding carbon-offsetting among German tourists.

H.2: There is a lack of knowledge among German tourists with regards to the concept of voluntary carbon-offsetting.

According to Mair (2011), demographic factors seem to have an influence on the voluntary carbon-offsetting behaviour of Australian and British tourists. The study suggested that those who already participated in such a compensation scheme are prone to be male, younger and better educated than those who are less likely to offset their air travel emissions. Therefore the third hypothesis is formulated as follows:

H.3: Young, male and educated German tourists are more likely to participate in a voluntary carbon-offsetting programme.

Each of the aforementioned hypotheses will be tested, and subsequently affirmed or neglected, by conducting quantitative research. The related research design and methodological procedure will be explained in the following.

2.2 Research Design

For the purpose of analysing the voluntary carbon-offsetting behaviour of German tourists, structured face-to-face interviews will be carried out at a German airport. The aim of this study is to receive statistical descriptions of attitudes and behaviours towards climate and mitigation options. For this reason, surveys are recommendable as they are used to seek for specific patterns of a population by collecting a great amount of data (Denscombe, 2010). The researcher decided on structured face-to-face interviews, which were carried out at the airport of Hamburg. A high response rate can be achieved by conducting an interview survey, because participants can be directly addressed and convinced to take part in the interview (O'Leary & Miller, 2003). In addition, structured interviews are remarkably useful because they can be accomplished in a very short timeframe (Altinay & Paraskevas, 2008). This is of high relevance for the current investigation, since it will be carried out at an airport; a location where people might be under time pressure to catch a flight and only have a limited amount of time available. Correspondingly, disadvantages have to be considered with respect to busy schedules of participants (Altinay & Paraskevas, 2008). Furthermore, limitations may arise in terms of receiving reliable data, as it is unlikely to achieve objective and consistent interview settings for each respondent (Denscombe, 2010). Respectively, care should be taken with respect to interviewer bias, as interviewees may be prone to please the interviewer and respond accordingly (Adams et al., 2007). Both researcher and respondents are confronted with prejudices and preferences of the counterpart, which may have an impact on their behaviour during the interview (Denscombe, 2010). Therefore, the interviewer has to adopt a neutral and reserved attitude towards the opinions and statements of the respondent (Denscombe, 2010).

Since the target population of German air travellers is unknown, it is not feasible to select participants on a random basis for this study. For this reason, the choice was made for convenience sampling, which belongs to the group of non-probability sampling techniques. This investigation involves tourists who are present at the airport of Hamburg in the particular timeframe. In order to minimise any sort of selection bias, interviews are conducted on three different weekdays at different times of the day in order to attain a wide range of diverse air travellers. Besides, the interviewer tries to select people by following a random pattern in order to minimise biased responses. Nevertheless, biased responses cannot be fully avoided but should be kept at a minimum.

2.3 Procedure

This paper aims to identify the flying behaviour of German tourists, which is why Hamburg airport was selected to represent the population of interest. The respondents of the survey investigation were interviewed between the 21st of February and the 2nd of March 2014 in the public area of terminal one and two, in the departure and arrival sections as well as on the viewing platform. Since the study aimed at analysing German air travellers, interviewees were chosen on the condition of having participated at least once in an airline flight and furthermore being a German citizen.

The structured interview did not last longer than ten minutes per person and covered a total of 22 questions, including short answer questions and closed questions. The interview template is based on a former study carried out by McKercher et al. (2010) who examined attitudes towards travel and climate change among Hong Kong residents. The survey questions were slightly modified and adapted for the purpose of this investigation. They can be divided into four parts covering different topic areas (based on McKercher et al., 2010). Part A aims to identify travel patterns over the past twelve months as well as the preferred mode of transport. Part B incorporates questions about the knowledge and awareness of environmental issues, trying to detect the respondent's level of concern and their pro-environmental behaviour. Information about tourism and the environment are obtained in part C, including the level of knowledge about carbon-offsetting programmes and the interviewees' willingness to compensate CO_2 emissions when travelling. Finally, interviewees were asked to give some information about standard demographic data in part D, including age, gender and education. The survey results were analysed using the Statistical Package for the Social Sciences (SPSS).

3 RESULTS

3.1 Demographics and Travel Patterns

A total of 100 tourists were interviewed at the Hamburg airport, of which 57% were female and 43% were male. With regards to age structure, the largest group with 32% are respondents aged 25 or younger. 18% are between 26 and 35 years old, while the smallest number of interviewees are aged between 36 and 45 years. People above 55 years include 21% of all respondents. Surprisingly, over half of the interviewees have achieved a university degree, which is understood as the highest educational level. Only 8% of the respondents went to the German secondary school ('Hauptschule'), which implies a nine-year course. Another type of secondary school ('Mittlere Reife') with one additional year, as well as apprenticeships, were each achieved by 10% of the respondents. Moreover, almost one fifth have completed their high school degree ('Abitur'). Note that people were asked about the highest level of education they have attained or are about to attain, therefore it is possible that some educational degrees have not been completed yet.

When it comes to travel patterns, tourists were asked about the number of domestic and international pleasure trips (lasting at least one night) they have taken in the last twelve months. On average 3.73 pleasure trips are done domestically within Germany, followed by 2.05 visits to other European countries and 0.32 trips to other continents. Hence, domestic holidays are the most frequent travel occasions, which may be due to the fact that people regularly visit friends and relatives in other German cities. With regards to the preferred transport facility, the majority of interviewees prefer to travel by airplane (76%). This is not surprising since the survey was conducted at the airport with a higher probability of meeting frequent air travellers. The car is ranked second with 42%, followed by the train, which is preferred by 20% of the respondents. The fact that air and car travel enjoys the highest popularity among German tourists suggests a desire for comfort and convenience when going on holiday, as also reported by Budeanu (2007).

3.2 Environmental Awareness and Concern

Interesting results were found about the respondents' level of awareness and concern with regards to environmental problems. Altogether 69% of German tourists are very or moderately concerned that changes to the environment will affect their lives, while only twelve respondents reported no concern at all. This is to some extent similar to McKercher et al. (2010), since they identified most of the Hong Kong residents to be very concerned about environmental changes in their lives. Furthermore, the results are being divided into male and female responses. It appears that women are more worried about changes in the environment than men. A total of 44 women and 25 men fall into the first two categories. Similar to Wells, Ponting and Peattie (2011) female travellers seem more likely to show a higher environmental awareness than men.

At a later stage, participants were asked to name major environmental problems affecting their hometown and the world. When it comes to local issues, land, sea, air and noise pollution are seen as the most serious problem, followed by extreme weather events, such as storms, flooding and droughts. These results are in partial agreement with Gössling et al. (2006), who found that tourists in Zanzibar judge extreme weather events as having the strongest impact on their destination. According to these findings, it is evident that tourists start to become conscious about the imminent consequences of climate change, which will not omit peoples' hometowns. Similar findings become apparent by regarding major environmental issues on a global scale.

The results are consistent with findings by Becken (2007), who reported that climate change is rated as being a major environmental crisis these days. Clear evidence for this aspect was also received by asking respondents directly about the perceived threat of climate change. 37% judged climate change as very serious, and almost half of the respondents as moderately serious. Only one respondent did not feel any threat by global warming.

Furthermore, interviewees were asked to state whether they see climate change as a major concern within the next twelve months and the next ten years. Overall, 61% do not consider climate change as a major threat within the next year. However, a different opinion was reported when it comes to the next decade, as almost 70% think that it will become a major concern.

3.3 Pro-Environmental Behaviour

The respondents of this study had to determine to what extent they would call themselves an environmentally friendly person. In this respect, a strong trend towards a positive self-assessment became evident. 85% of all interviewees answered this question with 'yes' or 'rather yes'. Only 15% did not see themselves as environmentally friendly persons. Nevertheless, it should be noted that people might be prone to answer in a social desirable way due to certain expectations of the interviewer (Colton & Covert, 2007; Schuman, 1972). For this reason, an open question was used to record specific measures that interviewees have taken in everyday life in order to reduce their negative environmental impact. Several answers were possible since it is an open-ended question.

The measurement with the highest frequency is waste management, which is carried out by 55 respondents (23.3%). Waste separation and avoidance were the most commonly mentioned actions in this respect. On the second rank, people named the avoidance of car usage and the switch to fuel-efficient cars. In terms of climate change, this is a very important approach to reduce CO_2 emissions. Noteworthy action was also taken with regards to energy savings and green electricity.

However, when it comes to changes in travel behaviour, only three respondents reported measures like local travel or the abandonment of air travel. Therefore, a first assumption can be made that people do not critically assess their travel behaviour with climate change issues. As stated earlier, the respondents indicate a great concern about the threat of the changing climate, which is expected to have serious impacts in the next ten years. However, it seems that this does not have implications for people's travel patterns. In order to support this fact, respondents were also asked directly about changes in their travel behaviour due to environmental concerns. The results show that only 14% of the respondents have changed their travel behaviour as a response to concerns about the environment.

Respondents were asked to further describe their changes in travel behaviour. Mentioned measures included local travel within Germany, the usage of public transport, car sharing and bike tours as well as a reduction in air travel and car usage in general. An important fact for the following results is the change in air travel behaviour, though only five interviewees reported such. Even though Hergesell and Dickinger (2013) connected general environmental friendliness in the everyday life behaviour with sustainable transport choices, the actual findings cannot support this correlation.

3.4 Voluntary Carbon-Offsetting Behaviour

Attitude-Behaviour Gap in Air Travel. This section reveals the key findings of the study, as the research aim is to identify the voluntary carbon-offsetting behaviour of German tourists. It was already established earlier that the majority of the respondents (86%) adjudge a certain threat towards climate change. Interestingly, only 4% have ever voluntarily participated in a carbon-offsetting scheme before. Similar results were published by McKercher et al. (2010) and Mair (2011), who found out that only a very small number of respondents have already taken part in compensation programmes. Identical to research by Mair (2011) as well as by

Prideaux, Coghlan and McKercher (2011), the study shows that even if travellers show pro-environmental attitudes, they do not automatically seek for ways to reduce their impact on the climate. Conclusions can be drawn that environmental concerns about global warming do not automatically lead to participation in offset programmes. With this obvious result, the assumption is maintained that German tourists indicate an attitude-behaviour gap when it comes to CO_2 compensation in air travel. Thus, hypothesis 1 can be supported, assuming that there is a gap between pro-environmental attitudes towards climate change and the voluntary carbon-offsetting behaviour of German air travellers.

However, one logical approach for the almost non-existent participation might be the unfamiliarity with the concept of CO_2 compensation (Becken, 2007). In order to prove this aspect, the interviewees were asked if they are familiar with the term 'carbon-offsetting'. The corresponding findings revealed that just under half of the tourists are familiar with the concept, while 30% have heard of it but do not know the meaning. About one quarter of all respondents (24%) are not at all familiar with the idea of compensating greenhouse gas emissions. Women tend to be slightly more aware of the concept than men. A further question examined the familiarity of respondents with airlines and other organisations that offer the possibility of voluntary carbon-offsetting. It is evident from the results that 21% could name such an organisation. The majority of those were familiar with airlines that cooperate with a specialised offset provider. The most frequently mentioned airline was Lufthansa.

According to these findings, over half of German air travellers disclose a lack of knowledge, similar to McKercher et al. (2010) who also highlighted a low awareness of voluntary carbon-offsetting programmes among their respondents. Hence, the second hypothesis can also be supported, stating that there is a lack of knowledge among German tourists with regards to the concept of voluntary carbon-offsetting. One possible explanation is the insufficient supply with related information by travel agencies, airlines, and other intermediaries in the booking process. There is still a possibility that a higher number of tourists would have compensated if they were better informed about voluntary compensation programmes. Hence, the gap between pro-environmental concerns and the missing translation of those into corresponding action can only be partially applied to the voluntary carbon-offsetting behaviour.

Willingness to Change Travel Behaviour. Another part of this study analysed tourist's willingness to change their travel behaviour in future. For this purpose, interviewees were asked whether they would make a contribution towards reducing the carbon output that was created during air travel, bearing in mind their income and travel expenses. The results reveal that over half of the tourists are willing to offset their emissions in future, while one quarter is not prepared to make an extra contribution. Despite of the critical attitude towards offsetting (Wehrli et al., 2011), German tourists indicate a surprising high willingness to participate in such.

The affirmative respondents were thereupon asked to name a percentage of their total flight costs they would be willing to donate. When regarding the average surcharge (mean), men (8.4%) are prone to contribute a higher amount than women (6.7%). However, the median of 5% is similar for both groups and also corresponds to findings of other studies (McKercher et al., 2010). In general, these are satisfying results with regards to the generosity of German tourists. Furthermore, it was found that 73% of the affirmative respondents indicated a preference for mandatory compensation programmes. This suggests that every passenger has to pay a premium amount when travelling. Many of them strongly believed that every person should be obliged to pay for carbon neutralisation.

Those respondents who were not willing to compensate their air travel emissions were asked for the major reasons. Analogous to past research (Becken, 2007; Wherli, 2011), the highest score was reached with regards to price. Exactly 50% of the cases reported that paying an extra amount for offsetting carbon emissions would be too expensive. In line with findings by Cohen, Higham and Reis (2013), the imbalance between environmental worries and personal restrictions, like the payment of premium prices, leads to the decision against a participation in offset programmes.

Another reason for not willing to compensate is the lack of information about compensation schemes. This fact supports the unfamiliarity with carbon-offset organisations, as discussed earlier. Besides, tourists also mentioned a lack of trust towards compensation providers, which implies a certain degree of deficient transparency and weak communication. As already stressed by Eijgelaar (2011), there is an urgent necessity to improve consumer education regarding carbon-offset schemes, since only a few providers offer proper information about emission reduction measures. Furthermore, consumers may also lose trust in airlines because they seem to misuse the compensation tool for the improvement of image and public reputation (International Ecotourism Society, 2012). Identical to findings by Becken (2007) some respondents (13,3%) saw the payment of carbon taxes as being the responsibility of others, especially the airline itself.

At a later stage, respondents were asked about other future changes in their travel behaviour. To begin with, the interviewer assessed whether respondents actually expect to pay a mandatory carbon tax in the future. Around 46% affirmed this prognosis. Prideaux, Coghlan and McKercher (2011) also reported in their study that many tourists are prepared to pay a compulsory extra amount in future. Some 23% of the interviewed tourists estimate the likeliness of paying such a tax as very low, while approximately 30% were unsure.

Furthermore, in terms of reducing greenhouse gas emissions of tourism, two important mitigation measures were addressed. First of all, tourists can make a major difference if they reduce their flying behaviour by switching to other means of transport. Interestingly, only 13% of the total participants are willing to travel less by plane. Certainly, these findings should be seen in relation to the travel frequency of individuals. Thus, a person that does not fly regularly will not indicate to travel less by plane. However, since the respondents seem to travel on a regular basis and 76% prefer the airplane for pleasure trips, one can assume that most of the tourists enjoy frequent air travel. Since 63% are not prepared to restrict their air travel behaviour, the willingness to relinquish travel habits, comfort and convenience in order to protect the environment is very weak among German air travellers.

Identical findings become apparent with regards to domestic holidays, which portrays yet another mitigation strategy. In case tourists increase their number of local holidays in Germany, long-distance air travels can easily be avoided, and simultaneously the emission of greenhouse gases. Unfortunately, over half of the respondents are not prepared to spend their holidays in Germany on a regular basis. For the sake of climate protection, only 26% are actually willing to spend their vacations in closer destinations.

Generally speaking, the willingness to participate in voluntary carbon-offsetting schemes is acceptably high, though German tourists are not as prepared to alter their travel patterns in general, for example by alternative mobility choices or travel destinations. The barrier of paying a premium amount for compensation seems lower than changing holiday habits and lifestyles. In good agreement with Cohen, Higham and Reis (2013), tourists rather tend to abandon or suppress concerns about the climate, than change habitual travel patterns.

Influence of Demographic Factors. The study further investigated whether demographic factors have an influence on the willingness of German air travellers to participate in voluntary carbon-offsetting programmes. As mentioned in previous results, around 57% are prepared to participate in compensation initiatives. The question is whether age, gender and level of education have an influence on this group of tourists.

Care should be taken with the interpretation of these findings, as the total number of respondents is unevenly distributed among the different age, gender and educational groups. Therefore conclusions should not be drawn by just regarding basic counts of each group. For a better evaluation, further numerical values were generated. These include the percentage of each count within the total age, gender or educational group of the respondent, as well as the expected count, which is a hypothetical parameter used as a kind of reference scale. It represents the expected value of each column by assuming that no correlation between the two variables would exist.

The influence of age on the willingness of German air travellers to compensate greenhouse gas emissions shows interesting results. Although interviewees aged 25 or younger hold the highest sum, they actually indicate the lowest percentage by comparing other counts in relation to their total number. That is the reason why respondents aged between 36 and 45 show a 100% willingness to compensate. An increasing willingness is visible with respect to the first three age groups. However, a clear pattern cannot be drawn regarding older age groups. In order to find out whether these results hold statistical significance, the Pearson Chi-Square test was applied using SPSS. It is used to detect whether there is a correlation between two variables (VanderStoep & Johnston, 2009), in this case the age of the respondent and the willingness to donate a compensatory fee. In either case, the test hypothesises that there is no dependence between both variables (null hypothesis). The asymptotic significance proclaims the probability of this hypothesis. In case its value is lower than 0.05, the probability of a correlation is over 95%, hence, the null hypothesis can be refused. However, the asymptotic significance displays a value of 0.267 and indicates that there is no correlation between age and the willingness to offset carbon emissions in air travel. A possible reason is the varying number of participants in different age groups. Based on these findings, it is not possible to affirm research by Mair (2011), who found that those who are more likely to compensate their air travel emissions are of younger age groups.

In the next step, the correlation between gender and tourists' willingness to compensate will be analysed using the same procedure as above. Past research suggests that men are more likely to participate in a voluntary carbon-offsetting programme (Mair, 2011), although women tend to show a higher environmental responsiveness (Wells, Ponting & Peattie, 2011). Results suggest that the influence of gender on the willingness to compensate is as follows: women (63.2%) show a higher tendency to participate in compensation programmes than men (50%). However, these results are questionable, since there are generally more female than male respondents in this survey, which could lead to distortions in the responses. Therefore, the Chi-Square test was used to detect whether there is a correlation between the two variables. The asymptotic significance (0.404) is very high and leads to the assumption that there is no dependence between age and the willingness to voluntarily offset greenhouse gas emissions.

Finally, it remains to determine whether the educational level of respondents influences their willingness to compensate air travel emissions. The research reveals that respondents who completed 'Mittlere Reife' (secondary school) (70%), university (63.5%) and 'Abitur/Fachabitur' (high school) (57.9%) show the highest willingness to purchase carbon-offsets. Apart from 'Mittlere Reife', those degrees belong to higher educational levels. People with university degree receive the highest absolute count, followed by high school graduates. Explicit evidence regarding the findings by Mair (2011) and Wehrli et al. (2011) is given with regards to the lower type of secondary school 'Hauptschule'. Only two respondents who attained this educational degree are prepared to offset carbon emissions in future. Results of the Chi-Square test confirm a correlation between level of education and willingness to purchase offsets. According to the asymptotic significance of 0.021, there is a 98% probability that the willingness of compensating is dependent on the level of education. On the whole one can conclude that German air travellers are more willing to purchase voluntary carbon-offsets in case they have attained a higher level of education.

Generally speaking, demographic factors will probably have certain influence on the willingness to neutralise air travel emissions, however, this could only partly be proven in this study. Evidence has not been accomplished with regards to the dependence of compensation behaviour on age or gender of the respondents. On the other hand, the study revealed that better-educated tourists show a higher willingness to CO_2 compensation. Hence, the third hypothesis can only partially be supported.

4 CONCLUSIONS

The aim of this study was to analyse whether the attitude-behaviour gap in terms of voluntary carbon-offsetting also accounts for German tourists. A gap between pro-environmental attitudes of tourists with respect to climate change and corresponding behaviour was indicated in past literature. Especially the willingness to offset greenhouse gas emissions of air travel has not enjoyed much attention in the past. Major reasons included a lack of price, time and information that impede the change to sustainable alternatives. Despite environmental concerns, peoples' personal needs often have a stronger influence over their actions. Since past studies focused on countries like Great Britain, New Zealand, Australia and Hong Kong, geographical reasons led to the choice of conducting research in Germany. The voluntary carbon-offsetting behaviour of German tourists was analysed by carrying out structured face-to-face interviews at the airport of Hamburg.

The findings demonstrated that German air travellers show a reasonable level of concern when it comes to general environmental issues, and in particular with regards to global warming. Next to pollution, climate change and extreme weather events were ranked among the top three environmental problems that will have future impacts on a local and global scale. Interestingly, tourists do not critically assess their individual travel behaviour with impacts on the climate. Although the majority of respondents display pro-environmental measurements in their everyday-life, attempts to change travel patterns have only been made by a minority of participants. This is especially true with respect to neutralising air travel emissions through carbon compensation. Identical to previous studies, only 4% have ever voluntarily participated in a carbon-offsetting scheme before. Thus, environmental concerns about climate change do not automatically lead to the willingness to offset the own travel emissions. Accordingly, the inconsistency between environmental attitudes and corresponding behaviour can also be supported for German tourists. However, the low participation rate possibly derives from a lack of awareness and familiarity with the idea of carbon-offsetting. Less than half of the respondents are familiar with the opportunity of compensating travel emissions elsewhere. This indicates a strong weakness in consumer education and communication.

Interestingly, ambivalent results became evident regarding the willingness to take future measures in travel behaviour. On the one hand, German tourists indicate a positive attitude towards compensating prospective air travel emissions. Over half of the respondents show a willingness to make an extra contribution, and most of them even encouraged mandatory compensation programmes. However, only a low willingness was shown in terms of other mitigation strategies. Just a small amount of the respondents considered to spend their holidays in Germany more frequently, and even less are prepared to reduce their flying performance. Hence, the barrier of paying a compensatory payment to neutralise emissions seems to be lower than changing holiday habits completely.

In good agreement with past research, the findings in this investigation indicated that better educated tourists tend to be more willing to purchase carbon-offsets in future. This could be explained by an enhanced knowledge about climate change with respect to people who enjoyed a higher educational level. Unfortunately, no significant results were reported in matters of age and gender of the respondents. Difficulties in this sense derived from the number of respondents and the unequal distribution between different gradations.

On the whole, behavioural change of tourists remains a major challenge in future. Despite great concerns about climate change and environmental friendly behaviour in the everyday life, German tourists have not shown many attempts to change their travel behaviour. The low participation rate in voluntary carbon-offsetting schemes does not only indicate a call for consumer education and instruction, but also requires the awareness of other stakeholders in the travel industry. Tour operators, travel agencies, airlines and other tourism organisations have a high potential to communicate compensation programmes and make consumers more acquainted to this opportunity. Furthermore, there remains a strong need for improvement in terms of carbon-offsetting itself. Trust and transparency needs to be built in order to provide consolidate collaborations. All in all, behavioural change can only be realised in case every stakeholder is committed to make a difference.

5   LIMITATIONS AND FUTURE RESEARCH

Several limitations have occurred during this study, among others the use of non-probability sampling. As a consequence, the sample must not be regarded as representative for the population of interest. Moreover, a higher number of respondents would have contributed to more reliable findings. This is particularly important with respect to demographic data, since strong variations appeared in terms of age and education. In addition, the study solely involved respondents at the airport of Hamburg. An inclusion of further locations would contribute to a better representation of German air travellers. Although it was assured that all of the respondents have taken a flight before, not everybody was actually travelling with the airplane at the interview day. It became evident that the last time a few of the interviewees have taken a flight was decades ago. Hence, a low awareness for compensation schemes is self-evident. This should have been considered in the survey as it might contribute to errors in the findings.

Future research may also imply the inclusion of supplementary methods of analysis since the current study only made use of frequency analyses. Applying correlation and regression analyses will lead to a higher significance of the survey results.

The paper predominantly emphasised environmental attitudes and concerns as being crucial determinants of sustainable tourist behaviour. Yet, there are many other variables that have not been covered in the survey, as this would have gone beyond the scope of this study. Nevertheless, the findings offer a first insight into the voluntary carbon-offsetting behaviour of German tourists. Compelling evidence was provided for the gap between awareness and action and may be seen as a starting point for future research. In this respect, it is highly recommended to conduct similar investigations on a larger scale, possibly at different locations in order to receive a good representation of German travellers. Also, the willingness of participating in a compensation programme could be linked to particular traveller segments, based on travel frequency, type of travel, income, and other demographics. An interesting approach would include a comparison between environmental attitudes and behaviours between different types of tourists, for instance railway users and air travellers. Furthermore, the comparison between offset purchasers and non-purchasers holds promise to understand different positions and motivations.

Moreover, a next stage might include an extensive analysis of the reasons for refusal in order to identify weaknesses and potentials for development. In this respect possible incentives for tourists to change their travel behaviour might also be explored.

REFERENCES

Adams, J., Khan, H., Raeside, R., & White, D. (2007). *Research Methods for Business and Social Science Students*. New Delhi: Response Books.

Ajzen, I., & Fishbein, M. (2005). The Influence of Attitudes on Behaviour. In D. Albarracín, B. Johnson & M. Zanna (Eds.), *The Handbook of Attitudes* (pp. 173-221). New York: Psychology Press.

Altinay, L., & Paraskevas, A. (2008). *Planning Research in Hospitality and Tourism*. Oxford: Butterworth-Heinemann.

Barr, S., & Prillwitz, J. (2011). Sustainable travel: mobility, lifestyle and practice. In P. Newton (Ed.), *Urban Consumption* (pp. 159-171). Collingwood, Australia: CSIRO Publishing.

Becken, S. (2007). Tourists' Perception of International Air Travel's Impact on the Global Climate and Potential Climate Change Policies. *Journal of Sustainable Tourism, 15*(4), 351-368.

Becken, S., & Hay, J. (2007). *Tourism and Climate Change. Risks and Opportunities*. Clevedon: Channel View Publications.

Bowen, D., & Clarke, J. (2009). *Contemporary Tourist Behaviour. Yourself and Others as Tourists*. Wallingford, England: CABI.

Broderick, J. (2009). Voluntary Carbon Offsetting for Air Travel. In S. Gössling & P. Upham (Eds.), *Climate Change and Aviation. Issues, Challenges and Solutions* (pp. 329-346). London: Earthscan.

Budeanu, A. (2007). Sustainable tourist behaviour - a discussion of opportunities for change. *International Journal of Consumer Studies, 31*, 499-508.

Cohen, S., Higham, J., & Reis, A. (2013). Sociological barriers to developing sustainable discretionary air travel behaviour. *Journal of Sustainable Tourism, 21*(7), 982–998.

Colton, D., & Covert, R. (2007). *Designing and Constructing Instruments for Social Research and Evaluation*. San Francisco, CA: Jossey-Bass.

Denscombe, M. (2010). *The Good Research Guide for Small-scale Social Research Projects* (4th ed.). Maidenhead: Open University Press.

DiPeso, J. (2007). Carbon offsets: Is the environment getting what you pay for?. *Environmental Quality Management, 17*(2), 89-94.

Eijgelaar, E. (2011). Voluntary Carbon Offsets a Solution for Reducing Tourism Emissions? Assessment of Communication Aspects and Mitigation Potential. *European Journal of Transport and Infrastructure Research, 11*(3), 281-296.

Gössling, S., Bredberg, M., Randow, A., Sandström, E., & Svensson, P. (2006). Tourist Perceptions of Climate Change: A Study of International Tourists in Zanzibar. *Current Issues in Tourism, 9*(4&5), 419-435.

Gössling, S., Broderick, J., Upham, P., Ceron, J. P., Dubois, G., Peeters, P., & Strasdas, W. (2007). Voluntary Carbon Offsetting Schemes for Aviation: Efficiency, Credibility and Sustainable Tourism. *Journal of Sustainable Tourism, 15*(3), 223-248.

Hergesell, A., & Dickinger, A. (2013). Environmentally friendly holiday transport mode choices among students: the role of price, time and convenience. *Journal of Sustainable Tourism, 21*(4), 596–613.

Hibbert, J., Dickinson, J., Gössling, S., & Curtin, S. (2013). Identity and tourism mobility: an exploration of the attitude–behaviour gap. *Journal of Sustainable Tourism, 21*(7), 999–1016.

IATA (International Air Transport Association). (2013). *Annual Review 2013*. Retrieved 11.02.2014 from http://www.iata.org/about/Documents/iata-annual-review-2013-en.pdf.

International Ecotourism Society. (2012). *Is Carbon Offsetting an Effective Tool for Sustainable Tourism?*. Retrieved 25.03.2014 from http://www.ecotourism.org/news/carbon-offsetting-effective-tool-sustainable-tourism.

IPCC (Intergovernmental Panel on Climate Change). (2013). *Climate Change 2013. The Physical Science Basis. Summary for Policymakers.* Retrieved 25.02.2014 from http://www.ipcc.ch/report/ar5/wg1/docs/WGIAR5_SPM_brochure_en.pdf.

Jenkins, I. (2013). Sustainability and Climate Change. In I. Jenkins & R. Schröder (Eds.), *Sustainability in Tourism. A Multidisciplinary Approach* (pp. 33-51). Wiesbaden: Springer Gabler.

Kennedy, E., Beckley, T., McFarlane, B., & Nadeau, S. (2009). Why We Don't "Walk the Talk": Understanding the Environmental Values/Behaviour Gap in Canada. *Human Ecology Review, 16*(2), 151-160.

Kind, C., Duwe, S., Tänzler, D., Reuster, L., Kleemann, M., & Krebs, J. (2010). *Analysis of the German Market for Voluntary Carbon Offsetting.* Dessau-Roßlau: Federal Environment Agency (Umweltbundesamt) Retrieved 05.03.2014 from http://www.umweltbundesamt.de/sites/default/files/medien/461/publikationen/climate_change_10_2010_kurzfassung_e1_0.pdf.

Kollmuss, A., & Agyeman, J. (2002). Mind the gap: Why do people act environmentally and what are the barriers to pro-environmental behavior?. *Environmental Education Research, 8*(2), 239-260.

Mair, J. (2011). Exploring air travellers' voluntary carbon-offsetting behaviour. *Journal of Sustainable Tourism, 19*(2), 215–230.

McKercher, B., Prideaux, B., Cheung, C., & Law, R. (2010). Achieving Voluntary Reductions in the Carbon Footprint of Tourism and Climate Change. *Journal of Sustainable Tourism, 18*(3), 297-317.

O'Leary, R., & Miller, R. (2003). Questionnaires and structured interview schedules. In R. Miller & J. Brewer (Eds.), *The A-Z of Social Research. A Dictionary of Key Social Science Research Concepts* (pp. 253-255). London: SAGE Publications.

Prideaux, B., Coghlan, A., & McKercher, B. (2011). Identifying Tourists' Likely to Adopt Voluntary Mitigation Activities. In K. Weiermair, H. Pechlaner, A. Strobl, M. Elmi & M. Schuckert (Eds.), *Coping with Global Climate Change. Strategies, Policies and Measures for the Tourism Industry* (pp. 41-59). Innsbruck, Austria: Innsbruck University Press.

Schuman, H. (1972). Attitudes vs. Actions Versus Attitudes vs. Attitudes. *Public Opinion Quarterly,36*(3), 347-354.

Strasdas, W., Gössling, S., & Dickhut, H. (2010).*Treibhausgas-Kompensationsanbieter in Deutschland.* Manuscript submitted for publication, HNE Eberswalde, Eberswalde, Germany. Retrieved 11.02.2014 from http://www.atmosfair.de/fileadmin/user_upload/Medienecke/Downloadmaterial/Vergleichende_Studien/VZBV_Studie_Eberswalde.pdf.

UNWTO (World Tourism Organization) & UNEP (United Nations Environment Programme). (2008). *Climate Change and Tourism. Responding to Global Challenges.* Retrieved 26.01.2014 from http://sdt.unwto.org/sites/all/files/docpdf/climate2008.pdf.

VanderStoep, S., & Johnston, D. (2009). *Research Methods for Everyday Life: Blending Qualitative and Quantitative Approaches.* San Francisco, CA: Jossey-Bass.

Wehrli, R., Egli, H., Lutzenberger, M., Pfister, D., Schwarz, J., Stettler, J. (2011). *Is there Demand for Sustainable Tourism? – A study for the World Tourism Forum Lucerne 2011.* Lucerne: Lucerne University of Applied Sciences and Arts.

Wells, V., Ponting, C., & Peattie, K. (2011). Behaviour and Climate Change: Consumer perceptions of responsibility. *Journal of Marketing Management, 27*(7-8), 808–833.

Outernet Technologies in Tourism: A Conceptual Framework and Applications for the Travel Industry

Paula Monteiro Harasymowicz

Salzburg University of Applied Sciences, Austria
paula.monteiroh@gmail.com

Abstract

The Internet is leaving its traditional cyberspace and is hitting the streets. The development of Outernet technologies, namely Radio-frequency identification, Near Field Communications, Quick Response Codes, Augmented Reality and Smart Wearable Devices, enable tourists to always stay connected with stakeholders on the go. These technologies also facilitate the interaction between travellers, the physical environment around them and digital information, diminishing the divide between the real and digital world. Although Outernet technologies, along with portable electronic devices, are nowadays intensively used in all phases of the travelling cycle, research on the term 'Outernet' and its adjacent concepts is still in nascent stages in the tourism academic literature. This research aims filling a conceptual gap by investigating the concept of the Outernet, structuring secondary data available in the topic and mapping relevant concepts in the context of tourism. The main result of this exploratory research is a suggested conceptual framework of the Outernet in the context of tourism. Managerial recommendations are provided.

Keywords: Outernet; etourism; Conceptual framework; Ubiquitous technologies; Augmented reality

1 INTRODUCTION

Technological advancement is widely accepted as a main fomenter for the development of tourism. As technology becomes more mobile, ubiquitous and user-focused, travellers progressively incorporate its usage in the pre, during and post stages of their travel cycle. Especially when *in situ*, portable electronic devices (PEDs) assist travellers to solve typical problems that appear while exploring a new destination, such as how to get around, which points of interest (POIs) to visit, how to book tourism services, among others (Brown and Chalmers, 2003). This leads to highly technology-enhanced experiences in tourism, in which travellers often chose to remain connected at all times (cf. Egger 2013; Neuhofer et al. 2013). The increase of Internet and PEDs usage by tourists enables them to interact with relevant tourism stakeholders that are close and far to their current location (Hannam et al., 2014). The possibility to have an incessant information flow between travellers and service providers creates both benefits and challenges for businesses. On the one hand, tourism businesses have more opportunities to reach out to customers with appropriate offers on site. On the other hand, they must make sure their offers are compatible to the traveller's location and personal preferences, in order to deliver the right offer at the right place and time. Furthermore, context and the environment surrounding the tourist are crucial factors in the decision making process, therefore should also be taken into consideration in the tourism offer (Buhalis and Foerste, 2013).

Tourism is known for being a highly competitive industry, where businesses often turn to innovation and information and communication technologies (ICTs) to gain competitive advantage (cf. Hjalager, 2010). In this sense, technologies that facilitate the interaction between businesses, consumers and physical environment will be crucial to fulfil the needs of technology-savvy travellers on the go. Technologies such as radio-frequency identification (RFID), near field communications (NFC), quick response codes (QR Codes), augmented reality (AR) and smart wearable devices have the ability to incorporate digital data to real world objects and scenes, diminishing the divide between people, objects and information. This link between online and offline spheres through technologies is denominated the 'Outernet' (Pesonen and Horster 2012; Marlinghaus and Rast 2013).

In spite of the current usage of Outernet technologies by both travellers and tourism service providers, the term 'Outernet' is still in a nascent exploration stage in the tourism academic research. In order to fill a literature gap on the topic, this exploratory paper presents a comprehensive review and analysis of secondary data available on the Outernet in the context of tourism. Through in-depth desk research, identification of key concepts, triangulation and soft falsification, the author of this paper attempts to structure the topic of the Outernet in tourism.

2 THEORETHICAL BACKGROUND

Technology and ICTs have evolved rapidly in the past years. From this evolvement, a significant change in the way individuals access and retrieve information took place. The Internet, once based in home desktops, left its traditional cyberspace and became accessible from a variety of portable smart devices. In the past two decades information was mainly available offline and in websites. Nowadays, data is retrievable from physical object, smart environments, wearable devices, among others (cf. Tussyadiah, 2014). Cisco, a technology-focused company, estimates that 50 billion devices will be connected to the Internet by 2020 (Evans, 2011). This indicates great interest of businesses to integrate physical objects and sights into the Web of Things. The facility of accessing information on the go from different sources, being them physical or digital, was a paradigm changer for the way individuals live, interact, communicate, do business and travel (cf. Sheller and Urry, 2006).

The tourism industry is known for its early and fast adoption of technology throughout the years (Buhalis, 2003). New terms emerged to describe the incorporation of ICTs and mobile technology in the tourism value chain, namely etourism and mtourism (Ibid; Huijnen 2006). The emergence of new technologies that allow a more fluid interaction between travellers, information and physical things, quickly caught the attention of tourism service providers. Outernet technologies provide travellers a great amount of autonomy and involvement while exploring a destination, allowing them to co-create their experiences on site (Prahalad and Ramaswamy, 2004). In this sense, an understanding of what the Outernet is and how it fits to the changing tourism environment becomes crucial for tourism suppliers to gain competitive advantage.

2.1 Outernet in academic literature

The term 'Outernet' is still in exploratory stages in the academic literature. To the knowledge of the author, the term was first mentioned by Pesonen and Horster (2012) in the context of tourism. In their article exploring possible applications of NFC technology for travel, the authors define the Outernet as being the "merge of offline and online world" (Ibid, p. 20). A number of business publications explore the topic of the Outernet with a practical approach, gathering knowledge from use cases of Outernet technologies and by interviewing experts.

Among the most significant publications is Marlinghaus and Rast's (2013) book, which outlined the main characteristics of the Outernet, identified its key drivers and listed its related concepts. These authors further provided recommendations for businesses on how to prepare for the changes to come when using technologies that connect physical things to information and people. AirPlus International (2014) recognized in a recent report, possible ways that the Outernet will affect tourism. The institution classifies the Outernet as a mega-trend that takes "the internet on to the streets through mobile apps and cloud computing" (Ibid, p. 8). Finally, TrendOne (n.d.) contributes to the topic by creating five theories of what the Outernet might trigger in society.

As a first step, it is important to understand what are the steering forces driving the Outernet into society. TrendOne (n.d.) identified four main forces deriving from information and technological changes in tourism: the development of technological information, the Internet and Web of Things, smart information processing and location-based information. Rehder (in Marlinghaus and Rats, 2013) builds up this logic by attributing increased competition and changes in customers' demand as further crucial factors for the integration of the Outernet into businesses and individuals' lives.

As for the main characteristics of the Outernet, three key elements were common among the analysed secondary data: location-based, ubiquitous and personalized. The first refers to the importance of identifying what is around the tourist aiming to provide location-relevant offers (Rehder in Marlinghaus and Rats, 2013). Accurate recognition of travellers' current location and 'smartization' of tourism POIs will be key to deliver relevant offers in travel recommendation systems (cf. Schiller and Voisard, 2004). The second characteristic indicates the ability of the Outernet (and its technologies) to be present everywhere, seamlessly integrated in real world scenes where the technical infrastructure is provided (Papagiannakis et al. 2008; Poslad 2009). The last distinctive trait of the Outernet, personalization, is an ongoing trend in both electronic and mobile tourism (Buhalis and O'Connor, 2005). Providing tailored offers in the Outernet context is possible through learning customer's behaviour patterns, collecting customer intelligence, identifying travellers' location and context, and learning from behaviour of similar customers (Höpken et al. 2008; Weaver 2011).

2.2 Outernet technologies in tourism

Outernet technologies are those able to interlink real world scenes and objects to people and to information available in the digital sphere (Rehder in Marlinghaus and Rats, 2013). Figure 1 provides an overview of existing technologies that are able to establish this complex interrelation. Acknowledging that upcoming technologies may also fit into the Outernet umbrella term, the author included a 'future technologies' box in the overview below.

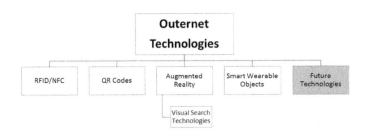

Fig. 1. Outernet technologies overview

These technologies are in different stages of maturity based on how long they have been in the market, their functionalities and application in tourism and other industries.

RFID transmits information wirelessly from a an RFID tag to an enabled reader, providing digital information about tagged objects' location, status, characteristics among other data

(Coskun et al. 2012). This technology has the potential to optimize services and processes in tourism and assist managers to track travellers' habits and preferences. Common use cases in tourism are new RFID tagged e-passports, information tags in POIs and RFID armbands in spas and ski passes.

NFC operates similarly to its preceding technology, however, it is considered an evolvement of RFID once it is safer and allows a two way communication between enabled objects and tags (Ibid). NFC can specially benefit travellers due to its ease of usage and ubiquity (Pesonen and Horster, 2012). In recent years, tourism managers and academics focused on investigating and trying NFC solutions in the tourism field. Main applications involve facilitating traveller payment on the go, faster access to tourism services, such as hotel rooms, spa areas, amusement parks, gathering and managing customer loyalty and couponing (Ondrus and Pigneur 2009; Swedberg 2012; Egger 2013). Improvement of service quality for tourists is a key benefit managers should be able to incorporate in the travel service providing with NFC.

QR codes are 2D barcodes that are able to encrypt large amount of information in a small machine-readable print area (Coskun et al., 2012). Widely used in tourism, QR codes provide "an analogue portal to the digital world" (Baik 2012, p. 427) that are attachable to any surface, easy to scan and manage. Similarly to NFC, tourism managers optimized customer benefits and loyalty programs by digitalizing traditional customer cards (Canadi et al. 2011). QR codes enable tourism suppliers to reduce costs by diminishing the production of physical customer cards and print material (Ibid). Furthermore, it facilitates customer intelligence gathering by monitoring travellers' behaviour towards specific offers (Ibid).

Augmented reality and smart wearable devices are relatively new when compared to other Outernet technologies. AR is defined as a system that "supplements the real world with virtual (computer-generated) objects that appear to coexist in the same space as the real world" (Azuma et al. 2001, p. 34). Location-based AR is a helpful tool to explore user's vicinities by indicating and navigating them to POIs. Examples of mobile apps that currently offer this functionality are the Wikitude, Layar, Tripwolf, Yelp, among others (Yovcheva et al. 2012). Other AR functionalities are slowly being introduced in the tourism sector such as clickable travel catalogues, AR simultaneous language translation, augmented sales staff on retail stores, augmented tour guides in museums, rendering of giant 3D models of famous sites (Yovcheva and Buhalis 2013; Wikitude n.d.).

Smart wearable apparatus are a wide range of technology-advanced devices, such as smart glasses, watches, clothing and even contact lenses, that travellers can wear at any time and any place (cf. Holloway 2014; Kelly 2014). Especially the development and popularization of smart watches and smart glasses represent one step ahead on the so called 'technology embodiment', which allows tourists to communicate on the go without the physical "interference" of PEDs (cf. Tussyadiah, 2014). The embodiment of technology enables travellers to take great control of co-creating their experiences on site (cf. Linaza et al. 2012; Yovcheva et al. 2012, Tussyadiah 2014).

These two Outernet technologies go hand in hand at this point in time. According to a recent AR and VR (virtual reality) report, "global dedicated devices augmented reality market is expected to reach $659.98 million by 2018" (Markets and Markets, 2014). The above mentioned applications of AR in tourism are yet to become mainstream, but in the near future it is expected that tourism suppliers will easily be able to contact travellers with location-based, context-aware and personalized offers through AR and wearable devices. Additionally, they will reach out for travellers in the precise point of times when they feel travellers will have the need for their offers, without disrupting the exploration of the destination (cf. Tussyadiah, 2014).

Table 1 summarizes the current main applications of the Outernet technologies in tourism per technology type, followed by relevant references available in academic literature.

Table 1. Outernet technologies by functionality in tourism

Outernet technology	Functionality	Reference in academic literature
RFID	Human tracking Assets tracking & management Control Systems (E-passports) Payment/Ticketing Information supply/retrieve Access management	Shepard (2005); Fuschi (2006); Bellotti et al. (2008); Öztayşi et al. (2009); Zeni et al. (2009); Hasan et al. (2010); Mishra and Mishra (2010); Hozak (2012); Ozkurt et al. (2012); Tsai and Chung (2012); Ginters and Martin-Gutierrez (2013).
NFC	Payment/Ticketing Couponing Access management Navigation Information supply/retrieve	Ondrus and Pigneur (2009); Borrego-Jaraba et al. (2010); Mitrokotsa et al. (2010); Ok et al. (2010); Ozdenizci et al. (2011); Coskun et al. (2012); Curran et al. (2012); Pesonen and Horster (2012); Egger (2013); Ronay and Egger (2013); Ronay and Egger (2014).
QR Codes	Couponing Payment/Ticketing Information supply/retrieve Link to URL/Digital data Customer card digitalization	Canadi et al. (2010); Canadi et al. (2011); Baik (2012); Emaldi et al. (2012); Fino et al. (2013).
Augmented reality	Payment/Ticketing Navigation Information supply/retrieve Search/Browse Provide Feedback	Azuma et al. (2001); Fritz et al. (2005); Papagiannakis et al. (2008); Portalés et al. (2009); Pence (2011); Kounavis et al. (2012); Linaza et al. (2012); Yovcheva et al. (2012); Buhalis and Yovcheva (2013); Fino et al. (2013); Puyuelo et al. (2013); Ahn et al. (2014).
Smart wearable objects	Payment/Ticketing Navigation Information supply/retrieve Object Recognition Search/Browse Provide Feedback Register scenes (photo or video)	Ehn and Linde (2004); Nilsson et al. (2004); Tussyadiah (2014).

2.3 Factors influencing Outernet incorporation in tourism

Tourism, as an industry, is highly focused in providing meaningful experience to travellers *in situ* (Neuhofer, 2014). Changes in technology and travellers' behaviours alter the requirements for what will be considered a great touristic experience. Nowadays, travellers are proactive, highly mobile, always connected and willing to share their experiences as they happen. This drives service providers to find innovative ways to reach tourists on the go. In this sense, Outernet technologies are likely to be incorporated in tourism for the following main reasons:

- Individuals' high mobility (Sheller and Urry, 2006);

- Tourist desire to always stay connected (Egger 2013, Tussyadiah 2014);

- Real time experience sharing (Tussyadiah, 2014);

- Need for ubiquitous, location-based and context-aware information (Höpken et al. 2008; TrendOne n.d.);

- Intensification of social media usage on PEDs (Cohen et al. 2013; Neuhofer et al. 2012) and

- Tourist desire to co-create experiences on site (Prahalad and Ramaswamy 2004, Neuhofer 2014).

2.4 Outernet from a tourism demand's perspective

Tourists' involvement with Outernet technologies happens exclusively at the visited destination. Travellers reach out for these technologies to retrieve information, navigate to POIs, purchase tourism products, register and share scenes, among other functionalities. Familiarity of travellers with Outernet technologies, as well as the structure provided by destination managers, will be key for developing a meaningful Outernet experience. Spontaneous decision making on site is common among generation X and Y travellers (cf. Cohen et al., 2013). These tourists, born between 1982 and 2002, are used to having technology supporting their decisions while travelling. Not only they search intensely for information, but also they communicate with peers, compare prices in multiple platforms and demand personalization and flexibility from suppliers (Buhalis and Law, 2008). Furthermore, generation X and early generation Y tourists have a high purchasing power on site, which means they are likely to splurge on unplanned offers they consider attractive when presented with the right approach and at the right context (Ibid).

Tourism suppliers, therefore, should strive to reach the new travellers with personalized, location-based and just-in-time offers through Outernet technologies.

2.5 Outernet from a tourism supplier's perspective

The Outernet allows businesses to increase value on their offers by reducing costs, improving service quality, delivering just-in-time products and enhancing customer-supplier relationship. Literature review indicates that the adoption of Outernet technologies in the travelling process will create additional touch points in the buying cycle of tourism products (cf. Rafat 2013; TrendOne, n.d.). Tagged physical objects and smart environments become 'hyperlinks' for digital data that can becomes easily accessible by PEDs (TrendOne, n.d.). This means tourism service providers have further channels, and therefore opportunities, to distribute their products on site. For that, suppliers must invest in setting up PEDs-friendly platforms where travellers can search, plan, book services, experience and share content on site.

Keeping up with the fast changing technology pace can be a challenge for tourism enterprises. Evaluation of which technologies to invest in, implementation of these technologies on existing business processes, building up staff knowledge and selecting appropriate strategies are some challenges tourism business might face. Despite the challenges, to lead in the competitive travel sector, suppliers must be aware of what the Outernet is and how it can benefit both businesses and travellers. By starting to evaluate Outernet solutions now, companies might face less competition and potentially find a 'Blue Ocean' of opportunities in tourism (cf. Kim and Mauborgne, 2009).

The following section will present the research methods and strategies chosen by the author in order to structure the revised literature in this exploratory research.

3 METHODOLOGY

This qualitative research adopted an exploratory approach towards the topic of the 'Outernet' in the context of tourism. This approach is justified by the current status of secondary data about the Outernet, on which little previous research has been carried by tourism scholars (cf. Brown, 2006).

As for the research methods adopted by the author, in-depth review of existing literature was done in order to identify the status quo of data on the subject. The author performed a detailed and systematic screening of academic articles, books, journals and conference proceedings in other to get a solid understanding of the theoretical background of what the Outernet is, its main functionalities and applications in tourism. Non-academic sources such as specialized journals, websites and interview carried with specialists were considered relevant by the author in other to get an understanding of practical use cases of Outernet functionalities and application of these technologies in the travel industry. Example of non-academic literature included Harvard Business Review articles, RFID Journal, technology industry reports and official documents produced by renowned companies in the technology and tourism fields, such as Cisco and AirPlus international. There were three main criteria established to select the examined literature: publishing date, language and relevance to the topics of the Outernet and tourism. Examined literature was primarily in English language with publishing year between 2000 and 2014.

In order to tackle non-falsifiability and overcome claims of lack of straightforwardness, which are reoccurring problems of conceptual papers (Popper 1959, cited in Xin et al. 2013), the author adopted a series of quality control techniques suggested by Xin et al. (2013), namely systematically reviewing peer-reviewed articles; soft falsification levels by providing several points of view on the discussed topics; skeptically questioning research elements; and finally, by triangulation of related concepts, ensuring consistency with the original problem.

Despite the appropriate questioning of conceptual investigations, Xin et al. (ibid) highlight the importance of research of this nature. They further emphasize the existence of a gap of conceptual studies in the tourism academic literature, which makes this paper of extreme value for the tourism literature. Some of the limitations of this study include a possible subjectivity and falsifiability of findings, as well as the language restriction of analysed secondary data. However, the author considers this exploratory paper a further step towards illuminating what the Outernet is and how it can be put into the context of the tourism industry.

4 RESULTS

An emergent nature of the term 'Outernet' was observed thought screening of relevant academic literature on the topic. There is a lack of consensus on what the Outernet actually is, being it referred at times as a mega-trend (AirPlus International, 2014) and other times as a phenomenon or Web 4.0 (TrendOne n.d; TrendOne 2011). The identification of common characteristics between RFID, NFC, QR codes, AR and smart wearable objects, being the most expressive their ability to link the physical and digital worlds, led the author to host these technologies under the umbrella term of 'Outernet technologies'. Adoption of these technologies in the context of tourism impact supply and demand in different ways, requiring adaptations from both sides.

4.1 Impacts of Outernet in tourism

Outernet technologies assist travellers to quickly obtain information from their surroundings through environment and object smartization. This means that tourists are able to quickly obtain information in order to reduce uncertainties and solve typical touristic problems. These technologies further facilitate the interaction with relevant stakeholders by giving tourists the possibility to communicate in real time, share information, book services, navigate to POIs and make cruising on destinations an Outernet-enhanced experience. The characteristic intangibility of tourism products are reduced by the possibility of always accessing information about them in real time and on site. This causes a considerable reduction of time between the moment the traveller first discovers the touristic offer and the actual experiencing of the product. Furthermore, the motivation for tourism stakeholders to adopt Outernet technologies vary between supply and demand. The author suggest, that both travellers and tourism service providers 'push-pull' for Outernet technologies and their functionalities based on identified factors influencing Outernet incorporation in tourism in section 2.3 of this paper. From a travellers' perspective, the Outernet influences how tourists search for information on site, make decisions, perform payments, communicate, share their experiences and cruise in destinations. High expectations towards technology-enhanced experiences come along the natural process of appropriating technology on individual's everyday (cf. Wang, 2013). Needless to say that providing Internet connections everywhere and enabling POIs and touristic destinations with Outernet technologies will be crucial to deliver meaningful experiences to travellers. Travellers' needs for just-in-time, location-based, context-aware and personalized information will create an on-site customer buying cycle. This will require advanced planning and preparedness from suppliers' side to manage unplanned and spontaneous booking of tourism services.

In another perspective, it is crucial to mention that, despite the fast technological advancements, there will still be tourists that will choose not to (or will not be able to) interact with Outernet technologies on site. Some reasons may include the lack of familiarity with these technologies, personal and financial limitations, or simply the desire to remain disconnected during the travelling time. For these tourists, the approach of touristic offer must be differentiated from the ones applied to the typical new tourist on site.

Tourism service providers, on the other hand, will face new challenges with the integration of Outernet functionalities by travellers on the go. The development of tourism product itself might be altered due to the emergence of new services, the hybridization of products and the concept of 'segment of one' (TrendOne, n.d.). Another impact is the radical shift of point of sale in tourism, traditionally hosted in websites in the past decades. TrendOne (n.d., p. 26) states that "the combination of Mobile Web and Web of Things will result in all objects becoming communication channels and selling spaces". This means that the placing of offers will become more malleable and competitive at the same time, on which tourism suppliers must come up with innovative solutions to deliver and communicate their message on the Outernet era. Timing will be a further challenge faced by businesses if they wish to reach customers at the right time and at the right place. A balance between proactive offering and non-intrusive communication will be key to influence travellers' decision making process on the go.

Among current holdbacks to mainstream adoption of Outernet technologies in tourism, the following can be highlighted: high cost of mobile data transfer and roaming fees, privacy and security issues, lack of intuitiveness of some systems, need to improve smart processing of information, among others (Egger and Buhalis 2008; Kim et al. 2013). Furthermore, developing appropriate platforms that are interoperable and compatible to multiple devices will be an important step to facilitate acceptance of Outernet technologies (cf. Wang and Xiang, 2012).

4.2 Conceptual framework

Frameworks are useful tools to help scholars explore topics in early research stage (cf. Pearce, 2012). A nascent nature of investigation of the Outernet in tourism was verified by the author in this exploratory paper. Qualitative studies, contrary to quantitative ones, do not require "clear identification of the variables and accurate measurement of the constructs" (Wang 2013, p. 47). In order to develop a conceptual framework explaining how tourism and Outernet relate to each other, it is important to identify the key concepts which will serve as a basis for determining this possible relationship (cf. Pearce, 2012). The following key concepts in this paper were obtained through the systematic review of secondary data available in academic literature: Outernet, Outernet technologies, Internet of Things, ubiquitous computing, high traveller mobility, experience co-creation, high traveller connectivity and new traveller. The conceptual framework below proposes the relationship between these key concepts of the Outernet in the context of tourism.

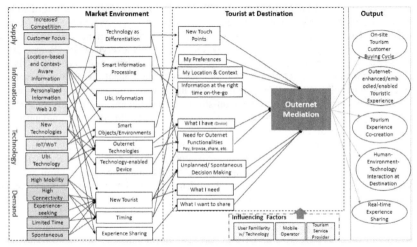

Fig. 2. Framework of proposed relationships between key concepts of the Outernet in tourism

The proposed conceptual framework is structured in three parts: market environment, on site environment (visited destination or POI) and possible outputs of these interactions with the intermediation of Outernet technologies. The first environment presents the main aspects of the transformed tourism market, where supply, demand, technology and information play a role. The second environment represents the *in situ* stage, where the tourist is at the destination or POI visited. In this second environment, travellers' needs and demands drive them to use Outernet technologies to solve typical touristic problems. An Outernet-enhanced experience is the output of using NFC, RFID, AR, QR codes and/or smart wearable objects to fulfil a desired task or need on site. The last environment of the framework suggests possible outcomes derived from the combination of the other two environments in the context of the Outernet.

Aware that the incorporation of Outernet-enabled environments require an appropriate set up by destination and attraction managers, the author considers their role determinant for creating an Outernet-enhanced experience on site. Equally important are the efforts of mobile service providers to deliver the necessary technical infrastructure, such as secure and fast Internet connection, at an affordable price for the traveller. Finally, the acceptance and familiarity of

Outernet technologies by travellers will be a deal maker or breaker for a long-lasting integration of the Outernet in the tourism industry. The author, based on the research findings, suggests the relationships drawn in the 'output' section of the framework. The remaining relationships, in the 'market' and '*in situ*' areas of the framework, represent those found in the literature review of secondary data.

5 CONCLUSION

The Outernet is referred as the "technical infrastructure of tomorrow" (Rehder in Marlinghaus and Rast 2013, p. 85) due to its ability to interconnect the physical world, digital data and people. The addition of time, place, context and personalization to touristic offers is able to suppress the logic of the Internet with Outernet technologies, therefore creating technology enhanced experiences in the travelling process. The new tourist relies on technology to obtain information, communicate, share data and solve several obstacles typically faced when travelling. Despite the increasing usage of Outernet functionalities at touristic POIs and destinations, tourism academics are still at initial stages of exploring the topic. The author of this paper, therefore, aimed exploring this nascent term by screening available academic research of the Outernet in tourism, structuring the topic, presenting use cases of Outernet technologies and suggesting a conceptual framework which identified the key concepts relevant to both tourism and Outernet topics. The nature of this paper, namely conceptual and exploratory, led to a subjective and interpretative analysis of the results. Validation and falsification problems were tackled by adopting rigorous and critical review of data, as well as soft falsification and triangulation of related concepts in the field of tourism, technology and the Outernet.

As for strategic recommendations, the Outernet is a highly fast, mutable and complex process that will continuously impact tourism, tourists and businesses. There is a definite need for tourism suppliers to start re-evaluating current business models and strategies in order to remain competitive and avoid a second wave of disintermediation. Inclusion of PEDs-friendly websites, apps and mobile and online shops are a first step that can be taken. Repositioning of brands as travellers' allies is a second measure to be taken. This means that tourism suppliers should strive to make marketing and sales a service to tourists, rather than an intrusive product selling approaches. Finally, tourism managers should evaluate how Outernet technologies can fit on their business processes and strategies. A fast integration of these technologies and 'smartization" of physical environments will be key to obtain travellers attention and influence their decision making on site.

As for further investigation of the topic, the author sees great potential for exploration as this is such a nascent and fast changing field. This paper is seen by the author as a first valuable step towards a clearer understanding of what the Outernet means to this industry. In particular, the author considers important deeper examination of the proposed conceptual framework, testing the relation between key concepts and applying the conceptual findings to real case studies that are sure to come.

REFERENCES

Airplus International, 2014. AirPlus International Travel Management Study 2014: A comparison of global trends, costs, and business travel management. Airplus International [Online]. Available at: <http://www.glomex.biz/Files/files/International_Travel_Management_Study_2014_-_part_1%20%281%29%281%29.pdf > [Accessed 16 September 2014].

Azuma, R. et al., 2001. Recent advances in augmented reality. *Computer Graphics and Applications*, IEEE, 21 (6), pp.34-47.

Baik, S., 2012. Rethinking QR code: analog portal to digital world. *Multimedia Tools and Applications*, 58 (2), pp.427-434.

Brown, B. and Chalmers, M., 2003. Tourism and Mobile Technology. *ECSCW 2003*, pp.335-354.

Brown, R. B. 2006. *Doing your dissertation in business and management: the reality of researching and writing.* London: Sage.

Buhalis, D., 2003. *eTourism: Information technology for strategic tourism management.* Harlow: Pearson Education.

Buhalis, D. and Egger, R., 2008. *eTourism Case studies: Management and Marketing issues in eTourism.* Oxford: Butterworth-Heinemann.

Buhalis, D. and Foerste, M. K., 2013. SoCoMo Marketing for Travel and Tourism. In: Z. Xiang and L. Tussyadiah, eds, 2014. *Information and Communication Technologies in Tourism 2014.* Wien: Springer. pp.175-185.

Buhalis, D. and Law, R., 2008. Progress in information technology and tourism management: 20 years on and 10 years after the Internet- The state of eTourism research. *Tourism Management*, 29 (4), pp.609–623.

Buhalis, D. and O'Connor, P., 2005. Information Communication Technology Revolutionizing Tourism. *Tourism recreation research*, 30 (3), pp.7-16

Canadi, M., Höpken, W. and Fuchs, M., 2011. Virtualisation of customer cards with 2D codes. In: R. LAW, M. Fuchs, M. and F. Ricci, eds. *Information and Communication Technologies in Tourism 2011.* Vienna: Springer. pp.215-227.

Cohen, S. A., Prayag, G. and Moital, M., 2013. Consumer behaviour in tourism: Concepts, influences and opportunities. *Current Issues in Tourism*, pp.1-38.

Coskun, V., Ok, K. and Ozdenizci, B., 2012. *Near Field Communication (NFC): From Theory to Practice.* West Sussex: John Wiley & Sons.

Egger, R., 2013. The impact of near field communication on tourism. *Journal of Hospitality and Tourism Technology*, 4 (2), pp.119-133.

Evans, D., 2011. The Internet of Things: How the Next Evolution of the Internet Is Changing Everything. Cisco Internet Business Solutions Group (IBSG). [Online]. Available at: <http://www.cisco.com/web/about/ac79/docs/innov/IoT_IBSG_0411FINAL.pdf.> [Accessed 27 June 2014].

Hannam, K., Butler, G. and Paris, C. M., 2014. Developments and key issues in tourism mobilities. *Annals of Tourism Research*, 44, pp.171-185.

Hjalager, A. M., 2010. A review of innovation research in tourism. *Tourism management*, 31 (1), pp.1-12.

Höpken, W. et al., 2008. Context-based Adaptation of Ubiquitous Web Applications in Tourism. In *Information and Communication Technologies in Tourism 2008.* Vienna: Springer. pp.533-544.

Holloway, C., 2014. Wearable tech from CES 2014. CNET [Online]. Available at: <http://www.cnet.com/news/wearable-tech-from-ces-2014/> [Accessed 8 June 2014].

Huijnen C., 2006. Mobile tourism and mobile government an inventory of European projects. European Centre for Digital Communication EC/DC April 2006 [Online]. Available at: <http://www.mgovworld.org/whitepapersandcasestudies/invenory-mobile-government.pdf> [Accessed 14 July 2014].

Kelly, W., 2014. Smartphones are fading. Wearables are next. CNN Money [Online]. Available at: <http://money.cnn.com/2014/03/19/technology/mobile/wearable-devices/> [Accessed 8 June 2014].

Kim, W. C. and Mauborgne, R., 2009. How strategy shapes structure. *Harvard Business Review*, 87 (9), pp.72-80.

Kim, M. J. et al., 2013. Motivations and Use Context in Mobile Tourism Shopping: Applying Contingency and Task–Technology Fit Theories. *International Journal of Tourism Research*.

Linaza, M. T. et al., 2012. Evaluation of Mobile Augmented Reality Applications for Tourism Destinations. *Information and Communication Technologies in Tourism 2012*. Vienna: Springer, pp.260-271.

Markets and Markets, 2014. Augmented Reality & Virtual Reality Market by Technology Types, Sensors (Accelerometer, Gyroscope, Haptics), Components (Camera, Controller, Gloves, HMD), Applications (Automotive, Education, Medical, Gaming, Military) & by Geography - Global Forecast and Analysis to 2013 - 2018 [Online]. Available at: <http://www.marketsandmarkets.com/Market-Reports/augmented-reality-virtual-reality-market-1185.html> [Accessed 13 March 2015].

Marlinghaus, S. T. and Rast, C. A., 2013. *Driving Impact: Value creation in the world of tomorrow*. Munich: MI Wirtschaftsbuch.

Neuhofer, B., 2014. The Technology Enhanced Tourist Experience. In: R. Baggio et al., eds. *eProceedings of Information and Communication Technologies in Tourism 2014*, Dublin. pp.90-96.

Neuhofer, B., Buhalis, D. and Ladkin, A., 2012. Conceptualizing Technology enhanced destination experience. *Journal of Destination Marketing & Management*, 1 (1), pp.36-46.

Neuhofer, B., Buhalis, D. and Ladkin, A., 2013. A Typology of Technology-Enhanced Tourism Experiences. *International Journal of Tourism Research*, 16 (4), pp.340-350.

Ondrus, J. and Pigneur, Y., 2009. Near field communication: an assessment for future payment systems. *Information Systems and E-Business Management*, 7 (3), pp.347-361.

Papagiannakis, G., Singh, G. and Magnenat-Thalmann, N., 2008. A survey of mobile and wireless technologies for augmented reality systems. *Computer Animation and Virtual Worlds*, 19 (1), pp.3-22.

Pesonen, J. and Horster, E., 2012. Near field communication technology in tourism. *Tourism Management Perspectives*, 4, pp.11-18.

Poslad, S., 2011. *Ubiquitous computing: smart devices, environments and interactions*. Chichester: John Wiley & Sons.

Prahalad, C.K. and Ramaswamy, V., 2004. Co-creation experiences: The next practice in value creation. *Journal of Interactive Marketing*, 18 (3), pp.5-14.

Rafat, A., 2013. The changed travel purchase cycle in a digital world. Skift [Online]. Available at: <http://skift.com/2013/03/29/the-changed-travel-purchase-cycle-in-a-digital-world/> [Accessed 10 July 2014].

Riley, R. W. and Love, L. L., 2000. The state of qualitative tourism research. *Annals of tourism research*, 27 (1), pp.164-187.

Schiller, J. and Voisard, A., 2004. *Location-based services*. San Francisco: Elsevier.

Sheller, M. and Urry, J., 2006. The new mobilities paradigm. Environment and Planning A, 38 (2), pp.207-226.

Swedberg, C., 2012. California Stores Pilot NFC System Providing Electronic Receipts. RFID Journal [Online]. Available at: <http://www.rfidjournal.com/articles/view?9174> [Accessed 15 June 2014].

Trendone, n.d.. The Outernet: Say hello to the wild world web. TrenOne [Online]. Available at: <http://www.trendone.com/outernet_english.pdf.> [Accessed 26 May 2014].

Tussyadiah, L. P., 2014. *Expectation of Travel Experiences with Wearable Computing Devices.* In: Z. Xiang and L. Tussyadiah, eds. 2014. *Information and Communication Technologies in Tourism 2014.* Switzerland: Springer. pp.539-552.

Wang, D. and Xiang, Z., 2012. The new landscape of travel: A comprehensive analysis of Smartphone Apps. *Information and Communication Technologies in Tourism 2012.* Vienna: Springer, pp.308-319.

Wang, D., 2013. *A framework of smartphone use for travel.* Unpublished thesis (PhD), Temple University.

Weaver, A., 2008. When Tourists Become Data: Consumption, Surveillance and Commerce. *Current Issues in Tourism*, 11 (1), pp.1-23.

Wikitude, n.d.. Boardshop.at – The interactive retail store. Wikitude. [Online]. Available at: <http://www.wikitude.com/showcase/boardshop/> [Accessed 13 March 2015].

Xin, S., Tribe, J. and Chambers, D., 2013. Conceptual research in tourism. *Annals of Tourism Research* 41, pp.66-88.

Yovcheva, Z, Buhalis, D, and Gatzidis, C., 2012. Overview of Smartphone Augmented Reality Applications for Tourism. *E-Review of Tourism Research*, 10 (2), pp.63-66.

Yovcheva, Z. and Buhalis, D, 2013. Augmented Reality in tourism: 10 unique applications explained. Digital Tourism Think Tank. [Online]. Available at: <http://thinkdigital.travel/wp-content/uploads/2013/04/10-AR-Best-Practices-in-Tourism.pdf.> [Accessed 26 May 2014].

The Evaluation of Augmented Reality in Practice: Enriching Tourists' Experience through Offline Media

Meng Zhang,

Wandi Zhang,

Yefei Liu, and

Yichen Zhao

Department of International Tourism Management, University of Surrey, UK
mz00069@surrey.ac.uk

Abstract

Augmented reality is a new concept introduced to the tourism industry. When it comes to the information search stage, different segments have different needs. Experience seekers, who have different personal characteristics and travel motivations than non-experience seekers, prefer to travel without planning (Lepp & Gibson, 2008; Plot, 1990). Consequently, this influences their perception in terms of three relative concepts: attitude, involvement and entertainment (Vorderer et. al., 2004).

Based on the research towards an augmented reality application, Layar, data was collected online and resulted in a sample of 1,193 usable questionnaires. Results show that regarding involvement and entertainment, experience seekers have more positive feelings in using Layar than non-experience seekers. In terms of general attitude, there were no significant differences between the two groups, and 90% have a positive attitude towards Layar. The factor that has the strongest correlation with the intention to use and the satisfaction generated is general attitude, followed by entertainment and involvement.

Results show that the tourism industry should view Layar as an innovative promotional tool to provide more multi-media enriched information. Layar should provide more travel related information for both the before-trip and during-trip stages.

Keywords: Augmented Reality; Attitude; Satisfaction (Involvement, Entertainment, and Intention to use)

1 INTRODUCTION

Information communication technologies (ICT) have transformed tourism globally, particularly after 2000, when the development of a series of attentive and adaptive technologies promoted interaction between tourists and destinations (Buhalis and Law, 2008). Research found that 93% of people make their own travel plan using online sources (Kim, 2008). However, travellers demand high requirements, including the flexibility and mobility of information systems, and, in particular, information sources. Therefore, a growing number of mobile applications have been produced to diversify interaction and ways of communication (Abowd et al, 1997). According to prior studies, a variety of concepts are introduced when discussing variable factors that influence technology acceptance, while attitude (Kraus, 1995), involvement (Richins and Bloch, 1986), entertainment (Zillmann and Bryant, 1994) emerge as significant parts of the technology adoption. Today, augmented reality is defined as a live view of a real-world environment whose elements are augmented by virtual technical objects (Azuma et al., 2001) to achieve a high level of interactivity and simultaneity. Through this, the information about the surrounding world of the user becomes interactive and digitally manipulative (Garau, 2014).

The usefulness of augmented reality (AR) apps for the tourism industry to a large extent depends on effective and usable design (Yovcheva et al., 2012). A number of studies deal with website design and design for other interfaces. Meanwhile, literature aiming at the requirements of different groups has been the focus of research, because people have distinct characteristics in terms of travel motivations, which results in diverse demands concerning what is perceived as a usable design (Venkatesh and Davis, 2000). However, there is little literature exploring the relation between AR apps and the requirements of different groups. Therefore, the purpose of this article is to contribute to this research gap by looking at Layar.

Layar is an example of an application that allows users to find various items based upon augmented reality technology. It mainly refers to an application bridging the gap between the print and digital worlds. With Layar, any images and print materials can be enhanced with digital content such as videos, links and slideshows (Layar, 2014). Different industries involving publishing, advertising and real estate can benefit from it. Particularly in tourism, Layar converses the form of travel experience by sharing panoramic views of destinations (Layar, 2014).

This article first introduces three relative concepts, 1) involvement, 2) entertainment and 3) general attitude. Further, the attitude towards Layar of two groups of respondents, experience seekers and non-experience seekers, will be examined based on these topics. Questionnaires will be used as the primary method to collect data. Through analysing the results of questionnaires, the relationships between respondents and each segment can be identified. Last, further implications regarding the tourism industry will be given to improve future utilisation.

2 LITERATURE REVIEW

2.1 General Attitude

Attitude is defined as disposition to respond to a range of objects in a particular way (Rosenberg, 1960). Thus, the core is the notion of evaluation along a dimension ranging from positive to negative (Petty et al., 1994). Satisfaction, as a possible result of evaluation, it is achieved when attitudes are consistent with behaviour in terms of time, target and context (Fazio and Olson, 2003). However, since Allport's (1935) revolutionary proposal, there has been a definite shift in universal way to thinking about the attitude. The refined concept (attitude) refers more to attitude-behaviour relationship, and the lack of strong correlations is considered as invalidate the attitude concept (Jawahar, 2003).

Attitude now is employed as the most accurate predictor of tourist decision (Ragheb and Tate, 1993) and buying behaviour (Berkman et al., 1986). Especially, attitude is one of the major concepts used in the analysis of electronic commerce (Vehovar et al., 2001). The relation between attitude and technology acceptance has been justified by Kim (2008) who provide sound prediction of technology usage by associating behaviours with attitudes. According to Teo et al. (2003), users' attitude plays an important role in determining their intention to use a technology system. Additionally, both elements have been identified as main drivers of adaptation and use of information technology (Wixom and Todd, 2005). The statement developed by DeSanctis (1983) indicates that prior positive attitude can contribute to increased possibility to perform behaviour otherwise it may reduce the willingness to act. While with the precise research towards literature review, implication is give that other relevant factors except attitude should be noticed to summarize the causes behind the behaviour performance.

2.2 Involvement

Users' involvement with the products describes the extent that people are engaged into the process of using applications (Richins and Bloch, 1986). Perceived personal relevance, which is the link between users' needs, objectives, self-knowledge and their knowledge or benefits toward products, is regarded as the essential characteristic of involvement, and the crucial factor deciding the level of involvement (Petty and Cacioppo, 1981; Zaichkowsky, 1985). The qualitative relationship between involvement and the degree of relevance is positive, which means a higher level of association between applications and users leads to the stronger feeling of involvement (Richins and Bloch, 1986).

Users' involvement for a subject emerges at certain situations and times. As Houston and Rothschild (1978) mention, it has two general sources: (1) social and physical aspects of environment; (2) intrinsic characteristics of the users. The first one is about situational sources that include various specific stimuli, cue and contingencies in environment. If these factors are strongly related to personal goals and values, or the representation of the factors of the situational sources are closely associated with significant consequences, such as objectives and values, then those specific stimuli, cue and contingencies are likely to affect users' involvement (Celsi and Olson, 1988). When users have a high level of involvement, they may generally feel appealing or interesting, while they may feel unappealing or boring overall if they are hardly involved (Celsi and Olson, 1988).

Many scholars discuss that the level of involvement of users can affect the attention and comprehension processes of users (Burnkrant and Sawyer, 1983; Cohen, 1983; Mitchell, 1979). Generally, users will have higher inspiration to attend and comprehend information when they experience greater involvement, for instance, in the information seeking process (Petty and Cacioppo, 1981). Furthermore, elaborate deeper meaning about salient environmental stimuli is likely to be created when consumers experience a higher degree of involvement (Richins and Bloch 1986). More precisely, people may form inferences about certain environmental stimuli and elaborate the information if they are motivated and able to understand those stimuli.

2.3 Entertainment

From the user's perspective, entertainment has not been understood as a product or a feature of a product, but rather as a response to it (Zillmann and Bryant, 1994), as the experience people go through while being exposed to the media or information sources (Vorderer et al., 2001). Most scholars have placed certain characteristics that are usually linked to positive terms such as enjoyment, pleasure and even delight, which embrace cognitive, physiological and affective components, as the crucial part of an entertainment experience (Bosshart and Macconi, 1998).

As different media are adopted in more abundant situations and contexts, their utilisation is logically expected to aim for entertaining purposes (Vorderer et al., 2001). For example, in order to satisfy various needs of customers, the development of the mobile telephone required evolution to a more multifunctional "fun device" rather than being a simple medium of telecommunication. Gamification, the application of game elements and digital game design techniques, has been increasingly used recently (Deterding, 2011). Additionally, there is a trend that the range of available entertainment products and the multidirectional integration of media corporations, such as Microsoft, will be expanded in the future. Audiences' appetite for new entertainment experiences is not indicated to decline (Wolf, 1999). Therefore, media entertainment, especially in augmented reality areas, seems to be on the rise (Costa and Melotti, 2012).

A significant prerequisite is the user's sense of being in actual scenes, which affects the occurrence of entertainment. More specifically, it is the user's sense of being transported to the site of the action, or the feeling of actually being there accompanied with those who participate in the action (Biocca, 2001).

In summary, media entertainment experience manifests itself in many different ways. It depends on factors influenced by audience: their readiness and ability to suspend disbelief, and their willingness to be entertained (Vorderer et al., 2004).The papers should be written in clear English and any technical jargon should be explained; complex issues should be defined.

2.4 Experience seekers & Non-experience seekers

According to Lepp and Gibson (2008), an experience seeker is a kind of sensation seeking tourist, who would like to travel without exact arrangement, and go freely for a more 'authentic' experience. Furthermore, sensation-seeking tourists depend more on Internet and technology (Shi et. al., 2011). Therefore, they often need to search for information during their trip. Non-experience seekers like to travel with the feeling of safety, so they always choose package tours or make plans before the trip (Plot, 1990), which means they search for detailed tourism information before the trip actually starts. Therefore, the characteristics of experience seekers and non-experience seekers are different from each other, which means they have different needs and different feelings when using information sources in general, and augmented reality in particular. Also, their general attitude, involvement with information sources, and desired entertainment level differs (Zaichkowsky, 1985; Vorderer et al., 2001).

Thus, based on previous literature, it is proposed that there are differences between experience seekers and non-experience seekers when it comes to (H1) general attitude towards Layar, (H2) Involvement with the augmented reality app Layar in a travel context, and (H3) the perceived entertainment factor. Finally, following Davis' (1989) finding, it is proposed that there is high correlation between general attitude and satisfaction (H4), and also between general attitude and intention to use (H5).

3 METHODOLOGY

Data was collected using an online questionnaire which was distributed worldwide. As an example of augmented reality, the mobile application Layar was used, as it is a newly developed product that is becoming increasingly popular (O'Reilly and Battelle, 2009). The questionnaire incorporated examples allowing respondents to try Layar before they answered the questions. All users where asked to download Layar and experience at least one of the provided examples, such as, the magazine cover, the photo of Kremlin, and a piece of newspaper. The first part of the questionnaire was about the general attitude of users towards augmented reality, for example, whether they had positive feelings towards using Layar, whether Layar made travel information searching more interesting, and whether they thought it was a good idea to utilise Layar in the tourism industry. Then, the questionnaire asked respondents if they felt involved when using the augmented reality app (Layar). They were asked whether or not they felt Layar was appealing, interesting, important, relevant, and exciting (Novak et. al., 2000). The third part of the questionnaire asked the respondents whether they felt entertained when using Layar, specifically whether or not they agreed that Layar was an entertaining app and whether or not it was fun using it. These items were adapted from Lastovicka (1983). The basis for these questions was Davis' paper (1989). As an answer scale, a 6-points Likert Scale from 1 (strongly agree) to 6 (strongly disagree) was used to identify the preference of respondents.

In order to analyse the data, frequency analysis was used to identify the respondents' profile. T-tests were carried out to identify significant differences between the two groups, experience seekers and non-experience seekers, about their general attitude, and their feeling about involvement and entertainment. Correlation analysis was conducted to examine if there was a correlation between general attitude, involvement, entertainment and satisfaction, and intention to use Layar.

4 RESULTS

4.1 Respondents' Profile

The online survey resulted in a sample of 1193 usable questionnaires from 82 counties. Fifty-six percent of the participants were female while 44% of them were male. In terms of education level, high school and university students accounted for 39%, while bachelor and master degree-holders represented 37% and 10% respectively. As for general technology skill, there were 77% who said they were highly skilled, and the other 23% thought they were lowly skilled. This situation is similar to their skills in mobile technology; 81% of respondents considered themselves as being highly skilled, and 19% thought they had only low skills. According to respondents' self-report, experience seekers accounted for 64% (768) of the sample were, while the other 425 (36%) were non-experience seekers.

4.2 Descriptive Results

It can be seen from Figure 1.1 and Figure 1.2 that both experience seekers and non-experience seekers show the same trend. From 28 types of media provided in the survey, websites were the most commonly used media for tourists to search travel related information, but this appeared to decrease slightly after people were introduced to Layar. Further, augmented reality apps, mobile applications and QR codes were the three media that increased the most after respondents used Layar. In other words, a considerable number of people would want to choose Layar as one of their information resources after having experienced it. Also, the introduction of Layar could increase the use of mobile applications and QR codes, which have something in common with Layar. Layar is one mobile application, and Layar can use scanning technology.

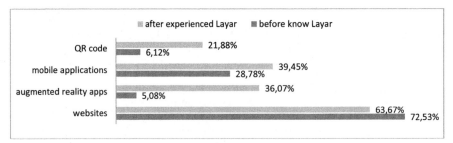

Fig. 1.1. The changes in which information resources *experience seekers* prefer for searching tourism information

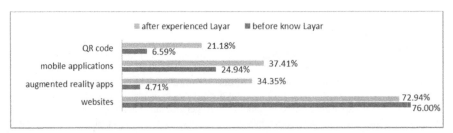

Fig. 1.2. The changes in which information resources *non-experience seekers* prefer for searching tourism information

Considering when people use Layar, it can be seen from Figure 2 that 60.2% of experience seekers and 64.47% of non- experience seekers would want to use Layar to enrich travel print media and search information before the trip. Further, 32.02% of experience seekers and 28.94% of non-experience seekers were more likely to use Layar during the trip. This data indicates that Layar is more often used before or during the trip. Moreover, experience seekers are more likely to use Layar during the trip when compared with non-experience seekers, while non-experience seekers more often use Layar before the trip.

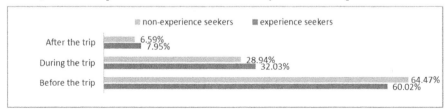

Fig. 2. Different people use Layar in different travel stages

4.3 Differences between Experience seekers and Non-experience seekers

General attitude (H1) The T-test identified no significant differences between experience seekers and non-experience seekers in terms of general attitude. See, for example, the questions asking whether they 'like Layar' and whether they 'think it is a good idea to use Layar in the tourism industry' (see Figure 3). Although the mean values of experience seekers are lower than that of non-experience seekers, 2 out of 3 questions are not considered significant since the p-value of the second and the third questions is bigger than 0.05.

	Variables	experience seekers means	non-experience seekers means	p-value	Support
General Attitude	I have positive feelings towards using Layar.	2.28	2.49	0.004	YES
	I think Layar makes travel information search more interesting.	2.27	2.35	0.171	NO
	It would be a good idea for the tourism industry to make use of Layar.	2.24	2.35	0.118	NO

Fig. 3. Differences between the two groups about General Attitude

In order to figure out they tended to agree or disagree with the questions, frequency analysis was used. It can be found that there were slightly more non-experience seekers who disagree with the questions that Layar makes travel information search more interesting and the industry should use it, compared to experience seekers (see Figure 4). However, almost 90% of both groups agreed with the questions, while only about 10% of respondents disagreed. Therefore, most respondents generally have a positive attitude towards Layar.

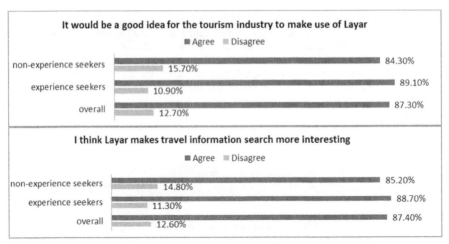

Fig. 4. Results of the frequency analysis of the two questions

Involvement (H2) The mean value of experience-seekers is lower than that of non-experience seekers. In other words, the mean value of experience-seekers is closer to 1 while that of non-experience seekers is closer to 6. It means experiences seekers are more agree with (have positive feeling) the questions comparing to non-experience seekers. Meanwhile, the p-values proved there were significant differences between experience seekers and non-experience seekers in terms of involvement (see Figure 5). The questions related to involvement show that experience seekers perceive Layar as more interesting, appealing, important, relevant and exciting when it comes to enriching travel print media with augmented reality.

	Variables	experience seekers means	non-experience seekers means	p-value	Support
Involvement	Appealing:Unappealing	2.23	2.43	0.006	YES
	Interesting:Boring	2.15	2.30	0.036	YES
	Important:Unimportant	2.77	2.99	0.005	YES
	Relevant:Irrelevant	2.47	2.64	0.016	YES
	Exciting:Unexciting	2.45	2.63	0.023	YES

Fig. 5. Differences between the two groups about Involvement

Entertainment (H3) The T-test identified significant differences between the two groups in relation to entertainment (see Figure 6). Experience seekers were more likely to feel entertained and to think it was fun to use the augmented reality app (Layar) than non-experience seekers.

	Variables	experience seekers means	non-experience seekers means	p-value	Support
Entertainment	I find Layar an entertaining app.	2.33	2.63	<0.001	YES
	Layar was lots of fun to use.	2.57	2.77	0.011	YES
	I thought Layar was clever and quite entertaining.	2.49	2.69	0.017	YES

Fig. 6. Differences between the two groups about Entertainment

4.4 Correlation Analysis

To figure out which concepts were most related to satisfaction and intention to use, correlation analysis was used. As shown in Figure 7.1, the concept that had the highest correlation with intention to use was general attitude, followed by entertainment and involvement. This rank can be applied to satisfaction as well. Furthermore, general attitude had a stronger correlation with satisfaction compared to intention to use.

The above correlation analysis results are appropriate for both experience seekers and non-experience seekers. Nevertheless, there are still differences between the two groups (see Figure 7.1 and Figure 7.2). Non-experience seekers show a stronger correlation in all aspects compared to experience seekers. For example, for non-experience seekers, general attitude has a stronger correlation with satisfaction; in contrast, the correlation to experience seekers is not as strong as that of non-experience seekers.

		Involvement	Entertainment	General attitude	Support
Overall	Intention to use	0.613	0.638	0.660	<0.0001（YES）
	Satisfaction	0.630	0.666	0.676	<0.0001（YES）
Experience seeker	Intention to use	0.572	0.590	0.631	<0.0001（YES）
	Satisfaction	0.585	0.619	0.635	<0.0001（YES）
Non-experience seeker	Intention to use	0.659	0.686	0.693	<0.0001（YES）
	Satisfaction	0.680	0.711	0.727	<0.0001（YES）

Fig. 7.1. Results of the correlation analysis

Variables	Experience seekers means	Non-experience seekers means	p-value	Support
Intention to use	2.46	2.73	<0.001	YES
Satisfaction	2.46	2.76	<0.001	YES

Fig. 7.2. Difference between the two groups about Intention to use and Satisfaction

5 DISCUSSION

5.1 Theoretical Discussion

Most respondents generally had a positive attitude towards Layar, which shows the high potential of augmented reality apps for the tourism industry. Besides, tourists' personal characteristics will influence the extent of involvement, which is in line with the findings of Celsi and Olson (1988). In this case, experience seekers are more involved in the use of Layar compared to non-experience seekers. Moreover, experience seekers and non-experience seekers have different opinions about entertainment. These results support the findings of Zillmann (1988), who states that people with different physiological and affective components will have different feelings about enjoyment and entertainment.

5.2 Managerial Implication

It is believed that Layar has potential and should invest more on promotion and marketing since the results from Figure 1.1 and 1.2 show that if more people tried Layar, its acceptance could expand.

Besides, different people use Layar in different time which suggests that Layar should develop two different branches in order to cater for different needs of various types of information seekers. This would improve the level of involvement of different segments. The before-trip-oriented branch should emphasise on detailed tour packages – providing in-depth travel information. Meanwhile, the during-trip-oriented branch should focus on instant information, making sure that tourists can instantly find useful information while en-route.

According to the definition, general attitude has the strongest correlation with satisfaction and intention to use (Davis, 1989). In other words, if Layar can improve the value and fulfil users' expectations, users will have more positive attitude towards using Layar and be more satisfied. Therefore, printed travel media should be enriched with multimedia, allowing users to actually experience and try such an app. Meanwhile, the industry should view augmented reality apps as an innovative promotional tool, which may help to improve information sources and entertainment factor.

Lastly, the application should use more gamification features to make it more entertaining, as entertainment is correlated with satisfaction and intention to use.

6   LIMITATIONS AND RECOMMENDATIONS FOR FUTURE RESEARCH

Future research should look into other groups such as people who have different levels of technology skills and their attitudes and feelings towards augmented reality apps. It would also be of interest to focus on the real tourism environment.

REFERENCES

Abowd, G.D., Atkeson, C.G., Hong, J., Long, S., Kooper, R. and Pinkerton, M., 1997. Cyberguide: A mobile context-aware tour guide. *Wireless networks*, 3(5), pp.421-433.

Ajzen, I., 1991. The theory of planned behaviour. *Organizational Behaviorand Human Decision Processes*, 50(2), pp.179–211.

Allport, G.W., 1935. Attitudes. In: C. Murchison, ed. 1935. *The handbook of social psychology.* Worcester: Clark University Press. pp.798-844.

Azuma, R., Baillot, Y., Behringer, R., Feiner, S., Julier, S. and MacIntyre, B., 2001. Recent advances in augmented reality. *The Institute of Electrical and Electronics Engineers*, 21(6), pp.34-47.

Berkman, H.W. and Gilson, C.C., 1986. *Consumer Behavior: Concepts and Strategies.* Boston: Kent Publishing Company.

Biocca, F., 2001. Visual touch in virtual environments: An exploratory study of presence, multimodal interfaces, and cross-modal sensory illusions. *Presence: Teleoperators and Virtual Environments*, 10, pp.247–265.

Bosshart, L. and Macconi, I., 1998. Defining 'entertainment'. *Communication Research Trends*, 18(3), pp.3-6.

Buhalis, D. and Law, R., 2008. Progress in information technology and tourism management: 20 ars on and 10 years after the Internet—The state of eTourism research. *Tourism management*, 29(4), pp.609-623.

Burnkrant, R.E. and Sawyer, A.G., 1983. Effects of Involvement and Message Content on Information Processing Intensity. In: R.J. Harris, ed. 1983. *Information Processing Re-search in Advertising.* Hillsdal: Lawrence Erlbaum Associates, pp.43-64.

Celsi. R.L. and Olson, J.C., 1988. The role of involvement in attention and comprehension processes. *Journal of consumer research*, 15(2), pp.210-224.

Cohen, J.B., 1983. Involvement and You: 1000 Great Ideas. In: R.P. Bagozzi and A.M. Tybout, eds. 1983. *Advances in Consumer Research*. MI: Association for Consumer Research, pp.325-328.

Costa, N. and Melotti, M., 2012. Digital media in archaeological areas, virtual reality, authenticity and hyper-tourist gaze. *Sociology Mind*, 2(1), pp.53-60.

Davis, F.D., 1989. Perceived Usefulness, Perceived Ease of Use, and User Acceptance of Information Technology. *MIS quarterly*, 13(3), pp.319-340.

DeSanctis, G., 1983. Expectancytheory as an explanation of voluntaryuse of a decision support system. *Psychological Reports*, 52(1), pp.247–260.

Deterding, S., Dixon, D., Khaled, R. and Nacke, L., 2011. From game design elements to gamefulness: defining gamification. *In Proceedings of the 15th International Academic MindTrek Conference: Envisioning Future Media Environments*, pp. 9-15.

Fazio, R.H. and Olson, M.A., 2003. Attitudes: Foundation, function and consequences. In: M.A. Hogg and J. Cooper, ed. 2003. *The Sage Handbook of Social Psychology*. London: Sage, pp.123-145.

Fesenmaier, D.R., Wöber, K.W. and Werthner, H. ed., 2006. *Destination recommendation systems: Behavioural foundations and applications*. Wallingford: CABI.

Garau, C., 2014. From Territory to Smartphone: Smart Fruition of Cultural Heritage for Dynamic Tourism Development. *Planning Practice and Research*, 29(3), pp.238-255.

Houston, M.J. and Rothschild, M.L., 1978. Conceptual and Methodological Perspectives in Involvement. In: S. Jain, ed. 1978. *Research Frontiers in Marketing: Dialogues and Directions*. Chicago: American Marketing Association, pp.184-187.

Jawahar, I.M., 2003. Personal and Situational factors as predictors of end user performance. *Advanced topics in end user computing*, 21(1), pp.58-75.

Kim, D., Park, J. and Morrison, A.M., 2008. A model of traveller acceptance of mobile technology. *The International Journal of Tourism Research*, 10(5), pp.393-407.

Kraus, S.J., 1995. Attitudes and the prediction of behavior: A meta-analysis of the empirical literature. *Personality and social psychology bulletin*, 21(1), 58-75.

Lastovicka, J.L., 1983. Convergent and discriminant validity of television commercial rating scales. *Journal of Advertising*, 12(2), pp.14-52.

Layar, 2014. [online] Available at: http://www.layar.com/ [Accessed: 14th December 2014].

Lepp, A. and Gibson, H., 2008. Sensation seeking and tourism: Tourist role, perception of risk and destination choice. *Tourism Management*, 29(4), pp.740-750.

Mitchell, A.A., 1979. Involvement: A Potentially Important Mediator of Consumer Behavior. In: W.L. Wilkie, ed. 1979. *Advances in Consumer Research*. MI: Association for Consumer Research, pp.191-195.

Novak, T., Hoffmann, D. and Yung, Y., 2000. Measuring the customer experience in online environments: a structural modeling approach. *Marketing Science*, 19(1), pp.22–42.

O'Reilly, T. and Battelle, J., 2009. Web squared: Web 2.0 five years on. *O'Reilly Media*, 20(1), pp. 1-13.

Oskamp, S., 1991. *Attitudes and Opinions*. 2nd ed. Englewood Cliffs: Prentice-Hall, Inc.

Perloff, R.M., 1993. *The Dynamics of Persuasion*. Hillsdale, NJ: Lawrence Erlbaum Associates Inc.

Petty, R.E. and Cacioppo, J.T., 1981. Issue Involvement as Moderator of the Effects on Attitude of Advertising Content and Context. *Advances in Consumer Research*, 8(1), pp.20-24.

Petty, R.E., Wegener, D.T. and Fabrigar, L.R., 1997. Attitudes and attitude change. *Annual Review of Psychology*, 48(1), pp.609-647.

Plot, S., 1990. A carpenter's tools: An answer to Stephen L. J. Smith's review of psychocentrism/allocentrism. *Journal of Travel Research*, 28 (4), pp.43-45.

Ragheb, M.G. and Tate, R.L. (1993) "A behaviour model of leisure participation, based on leisure attitude, motivation and satisfaction", *Leisure Studies*, 12, pp.61–67.

Richins, M.L. and Bloch, P.H., 1986. After the New Wears Off: The Temporal Context of Product Involvement. *Journal of Consumer Research*, 13(9), pp.280-285.

Rokeach, M., 1972. Organization and change within value-attitude systems. In: M. Rokeach, ed. 1972. *Beliefs, Attitudes, and Values*. Jossey Bass, Inc., pp.156-178.

Rosenberg, M.J. ed., 1960. *An analysis of affective-cognitive consistency*. Hovland: Yale University Press.

Shi, J., Chen, Z. and Tian, M., 2011. Internet self-efficacy, the need for cognition, and sensation seeking as predictors of problematic use of the Internet. *Cyberpsychology, Behavior, and Social Networking*, 14(4), pp.231-234.

Teo, H.H., Oh, L.B., Liu, C. and Wei, K.K., 2003. An empirical study of the effects of interactivity on web user attitude. *International Journal of Human-Computer Studies*, 58(3), pp.281-305.

Vehovar, V., Manfreda, K.L. and Batagelj, Z., 2001. Sensitivity of electronic commerce measurement to the survey instrument. *International Journal of Electronic Commerce*, 6(1), pp.31-51.

Venkatesh, V. and Davis, F.D., 2000. A theoretical extension of the technology acceptance model: four longitudinal field studies. *Management science*, 46(2), pp.186-204.

Vorderer, P., Klimmt, C. and Ritterfeld, U., 2004. Enjoyment: At the heart of media entertainment. *Communication Theory*, 14(4), pp.388-408.

Vorderer, P., Knobloch, S. and Schramm, H., 2001. Does entertainment suffer from interactivity? The impact of watching an interactive TV movie on viewers' experience of entertainment. *Media Psychology*, 3(4), pp.343–363.

Wixom, B.H. and Todd, P.A., 2005. A theoretical integration of user satisfaction and technology acceptance. *Information systems research*, 16(1), pp.85-102.

Wolf, M.J., 1999. *The entertainment economy. The mega-media forces that are re-shaping ourlives*. London: Penguin Books.

Yovcheva, Z., Buhalis, D. and Gatzidis, C., 2012. Overview of Smartphone Augmented Reality Applications for Tourism. *E-Review Of Tourism Research*, 10(2), pp.63-66.

Zaichkowsky, J.L., 1985. Measuring the involvement construct. *Journal of consumer research*, 12(3), pp.341-352.

Zillmann, D., 1988. Mood management: Using entertainment to full advantage. In: L. Donohew, H.E. Sypher and E.T. Higgins, ed. 1988. *Communication social cognition, and affect*. Oxford: Psychology Press.

Zillmann, D. and Bryant, J., 1994. Entertainment as media effect. In D. Bryant and D. Zillmann, ed. 1994. *Media effects: advance in theory and research*. Hillsdale, NJ: Erlbaum, pp.437-461.

The Acceptance of LBS in Tourism Destinations - Case Study: Wörthersee

Maximiliane Frey,

Bianca Hinterdorfer,

Julia Krippel, and

Anton Wrann

Salzburg University of Applied Sciences, Austria
bhinterdorfer.imte-m2013@fh-salzburg.ac.at

Abstract

Internet and information and communication technologies play a major role in today's society as well as in the tourism industry. Since the mobile phone has experienced an enormous growth in terms of user numbers, mobile applications offer various opportunities in the tourism industry. Tourists often encounter unfamiliar surroundings in their vacations and require information based on their current location. Therefore, this paper will deal with location based services in tourism destinations, which provide tourists with position-specific, up-to-date and personalized information referring to their context. This paper investigates the usage of portable, internet-ready devices in tourism destinations connected to location based services in the destination Wörthersee. The acceptance of location based services is measured with a questionnaire using the Unified Theory of Acceptance and Use of Technology 2 – Model. The results show, that the UTAUT2 model is an appropriate construct to measure consumer acceptance of LBS in a tourism destination. When it comes to the Wörthersee region, the study indicates that the offered LBS is still in its early phase and a majority of the guests is not aware about it, which implies further information campaigns of the destination. Nevertheless, a need for these provided services is confirmed, as almost all participants own Wifi-capable devices and have already used similar services on holidays before.

Keywords: LBS; Mobile Services; Technology Acceptance; UTAUT2; Wörthersee

1 INTRODUCTION

Information and communication technologies (ICT) have been a major contributor to the continuously changing character of the tourism industry over the last 20 years. This has an impact on business practices, projects and strategies in the industry (Buhalis & Law, 2008). Also the mobile phone has experienced a continuous growth in terms of users. According to eMarketer (2014) 4.55 billion people worldwide are expected to use a mobile phone in 2014. Mobile phone penetration will rise from 61.1% to 69.4% of the worldwide population between 2013 and 2017. A similar trend can be seen amongst smartphone users. In 2012 the 1 billion mark of smartphone users was surpassed. In 2014 already 1.75 billion people own a smartphone and use it at least once per month. Moreover, more than 2.23 billion people go online with their mobile phone at least once per month in 2014. This continuously rising trend offers various possible applications for the tourism industry such as location based services (LBS), which offer personalised and contextualised services based on the current geographical position of the users' mobile device. Tourists are often exposed to unfamiliar surroundings, which increase the need for orientation and information about the unknown (Berger, Lehmann, & Lehner, 2003; Groß, Groß, Freyer, & Freyer, 2006). As LBS is a growing trend, especially also in the tourism industry, more and more destinations are offering such services, like for example the tourism destination Wörthersee in Austria. However, few studies have yet explored the acceptance of LBS for tourists in tourism destinations.

The aim of the paper is to investigate the usage of mobile phones in tourism destinations, in particular the acceptance of LBS. An overview about different technology acceptance models is provided. Moreover, the study focuses on the case study of Wörthersee. Therefore, the project "Leuchtturm" is analysed in detail. Taking these aims into consideration the following research question has been developed and shall be answered within the empirical approach that is to be followed this paper:

How and to what extent is the acceptance of LBS assembled and currently accomplished with special regards to tourists in the Lake Wörthersee region?

2 THEORETICAL BACKGROUND

2.1 Mobile Services

Mobile services are booming amongst mobile phone users. In 2014 more than 2.23 billion people go online with their mobile phone at least once per month (eMarketer, 2014). Mobile communication is nowadays part of the everyday life. When on holidays, mobile devices can deliver location-based, up-to-date and personalized information (with LBS) in all stages of a holiday and ultimately improve the experience. (Egger & Buhalis, 2008).

2.2 Location Based Services

LBS are mobile applications, which are accessed by users through mobile devices and which are dependent on the location of the mobile device eg mobile phone, laptop, tablet, and so on. Therefore, the mobile device needs to have the ability to show the geographical location (Kushwaha & Kushwaha, 2011). LBS take the current geographical position of the user into consideration in order to provide personalised and contextualised services to each individual user. This includes the localization of persons, objects and places but also routing between them. Users may also search for specific objects in their vicinity or retrieve information about travelling conditions (Berger, Lehmann, & Lehner, 2003). The mobile device of the user has to be switched on, so that the user can be located and served with relevant information to his/her current location (Egger & Buhalis, 2008).

LBS can be subdivided into push and pull services. The first mentioned are automatically activated but depend on prior set conditions, e.g. news letters or weather services. The latter mentioned, pull services, are dependent on user-requests, e.g. using a navigation system (Kushwaha & Kushwaha, 2011). Especially in unfamiliar surroundings, which tourists are exposed to when being on holiday, the need for orientation and information about the unknown is increasing (Groß et al., 2006). Fronhofer & Lütters (2012) concluded that LBS in tourism seem to have an enormous potential in regards of service capacity and their use especially in non-urban destinations can act as coordinators of the touristic offers on site and increase the customer experience within the destination.

As this paper is concerned with the implications and the use of LBS along with their acceptance in practical use, a tourism destination was chosen. Ritchie & Crouch (2000) already claimed more than a decade ago, that the fundamental product in tourism is the destination experience. It is therefore a logical consequence that competition centres on destinations. In order to clarify the exact boundaries and contexts of destinations and their specific meanings some basic approaches need to be considered. According to Pike (2008) the destination product can be described as an amalgam of a diverse and often eclectic range of attractions, activities, people, scenery, accommodation, amenities and climate. It is a geographical space in which a cluster of tourism resources exist, rather than a political boundary. Beritelli and Bieger, (2013) added that the boundaries as such can vary, as they might also be dependent on the visitor's perception. Therefore a destination can be a resort, city, region, country or even a continent.

2.3 Case Study: Wörthersee Region

The area addressed in this paper is the Wörthersee destination. This lake-mountain region with long touristic history is situated in the Southern part of Austria, close to the Alps, the Italian and Slovenian border and lies in the federal province of Carinthia. In 2013 this touristic area generated a total of about 1.5 million overnight stays out of 357.000 arrivals, whereby approximately 85% were recorded in the summertime. The peak months are July and August (Tourismusstatistik Kärnten, 2013). The Wörthersee destination is characterized by a heterogeneous offering structure. Next to accommodation facilities, ranging from 5-Star hotels to simple bed and breakfasts, also a broad spectrum of infrastructure-related companies and service providers can be found.

At the end of 2013, tourism representatives of this area launched a new project with the name "Leuchtturm". The basic idea behind this concept is to create an innovative online experience hub, a so called virtual travel guide. As already outlined above, LBS shall enable tourists in the region to retrieve offers and services according to their position within the destination. Another aspect of this assignment is concerned with the orientation and guiding of guests along tracking routes and through staged sites with the help of GPS (Global Positioning System) in the Wörthersee region. In order to facilitate internet access the basis and pre-requisite for this project was the instalment of a destination wide free Wifi (Wireless Fidelity) which is now made available on different plots around the lake (Wörthersee Tourismus GmbH, 2013).

In addition of enhancing the customer experience on site this project shall also help in gathering information on guest behaviour with the help of a sophisticated CRM (Customer relationship management) module. Further initial aims were also to increase service and information quality, an enhancement in professional destination management and a re-evaluation of the image, coming alongside with the positioning. With the initiation in fall 2013 the final phase of the project is planned to be concluded in winter 2015 (Wörthersee Tourismus GmbH, 2013).

2.4 Technology Acceptance

Technology acceptance has been researched for decades from different perspectives and with various foci (Chuttur, 2009). Several technology acceptance models have been developed. The most prominent in literature are the theory of reasoned action (TRA), the technology acceptance model (TAM), innovation diffusion theory (IDT), unified theory of acceptance and use of technology (UTAUT) leading to a modification resulting in the UTAUT2. The characteristics will now be shortly outlined (Chuttur, 2009).

Theory of Reasoned Action. Developed by Fishbein and Ajzen (1975 as cited in Chuttur, 2009) almost four decades ago TRA proposes that the behaviour of a person could be understood by looking at their prior intention together with the users' opinions on and positions for the behaviour. Chuttur (2009) stated that this behaviour is subsequently split into two sections, the attitude of a person towards the behaviour driven by feelings (1) and the subjective norm associated with the behaviour, meaning the families and friend's influence on behaviour performance (2).

Technology Acceptance Model. Building on the fundamentals of the TRA, the technology acceptance model has been developed to understand the user acceptance of information systems better. "A key purpose of TAM, therefore, is to provide a basis for tracing the impact of external factors on internal beliefs, attitudes and intentions" (Davis, Bagozzi, & Warshaw, 1989, p. 985). Over time major changes have been undertaken to the model (Chuttur, 2009;

Yang & Yoo, 2004; Davis, Bagozzi, & Warshaw, 1989). The final version of the TAM indicates that external variables are influencing perceived usefulness, which describes the perception of the user that the productivity and the effectiveness of one's performance is enhanced and the ease of using a certain technology. Moreover, the perceived ease of use also influences the perceived usefulness, whereas both of these variables have an influence on the behavioural intention and finally also on the actual use of the system. (Chuttur, 2009; Davis, Bagozzi, & Warshaw 1989).

Innovation Diffusion Theory. As literature proposes, another influential model is the innovation diffusion theory (Zhang, Guo, & Chen, 2008). Innovation diffusion is interpreted as "the process by which an innovation is communicated through certain channels over time among the members of a social system" (Rogers, 1995 as cited in Lee, Hsieh, & Hsu, 2011, p. 126). Diffusion research as such aims to analyse the interplay of innovation characteristics, the practice of how information about innovation is communicated and finally also the time and nature of the social system where the innovation is introduced (Surrey & Farquhar, 1997). The IDT in specific comprises five substantial innovation characteristics: relative advantage, compatibility, complexity, trial ability and observability. Additionally, it argues that prospective users either adopt or reject an innovation by means of perceptions they form about an innovation. (Lee et al., 2011).

Unified Theory of Acceptance and Use of Technology. One of the most sophisticated models presented in literature is the UTAUT. It has various foundations building up on several models: TRA, TAM, motivational model (MM), theory of planned behaviour (TPB), decomposed technology acceptance and planned behaviour model (DTPB), model of PC utilization (MPCU), IDT and social cognitive theory (SCT) (No & Kim, 2013). The UTAUT model includes direct (Performance Expectancy (PE), Effort Expectancy (EE), Social Influence (SI), Facilitating Conditions (FC)) and indirect (Anxiety, Attitude towards using, Behavioural Intention (BI)) determinations of behaviour and outlines the organizational acceptance of technology. It is designed to explain employee's technology acceptance and consists of four key moderating variables, which are experience, voluntariness, gender and age (Carlsson, Carlsson, Hyvönen, Puhakainen, & Walden, 2006). With the need to switch the focus from an organizational context to the consumer perspective this model has been adapted, leading to the creation of the UTAUT2 model (Venkatesh, Morris, Davis, & Davis, 2003). Three moderating variables, age, gender and experience with the examined technology, have been added to create a relationship between the constructs incorporated: hedonic motivation (HM), price value (PV) and habit (HT) (Venkatesh, Thong, & Xu, 2012). For the context of measuring the acceptance of LBS in a tourism destination the UTAUT2 model seems most appropriate as it deals with factors addressing the consumer and by that also the user of the service provided. Even though other models show certain advantages, literature proves that UTAUT2 can be claimed as the right choice for the aim of this paper. The model can be seen in detail in Fig. 1.

3 METHODOLOGY

The study follows a deductive research approach. In the first phase information gathering in form of a collection of previous literature has been carried out. An intense desk research of books, journals and studies about the case study Wörthersee, LBS in tourism destinations and technology acceptance models served as a basis for this paper. The aim was to gain an overview and to determine the current research state of the topic (Bryman, 2012). After the detailed investigation, the implemented theoretical framework was applied in the case study Wörthersee in the form of a questionnaire, available in the three languages German, English and Italian. In order to guarantee, that the factors outlined in the UTAUT2 model were measured appropriately, questionnaires of previous research work applying this model were analysed. The underlying patterns were used for the creation of the questionnaire.

3.1 Research Model

In the research model, the postulations of moderating effects in UTAUT2 were followed and examined. The hypotheses model has been adapted according to Venkatesh et al. (2012). The paths from PE and PV are hypothesized to be moderated by age and gender. The path from FC to use behaviour is postulated to be moderated by experience and age. EE, SI, FC, HM and HT are hypothesized to be moderated by all three variables, gender, age and experience. The path between behavioural intention and use behaviour is not tested in this study.

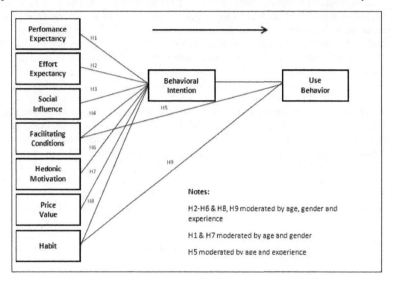

Fig. 1: Hypotheses Model (Adapted according to Venkatesh et al., 2012)

In addition to the above shown and developed hypotheses the following H10 has been developed: Moderating factors like age, gender and experience, have an influence on the determinants of BI.

3.2 Data Collection and Sample

The data has been collected through an online questionnaire available in the three languages German, English and Italian. The questionnaire has been designed according to the constructs of the UTAUT2 model. Participants were also asked about their possession of WiFi-capable mobile devices and the usage of the LBS provided in the Wörthersee region. This lead to a differentiation between those participants that have used LBS and those that did not use these services during their holiday in the Wörthersee region. In addition demographic questions and questions referring to the usage of WiFi-capable devices and the respondent's holidays in the Wörthersee region have been asked. Moreover, the questionnaire provided an introduction on what LBS is and how it can be used. The online questionnaire was sent out to the newsletter-database of the DMO of the Wörthersee region. The population of the study therefore were all tourists of the Lake Wörthersee region, who have signed up for the newsletter of the DMO. The sampling strategy was a self-selected one, as the online questionnaire was provided to all potential participants and those who responded are the sample of this study (Veal, 2006). The questionnaire has been sent out to a database of approximately 6000 guests. A response rate of 3.5% has been reached (n=206). After the completion of the data gathering, the results of the survey were analysed with SPSS.

3.3 Data Analysis

The questionnaire has been analysed using SPSS including three steps. First a statistical summary about the demographics and data about mobile devices was compiled. Secondly, the validity and reliability of the model was tested with Kaiser-Meyer-Olkin measures as well as Cronbach's Alpha and Inter-Item Correlation measures. This was followed by a regression analysis in order to further investigate the relationship between the diverse variables and hence leading to a result for stated the hypotheses. Pearson Correlation was adduced to explore the relationship between the independent variables and the moderating factors such as age, gender and experience ultimately providing an outcome for the 10th hypothesis.

4 FINDINGS AND DISCUSSION

4.1 Statistical Summary

Demographics		Tablet	53.2%
Sample Size	206	PDA	0.9%
Gender			
Male	55%	*Usage of free WLAN in previous holidays*	
Female	45%	Very Often	38.5%
Age		Often	13.8%
Mean	51.17 years	Sometimes	21.1%
<29	4.2%	Rarely	11.9%
30-39	16.2%	Never	14.7%
40-49	24.1%		
50-59	26.2%	Usage of free WLAN in the Wörthersee region	
60-69	21.5%	Yes	32.1%
<70	7.9%	No	67.9%
Nationality		Participants of the questionnaire that have	
Germany	50.2%	been in the Wörthersee region between May	
Austria	43.3%	and October 2014	
Switzerland	2.5%	in absolute figures	113
Italy	1.6%	in percentage	59.2%
Other	2.5%		
		Average Length of Stay	13.38 days
Mobile Devices (n=113)		Standard Deviation	34.819

Possession of a WiFi-capable mobile device
Yes 98.2%
No   1.8%

Possession of Mobile Devices
(Multiple Answers possible)
Laptop   62.4%
Mobile Phone   85.3%

Main Activities during the holiday
(Multiple Answers possible)

Swimming	76.1%
Excursions	55.0%
Hiking	42.2%
Boat Trip	31.2%
Cycling	28.4%
Specific Event	19.3%
Culture	10.1%
Wellness/Spa	7.3%
Golf	2.8%

Reasons for not using the free WLAN
(Multiple Answers possible)

Did not know that it exists	88.9%
Do not appreciate WLAN during holidays	9,7%
The WLAN did not work	5.6%
Did not want to use it	4.2%
Want to protect my privacy	2.8%
Do not know how to use it	1,4%
Do not trust free WLAN	1,4%

How did guests get aware of the free WLAN?
(Multiple Answers possible)

Hotel Personnel	41.9%
Website of the region	32.3%
Tourist Information	19.4%
In Restaurants	16.1%
Signage in the region	16.1%
From other guests or friends in the region	6.5%
From others travelling there before	3.2%

4.2 Validity

Kaiser-Meyer-Olkin (KMO), which measures the sampling adequacy, was applied first. According to Kaiser (1974 as cited in Field, 2013) a value greater than 0.5 can be accepted and a factor analysis is suitable for the data. The KMO-value for this study results in 0.767, showing that the sample size is alright and that factor analysis can be carried out.
According to Venkatesh et al., 2012 the 27 items used in the questionnaire were divided into 8 constructs. No further validity tests were undertaken, as the factors outlined in the UTAUT2 model were analysed carefully in previous research and have been proven already in various studies.

4.3 Reliability

In order to test the reliability of the results, derived from the Likert-scale questionnaire used in the context of this paper, a Cronbach's Alpha method and an Inter-Item Correlation matrix were applied. Table 1 outlines the Cronbach's alpha values for the constructs existing in the UTAUT2 model. According to (Gliem & Gliem, 2003) an excellent Cronbach's Alpha value is bigger than 0.9. Further standards are set as following: > 0.8 = Good, > 0.7 = Acceptable, > 0.6 = Questionable, > 0.5 = Poor, < 0.5 = Unacceptable. Therefore, PE, EE, SI, HM, HT and BI possess excellent internal consistencies of items. The facilitating conditions (.727) also fulfil the requirements for a satisfactory reliability. As the offered services in the addressed area are free of charge to the customer, the questionable alpha result for price value can be neglected and will not be considered further in this research.

Table 5: Cronbach's Alpha

Construct	Cronbach's Alpha	N of Items
PE	.897	4
EE	.961	4
SI	.994	3
FC	.727	4
HM	.947	3
PV	.535	2
HT	.894	4
BI	.951	3

The inter-item correlation, which measures the correlation among the constructs, is illustrated in Table 2. The values in general indicate a strong independence of the constructs, since the correlations are not close to 1.000. Due to the results of the previously conducted Cronbach's Alpha test, Table 2 does not include the price value variable anymore.

Table 6: Inter-Item Correlation

	PE	EE	SI	FC	HM	HT	BI
PE	1.000	.672	.267	.319	.842	.566	.640
EE	.672	1.000	.127	.296	.637	.538	.498
SI	.267	.127	1.000	.419	.278	.546	.498
FC	.319	.296	.419	1.000	.311	.455	.362
HM	.842	.637	.278	.311	1.000	.589	.660
HT	.566	.538	.546	.455	.589	1.000	.781
BI	.640	.498	.498	.362	.660	.781	1.000

4.4 Correlation

PE, EE, SI, FC, HM and HT were identified as potential determinants of Behavioural Intention to the utilization of LBS. Multiple regression analysis contributed to the testing whether the constructs were significant determinants of Behavioural Intention and if the stated hypotheses could be accepted. Table 3 shows the model summary, which also includes R-square, that represents extra validation and shows how well the collected data fit to the statistical model used in the research. The R-square is determined by the object that is measured and by the sample size. In this study the adjusted R-square is 0.606, which indicates that the independent variables (PE, EE, SI, FC, HM, HT) have 60.6% influence on the variation of the dependent variable BI. The other 30.9% of variation are explained by other factors.

Table 7: Model Summary

Model	R	R²	Adjusted R²	Std. Error of the Estimate
1	.831	.691	.606	.82051

The results for each predicting variable can be found in Table 4. The results of the regression in Table 4 demonstrate that PE, EE, HM, SI, FC and HM have no significant influence on the behavioural intention as the p-value (significance) is above 0.05. HT has the most significant impact, since its p-value is at 0,007 and the standardized coefficient is at 0.536. When considering the p-value of PE, EE, SI, FC and HM, the following hypotheses are not supported: H1, H2, H3, H4 and H6.

According to the collected data in this research, most of the UTAUT2 predictors for behavioural intention were identified to be non-significant determinants for the acceptance of LBS in the context of the destination Lake Wörthersee. This can be justified by the rather high significance-values in five predictors as well as the standardized coefficients, which are mainly below 0.2.

Table 8: Regression Coefficients for Predictors

Predictor	Unstandardized Coefficient	Standardized Coefficient	Standard Error	t	Significance
(Intercept)	.197		1.081	.182	.857
PE	.306	.172	.415	.736	.470
EE	-.060	-.040	.261	-.230	.820
SI	.101	.125	.122	.832	.414
FC	-.049	-.040	.169	-.292	.773
HM	.278	.203	.314	.886	.385
HT	.557	.536	.189	2.945	.007

To measure the influence of age, gender and experience on determinants of Behavioural Intention, Pearson correlations were applied. The results for these correlations can be found in Table 5. Indeed no significance could be found between the measured constructs and the age of the participants. Concerning the gender and the constructs, consisting of PE, EE and HM a significant correlation could have been detected. Moreover the participants' experiences displayed a significant correlation with the FC and HT constructs. Hence a strong interconnectivity between the constructs Facilitating Conditions as well as Habit and ultimately the usage intention of participants, who have already experienced the tool, was indicated. In conclusion, hypothesis 10 gets partially facilitated as experience shows in two cases a significant correlation with the UTAUT2 constructs, which are Facilitating Conditions and Habit. Moreover gender influences the Performance Expectancy, Effort Expectancy as well as Hedonic Motivation, whereas age has no influence on the constructs and hence Use Behaviour at all.

Table 9: Pearson Correlations (PC) of moderating factors (**significant at 0.01 level; * significant at 0.05 level)

	Age		Gender		Experience	
	PC	**Sig.**	**PC**	**Sig.**	**PC**	**Sig.**
PE	-.081	.676	-.635	.000**	.334	.077
EE	-.242	.207	-.379	.043*	.245	.199
SI	.138	.477	-.234	.221	.101	.603
FC	-.294	.122	-.179	.352	.381	.041*
HM	-.160	.408	-.518	.004**	.302	.112
HT	-.258	.177	-.364	.053	.514	.004**

4.5 Discussion of the Results

According to Table 6 the results show that H8 gets supported as Habit influences the Behavioural Intention and ultimately the Use Behaviour. H1, H2, H3, H4, H6 and H7 were not supported, as the constructs did not influence the Behavioural Intention. Moreover Price Value was treated very carefully, as the offered LBS system in the Wörthersee region is indeed for free and without any costs. Furthermore, H5 and H9 get partially supported, as Facilitating Conditions and Habit showed some significance with the moderating factor experience. This points out some evidence that these two factors might lead to a use behaviour of LBS. H10 is partially supported as some moderating factors have a significant influence on part of the constructs but not all were proven to have an effect.

Table 10: Hypotheses Testing

Hypotheses	Standardized Coefficient	Significance	Result
H1: PE influences the BI to use LBS.	.172	.470	Rejected
H2: EE influences the BI to use LBS.	-.040	.820	Rejected
H3: SI influences the BI to use LBS.	.125	.414	Rejected
H4: FC influences the BI to use LBS.	-.040	.773	Rejected
H5: FC influences the use behaviour of LBS.	-	-	Partially Supported
H6: HM influences the BI to use LBS.	.203	.385	Rejected
H7: PV influences the BI to use LBS.	-	-	Rejected
H8: HT influences the BI to use LBS.	.536	.007	Supported
H9: HT influences the use behaviour of LBS.	-	-	Partially Supported
H10: Moderation factors like age, gender & experience influence the determinants of BI	-	-	Partially Supported

4.6 Limitations of the Results

Generally seen, the significance might be rather low due to the defined time period, which was set from May to October 2014, when participants were supposed to be in the Wörthersee region in order to further continue the questionnaire. The participants, who have been to the Wörthersee region from May to October 2014 and have used the offered services where finally asked the relevant UTAUT2 questions. Indeed the sample size decreased thereof from 206 to 29, which makes a loss of 86%. A further reason for the drop out of participants might be the length and structure of the questionnaire. General information has been asked in the first part, followed by questions relevant for the UTAUT2 model. The authors tried to keep the participants motivated by attractive incentives to reply to all questions asked. Hence it is recommended to keep these facts in mind, when constructing and conducting a UTAUT2 questionnaire.

5 CONCLUSION

Mobile services and its varied possible applications such as LBS are offering the tourism industry various possibilities to distinguish from competitors and create value for their customers. The tourism destination Wörthersee has initiated a project for enabling guests to retrieve services and offers according to their position in the region based on LBS. Simultaneous in 2013 a destination wide free Wifi got installed on different spots around the lake. This enables all guests with mobile devices to make use of the provided LBS without facing higher costs that may arise due to roaming fees.

Understanding customers' acceptance of LBS is crucial. The successful use of LBS in the Wörthersee region depends on the factors that influence customer's intention to use, actual use and ultimately acceptance of LBS. The findings of this research are valuable for the tourism industry to gain further knowledge on how to launch LBS within a destination. Indeed the Wörthersee destination is the major beneficiary of this study, however, regions planning on adapting such a network might be able to apply this pre-knowledge and consequently diminish unpleasant results, ultimately reaching a magnificent acceptance of the customers by knowing strengths and weaknesses of the system. Subsequently, tourism institutions can set themselves apart by enhancing their uniqueness with the utilization of LBS hence creating an extraordinary network and customized experience for the tourist. Scholars are able to gain an overview of the various models applied in this specific context. Furthermore, certain obstacles when it comes to the execution of the study can be hereafter avoided as recommendations are given.

This paper has validated TAM and IDT in their original context and provides a better understanding of the UTAUT model, thus employee's possible perception and ultimately elucidates the UTAUT2 model, which originally elaborated out of the TAM and IDT. Hence according to the findings it can be stated that the UTAUT2 is the most suitable model in order to subsequently carry out the empirical research about the acceptance of LBS for tourists in tourism destinations and specifically in the region of the Wörthersee. This can be reasoned by the fact that the UTAUT2 model focuses on the customer and considers factors such as experience, age and gender.

While the merits of the UTAUT2 model got manifested, the findings of this paper provide great insight when analysing user's acceptance accompanied by their adoption of LBS in tourism destination. Even though some of the hypotheses were rejected, the results (Cronbach's Alpha, KMO, and Correlation) indicate that the UTAUT2 model is in general an appropriate construct to measure consumer's acceptance towards LBS in a tourism destination. The "Leuchtturm-project" at the Wörthersee destination is still in the start-up phase but the outcomes of the study reveal that there is an immense need of the services provided. Almost all of the participants surveyed (98.2%) possess a Wifi-capable device, whereby the biggest proportion is made up from mobile phones (85%) and laptops (62%). Furthermore, respondents also declared that while being on holiday, using the internet is important. 38.5% use it very often and 13.8% often. Concerning the investigated project nonetheless, a very significant outcome is that 88.9% of the respondents were not aware of the services provided. The remaining proportion was aware of the free "Seelan" and the accompanying features due to information of hotel personnel (41.9%) as well as the website from the DMO (32.3%). Therefore, and in order to increase the number of users for the service, those responsible should find appropriate means to raise awareness of the utilities offered. This may be concluded with an information campaign or signage within the destination.

5.1 Further Research

A follow up study, including the variables and measurements consistent in the UTAUT2 construct can be conducted at a different point in time to investigate the consumer behaviour towards LBS in the tourism destination further. This should ideally happen after the next peak season of tourists present at the given destination.

Furthermore, LBS systems in urban regions could be researched in further detail. The Wörthersee destination is rather rural and composed of small villages surrounding the lake. It might be interesting to see how LBS works in a huge entirety, such as a big city. The environment and users might be different than in the Wörthersee region. As in the mentioned target region mainly vacationers taking some time off their daily routine were targeted. Consequently it would be of interest to see how LBS is accepted in an urban environment. Conclusions about differences between urban and rural operators and consumers could be drawn.

Moreover, the future lies in networking and interconnectivity, hence continuing research in this field might support the tourism industry in satisfying the guest's stay even more by constructing a unique holiday experience.

REFERENCES

Berger, S., Lehmann, H., & Lehner, F. (2003). Location-Based Services in the Tourist Industry. *Information Technology & Tourism, 5*(4), 243–256. doi:10.3727/109830503108751171

Beritelli, P., & Bieger, T. (2013). From Destination Governance to Destination Leadership - Defining and Exploring the Significance with the help of a Systemic Perspective. *Tourism Review, 69*(1), 25–46.

Bryman, A. (2012). *Social Research Methods*. Oxford: Oxford University Press.

Buhalis, D., & Law, R. (2008). Progress in information technology and tourism management: 20 years on and 10 years after the Internet—The state of eTourism research. *Tourism Management, 29*(4), 609–623. doi:10.1016/j.tourman.2008.01.005

Carlsson, C., Carlsson, J., Hyvönen, K., Puhakainen, J., & Walden, P. (2006). Adoption of Mobile Devices / Services – Searching for Answers with the UTAUT. In *Proceedings of the 39th Hawaii International Conference on System Sciences* (Vol. 00, pp. 1–10).

Chuttur, M. (2009). Overview of the Technology Acceptance Mode : Origins , Developments and Future Directions. *Sprouts: Working Papers on Information Systems, 9*(37).

Davis, F. D., Bagozzi, R. P., & Warshaw, P. R. (1989). User Acceptance of Computer Technology: A Comparison of two theoretical models. *Management Science, 35*(8).

Egger, R., & Buhalis, D. (2008). *eTourism Case Studies: Management & Marketing Issues in eTourism*. Oxford: Butterworth-Heinemann.

eMarketer. (2014). Smartphone Users worldwide will total 1,75 billion in 2014. Retrieved May 18, 2014, from http://www.emarketer.com/Article/Smartphone-Users-Worldwide-Will-Total-175-Billion-2014/1010536

Field, A. (2013). *Discovering Statistics using IBM SPSS Statistics*. London: SAGE Publications Ltd.

Fronhofer, M., & Lütters, H. (2012). Chancen durch Location Based Services für den ländlichen Raum. *Tourismus Im Ländlichen Raum*, 292–315.

Gliem, J. A., & Gliem, R. R. (2003). Calculating , Interpreting , and Reporting Cronbach ' s Alpha Reliability Coefficient for Likert-Type Scales. In *2003 Midwest Research to Practice Conference in Adult, Continuing, and Community Education* (pp. 82–88).

Groß, M. S., Groß, S., Freyer, W., & Freyer, W. (2006). Mobilitätsverhalten im Tourismus: Methodenstudie zur Erfassung des Mobilitätsverhaltens von Touristen am Aufenthaltsort. *Zeitschrift Für Verkehrswissenschaft, 77*(1).

Kushwaha, A., & Kushwaha, V. (2011). Location Based Services using Android Mobile Operating System. *International Journal of Advances in Engineering & Technology, 1*(1), 14–20.

Lee, Y.-H., Hsieh, Y.-C., & Hsu, C.-N. (2011). Adding Innovation Diffusion Theory to the Technology Acceptance Model : Supporting Employees ' Intentions to use E-Learning Systems. *Educational Technology & Society, 14*(4), 124–137.

No, E., & Kim, J. K. (2013). Determinants of the Adoption for Travel Information on Smartphone. *International Journal of Tourism Research*. doi:10.1002/jtr

Pike, S. (2008). *Destination Marketing - An integrated marketing communication approach*. Oxford: Butterworth-Heinemann.

Ritchie, J. R. B., & Crouch, G. I. (2000). The Competitive Destination: A Sustainable Tourism Perspective. *Tourism Management, 21*(1), 1–7.

Surrey, D., & Farquhar, J. (1997). Diffusion Theory and Instructional Technology. *Journal of Instructional Science and Technology, 2*(1).

Tourismusstatistik Kärnten. (2013). Arrivals and Overnights for the year 2013. Retrieved May 14, 2014, from http://touris.kaernten.at/?siid=950&LAid=1&jid=so

Veal, A. J. (2006). *Research Methods for Leisure and Tourism - A Practical Guide*. Harlow: Pearson Education.

Venkatesh, V., Morris, M. G., Davis, G. B., & Davis, F. D. (2003). User acceptance of information technology: toward a unified view. *MIS Quarterly, 27*(3), 425–478.

Venkatesh, V., Thong, J. Y. L., & Xu, X. (2012). Consumer Acceptance and Use of Information Technology: Extending the Unified Theory of Acceptance and Use of Technology. *MIS Quarterly, 36*(1), 157–178.

Wörthersee Tourismus GmbH. (2013). *Lust auf virtuelles VIP-Service - Der Online-Urlaubsguide.*

Yang, H., & Yoo, Y. (2004). It's all about attitude: revisiting the technology acceptance model. *Decision Support Systems, 38*(1), 19–31. doi:10.1016/S0167-9236(03)00062-9

Zhang, N., Guo, X., & Chen, G. (2008). IDT-TAM Integrated Model for IT Adoption. *Tsinghua Science and Technology, 13*(3), 306–311.

The Digital Divide and User Experience of Blind and Visually Impaired Tourists

Zsofia Horvath,

Agnes Kraushofer,

Ekaterina Pok, and

Sina Wedl

Salzburg University of Applied Sciences, Austria
zhorvath.imte-m2012@fh-salzburg.ac.at

Abstract

This research project sets out to investigate the impact of the digital divide on the user experience of blind and visually impaired people when accessing tourism websites. Blind and visually impaired people are an important target group for tourism, however tourism webpages are hardly designed for their specific needs. This paper seeks to establish a better understanding of this issue. Therefore, a framework integrating the concepts of the digital divide and user experience has been developed. For empirical research, a multi-methodological approach was adopted, including an experiment with blind and visually impaired people, as well as distributing standardized questionnaires and conducting structured interviews. This paper presents the results that indicate the impact of age, usage and access on user experience, along with the practical and methodological challenges that occurred while working with this special target group. Finally, this paper concludes by providing suggestions for further research.

Keywords: Digital Divide; User Experience; Usability; Blind and Visually Impaired People; Accessibility

1 INTRODUCTION

It is generally acknowledged that the internet has revolutionised the tourism industry, as it, among other things, has facilitated the search for information and the vacation planning process (Buhalis and Law, 2008). However, not every segment of the population has reaped the same benefits from the use of Information and Communication Technologies (ICTs). Thus, researchers have been preoccupied with studying the phenomenon known as the digital divide, which refers to the barriers to accessing and using ICTs, in spite of its purported claims of universal availability and accessibility (Egger and Herdin, n.d.a.). Furthermore, the impact of ICTs on the disabled or more specifically, blind and visually impaired people has been twofold. On the one hand, the impact of disability has radically changed because the web has removed certain barriers to communication and interaction that people would ordinarily face in the physical world. Yet at the same time, when websites, web technologies, or web tools are badly designed, they can create barriers that exclude people from using them (Pühretmair and Nussbaum, 2011). Thus, much research and effort has been devoted to the development and application of "Web Accessibility Guidelines [WCAG]", in order to ensure that the disabled have access to the web. However, literature on the digital divide stresses the difference between internet access and internet use, ultimately highlighting the fact that having access is not synonymous with people being able to use technology properly/according to their needs (Minghetti and Buhalis, 2009; Selwyn, 2004; van Dijk and Hacker, 2003). This might be due to different reasons, such as a lack of knowledge, literacy, language skills, old age and disabilities (Minghetti and Buhalis, 2009).

While demographic, economic and regional factors have been widely explored in literature (Hargittai, 2003; Egger and Herdin, n.d.a.; Epstein, Nisbet and Gillespie, 2011), little is known about the degree of impact of the digital divide on people with visual disabilities. Correspondingly, there is a lack of research on the actual user experience of blind and visually impaired people when accessing a web page. As this target group is especially dependent on retrieving correct and accessible information on tourism webpages (Poria, Reichel, & Brandt, 2011; Small, Darcy, & Packer, 2011), this paper seeks to explore the impact of the digital divide on the user experience of blind visually impaired people when accessing tourism websites.

2 LITERATURE REVIEW

2.1 Tourism Webpages

Most of the current studies on tourist behaviour are focused on the use of web tools to buy touristic products and more specifically, on investigating and analyzing the degree of loyalty and trust that consumers have in their perception of a touristic package when they shop online (Kim, Forsythe, Gu, & Moon, 2002).

Tourists search for travel information on the web, where they can compare prices, design their own package tours and make their own reservations.

Sigala (2007) accounts for this tendency by explaining that internet-based technologies offer favourable ways for customers to do their research on what tourism businesses have to offer. The visitors searching on the tourism websites are able to find information related to their preferred destinations and compare offers from various suppliers, all of which can be done without leaving their armchair.

It has been suggested that successful websites are characterised by an abundance of information, clearly delineated and organized information threads, frequent updating, and interactive relationships with customers (LazarinisJanellopoulos, & Lalos, 2008). Law and Bai (2008) highlight that travel websites should put more emphasis on usability, functionality, search engine capabilities, e-mail and communication, and security related aspects. Only a pleasant e-experience can entice consumers towards visiting and revisiting tourism websites, thus leading to a surge in bookings.

2.2 Blind and Visually Impaired Internet Users

Blind and visually impaired people, a group that leads an active leisure and tourism lifestyle, are especially dependent on reliable and accessible information along the tourism service chain (Eichhorn and Buhalis, 2011). This is particularly relevant for website accessibility as well as for the presentation of reliable content on websites, as using the internet to search for information has been identified as the preferred means of trip planning for disabled people (Laburda and Smikac, 2009; Pühretmair and Nussbaum, 2011). Although ICTs and assistive technologies can be seen as gradually improving accessibility (Pühretmair and Nussbaum, 2011), problems of inaccessible or incorrect information still constitute a formidable barrier for visually impaired tourists and web users (Poria, Reichel, & Brandt, 2011; Small, Darcy, & Packer, 2011).

In order to improve and ensure webpage accessibility, one needs to adhere to the "Web Accessibility Guidelines [WCAG]" that were initiated by the "World Wide Web Consortium [W3C]" in 1999, which have undergone many revisions since then (W3C, 2011). This should be done by focusing on a range of issues including using alternative texts for pictures, alternative ways of presenting content, formatting and contrasting issues, how to make navigation easier with assistive technologies, how to minimize user error and maximize compatibility with various technologies (W3C, 2011). The last point is of special importance for blind and visually impaired web users, as a number of them rely on different types of assistive technologies, either by converting content into an audio format or providing content in Braille (Pühretmair and Nussbaum, 2011). Despite these initiatives, many webpages still do not abide by the WCAG and thus remain mostly inaccessible (Oertel, 2004 as cited in Pühretmair and Nussbaum, 2011).

2.3 Digital Divide

One of the most important aspects of ICTs is the availability and accessibility for everybody. But there exists a gap that is called the "digital divide", which refers to a not only technological, but also a social problem connected with inequality in abilities and opportunities of people with different socio-economic backgrounds, affecting their access and usage of ICTs (Fuchs, 2009).
Egger and Herdin state that the term digital divide is generally used to describe "the phenomenon of unequal distribution of information" (Egger and Herdin, n.d.a., p.4). Epstein, Nisbet and Gillespie (2011) offer another perspective on the notion of digital divide. They claim that the digital divide is not only about different types of inequalities, but it is also about the nature of the problems.

2.4 User Experience

Hassenzahl (2008, p. 12) defines user experience (UX) as "a momentary, primarily evaluative feeling (good-bad) while interacting with a product or service. Good UX is the consequence of fulfilling the human needs for autonomy, competency, stimulation (self-oriented), relatedness, and popularity (others-oriented) through interacting with the product or service (i.e., hedonic quality). Pragmatic quality facilitates the potential fulfillment of be-goals."
The importance of usability (Jokela, Iivari, Matero, & Karukka, 2003) is enshrined in ISO 9241, an index of standards/codes dealing with ergonomics requirements in workplaces (Abran, Khelifi, Suryn, & Seffah, 2003). In section eleven of this standard, usability is defined as "[t]he extent to which a product can be used by specified users to achieve specified goals with effectiveness, efficiency and satisfaction in a specified context of use" (ISO 9241-11, 1998 as cited in Bevan, 2009, p. 2). Usability, alongside with safety and flexibility, is also an important part of "quality in use" as outlined by ISO/IEC CD 25010.3 (Bevan, 2009). In both standards, the main components of usability are efficiency, effectiveness and satisfaction.

3 FRAMEWORK DEVELOPMENT

The framework below illustrates the concepts of the digital divide, user experience and usability. Based upon existing relevant concepts, it is a framework that integrates them into one coherent whole so as to enable the reader to better understand the interrelations and interdependencies between them.

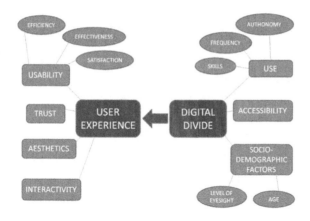

Fig. 1. Proposed framework for the study

Aspects of the digital divide, such as different levels of infrastructure development, different types of users (including differences in age, gender, disabilities, income and culture), as well as different knowledge and experience levels (Shneiderman, 1999), need to be taken into account when assessing/evaluating the user's experience of a webpage.

A number of studies examining the influence of socio-economic factors on web experience and usability have been identified. Already in 1999, Shneiderman reported based on findings from surveys, that issues reflecting the digital divide such as inadequate skills, experience or infrastructure, led to a decline in efficiency (wasted time) and effectiveness (perceived difficulty) of computer use (Shneiderman, 1999). Rodgers and Harris (2003) also reported differences in the levels of satisfaction and trust from users of online shopping websites. Furthermore, elderly users were found to have greater usability problems than younger users (Chadwick-Dias, Tedesco, & Tullis, 2004). Hence, the digital divide and the discrepancies that emerge stemming from socio-demographic factors, undeniably influence the user experience.

Shneiderman and Plaisant (2005 as cited Petrie and Bevan, 2009) in their 8 golden principles of good interface design, claim that an increase in the frequency of use results in greater user (quest for) efficiency. Moreover, literature on the digital divide stresses the relevance of possessing digital skills along with having access to ICTs infrastructure (accessibility) as important prerequisites to narrow the digital divide (Boeltzig and Pilling, 2007; Hargittai, 2003; Selwyn, 2004; van Dijk and Hacker, 2003). Thus, different dimensions such as the frequency of use or levels of user proficiency in ICTs will determine the nature of user experience.

The interdependency between accessibility, the digital divide, user experience and usability is still widely debated in literature. In the WAI guidelines, accessibility is a means to usability, being restricted to enabling certain user groups, such as people with impairments. This research paper focuses on the latter notion, believing that user experience is strongly connected with the phenomenon of digital divide which ensures that the website or technology is perceived as being usable by various user groups (Shneiderman, 2000, as cited in Lazar, Allen, Kleinman, & Malarkey, 2007) and thus narrows the gap between individuals with regards to their possibilities of using the internet, as outlined in the OECD definition of the digital divide. Hence it is assumed that an increase in user experience would result in a corresponding decline in the unequal access of online information. Moreover, Pühretmair and

Miesenberger (2005 as cited in Pühetmair and Nussbaum, 2011) mention that increased accessibility also has a positive impact on user experience, as it fosters satisfaction and loyalty.

4 METHODOLOGY

To derive an overview about the current state of the experience of the digital divide by blind and visually impaired people, an extensive literature review was carried out. Various theories related to the phenomenon of the digital divide, tourism webpages, and the user experience of blind and visually impaired people were examined and analyzed. From the acquired information, the authors developed a framework in order to link the different concepts together and highlight both the positive and negative interrelations.

With regards to the aim of the study to provide a holistic picture of the state of the digital divide within the target group of blind and visually impaired people, the authors decided to apply a multi-methodological approach (Bryman and Bell, 2011).

The core element of the empirical study was an experiment, comprising elements of both quantitative and qualitative research. This experiment was conducted in November 2013 with a group of five blind and visually impaired participants, who were found and contacted with the help of the Salzburg Federation of the Blind and Visually Impaired. According to Nielsen (2000) usability tests deliver best results with no more than five test persons. The sampling was based on Cluster Sampling. Sampling is often clustered according to geographical location or time period. The basis of our participant cluster was that they belonged to the blind and visually impaired group, all of them came from the area of Salzburg, and every one of them were in contact with the Federation of the Blind and Visually Impaired. The experiment took place at the Federation's Salzburg office, in rather small room which is used for computer training purposes and thus equipped with computers including relevant assistant technologies. All participants attended such trainings and thus were familiar with the setting. One of the participants executed the tasks on her own laptop.

For the experiment, the tourism web page www.salzburg.info was chosen. This webpage was pre-evaluated before the experiment by a short online accessibility test, due to the inability to obtain timely support from an experienced/professional blind/visually impaired Internet user. First, a general introduction to the aims of the study and the process of the experiment were provided. Then, several tasks were given to the participants of the experiment; for instance, concentrating on finding certain information on a tourism webpage www.salzburg.info; to open the webpage, to find out the opening hours of the Salzburg Museum, to read the description of the picture of the house in which Mozart was born, and to identify coffee houses and cafes located in the city center. Every person was asked to carry out these tasks. Furthermore all the participants were asked to continuously talk about what they were doing during the experiment, in order to document the whole user experience for scrutiny, which was recorded separately. The think-aloud method was chosen due to its great prominence in HCI research (Nielsen, Clemmensen & Yssing, 2002). Furthermore, its straightforwardness (Dix, Finlay, Abowd & Beale, 1997; Hackos & Redish, 1998) along with its ability to reveal participants' thoughts when interacting with the webpage are seen to be core benefits of the adaptation of this method (Nielsen, Clemmensen & Yssing, 2002). However, some main disadvantages, which partially also arose in the experiment, need to be acknowledged (Nielsen, Clemmensen & Yssing, 2002). According to XX, main issues include the potential insecurity of participants (e.g. feeling observed), their inability to voice their thoughts in the pace they occur as well as the possible excessive demand of speaking and navigating the page at the same time (Nielsen, Clemmensen & Yssing, 2002).

The whole experiment process was facilitated and documented by the Morae software that recorded every detail related to the user's interaction on the website (e.g. mouse click, duration of stay on the website, probands gestures etc.).

After the experiment, an interviewer-completed questionnaire was carried out which was recorded and written down by the interviewers as well. The questionnaire focused on the key elements of the digital divide and user experience outlined in the framework (socio-demographic factors of the participants, circumstances of their blindness, user experience during the experiment and their perception of the Salzburg Info website). This approach was chosen due to the relative ease of administration for the given target group, as well as for its potential to clarify questions and answers immediately. The duration of the experiment amounted to approximately one hour per participant.

With the support of Morae, quantitative data was obtained in the form of error rates, time spent on certain tasks and other factors defining usability as outlined by Nielsen (1994 as cited in Abran et al., 2003). Qualitative data was yielded in the form of the verbal protocol. After the data collection, the interviews were coded, and the information was classified and examined. Furthermore, a standardised user experience questionnaire that was included in the interview was analysed in a pre-defined Microsoft Excel template. These results were cross-checked against the interview answers and the Morae software.

5   RESULTS

5.1 General Findings on the Digital Divide Factors

As mentioned above in the study's framework, the analysis of the digital divide concentrated on factors such as variables related to usage (skills, frequency and autonomy), socio-demographics (age and level of eyesight) and accessibility. Table 1 shows the details of each participant's profile.

Table 1. Factors of digital divide per participant

Participant	Age Group	Level of eyesight	Age when losing sight	Internet experience	Av. Weekly internet use	Years of Internet Use	Autonomy
1 – "Frank"	50-59	Fully blind	37	Distinct	7- 10 hours	„since its existence"	Autonom use (Appart from minor things)
2 – "Ben"	50-59	58% of sight	52	Average	7-10 hours	10 years	Help needed
3 – "Ann"	40-49	Fully blind	12	Very limited	20 hours (work) 1-2 hours (leisure)	7-8 years	Help needed
4 – "Julia"	20-29	Fully blind	0	Very distinct	3-4 hours	8 years	Autonom use (Appart from minor things)
5 – "Tom"	30-39	10% of sight	2	Limited	1-2 hours	7-8 years	Totally independent

The three male and two female participants represented different age groups, with more than half the participants being above 40 years of age. Two of them were severely visually impaired; whereas the others were fully blind (only one of them from the time of birth). All participants were already fairly long-term internet users but weekly usage levels varied greatly, from one hour up to more than ten hours a week. Therefore, there were huge disparities in the level of internet usage proficiency, including two professional, one average and two limited users. Differences were also detected with regards to autonomy. One participant mentioned that he used the Internet autonomously; two only with little restrictions (e.g. CAPTCHA) and two were more dependent on external help.

5.2 General Findings on User Experience

Usability

Usability was assessed via looking at the variables of effectiveness, efficiency and satisfaction. **Effectiveness level** varied greatly among the different participants (see figure 2) and it is striking that no task, apart from opening the webpage, was fully completed by all participants. Likewise, the search function on the webpage was not always effectively used. The two visually impaired participants did not use it at all; for one participant it did not work properly and the fully blind participant refrained from using the website's search function but only used her assistive software. Overall, www.salzburg.info was perceived as user-friendly and the participants argued that their effectiveness level would probably increase if they used the website more often.

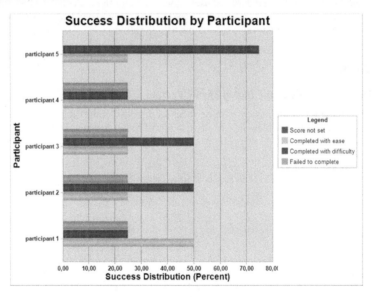

Fig. 2. Success distribution by participant

Efficiency

The concept of efficiency is closely related to the topic of effectiveness. The following table outlines the time needed to complete the respective tasks (see figure 3). One observes that these timings are rather long. This might be explained by the fact that blind users must read Web pages sequentially and that time needs tend to amplify if the assistive technology is not supported by the website or configured to the needs of the particular user. The inability to concentrate for a long period of time might have had a negative impact on both effectiveness and efficiency.

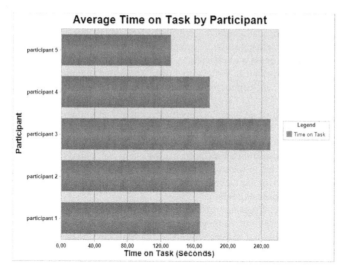

Fig. 3. Average time taken for each task by participant

Satisfaction

As for overall satisfaction, a generally high level was reported, provided that the participants were able to find everything they needed. Thus a certain connection between effectiveness and satisfaction was observed.

Trust

Like overall satisfaction, trust levels were also high. All information content was perceived extremely reliable and trustworthy. However, although not applicable to the study at hand, participants voiced some general concerns about having to register themselves somewhere or provide personal details.

Aesthetics

Almost no information was provided on the aesthetic component. This was more or less expected for the blind participants, as they do not perceive aesthetics-related elements. However, it was anticipated that the visually impaired might comment on this, which was not the case.

Interactivity

Interactivity with the webpage was also judged to be good, mainly because the usage of assistive technologies was possible. The visually impaired used the screen-magnifying software "Zoom" whereas the fully blind utilized "JAWS", as a screen reader. All software functioned without problems while on the webpage.

5.3 Impact of the digital Divide on User Experience

Based on the framework, three propositions concerning the impact of the digital divide on user experience were developed and examined. These linkages were found to exist in the general literature (pertaining to non-disabled users) and were adapted to the context of the present study.

Level of eyesight in combination with age influences user experiences

This experiment revealed a potential correlation between age and usability. The two younger participants were quicker in completing the tasks and also committed fewer errors. However, the identification of the majority of errors was based on the researchers' observations, as the software did not provide these details (see Limitations). The impact of age on usability could not be conclusively proven due to the different levels of media competence between the two youngest participants who embodied the two extremes, where one was a professional user while the other had rudimentary skills. More precisely, the impact of age seems to only have repercussions on effectiveness and efficiency, because satisfaction levels were quite constant within the group. The same is true for levels of trust, aesthetics and interactivity and therefore, it seems apparent that age influences aspects of usability, rather than having an overall impact on user experience.

With regards to the impact of various levels of eyesight as a factor, little variation was detected as the two fastest users represented both categories (fully blind and visually impaired). Therefore, it seems that age influences usability levels more so than different levels of eyesight. Nevertheless, indirect effects of the level of eyesight on the overall user experience might occur, due to the use of different assistive technologies that shape the users' perception and experience of the webpage.

Level of use influences user experience

High levels of autonomy, frequency of use and user skills were expected to impact overall user experience. In the experiment, these connections could not be observed clearly. This is mainly due to the fact that the researchers noted that participants tended to understate their skills. The most prevalent comment on their skills was: "For what I need my skills are enough, but they are far from perfect". In contrast to their statements, those with low skills performed not significantly worse than those who claimed their skills to be advanced. The same applies to levels of autonomy and frequency of use, where no considerable differences could be detected either. Therefore, no conclusive results were yielded and the impact of use on user experience cannot be judged. Moreover, for the observations at hand, it is also difficult to assess whether the potential impact of use is limited only to usability or if it equally applies to user experience as a whole, because participants were not always able to give a realistic and accurate self-assessment of their skills. Aesthetics, interaction and trust levels were rather constant among all usage levels.

Levels of accessibility influences user experience

Research on the use of ICTs by blind and visually impaired people strongly focuses on accessibility issues (W3C, 2011) and thus it was anticipated/postulated that a good perception of accessibility would positively impact user experience. Due to the fact that participants did not provide much detailed or in-depth information about accessibility in general and their specific requirements, there were limited possibilities of judging the impact of accessibility on user experience. Participants were regarded as a great source of information concerning this issue, but their answers were restricted to the following: "yes, for me it's rather accessible, because I could find, more or less, everything that I needed". One participant, showing an awareness of other groups of disabled users, stated: "for me it works well, but I don't know how the page is adapted for other disabled user groups, such as the deaf or the mobility impaired".

From the further comments that were informally provided during the experiment, the researchers gained the impression that accessibility was nevertheless important for user experience, especially for the component of interactivity. The participants emphasized that a prerequisite for them to judge a website as accessible, was that their assistive technologies had to be fully supported by the given webpage. Some evidence was also discovered that alluded to the connection between accessibility and satisfaction. Inaccessible web features such as CAPTCHAs or flash films, were cited as major factors of frustration and dissatisfaction. One participant complained: "I don't understand why they are not thinking about blind people when they install something like this" and another stated: "what do they expect a blind person to do with a flash film?"

In general, accessibility seems to continue being a rather elusive topic for the concerned target group. However, impacts on interactivity and satisfaction are rather evident.

6 DISCUSSION, CONCLUSION AND PRACTICAL IMPLICATIONS

Findings have suggested a connection between age and usability, which affirms reports from Abran (2003) and Shneiderman (1999), who emphasise the context of use and thus also the particular demographical profile of the user. No consistent results have been found with regards to the impact of use on user experience, as participants tended to understate their skills. This is unfortunate, because the linkage between use and user experience has been widely explored in literature. Examples include a focus on the impact of skills (Shneiderman, 1999; Adebesin, Kotzé & Gelderblom, 2010), the influence of use on satisfaction and trust (Rodger and Harris, 2003), as well as efficiency and use (Shneiderman and Plaisant, 2005 as cited in Petrie and Bevan, 2009). The participants from this study indicated a connection between accessibility and both interactivity and satisfaction, which reflects Shneiderman's notion (2000, as cited in Lazar et al., 2007).

Drawing from the results, the following advice can be given to tourism webpage operators. An essential point for blind and visually impaired users is that the websites must support their assistive technologies and that they can gain all the information they need. As these assistive technologies are strongly based on navigating through the structure of the websites, it has to be ensured that the websites are clearly and consistently structured. This eases the work both for the software and users, which is essential given their potential concentration problems. Furthermore, all disabling features, such as CAPTCHAS or flash films should be avoided. Lastly, blind and visually impaired people were found to have very high trust levels towards all information texts. This necessitates that all information that is provided online should be updated, correct and accessible (Poria et al. 2011; Eichhorn and Buhalis 2011).

6.1 Limitations and Further Research

The most important and formidable challenge was the process of convincing blind and visually impaired people to participate in the study. Although they were contacted by the Salzburg Federation of the Blind, interest was barely existent. Consistent follow-up ultimately led to a participation of five people. During the experiment, it became evident that fear/discomfort existed within the group, where there was the fear of being ridiculed because of the lack of ICT skills. Participants mentioned that they were always ready to help with (offline) research, but that the barriers on the internet are a topic that they do not readily talk about. Thus, future researchers should clearly focus more on creating and increasing awareness of people by showing them the benefits that they can (indirectly) gain from the work. What also needs to be mentioned are the level of investment and personal interest towards the research project. While some participants contributed a lot, others focused only on the quick execution of the tasks. Connected to this is the blunt and at times, negative/hostile reactions that were triggered by the standardized user experience questionnaire (Hinderks, Schrepp, Rauschenberger, Olschner, & Tomaschewski, 2012). One participant referred to it as "a waste of time and money" and almost all participants reacted the same way towards the control questions, commenting: "why are you always asking the same" or "how often have you now asked me the same question". Additionally, participants criticised some questionnaire items (e.g. attractiveness, creativity, innovativeness, etc.) as not appropriate or only partly suited for the blind and visually impaired. Consequently, the development of an adopted questionnaire for this target group should be a goal for further researchers. This would also make the tasks and questionnaire items more succinct and comprehensible, as difficulties arising from understanding questions have previously impeded the research at hand. A lot of inquiries were made, there was a great degree of hesitation and tasks as well as questions had to be frequently reiterated and re-explained. This might be due to lapses in concentration from the participants. Participants had difficulties concentrating in the new/different environment and this might have been aggravated by the length of the questionnaire and noise level in the room. For future research projects, care needs to be taken to provide adequate space and assistive technology, as well as to ensure the optimal continuous concentration of the participants. The nature of some of the tasks might have constituted complicated and unnecessary challenges for the participants. For some participants, searching for an "alt"-text made little sense, because their software did not provide much support in such matters. Moreover, parts of the webpage temporarily did not function, causing problems to one participant. In future, task selection should be done more carefully and with potential assistive technologies in mind. The Morae software was also a problem-zone itself. Although it is a user experience testing software, it was discovered that it is not suitable for any studies involving blind and visually impaired people. A main feature of the software is to calculate the time needed for the completion of a task or the number of errors made on the basis of mouse-clicks. As fully blind people do not use a mouse at all, Morae did not provide any suitable feedback/results. Furthermore, the change in screen size caused by "Zoom", was not reproduced in the software. Lastly, the absence of audio-outlets on the computers hampered the effective use of Morae. Based on experience, Morae cannot be recommended for further research on blind people and alternatives should be found. In general, sufficient pilot testing is highly recommended for further research. For the present study, this was not feasible, due to time constraints and a lack of access to qualified blind/visually impaired web users who could conduct such a test.

6.2 Methodological Limitations and Further Research

A number of methodological limitations can be identified as well. As the study only included the views of a limited number of participants, no conclusive, generalizable data could be obtained. Therefore, the results are solely meant to be interpreted as first insights or directions. Hence, further studies on a larger qualitative scale should be envisaged, in order to broaden our understanding of the issue. Moreover quantitative studies on a larger number of blind and visually impaired people are needed to investigate their user experience more precisely and thoroughly. However, an adaptation of the questionnaire as mentioned before, needs to be done first. A further limitation can be seen in the fact that the study focused on one single tourism webpage, namely www.salzburg.info. To gain a more complete view and to draw deeper, significant conclusions, more DMO websites should be examined and compared. Finally, the participants could be asked to perform a wider scope of tourism-related tasks, all of which must be feasible.

7 ACKNOWLEDGEMENT

We gratefully acknowledge the support of Roman Egger and Alexander Seymer for their valuable input.

REFERENCES

Abran, A., Khelifi, A., Suryn, W., & Seffah, A., 2003. Usability Meanings and Interpretations in ISO Standards. *Software Quality Journal*, pp. 323-336.

Adebesin, F., Kotzé, P., & Gelderblom, H., 2010. The Impact of Usability on Efforts to Bridge the Digital Divide. [online] Available at: <http://www.academia.edu/1040743/Impact_of_usability_on_efforts_to_bridge_the_digital_div ide> [Accessed 25 May 2013].

Bevan, N., 2009. Extending Quality in Use to Provide a Framework for Usability Measurement. In J. A. Jacko, C. Stephanidis, D. Harris, D. D. Schmorrow, M. Grootjen, B. T. Karsh AND I. V. Estabrooke, EDS. 2009. *HCI International*. San Diego: Springer. n.b.

Bryman, A., & Bell, E., 2011. *Business Research Methods* (3. ed.). Oxford: Oxford University Press.

Boeltzig, H., & Pilling, D., 2007. Bridging the Digital Divide for Hart-to-reach Groups. *IBM Center for the business of Government*. Leicestershire Country Council, UK.

Buhalis, D., & Law, R., 2008. Progress in information technology and tourism management. 20 years on and 10 years after the Internet-The state of eTourism research. *Tourism Management*, pp. 609-623.

Chadwick-Dias, A., Tedesco, D., & Tullis, T., 2004. *Older Adults and Web Usability: Is Web Experience the Same as Web Expertise?* CHI 2004: Late Breaking Results Paper.

Dix, A., Finlay, J., Abowd, G. & Beale, R., 1997. *Human-Computer Interaction*. Upper Saddle River: Prentice Hall.

Egger, R., & Herdin, T., n.d.a.. Beyond the Digital Divide: Tourism, ICTs and Culture - A Highly Promising Alliance. Unpublished Paper.

Eichhorn, V., & Buhalis, D., 2011. Accessibility: A Key Objective for the Tourism Industry. In D. Buhalis, AND S. Darcy, EDS. 2011. *Accessible Tourism. Concepts and Issues*. Bristol: Channel View Publications, pp. 46-59.

Epstein, D., Nisbet, C. E., & Gillespie, T., 2011. Who's Responsible for the Digital Divide? Public Perceptions and Policy Implications. *The Information Society*, pp. 92-104.

Fuchs, C., 2009. The Role of Income Inequality in a Multivariate Cross-National Analysis of the Digital Divide. Social Science Computer Review, 27(1), pp. 41-58.

Hackos, J. T. & Redish, J. C., 1998. *User and Task Analysis for Interface Design*. Hoboken: Wiley

Hargittai, E., 2003. The Digital Divide and What To Do About It. In D. C. Jones, ED. 2003. *New Economy Handbook*. San Diego: Academic Press, Printed Chapter.

Hassenzahl, M., 2008. User Experience (UX): Towards an experiential perspective on product quality. In e. Brangier, G. Michel, J.M.C. Bastien AND N. Carbonell, EDS. 2008. *IHM '08 Proceedings of the 20th International Conference of the Association Francophone d'Interaction Homme-Machine*. New York: ACM, pp. 11-15.

Hinderks, A., Schrepp, M., Rauschenberger, M., Olschner, S., & Thomaschewski, J., 2012. Konstruktion eines Fragebogens für jugendliche Personen zur Messung der User Experience. In German UPA, ED. 2012. *Proceedings of Usability Professionals 2012*. Stuttgart: German UPA., pp. 78-83.

Husing, T., & Selhofer, H., 2002. *The Digital Divide Index - A Measure of Social Inequalities in the Adoption of ICT. ECIS*. Gdansk, pp. 1273-1286.

Jokela, T., Iivari, N., Matero, J., & Karukka, M., 2003. The Standard of User-Centered Design and the Standard Definition of Usability: Analyzing ISO 13407 against ISO 9241-11. In C. Sieckenius de Souza, A. Sánchez, S. Barbosa, AND C. Gonzalez, EDS. 2003. *Proceedings of the Latin American conference on Human-computer interaction*. New York: ACM, pp. 53-60.

Kim, J.-O., Forsythe, S., Gu, Q., & Moon, S. J., 2002. Cross –cultural consumer values, needs and purchase behaviour. *Journal of Consumer Marketing*, 19(6), pp. 481-502.

Lamburda, A., & Smikac, H. (2009). Reispläne und Aktivitäten für einen Urlaub ohne Barrieren. [online] Available at: <http://www.ibft.at/upload/Ergebnisbericht_Umfrage-2008-09.pdf> [Accessed 19 February 2012].

Law, R., & Bai, B., 2008. How do the preferences of online buyers and browsers differ on the design and content of travel websites? *International Journal of Contemporary Hospitality Management*, 20(4), pp. 388-400.

Lazar, J., Allen, A., Kleinman, J., & Malarkey, C., 2007. What Frustrates Screnn Reader Users on the Web: A Study of 100 Blind Users. *International Journal of Human-Computer Interaction*, 3, pp. 247-269.

Lazarinis, F., Janellopoulos, D., & Lalos, P., 2008. Heurisitically Evaluating Greek e-Tourism and e-Museum Websites. *The Electronic Journal Information Systems Evaluation*, 11(1), pp. 17-26.

Minghetti, V., & Buhalis, D., 2009. Digital Divide in Tourism. *Journal of Travel Research*, pp. 1-15.

Nielsen, J., 2000. Why You Only Need to Test with 5 Users. [online] Available At: <http://www.nngroup.com/articles/why-you-only-need-to-test-with-5-users/> [Accessed 15 October 2014].

Nielsen, J., Clemmensen, T., & Yssing, C., 2002. Getting access to what goes on in people's heads? – Reflections on the think-aloud technique. In O.W. Bertelsen, ED. 2002. *Proceedings of the second Nordic conference of Human-computer interaction*. Aarhus: ACM, pp. 101-110.

Petrie, H., & Bevan, N., 2009. The evaluation of accessibility, usability and user experience. In C. Stepanidis, ED. 2009. *The Universal Access Handbook*. Boca Raton: CRC Press, n.b.

Poria, Y., Reichel, A., & Brandt, Y., 2011. Dimensions of hotel experience of people with disabilities: an exploratory study. *International Journal of Contemporary Hospitiality Management*, 23(5), pp. 571-591.

Pühretmair, F., & Nussbaum, G., 2011. Web Design, Assistive Technologies and Accessible Tourism. In D. Buhalis, ANS S. Darcy, EDS. 2011. *Accessible Tourism. Concepts and Issues*. Bristol: Channel View Publications, pp. 274-285.

Selwyn, N., 2004. Reconsidering political and popular understandings of the digital divide. New Media & Society, pp. 341-362.

Shneiderman, B., 1999. *Universal Usability: Pushing Human-Computer Interaction Research to Empower Every Citizen*. Insitute for System Research: Technical Research Report.

Sigala, M., 2004. The ASP-Qual model measuring ASP service quality in Greece. *Managing Service Quality*, 14(1), pp. 103-114.

Small, J., Darcy, S., & Packer, T., 2011. The embodied tourist experience of people with visual impairment: Management implications beyond the visual gaze. *Tourism Management*, 30, pp. 1-10.

van Dijk, J., & Hacker, K., 2003. The Digital Divide as a Complex and Dynamic Phenomenon. *The Information Society*, pp. 315-326.

Williams, R., Rattray, R., & Stork, A., 2004. Web site accessibility of German and UK tourism information sites. *European Business Review*, 16(6), pp. 577-589.

W3C., 2011. Accessibilty Principles. How People with Disabilities Use the Web. Available at: <http://www.w3.org/WAI/intro/people-use-web/principles> [Accessed 4 February 2012].

The Advantages of the "Great Place to Work" Award for Companies in the Tourism Industry and its' Role in Job Application and Job Choice Decisions of Applicants in the German-Speaking Countries

Ekaterina Pok

Salzburg University of Applied Sciences, Austria
pok.ekaterina@gmail.com

Abstract

This paper reports the findings of the study, which investigated the correlation between employer branding (EB) and the "Great Place to Work" (GPTW) award as its possible instrument. The author focused on the questions: "How companies in the tourism sector can benefit from the GPTW award?" and "To which extent its presence can influence the job application and job choice decision of applicants in the German-speaking countries?" Therefore, the topics of EB, the institution and the award GPTW, and job decision-making were explored. Expert interviews and the online survey for job seekers were conducted. The results of this study indicate that companies in the tourism industry are not usually using EB and the GPTW award often in their business to attract and retain employees. However, this study provides confirmatory evidence that the GPTW award has various advantages for companies and this award is perceived by job seekers as a signal of an employer with a good reputation and image, and thus, has an influence of the job application and job choice decision.

Keywords: employer branding; Great Place to Work; job application decision; job choice

1 INTRODUCTION

Nowadays there is a high competition on the labour market, and because of the changing nature of employment, workplace environment and labour shortages, organizations recognized the importance of human capital (the personnel) and started to believe in attraction of applicants as a vital part of success for companies (Wright et. al., 1995 cited in Turban and Greening, 1996), which led to their "jumping onto the great workplace bandwagon" (Levering, 2011). "Best Employer" and "A Great Place to Work" (GPTW) are statuses that more and more employers are currently looking for and would like to get (Alnıaçık and Alnıaçık, 2012), and plenty of companies can become such, regardless of the size and industry ("Why we do what we do", 2013). Organizations in tourism and travel industry are not exceptions in such competition for becoming great workplaces. During the last years, tourism has become one of the largest and fastest growing sectors in the world and turned into a key driver of socio-economic progress through export revenues, infrastructure development and also job creation. In the year 2012 1 job out of 11 was in the field travel and tourism (World Tourism Organisation, 2013). In organizations in the tourism and travel industry personnel is a crucial part that brings success to companies. According to Baum (1995, p.151 cited in Nickson, 2007, p.2) the nature of employment in the tourism industry is very diverse. Sometimes it could seem attractive, with good payment and working conditions and also the low level of the turnover. But on the other hand, the working conditions could be poor, with low payment and high personnel turnover (ibid). So, nowadays it is a challenge for many organizations in the tourism sector to recruit and keep employees.

To become attractive for applicants, a lot of organizations started to use branding principles and practices called EB (Alnıaçık and Alnıaçık, 2012), which aims at developing and upholding a "strong image of being a "great place to work" in the minds of the target group" (Grünewälder, 2007).

Although a significant amount of research has been recently conducted in the area of applicant attraction (Barber, 1998 cited in Ehrhart and Ziegert, 2005; Turban and Greening, 1996) and recruiting (Rynes, 1989; Breaugh and Starke, 2000; Rynes and Cable, 2003), most of it is done from the point of view of organisations. A small body of literature is dedicated to attraction of job seekers to organizations from applicants' perspective, focusing on individual decision–making and attitudes (Ehrhart and Ziegert, 2005). Also relatively little is known about companies with the GPTW award in the tourism sector, so there is a lack of academic research on the topic. It represents a gap in literature; therefore the author attempts to investigate the importance of the GPTW award and its interrelations with EB and decision–making of job seekers.

Therefore the aim of this study is to understand the importance of the GPTW award for companies in the tourism industry and to investigate its role in the job application and job choice decisions of individuals, paying special attention to the German–speaking countries.

2 THEORETICAL BACKGROUND

This part of the research paper lays the foundation by discussing the notions of EB, employer brand image and employer attractiveness. Also the institute and the award GPTW, with the examples of the best employers in the tourism industry, are closely examined. Then, the earlier research about job decision making is covered linking job application and job choice decisions and attraction.

2.1 Understanding employer branding

It is generally recognized that intellectual and human capital is the foundation of success, the source of competitive advantage and the tool of differentiating your organization from the others in the modern economy (Alnıaçık and Alnıaçık, 2012). Therefore, the contest among employers to attract and retain talented personnel takes place and it is a challenge for many organizations (Knox and Freeman, 2006). That is why, marketing principles, such as branding, were applied to HRM (Alnıaçık and Alnıaçık, 2012).

EB is a relatively young concept, but still has its origins in the 20th century (Rosethorn, 2009). The term *'employer brand'* was first introduced by Ambler and Barrow in the year 1996 (Barrow and Mosley, 2005, p.4), and they defined it as "the package of functional, economic and psychological benefits provided by employment, and identified with the employing company". EB is designed to create an image of a company that makes people want to work for this company (Sullivan, 1999 cited in Melin, 2005). It focuses on how the company is seen by current employees and job applicants and how the brand image is formed in their thoughts (Welsing, 2006). Suikkanen (2010) puts forward the view that EB practices use marketing tools and techniques in order organisations could become employers of choice and get the status of "great places to work" (ibid).

Today companies realize that business success depends on the employees in the company and their quality. That is why recruiting process is a crucial part of the HRM that has a function of attracting good personnel to the company. (Rynes and Cable, 2003). Companies nowadays should invest more in recruitment and applicant's attraction and compete to get the best people. Also, talented employees always have multiple job offers and organizations start to participate in the "war for talent" in order to get the best and highly qualified applicants. What is more, the demographic changes in the society, including the lack of young specialists, baby boomers and retirement of people, it would be not easy to find right people for the open positions in companies (Collins and Stevens, 2002). All these lead to the increasing significance and necessity in using EB nowadays. EB generates competitive advantage, helps employees to live the values of an organization, and, assists in creating a positive image of a company as a desirable and great place to work in the heads of current and potential employees (Dell and Ainspan, 2001). Thus, more and more organisations start to implement EB practices in their business activities. But what is important to take into consideration, is not only what a company is doing for it, but how it is done (Burchell and Robin, 2011). In other words, "employer branding focuses on winning the "hearts and minds" of staff" (ibid). So, the power of EB is in its ability to deliver organizational success by attracting and retaining employees, "providing an environment in which employees live the brand" (Fernon (2008, p.50 cited in Srivastava and Bhatnagar, 2010).

2.2 "The Great Place to Work" award

There are different approaches and channels how companies might bring their brand related messages to the public, for instance, traditional advertising, public relations activities, various kinds of publications. However, nowadays more and more popularity gain different surveys and awards, for example, "Best employer" survey conducted by the GPTW institution (Joo and McLean, 2006 cited in Love, 2011).

The GPTW is an organization that deals with human resources, consulting, advisory service and training, and helps to create and also identify and classify great workplaces around the world. The GPTW institution has different clients all around the globe; in the course of the year there could be around 5,500 companies with about 10 million employees. They are in different scopes of activities, various businesses and non-profit companies, governmental organizations in 45 countries of the world and all of them are ready to change and improve their workplaces, their culture and environment ("About Us", 2014).

The GPTW organization started with the book called "The 100 Best Companies to Work for in America" written by two journalists – Robert Levering and Milton Moskowitz. The book presents the core idea about to which extent trust is important and that building a high-quality relationships at the workplace, that are characterized by "trust, pride and camaraderie" is crucial to create a great workplace ("Our History", 2013). The role of trust is described as well in another book called "A Great Place to Work: What makes some employers so good – and most so bad". And after having written many books and articles about good and bad workplaces, in 1992 Robert Levering became a co-founder of GPTW Institution together with Amy Lyman. ("Why we do what we do", 2013).

The methodology of the GPTW Institute is tested and accepted by many business leaders and researchers in the world. The List of the Best Companies to Work For by the GPTW Institute present the recognition of a company as an employer-of-choice. Ratings and lists are a crucial part of the work of the institute. They collect all the data and research and it can be used further, as an example for other companies, some kind of a benchmark for the human resource management activities (Romero, 2004). What is more these lists create the reputation for the companies and make them recognized in the market ("FAQ", 2014). In order to be in the list a company should be first nominated for the Best Companies to Work For list. After this there is an application process where companies are chosen on the basis of the employees' response to the Trust Index Survey and Culture Audit done by managers. So, it surveys both employees and the management of the company to get a holistic view of each organization's HRM policies and practices and how these are perceived by the staff. All the gathered data is evaluated by the GPTW team. Companies who get the high number of points get the GPTW award and appear to be on the list, on the top are the companies with the higher score and it is formed in the descending order ("Best Place to Work Awards", 2014). Being recognized as one of the best workplaces has lots of advantages for companies. Many researchers suppose that implementing different HR practices in a company that would that support and improve the culture and lead to being one of the bests is a good investment (Joo and McLean, 2006 cited in Love, 2011). According to Joo and McLean (2006 cited in Love, 2011), Best Employer organizations tend to be more stable, offering something unique that makes them difficult to be imitated, and also provide a special and sustainable advantage in comparison with their competitors. Another positive outcomes of being a best employer include lower turnover rates (Douglas, 2007 cited in Love, 2011), the attractive employment brand of a company increases the number of applicants, employee's engagement is becoming higher that translates into better financial results for the company (ibid).

To sum up the author would like to point out that the GPTW institution evaluates the performance of a company from two perspectives – the employer's and the employees' and the awards by GPTW institution help organizations to transform and develop workplaces, to create great workplace environment and differentiate them from competitors. Moreover they create trust in an employer among clients and employees and make a company recognized on the market.

2.3 Job application and job choice decisions

Decisions play an important role in people's life because sometimes high costs are involved or it is a serious step in somebody's life or the outcome has far-reaching consequences, as, for example, job application and choice decisions (Verplanken and Svenson, 1997).

There exist plenty of job application decisions and organizational choice theories. These theories give the explanation of how decisions happen and what makes people to apply for a job and choose a job. Among the most widely used and known theories are the theory of reasoned action (TRA) (Fishbein and Ajzen's 1975, p.17), signaling theory (Barber, 1998; Rynes, 1991 cited in Ehrhart and Ziegert, 2009), Vroom's expectancy theory (Knox and Freeman 2006, p.701), image theory (Stevens, 1998 cited in Ehrhart and Ziegert, 2009), the generalizable decision processing model (Soelberg, 1967 cited in Ehrhart and Ziegert, 2009), objective factors theory (Behling, et al., 1968 cited in Harold and Ployhart, 2008), subjective factors theory (Behling, et al., 1968 cited in Harold and Ployhart, 2008). Many of these theories state that there is a positive effect of the reputation and image of a company on the applicant's attraction and decision making could be noticed. In addition to that different criteria, tangible and intangible attributes are usually important for applicants, for instance, location, size of a company, work policy, job fit, and many others.   All in all, the common focus of these theories involves how the processing of the available information about the company and job influences applicant's attraction to a company.

The author of this paper decides to adopt two theories for the current research: TRA and the signaling theory (Fig. 1. The role of GPTW in job decision-making process), explaining more detailed the connection between them.

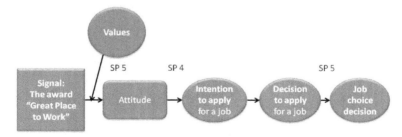

Fig. 1. The role of GPTW in job decision-making process (own creation).

The figure above shows how the two theories are combined. To put it in other words, one party is a sender – an organization. Another party is a receiver – a job seeker. An organization sends some information to a job seeker, some kind of a signal. And this signal is perceived and interpreted by the job seeker. (Holtbrügge and Kreppel, 2012). According to the signaling theory and the TRA, the GPTW award might be seen as a signal coming from a company that forms person's attitude. The attitude formation is effected by people's values that are formed by the society. The attitude depends a lot on what is important for a person when choosing a job. And the attitude affects the intention to apply for a job and the decision to apply and the final decision to choose a particular job.

Many authors emphasize the link between EB and psychology, examining different factors that may have the influence on company's attractiveness and how it is seen by potential employees (Corte et al., 2011). As the central aim of EB is creating a distinctive and superior image for the company so that it would attract jobseekers and current employees would not like to leave, psychology goes parallel, analyzing how exactly applicants choose an organization, which factors influence their decisions and why some companies seems more attractive for them than others. And the GPTW award, in its turn, could be a signal for a good image and reputation of a company that could possibly be an instrument of EB and would help to attract and retain employees.

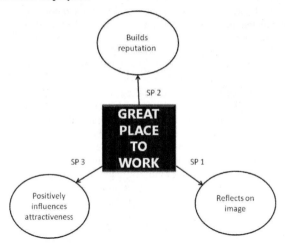

Fig. 2. Advantages of the GPTW award (own creation).

The image above (Fig. 2. Advantages of the GPTW award) shows how exactly the award GPTW could affect the organization, its image and reputation. The award GPTW reflects on the image of organization. It increases the media reception and awareness of people about this company. Also it makes the company more attractive and builds the good reputation.

The author has the main proposition for this research paper: The GPTW award could be used as an instrument of EB for attracting applicants and retaining employees. The main proposition includes the sub-propositions, which are the following:

SP 1: The presence of the award GPTW affects the image of a company as an employer in tourism and travel industry.

SP 2: The GPTW award builds a good reputation of a company as an employer in tourism and travel industry.

SP 3: The award GPTW makes a company in the tourism and travel industry more attractive as an employer.

SP 4: The presence of the award GPTW in a company is one of the key factors influencing the intention of job seekers to apply for a job.

SP 5: The signaling effects of the GPTW award positively influence the attitudes of job seekers and their job choice decision.

3 METHODOLOGY

As the main aim of this study is to provide a holistic picture of the state of the EB and the award GPTW in connection with job application and choice decisions, the author decides to apply a mixed methods approach.

The qualitative part of the research is represented by interviews with experts in the field of HR and EB and from the GPTW institution, as well as some representatives of the companies in the tourism industry, involving the discussion of topics of importance of the award for companies in tourism sector and employer branding, and how the award could be used to attract and retain employees. There were all in all 10 experts from Austria, Germany, Slovakia and Switzerland found. The interviews were held in April, May and June 2014 in Salzburg, Vienna and Bratislava. There were face-to-face interviews and the interviews conducted via Skype, each of them lasting from 15 up to 25. Interview plans have been established in order to ensure that the most important points are being covered. Each interview has been held in the English language and has been recorded by the author with a technical devise and also the most important issues have been written down, in order not to lose relevant information. All interview partners have been asked for permission to record the conversation, which was given by all.

In order to shed light on the subject matter from different points of views, in addition to the expert interviews, the author carried out a survey and a self completion questionnaire for employed and unemployed job seekers is developed. This questionnaire focuses on the key elements of decision making process in relation to job decisions and attractiveness factors that are important for the applicants when evaluating and choosing an employer in travel and tourism industry, taking into consideration the importance of the GPTW award for the job seekers. The questionnaire was offered to be filled online to people of different nationalities who are currently living and studying or working in Europe, mainly Germany and Austria. The sample is composed by 90 employed and unemployed job seekers, who are mainly students and graduates from Austrian and German Universities. All of them are more or less connected with the tourism industry, studying or working already in tourism related companies or considering working there. From the ninety returned responses 69 are used for data analysis.

4 RESULTS

Companies in German-speaking countries understand the necessity of using EB practices and there is a growing demand for it. However organizations in the tourism industry do not show a lot of interest in EB. Quite a similar situation is happening with the GPTW award. According to the experts, there are not a lot of companies in the German speaking countries which are trying to get the award and be certified as the best workplace. Although it is like this, the experts name plenty of benefits of the GPTW award for the organizations in the tourism and travel industry, such as applicant attraction, retention of the current employees, the positive influence on the image and the reputation of a company, pointing out the strengths and weaknesses, and easier recruiting through employee referrals.

The results of the questionnaire indicate that 3/4 of the participants from the German-speaking countries did not know about the GPTW award (Fig.3. Knowledge of the GPTW award).

Fig. 3. Knowledge of the GPTW award (own creation).

Even though the majority of the participants have not heard about the GPTW award and do not know exactly what this award is about, they have a positive image of it (Fig.4. Meaning of the GPTW award for people). They perceive companies with this award as employers with friendly work atmosphere, nice colleagues, working environment that supports the development of new ideas. Also participants suppose that in companies that are Great Workplaces have an opportunity to expand knowledge and skills, and good, fair salary. In addition to these, the GPTW is given to companies that have the image of a good employer, and have the good management, respecting their employees, and also providing various benefits and compensations.

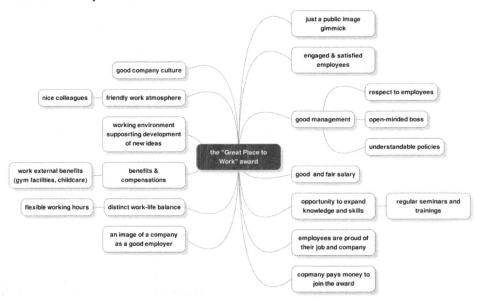

Fig. 4. Meaning of the GPTW award for people (own creation).

Concerning the decision making, the results of the survey show that the most important factors for the people when searching and applying for a job are the following:

- the interesting job (what is matching with the findings of the previous study by Posner (1981)),

- nice people and friendly atmosphere,

- good salary,

- career development opportunities.

The results indicate that the presence the GPTW award is the least important for the participants from the German speaking countries. Although it is like this, the majority of the individuals from the German–speaking countries perceive companies with the GPTW award as prestigious workplaces and would be proud to work for such a company (Fig.5. The perception of a company that is a great workplace by applicants from German-speaking countries).

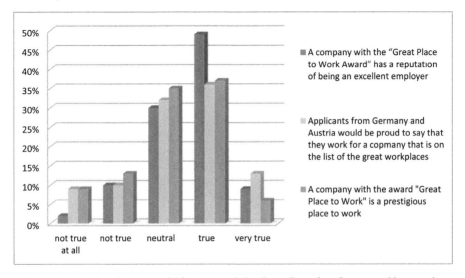

Fig. 5. The perception of a company that is a great workplace by applicants from German-speaking countries (own creation).

The results of the questionnaire differ from the opinions of the experts concerning the attractiveness issue. In general, it is supposed by the majority of the experts that there is a positive influence of the award GPTW on the applicants' attraction to a company, while the results of the survey indicate that the respondents do not consider it very important when applying for a job, and it would not make a company much more attractive. The author supposes that it could be due to the fact that 3/4 of all the participants form German speaking countries have not enough knowledge of the award GPTW, that is why they could not be completely honest and their answers cannot be considered fully accurate.

Moreover, the participants stated that they would choose a job in a company that is a Great Workplace (Fig.6. Applicants from Germany and Austria choose a job in a company that is a great workplace) and would accept a job offer from such a company (Fig.7. Applicants from Germany and Austria would accept a job offer from a company that is a great workplace).

Fig. 6. Applicants from Germany and Austria choose a job in a company
that is a great workplace (own creation).

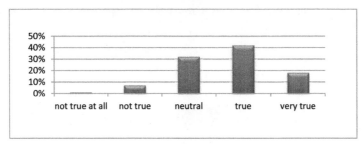

Fig. 7. Applicants from Germany and Austria would accept a job offer from a company
that is a great workplace (own creation).

All in all the findings of the expert interviews and the survey provide the author with important information about the importance of the GPTW award, the perception of the GPTW award among the applicants from the German-speaking countries and its role in the job related decision making process.

5 LIMITATIONS AND CONTRIBUTION

This paper has important theoretical and empirical implications. The author found out that in the EB, marketing and HRM literature little attention is paid to the GPTW institution and award, whereas from the research it is clear that this award is becoming more important nowadays and has a lot of advantages for companies. In addition to that, in the psychology literature about the decision making process there is not much known about the influence of such employer awards on job application and job choice decisions of individuals. That is why the contribution of this master thesis has been to clarify what is the essence of the GPTW award and its main activities. Moreover, this paper increases the awareness of job seekers about the existence of such an award and what exactly it is about. Besides, this master thesis provides the evidence of how the award GPTW is perceived by the job seekers and how it could influence their job application and job choice decisions.

The author of this master thesis would like to confess that this study is not without limitations. A weakness of this study is a not very high response rate to the online questionnaire. It means that the results could not be generalized. Thus future studies could reach higher validity by involving more participants. Moreover, many companies in the tourism sector refused to participate in the research and give expert interviews due to different reasons, for example, due to the lack of time, the company policy, or due to unwillingness to give any information,. It could be another limitation, because if the author had got more answers from the experts in the tourism industry, the results would have been clearer. What could also be mentioned is bias that experts have. The author supposes that experts from the GPTW and EB areas might be a bit subjective to the topic of the award GPTW, as they are working with it and are interested in its' success. That is why the answers which the experts gave during the interviews could have been affected by the bias and thus might be inaccurate.

A number of opportunities for the further research could be identified. First, as the gathered data shows, the award GPTW is not well–known and recognized by job seekers in Germany and Austria. That is why it would be appropriate to concentrate on the study about the GPTW award and its promotion and recognition among job seekers. It would also be useful to conduct the research of the GPTW with a more detailed study of its connection with the HRM, how this award could be applied by organizations during the recruitment process, for instance. Another suggestion for the further research could be to carry out a comparative study about the GPTW in the European context.

As a final point, the author would like to mention that although there are some limitations of this study, the author tried to minimize them. On the whole, this paper contributes to the understanding of the GPTW award as a possible instrument of EB in the process of individuals' job application and job choice decisions.

6 CONCLUSION

The research has determined the importance of the GPTW award for companies in the tourism industry and its role in the job application and job choice decisions of applicants from the German-speaking countries. The results demonstrated that there is a positive impression about the GPTW award itself among the respondents and they perceive companies with this award as employers with good reputation and would choose a job in such a company. It means that

- *The presence of this award in a company has a positive influence on company's image and reputation.*
- *GPTW award could be a signal that affects the attitudes of job seekers and their job application and job choice decisions.*
- *GPTW award might be used as one of the instrument of EB. It would help to build company's reputation as an employer of choice and create a strong employer brand.*

In general, it may be stated that the research has answered all research questions, has thrown more light on every proposition and explained them and also implemented its main aim of investigating the importance of the GPTW award for companies in the tourism and travel industry and its role in the job application and job choice decisions of individuals from the German speaking countries.

REFERENCES

Alniaçik, E. and Alniaçik, U., 2012. Identifying dimensions of attractiveness in employer branding: effects of age, gender, and current employment status. *Procedia – Social and Behavioral Sciences*, 58, pp. 1336-1343.

Barrow, S. and Mosley, R., 2005. *The Employer Brand. Bringing the Best of Brand Management to People at Work.* England: John Wiley & Sons Ltd.

Best Place to Work Awards, 2014. *Identifying best places to work: US and globally.* [online] Available at <http://www.greatplacetowork.com/best-companies> [Accessed 03 March 2014].

Burchell, M. and Robin, J., 2011. Introduction: The Value of Creating Great Workplaces. In: Burchell, M. and Robin, J., 2011. *The Great Workplace: How to Build It, How to Keep It, and Why It Matters.* San Francisco, CA: Jossey-Bass, pp. 1-26

Breaugh, J.A. and Starke, M., 2000. Research on employee recruitment: So many studies, so many remaining questions. *Journal of Management*, 26, pp.405-434.

Collins, C.J. and Stevens, C.K., 2002. The Relationship Between Early Recruitment-Related Activities and the Application Decision of New Labor-Market Entrants: A Brand Equity Approach to Recruitment. *Journal of Applied Psychology*, 87(6), pp.1121-1133.

Corte, V.D., Mangia, G., Micera, R., Zamparelli, G., 2011. Strategic employer branding: the brand and image management as attractiveness for talented capital. *China-USA Business Review*, 10 (12), pp.928-949.

Ehrhart, K.H. and Ziegert, J.C., 2009. Why are individuals Attracted to Organizations? *Journal of Management*, 31 (6), pp. 901-919.

FAQ (2014). *Quick links to frequently asked questions.* [online] Available at <http://www.greatplacetowork.net/our-approach/faq#Global_List> [Accessed 03 March 2014].

Fishbein, M. and Ajzen, I., 1975. *Belief, attitude, intention and behavior: An introduction to Theory and Research.* [e-book] MA: Addison-Wesley. Available through <http://people.umass.edu/aizen/f&a1975.html> [Accessed 18 April 2014].

Grünewälder, A., 2007. *Employer Branding. Marketing the company as an attractive employer.* Seminar paper, Germany. Munich: GRIN Publishing GmbH.

Harold, C.M., and Ployhart, R.E., 2008. What do applicants want? Examining changes in attribute judgments over time. *Journal of Occupational and Organizational Psychology*, 81, pp.191–218.

Holtbrügge and Kreppel, 2012. *Employer attractiveness of Chinese, Indian, and Russian firms in Germany. Signaling effects of HR practices.* LASER.

Keller, K. L., 1998. Conceptualizing, measuring, and managing customer-based equity. *Journal of Marketing*, 57(1), pp. 1–22.

Knox, S. and Freeman, C., 2006. Measuring and managing employer brand image in the service industry. *Journal of Marketing Management*, 22, pp. 695-716.

Leung, S.A., 2008. *Chapter Six. The Big Five Career Theories.* Netherlands: Springer, pp.115-132.

Levering, R., 2011. *A great place to work. What Makes Some Employers So Good (and Most So Bad).* [online] Available at <http://www.greatplacetowork.com/storage/documents/Publications_Documents/Preface_to_A_ Great_Place_to_Work.pdf> [Accessed 1 November 2013].

Love, L.F., 2011. Workplace branding: leveraging human resources management practices for competitive advantage through ''Best Employer'' surveys. *Journal of Business Psychology,* 26, pp. 175-181.

Melin, E., 2005. *Employer branding. Likeness and differences between external and internal employer brand images.* Master Thesis, Luleå University of Technology.

Nickson, D., 2007. *Human resource management for the hospitality and tourism industries.* UK: Elsevier.

Our history, 2014. *A quarter-century legacy.* [online] Available at <http://www.greatplacetowork.com/about-us/our-company/our-history> [Accessed 19 October 2013].

Romero, E.J., 2004. *Are the great places to work also great performers?* Academy of Management Executive, pp.150-152.

Rosethorn, H., 2009. Origins – Two Roots to the Family tree. In: ROSETHORN, H., ed. *The employer brand. Keeping faith with the deal*. England: Gower Publishing Limited, pp. 3-16.

Rynes, S.L., 1989. *Recruitment, Job Choice and Post-Hire Consequences: A Call for New Research Directions*. Working paper. New York.

Rynes, S.L. and Cable, D.M., 2003. Recruitment Research in the Twenty-First Century. In: Weiner, I.B. et.al. eds. *Handbook of Psychology*. New Jersey: John Wiley & Sons, pp. 55-73.

Schoenfelder, E. T. and Hantula, D.A., 2003. A job with a future? Delay discounting, magnitude effects, and domain independence of utility for career decisions. *Journal of Vocational Behaviour*, 62, pp.43-55.

Suikkanen, E., 2010. *How does employer branding increase employee retention*. Dissertation (BA), University of Lincoln, UK.

Srivastava, P. and Bhatnagar, J., 2010. Employer brand for talent acquisition: an exploration towards its measurement. *The Journal of Business Perspective*, 14 (1), pp.25-34.

Turban, D.B. and Greening, D.W., 1996. Corporate social performance and organizational attractiveness to prospective employees. *Academy of Management Journal*, 40 (3), pp. 658-672.

Verplanken, B. and Svenson, O. (1997). Personal Involvement in human decision making. Conceptualizations and effects on decision processes. In: Ranyard, R. and Crozier, W.R. eds. *Decision Making. Cognitive Models and explanations*. GB: Intype London Ltd., pp. 40-54.

Welsing, C., 2006. *HR Marketing: a new perspective on Human Resource Management*. Pearson Education Benelux.

Why we do what we do, 2014. *A Letter From Co-founder Robert Levering*. [online] Available at <http://www.greatplacetowork.com/about-us/why-we-do-what-we-do> [Accessed 18 October 2013].

World Tourism Organisation, 2013. Annual report 2013. UNWTO, Madrid.

The Glass Ceiling in the Hotel Industry

Marta Ortega Martínez

Universidad Rey Juan Carlos Madrid, Spain
marta.ortega.mtnz@gmail.com

Abstract

The 'glass ceiling' refers to the limitations that many women encounter to climb up the career ladder in different working circumstances or sectors. The aim of this paper is to study women's role in executive positions in the Spanish hotel industry and the impact that 'glass ceiling' has for women's careers in this sector. The lack of literature on the topic will also be shown. Quantitative research techniques have been used for gathering specific data through an on-line survey sent to three, four and five star hotels of the Autonomous Community of Madrid. A descriptive statistical analysis was used to obtain women's percentage by department in the hotels under scope. Among the main results, senior positions of departments like Housekeeping, Human Resources Management and Events are highly represented by women, whereas male prevail at executive post of departments such as General Management, Reception, Maintenance, Food & Beverage and Chef. Nevertheless, other departments like Finance and Administration show some change towards some preconceived patterns. Such tendency is better perceived in the Sales & Marketing Department.

Keywords: 'Glass Ceiling'; Tourism; Employment; Gender and Equity

1 INTRODUCTION

1.1 Reason for the Research

The world's economic data show the relevance the tourism sector has for the economies of most countries' economies. Due to tourism being the biggest industry in the world, it employs the highest number of human resources (Almeida & Antón, 2011). Nevertheless, such industry also implies negative aspects for the people employed, especially women (Faulkenberry, Coggeshall, Backman, & Backman, 2000).

The total contribution of Travel & Tourism to the GDP in 2011 reached 159.9 billion Euros, which corresponds to the 14.9% of the total GDP (World Travel & Tourism Council, 2012). In correlation, Travel & Tourism total contribution to employment was 12.7% of total employment, things equal, 2,304,500 jobs. Consequently, we could say that tourism provides relevant opportunities for both women and men. However, in order to build strong, stable and fair societies women should be empowered to participate at all levels of the economic development (UNWTO and UN Women, 2010).

Tourism is the most important sector in the Spanish economy. In 2012 these results have been 222.6 billion dollars in terms of the Travel & Tourism's total contribution to the GDP, which is a 14.9% share, and 488.4 jobs regarding the Travel & Tourism's total contribution to employment, which reflects a 12.7% share (World Travel & Tourism Council, 2012). In 2011, the 54% of the people in work within the tourism sector was male, whilst the 46% corresponded to women. Consequently, it is believed that male prevail in the tourism sector. However, when compared to the total economy, male positions represented the 55.2%, whereas in regards to the service sector they reached the 46.3% (IET, 2012).

The problem lies on the rift of women percentage in this sector which, although being diminished during the last few years, has suffered an increase as a result of the financial crisis that hit this sector in 2009. Likewise, the men percentage in the sector grew (0.4%), whilst the women percentage decreased a 2.5% (-4.3% in 2009). On the one hand, employed workers and people in work within the tourism sector, 53.8% and 54.9%, correspondingly, were predominately male in 2013, compared to the 46.2% and 45.1% represented by women. On the other hand, the number of unemployed women, 50.7%, was higher than men, 49.3% (IET, 2014).

The analysis carried out by the CCOO shows the following trend: as self-employment and management levels increase, woman's presence is slightly inferior: at a higher post and level of command, a higher masculinisation takes place. As a result, Spanish hotel industry management positions are solely occupied by women on the 32.65% of the cases, whose current position is determined by the 'glass ceiling', which limits their access to executive posts in this sector (CCOO, 2008).

The 'glass ceiling' is defined as: "the unseen, yet unreachable barrier that keeps minorities and women from rising to the upper rungs of the corporate ladder, regardless of their qualifications or achievements" (Glass Ceiling Commission, 1995, p. 4). Investigation towards the 'glass ceiling' is wide, although it is internationally limited in the tourism sector and almost non-existent in the case of Spain. This fact contrasts with the importance the tourism sector has for the Spanish economy (Segovia-Pérez, 2014).

In addition, compared with other sectors, it presents a higher tendency to gender stereotyping in specific labour posts. Furthermore, the Spanish hotel industry is the one with the lowest level of wages for women. In contrast, the need for innovation is essential in an increasingly competitive environment, where women can become an incentive for change. However, women's arrival to these executive posts is needed beforehand in order to make relevant decisions. Women's presence in the Spanish tourism sector is thereby essential. Despite this, it is in the executive posts where the problem appears, as it happens in other economic sectors. Women hardly go through the 'glass ceiling', as it is shown by its 10% of presence in executive positions. Vazquez (2008) highlights how previous investigations confirm the improvement of an enterprise's smooth running and profitability when the enterprise's 'Management and Administrative Board' is formed by both men and women, being diversity, creativity and company innovation among the improvement factors. The World Tourism Organization (UNWTO) is fully aware of this circumstance, as well as the positive consequences women have for the society and economy development. Consequently, one of its paramount objectives for the year 2015 is the abolition of gender inequality in tourism (UNWTO and UN Women, 2010).

For this reason, woman's situation in the tourism sector and an analysis of the factors which lead to the term coined as 'glass ceiling' in women executive posts need to be studied.

1.2 Objectives of the research

1.2.1 General Objective

The aim of this paper is to study women's role in executive posts in the Spanish hotel industry.

1.2.1 Specific Objectives

1. Define the term coined as 'glass ceiling'.
2. Prove the lack of tourism and 'glass ceiling' studies, especially in Spain, through the analysis of the literature.
3. Identify women's importance in executive posts, by women percentage, in three, four and five star hotels of the Autonomous Community of Madrid.

2 THEORETICAL BACKGROUND

For more than fifty years, women's rights have been on the daily's agenda of global development and international policies. In 1946, the CSW (Commission on the Status of Women) was created with the aim of preparing a single, comprehensive and international binding instrument to eliminate discrimination against women. However, in 1948, years before this binding instrument was established, the Universal Declaration of Human Rights took place, where the law entitlement to equality and enjoyment of human rights and fundamental freedoms was proclaimed: "without distinction of any kind, such as race, colour, sex, language, religion, political or other opinion, national or social origin, property, birth or other status" (United Nations, 1948, p. Art II). It was in 1979 when the Convention for the Elimination of all forms of Discrimination Against Women (CEDAW), was finally established (UNWTO and UN Women, 2010).

Gender equality has become a key issue in the UN Millennium Development Goals to 2015, where five of the eight goals are directly related to the women's role, assuming that gender equality and women's empowerment shape the basis for the achievement of the goals proposed (United Nations, 2000). According to UNIFEM (UN Development Fund for Women), 'gender' refers to "the array of socially constructed roles and relationships, personality traits, attitudes, behaviours, values, relative power and influence that society ascribes to the two sexes on a differential basis. Whereas biological sex is determined by genetic and anatomical characteristics, gender is an acquired identity that is learned, changes over time, and varies widely within and across cultures" (UNIFEM, 2010, p. 9).

A 'gender analysis' consists of systematically examine the different impact that "development, policies, programmes and legislation" have on women and men. It implies collecting "sex-disaggregated data and gender-sensitive information" regarding the population studied. 'Gender equality' is the freedom all human beings, both women and men, have "to develop their personal abilities and make choices without the limitations set by stereotypes, rigid gender roles, or prejudices", whilst 'gender equity' is the fairly treatment to men and women depending on their respective needs, considered equivalent "in terms of right benefit, obligation and opportunities" (UNIFEM, 2010, p. 9).

Another important definition is 'empowerment', explained as the capacity both women and men have for taking control over their own lives, by means of increasing their self-confidence, problem-soulution skills and the development of a feeling of self-reliance (UNWTO and UN Women, 2010). Last but not least, the term 'gender mainstreaming' should be closely looked at, understood as the assessing process of the array of implications any action planned, legislation, policy or programmes at any level might entail for women and men (UNIFEM, 2010). As a result, both women and men's concern and experiences must reflect an integral dimension in regards to the design, implementation, monitoring and evaluation of policy and programmes of any strategy to be taken whether in a political, economic, or social framework, in order to eliminate the inequality between women and men.

The term 'glass ceiling' was firstly coined by Gay Bryant, editor of Working Women, during an interview for a 1984 Adweek article (The Glass Ceiling & Gender Diversity Today, 2009) where she spotted: "Women have reached a certain point -- I call it the glass ceiling. They're in the top of middle management and they're stopping and getting stuck. There isn't enough room for all those women at the top. Some are going into business for themselves. Others are going out and raising families" (Frenkiel, 1984). This concept was also documented in the book written by the editors of Women Magazine: "the door to real power for women has opened. But it is just ajar. Women may already be in middle management, but the steps from there up to the senior hierarchy are likely to be slow and painstakingly small. Partly because corporations are structured as pyramids, with many middle managers trying to move up into the few available spots, and partly because of continuing, though more subtle, discrimination, a lot of women are hitting a 'glass ceiling' and finding they can rise no further" (Bryant, 1984, p. 19). Afterwards, this term appeared in a Wall Street Journal article, which talked about the barriers women were confronting at high levels of corporate power, which was widely read and popularized the 'glass ceiling' term, becoming part of the American lexicon (Schellhardt, 1986).

Consequently, the Department of Labour issued in 1991 a definition of it, stating that 'glass ceiling' is made up of "artificial barriers based on attitudinal or organizational bias that prevent qualified individuals from advancing upward in their organization into management-level positions" (Title II Civil Rights Act , 1991, p. 1). In that same year, the Federal Glass Ceiling Commission was established to gather information and study opportunities and barriers for women and minorities advancement in terms of management and decision-making positions, at the same time as issuing reports on the finding and conclusions, whilst making recommendations for the elimination of the 'glass ceiling' (Glass Ceiling Commission, 1995). Therefore, the following definition for the 'glass ceiling' concept was established: "It is the unseen, yet unreachable barrier that keeps minorities and women from rising to the upper rungs of the corporate ladder, regardless of their qualifications or achievements" (Glass Ceiling Commission, 1995, p. 4).

Whilst 'glass ceiling' can be metaphorical understood, the reality is that many women in their working places find this situation a reality. Taking a look to the meaning of 'ceiling', when it comes to ascending the corporate ladder, there is an implication of the existance of a limit that cannot be climbed. Along with this lies the implication of such barrier being a 'glass', expressing the idea that although it might be transparent or irrelevant to an observer, it is very real (Wallace, 2003).

Despite the different definitions proposed, the same pattern can be followed: the invisible barrier which prevents women from climbing up the career ladder.

The first written reference to gender in tourism appears in the 90s with the publication of three articles related to this topic (Ramos, Rey-Maquieira, & Tugores, 2002): Kinnardy and Hall (1994), a special volume of Annals of Tourism Research (1995) and Sinclair (1997). They set the conceptual framework for the analysis of gender issues in the tourism sector. In addition, some case studies on the effects of tourism development were presented. Despite the relevance tourism has in terms of development and job opportunities, there is a lack of literature analyzing its social effects, and especially the gender related ones. The educational parity and the change society's attitude experienced towards women and men roles during the last decades has lead to the presumption of women having access to the highest levels of management. However, that women would quickly climb up the career ladder has proved to be harder than expected, especially at the top, where male executives tend to perpetuate the 'glass ceiling' (Wirth, 2001). Such concentration of men at top professions, like supervisor, manager, executive, production supervisors and related posts, whilst women are usually over-represented in the lowest status paid professions like teachers, secretaries, nurses and childcare providers, is understood as 'sector segregation'.

In addition, within a given profession, women are predominant in the lower-ranked and lower-paid occupations (EQUAL, 2008). The difference between male and female earnings is regarded as 'gender pay gap' (Muñoz-Bullón, 2009). Women use to earn between 10 to 15% less than their male counterparts (World Tourism Organization UNWTO, 2011). Economists have realized that pay gaps get widen towards the top of the wage distribution, the already know 'glass ceiling' effect. According to Muñoz-Bullón (2009), the reason for differences in earnings between men and women relies on the 'occupational segregation', the concentration of low wages in some industries and the human capital theory. There is a clear correlation between qualification and wages. The qualification level required for the job is indeed a very important factor. The employment gender gap stands at 14.2% in the European Union, where both sector and occupational segregation continue to be the ultimate obstacles for the equal treatment accomplishment of women and men in employment and pay.

As pointed out by Muñoz-Bullón (2009), previous studies have proved to suggest women's 'horizontal and vertical employment segregation' as evident, reflected by the majority of female workers employed in subordinate posts and receiving lower levels of remuneration. The hotel industry is better characterized by horizontal segregation than vertical segregation. Occupational segregation increases as the size of the establishment grows, whilst decreases with the level of education. Therefore, occupational segregation is less common among workers with training contracts, whereas it is higher among part-time and seasonal workers (Campos-Soria, Marchante-Mera, & Ropero-García, 2011).

'Vertical segregation' is not only related to senior management. Many times the 'glass ceiling' is even predominant in the early stages of women careers, blocking their promotion by preconceptions and gender bias in recruiting processes. This situation appears frequently in those stages in where companies do not usually employ a mixed pool of management trainees. Besides, the posts below senior management are mostly in close relationship to the core production of the company, hardly accessible to women. This results in a lack of networking and credibility in this level of management, which triggers the circumstances of those traditional male sectors. Consequently, the development of women's leadership and the promotion of networks are of utmost importance (Glass Ceiling Commission, 1995).

Overcoming gender segregation in economic sectors and ocupations would valuably contribute to the diversification and improvement of the European working force skills, through "invest in knowledge to ensure the dynamism and vigour of the whole European economy" (EQUAL, 2008, p. 4). In this line, once this knowledge, based on human capital, research, education and innovation policies is realized by society, the potential growth will be boosted at the same time as the future preparation promoted. Concern towards traditional career choices and educating and training approaches has thereby risen, by emphasising female career ambitions from an early age, and encouraging their expectations of becoming senior managers. Nevertheless, this is also a consequence of the traditional gender stereotyped pattern which exists when it comes to study choices, which should be address at an early age by eliminating the prejudices and biases conceived towards a profession (EQUAL, 2008).

The benefits which would result from demolishing the barriers women encounter in the workforce would boost the Eurozone's Gross Domestic Product by at least 13% (R. Hausmann; L. D. Tyson; S. Zahidi, 2011). The positive correlation between gender diversity in top leadership managements and the company's financial results is an important economic motivation. Consequently, the pool of skill and talented women, which have lately been overlooked, taking part of the board members at larger numbers of companies, would have both social and financial benefits. In this way, the Federal Glass Ceiling Commision studied that "businesses committed to promoting women workers had an average annualized return on investment of 18.3 percent over a five-year period, in comparison with only 7.9 percent for those with the most shatter-proof glass ceilings" (Glass Ceiling Commission, 1995, p. 5). Companies with the highest proportion of women in senior management significantly outperformed others with the lowest proportion in both return on equity and total shareholder return. However, women face a very difficult situation.

Frequently they have to face the uncomfortable decision of following their career ambitions or forming a family. This is a very important step many women are forced to take. How to combine being ambitious at the same time as taking care of the family? Why this reflection is not share by men? Difficulty increases when due to their family tasks women are unable to attend training courses which would enable them to advance to senior roles. While many women regard the 'glass ceiling' as a real barrier to accessing male-dominated positions in business, there are others who claim that the existence of the 'glass ceiling' is a result of women's preference to focus more on family, eventually being unable to devote 100% to their careers. The current working force is not ready for the need of modern family, where both parents work and few working hours' flexibility is offered by senior positions. In contrast, women are the ones predominantly requiring flexibility for childcare which goes in detriment to their careers (The Guardian, 2011).

Besides, maternity leaves have decreased as a result of the economic situation. In this context, women are many times passed over for senior jobs, reinforcing the 'glass ceiling'. Nonetheless, women have to constantly demonstrate their value and abilities for a senior leadership position, with no feeling of entitlement to the company. Why do women with the same or better qualifications than men have to prove themselves and the rest to be better for a post that their male counterparts? Women's achievements are frequently underestimated and the effort, ability, skill or working time is often ignored (Wirth, 2001).

Women need individual empowerment in order to enter a male predominating sector or business. The European Employment Strategy, "encourages Member States to implement employment policies aiming at achieving full employment, improving quality and productivity at work, and strengthening social and territorial cohesion" (EQUAL, 2008, p. 3). Consequently, Norway, United Kingdom and Spain introduced different gender policies. Companies meeting this quota by 2015 would be compensated with priority status in the allocation of government contracts. Although there were no formal sanctions planned to apply, women proportion rose from 6.2% in 2006 to 11.2% at the beginning of 2011 (Abersoch, 2011).

Spain passed a gender equality law in 2007 by which public companies and IBEX 35 - quoted companies with more than 250 employees - were obliged to achieve a minimum of 40% share of each sex on the boardrooms within eight years (Abersoch, 2011). The Spanish Organic Law 3/2007, for the effective equality of women and men states: "Women and men are equal in human dignity and equal in rights and liabilities" (p. 12613). By this law, it is pretended to make effective the right to equal treatment and opportunities between women and men, especially through the elimination of women discrimination, whatever her circumstances or conditions might be, in whichever working atmospheres and particularly in the politic, civil, labour, economic, social and cultural aspects, in order to achieve a more democratic, fair and solidarity society. Among the aim of this law lies the inclusion of women in the board of directors of mercantile societies in order to achieve an equal representation of women and men by 2015 (BOE, 2007).

Despite the records obtained in the different countries, the financial situation has currently become a challenge in the promotion of gender and the composition of boards basically on legality. Nowadays, the highest echelons of businesses require an effective leadership and direction formed by the best and most talented candidates, whether male or female (Abersoch, 2011).

As regards to the tourism sector, women are generally well represented in formal tourism employment. Nevertheless, their average wage is lower than men as a result of being more likely to perform clerical level jobs and less likely than men to reach a professional-level tourism employment (UNWTO and UN Women, 2010). Around 50% of the total wage gap is the result of the contract held, the level of qualification and the area of employment (Muñoz-Bullón, 2009). Furthermore, the tourism sector still fosters the perceived image of those female posts like chambermaids and waiters, among others, which contribute to support those jobs as an extension of their home activities (Almeida & Antón, 2011). These jobs are mainly occupied by women whose remuneration is below other jobs of the same category, which would explain why despite the importance of women in the tourism industry their presence and work is sometimes not noticeable, overall in executive posts (Bolles, 1997). Although women occupy managerial positions in the tourism industry, these post are still gender segregated (Skalpe, 2007).

3 METHODOLOGY

Taking into account the three objectives identified, in order to answer the first and second objectives, correspondingly, define 'glass ceiling' and prove the lack of tourism and 'glass ceiling' studies, especially in Spain, an analysis of the existing literature was carried out. For this purpose, SCOPUS, the largest abstract and citation database of peer-reviewed research literature (ELSEVIER, 2015) served as a relevant searching tool for the literature review.

In order to identify women's importance in executive posts of three, four and five star hotels in the Autonomous Community of Madrid, the third objective, a quantitative statistical analysis has been elaborated. The technique employed in this quantitative research was the survey, by means of its tool, the questionnaire. For this reason, a census of the three, four and five star hotels of the Autonomous Community of Madrid has been undertaken.

As a result, this empirical analysis relies on the results of an on-line survey sent to all 'Hotel Managers' and 'Head of the Human Resources Management Departments' of the 236 hotel within the three, four and five star hotels range. In order to obtain a probability sample, the survey was sent to the 'universe'.

Such survey was organized in four blocks, the third of them being formed by four other parts, following the 'funnel theory'. It was in this third block where data from three, four and five star hotels was requested in terms of women's number employed in executive posts. This block itself was also divided into four other parts depending on different working areas (Management and Housekeeping; Marketing, Finance and Human Resources; Food & Beverage; Quality, ITCs and other Services) (Gonzalez & Talón, 1999). However, because of the diverse organization of the hotels within the Autonomous Community of Madrid, the composition of the working force had to be closely regarded. Consequently, not every hotel would have all the posts that were presented in the survey.

Due to the low rate of response to the survey, a follow-up was required, which enabled the response rate to considerably increase, allowing a sample of 64 hotels to be gathered. Because not all hotels managed to answer the survey, the response rate achieved the 27.83% of the population at the time the statistical data for the sample was done. Despite the rate being lower than 50%, the results obtained were considered a fair representation of the hotels of Madrid because all types of hotel and properties were included. Besides, these results were confirmed in the second part of the study (not shown in this paper), which allowed to obtain a higher responsive rate. Due to the results being in coherence with the ones presented herein, we considered the results presented at this first phase to be applicable.

The statistical data for the sample was divided into two sections depending on the category of the hotels, whether five, four or three star hotels, and on the type of hotel property, whether hotel chain or independent hotel. The reasons for this division rely, on the one side, on the difference among hotels of different category and property, and on the other side, on the easier analysis and description data approach, which shaped the Table presented below.

Table 1. Response by Hotel Category and Hotel Property

Number of Stars	Universe	Sample	%
5*	23	7	30.43
4*	124	39	34.45
3*	83	18	21.69
Total	230	64	

Hotel Property	Sample	%
Hotel Chain	44	68.75
Independent Hotel	20	31.25
Total	64	

The statistic descriptive analysis was analysed by means of the processing programme Excel 1997-2003, which allowed the study of the mean, percentiles, the mean absolute deviation, the population variance and the population standard deviation.

4 RESULTS

4.1 Total employees and women percentage

Taking a glance to the type of hotel category, we encounter different results depending on the number of stars when it comes to hotel size, total employees and women employees. As shown in Table 4.1., there is a remarkable difference between the number of women employed at independent hotels compared to hotel chains, which may be an indicator of the tendency to employ more women in independent hotel companies, whilst in the bigger ones the presence of the 'glass ceiling' might be higher.

Table 2. Total employees and women percentage

	Number of Rooms	Permanent Employees	Women Employees	% Women
5* Hotels	237	163.57	72.25	44.19%
4* Hotels	195	66.04	30.03	45.46%
3* Hotels	71	14.39	8.89	61.78%
Hotel Chain	187	67.42	30.00	44.46%
Independent Hotel	161	50.65	25.9	51.14%

According to the data, the 21% of executive post hold by women belongs to three star hotels, the 31% to four star hotels, while the rest correspond to five star hotels, which counts for the 48%. In the meantime, when the type of property is analysed, it could be stated that the 41% of the executive posts hold by women corresponds to hotel chains, while the 59% belongs to independent hotels.

4.2 Women percentage per department

Although the results obtained might give the impression of a very comfortable situation for women in the hotel sector, an analysis of the composition of management hotel posts must be described. Despite all hotel departments being under the scope of study, only the ones with meaningful results are hereby presented.

The General Manager position in five star hotels is only occupied by women in the 25.57% of the cases. However, as the hotel size decreases, there is a higher women representation. Despite this, independent hotels tend to have a higher number of female General Mangers than hotel chains. From the category point of view, the same tendency can be applied to the Assistance Management position. It is remarkable that all the three star hotels which have this position are held by women. Nevertheless, hotel chains employ more women in this position that independent hotels.

As shown in Table 4.2., the same pattern abovementioned do characterise the Reception Manager: women's percentage increases at the same time as hotel category decreases. On the contrary, Executive Housekeeping, one of the traditional female departments, women still prevail all executive posts. Despite this, there is also evidence of male Assistant Housekeepers in five star hotels from hotel chains. In contrast, the opposite happens in the Maintenance department where data shows the scarce number of women in senior roles. This position is held by women in very few cases within four star hotels belonging to independent hotels.

Table 3. Women Percentage by Hotel Department

Departments	% 5 * Hotels	% 4 * Hotels	% 3 * Hotels	% Hotel Chains	% Independent Hotels
General Manager	25.57%	32.43%	68.75%	38.10%	50.00%
Assistant Manager	25.00%	41.67%	100.00%	66.67%	25.00%
Reception Manager	28.57% %	34.29%	58.33%	42.11%	31.25%
Executive Housekeeping	100.00%	100.00%	100.00%	100.00%	100.00%
Assistant Housekeeper	83.33%	100.00%	NA	90.91%	100.00%
Maintenance Responsible	0.00%	3.23%	0.00%	0.00%	7.69%
Finance Manager	66.67%	46.15%	66.67%	69.23%	50.00%
Revenue Manager	60.00%	54.55%	50.00%	57.14%	50.00%
Sales & Marketing Manager	80.00%	63.64%	66.67%	69.23%	66.67%
Human Resources Manager	83.33%	60.00%	100.00%	76.92%	50.00%
Administration Manager	25.00%	71.79%	77.78%	61.29%	70.00%
FB Manager	33.33%	14.29%	0.00%	33.33%	0.00%
Chef	0.00%	3.57%	66.67%	7.41%	10.00%
Quality Responsible	66.67%	7.69%	NA	100.00%	0.00%
Events Manager	66.67%	83.33%	100.00%	92.31%	50.00%

Women's presence in financial positions is relatively higher in five star and three star hotels, as well as hotel chains, compared to four star hotels and independent ones. Notwithstanding, the Revenue Manager position would be fairly distributed between male and its female counterparts.

Nonetheless, the Sales and Marketing department is predominately occupied by women, especially in five star hotels. The same remains true for the Human Resources Management department, highly characterized by a strong women's presence. Interest is driven towards the Administration Manager's role in four and three star hotels, in comparison to five star hotels, which reflect a considerable lower percentage. This position tends to be commonly occupied by women both in hotel chains and independent hotels.

Vertical segregation is conceived as higher in restaurant or restaurant related activities. Food & Beverage Managers' male figure tends to be higher. The same tendency remains true for Chefs, determined by an overwhelming male representation. Not only is there a low percentage of women, but also they are sometimes non-present. Such profession, contrary to gender stereotypes, is predominantly occupied by men. Food & Beverage departments seem, according to the data, a traditional male department, where Maîtres' positions are frequently occupied by men.

The difference existing between five and four star hotels for the Quality Responsible position is very interesting. Whilst there is a higher presence of women in five star hotels, the pattern changes completely in the case of four star hotels. On the contrary, the Events Department is characterised by a very strong women representation.

5 CONCLUSIONS

This paper studied women's role in executive posts in the Spanish hotel industry. For this purpose, the term coined as 'glass ceiling' was defined as the invisible barrier which prevents women from climbing up the career ladder.

In reference to objective two, the lack of tourism and 'glass ceiling' studies (especially in Spain) was proved through the analysis of the literature. Such analysis shaped the content of the literature review, which required the use of a more global approach when referring to the term 'glass ceiling'. Therefore, international studies were covered and a wider general view was presented.

The hotel sector is highly represented by women in specific positions. However, this concentration of women does not correspond to women percentages in executive posts. Consequently, in order to identify women's importance in executive posts of three, four and five star hotels in the Autonomous Community of Madrid, a quantitative statistical analysis was done. However, the probability sample obtained was limited by the low rate response, which prevented more representative results to be withdrawn. These facts and figures are only a fair approximation to women and the 'glass ceiling' in the hotel sector. Notwithstanding, this paper set the framework for the need of more research towards this topic. This study was the first part of a wider research on 'glass ceiling in the hotel sector', in which the results of the second part were in coherence with the ones hereby presented.

Many of the hotel departments are characterized by a female or male traditional stereotype which is highly counterproductive to the desire of having the 'glass ceiling' shattered. Therefore, departments like Housekeeping, Human Resources Management and Events are highly represented by women in senior positions, whereas male prevail at executive post of departments such as General Management, Reception, Maintenance, Food & Beverage and Chef. Nevertheless, some other departments like Finance and Administration show some change towards some preconceived patterns. Such tendency is better perceived in the Sales & Marketing Department. However, there are very interesting differences depending on the category of hotels and whether they are hotel chains or independent hotels. A more in-depth analysis on the underlying reason triggering these decisions is also covered in the second part of this research.

Glass barriers are still predominant in senior leadership organizations. Diversity, the redefinition of the leadership business model, by means of shattering the popular image and biases popular media conceives of women and men. are proposed to defeat the gender discrimination and eliminate the 'glass ceiling'. Diversity has to be regarded as a must in the current financial situation, where CEOs, senior executives and board members should encourage leadership in order to create a new talented pool of candidates, formed both by women and men. In the event this does not occur, high-qualified women executives will continue to be ignored, which may negatively affect the professional quality workforce.

Evidence about the need for more research on the 'glass ceiling' topic has proved to be a social and economic challenge. For the improvement of future studies collaboration between universities and hotels from Madrid should be strengthen, given the benefits this might entail. Not only relations with hotels should be fostered, but also with corporate governments and agencies in order to maximize the results gathered, in an effective and two-flow approach.

Consequently, the importance of this research lies on the following factors: the limited existing research, the horizontal and vertical segregation and the need of innovation within the hotel industry in order to increase quality and avoid losing talent opportunities both for men and women.

REFERENCES

Abersoch, L. D. (2011). *Women on Boards*. UK.

Almeida, M. d., & Antón, J. M. (2011). *Turismo y Género*. Madrid: Síntesis.

BOE. (2007, 22 March). *Ley Orgánica 3/2007, de 22 de marzo, para la igualdad efectiva de mujeres y hombres*. Boletín Oficial del Estado.

Bolles, L. (1997). Women as Category of Analysis in Scholarship on Tourism: Jamaican Women and Tourism Employment. In E. Chambers (Ed.), *Tourism and Culture. An Applied Perspective*. Albany: State University of New York Press.

Bryant, G. (1984). *The Working Women Report, Succeeding in Business in the 80s.* New York: Simon and Schuster.

Campos-Soria, J. A., Marchante-Mera, A., & Ropero-García, M. A. (2011). Patterns of Occupational Segregation by Gender in the Hospitality Industry. (U. d. Málaga, Ed.) *International Journal of Hospitality Management, 30*, 91-102.

CCOO. (2008). La (des)igualdad de oportunidades entre hombres y mujeres en el caso de la hostelería: El caso español. *III Conferencia de Sindicatos de Turismo del Sur de Europa.* Malta.

ELSEVIER. (2015). *Online Tools.* Retrieved March 04, 2015, from Scopus: http://www.info.sciverse.com/scopus/scopus-in-detail/facts

EQUAL. (2008). *Widening vocational choices and breaking the glass ceiling for women's career advancement: Good practice and strategic lessons from Equal.* European Commission.

Faulkenberry, L. V., Coggeshall, J. M., Backman, K., & Backman, S. (2000). A Culture of Servitude: The Impact of Tourism and Development on South Carolina's Coast. *Human Organization, 59*(I), 86-95.

Frenkiel, N. (1984). The Up-and-Comers; Bryant Takes Aim At the Settlers-In. *Adweek.*

Glass Ceiling Commission. (1995). *A solid investment: Making full use of the nation's human capital.* Washington: Glass Ceiling Commission.

Gonzalez, L., & Talón, P. (1999). *Dirección hotelera: Operaciones y Procesos.* Madrid: Síntesis.

IET. (2012). *Empleo en el Sector Turísitco 2011.* Instituto de Turismo en España - TURESPAÑA. Madrid: Instituto de Estudios Turísticos.

IET. (2014). *Empleo en el Sector Turístico 2013.* Madrid : Instituto de Estudios Turísticos.

Instituto Nacional de Estadística. (2011). *Encuesta de Población Activa.* Retrieved May 21, 2012, from http://www.ine.es/

Muñoz-Bullón, F. (2009). The gap between male and female pay in the Spanish tourism industry. *Tourism Management, 30*, 638-649.

R. Hausmann; L. D. Tyson; S. Zahidi. (2011). *The Global Gender Gap Report.* Geneve: World Economic Forum.

Ramos, V., Rey-Maquieira, J., & Tugores, M. (2002). Análisis empírico de discriminación por razón de género en una economía especializada en turismo. *Annals of Tourism Research, 4*(1), 239-258.

Schellhardt, C. H. (1986, 24 May). The Corporate Woman (A Special Report): Cover --- The Glass Ceiling: Why Women Can't Seem to Break The Invisible Barrier That Blocks Them From the Top Jobs. *The Wall Street Journal.*

Segovia-Pérez, M. a.-D. (2014). Mujer y alta dirección: Soluciones para un futuro mejor. In M. Segovia-Pérez, & C. Figueroa-Domecq, *Mujer y alta dirección en el sector turístico* (pp. 15-29). Madrid: Síntesis.

Skalpe, O. (2007). The CEO gender pay gap in the tourism industry - Evidence from Norway. *Tourism Management, 28*(3), 845-853.

The Glass Ceiling & Gender Diversity Today. (2009). *THE GLASS CEILING.* Retrieved from http://glassceiling.info/about-glass-ceiling-info/

The Guardian. (2011, February 21). *Discrimination at work.* (G. Snowdon, Editor) Retrieved May 14, 2012, from Women still face a glass ceiling: http://www.theguardian.com/society/2011/feb/21/women-glass-ceiling-still-exists-top-jobs

Title II Civil Rights Act , Federal Glass Ceiling Commission (November 21, 1991).

UN Development Fund for Women (UNIFEM). (2010). *Women's Empowerment Principles: Equality Means Business.* United Nations Global Compact.

UNIFEM. (2010). *Women's Empowerment Principles: Equality Means Business.* United Nations Global Compact.

United Nations. (1948, December 10). *The Universal Declaration of Human Rights.* Retrieved from Article II: http://www.un.org/en/documents/udhr/history.shtml

United Nations. (2000). *Millennium Development Goals and Beyond 2015.* Retrieved from www.un.org/millenniumgoals

UNWTO and UN Women. (2010). *Global Report on Women in Tourism 2010.* Madrid: World Tourism Organization and United Nations Entity for Gender Equality and the Empowerment of Women.

Vázquez, S. (2008). El discurso de las mujeres líderes. In C. C. (dir.), *La segunda brecha digital* (pp. 185-219). Ediciones Cátedra, Instituto de la Mujer.

Wallace, O. (2003). *wiseGEEK.* Retrieved from What is the Glass Ceiling?: http://www.wisegeek.org/what-is-the-glass-ceiling.htm

Watson, J. (2003, May 20). Failure Rates for Female-Controlled Businesses: Are They Any Different? *Journal of Small Business Management, 41*, 262-277.

Williams, R. B., & Martin, L. (2010, May 15). *Wired for Success.* Retrieved May 14, 2014, from Why Hasn't The Glass Ceiling Been Broken?: https://www.psychologytoday.com/blog/wired-success/201005/why-hasnt-the-glass-ceiling-been-broken

Wirth, L. (2001). *Breaking through the glass ceiling: Women in management.* Geneva: International Labour Office.

World Tourism Organization (UNWTO) and United Nations Entity for Gender Equality and the Empowerment of Women (UN Women). (2010). *Global Report on Women in Tourism 2010.* Madrid: World Tourism Organization.

World Tourism Organization UNWTO. (2011, May 09). *Press Release.* Retrieved from UN Women's head commends tourism as engine for gender equality: http://media.unwto.org/en/press-release/2011-06-09/un-women-s-head-commends-tourism-engine-gender-equality

World Travel & Tourism Council. (2012). *Travel & Tourism. Economic Impact 2012. Spain.* London: World Travel & Tourism Council.

Online Hotel Reviews: Rating Symbols or Text… Text or Rating Symbols?
That is the Question!

Johanna Aicher,

Flavia Asiimwe,

Bujinlkham Batchuluun,

Miriam Hauschild, and

Martina Zöhrer

Salzburg University of Applied Sciences, Austria
jaicher.imte-m2013@fh-salzburg.ac.at

Abstract

This paper deals with the question of how hotel reviews impact the decision-making process when choosing a hotel accommodation and what role rating symbols play on hotel review and electronic booking intermediary websites. A potential customer's decision for or against a particular hotel may be influenced by the ratio of positive and negative reviews on hotel review platforms. Another crucial aspect is the importance placed on rating symbols in comparison to text items. Therefore, the aim of this paper is to identify whether the first look at a hotel review goes towards the rating symbols or the text. This research was conducted by means of a true experiment, making use of the eye-tracking technology (BeGaze 3.4). The findings show that high priority is given to rating symbols rather than text items and that the ratio of positive and negative reviews only partially influences an individual's decision for or against a certain accommodation. Furthermore, it offers tourism managers a general understanding of the importance of online hotel reviews.

Keywords: Eye-tracking technology; rating symbols; positive and negative (online) hotel reviews; decision-making process

1   INTRODUCTION

Resulting from the ongoing globalisation and the rise of Web 2.0, competition is more severe nowadays. The internet has not only complicated, but also intensified the tourism related decision-making process (cf. Soo et al. 2007). Nearly every aspect of people's day-to-day lives has been altered, starting from the ways of communication, attitudes of learning, working and playing, up to the means of how consumer products and services are purchased (cf. Lee and Tussyadiah, 2011). Browning et al. (2013) highlight the fact that tourism products, including holidays, are intangible and thus, are produced and consumed coincidentally and they are therefore not easy to rate prior to their actual consumption. The huge role electronic word-of-mouth captures within the tourism industry in these days is a prevalent fact and while the traditional face-to-face word of mouth can only be distributed orally, electronic word-of-mouth has the great advantage "of potentially conveying both verbal and visual information simultaneously; this advantage makes its impact even more powerful" (Lee and Tussyadiah, 2011: 351). Browning et al. (2013) emphasise the high importance searchers place on recommendations from friends and other travellers on review platforms rather than to the media including advertising and marketing campaigns. Characteristic of hotel review platforms are symbols. The online Oxford dictionary defines symbols as: "A mark or character used as a conventional representation of an object, function, or process" (oxforddictionaries.com). According to this definition, the researchers considered stars, overall ratings and pictures as rating symbols. An extensive amount of literature exists on the issue of hotel reviews, including aspects of electronic word-of-mouth and positive and negative reviews. However, there is a limited amount of research conducted with regard to the importance of rating symbols in hotel reviews and subsequently, this makes this paper vital in contributing to this existing gap in literature. Related to this, the following questions arise: How do hotel reviews impact the decision-making process when choosing hotel accommodation and what role do rating symbols play on hotel review and electronic booking intermediary websites? Do potential travellers first look at the actual hotel review, which means the written text, or the rating symbols? Is there a correlation between the ratio of positive and negative reviews and the potential travellers' perception of the product? The purpose of this paper is to address these questions. One major finding from the empirical study is that rating symbols are regarded as more significant than the written hotel review. The findings are considered as relevant for tourism managers since they show that potential guests mainly look at the rating symbols of a hotel review and not the actual written text. This means that a single negative review will not have a huge impact as the customers are primarily looking at the overall rating of a property. This research makes use of a true experiment by means of eye-tracking technology as a lot of tourism research lacks this approach so far.

2 LITERATURE REVIEW

Since the middle 20th Century, tourism developed parallel to technological progress and is currently credited as one of the biggest economies globally (Egger, 2010). Owing to the dependence of tourism on social systems of communication innate to travel, it is no wonder that technological advancements such as Web 2.0 have had a remarkable impact on Tourism as an industry (ibid). Sigala (2007a) defines Web 2.0 as internet tools that enable collaboration among users to generate, use and diffuse information through the internet. Social media sites that are a spinoff of the Web 2.0 phenomenon, plays an essential role, having turned into one of the most predominant tools that influence the tourism industry and consumer behaviour (cf. Cohen et al. 2013). Statistica (2014), records more than 1.6 billion social media users worldwide. Moreover, as of 2014, 40 percent of the European population was actively involved in accessing mobile social media (ibid). Fotis et al. (2012) maintain that social media plays a very important role during the travel process right from the pre-trip phase to the post trip phase. Xiang and Gretzel (2010) conclude that social media presents a platform where people cannot only share information, but where tourist experiences can be exchanged as well.

Most consider reviews as an important tool for deciding where to stay at a destination. Gretzel et al. (2007) state that incentives are needed so as to encourage consumers to use online hotel reviews in all stages of their travel-decision making process, not only before but also during the trip and after returning. "In the travel industry, online reviews (ORs) can be considered as electronic versions of traditional WOM [word-of-mouth] and consist of comments published by travellers on the tourism products, services, and brands they experience" (Filieri and McLeay, 2014: 44). Word-of-mouth is defined as the process of transmitting information from one person to another (Barreda and Bilgihan, 2013). Rasty et al. (2013) argue that the more a person is involved in the information search (which in this case is very often done through online hotel reviews), the more impact it will have on the decision-making. The available information is a key determinant in the decision-making process. Therefore, it is undeniable that hotel reviews affect this process. Rasty et al. (2013) characterize the involvement in the information search as a moderator in the process of decision-making. A survey conducted by an accommodation facility owned by Tui, known as Late Rooms.com, highlights the increasing demand for online reviews (Davies, 2012). The survey shows that among the 1,366 participants, 40 percent of them searched the internet purposely for reviews of former guests (ibid).

Further, Barreda, and Bilgihan (2013) state that through analysing the content of consumers' comments, managers gain a deep understanding of customers' feelings about their experiences at the hotel. Online hotel reviews are not only crucial for other potential customers of a hotel as a credible source of information but also for owners and managers of a hotel themselves. By means of reviews they clearly get a feeling what people think about the accommodation and what may need to be improved to increase customer satisfaction. Online hotel reviews are important for participants on each side of the chain so to say. They not only provide easy accessible information and a fast private and animus way of communication but above all, up-to-date and credible data for consumers and hotel owners and managers likewise. As a matter of fact, customers' judgement of the quality of purchased and experienced products and services is based on whether their expectations have been met or not (cf. Browning et al. 2013).

When considering the importance of online hotel reviews, it is also essential to deal with the question among those people writing reviews are actually producing helpful information for their peers. In their study about helpful reviewers on tripadvisor, Lee et al. (2011) found that reviewers are considered as helpful when they are frequent travellers and actively participate in posting reviews; those reviewers belong to no particular age and gender group and are rather giving lower hotel ratings. Not only do potential customers care about aspects like price, brand and the country of origin that allude to the quality of a product but reputation is another crucial issue, most of all when it comes to the question of how reputable a communicator of online information is (cf. Lee et al. 2011). However, the issue of trust and credibility of information on social media, and hotel reviews platforms in particular, and its effect on the decision making process is one that has caused divides among scholars. Yoo and Gretzel (2011); Purifoy (2007); Fotis et al. (2012); Barreda and Bilgihan (2013) contend that users find information generated by others trustworthy. Contrary, Cox et al. (2009) argue that social media reviews have a limited influence on the final decision of users owing to the issue of trust and credibility of the information as some of the posts can be faked by service providers. Additionally, Ayeh et al. (2012) also highlight the possibility of the credibility of hotel reviews being compromised by managers who masquerade as guests on hotel review platforms.

In general, positive messages can be helpful, but they alone are not a decisive factor, a few negative messages among several positive ones are not harmful according to Doh and Hwang (2009). With regard to traditional word-of-mouth, it is affirmed that negative reviews have a greater impact on readers than positive ones. Negative reviews should not be kept aside when dealing with online hotel reviews as they indeed have a great impact on consumers. Overall, a good review is qualified by being rational, rich in descriptions, detailed, balanced and critical and listing both pros and cons of a product in question (cf. Clare, 2010). In fact, negative reviews do not necessarily have to have a negative impact on customers as a certain negative aspect may not be relevant to every individual and thus, may not have a significant impact (cf. ibid).

3 RESEARCH METHODOLOGY

In choosing a methodology suitable for this particular study about online hotel reviews that amongst others aims at examining symbols and their values when it comes to the customers' decision-making process, the researchers decided on a not widely used method so far in the field of tourism: the method of eye-tracking. Predominantly employed in studies connected to marketing, psychological or most often medical issues, this method is "used to measure a person's point of gaze, which focuses on what a person [is] looking at and [on] find[ing] out the eye spot" (Ramakrisnan et al., 2012: 529). The researcher records the participants' eye movements while they are performing a given task in order to be provided with information about the cognitive process that occurs when completing the task as it is explained by Ramakrisnan et al. (2012). Here, amongst others the individual's eye-movements along a chosen webpage serves as information about focus areas of attention, areas or elements that are disregarded and elements by which the participants seem to be disturbed (cf. Tonbuloglu, 2013). Characteristically of qualitative data collection, the sampling of the participants for the study in question took part per random selection. It was not aimed at being representative as it would be the case in quantitative research. Nielsen and Pernice (2010: 22) state that a "basic qualitative usability study requires only five people to find many of the usability issues with a system." Sticking to these findings, this research was conducted with eight subjects per group so as to determine how people proceed when reading through hotel reviews. By means of a true experiment, the ratio of positive and negative reviews in relation to participants' decision for or against the hotel was analysed. According to Bryman (2012: 59): "[...] in order to conduct a true experiment, it is necessary to manipulate the independent variable in order to determine whether it does in fact have an influence on the dependent variable." A true experiment indeed is rarely seen in social sciences, but worked out well in this case as it was possible to manipulate the independent variable, which is not the case for most studies in social sciences (cf. Bryman, 2012). Due to the nature of a true experiment it was decided to manipulate the independent variable (the ratio of positive and negative reviews), while the dependent one (the participants' decision for or against the hotel) stayed the same.

To shortly describe the procedure of eye-tracking, the first step is the so-called calibration process to adjust the eye-tracking device to the actual participant. Then the participant is asked to start with the realisation of the given task, and then the researchers gain the exact data of the participant's performance, visually and recorded. The visual information includes a gaze plot, providing material on fixations (those moments when the eyes remain fairly static) and saccades (movements between one fixation to another) as well as a heat map, illustrating the participant's focus areas of attention by means of colours (cf. Ramakrisnan et al., 2012). In this particular project BeGaze 3.4 was used, which works exactly as just outlined. For the analysis of the data gained through the eye-tracking device, the researchers chose to stick to heat maps as well as to the first and last fixations of the individual participants, ways of analysis that will be discussed in the following chapters.

As a starting point for this research, a pre-study was conducted to find out about suitable hotel reviews. It was decided beforehand to only consider Austrian four star hotels as well as to go for both a city hotel, Holiday Inn Salzburg City, and a country hotel, Latini Hotel in Zell am See, both of which were randomly chosen. This was done to avoid any kind of bias people might have due to certain preferences for location and types of hotel. Moreover, the researchers aimed at having a more holistic and comprehensive approach with regard to the research questions. A collection of various hotel reviews, randomly taken from the hotel review platform tripadvisor, was prepared. This collection was handed out to 20 randomly selected participants who were asked to read it and to mark whether they considered the individual hotel reviews as positive, negative or neutral. Thus, this first step of research served as a guideline, which reviews people consider as positive and which as negative. The layout of tripadvisor was then used as a basis for the prototype for the actual eye-tracking experiment, as it is a commonly known hotel review platform. As a matter of fact, two prototypes were designed, each showing first hotel reviews of Holiday Inn Salzburg City and after that reviews of Latini Hotel. One contained more positive than negative reviews and the second one consisted of more negative than positive reviews. This was done in order to manipulate the independent variable (the ratio of positive and negative reviews). Due to the nature of the eye-tracking software (BeGaze 3.4), which only allows for pictures to be inserted, screenshots of the prototype were taken and inserted into the software to be able to put together the tasks for the participants. Finally, both prototypes comprised four pictures, two of Holiday Inn Salzburg City and two of Latini Hotel. This means that participants did not have the feeling of a webpage where one can scroll down. In the end, there were two tasks, or one could say two groups, one which was called "positive" and one called "negative", according to the amount of negative and positive reviews they included. Both tasks were compiled in the same way, including the same layout and the same hotel reviews as much as possible. Thus, some hotel reviews were used in both prototypes – naturally, in the positive prototype there were more positive ones and in the negative more negative ones. So it was only the ratio and the order of positive and negative reviews that was changed.

The 16 participants were chosen per random selection and their task was to read the hotel reviews of both Holiday Inn Salzburg City and Latini Hotel. While performing the tasks the participants were not limited by time and were able to choose by themselves how long to look at the individual pictures of the prototype. Afterwards they were asked to answer questions of a structured questionnaire posed by the researchers. However, the participants were not aware of the questions while performing the tasks. The questionnaire served as a backup-method to find out whether the participants would book a holiday in the hotels in questions or not. Further, the researchers wanted to determine why and how the participants came to their decision. The following questions were asked: (1) Which item first caught your attention? (2) Did you first look at the text or the rating symbols (stars)? (3) Why? (4) Would you make holidays in the hotels you just looked at? (5) Was your decision for or against the hotels influenced by the comments / hotel reviews? Why? (6) Any other comments?

When it comes to the development of the questionnaire, the questions asked were developed according to the conducted research and were simply used as a support of the chosen method of eye-tracking.

For a better understanding, the list below (Table 1) displays the Areas of Interest (AOIs) the researchers defined to conduct the eye-tracking procedure and succeeding analysis.

Table 1. List of AOIs

Positive Testing				Negative Testing			
Hotel	Pg.	AOI	AOI - Name	Hotel	Pg.	AOI	AOI – Name
Holiday Inn	1	1-001	Big Title, Name & Address	Holiday Inn	1	1-001a	Big Title, Name & Address
		1-002	Big Picture			1-002a	Big Picture
		1-003	Small Pictures			1-003a	Small Pictures
		1-004	Percentage			1-004a	Percentage
		1-005	Overall Review			1-005a	Overall Review
		1-006	First Positive Headline & Stars			1-006a	First Headline & Stars
		1-007	Text One			1-007a	Text One
		1-008	Second Headline & Stars			1-008a	Second Headline & Stars
		1-009	Negative Headlines			1-009a	Negative Headlines
		1-010	Text block			1-010a	Text block

4 FINDINGS

Table 2. First and last fixations

Name	Page	First Look	Last Look	Time / Seconds
		Positive Testing		
Sebastian	Holiday Inn 1st page	AOI 1-002 Big Picture	AOI 1-002 Big Picture	16,7
Manuel	Holiday Inn 1st page	AOI 1-006 First Positive Headline & Stars	AOI 1-005 Overall Review	16,6
Peter	Holiday Inn 1st page	AOI 1-006 First Positive Headline & Stars	AOI 1-001 Big Title, Name & Address	13,3
Mark	Holiday Inn 1st page	AOI 1-001 Big Title, Name & Address	AOI 1-003 Small Pictures	57,7
Michael	Holiday Inn 1st page	AOI 1-006 First Positive Headline & Stars	AOI 1-010 Text block	34,5
Axel	Holiday Inn 1st page	AOI 1-004 Percentage	AOI 1-005 Overall Review	19,2
Pia	Holiday Inn 1st page	AOI 1-006 First Positive Headline & Stars	AOI 1-007 Text One	16,3
Lasse	Holiday Inn 1st page	AOI 1-002 Big Picture	AOI 1-002 Big Picture	12
Results		AOI 1-002 Big Picture - 2 participants	AOI 1-001 Big Title, Name & Address - 1 participant	Average 23,2
		AOI 1-006 First Positive Headline & Stars - 4 participants	AOI 1-002 Big Picture - 2 participants	
		AOI 1-001 Big Title, Name & Address - 1 participant	AOI 1-003 Small Pictures - 1 participant	
		AOI 1-004 Percentage - 1 participant	AOI 1-005 Overall Review - 2 participants	
			AOI 1-007 Text One - 1 participant	
			AOI 1-010 Text block - 1 participant	

By means of the defined AOIs shown in Table 1 the researchers could precisely analyse the participants' first and last fixations on each page of the given task. Table 2, showing the individual participants' first and last fixations on the first page of the positive testing.

In order to visualise the findings, two videos have been converted and uploaded on one of the researcher's YouTube channel. These videos will give the reader a better insight into the actual way of analysing eye-tracking data by using scan paths:

Video 1: Scan path example 1 (negative task):
https://www.youtube.com/watch?v=F0gPJ4vKE0g&feature=youtu.be.
Video 2: Scan path example 2 (positive task):
https://www.youtube.com/watch?v=uVI2iTupS_o&feature=youtu.be.

Concerning the analysis of the eye-tracking data, the researchers' focus was on the first look of the individual participants on each page of the given tasks. As to that, the findings clearly display that participants frequently choose rating symbols as first item to look at. To be more concrete (to elaborate on this), when it comes to the first page of the positive task (Holiday Inn Salzburg City), four participants had a first look at AIO 1-006 (First Positive Headline & Stars), two of them preferred AIO 1-002 (Big Picture), one participant first focused on AIO 1-001 (Big Title, Name & Address) and one first dealt with AIO 1-004 (Percentage). On the second page of the positive testing (Holiday Inn Salzburg City), three participants started with looking at AIO 2-002 (Target Groups), two first looked at AIO 2-001 (Scoring) and each time one participant had a first glance at AIO 2-003 (Overall Rating), AIO 2-004 (Headline & Stars – Negative) and AIO 2-006 (Positive Reviews). Going on with the positive task, on the third page covering reviews of Latini Hotel, five participants first went for AIO 3-001 (Big Title, Stars & Address), two for AIO 3-002 (Big Picture) and one participant first had a look at AOI 3-004 (Percentage). On the fourth and last page of the positive task (Latini Hotel) the majority (five participants) went for AIO 4-001 (Scoring) and three for AOI 4-002 (Target Groups).

With regard to the negative testing, the analysis of the participants' first fixations shows quite the same pattern as with the positive testing. Again, on the first page of the negative task (Holiday Inn Salzburg City) the majority (three participants) had a first look at AOI 1-006a (First Headline & Stars). On the second page of this task (Holiday Inn Salzburg City) six participants went for AOI 2-001a (Scoring) and two for AOI 2-002a (Target Groups), which is quite similar to the results of the second page of the positive testing. Going on with the third and fourth page of the negative task (Latini Hotel), the majority here first looked at AOI 3-001a (Big Title, Stars & Address) in page three (four participants) and at AOI 4-001a (Scoring) on page four (six participants), which is again on par with the positive task.

When you look at these tasks as a whole, when it comes to the participants' first fixations, 13 of the participants first looked at the rating symbols when it comes to those pages covering reviews of Holiday Inn Salzburg City and the same is true for even 15 of them when it comes to the rest of the pages including reviews of Latini Hotel. Whereas the first fixations of the participants show a clear pattern and mainly involve rating symbols like stars and scoring, the last fixations do not show such a straightforward line but are quite mixed. In both testing procedures, positive and negative, the last fixations of the majority range from AOI 1-005 (Overall Review) with two participants on page one, AOI 2-004 (Headline & Stars – Negative) with four participants on page two, AOI 3-002 (Big Picture) with three participants on page three and AOI 4-002 (Target Groups) and AOI 4-003 (Overall Rating) with three participants each on page four in the positive task. Regarding the negative task, AOI 1-004a (Percentage) and AOI 1-005a (Overall Review) scored with two participants each on page one, AOI 2-002a (Target Groups) with three participants on page two, AOI 3-004a (Percentage) with three participants on page three and AOI 4-004a (Headline & Stars – Negative) with four participants on page four.

The structured questionnaires that served as back-up method to the eye-tracking procedure, showed similar results as the analysis of the eye-tracking data. Regardless of whether they took part in the positive or the negative testing, the majority of participants stated that the first items that caught their attention were either pictures (12 participants) or the overall rating symbol in form of a percentage (ten participants). This backs up the results of the eye-tracking procedure as 14 of the participants stated that they first looked at symbols rather than text items. As reasons for this, it was explained that symbols are outstanding, easy to spot and that they give an overview of the product (in this case the hotels). With regard to the two different tasks, positive and negative, this only partially influenced the participants' final decision for or against the two hotels. Six participants of the positive testing decided for both hotels and the remaining two participants stated that they would only decide for one of the hotels, one for Holiday Inn Salzburg City and the other one for Latini Hotel. As for the negative testing, one half of the participants would spend a holiday in both hotels and the other half would not do so in neither of them. When it comes to the second-last question whether their decision for or against the hotels had been influenced by the hotel reviews (meaning the actual text, either positive or negative) or not, interestingly enough half of the participants of the positive testing declared yes, respectively no. According to their answers, the hotel reviews (actual text) only partially influenced their decision-making process, but the overall rating symbol (percentage), pictures and personal preferences were also considered as important aspects in this regard. Six of the participants of the negative testing on the other hand clearly stated "no", illustrating that the actual text did not influence them at all but it was the overall rating symbol (percentage) that had the strongest impact on their decision-making.

In order to analyse the eye-tracking data, heat maps were used to visualise the findings. Heat maps utilise a particular colour spectrum to reveal the intensity of fixations of all 16 participants. Compared to scan paths, they provide a clearer level of visual overview (cf. Lorigo et al., 2008). The colours red, orange, yellow and green refer to the number of fixations in descending order. All findings listed in the previous paragraph were consistent with the heat maps, and contributed immensely to answering the research questions. As illustrated in Figures 1-4, the heat maps show fixations on the overall rating symbols as well as on the headlines. This is coherent with the findings that participants hardly looked at the text but rating symbols were much more appealing.

Fig. 1. Heat Maps Negative Task　　　　　　　**Fig. 2.** Heat Maps Positive Task

There are only a few fixations in all of the figures displayed above. A large number of fixations is considered an indicator of poor arrangements of objects in a stimulus (cf. Yusuf et al., 2008), thus, the objects in this particular setting were clearly arranged. In general, symbols are of utmost importance and this theory is in accordance with the outcome of the participant's interviews. When asked why they looked at the symbols, the most common answers were first of all convenience, and secondly, the possibility to gain a quick overview. It is therefore safe to assume that the participants consciously made the choice to first look at the symbols, as they seem to trust them and regard them as an important parameter when making a booking decision. The text items on the other hand have sometimes not even been read. This is partly due to their length. Participants claimed that the text was not properly arranged and that it was hard to read, so they decided to skip it and to fully rely on the symbols. What is more, the headlines of the text reviews proofed to be much more important than initially thought. Participants clearly did have a look on the headlines as indicated by the heat maps.

Generally speaking, the heat maps featuring the positive reviews and the ones featuring the negative reviews show similar patterns. Headlines and rating symbols were equally intensely looked at, whereas the text items did not attract the participant's interest. The pictures of the hotels merely played a secondary role and they were not a decisive factor for the participants' final decision for or against a certain hotel. At best, the pictures could be considered a supporting element. Regarding the first research question, the findings of the back-up questionnaire show that half of the participants declared that online hotel reviews indeed influence their decision for or against a hotel, but on the other hand, the other half of them stated that reviews do not impact their decision-making.

The findings of this research further illustrate that comments, meaning the text itself, only partially affect the final decision for or against an accommodation. Again, the analysis of the questionnaire proved that overall rating symbols, pictures and personal preferences also had a strong influence in the participants' final decision, irrespective of positive or negative reviews. The second research question refers to whether potential travellers first look at the actual hotel review, which means the written text, or at the rating symbol. As the findings present, this can be clearly answered by stating that rating symbols (stars & scoring) have a greater significance as first looks than text items, regardless of whether the participants took part in the positive or the negative group. Coming to the last question whether the ratio of positive and negative reviews influences the potential travellers' perception of the product, the findings show that this was only partially the case. Even though very negative reviews were included in the negative group, participants stated that they would stay in the represented hotels since mainly the overall rating symbol was considered which was not manipulated.

5 DISCUSSION AND IMPLICATIONS

Referring back to Xiang and Gretzel (2010), determining that social media displays a platform for people to share information as well as tourist experiences, this paper aims at providing hotel managers an insight into the issue hotel reviews, focusing on negative and positive ratings as well as on rating symbols. There are institutional rating organizations such as the British based AA ratings and Hotrec for countries in the European Union that are responsible for hotel rating systems that indicate that stars symbolize a yard stick for standards in quality service in the hospitality industry (Felix and Clever, 2014). Moreover, there is a correlation between hotel rating and the hotel quality actually perceived by guests (ibid). As highlighted by Scott and Orlikowski (2009), there is a difference in rating systems between institutional bodies like AA ratings and the ratings that exist on social media review sites. Social review sites like trip advisor use a different rating algorism based on factors such as traveller ratings, guidebook entries and media publications, disregarding the institutional rating (ibid). So to say, such sites create a harmonizing effect because hotels with different levels of quality service are able to compete with each other on the same review platform (ibid). Having this in mind, four star hotels might not necessarily get higher ratings by travellers on platforms like trip advisor. In light of these findings, managers of hospitality sites are given relatively equal opportunity through hotel review sites irrespective of their rating. Giving credit to Barreda, and Bilgihan (2013) again, hotel managers receive a profound impression of their customers' point of view and their experiences on-site when thoroughly analysing their reviews. If management of hospitality sites respond to customers' comments and thus, do their best to meet their needs, they stand high chances of receiving more positive reviews and therefore, may rank higher on review platforms than their competitors. Scott and Orlikowski (2009) further note that the business model of travel review sites is dependent on advertising and travel service links from suppliers. This presents an option for hotel managers to invest in advertising with travel review sites as this guarantees a large audience of review readers, commenters and comment generators.

The outcomes of this research with regard to positive and negative reviews correspond with the research of Vermeulen and Seegers (2008), which concludes that positive reviews are determinates of customer behaviour, and is in line with Clare (2010) as to the fact that negative reviews have less impact. Vermeulen and Seegers (2008) also comply with Doh and Hwang (2009) in declaring that negative reviews should not be attached too great importance to as long they positive and negative views balance each other. Just as Doh and Hwang (2009) reveal, positive reviews alone are not determining but some negative ones are needed as well to rise travellers' attention so to say. While negative reviews on the one hand may affect potential customers' attitude towards a hotel accommodation, they also have the potential to call customers' attention to hotels that would otherwise not be known or taken into consideration, be it in a positive or negative way (cf. Vermeulen and Seegers, 2008). Hotel reviews are not written without the bias of expectations, previous travel experiences, personality traits of different individuals and other factors like individual price ranges that may go beyond the control of establishment owners. A combination of all these factors mentioned may explain why readers of reviews may decide for booking a certain accommodation despite the fact that it contains negative viewpoints. It is again Clare (2010) who makes clear that a particular negative aspect may not be a crucial one for every potential customer and therefore, may not be counted as determining factor. The results of this paper's research show that the decision to book a hotel is based on symbols and ratings rather than the content of reviews. This is consistent with the conclusion of Bing and Lixuan (2009) that people are more drawn to images and symbols rather than to text because images reduce cognitive effort and increase customers' interest in a site. In a more practical context, all those findings suggest that booking platforms should put even more emphasis on the symbols by making them as visible as possible. In general, it is suggested by the researchers of this paper that the actual text of hotel reviews is not visible at first glance, so as to prevent potential customers who would be interested in certain reviews from being discouraged by overlong text items. In this sense, it would be an implication to only make the actual text of hotel reviews visible and accessible through a click on the respective rating symbol of a certain review. Further, on hotel review platforms there could be a limitation given with respect to the maximum amount of words the text of a review can consist of.

6 LIMITATIONS AND FUTURE RESEARCH

The findings of this study must be interpreted and analysed cautiously. Due to the qualitative nature of this research, both setting and findings may vary significantly. Firstly, manipulation of the original website was indispensable. The research setting deviated from a real-life scenario to that effect that participants could not scroll upwards and downwards on their own. Each participant was presented two pages per hotel, and since scrolling was not possible, the setting was partly perceived as artificial and simulated. Participants had to sit still and their movement radius was significantly limited. One researcher had to sit next to the participants to assist them, which made some feel rather uneasy. Unfortunately, this limitation depends on the software, and is therefore inevitable. Only the advancement of technology will allow researchers to eventually overcome this issue.

Moreover, the whole scenario had no effect on the participants because they were not asked to eventually book a vacation package. The hotels were preselected by the researchers. Therefore, some hotels might not have appealed to some participants due to simple reasons, such as discontent regarding location or other tourist amenities. As a matter of fact, most participants did not take the time to thoroughly examine the hotels, but merely skimmed through each page. Most decisions were made very fast after a first quick overview, and the follow-up interviews showed that these findings were coherent with the results from the eye-tracking analysis. Participants actively looking for hotel accommodation for themselves might act and react differently given these circumstances. It would be worth to explore if/to what extend external factors such as place and time play an important role as well. With these limitations in mind, future research should seek to integrate the role of the time component in detail. It was not included in this study because it was not part of the research questions in this context and would go beyond the scope of this study. Further, it would be worth to examine how long particular decisive fixations on a review or a symbol last. In addition, the time correlation might be worth exploring; measuring the amount of time participants spent looking at symbols on the one hand, and reviews on the other. Another interesting approach would be to evaluate whether the rating symbols fit to the actual written review and whether that would make a difference for participants or not. The same goes for headlines: one could take a closer look at whether the headlines reflect the content of the written review or not as well as whether hotel review readers are looking for specific key words in particular. Furthermore, also colour and font size of the symbols might play a crucial role; however, this is not clearly determined by this research. Moreover, all participants of this study were students who are approximately the same age. Future studies could be conducted in a quantitative way, thus paying attention to important factors such as gender, age, education and social status. This would provide an additional opportunity to analyse the importance of hotel online reviews and symbols in a broader and more generalizable context.

REFERENCES

Ayeh, K. J.; Au, N.; & Law, R. (2012): Predicting the Intention to Use Consumer- Generated Media for Travel Planning. In: Tourism Management, 35, 132-143.

Barreda, A.; & Bilgihan, A. (2013): An analysis of User-Generated Content for Hotel Experiences. In: Journal of Hospitality and Tourism Technology, 4/3, 263 – 280.

Bieger, T.; & Laesser, C. (2004): Information Sources for Travel Decisions: Toward a Source Process Model. In: Journal of Travel Research, 42, 357-371.

Bing, P.; & Lixuan, Z. (2009): An Eye Tracking Study on Online Hotel Decision Making: The Effects of Images and Number of Options. Travel and Tourism Research Association Conference.

Browning, V.; So, K. K. F.; & Sparks, B. (2013): The Influence of Online Reviews on Consumers' Attributions of Service Quality and Control for Service Standards in Hotels. In: Journal of Travel & Tourism Marketing, 30/1-2, 23-40.

Bryman, A. (2012): Social Research Methods (4th ed.). New York: Oxford University Press.

Cheng, V. T. P.; & Loi, M. K. (2014): Handling Negative Online Customer Reviews: The Effects of Elaboration Likelihood Model and Distributive Justice. In: Journal of Travel & Tourism Marketing, 31/1, 1-15.

Clare, C. (2010): Receiver Perspectives of the Determinants that Influence eWOM Adoption: An Exploratory Study. Research Institute for Business Management, Manchester Metropolitan University Business School, 1-15.

Cox, C.; Burgess, S.; Sellitto, C.; & Buultjens, J. (2009): The Role of User-Generated Content in Tourists' Travel Planning Behaviour. In: Journal of Hospitality Marketing and Management, 18, 743-764.

Cohen, S. A.; Prayag, G.; & Moital, M. (2013): Consumer Behaviour in Tourism: Concepts, Influences and Opportunities. In: Current Issues in Tourism, DOI: 10.1080/13683500.2013.850064.

Davies, P. (2012): Customers 'After the Truth' in Hotel Reviews, Finds Study. <http://www.travolution.co.uk/articles/2012/11/15/6195/customers-after-the-truth-in-hotel-reviews-finds-study.html>> [Accessed: 26.01.2015].

Dickinger, A.; & Stangl, B. (2011): Online Information Search: Differences Between Goal-Directed and Experiential Search.

Doh, S. J.; & Hwang, J. S. (2009): How Consumers Evaluate eWOM (Electronic Word-of-Mouth) Messages. CyberPsychology & Behaviour, 12/2, 193-197.

Egger, R. (2010): Theorizing Web 2.0 Phenomena in Tourism: A Sociological Signpost. In: Information Technology and Tourism, 12, 125-137.

Ekiz, E.; Khoo-Lattimore, C.; & Memarzadeh, F. (2012): Air the Anger: Investigating Online Complaints on Luxury Hotels. In: Journal of Hospitality and Tourism Technology, 3/2, 96 – 106.

Filieri, R.; & McLeay, F. (2014): E-WOM and Accommodation: An Analysis of the Factors that Influence Travellers' Adoption of Information from Online Reviews. In: Journal of Travel Research, 53/1, 44-57.

Felix, C.; & Clever, V. (2014): The Relationship Between Hotel Rating and Customer Outcomes: Customer Perceived Service Quality and Customer Satisfaction. In: Greener Journal of Business and Management Studies, 4, 146-156.

Fu, W. T.; & Pirolli, P. (2007): SNIF-ACT: A Cognitive Model of User Navigation on the World Wide Web. In: Human-Computer Interaction, 22, 355-412.

Fotis, J.; Buhalis, D.; & Rossides, N. (2012): Social Media Use and Impact During the Holiday Travel Planning Process. In: Information and Communication Technologies in Tourism. Proceedings of the International Conference in Helsingborg, Sweden. 1-11.

Gretzel, U.; Yoo, H.; & Purifoy, M. (2007): Online Travel Review Study: Role and Impact of Online Travel Reviews. In: Laboratory for Intelligent Systems in Tourism (by Tripadvisor), Texas A&M University, 1-70.

Huang, Y.; & Kuo, F. (2011): An Eye-Tracking Investigation of Internet Consumers' Decision Deliberateness. In: Internet Research, 21/5, 541-561.

Jeong, M.; & Lambert, C. U. (2001): Adaptation of an Information Quality Framework to Measure Customers' Behavioural Intentions to Use Lodging Web sites. In: Hospitality Management, 20, 129–14.

Kim, W. G.; & Kim, D. J. (2004): Factors Affecting Online Hotel Reservation Intention Between Online and Non-online Customers. In: Hospitality Management 23, 381-395.

Lee, G.; & Tussyadiah, I. P. (2011): Textual and Visual Information in eWOM: A Gap Between Preferences in Information Search and Diffusion. In: Information Technology & Tourism, 12, 351–361.

Lee, H. A.; Law, R.; & Murphy, J. (2011): Helpful Reviewers in TripAdvisor, an Online Travel Community. In: Journal of Travel & Tourism Marketing, 28/7, 675-688.

Lehto, X. Y.; Kim, D.; & Morrison, A. M. (2006): The Effect of Prior Destination Experience and Online Information search Behaviour. In: Tourism and Hospitality Research, 6/2, 160-178.

Lorigo et al. (2008): Eye Tracking and Online Search: Lessons Learned and Challenges Ahead. In: Journal of the American society for information science and technology, 59/7.

McCarthy, L.; Stock, D.; & Verma, R. (2010): How Travelers Use Online and Social Media Channels to Make Hotel-choice Decisions. In: Cornell Hospitality Reports, 10/18, 6-18.

Nielsen, J.; & Pernice, K. (2010): Eye tracking Web Usability. Berkeley: New Riders.

Oh, K.; Almarodeb, J. T.; & Tai, R. H. (2013): An Exploration of Think-aloud Protocols Linked with Eye-Gaze Tracking: Are They Talking About What They Are Looking at. In: Procedia - Social and Behavioural Sciences, 93, 184 – 189.

Oxford Dictionary, Language matters. <<http://www.oxforddictionaries.com/de/definition/englisch/symbol>> [Access: 26.01.2015].

Pantano, E.; & Di Pietro, L. (2013): From E-tourism to F-tourism: Emerging Issues from Negative Tourists' Online Reviews. In Hospitality and Tourism Technology, 4/3, 211-227.

Papathanassis, A.; & Knolle, F. (2011): Exploring the Adoption and Processing of Online Holiday Reviews: A Grounded Theory Approach. In: Tourism Management, 32, 215-224.

Ramakrisnan, P.; Jaafar, A.; Razak, F. H. A.; & Ramba, D. A. (2012): Evaluation of User Interface Design for Learning Management System (LMS): Investigating Student's Eye Tracking Pattern and Experiences. In: Procedia - Social and Behavioural Sciences, 67, 527 – 537.

Rasty, F.; Chou, C.; & Feiz, D. (2013): The Impact of Internet Travel Advertising Design, Tourists' Attitude, and Internet Travel Advertising Effect on Tourists' Purchase Intention: The Moderating Role of Involvement. In: Journal of Travel & Tourism Marketing, 30/5, 482-496.

Reutskaja, E.; Nagel, R.; Camerer, C. F.; & Rangel, A. (2011): Search Dynamics in Consumer Choice under Time Pressure: An Eye-Tracking Study. In: American Economic Review, 101, 900–926. (doi=10.1257/aer.101.2.900).

Sarma, M. K. (2007): Influence of Information Sources on Tourists: A segment-wise Analysis with Special focus on Destination Image. In: The Journal of Business Perspective, 11/1, 35-45.

Scott, V. S.; & Orlikowski, J. W. (2009): "Getting The Truth". Exploring the Material Grounds of Institutional Dynamics in Social Media. <<http://eprints.lse.ac.uk/26699/1/WP_177.pdf>> [Accessed: 26.01.2015].

Sirakaya, E.; & Woodside, A. G. (2005): Building and Testing Theories of Decision Making by Travellers. In: Tourism Management, 26/6, 815-832.

Sigala, M. (2007a): Web 2.0 in The Tourism Industry: A New Tourism Generation and New E-business Models. <<www.traveldailynews.com/pages/print/20554>> [Accessed: 26.01.2015].

Smallman, C.; & Moore, K. (2010): Process Studies of Tourists' Decision-Making. In: Annals of Tourism Research, 37/2, 397-422.

Soo, H. J.; Vogt, C. A.; & Mackay, K. J. (2007): Relationships between Travel Information Search and Travel Product Purchase in Pretrip Contexts. In: Journal of Travel Research, 45/3, 266-274.

Sparks, B. A.; & Browning, V. (2010): The Impact of Online Reviews on Hotel Booking Intentions and Perception of Trust. In: Tourism Management, 32, 1310-1323.

Sparks, B. A.; Perkings, E. P.; & Buckley, R. (2013): Online Travel Reviews as Persuasive Communication: The Effects of Content Type, Source, and Certification Logos on Consumer Behaviour. In: Tourism management, 39, 1-9.

Statistica.com. (2014): Statistics and Market Data on Social Media and User-Generated Content. <<http://www.statista.com/markets/424/topic/540/social-media-user-generated-content/>> [Accessed: 26.01.2015].

Susskind, A. M.; & Stefanone, M. A. (2010): Internet Apprehensiveness. An Examination of On line information seeking and purchasing behaviour. In: Journal of Hospitality and Tourism Technology, 1/1, 5-29.

Swanson, S. R.; & Hsu, M. K. (2009): Critical Incidents in Tourism: Failure, Recovery, Customer Switching, and Word-of-Mouth Behaviours. In: Journal of Travel and Tourism Marketing, 26/2, 180-194.

Tabbane, R. S.; & Hamouda, M. (2013): Impact of eWom on the Tunisian Consumer's Attitude Towards the Product. Advances in Business-Related Scientific Research Conference 2013 in Venice (ABSRC 2013 Venice), 1-12.

Tonbuloglu, I. (2013): Using Eye Tracking Method and Video Record In Usability Test of Educational Softwares and Gender Effects. In: Procedia - Social and Behavioural Sciences, 103, 1288 – 1294.

Vermeulen, I. E.; & Seegers, D. (2008): Tried and Tested: The Impact of Online Hotel Reviews on Consumer Consideration. In: Tourism Management, 30, 123-127.

Wong, J. Y.; & Yeh, C. (2009): Tourist Hesitation in Destination Decision Making. In: Annals of Tourism Research, 36/1, 6-23.

Xiang, Z.; & Gretzel, U. (2010): Role of Social Media in Online Travel Information Search. In: Tourism Management, 31, 179–188.

Yusuf, S.; Kagedi, H.; Maletic, J. (2008): Assessing the Comprehension of UML Class Diagrams via Eye Tracking. Department of Computer Science: Kent State University.

A Study of Web 2.0 Applications Usage in the Lake Constance Area Conference Venues' Marketing Strategies

Anja Gunz

SKEMA Business School, Austria

Abstract

The aim of this study is to explore how conference venues located in the Lake Constance area incorporate Web 2.0 applications in their communication strategies. Semi-structured interviews were conducted with marketing experts of seven different conference venues. Findings show that while some have comprehensively adopted Web 2.0 applications into their marketing plans, others are still investigating how to effectively use these tools. The paper concludes that there is a general uncertainty amongst venue professionals regarding the effectiveness and relevance of Web 2.0 applications in targeting B2B markets. However, their marketing potential as well as the increasing attention that these tools receive in organizations' marketing strategies was acknowledged. Although a number of barriers to adoption were identified, a strong confidence towards a wider incorporation of social media in the future prevailed.

Keywords: conference venues; Web 2.0 applications; social media marketing; Lake Constance area

1 INTRODUCTION

Over the past decade a whole new marketing logic has surfaced; one that is service-centered and hallmarked by interactivity, integration and customization (Vargo & Lusch, 2004). Marketing starts long before a product or service is actually being produced. The ultimate goal of marketing is not anymore to make a sale but rather to satisfy customer needs (Kimmel, 2010; Kotler, Wong, Saunders, & Armstrong, 2005). The current consumer landscape is undergoing a tremendous evolution. As Vargo and Lusch (2004) indicate, consumers are no longer merely passive receivers of marketing messages but play an important role in controlling the marketplace. New communication technologies such as Web 2.0 applications are interactive channels where the traditional top-down (B2C) marketing paradigm is being replaced by bottom-up (C2C) approaches (Kimmel, 2010; Mays, Weaver, & Bernhardt, 2011). The same principle applies to the meetings industry as results of a recent trend analysis on customer expectations have demonstrated. The study (Raith, 2014) reveals that corporate meeting planners primarily rely on peer recommendations as well as on the Internet when searching for a suitable event venue. The property's own website comes third.

The purpose of this study is first to assess how Web 2.0 applications are integrated in the communication strategy of selected conference venues. Secondly, it aims at describing the opportunities and challenges that meeting-venue marketing managers are faced with when using social media applications. Lastly, it provides recommendations on how conference venues can improve their social media strategies and therefore better manage and measure their activities online. Ultimately, this study uncovers how Web 2.0 tools are perceived and managed by marketing experts of seven different conference venues located in the greater Lake Constance area, which covers parts of Austria, Switzerland, and Germany. Specifically, the following research questions will be investigated: How are conference venues integrating Web 2.0 applications in their communication strategy? What are the barriers to their adoption by conference venues? Which opportunities and challenges do Web 2.0 tools create?

While the topic of social media marketing has received increasing attention in the academic literature during the past few years, little is known on how conference venue professionals use and benefit from Web 2.0 tools. This study therefore takes a further step towards closing this gap. It aims at achieving a better understanding for venue managers on how conference centers have embraced Web 2.0 applications in their marketing plans. The results are significant to those seeking an overview on how marketing managers of conference venues perceive benefits and challenges as well as the future of Web 2.0 tools. Moreover, this research can be useful for venue managers planning to add social media to their marketing portfolio.

2 LITERATURE REVIEW

2.1 The Web 2.0 Social Media Landscape

The origin of the term Web 2.0 is attributed to Tim O'Reilly who first described the Web 2.0 phenomenon in 2004. He looked at the web as a platform to 'harnessing collective intelligence' (O'Reilly, 2005) where "nobody knows everything, but everybody knows something" (Thackeray, Neiger, Hanson, & McKenzie, 2008). In marketing, social media is also referred to as user-generated content (UGC) (Muniz & Schau, 2011). Social media can be defined as "a group of Internet-based applications that build on the ideological and technological foundations of Web 2.0, and that allow the creation and exchange of user-generated content" (Kaplan & Haenlein, 2010, p. 61). Although providing a complete list of existing Web 2.0 applications lies beyond the scope of this paper, a number of categories that can be used to classify them were identified: blogs, Wikis, social networking services, content communities, user-gernerated review sites and podcasts (Ball, 2010; Kaplan & Haenlein, 2010; Kennedy, Dalgarno, Gray, Judd, Waycott, Bennett, Maton, Krause, Bishop, Chang, & Churchward, 2007).

2.2 Social Media Growth and its Importance in Marketing

According to a study by Pew Research Center's Global Attitudes Project (2012) that assessed popularity and usage of social media across 21 countries, "social networking has spread around the world with remarkable speed." This is reflected by the fact that once people have access to the Internet, they are likely to strongly get involved in social networking sites. On the other hand, less enthusiasm towards interacting on social networks is shown in economically more developed countries such as Germany and Japan. Although these two countries are regarded as highly connected, less than half of all connected people are using social networking sites. The social media population has increased by almost 2.5 times in the last years and is predicted to further grow in the upcoming four years. Although this growth is becoming more moderate, the number of social media users is still increasing faster than the growth of the online population (Miglani, 2013).

Even though in Europe social media marketing is approaching maturity, social spending will also continue to rise, predicts a recent study by Forrester Research (McDavid, 2013). This confirms also the exploratory investigation by Michaelidou, Siamgka, and Christodoulides (2011), which shows that 44% of B2B SMEs in the UK considered raising their budgets for social media marketing. In 2008, a study reported that 93% of social media users believe that companies should be present on social media (Cone, 2008).

2.3 ROI Measurement in Social Media Marketing

Rogers (2013) states that monitoring the effectiveness of online activities is vital for a social media strategy to be successful. This is done by evaluating online activities against pre-defined objectives. However, there is no such 'one size fits all' solution and it is difficult to systematically measure and follow-up the costs versus the effects of social media. This is one of the causes that contribute to the ambiguity and intricacy in the field of social media marketing (Lagrosen & Grundén, 2014). Michaelido et al. (2011) found that the majority of enterprises do not evaluate the effectiveness of using social media networks. One of the reasons lies in the managers' lack of knowledge with regards to possible metrics. Those who did measure social networking sites (SNS) effectiveness used mainly quantitative metrics such as the numbers of comments. There are a number of tools now available that can help managers to better measure their social media activities. Some of them can be used free of charge and include Hootsuite, Google Analytics, and Facebook statistic (Ball, 2013).

2.4 Challenges and Dangers

Davidson (2011) mentions the possible loss of control over content and the dissemination of information resulting from the users' increased ability to communicate directly with each other online. Furthermore, the boundaries get blurred not only between actual clients and producers but also between reality and *virtuality*. Specifically with applications that are based on user-generated content, a big issue regarding the abuse of intellectual rights arises. This includes the unauthorized use of copyrighted material such as videos, music etc. (Keen, 2007). Marketers are facing a new situation in which power over content, timing and frequency of information is shifted from producers to consumers. Web 2.0 applications put consumers more in control of how information is generated and shared than ever before (Schmallegger & Carson, 2008). The developments in social media are very fast. Features that may be up-to-date today could be outperformed tomorrow (Lagrosen & Grundén, 2014).

2.5 Social Media in the Meetings and Events Industry

Attendees are increasingly using Web 2.0 applications to buy tickets, network with other attendees and speakers, and talk about their experiences at the event (Spiess & Van Alphen-Schrade, 2013). In the context of the meetings industry, "social media form a natural extension […], as it facilitates an online extension of the offline discussions at a meeting" (ICCA International Congress and Convention Association, 2013, p. 5). As reported in XING EVENT's Social Media and Events Report 2013, 75% of event organizers valued social media as a very important marketing instrument for events. Facebook (78%), Twitter (56%) and LinkedIn (49%) are the top three channels that the surveyed organizers used for the promotion of their events (Spiess & Van Alphen-Schrade, 2013).

Integrating social media into meetings offers several benefits to organizers and can help them to increase the meeting's performance (ICCA, 2013): Broader reach and exposure, more intense contact with target group, Search Engine Optimization (SEO), increased networking opportunities, more involvement and influence from the organizer, increased amount of feedback. There is a strong confidence of event organizers towards social media marketing and its integration into meetings and events (82% indicated their intention to enhance online social activities in the future). At this point however it is important to mention that the main goal why most event organizers are integrating social media to their communication strategy is to increase awareness of the event (58%) and the brand (49%). Only 22% are striving for generating more leads and increasing ticket sales (20%). Despite the great potential of social media, 45% of event organizers identified 'lack of time' as the biggest obstacle to the implementation of social media.

2.6 Use of Social Media in Travel and Tourism

Travellers have widely adopted social media in order to support search, organize and share their travel experiences. Some of the most popular platforms include Bloggers, TripAdvisor,

Wikitravel, Flickr etc. (Xiang & Gretzel, 2010). In the World Travel Market 2011 Industry Report it was announced that more than one third of all leisure travellers in the UK select their accommodation based on reviews on social media sites (Koumelis, 2011).

Leung, Law, Van Hoof, and Buhalis (2013) reviewed the existing literature about the use of social media in the tourism and hospitality sector: Social media appear to play a vital role during the information search phase in the travel planning process. This can be explained by the fact that a tourism product's quality cannot be evaluated until the point of the actual consumption. Thus, in order to minimize the risk of making a wrong decision, travellers typically consult various platforms prior to their decision making (Jeng & Fesenmaier, 2002). Furthermore, it was found that no other information source is more effective in nourishing travellers with the desired knowledge than social media applications. The reason for this is simply the fact UGC is considered as trustworthy since it is created by people who reveal their personal experiences. Nevertheless, it is claimed that sometimes online content may not be reliable especially because it is often created anonymously and may be published by someone with a vested commercial interest (Yoo & Gretzel, 2011).

3 METHODOLOGY

According to a trend analysis study on customer expectations in the meetings industry, organizing meetings in rural areas is becoming more popular. The Lake Constance area and South Bavaria are the leading rural destinations for meetings in Germany (Raith, 2014). Beyond the author's personal interest for the region, this was the driving reason for investigating conference venues in the Lake Constance area.

3.1 Data Collection

A number of valuable research on the use of Web 2.0 and social media applications in marketing has been conducted on a qualitative basis (Davidson, 2011; Michaelidou et al., 2011; Riegner, 2007; Rothschild, 2011; Schultz, Schwepker, & Good, 2012) with often more than 100 responses. However, it was by no means the researcher's intention to obtain a large number of responses but rather to focus on conference venues located in a particular geographic area. Therefore, seven semi-structured interviews with venue marketers and managers in the Lake Constance area covering Germany, Switzerland, and Austria were conducted.

Qualitative interviewing differs in many ways form traditional questionnaires (quantitative research). Whereas with quantitative interviews the researcher is looking for answers that can be processed and coded quickly, unstructured or semi-structured interviews are more flexible in regards to the direction of the interview. The respondent can elaborate personal perspectives and opinions on certain topics. Besides that, it was found that managers are more willing to give interviews than to complete questionnaires, particularly if the topic is perceived as interesting. An interview may provide an opportunity to managers to reflect on topics that are relevant to their current work (McGehee, 2012).

Interviews were conducted face-to-face and a voice-recorder was used to record the conversations. In addition, the researcher took notes during the interviews to highlight specifically relevant points. An interview guide including the questions and main points to address was sent to the sample at least one week prior to the interview. The structure and the questions included in the interview guide were similar to those used by Davidson (2011) and Rothschild (2011). Interviews were audio-recorded, transcribed, and coded in order to better organize and analyse the qualitative data. In this study, the researcher first identified different categories. Along with the transcription of the interviews, bits of the original data were assigned to the relevant category. A colour-coding scheme was used to better distinguish the responses. Answers were treated anonymously and thus never put into relationship with the respective interviewee. In order to answer the research questions, results are summarized and compared with corresponding literature.

3.2 Sampling

A sample is described as a subgroup taken from the full set of cases, which is called population. Overall, there are two main approaches that a researcher may choose to select the sample. The first one is probability sampling where participants are selected randomly from the whole population (Veal, 2006). Common methods of this sampling technique include simple random sampling, systematic random sampling, stratified random sampling, and (random) cluster sampling (Cameron & Price, 2009; Saunders et al., 2012). The second method is called non-probability sampling and is largely based on subjective judgments of the researcher. Quota sampling, purposive sampling, volunteer sampling and haphazard sampling are examples for non-random sampling methods (Saunders et al., 2012). A decent number of qualitative investigators use purposive sampling to identify cases. This technique is commonly applied when collecting qualitative data from a small sample that illustrates some features, characteristics or processes, which the researcher is particularly interested in (Silverman, 2010).

In this study, a purposive sampling approach based on a number of characteristics was used to determine the sample. The target sample of this study comprised managers of conference venues in the Lake Constance area who are in charge of marketing their venues. The sample was first composed of venues that are located within an approximate radius of 100km around the Lake Constance area and that are members of the European Association of Event Centres (EVVC). With regards to the management of the venues, four are managed by a public company, two are managed privately, and one is operated by a combination of private and public partners.

Table 1. Participants of the study

Conference venue name	Location	Max. capacity largest room (theatre style)	Interview partner
Festspielhaus Bregenz	Bregenz, Austria	1700	Head of Marketing & Marketing Assistant
Kongresshaus Zürich	Zürich, Switzerland	600	Director
Messe Friedrichshafen	Friedrichshafen, Germany	4500	Marketing Coordinator
Messe / ICS Stuttgart	Stuttgart, Germany	5000	Senior Project Coordinator Marketing & Online Marketing Coordinator
Montforthaus Feldkirch	Feldkirch, Austria	1200	Director
Olma Messen St. Gallen	St. Gallen, Switzerland	3900	Head of Department, CongressEvents St. Gallen
Stadthalle Singen	Singen, Germany	910	Director / Marketing & Sales, SingenCongress

3.3 Data Handling

After an interview was conducted and recorded, it has to be transcribed, that means, reproduced as a written document (Saunders et al., 2012). This can be a time-consuming task, especially when using open questions, as responses often vary in length (Finn et al., 2000). Although producing complete verbatim transcripts is a laborious process, it can be of great value when analyzing the results (Veal, 2006). There are a number of alternative ways of reducing the time needed including voice-recognition softwares, special transcription machines etc. (Saunders et al., 2012). However, in this study no such technology was used. Interviews were conducted, respectively also transcribed, in German language.

Cameron and Price (2009) explain that once the interviews are transcribed, the next step is to code and analyze them. When analyzing qualitative data, "a code is a researcher-generated construct that symbolizes and thus attributes interpreted meaning to each individual datum for later purposes of pattern detection, categorization, theory building, and other analytic processes" (Saldaña, 2013). Veal (2006) remarks that a coding scheme should be able to transfer the meanings from answers to codes while not being too complex.

In this study, the researcher first identified different categories. Along with the transcription of the interviews, bits of the original data were assigned to the relevant category. Furthermore, for each interview a number as well as a different color were used. This helped the researcher to better distinguish the responses. However, answers were treated anonymously and thus never put into relationship with the respective interviewee. In order to answer the research questions, relevant results are summarized and compared with corresponding literature. Some of the results were supported by verbatim quotes of the experts and translated by the researcher to English. Moreover, tables were used whenever the researcher thought it was appropriate and helped to better report data.

4 RESULTS

4.1 Extent of Web 2.0 Application Use

Facebook is the most popular application; it is used by all seven venues. Xing, a professional networking site that is widely used in German speaking countries, comes second and has been embraced by five venues. Three respondents stated that they were using LinkedIn and YouTube, whereas in both cases two experts mentioned their interest towards introducing them. A similar scenario applies to Twitter and Google+ with three venues already using them and a further three considering their introduction. Blogs were not incorporated in any of the venues' marketing strategy. However, three out of seven are debating on setting up a corporate blog in the future.

Experts perceived blogs to be an appropriate application to communicate about the venue and its rental spaces as such rather than talking about events, for example that are already scheduled. Amongst the three underlying reasons why social media were integrated in the communication strategy, five venues mentioned the desire to engage in conversations with users and potential clients. Further factors such as monitoring what is said about the venue, to appear more modern and hip, as well as to take advantage of additional marketing opportunities were cited by experts to be amongst the three most important reasons that made them start using social media tools. Three respondents mentioned that a staff member's personal interest in social media played an essential role. Adapting to the current media situation and the urge of jumping on the bandwagon as competitors were using it as well were cited both four times.

4.2 Objectives for Using Specific Applications

Respondents were asked to match the applications with the precise objectives of using them. This helped to find out about the venues' goals behind the use of specific applications. Driving traffic to the venues own website was matched with all seven applications. Brand awareness and reinforcement and customer retention were matched six out of seven times and thus make them together with traffic generation the three most common objectives of using Web 2.0 applications in this study.

Besides that, communicating information and news about the venue, general public relations and customer acquisition received all a fair amount of priority. Facebook and Twitter appear to be the two applications in which experts invest most confidence as these two contribute to nine out of the ten objectives listed. Whereas LinkedIn and Xing are used primarily for professional networking, Facebook addresses a broader audience, which includes exhibitors, visitors in all age categories, journalists, speakers, locals, organizers etc. However, Facebook is mainly used for public relations and to communicate with people online. Five out of the seven respondents pointed out that it would be very optimistic to believe in acquiring new clients through or thanks to their presence on any social media application. It was said that Facebook makes it easier to see where people are, what they are interested in and at the same time to strengthen your brand. However, several experts argued that it is more 'person-related' and expressed their doubts about the willingness of people to follow companies on Facebook and the like. Experts were invited to reflect about the advantages, major challenges and disadvantages of using Web 2.0 applications.

The main points are summarized as follows:

Advantages:
- A cost efficient way of communicating and referencing.
- Depending on the target market, social media can support the acquisition of new clients.
- Makes the networking more efficient and helps to follow who is changing job positions.
- The possibility of spreading information within seconds and reaching a broad audience
- One receives immediate feedback and can get a glance at what users are interested in
- In case of public events, the end users can be approached directly.
- Good value for money if planned and managed correctly.
- The monitoring of what is being said about your events and your venue becomes easier.
- Social media applications provide good opportunities for entering into dialogs with users.
- The chance of entering special-interest channels and reaching very specific markets.
- The ability to respond immediately.
- Social media help to create word-of-mouth as well as strengthening the brand and the company's image.

Disadvantages and Challenges:
- Non-selective marketing: messages will reach users that are not part of the targeted audience e.g., especially on Facebook
- The overflow of information - as a result people might refuse to continue using the tools.
- Personal and property rights are very vague and missing guidelines of what is illegal.

- How to treat Xing and LinkedIn contacts e.g., should I add them as well to the mailing list?
- There is a lot of irrelevant information - takes time to filter the bits that one is interested in.
- A lot of uncontrolled and unverified content - possible loss of credibility of content.
- Social media are not a substitute but rather an addition and require extra resources.
- Especially in the business context, social media is not as relevant as it has become in our personal lives. Yet their value tends to get overestimated by meetings professionals.
- The definition and identification of the target audience is a difficult task.
- Difficult to prove the RIO e.g., the additional attendees attracted through social media.

Some of the above listed disadvantages and challenges are also the reasons why the venues are not using Web 2.0 applications as extensively as they could. One particular barrier clearly draws attention: "Lack of staff time" was indicated by four experts as the most important and by one more as the third most important reason for not using Web 2.0 application to a greater extent. A further significant barrier presents the difficulty to prove ROI. "Lack of staff expertise" was pointed out by four interviewees.

At this point, it is important to mention that some venues are using Web 2.0 more intensely for the promotion of their own events that are happening within their venues rather than the promotion of the location as such. This applies especially in cases of public fairs and other consumer events like concerts. Three out of seven professionals explained that besides the time needed there were no additional resources invested. This means that existing staff is taking care of social media as an extra duty. In another three cases, staff received internal (two instances) and external (one instance) training. Whereas in one venue it was decided to make social media the project for the trainees, another one is recruiting freelance staff to handle social media during more intense times. Moreover, one venue created a new position and recruited an additional team member plus one trainee to take care of online marketing activities.

4.3 Posting Behaviour and Type of Content

The content is always written in German, as the majority of users are German speakers. In two venues, respondents remarked that distinctive tones of voice are used to communicate in specific applications. On business networks such as Twitter, Xing, LinkedIn and Google+, the audience is addressed formally. On the other hand, Facebook tends to be more informal in the sense of how users are approached. Regarding the time when content is posted none of the respondents has indicated having precise timings.

The most popular type of content that is posted relates to news about the venue and includes images. Information about future events is very common amongst the published material. Furthermore, videos have a fair share and are used by five venues. Three out of the seven venues are regularly sharing industry-related news (e.g., company mergers, trend studies, etc.). Interviewees were invited to express their views about the future demand of so called collaborative marketing campaigns, which is referred to as co-promotion in this study. It was highlighted that depending on the particular role "the venue" is assuming in different projects, co-promotion could eventually play a role. Referring to the experts' point of view, the strategy behind co-promoting conferences only plays a valuable role if the conference is opened to the public or if the client wants the public to be informed. Experts have stated that they see a turn in events towards the co-promotion strategy. From their point of view, co promoting conferences will become common practice.

4.4 Social Media Planning and Measurement

Five of the seven interviewees stated that they have a plan rather than a specific social media marketing strategy. Some may plan it weekly, monthly, quarterly as it is hard to be planned biannually or annually – this is due to the fact, that social media marketing is something more spontaneous and can hardly be considered in long-term strategic plans. Measuring social media performance is a field for its own. In general it has been said, that measuring social media returns requires a lot of knowhow and time in order to be done properly.

The role of social media return measurements and evaluations is rather unsophisticated at this point in time. On the other hand, two of the seven experts do monitor the results weekly and try to see how their current activities have been accepted by their user base. Four out of the seven constantly monitor and observe how the acceptance is for their posts, but do not incorporate highly anticipated evaluations. One venue is effectively monitoring and evaluating their placement with three different tools (Hootsuite, Google analytics, and Facebook analytics).

4.5 The Future of Web 2.0 Applications

Another topic that has been identified is how the case of social media evolution will evolve in the future. In general, all have considered it as a difficult trend to predict due to the fact that it is still rather young in regards to being integrated in a corporate marketing mix. One of the respondents has referred to the topic of social media marketing in comparison to newsletters - 'if you do not have one you are not considered as a real company but who is actually still reading those newsletters?' Another point of view that was discussed was that Facebook might establish two different lines; one for private utilization and another arm focusing on corporate clients. One expert goes as far as stating that social media platforms will stay on the fringes (for the next five years) but will always be used by a certain span of clients.

Two theories have been used from one professional in order to explain her future outlook for social media platforms and their integration for marketing purposes in line with conferences. She was convinced that either two (Facebook and Twitter) or maximum three social media platforms will dominate the entire market and weaker platforms will disappear from the pool of useable platforms (e.g., Google+). The second theory was based on internationalization and the strengthening effect this has towards the integration of social media platforms within the daily business. LinkedIn and Xing will be further developed and accepted to be part of the standard communication channels within the business sphere. One interviewee considers it the normal evolution and closely links it to the ageing society and the new generation that will establish the marketing plans for the future. Overall they all see it as a hard topic to plan for the future and therefore want to observe how it will evolve over time. They don't want to lose out on the potential but they are not considering it as a key part of their marketing mix. Only one venue integrated social media on a professional level.

5 DISCUSSION AND CONCLUSION

The findings of this study indicate that venues have adapted at least two social media applications during the last years. This nicely confirms Davidson's study (2011) where the intensity and extent of usage of Web 2.0 applications was predicted to grow among venues. The majority of light-users recently recognized the potential of social media applications but is still uncertain about their effectiveness in the context of marketing conferences and business events. The indication from the sample is that many are still figuring out whether there is a strategic sense to incorporate such tools.

The findings also show that engaging in conversations with users and potential clients, and taking advantage of additional marketing opportunities are the two most common reasons why Web 2.0 tools became part of the venues' marketing mix. This points out the essential role of relationship marketing in the B2B sector and aligns with past evidence implying that new technology and the Internet could encourage and support it (Bauer, Grether, & Leach, 2002; Sharma, 2002). In a number of venues, the marketing potential of social media applications was recognized due to a staff member's interest in this field as opposed to being a strategically planned decision. However, most of the respondents mentioned the lack of staff expertise as a barrier for not using Web 2.0 more extensively.

Several interviewees pointed out that they were uncertain about how to effectivley make use of the opportunities presented by these channels. This resounds with what was suggested by the literature that marketers have to find ways to manage and adapt to the shift of power over content from producer to consumer (Schmallegger & Carson, 2008). The most significant barrier for further expanding in the domain of social media was found to be the time needed for a proper management of the channels. Resulting from the findings, experts highlighted the relative low above-the-line costs and modest effort that is need to create a presence on these applications. However, just as it resulted from the existing literature, additional staff time and training is required (Davidson, 2011).

Despite the growing pressure for marketing managers to show convincing evidence of the effectiveness of using such social media applications (Michaelidou et al., 2011), it was found that the majority of those interviewed do not systematically evaluate whether their online activities are successful. It was claimed that proving the real ROI is very difficult as appropriate metrics are missing. This confirms previous research (Dwyer, 2007; Hoffman & Fodor, 2010; Michaelidou et al., 2011; Rogers, 2013; Thackeray et al., 2008). Most professionals are used to place their success on numbers which is the common measure in the world of business. However, marketing involves more than numeric success and includes reach, brand awareness etc. (Hoffman & Fodor, 2010). The absence of well-grounded knowledge about the costs vs. effects of social media marketing contributes to the ambiguity in this field (Lagrosen & Grundén, 2014). Yet, given the increasing importance of social networks – as suggested in the literature review – organizations have to be creative in developing more customer-centered metrics. Rather than considering the return on the company's investment, it may seem more appropriate to measure the users'/customers' motivation and their social media investment to engage with the firm. Assessing user investment (e.g., time) in a social media relationship puts the focus on long-term payoffs as opposed to short-term results (Hoffman & Fodor, 2010).

If it is possible to generalize from the findings of this study, social media as a communication and marketing instrument is more popular in the field of B2C / public events. Therefore, examples of good practice in the field of entertainment (e.g., concerts, sports games etc.) could serve as a fruitful source to marketing managers of conference venue (Davidson, 2011). The experts have recognized the opportunities that are presented by social media and have generally appreciated the necessity to learn how to become part of online peer-to-peer conversations. The immediate feedback and the spontaneity resulted to be amongst the striking points of the medium which correlates with what was highlighted in the report by ICCA (2013) on how the meetings industry can benefit from social media. Also, this nicely correlates with the idea behind platforms such as Twitter as they deliver a snap shot of "the" moment – what is happening at this point in time.

The quality of content should be the first concern to marketers. While some of the investigated venues have a fairly clear idea which tools work and what content is appreciated by users, others are still in the earlier stages and have not taken full advantage of the additional marketing opportunities provided by Web 2.0 applications as of yet. Therefore, a number of recommendations are now pointed out. First and foremost, a marketer should consider several strategic key questions before launching a social media strategy. These should address the target population's preferences, the required resources, as well as the goals and objectives of the strategy. Secondly, setting up a social media strategy that includes the time and personnel requirement is vital.

A plan that lays out what content will be published over a specific period of time. However, there should be room for certain flexibility for spontaneous posts about topics that might pop up. The strategy has to go hand in hand with the overall marketing activities and should support the company's business objectives (ICCA, 2013). It is essential to measure and monitor the strategy's effectiveness against the pre-defined objectives in order to find out what works and what has to be changed (Rogers, 2013). Social media are interaction channels; interaction is time-consuming and needs competency.

As it results from the findings, respondents generally seem to be aware of what should be taken into consideration when publishing content on social media platforms. Yet, the great majority tends to not be as strict in the implementation. Lagrosen and Grundén (2014) provide some hands-on tips that could be of help to all those responsible for social media within an organization. Some of these recommendations were already applied by a few venues and were encouraged by the experience of those experts. Interesting content that triggers positive feelings is vital for attracting the users' attention. One expert pointed out that competitions always receive a fairly positive echo. Prizes can include free entrance tickets as well as goodies that relate to the topic of the conference. It was affirmed that creating a story around such campaigns helps to engage users even more as they can create meaningful links.

Depending on the social media channel the tone of writing when addressing the audience has to be adapted. When engaging with users on Facebook, it seems more appropriate to stay personal, yet always correct. On the other side, LinkedIn and Xing are generally used in a professional context and require a more formal and business like wording. Given the limited length (140 characters) of each tweet on Twitter it is recommended to use pictures to create feelings and impressions rather than conveying factual information about the product. Twitter, just as any other social media application should not be abused for hard selling but much more to maintain positive relationships with users and prospects as well as to provoke interest. In order to maximize a post's visibility, marketers are advised to think about the right timing when to publish content on which platform.

Late afternoon and evenings is usually the time where most people are online on Facebook. Twitter is often used as an alternative to the morning newspaper, thus planning tweets during coffee time is recommended. Instead of decreasing rates, venues could offer customer's to co-promote conferences/events via their social media channels and therefore add value to their product. Providing such a complementary service may help venues to accommodate the constant cry of "more for less."

Finally, the meetings industry associations have a certain responsibility to educate and train their members on how Web 2.0 tools can create value to them. The International Association of Conference Centers (IACC) has published a social media guide for conference centres, which reviews a rich number of different Web 2.0 applications. The paper is entitled 'A Guide to Social Media 2012' can be downloaded free of charge (IACC, 2012).

Meeting Professionals International (MPI) provides its members with a number of free white papers, articles and other informative material about social media and their relevance to the meetings industry. The findings highlighted the uncertainty of many experts in regards to the effectiveness of Web 2.0 applications related to the B2B marketing of their venues. While it was found that the choice of tools and content is fairly manageable, time constraints together with the lack of social media expertise are two factors withholding marketers of integrating these applications to a greater extent.

Besides few venues, the studied venues seem not to fully make use of the possibilities provided by social media. Although the Web 2.0 environment provides companies with additional marketing opportunities, it also presents them with new challenges. Marketers have to learn how they can create value from user-generated content and how to manage the shift of power from the producer to the consumer. From the result of the study it can be concluded that the interviewed experts seem to perceive the relevance of social media applications for the marketing of conference venues to be overestimated. Personal encounters and face-to-face meetings at industry related events, trade shows and sale visits remain without a doubt the most important interaction with customers and potential clients. Yet, social media have the power to support and enlarge professional networking.

The meetings industry has recognized the value of social media and has embraced these tools very quickly (Spiess & Van Alphen-Schrade, 2013). However, as the findings of this study show, there is still room for further developing the use of Web 2.0 applications in the conference venue sector. This statement was supported by 42% of the respondents who indicated to further integrate social media in their commercial strategies. Several experts acknowledged that Web 2.0 applications will become part of companies' communication plans and will therefore also further change the marketing strategies of conference venues in the future. However, changes will not only occur on part of the venues but also on the side of the platform and application operators. After all, as one professional argued, Facebook and all the other social media platforms are companies just as any other organization that offers a service to its clients. Additionally, marketers might well consider social media applications as a benchmarking tool to gasp how other venues with similar nature of business are taking advantage of this medium. Last but not least, the Web 2.0 provides collaborative platforms with which new research approaches can be developed in order to explore new research communities.

Although social platforms present rather new forms of data collection tools, researcher and marketers are becoming more confident at working with them (Cooke & Buckley, 2008). Today's competition in the conference venue sector is getting fiercer with new types of event localities popping up every day. Thus, there is an increasing pressure for venue owners to provide a reasonable ROI (Davidson, 2011). In the light of such conditions, venue marketers should recognize the recent addition of social media platforms as professional marketing instruments and therefore have to learn how to integrate said tools in their marketing mix.

This study presents a number of limitations. The research is based on qualitative methods carried out in one sector, the conference venue sector, and in one geographic location. Consequently, the generalizability of findings to other contexts is uncertain. Furthermore, some of conference venues that were originally identified are not included in this study because of time constraints on professionals or, in a few cases, because of the venue's unwillingness to participate. To follow-up on this exploratory qualitative study, a quantitative approach might be useful on a large sample of venue professionals. Furthermore, additional studies of this nature should be conducted in other cultural settings in order to compare the usage of social media marketing in different countries. Additional research could address the costs versus effects measurement of social media marketing, as this is still a topic of concern for marketers.

REFERENCES

Ball, C. (2010). *Social media - A new paradigm for meetings.* Retrieved June 4, 2014 from http://www.corbinball.com/articles_technology/index.cfm?fuseaction=cor_av&artID=6680

Ball, C. (2013). *Top technology trends transforming events - And what it mean for you!* From PowerPoint slides: http://www.corbinball.com/assets/trends-rcma.pdf

Bauer, H. H., Grether, M., & Leach, M. (2002). Building customer relationship over the internet. *Industrial Marketing Management, 31*(2), 155-163.

Cone. (2008). *Business in social media study.* Retrieved June 10, 2014 from http://onesocialmedia.com/wp-content/uploads/2010/03/2008_business_in_social_media_fact_sheet.pdf

Cooke, M., & Buckley, N. (2008). Web 2.0, social networks and the future of market research. *International Journal of Market Research, 50*(2), 267-292.

Davidson, R. (2011). Web 2.0 as a marketing tool for conference centres. *International Journal of Event and Festival Management , 2*(2), 117-138.

Dwyer, P. (2007). Measuring the value of electronic word of mouth and its impact in consumer communities. *Journal of Interactive Marketing, 21*(2), 63-79.

Hoffman, D. L., & Fodor, M. (2010). Can you measure the ROI of your social media marketing? *MIT Sloan Mangement Review, 52*(1), 41-49.

IACC International Association of Conference Centers. (2012). *A guide to social media.* From http://iacconline.org/content/files/iacc_socialmediaguide.pdf

ICCA International Congress and Convention Association. (2013). *Social media for meetings.*

Jeng, J., & Fesenmaier, D. (2002). Conceptualizing the travel decision-making hierachy: A review of recent developments. *Tourism Analysis, 7*(1), 15-32.

Kaplan, A. M., & Haenlein, M. (2010). Users of the world, unite! The challenges and opportunities of social media. *Business Horizon, 53*(1), 59-68.

Keen, A. (2007). *The cult of the amateur: how today's internet is killing our culture.* Doubleday, New York: Currency.

Kennedy, G., Dalgarno, B., Gray, K., Judd, T., Waycott, J., Bennett, S., Maton, K., Krause, K.L., Bishop, A., Chang, R. & Churchward A. (2007). The net generation are not big users of Web 2.0 technologies: Preliminary findings. Retrieved June 12, 2014 from http://www.ascilite.org.au/conferences/singapore07/procs/kennedy.pdf

Kimmel, A. J. (2010). *Connecting with consumers - Marketing for new marketplace realities.* Oxford, New York: Oxford University Press.

Koumelis, T. (2011). *Social media continues to play role in travel decisions.* Retrieved August 23, 2014, from http://www.traveldailynews.asia/news/article/46174/social-media-continues-tp-play

Kotler, P., Wong, V., Saunders, J., & Armstrong, G. (2005). *Principles of marketing* (4th ed.). Harlow, UK: Pearson Education.

Kwak, H., Lee, C., Park, H., & Moon, S. (2010). What is twitter, a social network or a news media? *19th International conference on World Wide Web*, (pp. 591-600). Raleigh.

Lagrosen, S. O., & Grundén, K. (2014). Social media marketing in the wellness industry. *The TQM Journal, 26*(3), 253-260.

Leung, D., Law, R., Van Hoof, H., & Buhalis, D. (20123). Social media in tourism and hospitality: A literature review. *Journal of Travel & Tourism Marketing, 30*(1), 3-22.

Mays, D., Weaver, J. B., & Bernhardt, J. M. (2011). New media in social marketing. In G. Hastings, K. Angus, & C. Bryant, *The SAGE handbook of social marketing.* London, UK: SAGE.

McDavid, J. (2013). *European social media marketing spending in good shape, upcoming legislation the major inhibitor.* Retrieved June 10, 2014 from Blogs Forrester: http://blogs.forrester.com/anthony_mullen/13-04-29-european_social_media_marketing_spending_in_good_shape_upcoming_legislation_the_major_inhibitor

McGehee, N. G. (2012). *Interview techniques*. In L. Dwyer, A. Gill, & N. Seetaram, Handbook of research methods in tourism - quantitative and qualitative approaches (pp. 365-376). Cheltenham, UK: Edward Elgar.

Michaelidou, N., Siamgka, N. T., & Christodoulides, G. (2011). Usage, barriers and measurement of social media marketing: An exploratory investigation of small and medium B2B brands. *Industrial Marketing Management, 40*(7), 1153-1159.

Miglani, J. (2013). *Social media spending In Western Europe is expected to reach 3.2 Bibllion euros by 2017, but there is a catch*. Retrieved June 10, 2014 from Blogs Forrester: http://blogs.forrester.com/jitender_miglani/13-03-04-
social_media_spending_in_western_europe_is_expected_to_reach_32_billion_euros_by_2017_
but_there_i

Muniz, A. M., & Schau, H. J. (2011). How to inspire value-laden collaborative consumer-generated content. *Business Horizon, 54*(3), 209-217.

O'Reilly, T. (2005). *What Is Web 2.0 Design patterns and business models for the next generation of software*. Retrieved June 3, 2014 from http://oreilly.com/lpt/a/6228

Pew Global Research Project. (2012). *Social networking popular across global*. Retrieved June 9, 2014 from http://www.pcwglobal.org/2012/12/12/social-nctworking-popular-across-globc/

Raith, J. (2014). Trendanalyse: Kundenerwartungen in der Veranstaltungswirtschaft. *Expodata. 4'14 March 2014*

Riegner, C. (2007). Word of mouth on the web: the impact of Web 2.0 on consumer purchase decisions. *Journal of Advertising Research, 47*(4), 436-447.

Rogers, T. (2013). *Events management: conferences and conventions*. Florence, KY, USA: Taylor and Francis.

Rothschild, P. C. (2011). Social media use in sports and entertainment venues. *International Journal of Event and Festival Management, 2*(2), 139-150.

Saldaña, J. (2013). *The coding manual for qualitative researchers*. London, UK: Sage.

Saunders, M., Lewis, P., & Thornhill, A. (2012). *Research methods for business students* (6th ed.). Harlow, UK: Pearson Education Limited.

Schmallegger, D., & Carson, D. (2008). Blogs in tourism: Changing approaches to information exchange. *Journal of Vacation Marketing, 14*(2), 99-110.

Schultz, R. J., Schwepker, C. H., & Good, D. J. (2012). Social media usage: An investigation of b2b salespeople. *American Journal of Business, 27*(2), 174-194.

Sharma, A. (2002). Trends in internet-based business-to-business marketing. *Industrial Marketing Management, 31*(2), 77-84.

Silverman, D. (2010). *Doing qualitative research* (3rd ed.). London, UK: Sage Publications.

Spiess, S., & Van Alphen-Schrade, M. (2013). *Social media & events report 2013*. Retrieved June 12, 2014 from http://www.amiando.com/fileadmin/Data/Info-Center/Reports/Social_Media_Report/EN_SMER_XING_EVENTS.pdf

Thackeray, R., Neiger, B. L., Hanson, C. L., & McKenzie, J. F. (2008). Enhancing promotional strategies within social marketing programs: Use of Web 2.0 social media. *Health Promotion Practice, 9*(4), 338-343.

Vargo, S. L., & Lusch, R. F. (2004). Evolving to a new dominant logic for marketing. *Journal of Marketing, 68*, 1-17.

Veal, A. J. (2006). *Research methods for leisure and tourism: A practical guide* (3rd ed.). Harlow, UK: Pearson Education.

Xiang, Z., & Gretzel, U. (2010). Role of social media in online travel information search. *Tourism Management, 12*(3), 233-248.

Yoo, K. H., & Gretzel, U. (2011). Influence of personality on travel-related consumer-generated media creation. *Computers in Human Behaviour, 27*(2), 609-621.

Small Medium Sized Hotels and Use of Social Media, the Case of Austria

Ali Gouhar

Salzburg University of Applied Sciences, Austria
gouharnoor@yahoo.com

Abstract

With the establishment of the internet and social media, travellers find tourism products and experiences quickly and conveniently. In addition, consumers have the ability to assess the tourism product or experience. The aim of this study is to explore the critical success factors of social media for small and medium hotels in Austria. The study focused approaches for small and medium hotels, which would make use of social media much more effective.

Mix method primary research combine to form the findings of this study. Fifteen small and medium hotels managers were interviewed to find out the critical success factors of social media. The study also focused on a survey. Fifty domain names were taken from the Austrian hotel association website. During the survey, participants were advised to visit each of the hotel websites, to assess social media strategies implemented by each hotel. In addition, participants were advised in the online questionnaires, to find out the characteristics of social media, after collecting the information, the data was analysed using spss version 16.

The results of the study are; social media play a significant role by creating interpersonal experience between suppliers and consumers. This study identified critical success factors of social media for small and medium hotels in Austria that includes; understanding and prioritizing benefits, identifying trends, deploying and employing certain characteristics, managing through social media, employing social media information, measuring return on investment, and staging interpersonal experience

In summary, the findings of this study provide an explanation of the critical success factors of social media that help to bring small and medium hotels operators, facilitating the travellers looking for information efficiently and affordably. Furthermore, social media support a hotel to become more visible in the global market.

Keywords: Social media; online reviews; internet; hospitality; e-word-of-mouth

1 INTRODUCTION

The aim of this study is to explore the critical success factors of social media for small medium hotels in Austria. This study acknowledges the potential of social media in driving business. For example, when travelers make a decision of booking a room in a hotel, most of the consumers have no prior information of the hotel. However, social media such as YouTube, Facebook, tripadvisor and Twitter can play a role in the purchase decision process for consumers. As a result consumers utilize opportunities offered by social media in buying decision process. Moreover, the aim of this study is to explore the importance of social media for small medium hotels in Austria, and to find out what challenges the owners of the SMHs are facing. This study explores approaches use by small medium hotels, which make the use of social media in much more effective ways. However, this study argue that, not all the SMH's in Austria do use the social media effectively. Therefore, this study aim to answer the question, what are the critical success factors of social media for small medium hotels.

Berne et al (2011) pointed out that, prior to the development of internet in the tourism sector, suppliers had no other choice to communicate with consumers but to use intermediaries, such as Travel Agencies and tour operators. However, with the development of web 2.0 and online social networking websites heavily affect today most of the online activities of both suppliers and consumers and their effect on tourism is obviously rather important (Milano et al., 2011). The fast development of information communication technologies (ICTs) and the expansion of the Internet have changed industry structures around the world (Ma et al., 2003). There is no question as to the benefits offered by technology-IT applications can reduce costs, enhance operational efficiency, and improve service quality (Alford and Clarke, 2009). Not only ICTs empower consumers to identify, customize and purchase tourism products but they also support the globalization of the industry by providing effective tools for suppliers to develop, manage and distribute their offering worldwide (Buhalis and Law, 2008).

The technological revolution experienced through the development of the Internet has changed dramatically the market conditions for tourism organizations (Buhalis and Law, 2008). As a result, new technologies have dramatically changed consumer's bookings and holiday behavior. The tourism product is perishable and intangible thus consumers have limited choices to experience the product before consumption. However, new technologies (ICTs and Social media) have dramatically changed buying behavior of the consumer. Nowadays consumers are empowered to buy, thus service providers have to attract consumers unlike traditional approaches because the development of ICTs (Information Communication Technologies) and particularly the Internet have empowered the "new" tourist to become more knowledgeable and is now able to seek exceptional value for money and time (Buhalis and Law, 2008).

With the introduction and the diffusion of the interactive Web 2.0 features and applications, tourism markets have become real conversations on one of the most thrilling subject for a human being (Milano et al., 2011). Therefore, Social network sites such Facebook, Myspace, Twitter, LinkedIn, YouTube etc. have recently gained enormous popularity for marketing communications (Maurer and Wiegmann, 2011). As a result, on travel review platforms, tourist can share their holiday experiences with the global community and travelers today can actively create and distribute travel information through social media (Law et al., 2011). Therefore, web 2.0 has made available some technologies that have changed the way users create, share, search for, and collect online information, and they offer new and more efficient ways of communication by enabling users to make their ideas and opinions available to a positional audience of millions of people (Chaves et al., 2011).

As a result online reviews posted in a travel related consumer review and rating website increase travelers' confidence during decision making, which reduce risk, assist them in selecting accommodation and therefore facilitate decision making (International Conference on et al., 2012). Thus, online consumer-generated opinions are especially important for hospitality and tourism (International Conference on et al., 2009). Many businesses, organizations, communities, and families are using social networking to promote themselves, to communicate better with others, and to engage with their audience (Peacock, 2010). Social media significantly engage customers and suppliers. Therefore, growing numbers of consumers take advantages of online opinions generated by experienced consumers, these new communication venues also create new opportunities for deception (International Conference on et al., 2009).

According to Thomas (2004) "There has been a flourishing of interest in a variety of issues relating to small business in tourism over recent years" (p.1). One of the most interested issues for small medium firms is social media marketing. According to Flynn (2012) "one new blog, the original social networking tool, is created every second among small medium sized companies, 69 percent use Facebook for business, 44 percent have a corporate presence on Twitter, 32 percent share video on YouTube and 23 percent connect via LinkedIn"(p.202). New internet communication tools, such as electronic data interchange and electronic commerce, make cross border networking easier and more practical for SMHs. Hence SMHs can reduce costs for potential consumers and improve a firm's visibility in global market (Organisation for Economic and Development, 2002).

2 LITERATURE REVIEW

Social media is a group of internet-based applications that build on the ideological and technological foundations of web 2.0 and that allow the creation and exchange of user generated content (Kaplan and Haenlein, 2010). Kaplan and Haenlein (2010) further point out the concept of social media is top of the agenda for many business executives today. Decision makers, as well as consultants, try to identify ways in which firms can make profitable use of applications such as Wikipedia, YouTube, Facebook, Second life, and Twitter. Hitz (2006) state that, the internet is changing the way that users can access fast, up-to-date, and interactive tourism information without any geographical and time constraints. Xiang and Gretzel (2009) point out that, many of these social media websites assist consumers in posting and sharing their travel-related comments, opinions, and personal experiences, which then serve as information for others. Social media is indispensable for small medium hotels in terms of presence in the global market.

Chaves (2011) point out that, web 2.0 has made available some technologies that have changed the way users create, share, search for, and collect online information, and they offer new and more efficient ways of communication by enabling users to make their ideas and opinions available to a potential audience of millions of people. Internet has developed communication tools, such as social media, which play a significant role as a source of information for consumers without time and money constraints.

Social media has reshaped the travel planning concept before the trip. Simon Wong and Gladys Liu (2010) mention that, travel guidebooks are used for a variety of purposes, mainly before travel takes place. However, reason for searching information before the trip is the perishable nature of the tourism product, thus consumer's constantly seeking information about the product by using several channels and social media is one of best channels, which has changed the process of seeking information before the trip. Blogs in tourism appears to be those from travelers who publish their travel stories and recommendations online. Consumers are consistently watching and interested to get information about a hotel before the trip from experience consumers rather than the service providers. Therefore, tripadvisor and other such websites are constantly getting popularity among the consumers.

According to Zhang et al (2010) the growing availability and popularity of web-based opinion platforms, online product reviews are now an emerging market phenomenon that is playing an increasingly important role in consumer purchase decisions. Customers could evaluate the product before the consumption process. Three-quarters of travelers have considered online consumer reviews as an information source when planning their trips (Ye et al., 2009). Thus consumers are getting much smarter than before, and customers know the sources of collecting information before the trip. Ye et al, (2009) further state that online user-generated reviews are an important source of information to travelers. However, Travel reviews have become valuable to both travelers and practitioners for various decision-making and planning processes. It's also a fact that, users are unable to read all available information because of overwhelming amount of information via internet (Rong et al., 2011). Nevertheless this study suggest that, social media has the abilities to cap overwhelming information into a package.

Vermeulen and Seegers (2009) mention that, exposure to online reviews enhances hotel consideration in consumers. In 2007 about 20 million people visit Tripadvisor to utilize other travelers' reviews every month (International Conference on et al., 2009). The amounts of online reviews are constantly increasing due to the reliability and validity of the contents. Recommendations of other consumers who have prior experience with a tourism product are not only the most preferred sources, but also the most influential sources for travel decision making (International Conference on et al., 2009). Therefore De Ascaniis and Morassol (2011) pointed out, tourism is an experience which needs to be communicated. In fact, be it wonderful or terrible, a travel experience is usually shared talking with others. Tourism is telling a story to others and social media has dramatically reshaped the way people telling or sharing their experiences with others. Ascaniis and Morassol (2011) further argues, that the fact that tourism is an experience worth to be communicated may reasonably be the main reason why travel reviews today flourish on the internet.

Law et al (2011) state that, with the unprecedented ability to empower travelers in producing and consuming travel information, Web 2.0 is fundamentally changing the way of traveler's information search behavior and affecting subsequent decision making. Therefore Rong et al (2011) suggested that, It is possible to turn customer data into profiling information, such as customer value, customer targeting information, customer rating, and behavior tracking, which is accessible by business. Thus all the information customers sharing through social sites would be a value tools for a hotel, it's no wonder even the customers might review a hotel critically but no doubt this review will definitely help a hotel to improve service and bring better product to market.

In today's marketplace, consumers are a different breed than they were even five years ago. They are much better informed, better educated, and more demanding in the products and services that they require, and they are more familiar with technology (Sharp, 2003). Therefore, effective use of Social media is helping to bridge a gap between customer's and service providers. Social media allow firms to engage in timely and direct end-consumer contact at relatively low cost and higher levels of efficiency than can be achieved with more traditional communication tolls (Kaplan and Haenlein, 2010). Effective use of social media is all about engaging with your customers rather explaining the product. Social media are all about sharing and interaction, so ensure that your content is always fresh and that you engage in discussions with your customers (Kaplan and Haenlein, 2010).

Wright (2006) mention that, the challenge for most companies who engage in customer conversation isn't obtaining feedback; it's how best to deal with the feedback, both positive and negative. To deal with customers an effective way, a hotel need effective way of using social media. After reviewing the literature, this study find the importance of social media for SMH's. This study further contribute to the literature towards critical success factors of social media for SMH's in Austria, which plays an important role for both academics and industry practitioners.

3 METHODOLOGY

To investigate the critical success factors of social media for small and medium hotels, a mixed method approach of qualitative and quantitative approaches were adopted. Such approaches can be used to describe and formalize the relation between qualitative and quantitative research (Flick, 2009). A qualitative approaches the interviews with small and medium hotels managers in Austria were conducted because interviews are the main types of qualitative research (Nykiel, 2007). Furthermore, interview is a main source of retrieving direct information from the participants, during open ended questions. A standardized interview was conducted with 15 managers of small and medium hotels in Austria. The aim of this interview was to find out the critical success factors of social media for small and medium hotels in Austria. The interview questions were sent to the hotel owners via emails 2 weeks before the interviews. After approval, an appointment was fixed with each hotel manager/ owner. Each manager was interviewed individually. The interview was conducted face-to-face. In the interview, total 8 questions were asked, the received data was also tape recorded for later evaluation.

This study also randomly selected 50 hotels domain names from the Austrian hotel association website, where almost every hotel is a member of the association. The domain names were selected from the Austrian hotels associations because the website is officially certified, and every hotel in Austria is the member of the association. This method was chosen based on content validity. However, no statistical evidence can be supplied for content validity (Thomas et al., 2010). In the domain names of the hotels, 25 small hotels with rooms up to 30, and 25 medium sized hotels with rooms up to 60 were selected. After taking the sample, we invited a group of 10 participants. However, only 5 participants participated in the survey. Later on all 5 participants were invited to the computer lab; the participants were the university students in Austria because they were familiar with the hotels, and they had prior knowledge about the use of social media.

In the survey each participant was assigned 30 minutes time and a computer, and a domain name of the hotel to find each hotel activities on social networks sites. Each participant found appropriate social sites of the hotel; each social network was evaluated for the characteristics of social media to identify the critical success factor of social media for small and medium hotels. After collecting the empirical data through the online questionnaire and qualitative data from entrepreneur's interviews and the literature review, the data was analysed via spss software.

4 FINDINGS

Table 1 provide detail information about active social network sites among SMH's in Austria. *Which one is an active social site among small medium sized hotels in Austria? Please select all that apply*

Table 1. Active Social networking sites

Measure	n	M	SD
Facebook	5	1.00	.000
YouTube	5	.28	.454
Twitter	5	.34	.479
Flicker	5	.08	.274
Google	5	.26	.443
Holidaycheck	5	.46	.503

Note. N= represent number of participants

Table 1 illustrates statistical analysis of question number one. Participates were asked, which one is an active social network site among SMH's in Austria. Therefore, total five participants participated in the electronic questionnaires survey. Therefore, valid percentage is (100%); the result indicates there is no missing value in the above table 1.

Taking further data into account, Mean 1.00 represent Facebook. This indicates each participant selected Facebook is an active social networking site among small medium hotels in Austria, while only 0.28 selected YouTube, 0.34 selected Twitter, 0.8 selected Flicker, 0.26 selected Google+ and 0.46 selected Holidaycheck, as an active social networking among SMH's in Austria. The participants were advised according to electronic questionnaires. In the questionnaires Facebook, YouTube, Twitter, Flicker, Google, None, Holidaycheck, and other were mentioned as an active social networking sites. This results indicate that, Facebook is favorable social network for Austrian SMH's hotels.

The following Figure 1 explain in detail the characteristic of social media, which is used by small medium hotels in Austria.

What are the characteristic of social media, which adopted by the hotel through social sites?

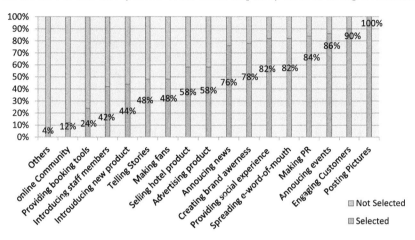

Fig. 1. The characteristics of social media among small medium hotels

Figure 1 illustrate a very clear result regarding the characteristics of social media among small medium hotels in Austria. Thus, it can be seen from the above figure 1, during the survey we found that (100%) small medium hotels do use social media as a tool of posting pictures. However, (90%) hotels can also be seen engaging customer in the conversation.

Moreover, it can be further seen that (86%) small medium hotels announcing events through social media. Thus, it can be seen as characteristics of social media among small medium hotels in Austria. It can be further described from the above figures that after announcing events, (84%) of hotels are involved doing PR through social media sites. Further, (82%) SMH's are also actively use social media as an active tool of spreading e-word of mouth.

Figure 1 further illustrate that after PR (82%) of small medium hotels do use social media a tool of providing social experience through social media sites of the hotels. After social experience, (78%) small medium hotels are also trying to create brand awareness through social media sits.

Figure 1 illustrates, that (76%) small medium hotels announce news through social media. Furthermore, (44%) hotels introduce new product through social networking sites. Moreover, (58%) small medium hotels are selling hotel products through social media. Furthermore, (48%) small medium hotels are making fans through social networking sites.

Figure 1 enumerate, (48%) small medium hotels telling stories of the hotel through social networking sites. Moreover, (44%) small medium hotels in Austria introduce a new product through social media networking sites. Furthermore, (44%) small medium hotels introduce staff members through social networking sites.

Figure 1 demonstrate only 24% small medium hotels provide booking tools through social networking sites in Austria. Furthermore, (12%) small medium hotels increase online community through social networking sites.

The following figure 2 explain managers interview, about critical success factors of social media.

What are the critical success factors of social media strategy for hotels?

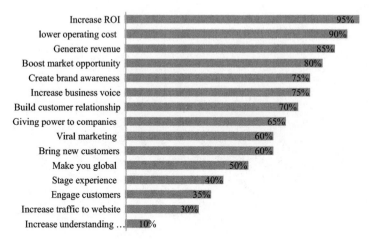

Fig. 2. Critical success factors of SMHs

Figure 2 illustrates the managers, emphasis that critical success factors of social media is an increase of return on investment (see figure 2) because the return on investment is not only economic benefits to an organization. However, managers, also emphasis to measure the return on investment of social media, then a hotel has to make sure many customers are leaving the positive comments about the hotel, handling complaints through the help of social media, and spreading electronic word of mouth is the return on investment. The managers also indicated that low operating cost is a critical success factors of social media because social media targeting a mass audience with minimal time and resources. According to Chaney (2009) when an organization know where a business audience lives online. An organization will be better equipped to choose delivery mechanisms that are the most cost effective. That is where the tools of social media can become a business ally as many of them require little or no investment of capital perhaps time.

Figure 2 demonstrates the managers considering one of the social media success factors is generating revenue because social media attract a mass audience with low cost, this result new target market and an increase in revenues. Social media are contingent revenue generator, for example, when customers leave the positive comments that leverage new customers, as a result, revenue of the hotel increases. Various customers are rating a hotel after the trip that result, indirect increase of revenue for a hotel. The managers stress social media success factor is to support and boost market opportunities because social media helps to bring small hotel in a position to compete with large chain hotels. The mangers further stress that various hotels were lagging behind attracting the new audience because of the high cost of traditional media. However, social media support small hotels to go global with low cost and high efficiency. Furthermore, social media enter the market via new types of content that drive adoption and validate emerging business models (Scharl and Tochtermann, 2007). The findings of the mangers interview further indicate, due to a new approach of social media and the development of new contents, this results boost marketing opportunities for small and medium sized hotels. Moreover, figure 2 illustrates the managers, consider one of the social media success factors is creating brand awareness because social media control a large numbers of loyal customers. As a result, these customers become electronic word of mouth, which helps a hotel to become known in the market. Tourism is an experience which needs to be communicated. In fact, be it wonderful or terrible, a travel experience is usually sharing talking with others and this conversation take place online. (International Conference on et al., 2011). As a result, a hotel brand becomes known to new customers due to the conversation. The managers also identified, social media help to increase an organization appearance in various platforms because social media help to provide different communication channels, where an organization communicate, and this communication increase an organization appearance

The managers indicated that social media helps a hotel to attract new customers because of electronic word of mouth. Customers tend to leave comments and evaluate a hotel that provides hands for a hotel to attract new customers. According to Chaney (2009) social sites has given birth, to a number of new customer service applications, which is known as idea aggregators. A customer can submit an idea, suggestions, questions, or complaints, and those are voting up or down by other customers can post and comments, this process creates opportunities to communicate.

5 RESULTS

It was important to find out which social network is much popular in Austria. Thus, first we found often useable social network for SMH's in Austria, which is Facebook and Holidaycheck (see table 1) and then we analyzed the activity of the hotels on each social network. We also asked. What are the characteristic of social media, which adopted by the hotel through social sites? Result of question number two (see figure 1) indicates social media is a main source of engaging customer in conversation. Hence, the result shows to start engaging customers. However, hotels have adopted characteristic of the social media that include posting pictures, announcing news, making PR, spreading e-word of mouth, provide social experience, creating brand awareness, announcing news, advertising product, selling hotel products through social media, making fans, telling stories about the hotel, introducing new product and staff members through social networking sites and provide opportunity to book a hotel room through social networking sites are the characteristic of social media.

The result of literature reviews provides useful data regarding the importance of social media and the critical success factors of social media. Therefore, researcher's emphasis social media assist consumers in posting and sharing their travel-related comments, opinions, and personal experiences, which then serve as information for others. Thus, theses information's are also helpful for small medium hotels to establish business relationship with customers, and to stage interpersonal experience. Furthermore, finding of the literature reviews emphasis; social media establish information and this information provide authenticity of the service providers, this help to bridge relationship between a hotel and a traveler.

Findings of the mangers interviews (see figure 2) illustrate return on investment, lower operating cost, revenue generation, provide marketing opportunity, create brand awareness, and increase business voice and to build customer relationship are the critical success factors of social media strategies. Moreover, giving power to companies, bring new customers, stage experience, and to engage customers were emphasis as the critical success factors of social media for small medium hotels in Austria.

Furthermore, return on investment, community monitoring, privacy concerns. Lacks of professional employees are social media challenges that small medium hotels in Austria are facing. Moreover, finding of the manager interviews show, best practice of social media for small medium hotels are to identify target market, identify goals, defining ethics, listen to implement customer feedback. Furthermore, Result indicates one of the critical success factors of the social media is return on investment. However, on the other hands, small medium hotels owners emphasis return on investment is not necessarily monetary value for a business because social media is indirectly increase sales growth, provide customer feedback, understanding customers' need, and to rectify customer complaints through social media are return on investment.

6 CONCLUSION

The thesis aim to explore the critical success factors for Austrian small medium sized hotels, the literature reviews describe, social media provide information, which is worth for both consumers and suppliers, as a result these information's enhance relationship between consumers and suppliers. Hence, the literature defines social media help to stage experience and provide interpersonal experience between suppliers and consumers. Literature reviews further mention, social media is a useful tool before and after the trip for consumers. Tourist are no longer waiting to read a hard printed brochures provided by a travel agents but rather preferred to go online and getting advises and discuss the trip in the online strange environment. However, in this regard small medium hotels in Austria are also playing a significant role by bridging relationship with consumers, as a result suppliers and consumers get closer. Thus, suppliers and consumers bypass third parties in order to develop personal relationship, this helps to avoid additional misunderstanding, and provide efficiency money and time wise. Moreover, literature reviews emphasis, the tourist tend to share their trip experience in front of friends and relatives. However, this discussion dramatically changed into online environment, where an experience tourist shares his trip experience in front of limitless strange groups, as a result this become a huge discussion among consumers. Furthermore, literature reviews suggest social media critical success factors, and provide and answer to the research question of social media critical success factor for small medium hotels in Austria. Thus, the result indicates staging experience is a main success factor of tourism. However, to stage tourism experience new technology particularly social media provide the opportunity to stage interpersonal experience between consumers and suppliers.

Literature reviews conclude an answer to the research question, what are the critical success factors for Austrian small medium sized hotel owners in establishing an effective social media strategy? Thus, effective social media strategies are staging interpersonal experience. When a social media stage interpersonal experience then, such experience develop further sub branches i.e. e-word of mouth, personal relationship, public relationship, brand development.

Furthermore, interview with SMH's managers explores the critical success factor, the result explores the findings of mangers interviews. One of the critical success factors is to increase return on investment. Hence lower operating cost, and to generate revenue these are the critical success factors of social media strategies for small medium hotels. Social media also help to boost market opportunity, and increase brand awareness. Moreover, to bridge customer relationship. Social media also empower small medium hotels, where SMH's raise vice in the global market, as a result such activities bring new customers to small medium hotels, and small medium hotels can compete with big chain hotels.

Furthermore, staging customers experience by engaging customers in the conversation. Customers have the vice to talk directly to the suppliers through the help of social media, as a result customers by pass third parties, which help to save time and money. Customers provide valuable feedback directly to the suppliers, this create online community, and online networking. Hence, such activities create harmony between suppliers and consumers, as a result customer's relationship develop between suppliers and consumers.

The literature reviews defines social media critical success factors. Staging interpersonal experience between suppliers and customers is a critical success factors, and result of manager's interviews and website contents analysis suggest, staging interpersonal experience between suppliers and consumer. Thus, the result of literature review, website content analysis and interview explored staging interpersonal experience is a critical success factor of social media, which further develop sub branches.

This study conclude, it is worth considering using social media as a marketing strategies for SMHs. However, this study also found barriers to SMHs that include lack of awareness towards social media strategies. SMHs perceive the required technology to be too expensive or complicated to run (Richardson et al., 2010). Furthermore, due to the limited resources and capabilities, SMHs find it difficult to focus on several e-commerce critical success factors. Therefore SMHs need to know what to focus in order to effectively support a budding outsourcing industry (Al-Qirim, 2004).

REFERENCES

AL-QIRIM, N. A. Y. 2004. Electronic commerce in small to medium-sized enterprises : frameworks, issues and implications, Hershey PA, Idea Group Pub.

ALFORD, P. & CLARKE, S. 2009. Information technology and tourism a theoretical critique. Technovation, 29, 580-587.

BERNE, C., GARCIA-GONZALEZ, M. & MUGICA, J. 2011. How ICT shifts the power balance of tourism distribution channels. Tourism Management.

BUHALIS, D. & LAW, R. 2008. Progress in information technology and tourism management: 20 years on and 10 years after the Internet"The state of eTourism research. Tourism Management, 29, 609-623.

CHANEY, P. 2009. The Digital Handshake: Seven Proven Strategies to Grow Your Business Using Social Media, Wiley.

CHAVES, M. S., GOMES, R. & PEDRON, C. 2011. Analysing reviews in the Web 2.0: Small and medium hotels in Portugal. Tourism Management.

DE ASCANIIS, S. & MORASSOL, S. G. The argumentative signiï¬ cance of tourism related UGC. 2011. Springer Verlag, 125.

FLICK, U. 2009. An introduction to qualitative research, Sage.

FLYNN, N. 2012. The social media handbook rules, policies, and best practices to successfully manage your organization's social media presence, posts, and potential [Online]. Hoboken: John Wiley & Sons. Available: http://public.eblib.com/EBLPublic/PublicView.do?ptiID=817869.

HITZ, M. 2006. Information and communication technologies in tourism 2006

proceedings of the international conference in Lausanne, Switzerland, 2006, Wien [u.a.], Springer.

INTERNATIONAL CONFERENCE ON, I., COMMUNICATION TECHNOLOGIES IN, T., FUCHS, M., RICCI, F. & CANTONI, L. 2012. Information and communication technologies in tourism 2012 proceedings of the International Conference in Helsingborg, Sweden, January 25-27, 2012 [Online]. Vienna; New York: SpringerWienNewYork. Available: http://dx.doi.org/10.1007/978-3-7091-1142-0.

INTERNATIONAL CONFERENCE ON, I., COMMUNICATION TECHNOLOGIES IN, T., HÖPKEN, W., GRETZEL, U. & LAW, R. 2009. Information and communication technologies in tourism 2009 : proceedings of the international conference in Amsterdam, the Netherlands, 2009, Wien, Netherlands, Springer-Verlag.

INTERNATIONAL CONFERENCE ON, I., COMMUNICATION TECHNOLOGIES IN, T., LAW, R., FUCHS, M. & RICCI, F. 2011. Information and communication technologies in tourism 2011 proceedings of the international conference in Innsbruck, Austria, January 26-28, 2011.

KAPLAN, A. M. & HAENLEIN, M. 2010. Users of the world, unite! The challenges and opportunities of Social Media. Business horizons, 53, 59-68.

LAW, R., FUCHS, M. & RICCI, F. 2011. Information and communication technologies in tourism 2011, Wien [etc.], Springer.

MA, J. X., BUHALIS, D. & SONG, H. 2003. ICTs and Internet adoption in China's tourism industry. International Journal of Information Management, 23, 451-467.

MAURER, C. & WIEGMANN, R. Effectiveness of Advertising on Social Network Sites: A Case Study on Facebook. In: LAW, R., FUCHS, M. & (EDS.), F. R., eds. Information and Communication Technologies in Tourism 2011, 2011 Innsbruck, Austria. Springer Verlag, 485.

MILANO, R., BAGGIO, R. & PIATRELLI, R. The effects of online social media on tourism websites. In: LAW, R., FUCHS, M. & (EDS.), F. R., eds. Proceedings of the International Conference, 2011 Innsbruck, Austria,. SpringerWienNewYork, 26-28.

NYKIEL, R. A. 2007. Handbook of marketing research methodologies for hospitality and tourism, Routledge.

ORGANISATION FOR ECONOMIC, C.-O. & DEVELOPMENT 2002. The OECD small and medium enterprise outlook. The OECD small and medium enterprise outlook.

PEACOCK, M. 2010. PHP 5 social networking create a powerful and dynamic social networking website in PHP by building a flexible framework [Online]. Birmingham: Packt Pub. Available: http://site.ebrary.com/id/10428655.

RICHARDSON, N., GOSNAY, R. & CARROLL, A. 2010. A quick start guide to social media marketing high impact low-cost marketing that works [Online]. London; Philadelphia: Kogan Page. Available: http://public.eblib.com/EBLPublic/PublicView.do?ptiID=622163.

RONG, J., VU, H. Q., LAW, R. & LI, G. 2011. A behavioral analysis of web sharers and browsers in Hong Kong using targeted association rule mining. Tourism Management.

SCHARL, A. & TOCHTERMANN, K. 2007. The geospatial web how geobrowsers, social software and the Web 2.0 are shaping the network society.

SIMON WONG, C. K. & GLADYS LIU, F. C. 2010. A study of pre-trip use of travel guidebooks by leisure travelers. Tourism Management, 32, 616-628.

THOMAS, J. R., NELSON, J. K. & SILVERMAN, S. J. 2010. Research methods in physical activity, Human Kinetics.

THOMAS, R. 2004. Small firms in tourism : international perspectives, Amsterdam; Boston, Elsevier.

VERMEULEN, I. E. & SEEGERS, D. 2009. Tried and tested: The impact of online hotel reviews on consumer consideration. Tourism Management, 30, 123-127.

WRIGHT, J. 2006. Blog marketing : the revolutionary new way to increase sales, build your brand, and get exceptional results, New York, McGraw-Hill.

XIANG, Z. & GRETZEL, U. 2009. Role of social media in online travel information search. Tourism Management, 31, 179-188.

YE, Q., LAW, R. & GU, B. 2009. The impact of online user reviews on hotel room sales. International Journal of Hospitality Management, 28, 180-182.

ZHANG, Z., YE, Q., LAW, R. & LI, Y. 2010. The impact of e-word-of-mouth on the online popularity of restaurants: A comparison of consumer reviews and editor reviews. International Journal of Hospitality Management, 29, 694-700.

The Impact of Longer Visits on Destination Image Perception: The Case of Exchange Students in University of Ljubljana

Konstantinos Vitoratos

University of Ljubljana, Slovenia
k.vitoratos@gmail.com

Abstract

This paper examines the connection between length of stay and destination image perception, resulting from a slow process of formation, establishment and, finally, alteration of the cognitive and affective destination image dimensions. The topic is first explored through the lens of some of the most widely-cited theories of tourism destination image, which help identify all the individual components of destination image perception and generate new research hypotheses. Subsequently, a new framework is suggested and tested through the case of exchange students, who lie in the middle of the continuum between tourists and residents in their host city, using a quantitative approach. As a result, the paper tries to answer how a lengthier visit in a destination can modify a country's perceived image for the traveler, as well as to provoke a conversation on how DMOs could potentially use student exchange and other long-term travel programs as a new way to boost tourism and project a new destination image through word of mouth and other information channels.

Keywords: destination image perception; image perception alteration; student travel; exchange programs; length of visit

1 INTRODUCTION

Tourism destination image is a thoroughly researched field of tourism studies, with many contributions on a global level and on different sub-topics, the first significant ones dating even back to the 1970's (Mayo, 1973; Hunt 1975). However, as with any other research field, it has research gaps, especially when combined with specific tourism markets or target groups. One of those markets is the student and youth travel market, which has grown significantly the past few years, reaching about 20% of the global tourism revenue worldwide, according to some scholars (Kim et al., 2007). Although expected to be very profitable in the next few decades, this market only recently managed to attract academic attention. Until now, little effort has been put into researching image perception of destinations for young travelers, with very few exceptions, like the study of Chen and Kerstetter (1999) on the opinion of exchange students on the image of rural Pennsylvania.

The current research is an effort to throw some more light into the complex phenomenon of alteration of destination image perception by using the case of an under-researched segment of travelers, such as exchange students, in order to answer the following research question: *"How does the length of visitation affect and modify a visitor's perceived destination image?"*

2 THEORETICAL BACKGROUND

The primary data collection and analysis process was based on previous relevant scholarly studies, most of which are considered cornerstones of destination image formation and modification studies.

The main issue that has been substantially addressed by scholarly research up to this time is the elements that compose a tourism destination image. By no means does this imply that there is general consensus on a definition of the term or the breakdown to its core elements. Nevertheless, a widely accepted definition of destination image would be the one by Crompton (1979), who claims that tourism destination image is "*the sum of beliefs, ideas and impressions that a person has of a destination*" (p. 18).

As far as the elements that compose tourism destination image are concerned, the debate on them seems to continue up to this day. However, the majority of scholars seem to be inclined towards the separation of destination image into a cognitive and an affective part (Dobni and Zinkhan, 1990; Baloglu and Brinberg, 1997; Baloglu and McCleary, 1999). The cognitive part is formed early during the evaluation stage, even before the destination is chosen, comprising of beliefs or fragments of knowledge on a destination and being much more logical in terms of formation. On the contrary, the affective part is more connected to feelings and external stimuli, which could affect the latter, thus needing more time to be formed and processed and tending to be less rational in their evaluations by the individual (Gartner, 1993; Baloglu and McCleary, 1999; Peter and Olson, 1999). Many scholars claim that cognitive and affective image as a whole create the holistic image that an individual forms about a destination. This concept can be found in literature under different names, such as *conative component* (Gartner, 1993; Pike and Ryan, 2004; Tasci et al., 2007), *overall image* (Baloglu and McCleary, 1999), or *complex image* (Fakeye and Crompton, 1991).

Destination image is formed through a long process, that starts even before the potential destinations are being evaluated (Gunn, 1972). According to more recent studies, the formation process is the result of a combination of personal and stimulus factors (Baloglu and McCleary, 1999) and information agents (Gartner, 1993). This means that the image is formed through both emotional and rational evaluations; however, the first have been very superficially studied by academics (Echtner and Ritchie, 1991). Regardless, the importance of information sources has been recognized by a large number of scholars, who support Gartner's theory (Bojanic, 1991; Hanefors and Mossberg, 2002; Molina and Esteban, 2006; McCartney et al., 2008).

In the last few years, some attention has been given to new forms of information sources, such as user-generated online material and social media (Schmalleger and Carson, 2007; Xiang and Gretzel, 2010). However, since this is a new phenomenon, only limited amount of research has been conducted on the topic. The current research will try to mix those elements to the suggested framework.

Since tourism destination image is a relatively complex construct, it is only expected to be affected by different factors and to be modifiable over time. Most of the earlier studies on image modification have focused on the effect of previous visit to a destination and the ways in which it can affect destination image (Phelps, 1986; Gartner and Hunt, 1987; Chon, 1991; Konecnik and Gartner, 2007). Other scholars have focused instead on creating and understanding particular typologies of tourists that travel for longer periods of time, the most prominent one thus far being travelers that visit friends and relatives, also known with the abbreviation VFR (Moscardo et al., 2000; Asiedu, 2008). This area of academic knowledge has further been expanded by a third group of scholars, who argue that the longer the visit is, the more accurate, solid and holistic the destination image perception becomes (Fakeye and Crompton, 1991; Baloglu and McCleary, 1999).

3   SUGGESTED FRAMEWORK AND HYPOTHESES

Of all the relevant academic and scholarly theories presented earlier, this study is mostly based on the theories of Baloglu & McCleary (1999) on information sources and that of Fakeye & Crompton (1991) on the effect of previous visitation on destination image. The paper's main effort is to combine these two theories and take them a step further by suggesting a new framework, which can add extra value to this particular field of tourism studies. The framework's validity is tested through the validation or rejection of several hypotheses, by applying them to the case of exchange students in University of Ljubljana. Schematically, the whole framework is presented in Figure 1.

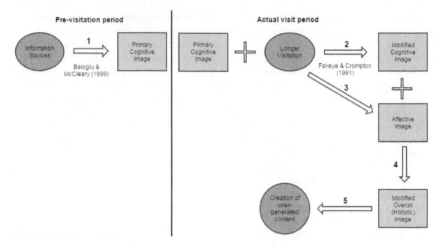

Fig. 1. Suggested framework of destination image modification

The suggested framework claims that a study exchange, as a form of a longer visitation to a destination, can significantly and positively affect tourism destination image of the host country. The process of image formation begins even before the destination is visited, when information agents are the main means to influence an individual's cognitive image of a destination (step 1 in Fig. 1). The variety of information sources is important, since different combinations of information agents have variable results for different individuals (Gartner, 1993; Baloglu & McCleary, 1999). It is assumed that an exchange student, before choosing a host university and country, is generally going through a larger number and variety of information sources than the average leisure traveler, as the risk of an exchange experience at this age is perceived as bigger and the significance of the trip much higher for the future development of the individual. Starting the visit already equipped with the primary cognitive image that the information agents helped them form, individuals get exposed throughout their stay to experiences and stimuli, which end up affecting their cognitive image but also help form their affective perceived image of the destination visited, as shown by steps 2 & 3 in Fig. 1. Those two elements end up modifying their holistic or overall image of the destination, comprising of the modified cognitive and the affective image, as shown in step 4, following the findings from Fakeye and Crompton's prior academic research (1991). In addition to all the above, this research tries to prove something additional that is completely missing from relative academic work realized so far on destination image: the association between longer-term travel abroad and the desire to create and share consumer-generated content on social media and other related Travel 2.0 applications, as shown in step 5 of Fig. 1.

The hypotheses used, in order to test the validity of this model, are as follows:

Hypothesis 1: A study exchange, as a form of longer visit in a destination, can make the cognitive image of the host country more positive for exchange students.

Hypothesis 2: A study exchange, as a form of longer visit in a destination, can make the affective image of the host country more positive for exchange students

Hypothesis 3: Exchange students that have received information from a larger number of different information sources have a more positive cognitive image of the host country in the first period of the study exchange experience.

Hypothesis 4: Exchange students with higher levels of cognitive and affective image perception are more likely to share material on social media and other web 2.0. based applications.

4 METHODOLOGY

The case of Slovenia as a destination for Erasmus exchange students was used, in order to test the validity of the model suggested. This particular group of travellers was favored, because exchange students lie somewhere in the middle of the continuum between tourists and residents, spending anywhere between 2-5 months in their host country. This study was realized with the use of a descripto-explanatory research design, trying to give answers to questions, based on causal relationships, as shown by the results of the primary data analysis process.

The use of questionnaires was preferred over other methods, based on vast literature on tourism destination image studies of the past that also utilized the same method (Chon, 1991; Fakeye & Crompton, 1991; Baloglu & McCleary, 1999; Konecnik, 2002; Kim & Yoon, 2003; Beerli & Martin, 2004). Two self-administered questionnaires were used, the first of which was handed to the respondents during the very first couple of days after their arrival in Ljubljana (pre-visitation), while the second was delivered to them after their departure from Slovenia at the end of the semester (post-visitation). The two questionnaires were necessary in order to measure the respondents' expectations from Slovenia before forming concrete first impressions and make comparisons with their final image perception after 2.5 months of stay in Slovenia. The preliminary questionnaire was handed to the students in person, at the beginning of their university classes and under the supervision of their professors and the researcher. The survey was not anonymous, so that the participants could be contacted again personally for the second and final round of the primary data collection process. The final questionnaire was handed to the students through email, because of distance and other constraints.

The questionnaires consisted of two parts: one common, static part, which measured opinion on 27 cognitive and 4 affective items on Slovenia's destination image and one part that was different between the first and second questionnaire. The cognitive items were all pulled from prior articles on relevant topics following a similar or identical method of primary data collection and their number was reduced by using factor analysis with the Varimax rotation procedure using the SPSS 16.0 software package for Windows. Only those variables that had factor loadings higher than 0.50 were retained in the final factor analysis. The remaining variables were then categorized in 5 different factors, which explained a total of 65.3% of the total variance. For the rating of the 27 cognitive image elements a seven-point Likert scale was used, following the example of previous relevant works in the field (Fakeye and Crompton, 1991; Baloglu and McCleary, 1999; Beerli and Martin, 2004; San Martin & Rodriguez del Bosque 2008). In the case of affective image, the adjective pairs picked are the same ones suggested by Russel et al. (1981) and later used for similar research purposes with the same measurement scale by many other researchers (Baloglu and McCleary, 1999; Konecnik, 2002; Beerli and Martin, 2008; Martin et al., 2008). A semantic-differential seven-scale rating system was used, with each one of the opposite adjectives of each pair being at each end of the rating line (Arousing-Sleepy, Pleasant-Unpleasant, Relaxing-Distressing and Exciting-Gloomy). Answers closer to 1 showed higher agreement with the positive adjective of the pair, whereas evaluations closer to 7 a higher agreement with the negative one.

In the second part of the questionnaire in the pre-visitation phase respondents were asked to name all the information sources they used before visiting Slovenia to familiarize themselves with the country, rating them in terms of importance, whereas in the post-visitation phase they were asked about their prior sharing, or willingness to share material or information about Slovenia on social media and other Web 2.0 travel applications.

The sample consisted of 78 non-Slovenian exchange students, who had spent overall less than a week in Slovenia – studying or visiting as tourists – by the time the pre-visitation questionnaire was handed out. These students represented almost the whole population of new exchange students at the Faculty of Economics of University of Ljubljana for the spring semester 2013. This particular faculty was chosen not only because it welcomes the highest number of exchange students in the country, but also because it partners with a great number of international universities and participates as a Consortium member in a joint international Erasmus Mundus master program, thus offering a much more culturally diverse population to research. More particularly, during this research the respondents were from 31 different countries in 4 continents. The average age of the respondents was 22.9 years, 65.4% of the sample being female. 61.5% of the initial respondents returned a fully completed questionnaire in the second phase of primary data collection.

5 MAIN FINDINGS

The answers of the 48 respondents who completed both parts of the survey were the ones to be analyzed from the whole survey population. The rest of the 30 questionnaires that remained from the first stage of the primary data collection, without being followed up by a response in the second stage were not taken into consideration in this part of the research, since it was impossible to track the change of attitude of these individuals throughout their semester in Slovenia.

The questionnaire results were processed by using SPSS 16.0 for Windows. The first, common part of both questionnaires (cognitive and affective image perception elements) was evaluated separately from the rest. The main test used to prove the hypotheses referring to this first part was a paired sample t-test, which allowed the comparison between the mean values of student evaluations of different questionnaire components before and after the visit was realized. For the second part of the questionnaires, which is relevant to information sources and social media, different methods and tests were used, depending on the case, since the measuring scales used were quite different and, thus, had to be approached in a different manner from one another.

It should be highlighted that, although the final sample of the survey equals more than 60% of the total population of exchange students at the Faculty of Economics of Ljubljana, which means that it is a quite representative portion of the total population studied, the final number of questionnaires as a total (N=48) is quite limited. This causes certain problems with the analysis of the results, especially given the limited power of the statistical tests. During the analysis of the results, this limitation was taken into consideration accordingly, before deciding if the initial hypotheses should be accepted, rejected, or accepted partially, with more research being needed to further decide on the result.

5.1 Cognitive, Affective & Overall Destination Image

The analysis showed that longer visits, in the form of an exchange experience, can significantly enhance cognitive evaluations of image perception, with 25 out of the 27 cognitive items in the questionnaire being evaluated higher in the second phase of the research (Table 1). Only "favorable climate for tourism" and "accessibility of Slovenia by air" were evaluated lower, the first one presumably because of the long and harsh winter, which lasted until the end of April 2013, and the second because of poor and expensive connections available from Ljubljana airport. Therefore, Hypothesis 1 was validated by the findings.

Table 1. Paired sample t-test results for cognitive items of the questionnaires

Component	Mean (Pre-visit)	Mean (Post-visit)	Std. Error (Mean)	t value	Sig. (2-tailed)
Favorable climate	4.96	4.94	0.243	0.086	0.932
Beautiful scenery	5.83	6.4	0.195	2.884	0.006
Unspoiled natural environment	5.25	6.17	0.195	4.704	<0.001
Beautiful lakes and mountains	5.94	6.4	0.186	2.466	0.017
Clean beaches	4.06	4.25	0.313	0.599	0.552
Outdoor activities & recreation	5.15	6.02	0.190	4.611	<0.001
Lovely small towns	5.23	5.5	0.195	1.391	0.171
Spa & wellness options	3.83	4.52	0.258	2.663	0.011
Good nightlife & entertainment	4.73	4.98	0.267	0.936	0.354
Cultural attractions	4.5	4.75	0.241	1.037	0.305
Interesting events and festivals	4.35	5.1	0.23	3.266	0.002
Restaurant & dining options	4.83	5.25	0.245	1.699	0.096
Good shopping options	4.29	4.54	0.339	0.738	0.464
Overall good value for money	5	5.25	0.277	0.903	0.371
High quality of accommodation	4.23	4.56	0.211	1.578	0.121
High quality of transport	3.96	4.04	0.273	0.306	0.761
Good tourism infrastructure	4.33	5	0.273	2.438	0.019
Good road accessibility	4.96	5.31	0.297	1.193	0.293
Good air accessibility	2.83	2.29	0.318	-1.704	0.095
Domestic transport network	4.02	4.35	0.289	1.153	0.255
Clean country	4.67	5.42	0.25	3	0.004
High standards of living	4.29	4.69	0.234	1.692	0.097
Safe country	5.44	6.21	0.227	3.392	0.001
Political stability	3.94	4.27	0.291	1.147	0.257
Interesting & unique cuisine	3.73	3.96	0.298	0.769	0.446
Interesting customs	4.27	4.35	0.284	0.294	0.770
Friendly & hospitable people	5.35	5.44	0.282	0.295	0.769

Additionally, it is interesting to point out the components with the highest and the lowest ratings (in a 7-point scale, 7 being very positive and 1 being very negative), thus showing Slovenia's strongest and weakest points in terms of cognitive image perception. These are presented in Table 2 below.

Table 2. Top-5 of Slovenia's highest and lowest rated cognitive items pre and post-visitation

Cognitive components rated highest (n=48) Pre-visit	Cognitive components rated highest (n=48) Post-visit	Cognitive components rated lowest (n=48) Phase I	Cognitive components rated lowest (n=48) Phase II
Lakes & Mountains **5.94**	Lakes & Mountains 6.40	Accessibility by air 2.83	Accessibility by air 2.29
Landscapes & Scenery **5.83**	Landscapes & Scenery 6.40	Unique local cuisine 3.73	Unique local cuisine 3.96
Safety of destination **5.44**	Safety of destination 6.21	Spa & Wellness offer 3.83	Quality of transport 4.04
Friendliness of locals **5.35**	Unspoiled environment 6.17	Political stability 3.94	Beaches for swimming 4.25
Unspoiled environment **5.25**	Outdoor activities 6.02	Quality of transport 3.96	Political stability 4.27

Contrary to the highly consistent results of the cognitive element analysis, the affective dimension analysis showed more mixed results (Table 3).

Table 3. Paired sample t-test results for affective items of the questionnaires

Component	Mean (pre-visit)	Mean (post-visit)	Std. Error (Mean)	t value	Sig. (2-tail)
Slovenia is relaxing/stressful	2.88	**2.52**	0.255	1.388	0.172
Slovenia is pleasant/unpleasant	2.23	**2.19**	0.166	0.252	0.803
Slovenia is exciting/gloomy	**2.79**	2.98	0.234	-.802	0.427
Slovenia is arousing/sleepy	**3.25**	3.50	0.257	-.973	0.336

Of the four items studied, only two had a lower mean grading in the second phase of the research, thus showing evaluations closer to the positive adjective in the continuum. This means that Slovenia was seen as more relaxing and pleasant in June than it was seen in March. On the contrary, the other two items were rated lower, Slovenia being seen as gloomier and sleepier in June, in comparison to the findings from March. Additionally, the significance levels of this part of the analysis did not permit for safe assumptions for most of the affective image elements. For that reason, Hypothesis 2 was only partially and tentatively confirmed as being valid, calling for further future research with a higher sample in order to finally accept or reject it.

5.2 Information Sources and Social Media

Before visiting, students seemed to use a large variety of information sources to learn more about Slovenia, word of mouth being the most popular (84,6% of respondents), thus validating Gartner's (1993) theory about the importance of unsolicited and solicited organic agents (Table 4). There was also found to be a positive correlation between the average rating of cognitive items and the number of information sources used, however with significance levels not being satisfactory on a statistical basis. For that reason, Hypothesis 3 was confirmed as valid but with a need of further research with a higher sample.

Table 4. Descriptive statistics of information source usage and importance before visiting Slovenia

Information source	Used by (% of respondents)	Importance avg. rating
Family & relatives	84,6%	4,38
YouTube/other video host	79,8%	3,85
Academic/school readings	79,8%	3,81
Social Media	79,5%	3,85
Wikipedia	78,2%	3,91
Slovenian Tourism Board Website	70,5%	3,33
Travel Guidebooks	67,9%	3,29
Tripadvisor	60,3%	2,77
Promotional Leaflets	56,4%	2,32
Travel TV shows	50,0%	1,81
Travel Magazines	48,7%	2,10
Other information source	23,1%	1,08

In the results of the second part of the second questionnaire, almost 60% of the students seemed to have shared material and impressions of Slovenia online, the vast majority (92,9%) of them having used Facebook. Students that had used social media seemed to have given higher evaluations to cognitive and affective items in the first part of the questionnaire than the ones that did not engage in such activity. However, because of the small size of the sample, plausible significance levels were not reached in all cases, allowing only the partial validation of Hypothesis 4, with a further need for future research.

6 CONCLUSIONS

From the research findings, it is obvious that destination image perception is a relatively complex concept and that, depending on the case studied, results of primary data analysis might vary, in some places confirming previous academic findings and in others rejecting popular and quite established ideas and theories. This particular study quite strongly confirmed that a longer stay at a destination can significantly improve the cognitive dimension of destination image perception. However, it could not solidly prove that the same experience could equally affect all elements of the affective dimension, which is a deeper, more emotional and esoteric one, thus being more easily influenced by feelings, attitudes and other unknown factors. As a result, it only partially managed to further support Fakeye and Crompton's (1991) earlier findings on the impact of longer visits on the holistic destination image. Additionally, the results generally align with Gartner's (1993) previous work on the importance of information agents in the formation of a pre-visitation cognitive destination image. More particularly, exchange students seem to prefer and trust more organic sources of information, like past travel experiences and advice from their family and friends, which was also the only item that showed satisfactory significance levels, as was the case in Baloglu and McCleary's (1999) study, that was used as a basis for the current research. Following word of mouth from friends and family, most of the other preferred agents like YouTube videos and Wikipedia articles mostly belong to the category of autonomous sources. This might imply either that the students are not reached by targeted tourism campaigns and commercials, which would be an interesting topic for future research, or that they simply prefer sources that are more easily accessible considering their lifestyle and daily habits (e.g. socializing with peers, browsing through videos or reading independent articles online in their free time).

This research faced a number of limitations that should be taken into consideration when evaluating its scope, applied methodology and results. The main one is the limited size of the sample, which was a result of unavoidable time and geographical constraints. Exchange students spend a long time in their new host country; as a result approaching more than one generation of exchange students throughout more than one semester would have prolonged this study's completion timeline to a period reaching almost a full calendar year. Another important limitation was the geographical distance between the respondents and the researcher during the post-visitation phase of the questionnaire completion. During that stage, the respondents were approached by email, something that was already explained to them before they replied to the pre-visitation questionnaire; however, the tendency of university students to travel for leisure purposes towards the end of their semester made the collection of answers from all the initial participants using this method impossible.

6.1 Main Contributions

This research contributed on three different levels to the fields of destination image and student travel, as sub-segments of the tourism studies field.

Firstly it provided a first insight into the inclusion of the pre-departure expectations and the post-experience promotion of the destination in the research of destination image. A long term visit, contrary to a short one, requires a lot more preparation in advance and concludes with a lot more knowledge and material to share at the end. Therefore, it is essential to start researching in more depth the connections between the phases and try to find the incentives which lead individuals to long-term visits to different places, as well as the ones that push them to share their experience with the world. Although the scope of the current research is relatively small, it is definitely good food for thought and a good base for future research, which could prove the suggested framework right and thus contribute vastly to the already existing literature.

Secondly, it threw some more light into the relatively under-researched segment of student travel. Exchange students are almost neglected by modern researchers, although the numbers of Erasmus exchange students in Europe are constantly growing, with the inclusion of new member and partner states in the European Union. Students not only are a profitable tourism segment, but also a very interesting one for research purposes, since today's students are going to be tomorrow's main earners and, therefore, the near future's main travelers. Understanding the changes in tourism behavior in young people could reveal a lot of trends in the tourism trends of the close future.

Lastly, this research focused on one of the less researched tourism destinations of Europe and the world. The aim of this research was to collect a little more information on this destination for the reader and to add some more insight to the quite limited existing literature on Slovenia.

6.2 Further Discussion and Recommendations

This research focused on Slovenia, a small European state facing very strong competition from geographically close countries, like Croatia in the sea, sun & sand tourism segment or Austria in the alpine tourism segment. The results adequately proved that the country, although not as well-known or as well-developed in terms of tourism infrastructure as its neighbors was overall seen as a very attractive and enjoyable destination by the niche market of exchange students. Future research could, therefore, focus more on examining the preferences of similar niche markets and try to suggest concrete solutions on how to better attract these tourism segments to destinations facing strong competition from their well-established neighbors.

Additionally it could be argued that the DMOs of destinations similar to Slovenia, instead of focusing on replicating successful strategies of their more well-known neighbors, should instead focus more on identifying their strongest and weakest points, in order to cater better to the needs of the niche markets that could potentially prove to be more profitable and accessible. The participants of this research particularly pointed out that they found Slovenia to be a relatively sleepy and slow-paced destination, thus implying the need for more youth-oriented cultural and sports events throughout the year, which could potentially help the country emerge into a hotspot for similar tourists in the future; this argument is further strengthened by the trust students show in word of mouth from peers when evaluating a new destination, as proven by the results of this research. A future research with a wider sample, focusing on different niche markets could possibly reveal more similar strengths and weaknesses that could be taken into consideration by the local tourism planning authorities.

Another topic of reflection that this paper raises is the profile of the average young or student traveler, as perceived by most tourism-related businesses and DMOs. From the answers received from exchange students in the two questionnaires, it was proven that contrary to popular belief students are not solely interested in mass tourism and traditional sea, sun & sand or party-oriented destinations. Throughout this study's cognitive item analysis exchange students rated Slovenia's alpine and lakeside landscapes, as well as the offered opportunities for outdoor activities much higher after the completion of the visit, thus supporting the Slovenian Tourism Board's efforts to promote the country primarily as an alpine, adventure and spa destination.

Further research with higher samples could potentially further support this study's suggested framework, thus confirming its findings more concretely.

REFERENCES

Asiedu, A. B. (2008). Participants' Characteristics and Economic Benefits of Visiting Friends and Relatives (VFR) Tourism – an International Survey of the Literature with Implications for Ghana. *International Journal of Tourism Research*, 10 (6), pp. 609-621.

Baloglu, S. and Brinberg, D. (1997). Affective Images of tourism destinations. *Journal of Travel Research*, 35 (4). pp.11-15.

Baloglu, S. and McCleary, K. W. (1999). A model of destination image formation. *Annals of Tourism Research*, 26 (4). pp.868-897.

Beerli, A. and Martin, J.D. (2004). Factors Influencing Destination Image. *Annals of Tourism Research*, 31 (3). pp.657-681.

Bojanic, D. C. (1991). The use of advertising in managing destination image. *Tourism Management*, 12 (4). pp.352-355.

Chen, P. and Kerstetter, D. L. (1999). International students' image of rural Pennsylvania as a travel destination. *Journal of Travel Research*, 37 (3). pp.256-266.

Chon, K. (1991). Tourism Destination image modification process. *Tourism Management*, 12 (1). pp.68-72.

Crompton, J. L. (1979). An assessment of the image of Mexico as a vacation destination and the influence of geographical location upon that image. *Journal of Travel Research*, 17 (4). pp.18–23.

Dobni, D. and Zinkhan, G. M. (1990). In search of brand image: a foundation analysis. *Advances in consumer research*, 17. pp.110-119.

Echtner, C. M. and Ritchie, J. R. (1991). The meaning and measurement of destination image. *Journal of Travel Studies*, 2 (2). pp.2-12.

Fakeye, P. C., and J. L. Crompton (1991). Image Differences between Prospective, First-Time and Repeat Visitors to the Lower Rio Grande Valley. *Journal of Travel Research* 30 (2). pp.10-16.

Hanefors, M., and L. Mossberg (2002). TV Travel Shows—A Pre-taste of the Destination. *Journal of Vacation Marketing*, 8 (3). pp. 234-46.

Hunt, J. D. (1975). Image as a Factor in Tourism Development. Journal *of Travel Research*, 13 (3). pp.1-7.

Gartner, W. C. (1993). Image Formation Process. *Journal of Travel & Tourism Marketing*, 2 (2-3). pp.191-216.

Gartner, W. C. and Hunt, J. D. (1987). An analysis of state image change over a twelve-year period (1971-1983). *Journal of Travel Research*, 26 (2). pp.15-19.

Gunn, C. (1972). *Vacationscape: Designing tourist regions*. Austin: Bureau of Business Research, University of Texas.

Kim, K., Oh, I. and Jogaratnam, G. (2007). College student travel: A revised model of push motives. *Journal of Vacation Marketing*, 13 (1). pp.73-85.

Kim, S. and Yoon, Y. (2003). The hierarchical effects of affective and cognitive components on tourism destination image. *Journal of Travel & Tourism Marketing*, 14 (2). pp.1-22.

Konecnik, M. (2002). The image as a possible source of competitive advantage of the destination – the case of Slovenia. *Tourism Review*, 57 (1-2). pp.6- 12.

Konecnik, M. and Gartner, W.C. (2007). Customer-based brand equity for a destination. *Annals of Tourism Research*, 34 (2). pp.400-421.

Mayo, E. J. (1973). Regional Images and Regional Travel Destination. In *Proceedings of the Fourth Annual Conference of Travel and Tourism Research Association*. Salt Lake City UT: TTRA. pp.211-217.

McCartney, G., Butler, R. and Bennett, M. (2008). A strategic use of the communication mix in the destination image formation process. *Journal of Travel Research*, 47 (2). pp.183-196.

Molina, A. and Esteban, A. (2006). Tourism brochures - Usefulness and image. *Annals of Tourism Research*, 33 (4). pp.1036-1056.

Moscardo, G., Pearce, P., Morrison, A., Green, D., O'Leary, J. T. (2000). Deceloping a Typology for Understanding Visiting Friends and Relatives Markets. *Journal of Travel Research*, 38 (3), pp. 251-259.

Peter, J. P. and Olson, J. C. (1999). Consumer behavior and marketing strategy. Boston: Irwin McGraw-Hill.

Phelps, A. (1986). Holiday destination image – the problem of assessment, an example developed in Menorca. *Tourism Management*, 7 (3). pp.168-180.

Pike, S. and Ryan, C. (2004). Destination positioning analysis through a comparison of cognitive, affective and conative perceptions. *Journal of Travel Research*, 42 (4). pp.333-342.

Russel, J. A., Ward, L. M. and Pratt, G. (1981). Affective quality attributed to environments – A factor analytic study. *Environment and Behavior*, 13 (3). pp.259-288.

San Martin, H. and Rodriguez del Bosque, I.A. (2008). Exploring the cognitive-affective nature of destination image and the role of psychological factors in its formation. *Tourism Management*, 29 (2). pp.263-277.

Schmalleger, D. and Carson, D. (2007). Blogs in tourism: Changing approaches to information exchange. *Journal of Vacation Marketing*, 14 (2). pp.99-110.

Tasci, A. D., Gartner, W. C. and Cavusgil, S. T. (2007). Conceptualization and operationalization of destination image. *Journal of Hospitality & Tourism Research*, 31 (2). pp.194-223.

Xiang, Z. and Gretzel, U. (2010). Role of social media in online travel information search. *Tourism Management*, 31 (2). pp.179-188.

Seeing, Feeling, Smelling, Hearing, and Tasting Austria:
A Qualitative Study of Austria's Destination Image

Andrea Ettinger

Vienna University of Economics and Business, Austria
andrea.ettinger@chello.at

Abstract

Managing a country's destination image is an increasingly important concept in tourism marketing to set a destination apart from the strong global competition. Therefore, it is surprising that the tourist destination Austria has not been the subject of larger destination image studies since the 1980s, especially not of qualitative studies. The present paper reports on the application of a particularly uncommon but highly useful research method with regard to destination image studies, namely 'brand fingerprinting' – the retrieval of respondents' sights, feelings, smells, sounds, and tastes when thinking of Austria as a tourist destination. Results show that the destination image of Austria mainly involves beautiful landscape, mountains, winter sports, sweet and hearty cuisine, historical buildings, fresh air, a peaceful atmosphere, a rich history, classical music, and a positive evoked feeling. Implications for the Austrian National Tourist Office and for tourism scholars are drawn, highlighting the importance of qualitative research in destination image studies.

Keywords: destination image; brand fingerprinting; qualitative research; tourism marketing.

1   INTRODUCTION

When tourists choose the destination they want to visit for their holidays, a big influence on their decision is the subjective, organic image they have of a destination (Schweiger and Wusst, 1988). Whether this image reflects the truth or not is irrelevant, as it is the destination image that will make the tourist decide to visit one destination rather than another. This subjective image might be a cliché, exaggerating certain image elements and neglecting others (Schweiger, 1992). Particularly, it might not necessarily represent the image that the tourist office of a destination would like potential tourists to have. Therefore, marketing communication from the tourist industry tries to establish, control, or change the organic image perceptions consumers have, to align them with the destination image desired by the tourist industry (Plummer, 1985). This communication from commercial sources, e.g. travel agents, brochures, or advertisements, is hoped to transform tourists' organic images derived from films, experience, or family accounts, for instance, into induced images (Gunn, 1988).

For Austria, research in destination image is quite dated, the last major, quantitative studies having been conducted in the 1980s, e.g. Schweiger (1988b). Therefore, this present research is expected to provide a relevant contribution to the body of knowledge in this field of tourism marketing. This paper aims at exploring the destination image of Austria among international students, retrieved through the so-far little employed technique of 'brand fingerprinting'. Hence, it brings destination image findings up to date with qualitative research. Moreover, practical implications for the Austrian National Tourist Office are derived from the findings.

The remaining part of the paper proceeds as follows: Chapter 2 examines the theoretical literature base of the concept of destination image and it provides an overview of the previous studies on Austria's destination image. Chapter 3 explains the methodology employed and Chapter 4 presents the findings of the research. In Chapter 5, these results are reflected upon and implications for Austria's tourism protagonists and academia are derived.

2 THEORETICAL BACKGROUND

In the last years, several developments have led to the increased importance of the concept of destination image in tourism. First, through globalisation, the choices for tourism destinations all over the world have increased for consumers, as more and more regions around the globe are developed for tourism. Second, an increasingly efficient transportation network provides the infrastructure needed to reach destinations more easily. Third, a rising income level and increased leisure time enable consumers to expand their consideration set of tourist destinations (Echtner and Ritchie, 2003). Fourth, the Internet and its vast possibilities, from detailed mapping of the world to booking holidays, also adds to the increased importance of destination image (Wenger, 2008). These developments render consumer decision-making more complex, presenting new challenges for tourism marketers (Echtner and Ritchie, 2003).

With the increased global competition for tourists it becomes necessary for destinations to position themselves in a way that favourably differentiates them from their competitors in the eyes of the consumers (Echtner and Ritchie, 2003). Important in this positioning process is the creation and management of a destination image that manifests the destination as being distinctive and attractive for tourists (Ekinci, 2003). Creating a powerful destination brand allows destinations to differentiate themselves, reduce consumers' perceived risks and lower the marketing costs (Prebensen, 2007). Furthermore, local tourist boards, hotels, or operators of tourist attractions benefit from a positive image. Hence, the measurement and management of this image is highly relevant practically and theoretically (Embacher and Buttle, 1989).

2.1 Destination Image

Destination image has become a very popular concept in tourism research (Pike, 2002). The first studies conducted on this topic originated in the 1970s and much attention has been given to the concept ever since (Hosany et al., 2006). For the purpose of this paper, the definition suggested by Crompton (1979), who saw destination image as "the sum of beliefs, ideas, and impressions that a person has of a destination" (p.18), is used.

Pikkemaat (2004) called destination image a "strategic weapon" (p.87) that is crucial for the description, promotion, organisation, and delivery of the destination. Like this, a set of expectations is created before a consumer actually experiences a destination. The stronger the positive brand image, the higher the likelihood to enter the consideration set and the travel decision process (Echtner and Ritchie, 2003). Destination image is a main component in the consumers' subsequent behaviour and destination choice process (Prebensen, 2007). For consumers, having an initial perception of a brand as being strong and positive leads to reduced search costs and minimised perceived risk (Hosany et al., 2006). It is against this image that consumers measure satisfaction on a visit to the destination (Pikkemaat, 2004).

Whether or not a destination tries to actively build a positive brand image with consumers, they will already have an image (Echtner and Ritchie, 2003). This general mental picture of a destination is called a 'destination stereotype' (Kurz, 1988) or an 'organic image' (Gunn, 1988). The more contact consumers have with information of any sort about the destination, the more individualised and unique the image becomes (Echtner and Ritchie, 2003), e.g. studying the country's history in school, their own experiences, personal accounts of friends and family, or media reports (Ekinci, 2003). Other information sources about the destination that lead to the construction of an image are travel brochures, a destination's promotional campaign that has reached the consumer, or books and films (Echtner and Ritchie, 2003). For managers, it is important to identify these image differences in people of different cultures, since understanding the (stereotypical) images prevalent in those cultures enables enlightened and targeted positioning and marketing strategies in those markets (Prebensen, 2007).

From a literature review of Pike (2002) and Echtner and Ritchie (2003), it becomes clear that researchers strongly prefer structured methodologies for their studies. Unstructured methodologies, such as open-ended questions, free association tasks, or projective techniques, do not pre-specify attributes of destination image for respondents (Echtner and Ritchie, 2003).

2.2 Previous Academic Studies on Austria's Destination Image

The organisation that takes care of Austria's national and international tourism marketing is the Austrian National Tourist Office (in German: Österreich Werbung). Reviewing the official website, it can be seen that Austria is mainly promoted as a destination featuring fantastic landscapes, nature, the possibility for summer and winter holidays, and fascinating culture and heritage. Depending on the season, either summer or winter activities are presented, for instance hiking, biking, and water sports, or skiing and snowboarding. Austria's culture is mainly represented through the historical heritage of Vienna and Salzburg, based on architecture, art, and classical music, but also through vineyards. The Austrian cuisine and the Austrian population itself are in the focus, too (Österreich Werbung, n.d., Wenger, 2008).

Probably still the most extensive research on Austria's country image abroad to date was conducted within the framework of a decade-long research project by the (formerly-named) Institute for Advertising and Marketing Research (WuM) under the leadership of Schweiger. The focus of the research project was Austria's country image abroad, with particular emphasis on Austria's economic image abroad. Schweiger (1988b) consists of three separate contributions by different authors working on the research project, each with a different focus. The first contribution by Schweiger and Wusst (1988) investigated to what extent country images are stable over time or whether they change with external developments, e.g. scandals. A historical analysis showed that Austria's image was clearly based on achievements of the last centuries (Schweiger and Wusst, 1988). The second contribution was by Kurz (1988). He revealed that Austria has a clear world image: Everywhere it is seen as a country of classical music, culture, classical architecture, tradition, and old customs. Less pronounced, due to the direct comparison with Switzerland and Germany, are the dimensions of Austria as a country of mountains, of winter sports, and its general attractiveness as a holiday destination. Moreover, the Austrian cuisine is seen as a strength internationally, and the Austrian population is considered friendly. Its economic image is rather weak, and Austria is not seen as being modern, compared to Switzerland and Germany. The third contribution by Schweiger (1988a) focused on the consequences of the derived country image of Austria on Austria's export economy, tourism, and foreign policy.

Embacher and Buttle (1989) investigated the destination images that English opinion leaders held of Austria as a summer destination, in comparison to Switzerland. Repertory grid technique was employed. Some of the results were that Austria possesses the image of being mountainous with attractive woodlands and impressive scenery. Austria is seen as clean, well-organised, economically well-developed but also old-fashioned.

A study on destination image was conducted by Pikkemaat (2004) who used questionnaires to discover Austria's destination image among Polish students. Twenty-six destination attributes were used, which were evaluated on a Likert scale. The strongest image associations concern cleanliness, safety, landscape, sports, and authenticity. The weakest associations were found for local cuisine, cultural facilities, contact with locals, and fair prices.

To the best of knowledge, no study has recently looked at Austria's destination image from a qualitative viewpoint. Hence, the research of this paper is justified, which is described below.

3 METHODOLOGY

For the elicitation of destination image a qualitative method, namely 'brand fingerprinting', was applied. Brand fingerprinting has as its goal to bring to light respondents' experiences and relationships with a brand, in this case a destination, and it is capable of uncovering metaphors, which represent unconscious associations (Supphellen, 2000). This technique "examines the thoughts and feelings held about [a destination] through the senses (sights, sounds, smells, tastes, touch and feelings)" (Morgan and Pritchard, 2000, p.111). Such a method dealing with metaphorical thinking and imagery is important, since imagery is indeed multi-sensory (MacInnis and Price, 1987), allowing the extracted destination image to be more complete. It is argued that in order to retrieve embodied brand knowledge, a method is needed that stimulates various senses, which were also involved in the creation of the brand knowledge (Von Wallpach and Kreuzer, 2013). As a projective technique, brand fingerprinting proves to be very adequate for marketing practice, as respondents can give answers to questions in an unthreatened and relaxed way (Will et al., 1996). However, to date there have not been many applications of brand fingerprinting, particularly not in a tourism context. The two main studies were done by Morgan and Pritchard (2000) for Las Vegas and by Prayag (2007) for South Africa and Cape Town.

The particular task for respondents in this study was to talk about their associations with the destination Austria 'one sense at a time'. The question posed was "When you now think of Austria as a tourist destination, what do you see in front of your eyes?" After that, respondents were asked what they feel, what they smell, what they hear, and what they taste when thinking of Austria as a tourist destination. This approach follows the recommendation of Supphellen (2000) who proposes to address each of the senses in succession and to employ the denomination 'feel' instead of 'touch'.

Two analysis techniques were applied, namely qualitative content analysis according to Mayring (2010) and frequency analysis. Central to qualitative content analysis is the construction and application of a system of categories. Converting pure text from transcribed interviews into meaningful and relevant chunks is done via data reduction (Miles and Huberman, 1994). Coding is the most important tool of data reduction. Similarly coded data become organised into categories that share certain characteristics and begin to form a pattern (Saldaña, 2009). The transcripts of this study were coded manually by three independent judges for all destination image aspects, to avoid interviewer bias and confirm performance of the analysis technique. Frequency analysis was applied, based on the categories derived through qualitative content analysis to get an indication of how common certain elements are. However, the main analysis tool remained qualitative content analysis and more frequently named elements were not considered more important in the interpretation of results. 'Word clouds' were chosen as means of data display, created through the free online tool "Wordle".

Research was conducted in Oslo, Norway (in the course of an exchange semester), with 32 student participants. Following the proposition of Supphellen (2000) to include users and non-users, both, people who had been to Austria and people who had not, were included in the sample. The interview sessions were audio-recorded and transcribed. To achieve the best possible degree of objectivity, the interviews followed a standardised procedure, which included the same interviewer giving every respondent the same information and task formulation, as proposed by Herz (2010).

4   RESULTS

4.1 Sample Description

The sample size of this study was 32, with 20 respondents being female and twelve male. The age range was 19 to 34. The participants were students of various subjects, representing 13 different nationalities from North and South America, Europe, and Asia.

4.2 Overall Image

The total of 292 individual elements extracted through this technique belong to ten categories, i.e. *geography* (63 elements), *culinary* (51), *atmosphere* (31), *country characteristics* (29), *people* (27), *activities* (25), *feelings* (23), *architecture* (22), *culture* (18), and *history* (3). The most often named category of the 32 respondents was *geography*, with 28 references, of which 22 referred to landscape or nature. Only 14 participants had the association of mountains. Nine interviewees commented on the quality of air. Animals were mentioned by five respondents. 17 subjects associated elements under climate, weather, or season. Winter (8 respondents) and snow (8) were common associations. 30 participants contributed to the *culinary* category, 27 referring to food and twelve to drinks. 27 interviewees also came up with image elements under specific dishes, types of food, or flavours. For instance, 16 respondents named sweet dishes. *Atmosphere* was commented on by 17 interviewees, eleven of which felt the atmosphere was peaceful. *Country characteristics* received mention from 18 respondents, with very varied elements that were not supported by many of the participants. 20 study subjects referred to the Austrian *people*, ten of them to the speech of the Austrians. *Activities* were named by 20 respondents, 13 of them associated winter sports with Austria. 25 of the 32 study participants expressed *feelings* Austria evoked in them. For 16 of them, these feelings were explicitly positive. *Architecture* was named by 17 interviewees, eleven of them referring to historical buildings. 13 participants associated *culture*, ten of them classical music. Four respondents considered Austria's *history* to be rich.

4.3 Sight

First, interviewees were asked what they saw in front of their eyes, when they thought of Austria as a destination. In total, 104 associations were named that are visualised in Figure 1. Most image elements for the sense of sight were linked to the *geography* category (30 elements), followed by *architecture* (22) and *activities* (21). The categories *culinary, people, culture, history,* and *atmosphere* contain ten or fewer elements, respectively. There were no elements mentioned to be sorted into the categories *feelings* and *country characteristics*.

Fig. 2. Sights evoked during the brand fingerprinting task

Of 32 respondents, 21 brought up *geography*-related elements, with landscape or nature receiving mention from 17 respondents. Twelve people named mountains as an association. Four respondents saw Austrian landscape or nature as beautiful. Vienna was pictured by four study participants in the sight association task. What was also a popular 'sight' for participants was winter (8 out of 32) and snow (6). Fewer people depicted a mountain village (1), sunshine (3), and grass (2). *Architecturally*, the most common association was historical buildings (10), including palaces (4) and castles (3). Three respondents saw beautiful buildings or nice architecture in front of their eyes. A concert hall was envisioned by three participants. Elements named by fewer people include ski cabins (2), green avenues (1), and bakeries (1). People engaging in all kinds of *activities* were pictured by 17 respondents. Eleven participants brought up people doing sports, especially skiing (9) and hiking (2). Generally, winter sports (10) was named more often than summer sports (3). Three participants had the association of somebody playing classical music. Other singular associations concerning activities were people yodelling (1), waltzing (1), or enjoying après ski (1). Only few people envisioned *culinary* items, of which hot chocolate was depicted by three respondents and coffee by two. Categorised under *people* were those associations that did not include persons engaging in an activity. For instance, healthy people (1) and stand-up artists (1) were named here. One interviewee saw "the mountains, and all the old-fashioned people in the Tyrol", which is definitely a noteworthy association. Not many associations were brought up concerning *culture*. Two respondents saw orchestras in front of their eyes, and another participant had images of the film "The Third Man" in his mind. Few people made references to *atmosphere*. One interviewee imagined night-time, yellow lights, and lots of glittery crystals. For another participant, the atmosphere described was idyllic. Concerning *history*, the only element named was Austria's (rich) history (5). One respondent verbalised this in the following way: "something like old castle, vintage, high class, of the old age".

Taking into account the participants who had (10) versus who had not visited Austria (22), some differences in image can be noted. While the previous visitors to Austria almost only mentioned winter sports (3), the associations under *activities* of the non-visitors included also non-sports activities such as playing classical music (3), yodelling (1), and waltzing (1), alongside winter sports (7) and summer sports (3). Previous visitors were able to name specific places or attractions under *architecture*, e.g. Schönbrunn (1). In contrast, non-visitors only generally mentioned historical buildings (5) and said they saw beautiful buildings (2) and nice architecture (3). In the other categories, both groups were balanced in their answers.

4.4 Feeling

The second task in the brand fingerprinting technique asked respondents to reply to what they felt or how they felt when they thought about Austria as a tourist destination. All responses from the brand fingerprinting task of feeling are visualised in Figure 2. Again, a little more than 100 elements were elicited. Most items concerned feelings about *country characteristics* (29), *feelings* (23), *atmosphere* (14), and *geography* (14). Feelings about *people* had ten items, and the other categories included even fewer associations, e.g. *activities* (4), *culinary* (2), *history* (3), and *culture* (2).

General evaluations concerning *country characteristics* were made by 19 out of 32 respondents. Austria was seen as a nice country by five participants and as a beautiful country by two participants. For four interviewees, Austria is a place they want to know more about. Several other evaluations, such as Austria being wealthy (2), similar to Norway (1), expensive (1), and not exotic (1) were named that referred to country characteristics. 22 respondents connected a *feeling* with Austria in this task. For instance, 16 interviewees felt positive when thinking about Austria as a tourist destination. Adjectives used to express this were, amongst others, comfortable (3), happy (3), relaxed (2), good (2), welcomed (1), and secure (1). Three respondents had a neutral feeling towards Austria. Five study subjects expressed the wish to visit Austria. Feelings concerning *atmosphere* were raised by ten respondents. Six of them felt Austria was peaceful. Words to describe this were relaxing (2), stress-free (1), not crowded (1), and quiet (1), e.g.: "very laid-back. And very… Not a lot of people, so relaxing. And enjoy life but not much to do". For another respondent, Austria is "a place that is very artistic". In the *geography* category the associations of feeling winter (4), nature (3), snow (2), cold (1), and ice (1) were named. One interviewee associated Vienna, feeling that it is "a great city to visit, although some parts of the city are fairly ghetto but besides that it's really cool". Feelings towards the Austrian *people* were expressed by seven respondents. The character of Austrians was described by adjectives, such as friendly (1), polite (1), helpful (1), social (1), happy (1), and formal (1). The Austrian dialect was considered as likable (1). As one of the few items mentioned in *activities*, skiing was named by four respondents. Other categories, such as *culinary*, *culture*, and *history* included only very few associations.

Fig. 3. Feelings evoked during the brand fingerprinting task

Comparing again the group of previous visitors to non-visitors, it is striking that of the ten previous visitors to Austria, eight expressed a positive feeling towards the destination. Of the non-visitors, only eight of 22 had this positive feeling, and three interviewees had a neutral feeling. Both groups of interviewees wished to visit or revisit Austria. As to the other associations and feelings towards Austria, both groups hardly differed.

4.5 Smell

For the third sense to be stimulated in the brand fingerprinting task, the question 'What do you smell when you think of Austria as a tourist destination' was asked. In total, only 45 individual associations were named (see Figure 3). All pertain to the category of *geography* (23), *culinary* (14), and *atmosphere* (7).

16 of 32 respondents came up with associations in the category of *geography*, most of them relating to the air (9 respondents). Eight participants said they could smell fresh air, followed by little pollution (2), thin air (1), and clean air (1), e.g.: "It's not really a smell but it's this fresh and clean air. It's not comparable to anything else. It's clean". Five interviewees could smell wood, "the wood of the forest, and of the traditional houses", two of them referred to trees. Three subjects smelled the grass. With regard to the smells of the city, only one respondent came up with an association, namely the smell of the underground, i.e. the sewers of Vienna. Climate or weather was mentioned by four participants, of which one said: "That smell of cold that happens […]. There is just a smell when it's really cold". Twelve study participants contributed associations to the *culinary* category. Four people smelled coffee, two hot chocolate, two wine, and one respondent mulled wine. Sweet dishes were also named,

such as baked goods (2), cake (2), apple strudel (1), and chocolate (1). The last category, *atmosphere*, was filled with associations from six participants. Among them are the smell of fire (1), of a Christmas tree (1), and of classical perfume (1). Noteworthy is the following association: "And I smell a bit, I don't want to be offending [...]. Smoke".

Fig. 4. Smells evoked during the brand fingerprinting task

Looking at the differences in answers given by previous visitors versus non-visitors, it can be detected that the smells of all sweet dishes were named by previous visitors. Many more associations for the smells of landscape or nature came from interviewees who had not been to Austria. What also has to be noted with this task is that four respondents could not come up with any association at all. Of these four persons, none had visited Austria before. The other responses are unremarkable in their origin.

4.6 Sound

As the next task, respondents were asked what they heard when they thought of Austria. 55 elements were named and are presented in Figure 4. Most of them belong to the category of *geography* (19 elements), *people* (11), *atmosphere* (10), *culture* (8), and *activities* (7).

Fig. 5. Sounds evoked during the brand fingerprinting task

With respect to *geography*, ten respondents said they heard nature sounds, e.g. animals (5), all five interviewees referring to birds and two to cows. The sound of water was heard by three persons. Four interviewees also heard the wind. One person heard "the crunching of snow when you walk in it. The crackling of the fire". The city was perceived by four participants, with sounds coming from water fountains (1), cars (1), or the tramway (1). 14 of 32 participants claimed they heard sounds stemming from *people*. For nine respondents, this was the sound of people talking. The German language was heard by two interviewees, while one heard "Austrian, the language". Two interviewees heard different languages. Other sounds heard were yodelling (2), singing (1), and laughing people (1). In the *activities* category, sports (4) were a common sound association, e.g. the noise of snow when skiing: "Maybe the scratching of the skis when you're around a root and then people are breaking [the root] and then it's just chr-chr-chr". One person heard the sound of partying and après ski. Sound associations referring to the *atmosphere* category were heard by eight respondents. Four said the atmosphere was quiet, three termed it peaceful. In the *culture* category, ten participants heard classical music, one of them an orchestra. Particular instruments named were the violin (2), piano (1), flutes (1), and harmonica (1). One person heard the Blue Danube Waltz.

There were hardly any differences in the images of those who had visited Austria and those who had not. This latter group heard water sounds, whether in nature or in the city. This sound was not named by any previous visitor. Non-visitors came up with a much broader variety of sound associations for people, including yodelling (2 out of 22) and singing (1). Moreover, the scope of instruments was broader with people who had not been to Austria. The other categories were evenly distributed in their image elements named by both groups.

4.7 Taste

The last question of the brand fingerprinting technique was what respondents tasted when they thought about Austria as a tourist destination. In total, 47 individual associations were made, which are displayed in Figure 5. The associations were found exclusively in the *culinary* sub-categories *food* (39 elements) and *drinks* (7).

Fig. 6. Tastes evoked during the brand fingerprinting task

27 of 32 respondents contributed to the sub-category *food*, 25 of them were able to come up with specific dishes, types of food, or flavours. In this latter group, the flavours sweet (15 respondents), spicy (3), sour (1), and bitter (1) were named. Dishes and types of food falling under the sweet category were chocolate (6), Kaiserschmarren (3), ice cream (2), applestrudel (2), and cake (1). Other dishes mentioned by name were Schnitzel (5), Semmelknödel (1), and sauerkraut (1). Meat was a fairly common association, too, brought up by six interviewees, who pictured sausages (3), pork (1), and rib eye steak (1), in particular. Six participants also made evaluative remarks, among them appetising (1), healthy (1), and value for money (1). Nine out of 22 respondents made remarks about the tastes of *drinks*. Wine and hot chocolate

were perceived by four subjects each. Beer was associated by three participants. Two respondents were unable to come up with any association concerning taste.

Contrasting the answers of previous visitors to Austria with those of non-visitors, it becomes obvious that the former were able to list many more Austrian dishes by name. The group who had not been to Austria rather named flavours and general types of food. The non-visitors also revealed more evaluations of the food than those who had visited Austria before. The two respondents who did not come up with any association had both not visited Austria before.

5 REFLECTION ON STUDY RESULTS

5.1 Discussion and Implications

Generally, there is large agreement among the previous studies of Austria in a tourism context and this study on destination image, despite the application of different methodologies. Moreover, the wealth of image elements derived through this research proves that destination image can indeed be a "strategic weapon" (Pikkemaat, 2004, p.87) that offers many opportunities to strengthen a positive brand image (Echtner and Ritchie, 2003, Hosany et al., 2006) and to influence tourists' travel behaviour (Prebensen, 2007).

Comparing the destination image studies previously carried out with respect to Austria, some differences in image can be detected, although it seems to be true that destination images are fairly stable over time (Schweiger and Wusst, 1988). The main dimensions of Austria as a country of classical music, culture, traditions, mountains, and winter sports were the most common image dimensions in Schweiger's (1988b) and the current study. The findings of Embacher and Buttle (1989) are mostly in line with the findings of this research, particularly its main results, a widespread image of Austria having mountains, forests, and lakes, as well as being old-fashioned. Comparing Pikkemaat (2004) with this study's findings also reveals some alignment. For instance, the strongest image associations in her research were cleanliness, safety, landscape, and sports, the latter two dimensions being common associations in this research, too. Safety, however, was not a common element in this study.

The results on Austria's destination image allow definite implications for tourism marketers.

The strongest destination image elements extracted for Austria across all image techniques are Austria's nature and mountains, its position as a winter sport destination, and its history and culture. Hiking, historical buildings, music, sweet dishes, wine, and a peaceful atmosphere are very strongly associated with the destination, too. For tourism marketers, these findings will not be surprising. While it is important to still actively communicate these USPs of Austria, the less obvious image elements, e.g. the cosiness and comfortable feeling, the smells of fresh air, grass, and wood, or the sound of water, should also receive attention.

These sensorial images raised in the brand fingerprinting tasks could also be used by tourism marketers in advertising campaigns, e.g. incorporating smells and tastes, differentiating Austria in a special way, as proposed by Prayag (2007). The more complete a destination image is, the better decisions concerning marketing strategies can be made (Echtner and Ritchie, 1993). It is the details that differentiate one destination from a similar one. For instance, Switzerland also has mountains, winter sports, and culture. But it is the not so obvious image elements, such as the character of the Austrians or the quality of Austrian wine, that allow differentiation from Switzerland, after all.

While a large number of positive image elements was elicited in this research, there were some negative or unfavourable image associations that need attention, e.g. the comment on cigarette smoke. For tourism marketers, these associations are particularly noteworthy, as negative associations could affect behaviour even more strongly than ignorance about the destination, as the image in that case might be neutral. The tourist office should actively try to counteract negative associations with appropriate communication campaigns. Considering Gunn (1988), it also becomes obvious that organic images built from various sources, e.g. films such as "The Third Man" that might well produce unfavourable associations, do indeed dominate a person's image if tourism marketing has not reached the person sufficiently.

Of interest are not only those image associations that were made but also those that were not made. For instance, certain senses did not produce any associations with some respondents. This has an implication for tourism marketers, as there might be serious shortcomings in the success of communication strategies in some markets.

This research also allows implication drawing for tourism scholars in an academic context with regard to methodological considerations. Brand fingerprinting proved efficient in arousing image associations, namely 292 individual elements from 32 respondents. Through addressing all senses, very unique affective, almost poetic image elements could be uncovered. Brand fingerprinting turned out to be very strong in extracting associations concerning atmosphere and feelings. The culinary category, too, was equipped with an impressive array of image elements, mostly generated through the smell and taste tasks. Also quality of air and sounds of nature were frequent associations. Therefore, brand fingerprinting is a highly successful technique and thus, complements other research methods optimally.

5.2 Limitations and Suggestions for Further Research

Like any study, particularly in qualitative research, this study has its limitations. First and foremost, findings of this research are not generalizable, due to the exploratory nature of the study and the rather small sample size under consideration. Moreover, the sample size only consisted of students. Of these 32 students, only the three Canadians were native speakers of English. For several others, the use of English as an interview language might have posed a language barrier to some degree. Another limitation is the possibility of response bias on the part of the interviewees, since all of them knew that the interviewer was an Austrian citizen.

Future research could be directed towards the quantitative validation of the destination image associations extracted in this study. In addition, studies with a similar methodology could be carried out in destinations that are seen as competitors to Austria, so that the fine image distinctions can be detected and used for tourism marketing campaigns. Such a study could then similarly pinpoint the competitive advantages for the destination Austria even more.

5.3 Conclusion

This research aimed at finding the current destination image of the tourist destination Austria. A round destination image could be elicited through the use of the qualitative 'brand fingerprinting' technique, making this study unique in the Austrian context with regard to the methodology used. It is thanks to these numerous and detailed associations that this study can serve as a new and current data base for future quantitative validity studies. The large number of singular image associations showed that destination images are indeed highly complex constructs, as already established in the literature. Tourism marketers must be aware of the actual image that potential and past tourists have of the destination, in order to detect weaknesses and find hints how to steer the actual image of these people as best as possible towards the desired destination image. Austrian tourism marketers must seek to distinguish their destination from the global competition to create a destination image that favourably stands out in the minds of consumers. After all, it does not matter whether the image that a person has of a destination is correct or not, since, in the end, it is the actual image of respondents that makes them choose one destination over another.

REFERENCES

Crompton, J. L., 1979. An assessment of the image of Mexico as a vacation destination and the influence of geographical location upon that image. *Journal of Travel research,* 17(4), pp.18-23.

Echtner, C. M. and Ritchie, J. B., 1993. The measurement of destination image: An empirical assessment. *Journal of travel research,* 31(4), pp.3-13.

Echtner, C. M. and Ritchie, J. B., 2003. The meaning and measurement of destination image. *Journal of tourism studies,* 14(1), pp.37-48.

Ekinci, Y., 2003. From destination image to destination branding: An emerging area of research. *e-review of Tourism Research (eRTR),* 1(2), pp.21-24.

Embacher, J. and Buttle, F., 1989. A repertory grid analysis of Austria's image as a summer vacation destination. *Journal of Travel Research,* 27(3), pp.3-7.

Gunn, C. A., 1988. *Vacationscape: Designing tourist regions,* New York: Van Nostrand Reinhold.

Herz, M., 2010. Exploring Consumers' Brand Image Perceptions with Collages -Implications on Data Collection, Data Analysis and Mixed Method Approaches. In: Mayerhofer, W. & Secka, M. (eds.) *Aktuelle Beiträge zur Markenforschung.* Wiesbaden: Gabler, pp.121-143.

Hosany, S., Ekinci, Y. and Uysal, M., 2006. Destination image and destination personality: An application of branding theories to tourism places. *Journal of Business Research,* 59(5), pp.638-642.

Kurz, H., 1988. Das Image Österreichs im Ausland. In: Schweiger, G. (ed.) *Österreichs Image im Ausland* Wien: NORKA, pp.62-119.

Macinnis, D. J. and Price, L. L., 1987. The role of imagery in information processing: Review and extensions. *Journal of consumer research,* 13(4), pp.473-491.

Mayring, P., 2010. *Qualitative Inhaltsanalyse - Grundlagen und Techniken,* Weinheim/Basel: Beltz.

Miles, M. B. and Huberman, A. M., 1994. *Qualitative data analysis: An expanded sourcebook,* Thousand Oaks et al.: Sage.

Morgan, N. and Pritchard, A., 2000. *Advertising in Tourism and Leisure,* Oxford et al.: Butterworth-Heinemann.

Österreich Werbung, n.d. Discover. [online]. Available at: <http://www.austria.info/uk/discover#fullscreen.> [Accessed 30 March 2014].

Pike, S., 2002. Destination image analysis—a review of 142 papers from 1973 to 2000. *Tourism management,* 23(5), pp.541-549.

Pikkemaat, B., 2004. The measurement of destination image: the case of Austria. *The Poznan University of Economics Review,* 4(1), pp.87-102.

Plummer, J. T., 1985. How personality makes a difference. *Journal of Advertising Research,* 24(6), pp.27-31.

Prayag, G., 2007. Exploring the relationship between destination image and brand personality of a tourist destination: An application of projective techniques. *Journal of Travel & Tourism Research,* 2(Fall), pp.111-130.

Prebensen, N. K., 2007. Exploring tourists' images of a distant destination. *Tourism Management,* 28(3), pp.747-756.

Saldaña, J., 2009. *The Coding Manual for Qualitative Researchers,* London et al.: Sage.

Schweiger, G., 1988a. Folgerungen für Österreichs Exportwirtschaft und Tourismus. In: Schweiger, G. (ed.) *Österreichs Image im Ausland.* Wien: NORKA, pp.120-128.

Schweiger, G., 1988b. *Österreichs Image im Ausland,* Wien: NORKA.

Schweiger, G., 1992. *Österreichs Image in der Welt: Ein Vergleich mit Deutschland und der Schweiz,* Wien: Service Fachverlag.

Schweiger, G. and Wusst, C., 1988. Länderimageforschung: Theorie, Methoden und Anwendung. In: Schweiger, G. (ed.) *Österreichs Image im Ausland.* Wien: NORKA, pp.21-61.

Supphellen, M., 2000. Understanding core brand equity: guidelines for in-depth elicitation of brand associations. *International Journal of Market Research,* 42(3), pp.319-338.

Von Wallpach, S. and Kreuzer, M., 2013. Multi-sensory sculpting (MSS): Eliciting embodied brand knowledge via multi-sensory metaphors. *Journal of Business Research,* 66(9), pp.1325-1331.

Wenger, A., 2008. Analysis of travel bloggers' characteristics and their communication about Austria as a tourism destination. *Journal of Vacation Marketing,* 14(2), pp.169-176.

Will, V., Eadie, D. and Macaskill, S., 1996. Projective and enabling techniques explored. *Marketing Intelligence & Planning,* 14(6), pp.38-43.

Film-Induced Tourism: The Use of Film as a Marketing Tool and its Impact on the Austrian Tourism Industry

Florentine Ramböck

Salzburg University of Applied Sciences, Austria
framboeck.imte-b2012@fh-salzburg.ac.at

Abstract

Film tourism is a rather new phenomenon and can be seen as the result of film successfully inducing tourists to visit a specific destination. This study examines the topic film-induced tourism by the use of an explorative research approach, with special regards on the evolving marketing opportunities especially for the Austrian tourism industry. It aims to show the background of film tourism and its positive and negative impacts on a destination. In order to identify the possible outcome of a successful implementation of film in the marketing strategy of a destination, literature review is conducted. Hereby, international and national best practice examples are considered in order to examine the role of so-called film commissions and DMOs in the realm of destination marketing. The resulting research propositions are the basis for semi-structured interviews with experts from different institutions within the field, which are sampled based on their knowledge and importance in terms of film tourism. Afterwards, the gathered data is evaluated through qualitative content analysis, which makes use of a pre-defined code system. Based on the results, there are recommendations and strategies suggested for the professional tourism and destination marketing context.

Keywords: film tourism; imaging tool; destination marketing strategies; new technologies; cross marketing

1 INTRODUCTION

In our modern times, people are exposed to advertisement on a daily basis and prospective clients, or in this case tourists, are not as easily influenced anymore by high-quality advertisements. However, this is usually one of the biggest parts of the marketing strategies of Destination Marketing Organisations, also called DMO's, all over the world. But instead of trying to push people by overwhelming them with TV advertisements and large billboards, the DMO's should induce the desire to travel to their destinations subconsciously.

One tool to achieve this is the use of film to showcase the respective destination. The phenomenon of tourists travelling to certain locations in order to experience what they have seen in movies is called film-induced tourism. Beeton (2005) defines it as "on-location tourism that follows the success of a movie made (or set) in a particular region." (p. 9). Examples where movies successfully influenced a destination's image are *The Lord of the Rings* and New Zealand or *The Sound of Music* and Austria. Especially New Zealand serves as best practice example and actively uses the *Lord of the Rings* and *The Hobbit* movies in their destination marketing (Beeton, 2005). Deborah Gray from Tourism New Zealand proves the success of film tourism by stating "New Zealand has seen a 52 per cent increase in visitor arrivals since *The Lord of the Rings* films. In 2000 we received 1.78 million visitors for the year, while by 2013 that had increased to 2.71 million" (2014, pers. comm.). The example shows that in recent years the awareness of the importance of film-induced tourism has increased rapidly, also in Austria.

Therefore, the DMO's have started to build film commissions within their organizations, which are responsible for marketing the destination as location for movie productions and for taking care of the producers and directors on-site (Tirol Werbung, 2013a). One example is Cine Tirol, which is a part of the local DMO Tirol Werbung. In 2013 they were able to reach more than 540 million viewers through TV series, movies and documentaries that were produced in Tyrol (König, 2014,p. 15). This number shows the huge potential of the film location Austria, that offers a picturesque landscape with mountains, lakes and rivers, but also big cities like Vienna, Graz or Salzburg.

The latter already benefits from film-induced tourism, due to the coincidental success of the movie *The Sound of Music* from 1965, which brings around 300.000 additional visitors to the region of Salzburg every year (Im and Chon, 2008). Ms Weszelka from *Tourismus Salzburg* emphasizes this by saying "The statistics show that every third Japanese who saw the movie and three quarters of the tourists from the US come to Salzburg because of the movie." (2014, pers. comm.). Even though this is a rather out-dated example, it still shows the long-lasting economic effect that a successful movie can have on a destination.

In the following paper the various factors for effective film-tourism will be discussed, as well as its backgrounds and the possible implementations for the tourism market.

2 THEORETICAL BACKGROUND

Initially, the theoretical concepts behind the film tourism phenomenon were examined in order to show the psychological and economic correlations. Therefore, the study made use of literature review and has drawn comparisons between various examples from the field. This preliminary analysis of the topic was of great importance for understanding the underlying research problem and the related propositions as well as for the development of categories in the further empirical research.

2.1 Definition of Film Tourism and its Concepts

The term of film-induced tourism is described in various ways within different papers or studies. During the literature review, it turned out that the definition by Beeton (2005), who described film tourism as "[…] on-location tourism that follows the success of a movie made (or set) in a particular region" is very accurate. This is especially true for this study, as it also takes into account television productions and series, which can also have an effect on tourism according to Beeton.

However, the research showed that the definition of a Hallmark Event fits to the concept of film tourism as well (Riley et al.,1998).

Major one-time or recurring events of limited duration developed to primarily enhance the awareness, appeal and profitability of a destination in the short and/ or long term. (Ritchie, 1984, quoted in Riley et al. 1998, p. 922)

This is due to the fact that a destination can also be inseparably related to a certain movie in the minds of the tourists. The research showed that this is in fact the case for New Zealand and the *Lord of the Rings* and the *Hobbit* movies, or for Salzburg and *Sound of Music*, which serve as best practice examples in this regard.

Besides, this also shows the economic importance of film tourism. The research suggests that film-induced tourism can bring big economic benefits to the tourism industry of a destination. However, those benefits are only indirect, as movies or series can only induce a growth in tourist numbers by increasing their awareness of a certain location. Hahm and Wang (2011) stated that film could be considered a "[…] fundamental factor in the decision making […] of the destination selection process of travellers."(p. 166).

Nevertheless, it needs to be added that film does not necessarily influence the tourists' decision to visit a destination depicted in a movie. Hudson and Ritchie (2006) defined the following five elements for effective film tourism:

1. Destination marketing activities
2. Destination attributes
3. Film-specific factors
4. Film commission and government efforts
5. Location feasibility
   (Hudson and Ritchie, 2006, p. 388)

These factors are considered as crucial in order to benefit from a growing tourist influx resulting from the success of a movie production. Furthermore, the concepts of authenticity, pilgrimage and celebrity involvement have been analysed in relation to movie-induced tourism. The first concept matches, because also film tourists are searching for the most authentic locations to visit and often identify themselves with a movie or a series. According to Steiner and Reisinger (2006) people identify themselves with their hobbies, the activities they engage in and their personal preferences. This leads to tourists searching for authentic and real places that represent in this case, a certain movie or series (Tooke and Baker, 1996). However, Beeton (2005) points out that in this regard there can also appear so-called 'mistaken identities', which occur when a movie is not shot in the same location as depicted. As a consequence, film tourists can be dissatisfied.

Subsequently, the concept of pilgrimage is closely linked to authenticity, as certain places, such as film locations, can be also seen as 'sacred' places for the tourists. This assumption was made by MacCannell (1973), who states that the reasons of pilgrims and tourists to travel are often similar.

Additionally, the concept of celebrity involvement implies that the effect of movies on the destination can even be enhanced by featuring famous actors or singers. Hence, the image of the celebrity can sometimes also be transferred to the destination. Yen and Croy (2013) state that while "[…] film plays a varying role as a tourist motivator, […] it may play a greater role for those that are celebrity involved" (p. 4). This means that fans of certain celebrities tend more to visit production sites of movies that featured their favourite actor.

The last important element in defining film tourism is its drawbacks and benefits. Just like every other phenomenon in tourism that attracts a big number of new tourists, also film tourism has some negative effects. Amongst others, the most significant problem is environmental issues, which arise when the destination's management is not able to regulate the stream of visitors.

In general, difficulties in coping with the rush of new visitors were identified as a drawback by most researchers. However, these negative effects are outnumbered by the benefits, which include positive economic impacts due to the increasing number of visitors and the enhanced destination image or brand due to the high credibility of the medium film (Hudson and Ritchie, 2006).

2.2 Important Marketing Strategies

In the realm of this study also the marketing strategies, which are involved in the concept of film tourism have been discussed. In order to understand the research propositions that will be explained in the following section, the most important findings about these destination marketing concepts were summarized.

Generally, destination marketing is used to attract visitors and tourists to a certain location or attraction. The UNWTO (2007) identified the following three objectives in destination marketing:

1. 'Cost leadership' (out-pricing competitors)

2. 'Focus' (Becoming specialists in a very focused area of activity)

3. 'Differentiation' (Offering clients a product, service or experience that has a unique value) (p. 41)

Research showed that film or television could be considered part of the last two objectives as it helps to give a destination a unique competitive advantage. Hereby, film particularly influences the destination's image and its product placement and branding. Beeton (2005) already stated that "visual media are considered to be the most powerful image-creators rather than marketing, especially [...] when they have not been primarily developed to achieve this goal." (p. 54). This statement goes in favour with the previous finding that film is a very credible and authentic tool for tourism marketing. Therefore, film can be seen as part of a pull-marketing strategy in the realm of destination marketing. This means that tourists are rather induced to visit a location instead of being overwhelmed with obvious advertisements. Macionis (2004) related film to the three main pull-factors "Place (location, attributes, landscapes, scenery), Personality (cast, characters, celebrity) [and] Performance (plot, theme, genre)" (Macionis, 2004, quoted in Yen and Croy 2013, p. 4). These factors are crucial to create an initial awareness among the prospective tourist, which can then influence their travel decision indirectly. Unfortunately the actual influence of film on tourist numbers still remains difficult to measure (Hahm and Wang, 2011). This is due to the fact that film tourists can barely be distinguished from ordinary visitors.

Furthermore, the most important assumption is that film is especially influencing the destination image, product placement and branding of a destination.

The first element is very important as it strongly affects the tourists' behaviour in terms of the decision-making process and the after-decision making behaviour, such as evaluations or interactions via social media or the website (Yen and Croy, 2013). Therefore one of the main tasks of a DMO should be the visual communication of the desired destination image (Ye and Tussyadiah, 2011). Film and television productions can be a very useful tool to achieve this goal, especially because they can transport experiences rather than just nice pictures of a certain location.

The second marketing element that is important in terms of film tourism is product placement and branding of a destination. These two factors are strongly correlated with each other and also with the destination image. Just like the latter, also product placement and branding aim to influence the travel decision process of prospective tourists. Therefore, a successfully branded destination can be a major asset according to the UNWTO (2007). Furthermore, the findings showed that product placement and branding are crucial for the differentiation of the tourism product of a destination. Hereby it is important for the DMO to create a trusted brand, which enhances the USPs of the destination. Hudson and Ritchie stated that in terms of film tourism, even a "[...] simple visual placement in the background can be as effective as a highly integrated placement." (p. 388). Nevertheless, the promotion of movies or series also after their release remains an important task of the DMO in order to ensure successful film tourism (Hudson and Ritchie, 2006).

However, research showed that film is not the only factor for successful destination marketing. Even though it can increase the awareness of a destination, tourist visitation still depends strongly on a good marketing mix.

3 METHODOLOGY

Due to the nature of the film tourism phenomenon, the study chose an explorative research approach, which seemed to be the most accurate. This enabled the researcher to develop six research propositions subsequently to the preliminary literature review, which became the basis for the conducted expert interviews as well as for the coding system used within the qualitative content analysis. Further details of the chosen research design will be explained in the following parts.

3.1 Research Design

In general, the choice of the research method strongly depends on the nature of the underlying research problem. Even though Silverman (2006) points out that there is no right or wrong method, each researcher has to find the appropriate method for their field and research problem. Consequently, this study chose a qualitative approach for obtaining and analysing data, because of the characteristics of the research question and the topic.

Besides, qualitative research is more explorative rather than explanative (Bortz and Döring, 2006). Also in this study an explorative approach was used, which can be a huge advantage for the very specific field of tourism research. Moreover, the film tourism phenomenon implies the use of a rather explorative research design, due to the difficulty in measuring its impacts appropriately, which supports the choice of a qualitative approach as well (Silverman, 2006).

Furthermore, the nature of the research problem itself also suggests qualitative methods over quantitative ones as it asks about 'how' film can be implemented successfully into marketing strategies. In order to examine the actual processes of destination marketing and the DMOs' strategies, close contact with experts from the field is necessary. With qualitative methods this is possible, whereas quantitative research barely involves such contacts (Silverman, 2006).

Lastly, the analysed phenomenon of film tourism itself needs to be mentioned as determining factor for the choice of the research design. Strauss and Corbin (1998) point out:

Qualitative methods can be used to obtain the intricate details about phenomena [...] that are difficult to extract or learn about through more conventional research methods. (p. 11).

Silverman (2006) supports their view as well by saying that "[t]he main strength of qualitative research is its ability to study phenomena which are simply unavailable elsewhere." (p. 43). This 'unavailability' of film tourism simply means the difficulty in measuring actual film tourism in the respective destinations. So far only few statistics on film tourism exist, which is due to the fact that film tourists can hardly be identified in a reliable and valid manner.

The qualitative research design is complemented with expert interviews that are used to obtain data, which were later analysed and evaluated using the qualitative content analysis method by Philipp Mayring (2004).

3.1 Expert Interviews

As previously mentioned, the study makes use of semi-structured expert interviews in order to obtain data from the field. Unlike other types of interviewing, expert interviews focus on the interviewees knowledge and experience about a field or topic rather than focusing on them as a person (Flick, 2009). Therefore, this form of interview facilitates the collection of reliable and valid data. Of course this makes it also necessary to choose the right experts and identifying the 'right' experts can bring up some difficulties. In this regard, Gläser and Laudel (2009) point out that, experts are not only people with a scientific knowledge but also people with a heightened affinity to a special topic (e.g. a hobby). Nevertheless, as Flick (2009) states, "[...] mostly staff members of an organization with a specific function and a specific (professional) experience and knowledge are target groups." (p. 166). Also the majority of the five different experts interviewed for this study belong to this group. They were purposefully sampled according to their experience in the field of film tourism or their function in the tourism industry. Hence, the researcher could ensure to cover both the point of view of the DMOs as well as of the film commissions. Additionally, one expert, who is not directly involved into the tourism business complemented the gathered data and provides a non-biased opinion about the film tourism phenomenon.

Furthermore, the five interviews were carried out either via telephone or in person and lasted approximately 25 minutes. Only the interview with the Tourism Board of New Zealand was held via email, due to the time difference.

3.3 Research Propositions and Research Question

The preliminary literature research has lead to six propositions, which are crucial for the further examination through qualitative content analysis. Moreover, the propositions were formulated in dependence on the underlying research question:

How is film successfully implemented as an imaging tool in the marketing strategies of Austrian tourism destinations?

In contrary to hypotheses, propositions are not operationalized, which means they are not measurable or testable. However, they can still be accepted or neglected after the data analysis. In this study four different categories originated from the previous literature review, which were then further distinguished into sub-categories in order to build the coding system. The propositions are already listed according to their respective category in the following.

Perspective on Destination Marketing
1. The implementation of film brings a measurable economic advantage to the Austrian tourism industry.
2. Destination marketing should shift its focus to more interactive and experience-oriented strategies.

The Role of Film Commissions
3. Film commissions should do movie-related promotion before, while and after the productions in order to maximize the outcome.
4. Film commissions need to work closely together with the local tourism and film industry in order to facilitate the production process and ensure quality.

Perspective on Cross Marketing
5. Austrian DMOs should consider cross marketing strategies for a holistic implementation of film.

Use of New Technologies
6. New technologies could enhance the tourist experience in Austrian destinations especially in relation to film tourism.

3.4 Evaluation and Interpretation Method

Consequently to the expert interviews, the researcher chose the method of qualitative content analysis to evaluate the gathered data. This involves the development of a coding system, which, in this case, is based on the already mentioned categories of the preceding research propositions, which were complemented with several subcategories. The coding scheme is then applied to the written text, which should be analysed. In this case, the text is generated by transforming the recorded interviews into transcripts.

In the next step, the information or content in the text is assigned and distributed to the appropriate codes. Hereby, the researcher focused on "[...] the way the theme is treated or presented and the frequency of its occurrence." (Spencer et al., 2003, p. 200). In practice this means that the relevant passages in the text were systematically listed according to the developed categories and sub-categories. Like this, the researcher gains a set of all relevant information, which could then easily be interpreted and compared in order to build concepts or models. These concepts were further used to answer the research question.

An important task within the qualitative content analysis is the constant revision of the developed codes. If necessary, they can be modified or reformulated in order to do justice to the research progress (Flick, 2009). In this manner, the author could ensure that the evaluation maintains its focus on the underlying research problem.

Besides, the analysis and interpretation followed an inductive approach (Bortz and Döring, 2006; Flick, 2009). This means that the expert interviews represent specific observations of the field, which are interpreted and thus transformed into generalizations that lead to broader theories about the topic and implementation of film tourism. In practice, this means that the researcher assigned the relevant passages from the interview transcripts to the according codes, in order to respond to the respective research propositions in a later step. This was done by the use of the software MAXQDA, which facilitates qualitative content analysis. Furthermore, the different passages could be easily compared and thus strategies for the tourism context could be formulated.

4 RESULTS AND IMPLICATIONS

During the evaluation process, the researcher's aim was to focus on the underlying research problem, which arose from the preliminary literature review and led to several research propositions. This goal was pursued by analysing each of these propositions separately and then combining the results, in order to get the whole picture of the potential of film as imaging tool for the Austrian tourism industry. In this regard, the relevant text passages were compared to point out the important facts suggested by the experts. Based on these results, the study then gives several implications for a successful use of film within the professional context as well as implications for further research.

4.1 Response to the Research Problem

Firstly, it needs to be emphasized again that the preceding propositions were all based on the research question and had the aim to examine the various elements of the research problem. The outcome of the analysis was that, apart from slight changes of some terms involved, all propositions could be accepted.

Consequently, after the evaluation of all propositions, there remained the question how these findings actually play together in the bigger picture of successfully implementing film as imaging tool. This can be answered by saying that there are various components and approaches involved, of which some are more important to implement than others.

The probably most important elements of a successful implementation, which were identified through the evaluation, are promotion and cooperation. Hereby it needs to be distinguished between the DMOs and the film commissions though. DMOs should focus on experience-oriented and interactive movie promotion to prospective tourists, whereas film commissions should promote the location to filmmakers in order to attract more movie productions. Furthermore, the research suggests that both DMOs and film commissions should try to collaborate as much as possible. This means that it is advisable for DMOs and film commissions to cooperate with each other, if they are not yet part of the same organization, as well as with the filmmakers. Collaboration with the latter is especially important concerning promotion and possible legal limitations that can be avoided by early contracts and agreements (David, 2014). Moreover, film commissions should also try to involve the local film industry. In the analysis it turned out that the experts, who represent the Austrian film commissions already see this as one of their organizations' tasks. Ms Urban from *Standortagentur Salzburg* states in this regard "It is our task to strengthen the movie industry and to include local industries (extras, drivers, etc.)" (Urban, 2014, pers. comm.).

Additionally, also cross marketing strategies can be used by the DMOs and film commissions to provide a holistic implementation of film. Even though it was found out that cooperation with the film industry could already be considered as cross marketing, this can be broadened by the inclusion of non-touristic partners. In this regard the interviewed experts also emphasized their efforts to collaborate with non-touristic partners, and hence gave some best-practice examples of cross marketing strategies. Among these suggestions were organized fan weeks (Koeck, 2014, pers. comm.), movie trails and exhibitions in museums (David, 2014, pers. comm.).

Lastly, it is also possible and advisable to use new technologies in order to successfully implement film in the marketing strategy. In this concern, it was found out that so far there are only few examples in Austria where such new technologies are already used, such as movie apps for film tourists in Tyrol (Koeck, 2014, pers. comm.). Nevertheless, it can be a powerful tool to enhance the tourists experience on-location, and also to make people aware of movies or series shot in the area (Gray, 2014, pers. comm.). Therefore, there is still a lot of potential and possibilities left to be used by Austrian destinations.

Concluding, it can be said that following at least some of these implications can bring a measurable economic advantage to the destination and ensures a successful implementation of film as an imaging tool within the different marketing strategies of Austrian DMOs and film commissions.

4.2 Implications for Further Research

The research within this study could not cover all the important relations concerning film tourism. First of all, even though it was intended to cover a wide range of related literature within the scope of the research, this is of course very time intensive and could therefore only be achieved to some extent. Additionally, the research only focused on a very narrow part of the tourism industry through the use of solely expert interviews in order to gather data. Therefore, future research could be done involving the point of view and the perceptions of the tourists or the film industry. Especially the perceptions of the tourists could be interesting in terms of experience-oriented marketing, which was already identified to be a big factor for film tourism.

Moreover, the use of quantitative research methods, including the use of questionnaires could be advisable for future researchers in order to further verify the results of this study in a quantitative way.

Additionally, future research could take into account series and documentation productions more than it was done for this study, where the focus was more on film and only to a small extent on series.

Lastly, it also turned out that there are some negative points, which shouldn't be disregarded. These could also be subject to further research about the film tourism phenomenon.

4.3 Implications for the Professional Context

In continuation to the implications for future research, there are also some recommendations for the professional context. The obvious aim of this study was to provide valuable insights about the point of views of both DMOs and film commissions in terms of movie-induced tourism. Therefore, also the results are probably most interesting for DMOs and film commissions, especially in terms of the possible outcome.

The study showed that despite the difficulties in quantifying the film tourism effect, there is actually a measurable economic advantage. This fact can be an incentive for tourism organizations to follow the above-mentioned propositions.

In this regard, the notions of incorporating experience-oriented marketing and cooperation could be of particular interest. The latter refers to cooperation between the film commissions and the DMOs as well as to collaborations with the production companies.

Furthermore, also the examples about movie-related promotion, involving cross marketing should be well considered by the DMOs.

Besides that, the examples of new technologies, which are not yet used to a big extent in Austria, could serve as possible ideas for complementing the experience-oriented marketing notion.

In general, film commissions and DMOs could both benefit from some of the examined propositions and therefore it is worth considering some of the ideas given by this study.

5 CONCLUSION

Having considered the theoretical background of the film tourism phenomenon, as well as the results of the empirical research, the study could come to the following conclusion.

First of all, it needs to be mentioned that film tourism involves several different concepts, which were listed within the realm of the literature review. Besides, there are also positive and negative effects on destinations that experience an increase in tourist numbers as the result of a movie or series production.

Nevertheless, it was found out that the possible positive outcome outweighs the downsides. Taking this fact into account, there are a number of destination marketing components, which are able to make use of movies as imaging tool. These marketing elements were elaborately examined within the first part of the study. From this first literature review and theoretical explanation of film tourism, there derived six research propositions, which were then subject to further evaluation through qualitative content analysis.

The propositions could be divided into four different categories, namely the *Perspective on Destination Marketing*, the *Role of the Film Commission*, the *Perspective on Cross Marketing* and *New Technologies*. Based on these categories, there were expert interviews conducted with the intention to gather qualitative data, which was then analysed. Through the evaluation and interpretation of this data, the study came to the result that the propositions could be approved, even though there had to be some things added or changed.

This means that film tourism actually has a measurable effect on destinations, given that their DMOs and film commissions cooperate effectively and incorporate an experience-oriented promotion.

Furthermore, the examples examined in the evaluation section could serve as implications for tourism organizations and film commissions, especially in terms of cross marketing and new technologies.

Concluding, it can be said that the results of the study could be of great interest for Austrian destinations, as there is still a lot of potential left, which was basically confirmed by all the experts interviewed. Hence, it can be claimed that film is already recognized to some extent by tourism organizations and will most probably gain even more importance as imaging tool for destination marketing in the future.

REFERENCES

Beeton, S. (2005) *Film-Induced Tourism.* Clevedon, Channel View Publications.

Bortz, J., Döring, N. (2006) *Forschungsmethoden und Evaluation.* (4th ed) Heidelberg, Springer Medizin Verlag.

David, Andrea (2014) Author of the Tourism Blog *Filmtourimus.de.* Interview with the author, 30 December. Personal communication.

Flick, U. (2009) *An Introduction to Qualitative Research.* (4th ed) London, SAGE Publications.

Gläser, J., Laudel, G. (2010) *Experteninterviews und qualitative Inhalsanalyse.* (4th ed) Wiesbaden, VS Verlag.

Gray, Deborah (2014) General Manager Corporate Affairs, Tourism New Zealand. Email to the author, 16 December. Personal Communication

Hahm, J., Wang, Y. (2011) Film-Induced Tourism as a Vehicle For Destination Marketing: Is it Worth the Efforts?. *Journal of Travel & Tourism Marketing,* 28, pp. 165-179.

Hudson, S., Ritchie, J.R.B. (2006) Promoting Destinations via Film Tourism: An Empirical Identification of Supporting Marketing Initiatives. *Journal of Travel Research,* 44, pp. 387-396.

Im, H. H., Chon, K. (2008) An Exploratory Study of Movie-Induced Tourism: A Case of the Movie *The Sound of Music* and Its Locations in Salzburg, Austria. *Journal of Travel & Tourism Marketing,* **24** (2-3), pp. 229-238.

Koeck, Johannes (2014) Head of Cine Tirol Film Commission. Interview with the author, 5 December. Personal communication.

König, S. (2014) Urlaub nach Drehbuch. *bulletin,* 2nd of March 2014, pp. 14-17.

MacCannell, D. (1973) Staged Authenticity: Arrangements of Social Space in Tourist Settings. *American Journal of Sociology,* 79 (3), pp. 589-603.

Mayring, P. (2004) Qualitative Content Analysis. In: Flick, U., von Kardoff, E., Steinke, I. eds *A companion to Qualitative Research.* London, SAGE Publications.

Riley, R., Baker, D. & Van Doren, C.S. (1998) Movie Induced Tourism. *Annals of Tourism Research,* **25** (4), pp. 919-935.

Silverman, D. (2006) *Interpreting Qualitative Data.* (3rd ed) London, SAGE Publications.

Spencer, L., Ritchie, J., O'Connor, W. (2003) Analysis: Practices, Principles and Processes. In: Ritchie, J., Lewis, J. eds. *Qualitative Research Practice.* London, SAGE Publications.

Strauss, A., Corbin, J. (1998) *Basics of Qualitative Research.* (2nd ed) London, SAGE Publications.

Steiner, C.J., Reisinger, Y. (2006) Understanding Existential Authenticity. *Annals of Tourism Research,* 33 (2), pp. 299-318.

Tirol Werbung GmbH. (2013a) *Tirol Inspiriert Filmtouristen.* [Internet]. Innsbruck, Tirol Werbung. Available from: <http://www.tirolwerbung.at/xxl/de/presse/_pressid/1912469/index.html> [Accessed 4 June 2014].

Tooke, N., Baker, M. (1996) Seeing is Believing: The Effect of Film on Visitor Numbers to Screened Locations. *Tourism Management,* 17 (2), pp. 87-94.

Urban, Edith (2014) Responsible for Filmlocation Salzburg department, Standortagentur Salzburg. Interview with the author, 11 December. Personal communication.

Weszelka, Birgit (2014) Press department, Tourismus Salzburg GmbH. Interview with the author, 29 December. Personal communication.

World Tourism Organization (2007) *A Practical Guide to Tourism Destination Management.* Madrid, World Tourism Organization.

Ye, H., Tussyadiah, L.P. (2011) Destination Visual Image and Expectation of Experiences. *Journal of Travel & Tourism Marketing,* 28, pp. 129-144.

Yen, C.H., Croy, W.G. (2013) Film Tourism: Celebrity Involvement, Celebrity Worship and Destination Image. *Current Issues in Tourism* [Internet], pp. 1-18. Available from: <http://dx.doi.org/10.1080/13683500.2013.816270> [Accessed 12 March 2014].

A Critical Analysis on the Implementation, Activeness and Level of Engagement of Destination Marketing Organisations across Social Media Platforms of YouTube & Google+

Sarah Nelum Rajika Wijesinghe, and

Magdalena Pozgaj

University of Surrey, UK
sarah_wijesinghe@yahoo.com

Abstract

The rapid penetration of social media platforms and escalating number of users offer a wide range of possibilities for Destination Marketing Organisations' (DMOs). Due to the high number of competitors, it is important for DMOs to be where the consumers are, therefore social media platforms are adequate to reach and build relationships with consumers. This study was conducted to explore and contribute to the website evaluation literature by developing a catalogue of dimensions based on previous literature, evaluating the implementation, activeness and level of engagement of 58 DMOs (33 European Travel Commission members and 25 Non-European travel commission members) on YouTube and Google+ platforms. The results of this research noted that DMOs still lack in terms of activeness and effectiveness and showcase a lack of understanding in adapting to the concept of social media. The paper contributes to existing theory by highlighting the weaknesses of DMOs in adapting to social media and providing specific insight into the platforms of YouTube & Google+. It also provides unique information and implications for DMOs and tourism marketers of the opportunities and potential of adapting and being proactive on YouTube and Google+ platforms to reach a global market.

Keywords: DMOs; Social Media platforms; Destination Marketing; YouTube; Google+

1 INTRODUCTION

As Popesku (2014) states, the development of the World Wide Web that lead to the creation of Web 2.0 has fundamentally changed the way tourists access information, the way they plan and book their travel and share their travel experiences. Furthermore, Lange-Faria & Elliot (2012) argues that, social media (SM) has become the modus operandi of the 21st century, making traditional marketing techniques less relevant to reach to a broader global market. Highlighting the growth of SM, Chan & Guillet (2011) states that travellers place a high degree of trust in destinations' social media networks. Therefore, a competitive advantage in the marketplace is reached by those DMOs that apply advances of SM platforms in order to formulate marketing strategy to engage with their potential consumers as early as possible in the decision-making process to earn a measurable return on investment (Popesku, 2014, p. 716).

SM has a unique significance for the activities of destination marketing organisations (DMOs), as destination marketers can use SM as a marketing platform before the travel, during the travel and after the holiday to inform, inspire, remember, share and engage (Popesku, 2014, p. 715). However, though SM serves as a highly competitive marketing platform for DMOs to build stronger relationships with consumers, Xiang & Gretzel (2010) and Kalpan & Haenlein (2010) argue that, SM should not be seen as yet another advertising channel (Chan & Guillet, 2011). It is a platform that should be proactively used to socialize and interact with consumers, thus it is not only essential for DMOs to be present on SM but also to be active and effective.

Although many studies have been conducted previously, investigating SM as a tourism marketing tool (Xiang & Gretzel, 2010; Buhalis & Wagner, 2013; Cantoni & Xiang, 2013, Chan & Guillet, 2011; Reino & Hay, 2011), there is still lack of research attempted to understand the use of YouTube and Google+ specifically in destination marketing.

As tourists are not able to test-drive a destination prior to purchase, Krippendorf (1987) & Urry (2002) state that decision to visit a destination is based on symbolic expectations established promotionally (Ribeiro, 2009; Jorgensen, 2004). In this case, YouTube known to be the second largest search engine in the world, serves itself as an essential SM platform for DMOs to provide tourists a real sense of the destination they desire to visit. Therefore, unlike traditional marketing methods and other SM platforms, YouTube offers unique opportunities for DMOs through the nature of the platform, which allows video sharing that is studied to have a much larger impact on consumers in marketing terms (Reino & Hay, 2011).

Whereas Google+, a newly launched SM platform in 2011 by Google, is argued to carry further opportunities for DMOs due to its connection with Google. Destinations are known to have spent large percentage of marketing budgets on Search Engine Marketing (SEM) & Search Engine Optimization (SEO) that allows them to be on the top results of Google search that in turn attract high clickthrough rates (Pan, 2015). Pan (2015) further argued that SEM is of high importance for DMOs to gain web traffics and revenue. However, though the importance of SEM and SEO for DMOs has been studied, the potential and power that Google+ holds in terms of contributing to this same benefits has yet not been given attention. Being present on Google+ as argued in the literature section of this study gives the benefit of being on top of Google search results, that as according to Pan (2015) study confirms is a tremendous advantage for DMOs in order to be visible & attract more consumers (Destination Marketing Association International, 2013; Pan, 2015).

Therefore, given the insufficiencies in the literature addressing the use of YouTube & Google+ platforms in destination marketing, this study aims to contribute & highlight the importance of these SM platforms in destination marketing. Data collected is statistically analysed and theoretically discussed in the results and discussion section after an in depth clarification of literature focusing on the importance of YouTube & Google+ for destination marketing and DMOs implementation, activeness and engagement on these SM platforms.

2 THEORETICAL BACKGROUND

2.1 Social media & tourism

Xiang & Gretzel (2010) discusses that it is impossible to regard marketing efforts in tourism without a significant SM component. As Schegg et al. (2008) and Wang et al. (2002) argue, tourism organisations that do not adopt to SM will lack a competitive advantage. Thus, today for a destination to be successful and gain the competitive edge, they must be able to provide information and experiences that the travellers demands and rely on in their decision making process, and as SM allows sharing of information across a global market, it is argued that maintaining some form of presence on SM is a must for tourism authorities or tourism related organisations, especially DMOs who markets the destination to a global market (Reino & Hay, 2011; Parker, 2012; Hays et al., 2012). However, as discussed earlier, decision of tourism providers to utilize SM, as Gretzel et al. (2006) states, must be accompanied by commitment and a proactive approach. The reason being as argued by Wang et al. (2002) and Stankov et al. (2010) is that, though a tourism organisation that do not adopt SM lack a competitive advantage; an organisation that do not understand the concept of SM and practices it in a poor manner could be directed to a much detrimental stage (Hays et al., 2012, p.3).

2.2 Social media as a tool for destination marketing

According to Destination Marketing Association International (2013), 85% consumers cite the Internet as their primary source of information for travel planning, visiting on average 17 different sites. This indicates the growing importance of SM to DMOs as discussed by Lange-Faria & Elliot (2012), to earn the competitive edge and return on investment. It is stated important for DMOs as Nguyen & Wang (2011) argues for reasons that, DMOs need to apply themselves where the visitors exist in order to remain relevant and useful to their potential target market in today's digital age. Thus due to the high adaptation rate of consumers to SM networks, it is highly relevant for today's marketer to be present and active in SM as a mode of engaging with their consumers to attract a global market.

As argued by Nguyen & Wang (2011), UNWTO & ETC emphasizes that, building appropriate marketing strategies on SM platforms allows DMOs' to see the immediate reaction of their target markets and also help to gain higher rank in search engines. This need for adaptation to SM is further argued by Munar (2012), Kierzkowski et al. (1996) and Pike (2008), who suggest that, to be successful in SM requires the DMOs to maintain updated and valuable content, learn about consumers through engagement, using feedback, discussion and other interactive media tools. Kierkowski et al. (1996) also states that DMOs need to offer information including those of the organisation, provide customizable Multilingual content to deliver user-friendly web pages that would foster sustained destination competitiveness (Nguyen & Wang, 2011; Munar, 2012; Chan & Guillet, 2011; Perttula, 2013).

Though there are major advantages of SM as Munar (2012) stresses, in terms of building customer relationship, accessing a global market and promoting the brand, Munar (2012) also states according to the findings of her study that many DMOs show weaknesses in utilizing SM strategies in terms of lack of user involvement, poor levels of participation and lack of dynamism (Munar, 2012, p.102; Nguyen & Wang, 2011). Therefore, as Gretzel et al. (2006a) state, the decision of DMOs to utilize SM must be informed and accompanied by proactive behaviour to commit and learn to address the continuing changes in the digital age.

2.3 The role of YouTube & Google+ in destination marketing

YouTube

Established in 2005 YouTube has experienced an astounding level of growth being the second largest search engine in the world after Google (Cheng et al., 2012). YouTube enables the communication between users and tourism businesses (DMOs) through video content that plays an important role in creating the destination image in consumer mind (Reino et al., 2011). Importance of YouTube in tourism marketing is growing for reasons that the static visual images of destinations offer less excitement to potential travellers compared to videos which deliver more emotional stimuli (Reino & Hay, 2011). YouTube also allows DMOs the opportunity to enhance positive brand image or fight negative perceptions of the destinations (Destination Marketing Association International (2013). Moreover, video contents increase the impact on tourism industry as more travel bookings are a result of online video sharing (Destination Marketing Association International (2013). King (2002) states that, nowadays, the consumers are those who decide when and how to reach the information and due to the fact that consumers have less time, YouTube brings these information anywhere they are at any time through creative content (Reino et al., 2011).

To understand the interactive features of YouTube, Cheng et al. (2012) & Wattenhofer (2012) state that the number of views a video has is important to measure as it reflects the popularity of the video and the destinations itself. However, though Miller (2011) agrees that total views can be used as a metric to measure the video success, it may be a false measurement to see if an organisation has accomplished the goals they have set out to achieve. Miller (2011) further discusses that comments may not constitute a hard metric, but it is a good representation of the degree to which the video engaged viewers in terms of gaining feedback. Adding to Miller (2011) argument, Colburn & Haines (2012) states that features such as rating, liking, comments, have a high potential to raise visibility of a given video throughout the social network. However, Rienhard (2009) observes that to achieve long-term success on YouTube, marketers have to consistently and frequently publish refreshing content that has intrinsic value for audiences online, he argues that, the failure to update and refresh their online content is one of the most frequent criticisms by consumers of online tourism information (Reino & Hay, 2011). Wattenhofer (2012) also argues that the approximate measure of YouTube channels popularity comes from the number of subscribers, explaining that there are channels that upload hundreds of videos, without subscribers and no interaction nor communication with the consumers.

Aside from the metrics such as number of subscribers or comments, there are still difficulties concerning the measurement of being effective on SM platforms. Though the general metrics of success are still not defined, most of the academics agree that the real value of sharing videos on YouTube is still mostly expressed by the 'eyeballs it has attracted' (Garfield, 2006).

Google+

Google+ is a newly developed SM platform launched by Google in 2011. Google describes it as a social layer, connected to all Google properties including Google search. This integration into Google search, "Search+ Your World," may be the most impactful aspect of Google+ (Destination Marketing Association International, 2013). One of the major benefits highlighted for DMOs' to be present and active on Google+ are that, being part of the Google+ community means that the brand is weighted heavier in the top-secret algorithm Google uses to determine where a company or site lands in search engine results. Thus, in short being present on Google+ helps DMOs to be on top of Google search results (Destination Marketing Association International, 2013). This is important as DMOs can easily track consumer behaviour on their website and gain revenue through direct sale. As Pan (2015) argued in his study, DMOs can also benefit in terms of evaluating Return on Investment (ROI) of marketing efforts by monitoring the CTR (Pan, 2015). In comparison with YouTube which is primarily a video sharing platform, Google+ platform is more similar to Facebook and the study conducted by Motamedi et al. (2013:6) showcases that users on Google+ and Facebook share similar activity rate, which positions Google+ as a relevant platform among users.

Other major benefits of Google+ include, availability of innovative tools to communicate with consumers such as Google+ Hangouts which can also be recorded to YouTube (Stay, 2012). However Stay (2012) also argues that though being on Google+ has its benefits, just being present and without being active or utilizing the many tools the platform offers may not help an organisation be ranked at top search results. Therefore, he argues that it is essential to adapt, engage and be active proactively. One of the features that Google+ has in comparison with YouTube is the 'share' option, where users share the posts they like, turning the platform into virtual word-of-mouth. Every share on SM platforms can attract and engage more users, which is important because it increases brand awareness and content visibility, as well as attracts higher number of followers. Furthermore, the messages are virally disseminated, reaching more and more consumers, making it easier for DMOs to communicate their destination brand (Sabate, 2014). However, though Bakshy (2011) points out that the influence of posts is still generally unobservable and difficult to define, with lack of understanding whether the quantity of uploaded content on SM platforms is more important than the quality and vice versa, it can be argued that through observing the interaction of user to the DMOs content (features such as comments, likes, views) has the ability to showcase how effective their marketing efforts are on Google+ which can be further confirmed through CTR on Google search.

3 RESEARCH METHODOLOGY

This study aims to understand the extent to which DMOs use the social media platforms of YouTube & Google+ in their marketing efforts. The study is conducted as an exploratory research with an inductive approach. The first step was identifying the official websites of the DMOs and further identifying their YouTube & Google+ presence based on the hyperlinks provided in the official webpages. A well-defined criteria catalogue was designed based on consolidating previous website evaluation literature at the primary phase which was later utilized for data collection for this study. The criteria catalogue for evaluation consisted of 78 sub categories spread under 13 main dimensions for YouTube platform and 64 sub categories under 12 main dimensions for Google+ platform. The 13 dimensions by which the data was collected are as follows: Channel Existence, Authority, Availability, Content Information, Communication, Customization, Outcome Criteria, Interactivity, Interface Design, Navigation, Mash ups and Web 2.0 features and were developed based on literature of following journals - Journal of Travel and Tourism Marketing, Journal of Travel Research, International Journal of Information Management, Electronic Journal of information system Evaluation, etc. Further to the academic journals, the authors further investigated the specific features of the two SM platforms that was added into the criteria catalogue.

Destinations explored for this research are chosen based on the 'UNWTO, Tourism Highlights 2014' report, which is a total of 33 ETC members and 25 Non-ETC members. This nations were further investigated in the study according to the World's Top 10 tourism destinations. Data collected in phase 1 of the study through the criteria catalogue was used to analyse and interpret the DMO presence, activeness and their level of implementation on SM platforms of Google+ and YouTube. Out of 58 DMOs, the total DMOs present on YouTube is 43 and 35 in Google+. Results were analysed across ETC & Non-ETC and also discussed in terms of top 10 destinations and international arrival statistics in 2013 as showcased by UNWTO Tourism Highlights. The analysis was then utilized to test the developed hypothesis to clarify the relationship between variables as well as to determine the dominant DMOs across the social media platforms. The results of this study are discussed under the before holiday - inspire, inform and engage stages (see Section 2.3) of the e-destination benchmark suggested by Buhalis & Wagner (2013).

Hypothesis

H1: There is a significant impact of number of total posts (post frequency in October) on the number of total followers on Google+

H2: There is a positive relationship between the date channel was created on YouTube and the number of total subscribers on YouTube

H3: There is a positive relationship between number of total videos & total views on YouTube channel

4 RESULTS AND DISCUSSION

The objective of this study was to provide insight of the current practice of social media by DMOs. The analysis of this study serve as a means to provide detailed understanding of DMOs implementation, activeness, and level of engagement in SM platforms of Google+ and YouTube.

Table 1. DMO Presence across Social Media Platforms

European Travel Commission Member	Social Media Presence (1=Yes, 0=No)				
	YouTube	Facebook	Google+	Instagram	Twitter
33	91%	100%	64%	55%	85%
Non-European Travel Commission Members					
25	52%	84%	56%	24%	76%
58	74%	93%	60%	41%	81%

Analysis was conducted as of the first phase in this study to verify which DMOs are present on YouTube & Google+. The results suggested that the most widely used platforms across both ETC members and Non-ETC members are as follows, Facebook (93%; n=54), Twitter (81%; n=47), YouTube (74%; n=43), Google+ (60%; n=35) and Instagram (41%; n=24). However, it indicated that overall ETC members are more present across the SM platforms than Non-ETC members. Similar to the results of the study conducted by Alizadeh & Isa (2014), the results of this research showcase that Facebook is the leading social networking site in the world with the highest rate of adaptation among DMOs; and though YouTube is also known for its high adaptation and popularity since 2005 as a SM platform, it is noticed that the presence on the platform is relatively low. And, though Facebook, Twitter & YouTube which are known as the most renowned SM platforms for tourism marketing, it is observed that there still are DMOs who has not adapted to Facebook (7%), Twitter (19%) & Youtube (26%) with no official presence on the platform. According to Table 4.1, from the total of 58 ETC and Non-ETC member countries, a total of 43 DMOs are present on YouTube and a total of 35 present on Google+ showing great room for adaptation to effectively use SM as a marketing tool to reach the global consumer.

4.1 Hypothesis Testing

H1: There is an impact between the number of total posts (post frequency in October) and the number of total followers on Google+

Table 2. Correlation Test results for H1

Correlations

		Posts Frequency	Total Followers
Posts Frequency	Pearson Correlation	1	.637**
	Sig. (2-tailed)		.000
	N	35	35
Total Followers	Pearson Correlation	.637**	1
	Sig. (2-tailed)	.000	
	N	35	35

**. Correlation is significant at the 0.01 level (2-tailed).

Correlation test shows a strong positive correlation between the two variables with a p value of 0.001 (see Table 4.3). R value in regression analysis is 0.6 indicating a strong relationship between the two variables as well and the coefficient of determination (R^2) is 0.40 indicating that 40% of changes in total followers in explained by number of total posts. Beta value of 0.360 indicates a significant impact of post frequency showing that for each unit of uploaded post, the number of followers' increases by 36%.

H2: There is a positive relationship between the date channel was created on YouTube and the number of total subscribers on YouTube

Table 3. Correlation Test Results for H2

Correlations

		Joined Date	Total Subscribers
Joined Date	Pearson Correlation	1	-.350*
	Sig. (2-tailed)		.021
	N	43	43
Total Subscribers	Pearson Correlation	-.350*	1
	Sig. (2-tailed)	.021	
	N	43	43

*. Correlation is significant at the 0.05 level (2-tailed).

As shown in Table 4.4, there is a negative correlation (-0.350) indicating a negative relationship between the two variables showcasing similar results as to the study conducted by Alizadeh & Isa (2014). P value is at 0.021, therefore, it is significant (p<0.021). The significant negative relationship between the variables indicate that the date DMO channel was created on YouTube has no impact on the number of followers (i.e. Switzerland joined in 2006 and has only 5,321 subscribers whereas Discover America channel joined in 2012 and has over 10,236 subscribers) and it is still not late for absent DMOs to adopt to the platform.

H3: There is a positive relationship between number of total videos & total views on DMO YouTube channel

Table 4. Correlation Test Results for H3

Correlations

		Total Videos under the Channel	Total Views
Total Videos under the Channel	Pearson Correlation	1	.292
	Sig. (2-tailed)		.058
	N	43	43
Total Views	Pearson Correlation	.292	1
	Sig. (2-tailed)	.058	
	N	43	43

Table 4.5 indicates that there is a weak positive relationship (0.292) between the two variables as the correlation is below 0.5. The p value is at 0.58 (p> 0.58) indicating that the relationship between the variables is insignificant. Statistically, it indicates that uploading new videos does not necessarily generate more views on DMOs' channels and that they not only need to post videos but also need to communicate and engage with their subscribers more attentively. This aligns with Miller (2012) argument that quality of content is important and not only the content to attract the consumer.

4.2 Inspire Stage

Table 5. DMO Activeness on YouTube & Google+

European Travel Commission Member	Total Videos/Posts in October		Total Videos	Total Subscribers/Followers		Total Views	
	YouTube	Google+	YouTube	YouTube	Google+	YouTube	Google+
Croatia	1	24	94	3,708	9,649	5,102,278	2,892,523
Czech Republic	0	1	86	1,424	-	3,791,852	-
Cyprus	1	1	53	852	44	398,281	4,368
Germany	3	3	44	1,007	110	740,169	10,669
Greece	5	100	179	6,749	1,641,930	5,357,858	30,593,200
Hungary	0	60	74	2,288	-	1,102,930	-
Iceland	2	2	22	1,130	4	607,856	35,683
Ireland	0	-	49	2,600	-	1,000,080	-
Italy	2	52	382	2,685	175,130	861,552	60,518,525
Malta	1	1	118	1,863	103	1,853,531	22,986
Norway	7	4	132	4,204	11,904	4,776,422	1,730,677
Turkey	3	0	59	3,118	102,970	9,601,404	24,154,199
Total ETC Members: 12	Total: 25	248	1,292	31,628	1,941,844	35,193,713	119,962,830
Non-European Travel Commission Members							
Belarus	0	-	172	205	-	156,173	-
China	-	-	-	-	-	-	-
France	-	1	-	-	510	-	93,805
Georgia	0	21	48	494	903	61,248	1,740,142
Kyrgyzstan	-	-	-	-	-	-	-
Russia	-	-	-	-	-	-	-
Thailand	1	126	469	5,126	287,537	1,642,120	70,539,852
The Netherland	0	1	158	3,336	282	2,606,485	155,772
United Kingdom	3	-	97	5,169	-	2,295,947	-
United States	30	32	490	9,522	76,765	11,717,316	729,067
Total Non-ETC Members: 10	Total: 34	181	1,434	23,852	365,997	18,479,289	73,258,638
22	Total: 59	429	1,434	55,480	2,307,841	53,673,002	193,221,468

The results under this stage presents that a majority of DMOs provide the content in English. However, it is noticeable that on Google+ it is considerably low with only 65% providing a homepage in English. As argued earlier according to Kierzkowski et al. (1996) multilingual content with the dominant language of English should be applied in to provide consumers with user-friendly website. Yet in this study it is found that only 43% of DMOs provide multilingual content on their Google+ pages to communicate with their consumers. The tendency to use non-English, native language content is higher on Google+ compared to YouTube that aligns with results of the studies on Facebook and Twitter conducted by Alizadeh & Isa (2014) & Roque & Raposo (2013). Due to the nature of YouTube as a video sharing SM platform. DMOs have to provide videos that will promote the destinations, which is an expensive type of advertising. Therefore to target the wide market area, English as a commonly spoken language is used. On the other hand, the use of native language is noted mostly among DMOs that have adopted the Google+ platform. The same patterns of usage in language can be observed in the DMOs Facebook pages as well.

Taking the first 3 years after the platform launch date, the DMOs were slower in joining YouTube platform (2005-2008; n=15) compared to Google+ (2011-2013; n=28). One of the possibilities that might have affected faster adoption of Google+ platform lies in already stagnant practice of SM usage, while other can be referred to better SEO rankings through Google search (Stay, 2012). The authors found in their study conducted on NTOs on Facebook that a longer presence on the platform does not necessarily lead to a higher number of followers. Similarly this study indicated a negative correlation (-0.350) indicating a negative relationship between the two variables with the p value at 0.021 therefore it is significant ($p<0.021$) (see H2).

As Soininen et al. (2012) & Sigala et al. (2012) argued huge networks of people or communities are created by linking SM channels to each other. It is also emphasized that links to official website is important to increase the level of interactivity and connectivity (Cantoni & Xiang, 2013). In this study it is found that the most linked SM pages are accordingly as Google+, YouTube, Facebook and Twitter, other SM platforms linked are provided by a selective number of DMOs. Link to official website is provided by a majority of ETC members in both platforms while for Non-ETC members, though there is a high percentage of DMOs providing the link to official website on YouTube, there is a relatively low percentage (66%) providing official site links on Google+ which as argued earlier indicates a disadvantage, because providing this links to the official site on Google+ has high SEO value in terms on Google search results.

In terms of measuring the effectiveness of SM pages Alizadeh & Isa (2014) state that one measure is the number of fans it has attracted. However in this study, it indicates a big gap between the highest and the lowest number of followers on both platforms, for instance, Bulgaria that has over 500 videos, however their total subscribers are at 2,192. Another factor observed here is that ETC members have more total subscribers and followers on both platforms than Non-ETC members (see Table 4.2).

According to Kierzkowski et al. (1996) companies should try to provide a fresh but still valuable and engaging content to the consumers. It is argued by Rienhard (2009) that to achieve long term success on SM, marketers have to consistently and frequently publish refreshing content (Reino & Hay, 2011). The study conducted by Chan & Guillet (2011) found that 13 out of 48 hotels updated their SM sites infrequently. Similarly this study results showcase that, the interaction through updated content is higher among ETC, than Non-ETC members which is also due to the higher presence on SM. For example top 10 countries such as Italy and Spain has no content update in October showing infrequency in updating content. The results of H1, indicate that there is indeed a relationship between the post frequency and the total numbers of subscribers, thus it can be concluded that engaging and providing valuable information to consumers through content on Google+ leads to increased rate of consumer interest, thus a higher rate of subscription.

Georgia, Kazakhstan and Russia are some of the Non-ETC countries that had the highest and significant change in terms of international tourist arrivals in 2012-2013 (UNWTO, 2014). However the results of this study indicate that they are not present or active on YouTube and Google+. As of the top 10 destinations, research indicates significant gaps in post frequency in content posting and overall engagement with users (see Table 4.1). Munar (2012) found on her study that many DMOs do not have enough knowledge in utilizing SM. As can be concluded on Thailand's YouTube channel though there is a high post frequency, it can be noted that there are poor levels of user participation through observing their total views and total subscribers (see Table 4.2).

Pearson correlation test conducted to test H3 indicated an insignificant weak positive correlation (.292) between the two variables. To clarify, Spain and Turkey are some of the examples which confirm that the number of total views does not necessarily depend on the total number of posted videos (see Table 4.2), as agreed by Miller (2011) stating that total views can be a false measurement in analysing if an organisation has achieved the set out goals.

4.3 Information Stage

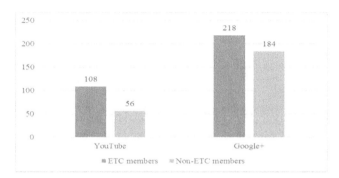

Fig. 1. Total number of Video/Posts in October

Figure 4.1 shows the total number of posts by ETC and Non-ETC members in the month of October. Content frequency on Google+ is higher by ETC members (n=218) compared to Non-ETC members (n=184), the same applies to YouTube where ETC post frequency is at 108 and Non-ETC is at 56. As it is shown in the Figure 4.1, Non-ETC members are less active on YouTube platform, showcasing a total of 56 video uploads throughout the month of October (n=56) posts. A study conducted by Chan & Guilett (2011), states that, for an organisation to convey the distinctive identity they should share valuable information with their consumers. In their study they pointed out that 20 out of 48 researched hotels on SM provide minimal amount of organisations' information. However, this study showcases that though 84% (n=36) of DMOs on YouTube provide a page description, only 56% (n=24) of them have provided their contact information (i.e. e-mail & telephone) under the "About" section in YouTube . In contrast, it is incated that a lower percentage of DMOs provide information, 74% (n=26) of DMOs provide a page description on their Google+ pages, with 69% (n=24) providing contact information. Overall a majority of DMOs on both Google+ and YouTube provide information on their SM pages while there is still a minority of DMOs who need to adapt. For example, out of the top 10 destinations in the world, the USA, Thailand & Turkey provide descriptive information and contact details, while Germany, for instance, does not showcase any information on the page.

4.4 Engagement Stage

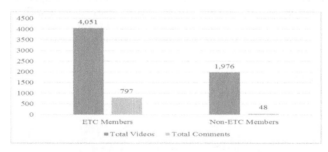

Fig. 2. Total number of Videos and Comments on YouTube DMOs' channels

Miller (2012) states that though comments may not constitute a hard metric, it is a good representation of the degree to which the content has engaged viewers. As seen in Figure 4.2, according to the number of total videos and total comments on channel, DMOs and users are more engaging on ETC YouTube channels (n=797) than on Non-ETC members' YouTube channels (n=48). The countries with the highest number of total videos are Switzerland (n=525) and Bulgaria (n=592) and the highest number of total comments are Sweden (n=125), Croatia (n=102) and Ireland (n=98). Of Non-ETC members the highest number of total videos is noted in the USA (n=490) and Thailand (n=469). However, none of the two destinations have any comment, showcasing lack of communication.

Data collected in terms of utilizing communication tools available on the YouTube shows that only 50% out of the 43 DMOs on YouTube try to arouse interactions among users in the community using feedback and enquiry tools. Other 50% of total DMOs fail to interact or to facilitate communication tools in order to interact with their subscribers. As for Google+, where innovative communication tools such as Google Hangouts are provided, only 3 countries (Germany, Iceland and San Marino) was observed to have utilized this feature, therefore showing a lack of adaptation in utilizing communication tools provided in the SM platforms to enhance interaction between users and DMOs. However, in this study it is indicated that there exists a big gap in terms of number of videos posted on YouTube and the total comments on channel. For example Switzerland has over 525 videos posted on their channel, however their total comments on the channel is 44, with a total number of views at 140,682, showing that the engagement of users is not high on the content posted. It is showcased that many DMOs (Azerbaijan, Liechtenstein, Macedonia, Thailand, & USA) have no comments on their YouTube channel, though videos have been posted, also showcasing a lower number of total views as shown in Table 4.1 (n=73,745,370) compared to ETC members (n=125,132,992).

5 CONCLUSION AND MANAGERIAL IMPLICATION

In conclusion, the results and findings of this study indicate that many DMOs some of whom are top destinations in the world such as France and the UK are still lagging behind in terms of adaptation to platforms of YouTube and Google+. Therefore it presents that many are still not aware of the opportunities and scale of potential SM has to offer. Yet another negative factor found in this study is that DMOs that are currently present across SM platforms there still is great room for improvement to fully take advantage of SM opportunities, showing major weaknesses in terms of maintaining consistency across SM platforms, activeness, usage of innovative tools, engagement and etc.

In this study it is indicated that though a majority of DMOs are present on Google+ (60%) and YouTube (74%), there is still a large number of destinations lagging behind such as Latvia, Montenegro, Monaco, Armenia, Kazakhstan, Kosovo, Kyrgyzstan, Moldova, Russia, Tajikistan, Turkmenistan who are not present on both platforms and major top 10 destinations such as the UK, who has yet no presence on Google+ and France who yet has no presence on YouTube. However, statistics has shown the increase in SM penetration over the years (1,856,680,860 active social networking users as of 2014) showing the great importance for DMOs to be present on the SM platforms to reach the global market (wearesocial, 2014). It is also indicated that countries such as Kazakhstan & Belarus have increasing international arrivals, but no official presence on these platforms. As among travellers, word-of-mouth has a big impact on holiday planning that can create various positive and negative destination images, therefore, the destinations that are not present across SM platforms do not have the control of tracking and consequently changing negative consumers' impressions. Therefore, it is recommended for them to adapt to SM to earn the competitive advantage, build consumer relationship and brand awareness and enhance positive brand image. The data also presented that top 10 destinations such as France, the UK and Germany show low activeness levels and engagement levels with user. Therefore it is recommended that being top destinations in the world in international tourists arrivals it is argued as important for them to be present and active on SM to build a positive image among their consumers and provide information for their consumers across a global market.

Many DMOs such as UK, Finland, Czech Republic, Austria, Ireland, Bulgaria, etc. are yet not actively present on Google+ or not active at all. However as argued earlier being part of the Google+ community is important as it means that the brand is weighted heavier in the top-secret algorithm Google uses to determine where a company or site lands in search engine results. In short being present on Google+ helps to be on top of Google search results, which is as stated by Pan (2015) of utmost importance because it increases business revenues and ensures competitiveness between destinations. Therefore, these DMOs not present on Google+ lack a major competitive advantage. Thus it is recommended that they adopt and apply themselves proactively on Google+.

It is noted that through the results of this study that many DMOs who are present across a wide range of SM platforms are not active across their pages showing inconsistency. Thus this study recommends that, due to the limited resources available to DMOs, they should prioritise in which SM platforms it is important to be present in according to the current trends of social media and also mainly according to the behaviour patterns of their specific target group to which they want to communicate with.

While this study contributes to existing theory to understand the importance of social media in destination marketing and has developed new insight providing specific knowledge in terms of YouTube and Google+ platforms, the study has some limitations due to the ever evolving nature of SM. Due to this scenario it is indicated that this research can only offer a snapshot of the current situation of the use of SM by DMOs as to the data collected was initiated through a month period in October, 2014. Therefore it is recommended that future research adopt a longitudinal approach to further examine the use of SM by DMOs including a wider range of DMOs across different continents. This analysis across different continents would allow future research to understand the various strategies adapted by DMOs across the world. The dimensions developed in this study could be further utilized in accordance to the technological advances over time in SM platforms to gather in depth information on the changes over time, also further research could focus on a specific dimension of the platforms i.e. interactivity to provide in depth information about the gaps, lacking points and ways of improving and addressing these gaps.

REFERENCES

Alizadeh, A. & Isa, R. M. (2014) *An examination of use of social media in destination marketing.* Singapore, Proceedings of the First Asia-Pacific Conference on Global Business, Economics, Finance and Social Sciences.

Bakshy E., Mason W. A., Hofman J. M. & Watts D. J. (2011) *Everyone's an Influencer: Quantifying Influence on Twitter.* Proceedings of the fourth ACM international conference on Web search and data mining. Hong Kong. February 2011. New York: ACM.

Buhalis, D. and Wagner, R. (2013) E-destinations: Global Best Practice in Tourism Technologies and Applications. In: L. Cantoni and Z. Xiang, ed., *Information and Communication Technologies in Tourism 2013*, 1st ed. Cham: Imprint: Springer, pp.119-131.

Cantoni, L. & Xiang, Z. (2013). *Information and Communication Technologies in Tourism 2013*: Proceedings of the International Conference in Innsbruck. Austria: Springer Science & Business Media.

Chan, N. L. & Guillet, B. D. (2011) Investigation of Social Media Marketing: How Does the Hotel Industry in Hong Kong Perform in Marketing on Social Media Websites?. *Journal of Travel & Tourism Marketing,* 28(4), pp. 345-368.

Cheng, X., Liu, J. & Dale, C. (2012) Understanding the Characteristics of Internet Short Video Sharing: A YouTube-Based Measurement Study. *IEEE TRANSACTIONS ON MULTIMEDIA,* 15(5), pp. 1184-1194.

Colburn, S. & Haines, L. (2012) Measuring Libraries' Use of YouTube as a Promotional Tool: An Exploratory Study and Proposed Best Practices. *Journal of Web Librarianship,* 6(1), pp. 5-31.

Destination Marketing Association International (2013) *DIGITAL & MOBILE MARKETING TOOLKIT,* s.l.: Destination Marketing Association International.

Garfield B., (2006) YouTube vs. Boob Tube. *Wired.* December. Avaliable from: http://www.wired.com/wired/archive/14.12/youtube.html [Accessed: 15th December 2014]

Gretzel, U., Christou, E. & Sigala, M. (2012) *Social Media in Travel, Tourism and Hospitality: Theory, Practice and Cases.* s.l.:Ashgate Publishing Ltd.

Hays, S., Page, S. J. & Buhalis, D. (2012) Social media as a destination marketing tool: its use by national tourism organisations. *Current Issues in Tourism,* pp. 1-30.

Jarboe, G. (2011) *YouTube and Video Marketing: An Hour a Day.* 2nd ed. s.l.:John Wiley & Sons , Inc.

Jarrett, K. (2008) Beyond Broadcast Yourself ™: The Future of YouTube. *Media International Australia,* Issue 126, pp. 132-156.

Jørgensen, L. G. (2004) *An analysis of a destination's image and the language of tourism,* Singapore: The Aarhus School of Business.

Kierzkowski, A., Mcquade, S., Waltman, R. and Zelsser, M. (1996) 'Marketing to the Digital Consumer', McKinsey Quarterly 79(3): 5–21.

Lange-Faria, W. and Elliot, S. (2012) Understanding the role of social media in destination marketing. Tourismom: An International Multidisciplinary Journal of Tourism, 7(1), pp.193-211.

Miller, M. (2011) *YouTube for Business: Online Video Marketing for Any Business.* 2nd ed. Indiana: Que Publishing.

Motamedi R., Gonzalez R., Farahbakhsh R., Cuevas A., Cuevas R. & Rejaie R. (2013) What OSN should I use? Characterizing user engagement in major OSNs. Universidad Carlos III de Madrid. Available at: http://www.it.uc3m.es/~rgonza1/pubs/whatOSN.pdf

Munar, A. M. (2012) Social Media Strategies and Destination Management. *Scandinavian Journal of Hospitality and Tourism ,* 12(2), pp. 101-120.

Munar, A. M., Gyimóthy, S., Cai, L. & Jafari, J. (2013) *Tourism Social Media: Transformations in Identity, Community and Culture.* Volume 18 of Tourism Social Science Series ed. s.l.:Emerald Group Publishing.

Nguyen, V. H. & Wang, Z. (2011) *Practice of Online Marketing with Social Media in Tourism Destination Marketing,* Huddinge, Sweden: Södertörns University, Department of Business Studies.

Pan B. (2015) The power of search engine ranking for tourist destinations. *Tourism Management,* 47, pp. 79-87

Parker, R. D. (2012) The Evolving Dynamics of Social Media in Internet Tourism Marketing. *Journal of Tourism Research & Hospitality,* 1(1), pp. 1-2.

Pentina, I., Koh, A. C. & Le, T. T. (2012) Adoption of social networks marketing by SMEs: exploring the role of social influences and experience in technology acceptance. *Int. J. Internet Marketing and Advertising,* 7(1), pp. 65-82.

Perttula, M. (2013) *SOCIAL MEDIA AS A MEANS OF TOURISM MARKETING,* Karleby, Finland: CENTRIA UNIVERSITY OF APPLIED SCIENCES.

Pike, S. (2008) Destination marketing. Amsterdam: Butterworth-Heinemann.

Popesku, J. (2014) *SOCIAL MEDIA AS A TOOL OF DESTINATION MARKETING ORGANIZATIONS,* Serbia: Sinteza 2014 - Impact of Internet on Business Activities in Serbia.

Reino, S. & Hay, B. (2011) *The Use of YouTube as a Tourism Marketing Tool,* London, Ontario : Proceedings of the 42nd Annual Travel and Tourism Research Association Conference.

Ribeiro, N. F., (2009) Tourism Representation and Semiotics –Directions for Future Research. *Journal of Tourism Studies,* 2(2), pp. 7-14.

Roque, V. & Raposo, R. (2013) Social Media as a Communication and Marketing Tool: An Analysis of Online Activities from International Key Player DMO. Marketing Places and Spaces: Shifting Tourist Flows. Portugal. October 2013. Portugal: Faculdade de Economia da Universidade do Algarve.

Sabate F., Berbegal-Mirabent J., Canabate A. & Lebherz P. R. (2014) Factors influencing popularity of branded content in Facebook fan pages. *European Management Journal.* 32 (5). p. 1001-1011

Sigala, M. (2012) Social media and crisis management in tourism: applications and implications for research. *Information Technology and Tourism,* Vol. 13, No. 4, pp. 269 – 283

Stay, J. (2012) *Google+ Marketing For Dummies.* s.l.:John Wiley & Sons.

theguardian (2014) *YouTube for marketing: how do you make it work?.* [Online] Available at: http://www.theguardian.com/technology/2014/jan/08/youtube-for-marketing-how-do-you-make-it-work [Accessed 29 November 2014].

UNWTO (2014) Tourism Highlights 2014. [online] Available at: http://mkt.unwto.org/publication/unwto-tourism-highlights-2014-edition [Accessed: 21st December 2014].

Wattenhofer M., Wattenhofer R. & Zhu Z. (2012) *The YouTube Social Network.* Proceedings of the Sixth International AAAI Conference on Weblogs and Social Media. Ireland. June 2012. California: The AAAI Press.

wearesocial (2014) *GLOBAL DIGITAL STATISTICS.* [Online] Available at: http://etonpreneurs.com/uploads/Global%20Social,%20Digital%20&%20Mobile%20Statistics, %20Jan%202014.pdf [Accessed 7 December 2014].

Xiang, Z., & Gretzel, U. (2010) Role of social media in online travel information search. Tourism Management, 31(2), 179-188.

Yoganarasimhan, H. (2012) Impact of social network structure on content propagation: A study using YouTube data. *Quant Mark Econ,* Volume 10, pp. 111-150.

Zimmerman, J. & Ng, D. (2012) *Social Media Marketing All-in-One For Dummies.* 2nd ed. s.l.:John Wiley & Sons.

Competitiveness of a Travel Destination – A Case Study of Montenegro in Relation to Relevant Models of Competitiveness

Marija Cimbaljević, and

Anđela Bučić

Faculty of Science, University of Novi Sad, Serbia
maja_0206@hotmail.com

Abstract

Destination competitiveness is a growing theme in travel destination marketing and management. In the literature, competitiveness is defined as a very important factor for the success of a tourist destination. The number of papers that deal with matters of competitiveness increases constantly. This paper debates the competitiveness of a travel destination and relevant models of competitiveness, with special reference to Montenegro. The increase of competitiveness and profiling on the international market is currently an attractive theme for Montenegro.

The purpose of the paper is to represent the competitive position of Montenegro according to TTCI, as well as the model of destination competitiveness and results of research, based on indicators associated with the model. The results of the research based on the attitudes of tourism offer holders show that the main advantage of Montenegro is the variety of offer on a small space, cultural and historical heritage, as well as climate and geographical position.

Keywords: Destination competitiveness; competitiveness models; Travel & Tourism Competitiveness Index; Montenegro

1 INTRODUCTION

A travel destination represents the central part of the tourist offer. The degree to which a country can benefit from the tourist industry to a large extent depends on its competitive position in the international market. A basic determination of competitiveness informs us that it is the capability of a destination to attract a greater number of tourists through available attractions, alongside the other elements of the offer, providing them with a unique experience, and that, with an innovative politics of matters, it enhances its competitiveness in relation to other destinations. Thus, for a destination to become competitive, it has to strategically promote its specific characteristics by differentiating them from similar destinations, or by establishing competitive and comparative advantages (Pyo, 2005; Crouch, 2011).

Tour operators, travel agencies, experts in the field of tourism, beside the independent travelers, are also becoming aware of certain destinations (Kim and Perdue, 2011). Montenegro as a travel destination has determined comparative advantages, especially in terms of resources. In this paper, competitiveness of the travel destination is observed from the aspect of tourism offer holders (DMO, travel agency, catering facilities). In order to review the past analysis of designating components of Montenegro's tourism offer regarding the tourism offer holders attitudes that are very authoritative in their rating, and on the other hand are directly or indirectly included in providing services at the destination, a research was conducted to serve as an indicator of a subjective rating about the current condition of the tourism product and tourism offer of Montenegro.

As a result, starting point was the general assumption that the tourism product of Montenegro is to a large scale determined by a combination of natural beauties, diverse anthropogenic characteristics and development of key resources that require protection and enable long-term tourism development and ensure a strategic competitive advantage of the destination. The data for this study was collected by using Crouch and Ritchie (2003) Integrated Model of Destination Competitiveness. The research purpose is to see if the differences between the tourism offer employees are significant, as well as to analyze these findings from the aspect of the destination competitiveness. On the basis of that analysis we will get a wholesome view of the set subject of the research. This paper presents preliminary results of research dealing with the attitudes of employees in the tourism sector concerning tourism product and competitiveness of tourism in Montenegro.

The paper is structured in the following manner. After the introduction, the second part provides an overview of the literature related to competitiveness of a travel destination, as well as about the models of travel destination competitiveness. In the third section is shown the analysis of competitive position of Montenegro as a travel destination, with the reference to WEF Travel & Tourism Competitiveness Index. The fourth section provides an overview of research about the indicators of Montenegro's competitiveness from the tourism offer holders' point of view. This research was part of the broader competitiveness indicators' study. Section five introduces some concluding remarks.

2 LITERATURE REVIEW

In the sector of tourism it is not possible to have a unique definition of competitiveness. Nowadays, even though the term competitiveness has a wide utilization, its meaning varies according to the standard applied in the evaluation, whether it is applied in industry, service sector, countries, regions, or cities. To be competitive means to attain superiority in quality. However, attempts at measuring competitiveness come across difficulties in defining it, because competitiveness, on one hand, is a relative concept (superiority to what/whom?) and is mostly multidimensional (which are the emphasized qualities of a destination?) (Crouch and Ritchie, 1999).

Competitiveness of a destination might be connected to its ability to deliver a tourist experience that provides a greater pleasure to visitors than the pleasure provided by other destinations (Vengesayi, 2003), and in those aspects that are of importance to tourists (Dwyer and Kim, 2003). Accordingly, there are two different perspectives – the perspective of tourist, which focus their decisions about travelling on the attractiveness of destinations, and the perspective of the destinations themselves, which tend to provide conditions for accomplishing good results through strengthening the competitiveness. Factors of the tourist demand and factors of the tourist offer provide assistance in creating an environment in which tourism can develop and create visitors' satisfaction (Vengesayi, 2003). Furthermore, competitiveness of a destination refers to the ability of a destination to attract visitors, whether they visit for the first time, or repeated visits are in question, for maintaining its position on the market and a possible improved position over time (d'Hauteserre, 2000).

Determining the concept of competitiveness of a destination is possible if the destination's measures of performance are discussed too (Mazanec, et al., 2007). However, the attempts of performance measuring are often limitative (Vengesayi, 2003). Some authors (Cracolici, et al., 2008) consider that the performances of a travel destination can be rated through its ability to transform its inputs (material and human resources) through the so-called virtual tourist "manufacturing process" into a maximal output (arrivals, overnight stays, employment, customer satisfaction, additional value, etc.).

In the other hand, destination's competitiveness can be measured qualitatively and quantitatively. The elements concerning the qualitative competitiveness include attributes that the visitor during the stay at the destination likes the most or the least. It is an assumption that a tourist will compare these elements in terms of his experiences at other destinations (Kozak and Rimmington, 1999). However, there is a need to consider the relevant quantitative aspects of the destination's competitiveness too. Quantitative performance of a destination can be measured through the data overview of arrivals and overnight stays of tourists and tourist incomes (Kozak and Rimmington, 1999; Hassan, 2000). According to Crouch (2011) these measures of the destination's competitiveness are inadequate, but appropriate for representing the ability of a destination to accomplish a line of set tasks that often contain economic, social, and the results related to preserving and improving the environment, and that, among others, include those related to the scope of tourist demand (arrivals, overnight stays, incomes).

A large number of authors have contributed to the understanding and practical research of competitiveness of travel destinations, from the other, different or more specific aspects (Ritchie and Crouch, 1993; Hassan, 2000; Mihalic, 2000; Lee & King, 2009; d'Hauteserre, 2000; Kozak, 2001; Claver-Cortés, Molina-Azorín and Pereira-Moliner, 2007; Omerzel Gomezelj and Mihalič, 2008; Cracolici and Nijkamp, 2009; Chin et al., 2014).

According to Lee and King (Lee & King, 2009), models of destination competitiveness are not adequate to determine the competitiveness of individual tourism sectors or types of tourism, such as spa tourism sector, but are focused on the competitiveness of entire countries, and have developed a special model of competitiveness of tourism sectors, related to sources of hot water in Taiwan. Hassan's model (2000) emphasizes the importance of a sustainable environment as one of the four determinants of tourism competitiveness. d'Hauteserre (2000) discusses the factors of competitiveness in the case of a Casino Resort. On the other side, Claver-Cortés, Molina-Azorín and Pereira-Moliner (2007) point out in the case of Benidorm (Spain) that improving the competitiveness of certain factors, mass tourism destinations can avoided phase of decline and remain competitive. Model of Omerzel Gomezelj and Mihalič (2008) is applied on particular destination with the aim of analyzing their competitive position.

The complexity of the term ''competitiveness'' becomes clear once we try to define and measure competitiveness. Among the first and most famous theoreticians in the field of competitiveness that stands out is Porter (1990). His analyses which are mainly directed towards the traditional industries are yet also applicable to tourist economy, more accurately the travel destination, and his model of competitiveness is based on the national diamond of competitiveness. There are many models that were created with the intention to measure competitiveness as a unique phenomenon. This paper will give an overview of two most influential models which were applied in determining the competitiveness of Montenegro as a travel destination. One is the Integrative Conceptual Model by Ritchie and Crouch, and the other is model developed by the World Economic Forum for the needs of creating The Travel & Tourism Competitiveness Index – TTCI. TTCI has as a goal to measure the factors and policies which make the development of the tourism sector and trips attractive to different countries.

2.1 Relevant Models of Travel Destinations' Competitiveness

Crouch and Ritchie started researching the nature and structure of destinations' competitiveness in 1992 (Crouch and Ritchie 1994, 1995, 1999; Ritchie and Crouch 1993, 2000). Their goal was to prove that models of economic competitiveness, such as Porter's model, can be applied on the level of destination. Crouch and Ritchie claimed that the most competitive destination was the one who brought most success; it is the destination that creates a wellbeing for their inhabitants on sustainable grounds. Considering that they intended to include all of the relevant factors of competitiveness, in later years Crouch and

Ritchie revised their model, in order to finalize its form in 2003 as an integral model of destination competitiveness.

This model is shown in a scheme on Figure 1, and it contains five groups of factors – the main factors of competitiveness and 36 sub-factors. Each of the model's components contains various attributes to the competitiveness of a destination. 1) *Fundamental resources and attractions* include the deciding elements in choosing destination. Those are the main reasons for potential visitors to select determined destination among others. The attributes included in this model component are organized into 7 categories: physical geography and climate, culture and history, a mix of activities available at the destination, special events, entertainment, tourist supra-structure and business, family, and other relations of the destination to the sources of demand. Other components of the model expand determinants of competitiveness of a tourist destination by including a wider spectrum of attributes that help connect the attractions of a destination to the factors more often found in studies of generic business competitiveness (Enright & Newton, 2005). 2) *Support factors and resources* are factors creating the basis on which a successful tourist industry can be founded. They include infrastructure, availability, production resources, hospitality, entrepreneurship, policy will. 3) *Politics, planning and development of a destination* include defining of systems, comprehension/value, vision, positioning/branding, development, analysis of competitiveness/cooperation, control and rating, revision. The next component 4) *destination management* is focused on activities which are based on policy implementation and planning a frame for the improvement of key resources and attractions, upgrading the quality and effectiveness of supporting factors. According to these authors, destination management consists of organisation, marketing, quality of services/experience, awareness/research, managing human resources, financial and business capital, managing visitors, managing resources, crisis management. The last component, 5) *determinants of qualification and expansion,* includes factors that can modify, possibly in a negative sense as well, the effects of other components/ So, they can possibly limit the ability of destination to attract and please potential tourists and thus endanger its competitiveness. This component includes location, safety/security, expenses/benefits, interdependence, importance/image, carrying capacity (Ritchie and Crouch, 2003).

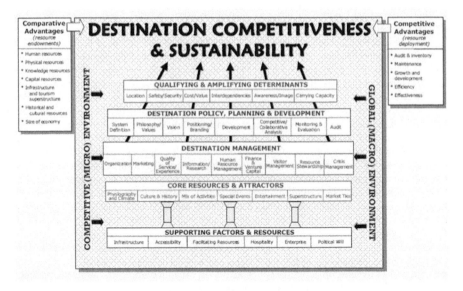

Fig. 1. Integrated Model of Destination Competitiveness, pp.1051
(Source: Ritchie, J. R. B., Crouch, G. I., 2010.)

The model takes into consideration the influences of global forces that come from the macro-surrounding, as well as the influences of the competitive (micro) surrounding. It also allows communication among stakeholders included in managing tourist destinations and can be used as a basis for creating an insight into the characteristics of certain destination. In accordance with certain elements of destination competitiveness through 36 features suggested by this model, the study unites experience, knowledge, and perceptions of managing a tourist destination, researchers and those who are interested into building and understanding the competitiveness of a destination.

2.2 Competitiveness of Montenegrin Tourism Measured by TTCI

A model of competitiveness of tourism and travel according to which TTCI is calculated represents a model which is the base of comparing the competitiveness of world countries in tourism and is one of the most significant indicator of performances in tourism. The Travel and Tourism Competitiveness Index (TTCI) was developed by The World Economy Forum. It is based on three categories summarized in three sub-indexes: sub-index of the regulatory scope of tourism and travel, sub-index of business environment and tourism and travel infrastructure, and sub-index of human, cultural and business resources. These sub-indexes are made up of 14 columns of competition: 1) policy rights and regulations, 2) environmental sustainability, 3) safety, 4) health and hygiene, 5) giving priorities to travel and tourism, 6) air traffic infrastructure, 7) land traffic infrastructure, 8) tourist infrastructure, 9) infrastructure of information and communication technology, 10) price competitiveness, 11) human capital, 12) preference of travel and tourism, 13) natural resources, 14) cultural resources (http://www3.weforum.org).

Diversity that exists among tourist destinations makes it difficult for them to be categorized in a same group and ranked by a certain criterion from the best/most competitive to the weakest/least competitive (Kozak, 1999). When destinations are compared it is important to determine which destinations are competitors (Kozak and Rimmington, 1999; Enright and Newton, 2004).

In the context of previous facts, it would be necessary to determine the competitors of Montenegro and represent its position in relation to other selected countries. In the lack of research we will stick to those countries which are implicitly emphasized in the Tourism Development Strategy of Montenegro (Italy, Greece, Albania, Slovenia, Croatia) and, also, other countries in the surrounding will be debated too (Hungary, Bulgaria, Romania, Macedonia, Serbia, Bosnia and Hercegovina).

Table 1. Position of Montenegro compared to neighboring countries according to the Index of Travel and Tourism Competitiveness in 2013, 2011, 2009 and 2008

	2013	2011	2009	2008
Italy	4.90 (26 place)	4.87 (27 place)	4.78 (28 place)	4.84 (28 place)
Croatia	4:59 (36 place)	4.61 (34 place)	4:54 (34 place)	4:59 (34 place)
Slovenia	4:58 (36 place)	4.64 (33 place)	4:53 (35 place)	4:49 (36 place)
Greece	4.75 (32 place)	4.78 (29 place)	4.91 (24 place)	4.92 (22 place)
Montenegro	4:50 (40 place)	4:56 (36 place)	4:29 (52 place)	4:15 (59 place)
Albania	3.97 (77 place)	4:01 (71 place)	3.68 (90 place)	3.60 (92 place)
Hungary	4:51 (39 place)	4:54 (38 place)	4.45 (38 place)	4.60 (33 place)
Bulgaria	4:38 (50 place)	4:39 (48 place)	4.30 (50 place)	4:36 (43place)
Romania	4.04 (68 place)	4:17 (63 place)	4.04 (66 place)	3.88 (69 place)
Macedonia	3.98 (75 place)	3.96 (76 place)	3.81 (80 place)	3.68 (83 place)
Serbia	3.78 (89 place)	3.85 (82 place)	3.71 (88 place)	3.76 (78 place)
Bosnia and Herzegovina	3.78 (90 place)	3.63 (97 place)	3:44 (107 place)	3.45 (105 place)

(Note. These data are obtained from the WEF TTCI report for 2013, 2011, 2009, and 2008 (Blanke and Chiesa, 2013, 2011, 2009, and 2008)

According to the reports of the World Economic Forum (2013) Montenegro is 40th in the world in terms of tourism and travel sector competitiveness (TTCI). The rank is a bit lower compared to 2011 (36th place), but still represents a progress, considering that it was in the 59th place in 2008. In relation to 140 ranked countries, in terms of the regulatory frame of tourism and travel, Montenegro is in 34th place, in terms of the business surrounding and tourism and travel infrastructure it is in 50th place, and in 47th place in terms of human, cultural, and natural resources. Montenegro notes a good rank in the sector of tourism related to preference of tourism and travel, more precisely, related to openness of people to tourism it is in 7th place. Montenegro has a specifically bad ranking in the field of traffic infrastructure where in terms of road quality it is in 92nd place, in terms of port infrastructure quality in 101st place, and in terms of the number of airports in 107th place. In general, according to the report of the World Economic Forum, the main flaws of Montenegro are related to the field of cultural resources, where in terms of the number of sights of world cultural heritage it is in 109th place, in terms of the number of international fairs and exhibitions organized in 111th place, while in terms of creative industry it is in 117th place. However, what it possible to notice is the fact that Montenegro, in very short period of time, managed to accomplish a great improvement from the 59th place to the 40th, which shows that this country has significantly improved its competitive position.

In order to further analyze the competitive position of Montenegro as a tourist destination from the aspect of tourism offer holders (tourist organisations, travel agencies, and catering facilities), some of the key pointers of competitiveness were analyzed, on the grounds of further research.

3 METHODOLOGY

Primary goal of the research was to compare the factors of tourism competitiveness in Montenegro and from the aspect of tourism offer holders. The author decided that the research should be conducted among the tourism sector employees, and not among tourists, because it is considered that the tourists may value these components of the attractiveness of a destination among the services they consume. However, the chances for them to give a precise evaluation of the factors in the basis of those services and that influence competitiveness are not so encouraging, especially because of their visitor status (Enright and Newton, 2004).

Thus, the sample research consisted of employees in tourist organisations, travel agencies, and catering facilities, since they are the main carriers of the tourism offer. Their knowledge of portfolios of competitive resources of a destination may help discover the values of a tourist destination appropriately. The sample was selected on the basis of a list of all tourist organisations in 21 municipalities in Montenegro, travel agencies and hotels that are on the web portal http://www.portal-crnagora.com.

Integrative conceptual model of destination competitiveness developed by Crouch and Ritchie (1999), and which was further revised (Ritchie and Crouch, 2003) was the basis for this research. The model identifies 36 attributes of competitiveness which are grouped into 5 main factors. In this group, a question that assessed parking zones in Montenegro was also added.

When destinations are compared, it is important to determine the competitive destinations (Kozak and Rimmington, 1999; Enright and Newton, 2004). In that context, it is necessary to determine the competitors of Montenegro, and to represent its position towards selected countries. The examinees had a task to, according to their own opinion, determine the head competitors and in that group Italy, Slovenia, Greece and Albania stood out. According to that, the greatest competitors of Montenegro are the surrounding countries with similar natural characteristics, so they have the same or similarly developed forms of tourism, such as coastal, mountain, rural tourism.

Participants of the poll research had the task to rate 37 competitive indicators on a 5-degree Likert scale (from 1=very below the competitor to 5=great advantage of Montenegro), comparing Montenegro with the most competitive country among the listed. The research resulted in 76 questionnaires.

4 RESEARCH RESULTS

Out of 230 questionnaries sent, 76 were returned. The sample of the research included 29% of the employees in tourist organisations, 40% of the employees in travel agencies and 31% of the employees in catering facilities. Sample characteristics are shown in Table 2.

Table 2. Socio-demographic characteristics of respondents

Tourist enterprise	Percentage	Work experience	Percentage	Position	Percentage
Tourism organisations	29%	1-11 months	3%	Owner/Director	20%
Travel agencies	40%	1-10 years	75%	Manager	18%
Catering establishments	31%	11-20 years	13%	Marketing Manager	5%
Age group		21-30 years	7%	Sales Agent	22%
18-30	51%	31-40 years	1%	Implementer of tourist trips	12%
31-40	24%	41-50 years	1%	Other	23%

41-50	15%	**Gender**			
51-60	9%	Male	32%		
More than 60 years	1%	Female	68%		

(Source: Data obtained by survey research)

The research sample was comprised of 75% of tourism workers employed in tourism industry for 1 to 10 years, 13% from 11 to 20 years, 7% from 21 to 30 years, 3% from 1 to 11 months, and only 2 examinees with the working experience over 31, i.e. 41 year. Most of the examinees were young people in between 18 and 30 years old (51%), age category of up to 40 years took up 24%, then 15% in the age category in between 41 and 50, while the least number of employees was the age from 51 to 60. The sample consisted of much more female (68%) than male respondents (32%).

4.1 Competitive Ranking of Montenegro as a Travel Destination

Professional literature, as well as analysis of secondary sources of information about Montenegro, such as the Tourism Development Strategy of Montenegro, the Master Plan of Montenegro, the Mountain Tourism Development Program in Montenegro, have given us a large number of information about the potentials and values projected by the tourist destination. It is also important to take into consideration the specific attributes that characterize the destination individually. Montenegro is known on the tourism market by its natural beauties, rich cultural and historical heritage, culinary specialties which make a unique blend of oriental and Mediterranean cuisine, and products that represent a brand of their own (smoked ham, cheese, Vranac wine, olive oil, etc.). However, it was important to look into other elements concerned with strategic activities on the scale of planning and managing the destination, research and awareness, development of human resources, factors of location, safety, security, and others. Taking into account the already mentioned determinants on primary domain of research, the work can start from the following general hypothesis.

Ho: The tourism product of Montenegro is largely determined by combination of natural beauty, diverse anthropogenic characteristics and development of key resources that should be preserved and thus ensure long-term tourism development, provide strategic competitive advantage destinations, and holders of the tourist offer on the state of Montenegrin tourism product in relation to its competitors share the same opinion.

Due to the fact that we are interested in different interpretations of Montenegrin competitiveness from the perspective of employees in the tourist sector, we will provide results comparatively in columns in Table 3. if there are any differences and where they are shown.

Table 3. Comparative overview of competitiveness of Montenegro as a tourist destination

Indicator	Tourism organisations	Travel agency	Catering establishments	Significance (sig)
	Mean	Mean	Mean	Between groups
The geostrategic position	2.3182	3.6000	4.5833	.000
The level of personal and commercial security	2.0455	4.4000	4.6667	.000
Quality of service is in accordance with the price	1.5909	2.4000	3.8333	.000
Strategic relationships between tourism enterprises	1.7727	2.9000	3.8333	.000
The awareness of the tourism industry about the importance of quality tourism brand	1.8636	2.7000	3.8333	.000

Strong seasonality	1.7727	2.9667	4.5000	.000
The efficiency of the tourism business	1.7727	3.0000	3.7500	.000
The prioritization of the tourism and travel	2.1364	3.1333	4.2500	.000
Awareness of the government and tourism industry about the importance of long-term sustainable tourism development	1.5455	2.9333	4.2917	.000
Development and promotion of the brand and new tourism products	1.7727	3.1333	4.2500	.000
The existence of strategic and planning documentation for tourism development	1.8182	3.2333	4.4167	.000
Cooperation with other countries and project partnerships	1.8636	3.1333	4.2500	.000
Research for tourism policy and planning	1.5455	2.7000	3.5833	.000
The optimal coherence of development objectives at the national, regional and local level	1.4091	2.4000	3.5417	.000
An organized destination management	1.5455	2.3333	3.5417	.000
The application of information technology in tourism promotion	2.2727	3.2000	4.3333	.000
Information about attractions, services, products and activities in foreign languages	2.3636	3.7000	4.2917	.000
The quality of complementary services and public transport	1.7273	2.8667	3.5833	.000
The quality of the educational structure of tourism workers	1.4091	2.5333	3.7500	.000
The participation of foreign capital in the tourism sector	2.3636	3.7000	4.3750	.000
The level of satisfaction of tourism needs in tourist enterprises	2.0909	3.0333	4.0833	.000
The awareness of the local population about the importance of preserving the natural and cultural heritage	1.4091	2.3667	3.5833	.000
Compliance of tourism development with overall national development	1.6818	2.7000	3.8333	.000
Climate and geographic location	3.5000	4.6000	5.0000	.000
Cultural and historical heritage	3.3182	4.4333	5.0000	.000
Diversity of the offer in a small area	3.5000	4.9000	5.0000	.000
Presence of selective forms of tourism (eco-tourism, adventure, hunting, rural)	2.2727	3.8000	4.9583	.000
Entertainment and nightlife	3.1818	4.3000	5.0000	.000
The quality and diversification of catering facilities	2.4091	3.1333	4.1667	.000
The impact market relations to tourism development (family, religious, sports, business...)	2.6364	3.0667	4.1667	.000
Tourism infrastructure	1.6818	2.7000	3.6667	.000
Availability from other countries	2.1364	3.5333	4.1667	.000
Availability within the country	2.1818	3.3000	4.2917	.000
Parking zones	1.2727	2.1000	3.3750	.000
The hospitality and kindness of the local population	1.8636	3.4333	4.4167	.000
The local gastronomy and its use as a tourism product	2.4545	3.8000	4.8750	.000
Active participation of government in the creation of tourist products	1.7727	2.8667	4.0417	.000

(Source: Data obtained by survey research)

The general hypothesis (arithmetic mean of the three mentioned groups are equal), will be accepted if the values observed in the last column in Table 3 are greater than 0.05. In our case, as the value of *sig* for all elements is less than 0.05 we reject the general hypothesis and thus emphasize that there is a significant difference in attitudes between the three groups of respondents of the tourist product of Montenegro (relative to competitors), and obtain estimates of the tourism offer are diversified.

4.2 Attitudes of employees in tourist organisations

Employees in tourist organisations agree firmly that the key competitive advantages of Montenegro as a destination are: "the diversity of offer on a small space" (3.50), "climate and geographic position" (3.50), "cultural and historical heritage" (3.32), "entertainment and night life" (3.18). The main strategic goals chosen to be focused on when accomplishing the competitive advantage of Montenegro are quality accommodation capacities (2.41), tourism offer not dependent on the season (1.77), qualified professional staff (1.41), strengthening of marketing measurements (2.27) and others (Tourism Development Strategy of Montenegro, 2008).

Those element were emphasized by employees in tourist organisations as well, whose rankings clearly show that it is necessary to work on eliminating the determined weaknesses of the tourist system. Especially low ranking was given to following elements of Montenegrin competitiveness: "parking zones" (1.27), "local people's awareness of the importance of preserving the natural and cultural heritage" (1.41), "quality of educational background of tourism workers" (1.41), and "quality of service in accordance with price" (1.59).

4.3 Attitudes of employees in travel agencies

When the tourism employees of travel agencies are asked about the key elements of destinations' competitiveness, the expected answer is realistic and based mainly on working experience in the country where they are employed and on the other hand, on the knowledge the tourism offer of a large number of other destinations. The degree of accordance in travel agencies with the mentioned elements is pretty equal (standard deviation for all elements is less than one) and to a certain degree larger comparing to the one with employees in tourist organisations.

Out of 37 elements of competitiveness, tourist agencies firmly agree that the key advantage of Montenegro is "diversity of offer on a small space" (4.90). Smaller percentage of accordance is noted for elements of "climate and geographic position" (4.60), "cultural and historical heritage" (4.43). Thus it can be said that according to the opinion of the employees in these companies, these are the key competitive advantages of Montenegro. It is interesting that the higher rank than the one given by tourist organisations was given to "the level of personal and commercial security" (4.40). There we can note a discrepancy in the way Montenegro is perceived by two groups of tourism workers. It is very possible that better knowledge of other countries due to sojourn and the possibility of subjective comparison of Montenegro with those countries influenced such a comment from travel agencies.

Especially low ranking was given to further elements: "parking zones" (2.1), "organized management of the destination" (2.33), "awareness of local people of the importance of preserving the natural and cultural heritage" (2.36), "optimal accordance of development goals on a national, regional, and local level" (2.40), and "quality of service in accordance with price" (2.40). Average ranks given tell us that the listed flaws are to be corrected in order to improve the tourist activity of the country and, furthermore, its competitive position.

4.4 Attitudes of employees in catering facilities

In catering facilities, the opinions regarding the marks of Montenegrin competitiveness were different than the other two categories of examinees. The main difference was that in the ranking of three elements there were no gaps in the percentage of agreement, i.e. the elements "climate and geographic position", "diversity of offer on a small space", and "entertainment and night life" got the highest ranking as competitive advantages of Montenegro (5.00). "Presence of selective forms of tourism" was also given a high rank (4.96). It is noted that the higher ranking by the employees in catering facilities was given to "local gastronomy and its usage as a tourist product" (4.88) in relation to employees in other tourism businesses.

Another notion is that this group of examinees gave less negative rankings to elements of competitiveness of Montenegro, unlike tourist organisations and travel agencies. Yet, the lowest rankings were in this case also directed to destination management, i.e. "organized managing of the destination" (3.54), "optimal accordance of development goals on a national, regional, and local level" (3.54), and a great disadvantage emphasized was the "quality of complementary services and public transportation" (3.58).

5 CONCLUSION

Competitiveness of a tourist destination represents a multidimensional concept that includes social, cultural, ecological, economic, political, and technological advantages. One of the key matters of tourist destination competitiveness is concerned with the importance of certain factors of competitiveness and their mutual relations in a certain time frame, as well as the relation with various competitors. Development of tourism in Montenegro is a great chance for overall economy development of the country, however, the current competitive position in the market is not satisfactory. Thus, the purpose of this research was to determine the weakest spots of Montenegrin tourist competitiveness based on the results shown in the TTCI report for Montenegro (2008, 2009, 2011, and 2013), as well as the application of the Integrative Conceptual Model of Competitiveness. According to TTCI, generally observed, Montenegro has a pretty weak competitive position, but in relation to other surrounding countries its position is significantly better in most of determinants, except for Italy, Croatia, Greece, and Slovenia. However, it should be pointed out that certain destinations are not always direct competitors because of the fact that one destination might have a very wide tourism offer portfolio. According to that, the season might be an important factor in determining competitiveness. So, e.g. Montenegro and Greece are competitors in summer tourism, but not in winter.

Based on the conducted research, it was noted in the percentage of accordance with listed elements of Montenegrin competitiveness that there are discrepancies from middle values which were expressed by standard deviation (Table 3). Observing each variable individually, it was noted that the arithmetic middles of all three groups differ significantly. Thus, we can point out that the attitudes of examinees in tourist organisations, travel agencies, and catering facilities have different oppinions about which elements represent the competitive advantage of Montenegro as a tourist destination. However, what most off examinees consider as a great advantage (the largest percentage of ranks given) among the 37 elements of competitiveness is concerned with the diversity of offer on a small space, cultural and historical heritage offered by Montenegro, as well as the climate and geographical position.

What can be concluded from the examinees' attitudes thus far about the condition of tourism and tourist product of Montenegro is the attitude that, in order to develop tourism product, infrastructure of a good quality is required, primarily traffic, and then water supply, energetic, and accommodation. Afterwards, the tourism product of good quality can be developed. What represents another issue for Montenegro in improving competitive advantages is the low level of tourist offer development, disagreement of priority goals on a local, regional and national level, as well as the disagreement of tourism development with the total national development, noted by the employees in the tourism sector. On the other hand, the unique blend of natural resources and cultural values on a small space should be emphasized, which are the great advantage for a high rank of Montenegro in international market.

This research represents only one step in the analysis of competitiveness of Montenegro as a tourist destination.

REFERENCES

Alavi, J., Yasin, M. M., 2000. A systematic approach to tourism policy. *Journal of Business Research,* 48(2), pp.147–156.

Blanke, J., Chiesa, T.,2008, The Travel and Tourism Competitiveness Index 2008: Measuring Key Elements Driving the Sector's Development.in J. Blanke and T. Chiesa (Eds.), The Travel and Tourism Competitiveness Report 2008: Balancing Economic Development and Environmental Sustainability (pp.3-26), World Economic Forum, Geneva, Retrieved January 10, 2015, from http://www3.weforum.org/docs/WEF_TravelTourismCompetitiveness_Report_2008.pdf

Blanke, J., Chiesa, T., Trujillo Herrera, E., 2009. The Travel and Tourism Competitiveness Index 2009: Measuring Sectoral Drivers in a Downturn, in J. Blanke and T. Chiesa (Eds.) The Travel and Tourism Competitiveness Report 2009: Managing in a Time of Turbulence (pp. 3-38), World Economic Forum, Geneva, Retrieved January 10, 2015, from http://www3.weforum.org/docs/WEF_TravelTourismCompetitiveness_Report_2009.pdf

Blanke, J. Chiesa, T., 2011. The Travel and Tourism Competitiveness Index 2011: Assessing Industry Drivers in the Wake of the Crisis, in J. Blanke and T. Chiesa (Eds.), The Travel and Tourism Competitiveness Report 2011: Beyond the Downturn (pp. 3-33), World Economic Forum, Geneva, Retrieved January 10, 2015, from http://www3.weforum.org/docs/WEF_TravelTourismCompetitiveness_Report_2011.pdf

Blanke, J., Chiesa, T., 2013. The Travel and Tourism Competitiveness Report 2013: Contributing to National Growth and Employment, in J. Blanke and T. Chiesa (Eds.) The Travel and Tourism Competitiveness Report 2013 : Reducing Barriers to Economic Growth and Job Creation (pp. 3-41), World Economic Forum, Geneva, Retrieved January 10, 2015, from http://www3.weforum.org/docs/WEF_TT_Competitiveness_Report_2013.pdf

Claver-Cortés, E., Molina-Azorín, J. F. & Pereira-Moliner, J., 2007. Competitiveness in Mass Tourism. Annals of Tourism Research, 34 (3), pp. 727–745.

Chin, C.H., Lo, M.C., Songan, P., Nair, V., 2014. Rural tourism destination competitiveness: A study on Annah Rais Longhouse Homestay, Sarawak. Procedia - *Social and Behavioral Sciences*, 144, pp. 35-44.

Cracolici, M. F., Nijkamp, P., 2009. The attractiveness and competitiveness of tourist destinations: A study of Southern Italian regions. *Tourism Management*, 30(3), pp.336-344.

Cracolici, M.F., Nijkamp, P., Rietveld, P., 2008. Assessment of Tourist Competitiveness by Analysing Destination Efficiency. *Tourism Economics*, 14(2), pp.325-342.

Crouch, G. I., 2011. Destination competitiveness: An analysis of determinant attributes. *Journal of Travel Research*, 50, pp.27–45.

Crouch, G, Ritchie, JRB., 1995. Destination competitiveness and the role of the tourism Enterprise. Proceedings of the Fourth Annual Business Congress, Istanbul, Turkey, July 13-16 (pp. 43-48).

Crouch, G, Ritchie JRB., 1994. Destination competitiveness: Exploring foundations for along-term research program, Proceedings of the Administrative Sciences Association of Canada Annual Conference, Halifax, Nova Scotia, June 25-28, 1994 (pp. 79-88).

Ritchie JRB., Crouch, G., 2010. A model of destination competitiveness sustainability: Brazilian perspectives, RAP Rio de Janeiro 44(5), (pp. 1049-1066).

Crouch, G. I., Ritchie, J.R.B., 1999. Tourism, Competitiveness, and Societal Prosperity. *Journal of Business Research,* 44(3), pp.137–152.

d'Hauteserre, A. M., 2000. Lessons in managed destination competitiveness: the case of Foxwoods Casino Resort. *Tourism Management,* 21(1), pp.23-32.

Dwyer, L., Kim C., 2003. Destination Competitiveness: Determinants and Indicators. *Current Issues in Tourism,* 6(5), pp.369-414.

Enright, M. J., Newton J., 2004. Tourism destination competitiveness: a quantitative approach. *Tourism Management,* 25(6), pp.777-788.

Gomezelj, D. O., & Mihalič, T., 2008. "Destination Competitiveness - Applying different models, the case of Slovenia". Tourism Management,29 (6), pp. 294-307.

Gooroochurn, N., Sugiyarto, G., 2004. Measuring competitiveness. Discussion Paper, TTRI. Nottingham University Business School. University of Nottingham.

Hassan, S. S., 2000. Determinants of market competitiveness in an environmentally sustainable tourism industry. *Journal of Travel Research,* 38, pp.239-245.

Johns, N., Mattsson, J., 2005. Destination development through entrepreneurship: a comparison of two cases. *Tourism Management.* 26, pp.605-616.

Kim, D., Perdue, R. R., 2011. The influence of image on destination attractiveness. *Journal of Travel and Tourism Marketing,* 28, pp.225–239.

Kozak, M., 2001. Repeaters' behavior at two distinct destinations. *Annals of Tourism Research,* 28(3), pp.784–807.

Kozak, M., Rimmington, M., 1999. Measuring Tourist Destination Competitiveness: Conceptual Considerations and Empirical Findings. *International Journal of Hospitality Management,* 18(3), pp.273-283.

Lee, CF. & King, B., 2009. A determination of destination competitiveness for Taiwan's hot springs tourism sector using the Delphi technique. Journal of Vacation Marketing, 15 (3), pp. 243-257.

Mazanec, J.A., Wöber, K., Zins, A.H., 2007. Tourism Destination Competitiveness: From Definition to Explanation? *Journal of Travel Research,* 46, pp.86-95.

Melian-Gonzalez, A., Garcia-Falcon, J. M., 2003. Competitive potential of tourism in destinations. *Annals of Tourism Research,* 30(3), pp.720-740.

Mihalic, T., 2000. Environmental management of a tourist destination A factor of tourism competitiveness. *Tourism Management* 21(1), pp.65–78.

Pyo, S., 2005. Knowledge map for tourist destinations—Needs and implications. *Tourism Management,* 26, pp.583–594 .

Ruhanen, L., 2007. Destination competitiveness. In A. Matias, P. Nijkamp, P. Neto, eds. 1993. *Advances in modern tourism research* 1993. Heidelberg: Physika- Verlag. pp. 133–152.

Ritchie, B. J. R., Crouch, G. I., 1993. Competitiveness in international tourism-a framework for understanding and analysis. Reports on 43rd Congress, 35, pp.23–71.

Ritchie, J. R. B., Crouch, G. I., 2000. The competitive destination, a sustainable perspective. *Tourism Management,* 21(1), pp.1–7.

Ritchie, J. R. B., Crouch, G. I., 2003. *The competitive destination, a sustainable tourism perspec-tive*. Cambridge: Cabi Publishing

Thomas, R., Long, J., 2000. Improving competitiveness: Critical success factors for tourism development. *Journal of the London Economic Policy*, 4, pp.313-328.

Vengesayi, S., 2003. A Conceptual Model of Tourism Destination Competitiveness and Attractiveness. Paper presented at the Proceedings of Australian and New Zealand Marketing Academy Conference - ANZMAC 2003. Adelaide (pp. 637-647).

Service Design for Product Development in Tourist Destinations

Janosch Untersteiner

Management Center Innsbruck, Austria
janosch.untersteiner@mci.edu

Abstract

The purpose of this paper is to explore relevant issues regarding product development in alpine destination management and to generate a first dataset for the application of service design methods and tools in tourist destinations on the example of Austrian destinations. The conceptual framework of this paper thoroughly reviews relevant literature regarding service and product development in tourist destinations. The empirical part surveys all Austrian tourist destinations (full survey) with a standardized online questionnaire regarding product development and the application of twelve selected service design methods and tools to finally deduce recommendations for destination management. The results of the survey assert a high degree of product development performance among Austrian tourist destinations. The average degree of use of the selected service design methods and tools increase in a highly significant way, if the destination applies a service design focused product development approach. This survey comprises exclusively Austrian tourist destinations. Future research should foster empirical studies to validate the results outside of Austria.

Keywords: Destination Management; Product Development; Service Design

1 INTRODUCTION

Despite global economic challenges, international tourist arrivals in 2013 reached a new record of 1,087 million arrivals and UNWTO forecasts further growth (UNWTO, 2014). Despite the positive external effects[2] of the tourism industry, the increasing demand grants attractiveness within the sector and results in an on-going increase in capacity within single tourism destinations. Due to a liberalization of the markets and the progression of globalization also new destinations enter the market (Vanhove, 2012) often ending up in intense price competition (Pechlaner and Raich, 2007; Bieger and Beritelli, 2013). During the last decades the development of destination management organizations (thereinafter DMOs) focused primarily on structure, organization and marketing tasks. „While all destinations engage in marketing and promotion, a much lower proportion focus their attention on the development and delivery of the various attractions and activities that make up the tourism product" (UNWTO, 2011, S.XI). Therefore, increasing attention on process and product issues is demanded by DMOs of the *"new generation"* (ÖHV, 2010; UNWTO, 2011; Bieger and Beritelli, 2013). The special characteristic, the complexity and interdisciplinary nature of the tourist product calls for methods and instruments allowing DMOs to analyse and to innovate processes along the service value chain and to optimize and adapt products regularly (Peters and Weiermair, 2000). A quite new and young discipline meeting these high expectations of tourist product development is the customer-oriented and iterative approach of Service Design. This interdisciplinary method enables entrepreneurs and innovators to design products and services best possible for their customers (Stickdorn and Schneider, 2011).

---

2 The tourism industry can influence economies positively by increasing regional competitiveness, balance of payments, employment, income, domestic products, etc. The tendency of tourism towards peripheral areas opens possibilities to set economical impulses affecting industries which could not exist without tourism. Therefore, tourism could be seen as a favorable starting engine for structurally weak areas.

2 THEORETICAL BACKGROUND

2.1 Destination

Following Bieger and Beritelli (2013), a destination is a geographical area consisting of all the services and infrastructure necessary for the stay of a specific tourist or tourism segment. Destinations are the competitive units of incoming tourism and must be managed as a strategic business unit. DMOs have to manage complex tasks and act – especially in alpine regions – as a form of cooperation management (Scherhag and Menn, 2010). According to Bieger and Beritelli (2013) the management of a destination encompasses (1) *planning* (strategy, development, implementation and controlling of all activities) (2) *coordination of products* (information, design and/or support of products and service quality), *players* (participating actively to enhance the destinations attractiveness), *processes* (as interface between companies to enhance cooperation) and *pricing*, (3) *marketing* (promotion) as well as (4) *representation of interests* (touristic, population, local and regional policy). Driven by new technologies, increasing competition and cost-effecting pressure as well as changing customer requirements Bieger et al. (2011) articulate a managerial approach, which concentrates on individual target markets and their requirements, professional customer service centres and authority on product development and distribution. According to Poon (1993), UNWTO (2011) and Bieger et al. (2011) the destination's potential is closely linked to product development and delivery. Specialities regarding the strong service character (Freyer, 2009; Bieger and Beritelli, 2013), bundle of components delivered by several providers as one product (Ritchie and Crouch, 2003; Bieger and Beritelli, 2013) or a new tendency versus experience economy (Grötsch, 2001), the tourism product requires a different approach regarding process and product development.

2.2 Product Development

Product development can either be business related or market driven and new idea-findings often happen coincidently or spontaneous. Nevertheless, the product development process has to be cultivated in a concentrated manner up to marketability (Peters, 2009). A variety of models try to sequence the product development process into single logic steps. While Cooper's (2001) "new product development (NPD)" model sequences the steps in linear ways, Johnson et al. (2000) point out the different nature of services proposing a-linear and iterative product development models. A growing focus on the development of services can be observed over the last decades (Brown, 1994; Johnston, 1999) focussing on subject areas like *New Service Development* (Fitzsimmons and Fitzsimmons, 2000; Edvardsson et al. 2013), *Service Design* (Shostack, 1984, Kimbell, 2009), *Service Innovation* (Gallouj and Weinstein, 1997; Bitner et al. 2008), *Service Quality* (Parasuraman and Zeithamel, 1984; Gummesson, 1991) and *Service Experience* (Pine and Gilmore, 1998; Zomerdijk and Voss 2010;) gain more and more insides underpinning a customer-centred logic. Vargo and Lush (2004) indicate a transition into a service area, as all economies are (at least in parts) service economies with the need to evolve a "*service dominant logic*". To create sophisticated services "we have to go beyond superficial service/goods characteristics and down to the generic elements of the design and production/delivery of the service" (Gummesson, 1991, p.10). In Gummesson's (1994) view "the development and use of service design methodology is a key, maybe even the key to the future of service management" (p.86).

2.3 Service Design

Nowadays, many practitioners and scholars from different disciplines provide insights into the practice of service management and still "service design is not yet an established area of practice or theory" (Kimbell, 2009, 158). According to Ostrom et al., (2010, p.17) service design ideally "is a collaborative, cross disciplinary activity that, at times, crosses marketing, human resources, operations, organizational structure, and technology disciplines. Service design involves the orchestration of clues, places, processes, and interactions that together create holistic service experiences for customers, clients, employees, business partners, or citizens". Birgit Mager (2009) explains, that service designers visualize, formulate and choreograph solutions still not invented. They interpret necessities and behaviours, transforming them into possible future services by explorative, generating and evaluating instruments and tools. Moritz (2005) points out, that service design can be seen as a mediator between the desires of the client and the desire of the company, differing from other approaches by truly representing clients perspectives, addressing the characteristics of services, integrating expertise by crossing disciplines, interactivity and iterative processes. Following Stickdorn and Schneider (2011) the nature of a service design process is basically iterative by repeating every step as long as failures arise. In doing so, service designers have to involve the entire environment (holistic), sequencing (interdisciplinary) and documenting/visualizing (evidencing) problem statements in a user-centred and co-creative way.

2.4 Service Design in Tourism

Service design is already applied and discussed in a tourism context among practitioners and scholars. *Tourism consultants* (tourismusdesign, 2013; TRAVEL2.0, 2013), *blogs* (Tourismuszukunft, 2013; blog.austriatourism, 2014), *conferences* (SDT, 2013; SDN, 2014) and *tourism business studies* (Management Center Innsbruck, 2015; FH Krems; 2015) integrated service design in their portfolio. A first service design contact point has been installed at Upper Austria Tourism on DMO level, supporting shareholders interested in the topic of service design (ooetm, 2015). While practitioners are already lively applying and adapting service design methods and tools, tourism scholars still exercise restraint. Only few scholars (Faché, 2000; Lally and Fynes, 2006; Zehrer, 2009; Stickdorn and Zehrer, 2009; McCabe, et al., 2012) attempt to link service design methods and tools to the tourism industry. According to Stickdorn and Frischhut (2012, p.50) service design in particular "provides processes and methods to create organizational structures and understand the culture required to deliver superior customer experiences within a complex ecosystem of both public and private organizations such as tourism destinations".

2.5 Service Design Process

An essential condition regarding the implementation of a service design process is a service strategy (Goldstein, et al., 2002, Edvardsson et al., 2013). The authors propose a multi-dimensional service concept as a central component and key driver in designing services along all planning levels. The service strategy should determine *"what"* services to develop whereas the service delivery system carries out the design (*"how"*) of service delivery. Goldstein et al. (2002) also recommend the implementation of performance measuring systems. Within a destination, especially Dwyer and Kim (2003) and Becher (2007) present a set of competitiveness indicators as a valuable tool to identify overall destination performance.

The service design process should be divided into different stages to systematically identify tasks that need to be undertaken. Moritz (2005) has identified six grouped stages:

Stage (1) *Service Design Understanding* provides insights into clients, contexts, providers, and relationships recommending analysis methods like *contextual interviews* (interview in familiar surroundings to gather relevant information and to observe or test reactions) (Stickdorn and Schneider, 2011) and *mobile ethnographies* (geographically independent ethnographic research where users define and rate personal touch points recording real (customer) journeys in real-time) (Stickdorn and Frischhut, 2012).

Stage two is named (2) *Service Design Thinking* and addresses the strategic direction (defining) in a service design process by identifying criteria, setting objectives, planning feasibility, analysing information from stage one and establishing time plans, guidelines, team setups and specifications. For this stage Moritz (2005) recommends a variety of creative and structural tools. Methods enhancing creative and structural thinking are *affinity diagrams* as an effective technique to gather, cluster and connect big and complex data (Charantimath, 2009) as well as *priority matrixes* allowing to categorise tasks related to importance and urgency.

In stage three, (3) *Service Design Generating*, it is proposed to develop relevant, intelligent and innovative ideas to generate creative problem solutions and experiences. This stage demands professional creativity by applying tools, which allow visualizing ideas and making them tangible. According to Moritz (2005), an explorative tool like the *"What if..."* method could be used to develop and explore innovative scenarios. To create real perspectives the method of *co-creation* could be applied. This user-centred method allows integrating share- and stakeholders by making them to active producers. To visualize and steer developed ideas *customer journey map* are recommended. Customer scripting techniques support developers in planning and steering experiences for customers and providers to minimize mistakes during the service delivery.

In stage four, (4) *Service Design Filtering,* best ideas and concepts should be identified and selected and criteria regarding performance and quality should be examined, evaluated, measured and fixed. Following Moritz (2005), a set of evaluation methods like STEP[3], SWOT[4] analysis, feasibility checks, etc. could be used. To facilitate a personal relation regarding a target group it is recommended to create fictive characters (*personas*) reflecting the target groups' interests and emotions to provide feedback to developers (Stickdorn and Schneider, 2011). A special tool for testing developed ideas is the development of hypothetic but detailed tales, so called *design scenarios*. This can happen descriptive, in form of storyboards or videos. To evaluate possible products from different perspectives it is recommended to apply a heuristic method called *pluralistic walkthrough*. This method is often used in the IT industry and allows evaluating prototypes from customers', employees', managing staff's and experts' perspective by documenting processes and itineraries incrementally.

The goal of stage five (5) *Service Design Explaining* is to visualize developed ideas, processes, interactions and experiences for all senses, giving decision makers and other stakeholders access to abstract future concepts with the aim to create a shared understanding of the topic. In their paper *"Experience Prototyping"*, Buchenau and Suri (2000) present a method emphasizing the experiential aspect with "any kind of representation, in any medium, that is designed to understand, explore or communicate what it might be like to engage with the product, space or system we are designing" (p.425). *Service and experience prototypes* are therefore useful to simulate sceneries or service experiences by designing physical touch points, using requisites just as on a stage (Stickdorn and Schneider, 2011).

The last stage, (6) *Service Design Realising*, is concerned to take the service to the market. This stage is characterized by the development of specific and practicable solutions in form of business plans, guidelines and conduct trainings. The *service blueprint* developed by Lynn Shostack (1984) is a method, which allows to specify and to accurately reproduce every individual aspect of a service by dividing processes by a line of visibility. This enables service

---

3 Sociological, Technological, Economical, and Political Change-Analysis

4 Strengths, Weaknesses, Opportunities, and Threats-Analysis

developers to specify visible parts of a service (line of interaction) and invisible parts of a service (backstage) as a model to implement existing and new services considering the service concepts strategy and delivery system. The service blueprint provides a clear plan for employees and managing staff of what has to be delivered and how. At the same time, the service blueprint can be basis for trainings, guidelines, drafts, instructions and specifications.

3 METHODOLOGY

3.1 Research question

For conducting the study, research questions are subsequently deduced from the above described conceptual framework serving as basis for a standardized online questionnaire.

Due to the high development level of Austrian destinations (ÖHV, 2010), it is supposed that they focus on and apply product development. Ideally, DMOs do have a product development department, employ a product manager, or a responsible people for product development (Bieger et al. 2011). In the tourism industry product development might happen also related to marketing (Freyer, 2009; Bieger and Beritelli, 2013). Furthermore, adequate financial resources have to be budgeted for product development to cover raised product development costs (ÖHV, 2010). Therefore, the first research question is: *To what extent do Austrian DMOs anchor and apply product development?*

Today's DMOs have to be able to develop products, which meet or even exceed the customers' demand. Due to the complex and interdisciplinary nature of tourism and a tourist destination the development of tourist product calls for an approach, which allows to analyse and to innovate processes and products along the service value chain from a customers' point of view (Peters and Weiermair, 2000). The application of service design methods and tools could maybe be the key for success (Gummesson, 1994). The second research question is: *Do Austrian DMOs know or apply the concept of service design by using predefined service design tools and instruments?*

3.2 Sample and data collection

The survey has been carried out and exported via the online software EFS Survey (8.0) and analysed by SPSS Statistics.

Table 1. DMOs in Austria

DMOs in Austria	
Federal State Level	**Regional Level**
Burgenland (1)	3
Carinthia (1)	13
Lower Austria (1)	6
Upper Austria (1)	7
Salzburg (1)	16
Styria (1)	9
Tyrol (1)	28
Vienna (1)	
Vorarlberg (1)	6
9	88

Source: Own representation based on ÖHV, 2013

A standardized (pretested) online questionnaire has been sent out to 97 DMOs (full survey) all over Austria (ÖHV, 2013) between the 3rd of July and the 16th of July via email. The author investigated all email addresses, focusing mainly on personalized addresses from CEOs or product development departments. 65 of 97 DMOs (67%) completed the questionnaire.

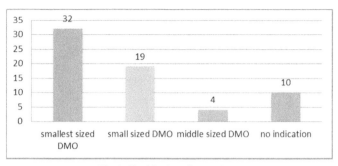

Fig. 1. Classification of respondents
Source: Own representation, n=65

Based on Kohl & Partner (2010) classifying DMOs by overnight stays and based on European Commission's (2006) SME classification regarding budget and number of employees it was possible to classify respondent DMOs by encountering at least two out of three variables. Following this classification 32 (49%) smallest sized, 19 (29%) small sized and 4 (6%) middle-sized DMOs completed the questionnaire. 10 (15%) abstained from specifying.

4   RESULTS

As mentioned in chapter 2.1 especially alpine destinations executed essential reform steps over the last decades by consolidating small tourism associations into bigger DMOs. The basic idea towards stronger cooperation and bundling of resources is nowadays established all over Austria by consolidating small tourism organisations into powerful DMOs (ÖHV, 2010). Besides the exception of Vienna as special case, Tyrol for instance has one of the strictest destination structure by consolidating 247 local tourism organisations into nowadays 34 regional DMOs with management structures and authority on destination and local level with one umbrella organisation on federal state level (Tirol Werbung, 2005; ÖHV, 2010).

4.1 Product development among Austrian DMOs

Austrian DMOs where asked on which level the task of product development is anchored within the organisation.

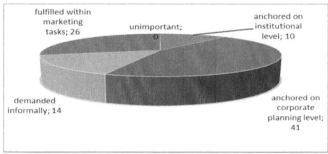

Fig. 2. Product development in your institution is...
Source: Own representation, n=65

Within the possibility of multi-selection 10 DMOs (15%) anchored product development on institutional level (statutes), 41 DMOs (63%) anchored product development on a corporate planning level and 14 DMOs (22%) demand product development informally. 26 DMOs (40%) fulfil product development within marketing tasks. No DMO sees product development as unimportant. Further Austrian DMOs where asked if they have a product development department, employ a product manager, or a responsible people for product development and/or budget financial resources for product development.

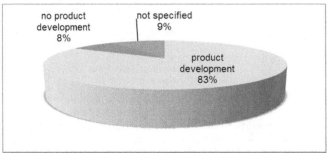

Fig. 3. Product development among Austria's DMOs
Source: Own representation, n=65

Due to affirmations regarding the extent of product development among Austria's DMOs, the study revealed that under the condition of multi-selection 25 DMOs do (38,5% n=65) dispose of a product development department, 43 DMOs (66,2% n=65) dispose of a budget for product development, 52 DMOs (80% n=65) have employees responsible for product development and 14 DMOs (21,5 n=65) apply product development related to marketing. Thus, it appears that 54 DMOs (83,1% n=65) in Austria apply product development within the organisation. Six DMOs abstained from voting. Austrian DMOs on average employ 3.3 (n=65) employees in charge of product development. 83% of DMOs employ at least one responsible person and 22% of DMOs employ at least three employees in charge for product development. Regarding the question of who is responsible for product development within the region the respondents assign local and regional DMOs under the condition of multi-selection the highest degree of responsibility (83%; n=65) followed by touristic providers themselves (80%; n=65).

4.2 Service Design among Austrian DMOs

To assess if Austrian DMOs know or apply the concept of service design by using predefined service design tools and instruments the author operationalized the data by frequency (Schnell, 2011). The application of the twelve service design methods and tools was measured using a five-point Likert-type scale ranging from "very often" to "unknown". The subjects applying service design methods and tools were reviewed. The minimum use of instrument was 0 and the maximum 12. The calculated median of 5 allowed to identify two groups (n=54). *Group A* (thereinafter *group noSD*) applies up to five service design methods and tools and is assumed to not apply a service design focused product development. *Group B* (thereinafter *group SD*) applies at least 6 methods and tools and is assumed to apply a service design focused product development.

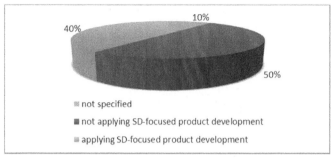

Fig. 4. Service Design focussed product development
Source: Own representation, n=60

Both groups have been tested in a *cross-classified table* regarding all 12 surveyed service design methods and tools. The results of the data reveal that *24 DMOs* (40% n=60) *apply a service design focused product development*. On the other hand *30 DMOs* (50% n=60) do *not apply a service design focused product development*. 6 DMOs (10% n=60) abstained from voting. A closer look into group noSD reveals that this group does not use most defined service design methods and tools. Top three used tools of this group are the priority matrix (used by 14 DMOs), co-creation (10 DMOs) and the contextual interview as well as the customer journey map (used by 9 DMOs). Even though twelve DMOs apparently know the service blueprint, no respondent of this group uses this tool. On the other hand a closer look into group SD reveals that this group uses most defined service design methods and tools. Top three used tools of this group are again the priority matrix (used by all DMOs), the customer journey map (21 DMOs) and the contextual interview (21 DMOs).

The author decided to apply a Spearman's Rank Correlation test showing throughout a negative correlation attesting a clear correlation between the application of contextual interviews, mobile ethnography, affinity diagram, priority matrix, customer journey map, pluralistic walkthrough, service and experience prototype, service blueprint and a moderate correlation between the application of co-creation, what if…, personas, and design scenarios within the groups noSD and SD (n=54). All correlations are significant (both sides) on a 0,01 level. According to the collected and evaluated data the author interprets that the *average degree of the application of service design methods and tools increases if a DMO strives for a service design focused product development.*

5 CONCLUSION

DMOs largely focused on marketing and promotion while the supply of attractions and activities does represent the proper core element of a tourism product satisfying customer's wants and needs. Due to the increasing competition, DMOs are expected to focus on product and process development in the future to not end up in price competition. Tourism is a service-intensive industry urging for methods and tools considering the specialities of the tourism product in terms of services and in terms of individual providers supplying experiences rather than simple products. The user-centred and iterative approach of service design is quite a young discipline considering the specialities regarding tourist product development, enabling entrepreneurs and innovators to design products and services best possible for their customers.

The survey of this paper reveals that the majority (83%) of Austrian DMOs apply product development. This reflects postulated requirements regarding product development on DMO level (Poon, 1993; UNWTO, 2011; Bieger et al. 2011; Bieger and Beritelli, 2013). Additionally the operationalization of the data show, that 40% of Austrian DMOs are already applying a service design focused product development within their organisation.

The results of the conceptual framework stress a systematic product development approach on strategic and operational level to enable the development of sophisticated, user-centred and experience oriented products to not only satisfy but to fill tourists with enthusiasm. Service design understands itself as multi-disciplinary approach, providing a vast selection of interdisciplinary, explorative, generating and evaluating methods and instruments, which could be applied to the different service design stages during a product development process. The results of this study show that, in particular, chosen service design methods and tools are already commonly known and used among Austrian DMOs, especially from DMOs striving for a service design focused product development.

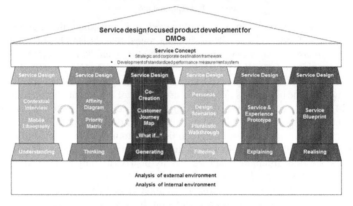

Fig. 5. Service design focused product development for DMOs
Source: Own representation, n=60

Figure 5 illustrates a recommended guideline for the use of service design by visualizing the concept and process of service design. Knowledge about the external and internal environment is crucial for every venture and can be seen as the basement. It is crucial to implement a service design concept establishing service strategies and service delivery systems norming the "what" and the "how" of service delivery accompanied by a set of competitiveness indicators in form of a standardized performance measurement system. The six pillars represent different stages within a service design process. They are filled with different recommended instruments and tools to reach single stage goals. As mentioned service design offers a variety of different methods and tools, which can be used depending on the type of task and goal. The resemble spirals symbolise the iteration of a service design process, which should be repeated at regular intervals to be successful in the long term.

This paper provides a first dataset for the application of service design methods and tools in tourist destinations on the example of Austrian destinations. The nature of full surveys is an extreme case of non-random data causing restrictions regarding random human behaviour influenced by external factors providing at times inexplicable actions. Moreover, it has to be considered that 65 out of the 97 DMOs have completed the survey, leaving a lack of 32 datasets. The survey only encompasses Austrian DMOs. To which extent the results can be deduced to DMOs from other alpine countries has to be further researched. The non-exhaustive list of various service design methods and tools represents strong constraints due to the strictly selected and limited choice of methods and tools. Lastly, the operationalization of data influences the results of the study significantly. Future research with different operationalization approaches could evidence if the results are comparable.

REFERENCES

Becher, M., 2007. Entwicklung eines Kennzahlensystems zur Vermarktung touristischer Destinationen. Wiesbaden: Gabler Edition Wissenschaft.

Bieger, T., Laesser, Ch. And Beritelli, P., 2011. Destinationsstrukturen der 3. Generation: Anschluss zum Markt. St. Gallen: Universität St. Gallen.

Bieger, T. and Beritelli, P., 2013. Management von Destinationen. 8. Auflage. München: Oldenbourg Wissenschaftsverlag.

Bitner, M.J., Ostrom, A., and Morgan, F., 2008. Service Blueprinting: A Practical Technique for Service Innovation. *California Management Review*, 50 (3), pp.66-94.

blog.austriatourism, 2014. Service Design im Tourismus am Beispiel Allgäu. [online] Available at: http://blog.austriatourism.com/2014/03/service-design-im-tourismus-am-beispiel-allgaeu/ [Accessed 04th of February, 2015].

Brown, S.W., Fisk, R.P. and Bitner, M.J., 1994. The Development and Emergence of Services Marketing Thought. *International Journal of Service Industry Management*, 5(1), pp.21-48.

Buchenau, M. and Fulton Suri, J. F., 2000. Experience prototyping. In. Boyarski, D. and Kellog, W. A., eds. 2000. *Proceedings of DIS2000*. New York: ACM Press, pp.424-433.

Charantimath, P.M., 2009. Total Quality Mangement. Singapore: Pearson Education.

Cooper, R.G., 2001. Winning at New Products. Accelerating the process from idea to launch. 3th edition. New York: Basic Books.

Dwyer, L. and Kim, C., 2003. Destination Competitiveness: Determinants and Indicators. *Current Issues in Tourism*. 6 (5) pp.369-414.

Edvardsson, B., Meiren, T., Schäfer, A. and Witell, L., 2013. Having a strategy for new service development- does it really matter? *Journal of Service Management*, 24 (1), pp.25-44.

European Commission, 2006. Die neue KMU-Definition. . [online] Available at: http://ec.europa.eu/enterprise/policies/sme/files/sme_definition/sme_user_guide_de.pdf [Accessed 13th of March 2015].

Faché, W., 2000. Methodologies for innovation and improvement of services in tourism. Managing Service Quality, 10 (6), pp.356-366.

Fitzsimmons, J.A. and Fitzsimmons, M.J., 2000. New Service Development: Creating Memorable Experiences, Thousand Oaks: Sage Publications Inc..

FH Krems, 2015. Detail zum Studium. [online] Available at: http://www.fh-krems.ac.at/de/studieren/master/tourism-and-leisure-management/details-zum-studium/ [Accessed 04. Februar 2015]

Freyer, W., 2009. Tourismus- Einführung in die Fremdenverkehrsökonomie. 9., überarbeitete Auflage. München: Oldenbourg Wissenschaftsverlag.

Gallouj, F. and Weinstein, O., 1997. Innovation in Services. *Research Policy*, 26, pp.537-556.

Goldstein, S.M., Johnston, R., Duffy, J. and Rao, J., 2002. The service concept: the missing link in service design research? *Journal of Operations Management*. 20, pp.121-134.

Grötsch, K., 2001. Psychologische Aspekte von Erlebniswelten. In: Hinterhuber, H., Pechlaner, H. and Matzler, K., eds. 2001: *IndustrieErlebnisWelten- vom Standort zur Destination*. Berlin: Erich Schmidt Verlag, pp.69-84.

Gummesson, E., 1991. Truths and Myths in Service Quality. *International Journal of Service Industry Management.* 2 (3), pp.7-16.

Gummesson, E., 1994. Service Management: An Evaluation and the Future. *International Journal of Service Industry Management.* 5 (1), pp.77-96.

Johnson, S. P., Menor, L.J., Roth, A.V. and Chase, R.B., 2000. A Critical Evaluation of the New Service Development Process. In: Fitzsimmons, J. A. and Fitzsimmons, M. J., eds. 2000. *New Service Development: Creating Memorable Experiences.* Thousand Oaks: Sage Publications Inc., pp.1-32.

Johnston, R., 1999. Service operations management: return to roots. *International Journal of Operations & Production Management.* 19 (2), pp.104-124.

Kimbell, L., 2009. The turn to service design. In: Julier, G. and Moor, L., eds. 2009. *Design and Creativity: Policy, Management and Practice.* Oxford: Berg, pp.157-173.

Kohl & Partner, 2010. DestinationCompass 2010. [online] Available at: http://www.kohl.at/?main=5&subm=15&id=3 Abfragedatum. 20.07.2013 [Accessed 13th of March, 2015].

Lally, A.M. and Fynes, B., 2006. Articulating service concept to enhance tourism experience design. *Irish Academy of Management*, pp.1-25.

Mager, B. and Gais, M., 2009. Service Design. Bern/Stuttgart/Wien: UTB Haupt Verlag

McCabe, S., Sharpless, M. and Foster, C., 2012. Stakeholder engagement in the design of scenarios of technology-enhanced tourism services. *Tourism Management Perspectives*, 4, pp.36-44.

MCI, 2015. Process & Service Design. [online] Available at: https://www.mci.edu/de/?Itemid=2037 [Accessed 4th of February, 2015].

Moritz, S., 2005. Service Design- A Practical Access to an Evolving Field. London: KISD.

ÖHV, 2010. Österreichs Destinationen im Vergleich. Wien: ÖHV.

ÖHV 2013. Österreichs Destinationen im Vergleich. Jahresvergleich 2010- 2011. Wien: ÖHV.

Ostrom, A.L., Bitner, M.J., Brown, S.W., Burkhard, M.G., Smith-Daniels, V., Demirkan, H. and Rabinovich, E., 2010. Moving Forward and Making a Difference: Research Priorities for the Science of Service. *Journal of Service Research*, 13(1), pp.4-36.

ooetm, 2015. Service Design. online] Available at: http://www.oberoesterreich-tourismus.at/wir-fuer-sie/ansprechpartner/details/ansprechpartner/39/sylvia_prunthaller.html [Accessed 04th of February 2015].

Parasuraman, A., Zeithaml, V.A. and Berry, L.L., 1985. A Conceptual Model of Service Quality and Its Implications for Future Research. *Journal of Marketing*, 49, pp.41-50.

Pechlaner, H. and Raich, F., 2007. Gastfreundschaft und Gastlichkeit im Tourismus-Kundenzufriedenheit und –bindung mit Hospitality Management. Berlin: Erich Schmid Verlag.

Peters, M. and Weiermair, K., 2000. Tourist Attractions and Attracted Tourists: How to satisfy today's „fickle" tourist clientele? *The Journal of Tourism Studies,* 11 (1), pp.22-29.

Peters, M., 2009. Strategische Produktentwicklung und Unternehmertum. In: Pechlaner, H./ and Fischer, E. eds.2009. *Strategische Produktentwicklung im Standortmanagement. Wettbewerbsvorteile für den Tourismus.* Berlin: Erich Schmid Verlag, pp.31-46

Pine, J.B. and Gilmore, J.H., 1998. Welcome to the Experience Economy. *Harvard Business Review.* July- August, pp.97-105.

Poon, A., 1993. Tourism, Technology and Competitive Strategies. Wallingford: C.A.B. International.

Ritchie, J.R. and Crouch, G., 2003. The Competitive Destination- A Sustainable Tourism Perspective. Wallingford: Cabi Publishing.

Scherhag, K. and Menn, A., 2010. Polaritäten im Überblick. Polaritätsfelder im Destinationsmanagement. In: Egger, R. and Herdin, T. eds 2010. *Tourismus im Spannungsfeld von Polaritäten*. Münster: LIT Verlag, pp.11-24.

Schnell, R./Hill, P.B./Esser, E. (2011): Methoden der empirischen Sozialforschung. 9. Auflage. München: Oldenbourg Verlag

SDN, 2014. Innovation durch Service Design – Erstes österreichisches Service Design Symposium. [online] Available at: http://www.service-design-network.org/innovationen-durch-service-design/ [Accessed 04th of February, 2015].

SDT, 2013. SDT Service Design in Tourism. [online] Available at: http://www.sdt2013.org/ [Accessed 04th of February, 2015].

Shostack, G.L., 1984. Designing Services That Deliver. *Harvard Business Review*, January- February, Nr.84115, pp.132-139.

Stickdorn and Zehrer, 2009. Service Design in Tourism: Customer Experience Driven Destination Management. First Nordic Conference on Service Design and Service Innovation. [online] Available at: http://www.aho.no/PageFiles/6819/Stickdorn_Zehrer.pdf [Accessed 12th of July, 2013].

Stickdorn M. and Schneider, J., 2011. This is Service Design Thinking. Basics- Tools- Cases. Amsterdam: BIS Publishers.

Stickdorn, M. and Frischhut, B., 2012. Service Design and Tourism. Case Studies of Applied Research Projects on Mobile Ethnography for Tourism Destinations. Norderstedt: Books on Demand.

Tirol Webung, 2005. Leitfaden zur Destinationsentwicklung. Innsbruck: Tirol Werbung.

tourismusdesign, 2013. Service Design. [online] Available at: http://www.tourismusdesign.com/service-design/ [Accessed 12th of July 2013].

TRAVEL2.0, 2013. We are a service design consultancy for tourism organisations. [online] Available at: http://travel2dot0.com/ [Accessed 12th of July 2013].

Tourismuszukunft, 2013. Mehr Kundenzufriedenheit im Tourismusbereich durch „Service Design" [online] Available at: http://www.tourismuszukunft.de/2013/08/service-design/ [Accessed 12th of July 2013].

Vanhove, N., 2012. The Economics of Tourism Destinations. Second Edition. New York: Routledge.

Vargo, S.L. and Lusch R.F., 2004. Evolving to a New Dominant Logic for Marketing. *Journal of Marketing*, 68, pp.1-17.

UNWTO, 2011. Handbook on Tourism Product Development. Madrid: UNWTO.

UNWTO, 2014. Facts & Figures edition page. [online] Available at: http://www2.unwto.org/facts/eng/vision.htm [Accessed 12th of July 2013].

Zehrer, A., 2009. Service experience and service design- concepts and application in tourism SMEs. *Managing Service Quality*, 19 (3), pp.332-349.

Zomerdijk, L. G. and Voss, C.A., 2010. Service Design for Experience-Centric Services. *Journal of Service Research*, 13 (1), pp.67-82.

Local Entrepreneurs' Perceptions of Cruise Tourism's Economic Impacts: The Case of Kavala (Greece)

Nikolaos Chrysanidis

University of Surrey, UK
chrysanidisn@gmail.com

Abstract

The aim of this study was to investigate an entrepreneurial community's perceptions of cruise tourism's economic impacts on their region and offer stakeholders recommendations for sustainable development. Kavala, a growing cruise destination located in North-Eastern Greece, was chosen as study area. Primary data collection involved interviews with local entrepreneurs from various business segments. In order for a more balanced overview to be achieved, the representatives of two local authorities involved in decision making were also interviewed. Findings illustrated that Kavala's entrepreneurs perceive cruise tourism as beneficial for their businesses and particularly local economy. However, they believe that there is still room for improvement towards sustainability and their level of participation in decision making remains low. Apart from the latter point where there was an opinion divergence, the views of local authorities were found to be quite similar to those of entrepreneurs. In order to capitalise on this positive climate and common ground, policy makers should insist on the development of cruise tourism, communicate the potential economic benefits to entrepreneurs and give them more space in decision making. On the other hand, in order to maximise their benefits from cruise tourism, entrepreneurs should try to adapt to the requirements of this type of tourism, while asserting a stronger participation in planning and development.

Keywords: cruise; tourism; impacts; perceptions; Kavala

1 INTRODUCTION

This paper deals with cruise tourism and how the entrepreneurial community of Kavala (Greece) sees its economic impacts on the region. The above topic was chosen because the triptych *impacts – sustainability- residents' perceptions* constitutes a contemporary aspect of tourism research. However, although cruise tourism is the fastest-growing segment of leisure tourism (Weeden et al., 2011), it still remains a relatively under-researched area (Brida et al., 2011). In this introductory section, the structure of this study is outlined. Section 2 starts with a brief literature review around tourism impacts, the importance of their management on a long-term basis, as well as residents' vital role. Then it focuses on the theory around the economic impacts of cruise tourism and port communities' perceptions and attitudes. Finally, it provides important information about the cruise destination chosen as study area. Section 3 presents the aim and objectives of this study, as well as the data collection methods adopted by the author. This is followed by section 4 where findings are presented and analysed under a critical scope and in relation to the existing theory. The last section summarises the key findings and offers recommendation to local authorities and entrepreneurs towards the sustainable development of cruise tourism in the region.

2 LITERATURE REVIEW

2.1 Tourism Impacts, Sustainability, and Residents' Perceptions

Since tourism is one of the fastest-growing industries in the world ([1]UNWTO, 2014), it has inevitably been associated with a number of impacts on destinations (Wall and Mathieson,

2006). According to the most common classification, these impacts can either be positive or negative and they fall into three main and often interrelated categories: economic, environmental, and sociocultural (UNEP, 2014). Tourism impacts have extensively been investigated by researchers. Table 1 summarises the key findings:

Table 1. The impacts of tourism on destinations

	ECONOMIC	ENVIRONMENTAL	SOCIOCULTURAL
POSITIVE	• national and local economic growth • generation of income and employment through direct, indirect, and induced spending • business and investment opportunities • better infrastructure • better standard of living	• promotion of the conservation of natural and manmade environment • increased public awareness of environmental issue	• social prosperity • pride of locals • preservation of cultural heritage • revitalisation of arts and crafts • promotion of intercultural contact
NEGATIVE	• higher taxes and value of products, services, and land • higher cost of living • revenue leakages • unfair distribution of economic benefits • over-dependence on the sector low-paid employment, and underemployment due to the industry's intense seasonality	• direct damage of ecosystems and environmental integrity • worsening of already existing problems, such as pollution (e.g. water, air, land, noise, aesthetics) • over-exploitation of certain natural resources (e.g. drinkable water, land, fuels, and energy)	• overcrowding and social stress • erosion of local values and morals • changes in traditional lifestyle and behaviour patterns (e.g. demonstration effect) • accentuation of socially undesirable activities (e.g. crime and prostitution) • commercialisation of culture • lack of authenticity • acculturation in the long run

(Source: Adapted from Brunt and Courtney, 1999; Gjerald, 2005; Wall and Mathieson, 2006; Aref, 2010; Vehbi and Doratli, 2010; Assante et al., 2012; Marzuki, 2012; Kim et al., 2013; Moyle et al., 2013; Siu et al., 2013; Vareiro et al., 2013)

The continuous assessment of the aforementioned impacts, the maximisation of benefits and the minimisation of associated costs enable tourism policy makers to ensure destinations' sustainability, in other words viability in the long-run (Ştefănică and Butnaru, 2013). However, impact assessment is a quite complex process because some changes (particularly the environmental and sociocultural ones) can also be attributed to other factors, non-related to tourism (Fischer, 2004). Wall and Williams (2006) distinguish between actual and perceived impacts. Since tourism industry involves many stakeholders with different and often conflicting interests and objectives, their perceptions of impacts and attitudes towards tourism development may vary significantly (Kuvan and Akan, 2012). Byrd et al. (2009) suggest that stakeholders' perceptions should be investigated and compared between each other. In this way, decision makers can reduce conflict and find common ground to implement future tourism policies. Residents' perceptions of tourism impacts have drawn much academic attention in recent years (Aref, 2010). That is because local communities' involvement and active support are considered as vital to sustainability and success of tourism development (Vareiro et al., 2013). According to certain theoretical frameworks developed, such as Doxey's Irridex and Butler's TALC, residents usually perceive tourism development as beneficial and support it during its initial stages. Later, as the destination evolves and approaches its saturation point (carrying capacity), they take benefits for granted and become more sensitive to the long-term impacts of tourism (Wall and Mathieson, 2006; Diedrich and García-Buades, 2009). However, the aforementioned frameworks ignore that communities' perceptions and attitudes depend on many other factors, either extrinsic (e.g. state of economy) or intrinsic (e.g. involvement with tourism) (Falkner and Tideswell, 1997; Brida et al., 2011). Ap (1992) suggests that tourism is a social interaction which involves both positive and negative outcomes. Thus, when residents perceive more benefits than costs they tend to adopt a more favourable overall attitude (Lee, 2013). From this point of view, residents' involvement with the sector, which possibly leads to individual economic benefits, can be determinant to positive cost-benefit evaluation and active support of tourism development.

2.2 The Economic Impacts of Cruise Tourism on Destinations

Cruise tourism is considered to be an increasingly important sector of the tourism industry. It emerged in the late 1960s – early 1970s (Rodrigue and Notteboom, 2013) and soon became the fastest-growing segment of leisure tourism worldwide (Klein, 2011). Since 1990, cruise tourism's annual growth rate has consistently remained above 7% and further growth is expected by 2018 (Cruise Market Watch, 2014). North America and Europe are the largest source markets while Caribbean and Mediterranean remain the most popular destination markets (Rodrigue and Notteboom, 2013).

The Impact of Cruise-Related Expenditure on Local Economies. The direct, indirect and induced expenditure arising from cruise activity contributes to income and employment generation for port communities (Dwyer and Forsyth, 1998). Cruise-related expenditure can be broken down into cruise line and passenger/crew expenditure. Cruise line spending refers to the cruise companies' payments for the use of port facilities and cruise terminals (e.g. agency fees) (Brida and Zapata, 2010a). It also includes the money spent for the purchases of goods and services at destinations (e.g. fuels), as well as the payments to residents who are directly hired by cruise lines (Dwyer and Forsyth, 1998). The expenses made by cruise companies assist national and local governments to fund the construction/expansion of cruise terminals and therefore, improve the level of investments and infrastructure around ports. However, as Klein (2011) highlights, these expenses are often not enough to ensure the viability of the projects undertaken. That is not only because of wrong financial planning, but also because cruise lines sometimes abuse their negotiation power adopting practices that do not constitute a responsible attitude (e.g. arbitrary changes in itineraries). Passenger/crew spending is thought to be another major source of economic benefits for port communities. European destinations, for example, enjoyed EUR 3.63 billion wages from passenger and crew purchases during 2012 (CLIA, 2013). Table 2 summarises the business segments that benefit from this spending category.

Table 2. Destinations' business segments that benefit from passenger and crew spending

Categories of Passenger and Crew Expenditure			
1	Shore Excursions	8	Retail Purchases of Liquor
2	³F&B at Restaurants and Bars	9	Entertainment and Nightclubs

3	Clothing	10	Telephone and Internet
4	Local Crafts and Souvenirs	11	Electronics
5	Taxis/Ground Transportation	12	Other Purchases
6	Watches and Jewellery	13	Lodging (Only applicable for homeport passengers)
7	Perfumes and Cosmetics		

(Source: Adapted from FCCA, 2012)

Apart from the economic benefits mentioned above, the literature also presents some areas of concern regarding the impact of cruise tourism on local economies.

Cruise Tourism and Land-Based Tourism. Various studies (Wilkinson, 1999; Brida and Zapata, 2010a; Larsen et al., 2013) suggest that cruise tourism definitely contributes to the generation of employment and income, but not as much as land-based tourism does. Tourism policy makers are often aware of this fact. However, they keep investing in cruise tourism in order to turn passengers into stay-over tourists in the future (Wilkinson, 1999). Although there is a positive relationship between passenger satisfaction and intention to return to a destination and recommend it to others (Brida et al, 2012a), the actual results are often far below the expectations (Klein, 2003; Marušić et al., 2008). However, some advantages of cruise tourism against land-based tourism do exist (e.g. lower marketing and [2]R&D costs) (Macpherson, 2008). Moreover, cruise tourism can assist the development of land-based tourism (e.g. by enhancing the image of luxury and modernity for destinations) (Figueira de Sousa, 2001).

The Enclave Nature of Cruise Tourism. Cruise industry has often been accused of operating at the expense of cruise destinations and local economies. That is because cruise lines try to maximise their revenue offering a huge variety of on-board facilities, activities, and entertainment options (e.g. bars, restaurants and casinos). As a result, the majority of passenger expenses are captured within the ship (Rodrigue and Notteboom 2013). In order to fully enjoy the appealing options offered on-board, some passengers do not even disembark at ports of call. However, this behaviour also stems from the passengers' desire to spend most of their time within a safe, convenient, and pleasant environment. Besides, not all passengers have the same spending profile (Brida et al., 2013), while the ports of call often play a secondary role in overall consumer experience (Weeden et al, 2011). Thus, accusing cruise lines of "*trapping*" passengers on the ship may be a one-sided approach. However, this is not to argue that cruise companies are blameless. Far from that, they often establish practices that leave port communities with little or no benefit. These practices include excessive commissions charged on shore excursions, preferential agreements with entrepreneurs, and the ownership of cruise terminals, beaches or even entire islands which serve as artificial destinations (Klein, 2011).

Hidden Economic Costs. Cruise activity also involves some negative economic effects which may not be apparent on the first sight. Gross expenditure includes some important revenue leakages which, if subtracted, lead to a lower net economic benefit (e.g. sales of imported goods). Furthermore, while some sectors benefit from the intense cruise activity, others may suffer from lack of funds and production factors (e.g. labour), increased prices (e.g. expensive waterfront land), or reduced competitiveness (e.g. decline in fishing industry) (Dwyer and Forsyth, 1996). The economic benefits sacrificed on the altar of cruise activity, can be defined as the opportunity costs of cruise tourism (Brida and Zapata, 2010a). Finally, the loss of income arising from environmental (e.g. degradation of a cruise destination's image due to water pollution) and sociocultural issues (e.g. overcrowding, port homogenisation) should also be considered (Brida. and Zapata, 2010b).

2.3 Port Communities' Perceptions and Attitudes

While research on tourism and residents' perceptions and attitudes has been extensive, cruise tourism still remains an under-researched area. Only a few studies have been conducted to examine port communities' perceptions of cruise tourism's impacts (Brida et al., 2011). Overall, cruise destinations' residents recognise that cruise tourism benefits their economies regarding income and employment (Gibson and Bentley, 2007; Stewart et al., 2011), investment attraction (Brida et al., 2011), upgrade of port infrastructure (Brida et al., 2012b) and promotion of their destination (Marušić et al. 2008; Peručić and Puh, 2012). However, in some cases concerns over negative effects do exist and better destination management is expected. Inflation and unfair benefit distribution (Brida et al., 2011), loss of income due to excessive on-board spending (Hritz and Cecil, 2008), environmental degradation of fragile areas (Diedrich, 2010), and disturbance of tourists due to overcrowding (Marušić et al. 2008) are some of the negative impacts identified by locals. Finally, regarding the factors that influence communities' perceptions and attitudes, most of studies (e.g. Brida et al., 2012b and Brida et al., 2012c) have confirmed that involvement with the sector is among residents' strongest motives for adopting a positive attitude towards cruise tourism development.

2.4 Kavala: A Greek Growing Cruise Destination

Kavala, a coastal city located in the Nort-Eastern part of Greece, was chosen as the investigation area. This place combines features which give it great potential as a tourist destination (e.g. historic sites, monuments, crystal beaches, port and airport). Local authorities realise the importance of tourism for the region and try to promote it through a number of initiatives. Since Greece is the third most preferred cruise destination after Italy and Spain on a national scale (CLIA, 2013), Kavala's authorities have decided to invest in this type of tourism spending approximately EUR 20 million to upgrade the port facilities (e.g. pier expansion) (Municipality of Kavala, 2014) and advertising the potential of the city as a cruise destination more intensively (e.g. participation in international cruise fairs) ([1]PBOK, 2014). Kavala's port is only operating as a port of call at the moment enjoying an increase in passenger volume during the last four years (Hellenic Ports Association, 2013). Local authorities are optimistic that cruise traffic will keep increasing in the future. Cruise-related expenditure arises from navigation and mooring fees, payments for waste disposal, and passenger spending (guides, attractions, excursions primarily to [2]Philippi, taxis, F&B, souvenirs, and convenience stores) (PBOK, 2014). Regarding residents' perceptions, locals have adopted a positive attitude towards tourism development in general (Stylidis and Terzidou, 2014; Stylidis et al., 2014). Due to the latest severe economic crisis in Greece, Kavala's residents, particularly those involved with the sector, were found to have strong perceptions of tourism's economic benefits, while being less sensitive over environmental issues (Stylidis and Terzidou, 2014). Although the aforementioned studies form a general picture, no research has yet been conducted with a particular focus on residents' perceptions of cruise tourism's impacts and their attitudes towards cruise tourism development.

3 METHODOLOGY

3.1 Research Aim and Objectives

Given the importance of residents' views and attitudes to the sustainable development of destinations, the aim of this exploratory study was to investigate [3]local entrepreneurs' perceptions of cruise tourism's economic impacts on Kavala (Greece) and offer stakeholders recommendations for the sustainable development of cruise tourism in the region. In order to achieve this aim, the author set four basic objectives: **(a)** to examine to what extent local entrepreneurs perceive cruise tourism as beneficial (or not) for their businesses and Kavala in general; **(b)** to examine how entrepreneurs evaluate the policies implemented by local authorities; **(c)** to compare entrepreneurs' perceptions and views to those of local authorities in order to identify similarities and differences, and **(d)** to offer local authorities and entrepreneurs recommendations which can possibly bridge these differences and contribute to cruise tourism's sustainable development.

3.2 Data Collection

The above objectives were achieved through the collection of both secondary and primary data. The author critically evaluated and used different sources of secondary data in order to formulate a solid theoretical framework. However, due to the fact that secondary data have been collected for a different purpose than the research purpose, they have a number of drawbacks [e.g. no control over the data quality (Saunders et al., 2012)]. Thus, the author also collected primary data in order to achieve an in-depth investigation of the perceptions and views of local entrepreneurs and authorities. Due to the exploratory nature of this study, the author decided to employ qualitative methods of data collection, and specifically face to face semi-structured interviews. That is because this type of interviews is ideal for achieving conversation flexibility, asking purposeful questions, listening to the answers, and investigating them further (Saunders et al., 2012). In order to approach information-rich participants the author used purposive and snowball sampling. Plus, in order to maximise sample heterogeneity, he split the study population into five distinct business groups (**a.** shore excursions and transports, **b.** F&B and entertainment, **c.** service providers, **d.** retailers, **e.** accommodation). Since this dissertation aimed to examine a heterogeneous population, the number of participants interviewed should not have been below 12 (Guest et al., 2006). Thus, 16 entrepreneurs and the official representatives of PBOK and Kavala Port Authority were interviewed for this study. Two [1]slightly different sets of questions were used in order to examine participants' views and perceptions over three major areas of cruise tourism's development in Kavala: **(a)** benefits **(b)** negative effects **(c)** policies implemented. The data collected were transcribed and grouped into analytical categories in order to be critically discussed in relation to the existing theoretical framework. Finally, it has to be mentioned that all ethical issues (e.g. access, confidentiality, anonymity) were considered before any data collection.

4 RESULTS AND ANALYSIS

4.1 The Contribution of Cruise Tourism to Income and Employment

The interviews conducted illustrated that cruise tourism is seen as a positive economic force for the city of Kavala by the local business community. The majority of entrepreneurs perceive cruise tourism as beneficial (even if potentially) for their businesses. Income generation was identified as the dominant individual benefit arising from cruise-related expenditure (particularly from passenger spending). Although the methods adopted do not allow any generalisation, a general observation is that entrepreneurs dealing with shore excursions, transports, and provision of services gain the most from cruises. However, the possibility of establishing Kavala as a homeport in the future has made entrepreneurs of the all five segments optimistic that their income will increase. On a collective basis, Kavala's entrepreneurs were found to have even stronger perceptions of cruise tourism's contribution to income and employment. The fact that many of them enjoy limited or zero direct benefit at this stage has not discouraged them from supporting cruise tourism development. That is not only due to their willingness to gain direct benefits in the future, but also due to the importance of the benefits accruing from induced spending (Dwyer and Forsyth, 1998). This strong sense of collectivism is apparently intensified by the on-going economic crisis which forces entrepreneurs to see beyond their direct benefit and appreciate even the minimum amounts of money injected in the local economy ("*even one Euro coming from outside is precious*..."[Clothe Shop Owner]). This confirms Stylidis and Terzidou (2014) who identified a positive relationship between the current recession and Kavala residents' favourable attitude towards tourism development. Local authorities' representatives agreed that cruise-related expenditure in Kavala have an "*a priori*" positive impact on income and employment (e.g. attraction fees). However they admitted that passenger spending has not reached its full potential yet and they noted that Kavala's entrepreneurs should try to adjust better to the requirements of cruise tourism (e.g. working hours).

4.2 The Contribution of Cruise Tourism to Infrastructure and Investments

Apart from a few cases, respondents identified a positive relationship between cruise tourism development, infrastructure upgrade and investment attraction. This confirmed the findings of previous studies where residents perceived a positive influence of cruise tourism on these economic indicators (e.g. Brida et al., 2011). However, several interviewees expressed their scepticism whether infrastructure and investment should precede the development of cruise tourism. At the same time, local authorities seemed to be more enthusiastic about this relationship. Such a finding is natural in the sense that local authorities are those who are responsible for planning and implementing important projects around port. Finally, no fears were expressed regarding the viability of the projects undertaken. That is because these projects do not depend exclusively on cruise line spending, while they serve the broader purpose of enhancing Kavala's port, which is considered to be the core of the local economy.

4.3 The Impact of Cruise Tourism on Land-Based Tourism

The findings suggest that both entrepreneurs and local authorities consider the impact of cruise tourism on land-based tourism to be positive. Some of the entrepreneurs stated that "*cruise passengers can return to Kavala as overnight tourists in the future*", although such a possibility is not well-supported by the literature (see section 2.2). Respondents also indicated that cruise passengers' satisfaction from their experience in Kavala can possibly lead to positive recommendations for the destination and, hopefully, to a future increase in stay-over tourist arrivals. Furthermore, the view that cruise tourism is perceived as an attraction for other types of tourism supports the argument of Figueira de Sousa (2001) who noted that cruises help destinations to market themselves as upscale and worthy-to-visit places. The above findings confirm previous studies where residents were found to perceive cruise tourism as a valuable promotion tool for their area (e.g. Hritz and Cecil, 2008). Adverse impacts on land-based tourism such as the disrespectful behaviour of cruise travellers towards tourists with particular interests (Hritz and Cecil, 2008) or disruption of tourists' holiday experience (Marušić et al., 2008) were not reported in the case of Kavala. As also expected from the literature reviewed (e.g. Larsen, 2013), Kavala's entrepreneurs indicated that land-based tourism constitutes a more profitable market-segment than cruise tourism, primarily because tourists spend more time and therefore money in the region. However, despite this note, the majority did not reveal any particular preference between the two groups, in the sense that all types of tourism, even the least profitable ones, can benefit the region. This euphoria for tourism development regardless of its type and features is possibly associated not only with the early development stage of Kavala (see section 2.1), but also with the current poor state of economy, which makes them even more enthusiastic (Stylidis and Terzidou, 2014).

4.4 The Negative Impacts of Cruise Tourism on the Local Economy

The enclave nature of cruise tourism was identified as a negative influence on local economy by local authorities and partially by entrepreneurs. The former criticised the *"imperialistic"* and *"arrogant"* attitude of cruise companies that arises from their negotiation power, noting however that *"compared to other Greek ports Kavala is still in a relatively good position"*. This view comes in line with Klein's (2011) argument that cruise lines often abuse their power behaving irresponsibly towards destinations. On the other hand, those entrepreneurs who were critical about this aspect, focused on the way that cruise companies structure their passengers' schedule in order to maximise their on-board spending and prevent them from spending ashore (e.g. limited time ashore, directed excursions outside Kavala, and provision of insufficient information about the city). These views confirm previous researchers (e.g. Weaver, 2005) who observed that companies endeavour to keep passengers within their enclave and *"squeeze"* them. However, neither commission policies nor preferential agreements as those presented in section 2.2 were reported. On the other hand, half of the entrepreneurs interviewed did not seem to consider cruise lines responsible for any problems arising for the local economy. They argued that some passengers may not spend a lot because they are simply *"stingy"* or belong to nationalities which *"traditionally spend less"*. This finding confirms Brida et al. (2013) who noted that there may be significant differences between cruise travellers' spending behaviour. Finally, Kavala's entrepreneurs were found to consider the reaction of local business community to be more important than the enclave tourism itself, in the sense that entrepreneurs can avoid unprofessional practices and protect the local tourist product. This view evinces once more the business community's optimism that Kavala can make the most out of tourism resisting to potential threats. This tendency becomes even more apparent from the confidence expressed that cruise tourism cannot harm the local economy or other sectors in the ways presented in section 2.2 (e.g. revenue leakages, prices increase, and funds/resources drain) (Dwyer and Forsyth, 1998). Furthermore, no negative economic implications arising from environmental or sociocultural problems were reported by respondents. In general, they agreed that cruise tourism does not constitute a serious environmental threat. They also claimed the arrival of cruise passengers can only bring sociocultural benefits for the city (e.g. social status and cultural contact). Therefore, perceptions of negative cruise tourism's outcomes, such as those mentioned in section 2.2 were not found in this case. Such a result was rather expected, not only because Kavala is going through an early development stage combined to a severe economic crisis (Stylidis and Terzidou, 2014), but also because the social group examined is considered to be economically dependent on tourism in general. Consequently, entrepreneurs' personal benefit from tourism makes them more tolerant to the negative outcomes mentioned above and pushes them to adopt a favourable attitude towards tourism development (Ap, 1992; Lee, 2013). Besides, this theory has been confirmed in the cruise tourism context as well (e.g. Diedrich, 2010; Brida et al., 2011; Brida et al., 2012b).

4.5 Policies and Sustainability

Evaluating the sustainability of tourism development is far from easy, in the sense that this assessment depends on whether the actual or perceived impacts are taken into account (Wall and Mathieson, 2006). Provided that this study focused on a social group's perceptions of impacts, from this point of view, the development of cruise tourism in the region could be considered as *"sustainable"*. That is because this social group (entrepreneurs) identified economic benefits for Kavala, while refusing the existence of negative impacts on local economy, environment, social, and cultural life. When asked to evaluate local authorities' policies, most of entrepreneurs seemed to appreciate the efforts made to increase cruise traffic in the region. However, the general view was that there is still room for improvement in order for Kavala to reach its full potential as a cruise destination. Therefore, a number of suggestions were made towards this direction, primarily regarding the enhancement of port infrastructure and promotion of local traditional products. On the other hand, local authorities also agreed that some improvements should take place (also mentioned port infrastructure). However, they set the discussion on a realistic basis, claiming that for a number of reasons (e.g. financial difficulties, destination's special features) the local community should not expect drastic changes to happen. As said actually, the objective goal is *"to achieve a steady rise of ship arrivals within the forthcoming years"*. Despite some differences in the future development rationale, the fact that both sides identify benefits and want cruise tourism to keep growing in the region could be considered as a very positive element in terms of sustainability (Byrd et al., 2009). Another positive element is the fact that entrepreneurs realise that the success of cruise tourism development in Kavala depends not only on the actions of local authorities, but also on their own attitude (e.g. professional behaviour, quality of products and services, adjustments to the cruise schedule, reasonable prices). Therefore, they understand that their role in sustainable development is more than important. This is also supported by local authorities who suggested that entrepreneurs should become more flexible in order to take full advantage of passenger spending. Furthermore, local authorities understand the importance of taking entrepreneurs' views under consideration, even if indirectly via the Commercial Chamber of Kavala and various unions. However, apart from a few entrepreneurs who stated that they have experienced this indirect participation, most of respondents described their level of participation as *"low"*. Therefore, here there is an opinion divergence. This gap can possibly be attributed to the lack of organisation or communication between the three actors: local authorities, intermediate bodies, and entrepreneurs. Additionally, the fact that some of the entrepreneurs illustrated their unwillingness to actively participate should also be underlined. In the long run, such an attitude would act as one step back, since it would lead to their absolute exclusion from decision making and their establishment as passive recipients of the policies implemented. Finally, another critical point was the statement of local authorities that *"long-term impact assessment does not take place in the case of cruise tourism due to economic and political issues"*. Considering that the continuous recording and assessment of actual and perceived impacts is the core of sustainable tourism development (Ştefănică and Butnaru, 2013), a strategy based exclusively on short-term decisions may threaten the future growth of Kavala as a cruise destination.

5 CONCLUSION AND MANAGERIAL IMPLICATIONS

5.1 Key Findings

The key findings of the study can be summarised as follows: **(a)** Overall, Kavala's entrepreneurs were found to perceive cruise tourism as beneficial for their businesses. Even those who do not enjoy many individual benefits at this stage support the development of cruise tourism recognising the indirect and potential gains. Apart from some concerns over enclave tourism, no negative effects on the economy were identified, including those possibly arising from the environmental and sociocultural aspect. **(b)** This study revealed that Kavala's entrepreneurs recognise the efforts made by the local authorities to develop the city as a cruise destination. However, they believe that there is still room for improvement, particularly regarding the upgrade of the port infrastructure. They also believe that the entrepreneurs' level of participation in decision making is still low. **(c)** The comparison of local entrepreneurs' views with those of local authorities revealed that there is common ground in most of the aspects examined. Nevertheless, local authorities were found to be a bit more enthusiastic regarding the impact of cruise tourism on infrastructure and investments. They were also found to have a milder approach to future changes and improvements.

Finally, contrary to entrepreneurs, they recognised business community's participation to be strong via intermediate bodies.

5.2 Recommendations for Local Authorities

(a) Insist on cruise tourism development and communicate intensively the potential economic benefits for the region to local entrepreneurs. Provided that entrepreneurs perceive cruise tourism as beneficial for their businesses and local economy, authorities should pursuit the further development of Kavala as a cruise destination. The enhancement of port facilities could be an area of focus as underlined by both entrepreneurs and authorities. At the same time, the effort to establish the city as a homeport should not be abandoned, since it acts as a source of hope for local entrepreneurs that benefits for the region will multiply. It is also very important for local authorities to keep communicating and advertising the potential benefits to the local business community in order to ensure its active support for further development. This can be achieved through regular informative events, such as fairs, workshops, seminars or face to face discussions between tourism consultants and entrepreneurs.

(b) Increase entrepreneurs' level of participation in decision making by improving indirect and direct communication. Despite local authorities' perception that entrepreneurs participate actively in decision making for cruise tourism development, this does not seem to be the case considering the opposite side's opinion. This gap can possibly be bridged in two different ways. First, by organising better the communication and flow of information across the network Authorities – Commercial Chamber/Unions – Entrepreneurs. Authorities should ask from the intermediate bodies to adopt a more responsible stance and collect their members' views and suggestions on a more regular and consistent basis. **Second**, by establishing channels for direct interaction with entrepreneurs (e.g. a website, e-mail, or phone line dedicated to cruise tourism, quarterly or biannual open discussions with business people from different sectors). These new channels can act supplementary to the traditional information flow without diminishing the role of existing bodies. In this way, various suggestions can be collected and subjected to feasibility assessment in a more efficient way.

(c) Develop and implement a long-term impact assessment plan. There is no doubt that the total absence of long-term impact assessment projects jeopardises the sustainable development of Kavala as a cruise destination. Therefore, it becomes urgent for local authorities to organise and implement a project for the assessment of the economic, environmental, and sociocultural impacts of cruise tourism on Kavala (both actual and perceived). Furthermore, provided that entrepreneurs' perceptions of impacts may change over time, this assessment should take place on a periodical basis. It is understandable that the current economic recession has limited the allocation of funds for such projects. However, given the benefits accruing for Kavala, authorities should add more pressure to the national government to get as many funds as possible for this purpose. Finally, authorities should set the need for long-term planning and sustainability above any political cost.

5.3 Recommendations for Local Entrepreneurs

(a) Adapt to the requirements of cruise tourism and behave responsibly. As entrepreneurs stated, cruise passenger satisfaction can upgrade Kavala's reputation as a destination and strengthen its position in the tourist map. Therefore, it becomes imperative for them to adapt to the requirements of cruise tourism (e.g. working days and hours) and adopt a responsible attitude towards cruise tourists (e.g. professionalism, quality of products and services, reasonable prices). Besides, that was underlined not only by the local authorities, but also by a number of entrepreneurs.

(b) Assert a more active participation in decision making. The tendency of some respondents to abstain from participation in the decision making for cruise tourism development, in the sense that *"local authorities know better"*, could become a serious threat for sustainability in the long run. Entrepreneurs should try to get more involved with cruise tourism and add pressure to their elected representatives to forward their views to local authorities with consistency and accuracy. Especially those who were found to realise the great importance of entrepreneurs' participation, should lead this initiative and convince their hesitant colleagues to adopt a more active attitude.

5.4 Limitations and Recommendations for Future Research

This study involved a number of limitations primarily associated to the research methods adopted: **(a)** The sampling methods adopted did not allow statistical generalisations for the whole population (Patton, 2002). **(b)** Snowball sampling may have led to participants who had limited variety of information to offer (Saunders et al., 2012). **(c)** The merge of business segments into five distinct groups was arbitrary made by the author. **(d)** Certain geographical regions of Kavala (e.g. Old Town) were not represented at all. **(e)** During the interviews, the author tried to express the questions as neutrally as possible to minimise interviewer bias. However, interviewee bias may have arisen to a certain extent from some participants' tendency to embody a socially desirable role (e.g. entrepreneurs being actively involved with unions) (Saunders et al., 2012). **(f)** It is well-understood that there is a wide range of stakeholders regarding cruise tourism in Kavala (residents, entrepreneurs, authorities, the Commercial Chamber of Kavala, business unions, cruise lines etc.). However, due to size restrictions recommendations have been given only to those involved in this study (local authorities and entrepreneurs). Considering these limitations, a suggestion for future research could be a study of entrepreneurs' perceptions and attitudes towards cruise tourism's development, using quantitative methods (e.g. questionnaires), a larger sample, as well as sampling methods that enable statistical generalisations and a more consistent representation of different business segments and geographical areas. In this way, researchers will be able to record entrepreneurs' views more accurately, and identify to what extent these views are influenced by various factors (e.g. demographics, type of business, and distance of the business from the port). Additionally, a qualitative study including a wider range of stakeholders could also be conducted, in order to investigate a greater variety of opinions and give recommendations accordingly.

REFERENCES

Ap, J. (1992) "Residents' perceptions on tourism impacts." *Annals of Tourism Research*, 19 (4), pp. 665-690.

Aref, F. (2010) "Residents' Attitudes Towards Tourism Impacts: A Case Study of Shiraz, Iran." *Tourism Analysis*, 15 (2), pp. 253-261.

Assante, L.M., Wen Hsing, I., and Lottig, K.J. (2012) "Conceptualization of Modelling Resident Attitudes on the Environmental Impacts of Tourism: A Case Study of Oahu, Hawaii." *Tourism Planning & Development*, 9 (2), pp. 101-118.

Brida, J.G. and Zapata, S. (2010a) "Economic Impacts of Cruise Tourism: The Case of Costa Rica." *Anatolia: An International Journal of Tourism & Hospitality Research*, 21, (2), pp. 322-338.

Brida, J.G. and Zapata, S. (2010b) "Cruise tourism: economic, socio-cultural and environmental impacts." *Lesiure and Tourism Marketing*, 1 (3), 205-226.

Brida, J.G., Pulina, M., Riaño, E., and Zapata-Aguirre, S. (2012a) "Cruise visitors' intention to return as land tourists and recommend a visited destination." *Anatolia: An International Journal of Tourism and Hospitality Research*, 23 (3), pp. 395-412.

Brida, J.G., Del Chiappa, G., Meleddu, M., and Pulina, M. (2012b) "The perceptions of an island community towards cruise tourism: A factor analysis." *Tourism (Croatia, Zagreb)*, 60 (1), pp. 29-42.

Brida, J.G., Del Chiappa, G., Meleddu, M., and Pulina M. (2012c) "A Comparison of Residents' Perceptions in Two Cruise Ports in the Mediterranean Sea" *International Journal of Tourism Research*, 16 (2), pp. - . [Online] ResearchGate. Available at: http://www.researchgate.net/profile/Giacomo_Del_Chiappa/publications (Accessed: 15 March 2014).

Brida, J.G., Pulina, M., Riaño, E., and Zapata-Aguirre, S. (2013) "Cruise Passengers in a Homeport: A Market Analysis." *Tourism Geographies*, 15 (1), pp. 68-87.

Brida, J.G., Riaño, E., and Zapata Aguirre, S. (2011) "Residents' attitudes and perceptions towards cruise tourism development: A case study of Cartagena de Indias (Colombia)." *Tourism and Hospitality Research*, 11 (3), pp. 181-196.

Brunt, P. and Courtney, P. (1999) "Host perceptions of sociocultural impacts." *Annals of Tourism Research*, 26 (3), pp. 493-515.

Byrd, E.T., Bosley, H.E., and Dronberger, M.G. (2009) "Comparisons of stakeholder perceptions of tourism impacts in rural eastern North Carolina." *Tourism Management*, 30 (5), pp. 693-703.

CLIA (2013) *THE CRUISE INDUSTRY: Contribution of Cruise Tourism to the Economies of Europe*. Available at: http://www.europeancruisecouncil.com/content/CLIA%20Europe%20Economic%20Impact%2 0Report%202013%20Edition.pdf (Accessed: 17 February 2014).

Cruise Market Watch (2014) *Growth of the Cruise Line Industry*. Available at: http://www.cruisemarketwatch.com/growth/ (Accessed: 3 May 2014).

Diedrich, A. (2010) "Cruise ship tourism in Belize: The implications of developing cruise ship tourism in an ecotourism destination." *Ocean & Coastal Management*, 53 (5-6), pp. 234-244.

Diedrich, A. and García-Buades, E. (2009) "Local perceptions of tourism as indicators of destination decline." *Tourism Management*, 30 (4), pp. 512-521.

Dwyer and Forsyth (1998) "Economic significance of cruise tourism." *Annals of Tourism Research*, 25 (2), pp. 393-415.

Faulkner, B and Tideswell, C (1997) "A framework for monitoring community impacts of tourism." *Journal of Sustainable Tourism*, 5 (1), pp. 3-28.

FCCA (2012) *Economic Impact of Cruise Tourism*. Available at: http://www.f-cca.com/downloads/2012-Cruise-Analysis-vol-1.pdf (Accessed: 30 April 2014).

Figueira de Sousa (2001) "The tourist cruise industry" *Portus (September)*, pp. 6–13.

Fischer, D. (2004) "The Demonstration Effect Revisited." *Annals of Tourism Research*, 31 (2), pp. 428-446.

Gibson, P. and Bentley, M. (2007) "A Study of impacts-Cruise Tourism and the South West of England." *Journal of Travel & Tourism Marketing*, 20 (3-4), pp. 63-77.

Gjerald, O. (2005) "Sociocultural Impacts of Tourism: A Case Study from Norway." *Journal of Tourism and Cultural Change*, 3 (1), pp. 36-58.

Hellenic Ports Association (2013) *Επιτροπή Λιμένων Κρουαζιέρας [Cruise Ports Committee]* Available at: http://www.elime.gr/index.php/2011-09-16-08-32-09/2011-09-16-08-28-40/107-2011-09-16-06-54-41 (Accessed: 20 March 2014).

Hritz, N. and Cecil, A.K. (2008) "Investigating the Sustainability of Cruise Tourism: A Case Study of Key West." *Journal of Sustainable Tourism*, 16 (2), pp. 168-181.

Kim, K., Muzaffer, U., and Sirgy, M.J. (2013) "How does tourism in a community impact the quality of life of community residents?" *Tourism Management*, 36 (June 2013), pp. 527-540.

Klein, R.A. (2003) Charting a course: *The Cruise Industry, the Government of Canada, and Purposeful Development*. Halifax: Canadian Center for Policy Alternatives.

Klein, R.A. (2011) "Responsible Cruise Tourism: Issues of Cruise Tourism and Sustainability." *Journal of Hospitality & Tourism Management*, 18 (1), pp. 107-116.

Kuvan, Y. and Akan, P. (2012) "Conflict and agreement in stakeholder attitudes: residents' and hotel managers' views of tourism impacts and forest-related tourism development." *Journal of Sustainable Tourism*, 20 (4), pp. 571-584.

Larsen, S., Wolffa, K., Marnburgb E., and Øgaardb, T. (2013) "Belly full, purse closed: Cruise line passengers' expenditures." *Tourism Management Perspectives*, 6 (1) pp. 142–148.

Lee, T. H. (2013) "Influence analysis of community resident support for sustainable tourism development." *Tourism Management*, 34 (February 2014), pp. 37-46.

Macpherson, C. (2008) "Golden goose or Trojan horse? Cruise ship tourism in Pacific development." *Asia Pacific Viewpoint*, 49 (2), pp. 185-197.

Marušić, Z., Horak, S., and Tomljenovic, R. (2008) "The socioeconomic impacts of cruise tourism: A case study of Croatian destinations." *Tourism in Marine Environments*, 5 (2-3), pp. 131–144.

Marzuki, A. (2012) "Local residents' perceptions towards economic impacts of tourism development in Phuket." *Tourism (Zagreb, Croatia)* (1332-7461), 60 (2), pp. 199-212.

Moyle, B.D., Weiler, B., and Croy, G. (2013) "Visitors' Perceptions of Tourism Impacts: Bruny and Magnetic Islands, Australia." *Journal of Travel Research*, 52 (3), pp. 392-406.

Patton, M.Q. (2002) *Qualitative Research and Evaluation Methods*. Thousand Oaks, California: Sage Publications Inc.

PBOK (2014) E-mail sent to author. *Στοιχεία για έρευνα για την ανάπτυξη του τουρισμού κρουαζιέρας στην Καβάλα [Data provided for the research for the development of cruise tourism in Kavala]*, 6 March 2014.

Peručić, D. and Puh, B. (2012) "Attitudes of Citizen of Dubrovnik towards the Impact of Cruise Tourism on Dubrovnik." *Tourism and Hospitality Management*, 18 (2), pp. 213-228.

Rodrigue, J.P. and Notteboom, T. (2013) "The geography of cruises: Itineraries, not destinations." *Applied Geography*, 38 (3), pp. 31-42.

Saunders, M, Lewis, P., and Thornhill, A. (2012) *Research Methods for Business Students*. 6th edn. Harlow: Pearson Education Limited.

Siu, G., Louisa, Y.C.L., and Leung, D. (2013) "Residents' Perceptions Toward the "Chinese Tourists' Wave" in Hong Kong: An Exploratory Study." *Asia Pacific Journal of Tourism Research*, 18 (5), pp. 446-463.

Ștefănică, M. and Butnaru, G.I. (2013) "Approaches of durable development of tourism." *Revista de Turism - Studii si Cercetari in Turism*, 15, pp. 41-47.

Stewart, E.J., Dawsonb, J., and Draperc, D. (2011) "Cruise Tourism and Residents in Arctic Canada: Development of a Resident Attitude Typology." *Journal of Hospitality and Tourism Management*, 18 (1), pp. 95–106.

Stylidis, D. and Terzidou, M. (2014) "Tourism and the economic crisis in Kavala, Greece." *Annals of Tourism Research*, 44 (January 2014), pp. 210-226.

Stylidis, D., Biran, A., Sit, J., and Szivas, E.M. (2014) "Residents' support for tourism development: The role of residents' place image and perceived tourism impacts." *Tourism Management,* 45 (December 2014), pp. 260-274.

UNEP (2014) *Impacts of Tourism.* Available at: http://www.unep.org/resourceefficiency/Business/SectoralActivities/Tourism/FactsandFiguresa boutTourism/ImpactsofTourism/tabid/78774/Default.aspx (Accessed: 6 March 2014).

Vareiro, L.M.C., Remoaldo, P.C. and Cadima Ribeiro, J.A. (2013) "Residents' perceptions of tourism impacts in Guimarães (Portugal): a cluster analysis." *Current Issues in Tourism*, 16 (6), 535-551.

Vehbi, B.O. and Doratli, N. (2010) "Assessing the Impact of Tourism on the Physical Environment of a Small Coastal Town: Girne, Northern Cyprus." *European Planning Studies, 18 (9)*, pp. 1485-1505.

Wall, G. and Mathieson, A. (2006) *Tourism: change, impacts, and opportunities*. 2nd edn. Harlow: Pearson Prentice Hall. MyLibrary [Online]. Available at: http://lib.myilibrary.com/Open.aspx?id=133376&src=0 (Accessed: 17 February 2014).

Weaver, A. (2005) "Spaces of Containment and Revenue Capture: 'Super-Sized Cruise Ships as Mobile Tourism Enclaves." *Tourism Geographies*, 7 (2), pp. 165-184.

Weeden, C., Lester, J.A., and Thyne, M. (2011) "Cruise Tourism: Emerging Issues and Implications for Maturing Industry." *Journal of Hospitality and Tourism Management*, 18 (1), pp. 26-29.

Wilkinson, P.F. (1999) "Caribbean cruise tourism: delusion? illusion?" *Tourism Geographies*, 1 (3), pp. 261-2

Luxuy Tourism and Destination Branding: A Case Study of the Tourism Destination Vienna

Catherine S. Latzenhofer

Modul University Vienna, Austria
catherine.latzenhofer@gmail.com

Abstract

Latest trends such as the increase in annual disposal income of emerging markets and the increase in demand for luxurious self-fulfilment is contributing to the desire for a sophisticated travel experience. Hence, an emergence of the luxury travel segment is noticed and the tourism industry is faced with different challenges on how to serve this segment. By using several in-depth interviews with diverse stakeholders and a conduction of a SWOT analysis, the dissertation's aim was to understand how a tourism destination could integrate the concept of luxury tourism into their branding strategies. Therefore, this study scrutinized the possibilities for Vienna to be perceived as a luxury tourism destination. The results indicate that Vienna has the potential to be perceived as a luxury destination in the long-term. Conclusively, it has been agreed that this destination image has to be ensured by an increase in luxury destination suppliers, dynamic package design together with personalization. Finally, all stakeholders involved have to provide a luxury ambience throughout the entire service-delivery process.

Keywords: luxury tourism; destination branding; stakeholder management; case study

1 INTRODUCTION

Recently there have been developments that have heightened the interest in luxury tourism. Firstly, economical shifts as well as changes in demographics and lifestyle patterns are heavily influencing the demand for luxury travel experiences. Primarily, the growth of the global wealth has been thought of as a key factor in the increasing interest in luxury tourism. Capgemini and RBC Wealth Management (2013) were demonstrating that in 2012 a global growth in wealth of 10% for 'high-net-worth individuals' (HNWIs) has been measured. Moreover, the second aspect extracted from the demand-side is the shift in travel behaviour and lifestyle fulfilment. Euromonitor International (2012) claims that ordinary travel experience is exceeded by the desire for a more experiential as well as authentic adventure in luxury tourism. In addition, the last main aspect is driven from the supply side. The International Luxury Travel Market (2007) states that in recent years, there has been an increasing interest and subsequent intensified supply of upscale hotel brands and similar exclusive travel suppliers. However, to date there has been little agreement on an integrated definition of 'luxury tourism'. Nonetheless, recent evidences suggest that luxury tourism incorporates emotional benefits, authenticity, personalization, and creativity (e.g. Page, 2009; Horwath HTL, 2011). Moreover, research lacks an understanding of how stakeholders perceive the concept of luxury tourism, integrate it into their marketing strategies and aim to develop future strategies. Given the emergence of the luxury sector, research as well as practice needs to start understanding its implications. Therefore, this paper aims to understand the concept of luxury tourism in the light of city tourism while aiming to address the following research question: What are the possibilities for the city of Vienna to develop and execute the concept of luxury tourism?

Subsequentyly, the paper's aim is twofold; i) to critically examine the components of the travel experience that contribute to a luxury destination branding, and ii) to understand the stakeholders perceptions and contribution to the concept of luxury tourism. Therefore, the main aspects from the demand as well as supply side will be analysed in order to demonstrate the relevance of the luxury tourism market. Finally, this paper reviews the opportunity for a destination to being branded as luxurious after identifying and analysing the impact of several stakeholders involved in the entire process.

The research paper is organized as follows. First the main literature streams are introduced. Then, a case study of Vienna and the different methods used are discussed. Subsequently, the results will be presented followed by concluding remarks.

2 THEORETICAL BACKGROUND

The purpose of the following chapter is to give a synopsis about relevant literature in terms of theories of branding, stakeholder management, luxury tourism, as well as it will indicate significant travel behaviours of this niche segment.

2.1 Branding

According to the definition provided by the World Tourism Organization and European Travel Commission (2009) the main purpose of a brand is to establish a unique identification among other competitive products or services. Subsequently, a brand comprises core values of the product or destination that differentiate it from its counterparts. Kolb (2006) continues that the main goal of establishing a destination brand is to reflect the attributes and core values of a place together with the destination name. In addition to the core values, a place brand indicates the collectivity of personal emotions, thoughts and assumptions an individual perceives about a particular place. Hence, the destination's reputation, its unique characteristics as well as its specific set of values represent its competitive components (Baker, 2012). Moreover, Kolb (2006) points out that a brand should not be confused with visual applications such as product designs, logos, or slogans. The branding procedure itself solely involves intangible applications such as the creation of an image together with pushing the awareness about the destination's features and benefits. However, the brand can then be visualized and communicated by the destination's logo, mission statement or slogan (Kolb, 2006). Furthermore, the brand values are perceived individually. Therefore, in the destination management context a dynamic exchange exists between the destination as the product and the potential tourist as the audience (World Tourism Organization and European Travel Commission, 2009). In general, in a marketing context, a 'product' is considered to be a physical and therefore tangible good, or an intangible product such as an experience or service encounter. The latter is concerning the destination product as the place. Hence, during the travel purchase process, the tourist is gaining an intangible service and experience rather than a physical core product (Kolb, 2006).

By virtue of the intangibility of a destination, a destination brand should act as an assurance of travel experience of what the potential tourist will encounter at the destination (World Tourism Organization and European Travel Commission, 2009). Two main elements are crucial within the destination brand building process. First, the brand identity that is consistent of the mission and vision, the core and augmented values, as well as the favoured image of the brand, which is desired by the organization. Second, the actual brand image perceived by the market and lastly the brand positioning is then the combining component that can be controlled by a destination management organization (DMO) (Aaker, 1996).

2.1 Stakeholder Management

Throughout the entire tourism destination planning and branding process, several stakeholders are involved. The stakeholders are able to affect the tourism destination to various extents. According to a definition in the context of business management provided by Stoner et al. (1995, p.63), "stakeholders are those groups or individuals who are directly or indirectly affected by an organization's pursuit of its goals." In the tourism context, stakeholders are the suppliers who deliver products and services for tourism to a respective destination. Nonetheless, they also act as customers who are permanently integrated in the whole stakeholder management procedure. Thus, the highest aim is to find a consensus of every stakeholder's needs and desires within the tourism planning and destination-branding phase (Page & Connell, 2006). Coherently the DMOs role is to assemble various stakeholder objectives in order to develop the destination brand imagery with adequate core and augmented products. Moreover, Robinson et al. (2013) argue that DMOs have essential power over tangible features within the destination. Therefore, establishing a partnership with stakeholders who have similar interests in the impact of tourism in the respective destination enhances destination competitiveness, according to Pike (2008). However, DMOs can steer ownership control among destination stakeholders according to their responsibilities (Robinson et al., 2013). The DMO's challenge is thus on the one hand to give stakeholders full responsibility within the decision-making processes; and on the other hand, negotiate the importance of individual components participating in the final decision (Murphy & Murphy, 2004). Hence, stakeholders' management in a tourist destination is a dynamic process that needs to be monitored on a regular basis by the DMO.

2.3 Defining Luxury Tourism

According to Kivetz & Simonson (2002) cited in Hansen & Wänke (2011), the purchase of luxury goods includes items that are exceeding an individual's necessity of needs and wants. Moreover, Hansen & Wänke (2011, p.790) refer to Houghton Mifflin Company (2000) and their definition of the 'American Heritage Dictionary of the English Language' that defines luxury as "something inessential but conducive to pleasure and comfort" or "something expensive or hard to obtain". Therefore, when referring to luxury in tourism, it may be categorized to 'conducive to pleasure' that stimulates luxurious hedonic travel experiences as recently outlined by Ghosh & Varshney (2013).

Moreover, 'luxury tourism' is a term frequently used in the literature, but to date there is no consensus about a common definition. In the past, between the eighteenth to the twentieth century, luxury tourism referred to a travel experience that was portrayed as being high-priced and excellent in quality at the same time. Showpieces for past luxury travels are cruise and scheduled airline carriers. Recently, there has been a shift to more accessible, newly established luxurious arguments within the tourism context (Page, 2009). For instance, the stay at a luxury hotel accommodation has become more affordable than ever before. Therefore, the luxury tourism market is becoming more accessible to the main population (International Luxury Travel Market, 2007). Researches claim that the emotional benefits in tourism will be leading drivers in the long-term. The luxury tourism consumption requires elements of authenticity, uniqueness, personalized service, quality, comfort, and much more (e.g. Page, 2009;Horwath HTL, 2011). In detail, Horwath HTL (2011) argues that the term 'luxury' itself comprises two main elements. On the one hand is the uniqueness of a product or service such as quality, selectivity, creativity, and limitation. On the other hand is the brand imagery such as the brand values and the selective communication (Horwath HTL, 2011).

According to a definition provided by the International Luxury Travel Market (2007), 'luxury tourism' is differently defined between two major market origins. Firstly, wealth market origins such as the US and main parts of Europe identify luxury tourism as a 'fancy' travel experience that comprises authentic, unique, and personalized components. Whereas, emerging market origins as well as young generations perceive luxury tourism as a remarkable and extravagant travel experience (International Luxury Travel Market, 2007). Having defined the market origin of a potential luxury traveller, the segmentation categories of the luxury audience, as well as the demographic shifts in luxury tourism, the detailed profile of a luxury tourist can be defined. Horwath HTL (2011) examined four main profiles of the luxury tourism clientele. The first profile is comprised of travellers who seek for an authentic and active leisure experience.

Due to limited leisure time available, the maximum of adventure has to be achieved. That clientele is characterized as highly educated and enthusiastic. The second major profile consists of luxury travellers, known as explorers, who are willing to pay a reasonable price for luxury in return for high emotional benefits. Travellers seeking contentment and high quality characterize the third profile of high-end travellers. Lastly, the intelligent buyers who pursue extravagant travel experiences through online research with less financial assets available.

This profile is comprised of mainly younger luxury travellers, which are concerned about receiving value for money (Horwath HTL, 2011). In order to understand the segments of luxury tourists, the coherent travel behaviour will be explained in the following section.

2.4 Travel Behaviour in Luxury Tourism

The first trend concerns the desire for short trips and frequent travels at the same time. Subsequently, luxury short travel trips are increasing especially to popular city hotspots. Moreover, the expansion of low-cost carriers is enhancing the travel network to small cities and places. This has a subsequent impact on luxury traveller interests, since high-end visitors might prefer to travel with low-cost airlines but still insist on a luxury hotel accommodation. Hence, value for money is still relevant for HNWIs (International Luxury Travel Market, 2007). Moreover, a recent study by Horwath HTL (2011) reports that 33% of the luxury audience take short trips about four times annually. The second development might contradict the former finding, since there is also a growth in long-stay travels observed. However, this trend is mainly affecting long-distance travels by primarily Baby Boomers with higher disposable leisure time (International Luxury Travel Market, 2007). Subsequently, Horwath HTL (2011) indicates that 75% of luxury travellers take long-stay travels one or two times annually. Moreover, the third main change in travel behaviour affects the lifestyle encountered during a luxury trip. Hereby, the longer the travel is, the more an authentic and extraordinary luxury travel experience is desired. In addition to authenticity as well as philanthropy, adventure and action is intended. Therefore, sustainability in terms of a destination's environmental setting, cultural heritage, as well as welfare of locals, is crucial in luxury travel behaviour developments (International Luxury Travel Market, 2007). In addition to that, social responsibility of a tourism destination is in favour of the luxury clientele. Hence, travel suppliers of the luxury tourism market are adjusting the core product with organic and sustainable enhancements (Horwath HTL, 2011).

Euromonitor International (2012) concludes that adventurous and sustainable travel experiences are leading factors among the luxury audience preferences besides the basic desire of high service quality and contentment. Next to the sustainable aspects, particularly Baby Boomers seek an authentic education during their luxury holidays. Trends range from attending cooking classes to wine tastings and even language trainings are prevailing in the luxury travel experience (International Luxury Travel Market, 2007). Lastly, a study by Horwath HTL (2011) explicitly indicates the dominant position of Europe (41%) as a key destination for luxury inbound travellers.

3 METHODOLOGY

3.1 Case Vienna

By the use of a case study this paper effectively analyses the tourism destination Vienna in the light of luxury tourism and branding strategies.

Vienna as the capital of Austria enables around 1,741,246 inhabitants a living space across 41,487,1h, measured in the beginning of the year 2013. In 2010, Vienna contributed with 26,4% as €75,503 million to the overall Austrian gross regional product as of 286,397 (Vienna City Administration, 2013).

Destination Management and Branding of Vienna

The Vienna Tourist Board [1] (2014,p.1) defines itself as "the official destination marketing agency for the tourism sector of the city. It provides many service offers, tips and much information for Viennese tourist businesses". Moreover, additional responsibilities comprises touristic data maintenance, tourism destination promotion and marketing activities, assistance in market research execution, and similar (Vienna Tourist Board [1], 2014).

According to the Vienna Tourist Board the following five main brand attributes are creating Vienna's unique brand identity: "imperial heritage, profusion of music and culture, savoir vivre functional efficiency, balance of urban and green areas" (Vienna Tourist Board [2], 2010, p.6). Moreover, the Vienna Tourist Board highlights on four principle brand values that are contributing to the overall destination image: "sensuous, timeless, cultivated, premium quality" (Vienna Tourist Board [2], 2010, p.24).

Current Tourism and Hospitality Market in Vienna

In 2012, total bed nights of 12,262,828 were measured in Vienna. In detail, 2,240,750 were considered as domestic arrivals as well as 10,022,078 as total foreign arrivals. The table below indicates that Vienna is leading in tourism overnights by far at national level (Vienna City Administration, 2013). Furthermore, on a European capital city level, in 2011, Vienna was ranked inside the top ten cities with the highest estimated tourism bed nights by domestic as well as foreign inbound travel market (Vienna City Administration, 2013).

Current Luxury Tourism in Vienna

Luxury in Vienna starts already upon arrival at the Vienna International Airport, while purchasing a VIP package including luxury services at the airport. Arriving in Vienna, several destination components are able to delight the luxury tourism audience. Besides the exquisite accommodation sector, Michelin star nominated restaurant cuisines, high-end fashion label flagship stores, exclusive cultural heritage facets, together with former 'k.u.k. Hoflieferanten' suppliers, are all capable in warming the heart of the luxury traveller (Vienna Tourist Board [3], 2013). The luxury five-star hotel market in Vienna is steadily increasing. Besides prior historic and exquisite luxurious hotel properties such as the Hotel Sacher or Hotel Imperial, there is an upwards trend observed in the establishment of exclusive five-star hotel properties from high-class international brands such as the Ritz Carlton, the Kempinski as well as the Park Hyatt, together with other prospect branded properties in the near future.

Moreover, the following *Figure 1* visualizes the bed as well as room capacity of the five-star hotel market in Vienna. A significant increase can be observed during 2009 to 2014.

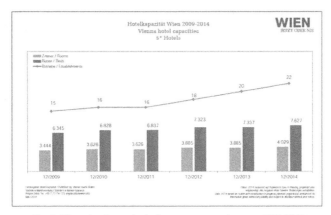

Fig. 1. Vienna hotel capacity in five-star segment, between 2009-2010
(Vienna Tourist Board [4], 2014, p.2)

3.2 Qualitative Research

A significant supplement for the case study approach of Vienna was the use of qualitative interviews. In the course of this study, interviews were conducted with diverse destination stakeholders representing the brand of the city of Vienna. This allowed critical analysis on the gathered valuable subjective judgments about components that are able to contribute to a luxury destination branding for Vienna.

Therefore, five individual interviewees were selected in order to represent one significant tourism sector that is able to contribute to a luxury destination brand.

Namely, i) management personnel of the *Vienna Tourist Board*; ii) owner's representative of two five-star properties of the Viennese *JJW Hotels*; iii) marketing personnel of *Austrian Airlines*; iv) restaurateur of *Steirereck*; v) managing director and expertise of *Zolles & Edinger GmbH*. Decisively, the above-mentioned significant interview partners and their assumptions as well as judgments were considered to serve the current study well due to their crucial influence on the local tourism industry, which was essential for targeting the outlined research aim and objective.

Four out of five interviews were conducted in a face-to-face setting, whereas one interview was conducted online on a written basis. This study used semi-structured interviews adjusted to the respective stakeholder's role, which was directly applied to the case study of Vienna. Subsequently, one set of questions was standardized and another will was conformed to the specific tourism industry sector. The main topics discussed were i) luxury tourism, ii) current luxury in Vienna, iii) luxury destination branding for Vienna, and iv) future of luxury tourism in Vienna. Each topic was divided into different subsections. Moreover, the application as an exploratory research was strategically assisting in approaching the main research objective by collecting insight knowledge.

The design of the interview questionnaire was mainly based on open questions in order to encourage the selected research contributors to respond in a detailed manner. In the end, the qualitative outcome was preceded systematically by first summarizing the interview questions in bullet points and a subsequent categorization into thematic sections were then following.

3.3 SWOT Analysis

Besides the conduction of a qualitative research, it was considered that the additional conduction of a SWOT analysis would be highly beneficial for effectively targeting the research aim. The comprehensive character of this approach would serve the main research objective well in order to gain a holistic view on the issue. Therefore, during the conduction of the qualitative research, the interview questionnaire of all selected interviewees included the question to briefly describe possible opportunities, threats as well as strengths and weaknesses the tourism destination Vienna is facing while establishing a luxurious destination brand as a 'Premium Destination'. The following SWOT analysis is based on the responses to the respective question together with other relevant content of the interview outcome. Consequently, the SWOT analysis was conducted based on subjective knowledge as well as expertise judgments produced by the interviewed destination stakeholders. A consensus might be observed among certain aspects, whereas discrepancies or divergent opinions on other assumptions.

4   RESULTS

4.1 Qualitative Research

4.1.1 Luxury Tourism

First of all, one significant interviewee defines a 'luxury tourist' as a traveller that is staying at a five-star hotel accommodation during his travel to Vienna. Coherently, one interviewee states that the service aspect is an essential component during a luxury hotel stay while indicating, *"in the hotel industry, luxury is the attention of service."* Secondly, different interviewees commonly argue that there is no limit in creating a luxury tourism experience for the luxury traveller audience. Thirdly, they all state that luxury derives from the unexpected experience encounter. Hence, some discrepancies can be found. For instance, one interviewee indicates the monetary aspect of luxury travel behaviour, claiming the following *"the luxury traveller is an individual who is in the position and able to spend a great amount of money during the trip."* Whereas another interviewee counters this argument, arguing that luxury tourism is not 'materialism' however luxury in travel signifies the importance of time. Finally, another interviewee complements the previous by indicating values of "flexibility, freedom, and comfort" comprehending the luxury tourism definition.

Motivations of the Luxury Traveller
Overall, contributing stakeholders state that various components, such as high-class accommodation and exclusive restaurants, exclusive shopping facilities and local cultural heritage, contribute to the purchase-decision process. Therefore, those values are able to motivate a luxury traveller. Significantly, one interviewee claims that special events held in the city are decisive components (i.e. the Opera Ball, the Philharmonic Ball, or the Life Ball).

Demand of the Luxury Traveller
All interviewees argue that they will be able to responds to the given needs and wants of the luxury tourist. Diverse contributors maintain that a fast and smooth service-delivery procedure is the 'lifeblood' of satisfying the demand of the luxury guest. Moreover, all confirm that next to unique service procedures, the personalization aspect is most crucial for a positive experience for the luxury tourist. One interviewee emphasizes the following: *"The service delivery has to be fulfilled in a very elegant, pleasant, and perfect way."* Another interviewee suggests the concept of authenticity. In this case authenticity may be ensured by authentic services or by travelling to an 'untouched' tourism destination. Conclusively, the agreement can be found in the fact that during all kinds of service experiences that are encountered throughout the travel, the quality and the comfort have to beat the price in order to satisfy the luxury traveller.

Market Origin of Luxury Inbound Tourists

Different interviewees mention that most of the Asian markets include a high potential for luxury outbound tourists. In addition, the US, Latin America, Mexico, and Brazil are indicated as potential luxury markets to target. Furthermore, UK or Switzerland travellers are discussed as European target markets for the luxury segment. One contributor indicated that besides the BRIC markets, markets such as Indonesia, Thailand, Taiwan, Middle East and the Emirates are forecasted to gain the highest increase in income in the future. Another interviewee states that the current crisis of Eastern countries will impact tourist arrivals especially for the luxury travel segment; *"The demand of the Ukrainian and Russian market is declining; therefore, respective travellers from the concerned market origins are expected to execute a longer purchase-decision process."*

4.1.2 Current Luxury Tourism in Vienna

Importance of Luxury Tourism to Vienna

All interviewees agree on the fact that 'luxury tourism' is highly relevant in the near future globally as much as for the city of Vienna. One interviewee concludes the following: *"In the past it was not that important, but now it is becoming very important for Vienna."* Especially the current increases in the upscale accommodation sector together with an increase in luxury flagship store establishments to Vienna proves this, as highlighted by one contributor. Similar to the fact, that there was a 50% bed-capacity increase in the five-star hotel segment in Vienna. Hence, one interviewee conveys that Vienna has already achieved the image of a 'luxury tourism destination', stating that *"Vienna is limited and every product that is limited is perceived as luxury."* Other interviewees justified the latter by explaining that Vienna is limited in terms of space, since the city is perceived as 'narrow' and the heart of the city is tightly structured. Besides, the importance of this niche market is brought up as a 'spill over effect' for different stakeholders in the city (i.e. popularity of extravagant restaurant, optimum capacity of transportation, high occupancy in upscale hotels, and similar).

Luxury Hotel Market in Vienna

Based upon the previous discussion, one interviewee argues that the growth of the luxury five-star hotel market is a major opportunity to the existent upscale market, stating it as *"competition drives business forward."* Nonetheless, one interviewee perceives besides this opportunity there are also some threats. Respective issues include price dumping and saturation of this segment. Hence the most crucial aspect mentioned is the equal labour market as before. Finally, all interviewees agree that in the mid-term and long run luxury tourism is definitely an opportunity for Vienna. However, in the short-run it is a threat indeed. One interviewee concludes on the latter as followed, *"the process is about time, since every market will adapt to changes in the end."*

4.1.3 Luxury Destination Branding for Vienna

Current Image of Vienna

One interviewee clarifies that currently the international tourism audience perceives Vienna as a *"beautiful, kind of romantic, pleasant, secure, and clean destination."* On the contrary, another interviewee raised his concerns by claiming that Vienna was not enough dynamic yet. Furthermore, another interviewee adds that Vienna can still be developed in terms of *"innovation, creativity, and cheeky spirit."* Given the fact that Vienna is ranked as number one in living conditions at the MERCER study, supports a highly positive image of the city. In addition, the local tourist board integrates the attributes of 'cultivated, hospitable, and appealing' to their brand manual. Decisively, all contributors agree that the attributes of 'exclusive and high-quality' can support the development towards a luxurious destination brand.

Destination Branding

One interviewee acknowledges that the Vienna destination brand has different brand building blocks that can significantly contribute to the luxury travel market. Examples given are, the 'imperial heritage' together with "premium architecture and city space" as well as 'music and culture' together with "iconic world-famous institutions, in the city of music", lastly, 'culture of pleasure' together with "Viennese coffeehouse culture and cuisine." All interviewed stakeholders are convinced that one of the core values as 'premium quality' represents the whole travel experience in Vienna thus helping to brand the destination as a luxury destination.

Stakeholder Management

The local tourist board is in charge of *"international advertising of the destination together with influencing the overall brand perception"* while establishing a luxurious destination brand. Diverse interviewees discuss the importance of the creation of a committee consistent of respective stakeholder representatives who are then responsible for assisting the luxury destination branding process. Therefore, this committee should act as a strategy group including representatives from various tourism sectors, such as the accommodation sector, cultural institutions, shopping facilities, and further. The interviewee representing the restaurant sector indicates that this branch is able to attract the luxury 'gourmet' traveller. Therefore, the Viennese restaurant sector might act as a reliable motivational factor for the luxury audience. The interviewee representing the transportation stakeholder argues that this sector is *"inevitable from the entire tourism consumption."* The respective interviewee continues that the luxury experience can already be started during the transport until reaching the 'Premium Destination Vienna'. Lastly, the representative for the accommodation sector proclaims that luxury hotels in Vienna are able to assist the luxury destination branding by valuable public relations (PR) activities.

The interviewee emphasizes on the following, *"If the destination would not have such properties, then the whole destination would not be perceived as luxury."* Hence, all stakeholders agree that Vienna together with destination stakeholders and a proper stakeholder management can effectively contribute to a luxurious brand.

4.1.4 The Future of Luxury Tourism in Vienna

All interviewees commonly agree that there is a long-term trend in luxury tourism on the global level. Coherently, all are convinced that Vienna can be perceived as a 'Premium Destination' in the long-run. Distinctively, one interviewee points out that the increasing gap between two classes will be crucial in the future. Nonetheless, an increase in HNWI will provide more money to spend in the market. In respect to Vienna, a different interviewee adds that further investigations are necessary for developing a luxury brand for Vienna, such as in-depth studies and further market research. They all agree on the fact that the demand in luxury tourism will always exist, same for the local tourism market. However, one interviewee states that the definition of luxury tourism has to be revised while arguing the following: *"Time will be the new luxury; sustainability and authenticity will be major values; as well as dynamic product arrangement will gain high prioritization in this specific market."* Conclusively, all interviewed stakeholders assume that there is an opportunity for Vienna to be perceived as a 'Premium Destination' in the long-term.

4.2 SWOT Analysis

The final section of this paper addresses the implementation of a SWOT Analysis. Applying the given suggestions and expertise knowledge from the conducted interviews, a SWOT Analysis is employed indicating the possibilities for Vienna to be developed towards a luxury destination, as presented in *Table 1*.

Table 1. SWOT Analysis 'Vienna as a Luxury Destination'

Strengths	Weaknesses
Vienna is an exclusive and exquisite tourism destination	Poor opening hours of shops
Cultural offer and imperial heritage	Vienna is relying on historic facilities and
'Culture of pleasure'	attractions
High-class international hotel brands situated in Vienna	Lack in dynamic city attributes
General good image	Lack in creativity, innovation and 'cheeky
Quality of living (MERCER study)	spirit'
Cleanliness of the city	Poor nightlife in Vienna
Security in the city	Lack in friendliness of the residents
Green city	
Good institutional facilities	
Good accessibility	
High service quality from stakeholders	
Personalized services by stakeholders	
High quality in the restaurant sector	
Current enhancement in the shopping sector	
High density of luxurious events and balls	
Expansion of Vienna International Airport	

Opportunities	Threats
Increasing demand in luxury tourism	Risk of niche
Luxury will always be persistent	Luxury niche market is quite small
Global steady increase in disposal income	High density of five-star hotels in the
International luxury hotel brand establishment in Vienna	Viennese hotel market
Competition drives local business forward	Market cannot adapt consistently, price
Enhancement in the alternative luxury accommodation sector	dumping and saturation of the five-star market
Head-quarter city	Danger of losing authentic aspects
Merge traditional destination features with modern luxurious aspects	Vienna is no 'untouched' destination
Raise Vienna to a more contemporary tourism destination	No standardized urban design (signage, billboards, and further)
Vienna is limited in space	All shops are closed on Sundays
Dynamic package design for the luxury niche market by various destination stakeholders	Vienna is not a 'fashion city'
PR activities by single stakeholders	The city is not dynamic enough yet
High opportunity in diverse luxury market origins	Danger if not all encountered stakeholders within the service-delivery process are
The luxury travel segment is in general resistant to crisis	ensuring a luxury atmosphere
Transportation sector can provide luxury and authentic service creation before arrival	Current crisis in Russia and Ukraine
	Not enough investigations done yet for establishing a luxurious destination brand for Vienna

5 CONCLUSION

This research paper aimed to investigate how the components of the overall travel experience are able to contribute to the development of a luxury destination brand. This study focused on the city of Vienna, Austria. Diverse significant stakeholders have been interviewed also a subsequent SWOT analysis has been conducted. First of all, the current study maintains the idea that luxury implements in tourism when the necessity is exceeded. It derives from the unexpected travel experience encounter. Contemporary luxury tourism comprises key facets as 'time, flexibility, freedom, and comfort'. Core values of Vienna such as 'imperial heritage' or 'music and culture' are currently pleasing the luxury traveller audience. Moreover, the city of Vienna can be symbolized as limited, exclusive as well as is perceived as a high-quality destination. The previous due to the limited space available and the latter in regards to the leading position within the MERCER study in a row.

Besides, the findings indicate that the local tourist board defines a 'luxury tourist' as a traveller staying in a five-star hotel. Subsequently, a current fifty percent increase of bed-capacity in the upscale accommodation market fosters the feasibility for Vienna to attract even more luxury travellers.

The relevance of profound stakeholder management is clearly supported by the finding that every stakeholder within the service-delivery process is in charge of ensuring a luxury atmosphere from arrival to departure. Thereupon, service examples in Vienna include: high-cuisine restaurant's ability to attract the luxury 'gourmet traveller'; the transportation sector's adaptation to given luxury desires before arrival; as well as exclusive personalization intelligence by the luxury hotel industry. The previous patterns are able to act as reliable motivational factors together with assistance in PR activities that will boost the awareness as a 'premium' destination followed by an increase in luxury inbound travellers. All interviewees emphasized on the diversity of potential market origins in this segment, ranging from the United Kingdom, Switzerland to Middle East and South-East Asia besides the BRIC states.

The most obvious findings to emerge from this study are opportunities including density in luxury five-star properties, dynamic package implementation by various stakeholders as well as the increase in luxury tourism suppliers, such as luxury flagship store establishments. One interviewee concludes smartly on global luxury travel trends by stating that *"time will be the new luxury; sustainability and authenticity will be major values; as well as dynamic product arrangement will gain high prioritization in this specific market."*

Conclusively, the findings from this study revealed diverse significant possibilities for Vienna to develop luxury tourism as well as how to adapt effectively and efficiently to universal trends in this niche segment. All interviewed stakeholders assume that Vienna can be perceived as a 'Premium Destination' in the long-term. Luxury tourism is highly relevant and will always be persistent as disposal incomes together with HNWIs are constantly increasing. Vienna is currently reacting to the luxury travel desires by steady developments in the luxury hotel sector, dynamic package design or with merging Viennese imperial heritage values together with contemporary features. Finally, it is anticipated, that Vienna will be perceived as a 'Premium Destination' by 2020.

Limitations

The findings in this paper are subject to a set of limitations. Firstly, the most important limitation lies in the fact that not entirely all stakeholders that would contribute to a luxury destination branding for Vienna could be interviewed. Secondly, the study was unable to analyse the demand side by the conduction of a survey or similar.

Therefore, further research should concentrate on a holistic approach while considering both demand as well supply side equally. Thirdly, the current investigations on luxury tourism were based on limited literature due to the lack in prior research published about this niche segment. The last source of weakness, which could also affect the measurement, is that no consensus in defining 'luxury tourism' is yet dominant neither in the literature, nor has been deriving from the qualitative approach. Conclusively, there are different avenues for future research to consider, such as the development of solid definition of luxury tourism or the analysis of luxury demands (i.e. customer perspectives) in order to understand this emergent topic even better.

REFERENCES

Aaker, D.A., 1996. *Building Strong Brands*. New York: Free Press.

Baker, B., 2012. *Destination Branding for Small Cities*. 2nd ed. Oregon, Portland , USA: Creative Leap Books.

Capgemini and RBC Wealth Management, 2013. *The World Wealth Report*. [Online] Available at: http://www.worldwealthreport.com/sites/default/files/RBC_Wealth_infographic_EN.pdf [Accessed 14 January 2014].

Euromonitor International, 2012. *Luxury Travel: Experiencing The Best*. The WTM Euromonitor Report. London: World Travel Market Euromonitor International.

Ghosh, A., Varshney, S., 2013. Luxury Goods Consumption: A Conceptual Framework Based on Literature Review. *South Asian Journal of Management*, 20(2), pp. 146-159.

Hansen, J., Wänke, M., 2011. The Abstractness of Luxury. *Journal of Economic Psychology,* 32, pp. 789-796.

Horwath HTL, 2011. *The Future of Luxury Travel: A Global Trends Report, First Findings for ILTM Asia*. Global Trends Report. Asia: International Luxury Travel Market ILTM.

International Luxury Travel Market, 2007. *ILTM Industry Report 2007*. Industry Report. Cannes: International Luxury Travel Market ILTM. ILTM commissioned this report from bgb research/global travel industry research expert Nancy Cockerell from August 2007 - October 2007.

International Luxury Travel Market, 2012. *Luxury Futures: A Global Snapshot of New and Emerging Trends in the Luxury Travel Market*. Cannes: ILTM The Future Labratory.

Kolb, B.M., 2006. *Tourism Marketing for Cities and Towns: Using Branding and Events to Attract Tourists*. Oxford : Elsevier Inc..

Murphy, P.E. & Murphy, A.E., 2004. *Strategic Management for Tourism Communities: Bidging the Gaps*. Clevedon: Channel View Publications.

Page, S.J., 2009. *Tourism Management: Managing for Change*. 3rd ed. Oxford: Butterworth-Heinemann; Elsevier Ltd.

Page, S.J. & Connell, J., 2006. *Tourism: A Modern Synthesis*. 2nd ed. London: Thomson Learning.

Pike, S., 2008. *Destination Marketing*. First Edition ed. Oxford: Elsevier Inc..

Robinson, P., Lück, M. & Smith, S., 2013. *Tourism*. Oxfordshire : CABI International.

Stoner, J.A.F., Freeman, R.E. & Gilbert, D.R., 1995. *Management*. NJ: Prentice Hall.

Vienna City Administration, 2013. *Vienna in Figures 2013*. Vienna Figures. Vienna : Vienna City Administration Economical Affairs, Labour and Statistics; Responsible for the contents: Klemens Himpele. Editorial Office: Section Statistics Vienna; Editors: Michaela Lukacs & Christan Fendt;.

Vienna Tourist Board [1], 2014. *B2B Service for the Tourism Industry, The Vienna Tourist Board : About Us*. [Online] Available at: http://b2b.wien.info/en/viennatourism/aboutus [Accessed 2 June 2014].

Vienna Tourist Board [2], 2010. *Brand Manual*. Manual. Vienna: Vienna Tourist Board.

Vienna Tourist Board [3], 2013. *B2B Service for the Tourism Industrie, Media Services: Press Texts: Luxury in Vienna*. [Online] Vienna Tourist Board Available at: http://b2b.wien.info/en/press-media-services/reports [Accessed 7 June 2014].

Vienna Tourist Board [4], 2014. *B2B Service for the Tourism Industrie, Statistics & Market Research: Hotel Capacity & Occupancy: 5-star category*. [Online] Vienna Tourist Board Available at:

http://b2b.wien.info/en/statistics/data/bed-capacity-and-occupancy [Accessed 7 June 2014]. Data Source: MA 23 - Dezernat Statistik Wien; Notice: Data 2014 based on hotels with construction in progress, planned, projected or announced. All information given without any liability and subject to alteration without prior notice.

World Tourism Organization and European Travel Commission, 2009. *Handbook on Tourism Destinations Branding*. Madrid: World Tourism Organizatin and European Travel Commission.

Paris Destination Image from the Point of View of Asian Students

Claire Dupain, and

Olga Novitskaya

Glion Institute of Higher Education, Switzerland
claire.dupain@laureate.net

Abstract

Studies about the destination image of Paris revealed that the French capital has a strong destination brand associated with romance and the art of living; however, a number of media sources have recently described an issue of insecurity that Asian people are experiencing when traveling to this destination. The Paris Syndrome, a condition experienced by Japanese and Chinese tourists, indicates that Paris may convey a distorted image as a result of changes that have taken place in the last few years. The aim of the study was to understand how Asian students, given the current situation, perceive the image of Paris as a destination. The mixed method was adopted in order to analyze the characteristics that impact the respondents' perception of a city, and to measure the destination image of Paris by taking into account the holistic dimension of images. The results confirmed the assumptions related to recent media reports. Findings show that Paris has destination image difficulties linked to the feeling of insecurity in the large city and the general unwelcoming atmosphere.

Keywords: Paris; The Paris Syndrome; Destination Image; Competitiveness; Asian tourists

1 INTRODUCTION

Over the past few decades, the tourism industry has significantly expanded worldwide and today represents about 9% of the global GDP, a fact which helps countries to stimulate economic growth and development despite the global economic crisis (UNWTO, 2014). The growth of international trade among nations and other socio-demographic factors such as leisure time, higher incomes, and new trends encourage people to travel more for both personal and professional purposes (Armstrong & Kotler, 2013). This phenomenon has given new meaning in today's marketing rules, and it has also turned all destinations into competitive marketable brands. Major cities are now developing a strategic plan to control their image and to build their own destination brand in order to reinforce their competitiveness.

Studies have been carried out to understand how marketing tools are used to manage a city's image, and previous studies explain what factors influence the formation of a Destination Image (DI). In 2013, the region Ile de France regained its position as one of the most popular destinations in the world with 33 million tourist arrivals, of which 48% came from abroad (Poirier, 2013). The image of the city of lights has evolved over the years and Paris is now competing with many other trendy destinations. Despite a significant decline in the number of North American visitors, Paris continues to gain the interest of the growing Asian market from where arrivals on French territory increased 12,9% between 2012 and 2013 (Amirou, Pauget, Lenglet, & Dammak, 2011; Fabius, 2014). Although the dynamic tourism sector generates about 10% of the region's gross domestic product thanks to the country's good reputation and cultural values, Paris's response to tourism sometimes conveys a strong negative image and Olivier Magny (2010) draws a clear picture of it in his book Draw me a Parisian. The rudeness of local people has been commented on in well-known newspapers such as The New York Times and Le Figaro, and the French capital has been ranked fourth in the annual top 10 "least pleasant cities in the world" (Masson, 2014). A sense of general insecurity is spreading among tourists and French citizens alike, and this has encouraged Chinese authorities to dissuade people from staying more than few days in the capital (Alderman, 2013). As this problem has become more persistent, the Chinese police decided to accompany large groups of tourists last summer in order to avoid thefts and to ensure the protection of their people in the most popular attractions. Indeed, Asian tourists have a reputation for having cash in their pocket which marks them as the target audience for thieves (Irish, 2014; Zilberstein, 2013). In a recent article from the New York Times, a Chinese citizen states that people are told that Paris is pictured as a romantic and mysterious city; however, she quickly realized during her trip that this image was nearly a myth and she expressed her astonishment by saying: "Once I realized that the Parisians were indifferent, I made the decision: Try to make the most of this trip, but never come back to Paris again" (Bilefsky, 2014, para. 3). It is principally the actual news about this contemporary topic and a deep interest in the city that have encouraged the researcher to write about the Paris DI. Even if the beauty of France is considered as a major asset for the tourism industry, the French Ministry of Foreign Affairs has not hesitated to stress that this competitive advantage is not sufficient anymore (Fabius, 2014).

Studies about DI and its impacts on Tourism have been carried out, demonstrating that tourist perception is an extremely broad notion. Consequently, it is essential to understand how images are formed because this will influence travelers in their decision making process when choosing a destination. Since the number of Chinese visitors is increasing every year, it would be reasonable to believe that the Asian community has a relatively positive picture of the powerful Paris brand. Therefore, understanding how other large cities manage their reputation so as to not push people away is crucial. Although a lot of research has been made on the Paris DI, little of it has taken into consideration the large number of media reports about Parisians' unfavorable behavior towards tourists. Moreover, existing literature does not mention the Paris Syndrome disorder, a condition that occurs when the gap between experience and expectations is too high, which was recognized by a Japanese psychiatrist who lives in France (Fagan, 2011). Most of the researchers studied DI by using a quantitative method based on pre-selected individual attributes measured with a Likert Type scale; however, studies have shown that this structured methodology is not adequate to understand the holistic or global impression people may have of a destination. This important gap in existing literature allowed the author to measure Paris DI in a comprehensive manner based on Echtner & Ritchie's (2003) conceptual model, which includes all aspects of images.

2 LITERATURE REVIEW

The concept of DI has been extensively studied by Gunn (1972), Mayo (1973) and Hunt (1975), for its subjectivity and elusive nature. The growth in the number of international tourists has become a challenge for tourism marketing because destinations try to differentiate from competitors in order to attract the largest number of visitors. Some people interpret a destination as a set of attributes while others give more a sense of "cultural and subjective meaning" (Morgan, Pritchard, & Pride, 2011, p. 4). Lawson and Baud Bovy (1977) define a DI as "*the expression of all objective knowledge, impressions, prejudice, imaginations, and emotional thoughts an individual or group might have of a particular place*" (Jenkins, 1999, p. 1). In this research destination refers to "*large entities*" (Echtner & Ritchie, 2003, p. 38) such as major cities or countries, and the concept of image can be defined as the mental representations associated with a destination. For many years, researchers have been using the terms DI and destination personality as concepts having the same meaning; however, recent studies state that DI is composed of several components while destination personality refers more to "*the set of human characteristics associated to a brand*" (Hosany, Ekinci, & Uysal,

2006, p. 639). According to Baloglu and Brinberg (1997), the subjective meaning of DI results from its two distinct but interrelated rational and emotional dimensions, which are both formed by the cognitive and affective functioning of human beings (as cited in Stepchenkova & Mills, 2010). The cognitive components refer to the mental representations and ideas a tourist may have about the physical attributes of a destination, whereas the affective components relate to the positive, negative or neutral feelings this person may associate with those attributes (Stepchenkova & Mills, 2010). In order to measure DI it is necessary to understand the image formation process, its components, and its general impact on tourists' behavior.

Gunn (1988) has developed a model containing seven phases which visitors may go through during their travel experience. Each phase depends on different kinds of information sources to which people are exposed during their life, including literature, other people's opinions, and the mass media. According to Gunn (1988), there are three major phases that truly impact DI. The first phase refers to the organic image including all the mental pictures of a place someone may have from external sources, and those pictures exist without an individual having made any specific research about the destination. Most of the time, these images depend not only on word of mouth, but also on general media sources and things learned during school education (Echtner & Ritchie, 2003). The second phase allows the organic image to become an induced image based on specific researches about the place. The use of brochures, books, websites, and travel agents would therefore increase the accuracy of the first image. Finally, the modified-induced image results from the individual's actual experience with the destination, which allows people the opportunity to compare their initial expectations with the actual reality (Echtner & Ritchie, 2003). Indeed, previous studies show a correlation between human beings' satisfaction during a visit and their intention to visit the place again (Chen & Tsai, 2007; Park & Njite, 2010).

Destination images influence tourists' decision making-process and tourists' behavior when experiencing and returning to the destination. In previous research, a positive correlation has been made between destinations having a positive image and the high number of tourists traveling to these places; the formation of images would therefore impact the benefits and overall value expected before visiting a place. Conversely, Stabler (1988) separates the supply and demand factors that influence the formation of DI in nine categories, including *"perceptions, psychological characteristics, personal experiences, hearsay, destination marketing, media, education, socio-economic characteristics and motivations"* (as cited in Jenkins, 1999, p. 2). Gunn (1988) supports this idea and argues that the demand factors are associated with the organic image formation stage whereas the supply factors relate to the induced-image phase previously stated. While some people believe that DI develops mainly during the pre-visit stage with the help of secondary sources of information, others such as Gunn (1988) believe that DI evolves and becomes rational only after the post-visit experience or during the modified-induced image (as cited in Buhalis, 2012). In that sense, any kinds of experiences lived by a young person will subsequently affect his choice of destination later on (Kim, Hallab, & Kim, 2012; Nyaupane, Paris, & Teye, 2011). Beerli & Martin (2004) established two main factors influencing DI formation, including information sources, also called stimulus factors by Baloglu & Mcleary (1999), and the personal factors. Individuals are constantly exposed to different primary and secondary sources whether intentionally or not. Primary sources cover all personal experiences whereas secondary sources refer to the promotional and non-promotional information to which people are exposed. The country's history and its economic and political situation may also play a significant role in the perception of images. According to McCartney, Butler & Bennett (2008), information sources seem to play a key role in the formation of images. Differently, personal factors combine the socio-demographic characteristics of an individual, vacation experiences and all elements which constitute his distinctive personality such as personal motives, values and lifestyle (Beerli & Martín, 2004). Most of those forces apply to Baloglu and McCleary's (1999) rational and emotional dimensions, which suggest that the formation of images results from stimulus factors including information sources and personal elements (as cited in Buhalis, 2012). Information sources represent all primary and secondary sources whereas personal factors refer to the individual's personal characteristics such as gender, age or social class, meaning that images can be interpreted and experienced differently. Moreover, Stepchenkova & Mills (2010) argue that individuals who have already visited a place tend to have a better image than those who have not. If images evolve through the lifetime depending on many factors, then it is important to understand what they are composed of.

Martineau (1958) introduced the notion of functional and psychological characteristics to differentiate the attributes that can be perceptible or measured, and those depending on each individual's feeling. The functional characteristics incorporate all measurable traits by which cities could be compared such as climate, infrastructures and prices, whereas the psychological characteristics refer more to abstract concepts based on individuals' experiences.

Echtner and Ritchie (2003) suggested a conceptual model including both functional and psychological characteristics, allowing the transformation of a list of single attributes into a holistic construct. Indeed, most of the researchers have always conceptualized DI based on the rating of attributes and not in terms of global feelings and impressions. Instead of focusing only on "attribute-based components" (Echtner & Ritchie, 2003, p. 42), they revealed the importance of considering the unique and global mental picture induced from the different functional and psychological characteristics. Figure 1 presents the conceptual model on which the current research is based.

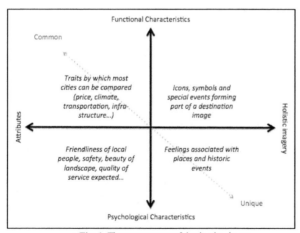

Fig. 1. The components of destination image
Source: Composed by author based on Echtner & Ritchie (2003, p. 43)

The conceptual model implies that DI is not only composed of general attributes that can be rated, but also unique and holistic components which could constitute the destination's real differentiating factors. The "holistic impression" (Echtner & Ritchie, 2003, p. 43) made by a destination is extremely important since the global perceived image certainly impacts visitors' decision making process when choosing a destination. In their research, Echtner & Ritchie (2003) differentiate imagery from discursive processing that can be defined as two ways to process and stock information about a destination. For example, a person who wants to travel to a sunny destination might first compare the different functional and psychological attributes of different places with a hot weather to make the final decision based on the most positive holistic image he has about one of them: this would refer to the discursive processing suggested by MacInnis & Price (1987). On the other hand, people using imagery processing would first reduce the number of alternatives based on the holistic perception they have about a selected set of destinations and base their final decision by comparing different single attributes. Echtner & Ritchie's (2003) concept of imagery processing highlights the importance and the challenges for cities to project a positive overall and unique image to potential visitors. The attributes-based and holistic imagery variables explained above allow individuals to formulate the full picture of a destination based on both personal knowledge and feelings. Although the concept shown in Figure 1 separates the components of an image in four different parts, the arrows going top-down-right-left suggest that each component depends on one another. The holistic impression depends on the value placed on several attributes, but the overall value placed one those attributes may also be influenced by global impressions.

2.1 The perception of Paris

According to Catherine Becker (2011), Paris is strongly associated with romanticism and poetry from most of Asian people's point of view. Based on Echtner & Ritchie's (2003) model, romance would refer to the unique aura or unique atmosphere of the place; however, she argues that people's image of the city lies more with *"arts rather than action"* (Becker, 2011, p.48), and that developing an image based on imaginary romanticism is not sufficient enough to build a strong positive holistic image and most especially in Asia where people are constantly moving and innovating. In order to describe the main attributes used by French tourist offices to advertise the City of Lights, the researcher referred to existing academic publications as well as promotional booklets and technical publications produced by the French tourism development agency.

It is essential to understand that a city's image necessarily relates to its country of origin's image. For example, Margot-Duclos (2011) believes that it is mainly the French famous luxury brands such as Dior, Channel, and Louis Vuitton that attract tourists and foreign investors who visit Paris. Although the country's industrial resources are mainly located in the provinces, Asian people tend to relate French brands and products to its capital because it is the place where they can purchase almost everything; however, each city has its own trajectory, and the elements that create the Paris image make the city quite unique in people's eyes. Paris is also known for its architecture, and particularly for its *"national symbol"* (Berger, 2013, p. 84), the Eiffel Tower, which is a famous and unique feature frequently evoked by tourists. Brochures and books take advantage from common functional characteristics when advertising Paris because the city benefits from a wide range of tourism attractions, shopping facilities, touristic sites, exhibitions, and festivals. In a previous study made by Roland Berger Strategy Consultants (2012), the functional and psychological attributes related to Paris are generally positively rated, while the degree of friendliness and competences of local staff are not high enough as compared to expectations. The Paris DI may have also been affected by the recent political turmoil and the economic crisis, and a report has been produced on *"how to improve French competitiveness"* (Lequesne, 2013, p. 46). Although a large number of studies on Paris clearly analyze the functional attributes of the city, few of them have focused on psychological attributes such as hospitality or friendliness and they have not been able to provide the holistic impressions made by the French capital. As explained previously, conveying a positive picture of a destination is extremely important since this unique global image will impact tourists' destination choices in the future. Margot-Duclos (2011) states that Paris is perceived as the World Capital of Romanticism, art of living, luxury, and culture over other European cities such as London or Frankfurt which are considered to be more business and technology orientated. It is additionally crucial to understand that local cultural dimensions also form a destination's identity, and Paris has an international cultural reputation for its many revolutions throughout history as well as its desire to change the world (Buhalis, 2012; Dinnie, 2011). This intangible facet of Paris image described by Margot-Duclos (2011) could eventually be integrated into the holistic dimension of Echtner & Ritchie's (2003) model.

As explained previously, the perception of a destination is influenced by different factors and Aramberri & Liang (2012) explain how travel magazines present Paris to the Chinese market. The French city is described as a shopping mall full of "art and history made by grand personalities" (Aramberri & Liang, 2012, p. 295), and this perceived image results from the numerous movies and books that made great impressions in China such as Da Vinci code with the Louvre, or The Fabulous Destiny of Amelie Poulain in Montmartre. Travel magazines use mainly functional attributes, special icons and symbols to market the city since those attributes are considered as being the driving force of the French capital. The analysis exploring the tourism potential of the Chinese middle class established by Delom et al. (2012) shows that visitors' perception of the city was deteriorated after their first visit. This study states that Chinese visitors associate Paris with romance, luxury and night parties, but also with the Eiffel tower, the Louvre and the Seine when it comes to objects and cultural symbols. These associations refer to the uniqueness of the city and the holistic impressions of Echtner & Ritchie's (2003) model. According to Delom et al. (2014), Paris has different strengths and weaknesses that are listed in Table 1 below:

Table 1. Paris strengths and weaknesses

Strengths	Weaknesses
• High number of touristic attractions • Cultural heritage • Variety of offers and activities • High quality of food • Good location to do shopping	• Language barriers • Quality of service below expectations • Insecurity • Expensive • Insufficient adaptation to Asian needs and habits • Complicated process to get a visa

Source: Adapted from Delom et al. (2014, p. 59)

The impressions of Paris visitors will remain in their mind as one integrated positive or negative experience. Within this global experience, people can rate individually different functional and psychological attributes that can then shared on blogs, mainstreams and forums (Fabry & Lespinasse-Taraba, 2014) creating an image of Paris for those who did not visit it yet.

3 METHODOLOGY

Different approaches have been used in previous studies to measure DI, and most of them focused on quantitative methodologies to easily compare structured answers rather than generalizing a small group of people's feelings (Echtner & Ritchie, 2003). The qualitative stage of DI measurement is often applied to find relevant constructs and attributes that can be measured through the quantitative phase. In this study, the researcher used a mixed method in order to achieve the objective in a rational manner. The assciated questionnaires were used to define Asian students' perception of Paris as a vacation destination. The main reason for using a mixed method was to provide a deeper insight of the issue by interpreting the quantitative data collected, and to "*explain relationships between variables emerging from the other*" (Saunders et al., 2012, p. 169).

The author designed an online questionnaire using the online survey tool *Survey Monkey*, which allowed the comparison of motives and different perceptions of functional and psychological attributes regarding the Paris DI between Asian students who have visited the city and those who have never been there. A sample of 87 Asian students, of which 54 have been to Paris and 33 who have never visited the city, agreed to answer the survey. Selecting young people was the key point of the research since this generation will be the one deciding on their travel destinations in the future.

The appropriate attributes were selected from previous studies about the Paris DI and media sources. The questionnaire was designed in English only in order to facilitate the analysis of the data collected. According to Echtner & Ritchie's (2003) framework, capturing the whole picture of a city's image requires closed-ended and open-ended questions. The questionnaire was separated into three sections. The first part aimed at collecting socio-demographic information about the respondents as well as the characteristics that influence their perception of a city. The second part, consisting of closed-ended questions, included the relevant attributes selected for the research on a standardized Likert scale. Different types of questions such as yes-no questions, multiple choice, rating scales, and open-ended questions have been designed strategically to truly understand the respondents' holistic perception of Paris (Matthews & Ross, 2010). The open-ended questions in the last part of the questionnaire were essential to capturing the unique imagery of Paris and to allow respondents to express their feelings with their own words. The three open questions were adapted from Reilly's (1990) research, in which the author suggests that "*free elicitation and descriptive adjectives*" (Reilly, 1990, p. 21) provide deep insight when assessing images.

A Japanese student who lives in Paris agreed to answer the questionnaire in order to verify the questions. This critical phase of the process aimed at ensuring that the questions would be well understood by the potential respondents. Any problem areas identified were corrected at this stage.

A non-probability snowball and self-selection sampling method was used within this study in order to perform deeper and not broader research, identifying the holistic side of the model.

4 RESULTS AND DISCUSSIONS

The 87 respondents who agreed to complete the questionnaire were from different countries, and the Figure 2 shows their countries of origin.

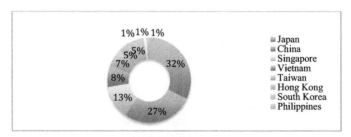

Fig. 2. Respondents' countries of origin

As previously stated, there are many socio-demographic factors that affect a person's perception of a city. Of the respondents, 59% Japanese or Chinese so these two nationalities demonstrated higher interest in this research. These results align perfectly to the recent articles in the news media talking about the Paris Syndrome, which affects mainly tourists from Japan and China. Out of the 87 students, 55% were females and 45% were males. The average age was 22 for the entire sample, and 39% of the respondents were currently studying in Europe. This information was necessary in order to determine if the fact that they live in Europe, and therefore know the European culture, might eventually affect their perception. In the first part of the questionnaire, the author was interested in knowing if the respondents had already been to Paris since previous experiences influence people's image of a city according to Gunn (1988). The third stage of Gunn's (1988) model implies that the students who have visited Paris have a modified-induced image, meaning that their perception is more accurate and closer to reality than those who have not. Among the different information sources established by Beerli & Martin (2004), secondary sources are an important factor influencing individuals' choices of destinations. If destinations have to market themselves as any other product, then it is important to know what kind of information sources the new generation uses the most. Figure 3 shows the frequency with which people use the common sources of information presented in the literature review.

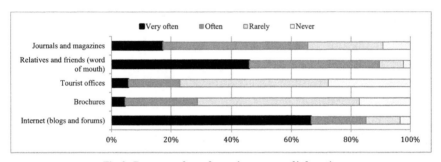

Fig. 3. Frequency of use of secondary sources of information

The results indicate clearly that students use primarily the Internet. This finding justifies the reason why Fabry & Lespinasse-Taraba (2014) have identified the most popular blogs and forums used by the Chinese community, as well as the importance of conveying a positive image so that travellers can post positive comments about a their trip. Of the respondents, 46% attached great important to word of mouth, and this form of secondary sources would consequently impact the quality of blogs and forums' content. Journal and magazines have been identified as the third support of communication used the most, which justifies the importance of having good reviews and articles in the news. Journals such as the New York Times or Le Figaro can be consulted through the Internet, and most of the articles evoked in the introduction and the literature may be accessed on the Internet. As anyone can now book a trip through the Internet and get hundreds of feedbacks from real experiences, tourist offices and brochures are less and less inclined to impact individuals' destination travel choices according to the survey respondents.

In order to compare the factors that motivate respondents when choosing a destination with the image they have from Paris, the author used a two-step method. To measure the importance of attributes, the respondents were asked in a first part (Table 2): *How important these attributes are when choosing a holiday destination?* In the second part (Table 3) of the questionnaire, the same attributes have been rated in relation to Paris.

The means presented in the three last columns of Table 2 correspond to global average evaluation scores, and show the importance attached to the different selected attributes by the respondents when choosing a destination. As explained by Beerli & Martin (2004), personal factors such as socio-demographic characteristics influence people's perception of a destination. Therefore, the researcher compared the scores between males and females in order to understand how gender affects personal motives. The results generally indicate that such factors as welcoming atmosphere, the attractive culture, and the city's general safety environment are very important for the respondents. If these students were to perceive Paris as an unsafe place, then they would more likely travel to another city. The comparison between males and females also showed surprising facts; males place more importance to the notion of value for money, as well as the shopping experience. The average scores for males are generally higher than for females, meaning that men have higher expectations and are more difficult to convince.

Table 2. Motivation factors of respondents

	Not important at all	Somewhat important	Important	Very important	Total	Mean	Mean Female	Mean Male
Local people speak English	16	27	28	16	87	2,5	2,2	3,0
	18%	31%	32%	18%	100%			
The city offers good value for money	8	21	40	18	87	2,8	2,5	3,2
	9%	24%	46%	21%	100%			
High number of touristic attractions	10	23	28	26	87	2,8	2,6	3,2
	11%	26%	32%	30%	100%			
Shopping experience	16	26	22	23	87	2,6	2,5	2,8
	18%	30%	25%	26%	100%			
City not too crowed	23	27	26	11	87	2,3	2,1	2,7
	26%	31%	30%	13%	100%			
Welcoming atmosphere	4	11	40	32	87	3,1	2,8	3,7
	5%	13%	46%	37%	100%			
Cleanliness of the streets	6	17	47	17	87	2,9	2,4	3,6
	7%	20%	54%	20%	100%			
Safe to visit	1	6	32	48	87	3,5	3,1	4,1
	1%	7%	37%	55%	100%			
Attractive culture	3	10	35	39	87	3,3	2,9	3,8
	3%	11%	40%	45%	100%			
Political stability	6	27	32	22	87	2,8	2,6	3,1
	7%	31%	37%	25%	100%			

Table 3 summarizes the average scores of each attribute relating to the city of Paris in comparison to the motive factors of the respondents. Among the 87 participants, 54 respondents had already visited the city and only 33 students had never been to Paris. In previous studies mentioned in the literature, it was found that visitors' perception of the city deteriorated after their first visit so it was important to target two samples to compare the differences of rating for each attribute. The first column recapitulates how much importance is attached to the attributes when selecting a destination. As clearly indicated in Table 4, results show that students attach importance to local culture, safety, and its general atmosphere. Paris average evaluation scores in comparison to the first column suggest what the main strengths and weaknesses of Paris are. The most important thing emerging from this table is that the culture, the shopping facilities and the tourist attractions constitute a real competitive advantage for the city of Paris whereas the personal safety element and the attitude of Parisians towards tourists influence the global image negatively. Therefore, it is principally the functional characteristics of the product Paris that constitute the strength of the French capital, whereas important psychological characteristics such as friendliness, atmosphere and personal safety affect negatively the city's image.

Table 3. Paris Destination Image

	Importance of attributes	Attributes associated to Paris	Attributes associated to Paris (VISITED PARIS)	Attributes associated to Paris (NOT VISITED PARIS)
Local people speak English	2,5	2,6	2,7	2,4
Value for money	2,8	2,9	3,0	2,8
Touristic attractions	2,8	4,3	4,4	4,4
Shopping facilities	2,6	4,4	4,4	4,3
City not too crowed	2,3	2,3	2,0	2,6
Welcoming atmosphere	3,1	2,4	2,4	2,4
Cleanliness	2,9	2,4	2,4	2,5
Personal safety	3,5	2,6	2,5	2,7
Attractive culture	3,3	4,2	4,5	4,2
Political stability	2,8	3,3	3,4	3,2

The results presented in Table 3 could be also analyzed through an Importance-Performance Matrix suggesting the gaps between importance of certain attributes and their performance. Figure 4 shows that an attractive culture has both high importance as well as high performance in Paris, while such factors as welcoming atmosphere and safety represent areas in need of improvement. These finding are also in line with Delom et al. (2014), highlinting the main strengths of Paris in attracions, shopping, and political stability. The major difference in perception of studied factors between those have already visited Paris and whose who did not were not observed. This fact could be explained by well communicated experiances to the rest of the population by Internet or word of mouth.

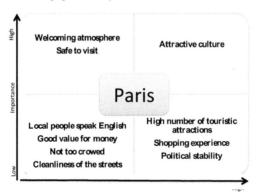

Fig. 4. Importance-Performance analysis of Paris
Source: Composed by author

Echtner & Ritchie's (2003) model underlines also the importance of the holistic image of a destination when measuring DI. The third part of the questionnaire was open-ended questions to allow respondents to express themselves freely as Reilly (1990) suggested. The first question related to the image or characteristics that came to the respondents' minds when they thought about Paris. The second open-ended question focused on the description of the atmosphere of the city and the third one on its unique features and attractions. The four following tables summarize the terms used by Asian students, and results show that Paris image is quite controversial as some of them are radically opposed. When answering the first open question, which was "*what images or characteristics come to mind when you think of Paris as a vacation destination?*", respondents referred to many different terms that have been categorized according to their meaning (Table 4).

Table 4. Images of Paris categorized

Shopping - Fashion	20%	Culture	14%
Attractions	19%	Food & Beverages	7%
Love - Romanticism	19%	Social	5%
Descriptive adjectives	15%	Weather	1%

Out of the 110 words analyzed, 20% fit into the category shopping-fashion such as Luxury, Chic, Glamorous, Louis Vuitton ... The second category regroups 19% of the analyzed content, which refers to local attractions, architecture and famous monuments. In the third category, the words romantic, love, dream and light demonstrate that the images associated with the city are quite positive and that magic is still at the heart of the destination product. The students also referred quite often to French food and restaurants, so culture represents an important component of Paris image and the city should take advantage of it when marketing the destination as it is considered as a revenue earner that is central to destination branding (Anholt, 2005); however, some negative terms such as expensive, dirty, crowdedness, or pickpocket are evoked and these images are in line with the results analyzed in the evaluation of the selected attributes.

In the second open-ended question, students were given the possibility to describe the general atmosphere they have experienced or would expect to experience in Paris. Apart from the recent media reports, people have not been able to express their feelings with their own words. This question reveals the existence of new attributes that may eventually be rated by in future research, and Table 5 summarizes the adjectives used by Asian students. Asian students have generally a positive image of Paris as explicitly showed in their answers; however, the negative adjectives should also be considered and strategies should be implemented to overcome possible image degradation in the future.

Table 5. Adjectives used to describe the atmosphere of Paris

Romantic	15	17%	Captivating	1	1%
Unfriendly	9	10%	Chic	1	1%
Stressful	8	9%	Cute	1	1%
Beautiful	7	8%	Dangerous	1	1%
Overcrowded	6	7%	Exciting	1	1%
Relaxing	5	6%	Grumpy	1	1%
Fun	3	3%	Hectic	1	1%
Magic	3	3%	Intriguing	1	1%
Sad	3	3%	Passive	1	1%
Unsafe	3	3%	Peaceful	1	1%
Cold	2	2%	Safe	1	1%
Cosmopolitan	2	2%	Stimulating	1	1%
Lovely	2	2%	Touristy place	1	1%
Welcoming	2	2%	Vigorous	1	1%
Amazing	1	1%	Weird	1	1%
Artistic	1	1%	**Total adjectives**		87

The answers to the third open question proves that Paris offers many different attractions since there is a large number of different words that have been mentioned only once. These findings confirm Berger's (2013) statement, asserting that the Eiffel Tower is the national symbol of Paris since 42% of respondents mentioned it. The Louvre, Champs Elysées, Montmartre, and the Arc de Triomphe are the next most common words evoked by the students. The variety of attractions shows that answers were very specific and the exact formulation of certain places such as the Musee de l'Orangerie or the Pere Lachaise Cemetery suggest that some students have a profound knowledge of the city. Table 6 presents the tourist attractions that have been given by respondents.

Table 6. Images of Paris

Romantic	14	17%	Fashion	2	2%	Mona Lisa	1	1%
Eiffel Tower	13	16%	Museums	2	2%	Old	1	1%
Beautiful	6	7%	Accessible	1	1%	Pickpocket	1	1%
Culture	6	7%	Champs Elysées	1	1%	Pretentious people	1	1%
Expensive	6	7%	Chic	1	1%	Restaurants	1	1%
Luxury	6	7%	Coco Channel	1	1%	Smokers	1	1%
Shopping	7	9%	Cosmopolitan	1	1%	Snow	1	1%
Food	4	5%	Crowdedness	1	1%	Social diversity	1	1%
History	4	5%	Disneyland	1	1%	Versailles	1	1%
Love	4	5%	Dream	1	1%	World heritage	1	1%
Art	3	4%	French bakery	1	1%	Amazing	1	1%
Louis Vuitton	3	4%	Galleries Lafayettes	1	1%			
Architecture	2	2%	Glamorous	1	1%	**Total words**		**110**
Café	2	2%	Light	1	1%			
Dirty	2	2%	Magic	1	1%			

These findings confirm that Stepchenkova & Mills's (2010) theory, stating that people who have already visited a place tend to have a better image than those who have not, is valid since the global average score for Paris is slightly higher for the respondents who have already been to Paris. The Paris DI remains quite positive in general, but it has definitely been affected by some factors for the opinions and descriptions to be so contrasted. The images fitting in the category of Shopping and Fashion from Table 4 confirm Margot Duclos' (2011) opinion that the Paris image is mainly associated with the country's luxurious and famous brands, which taken together form a segment of the destination brand. The negative terms that emerged from the open-ended questions reveal that there is a whole aspect of the city that needs to be improved, especially on a social and security level. The terms used are quite relevant as they oppose each other. Although respondents associate Paris with romanticism, the adjectives such as unfriendly, overcrowded, sad, or dangerous are clearly to the contrary of an atmosphere full of love and magic. The adjective sad has come to the researcher's attention because the word is very meaningful and completely opposed to the cosmopolitan atmosphere described by other respondents. Nonetheless, this approach offered a holistic way to measure the Paris DI and to realize that the city has generally quite a positive image.

Although 63% would recommend Paris to their relatives and friends, the 37% remaining represent a significant part of the sample that can't be ignored. This last question was asked because it reveals much of the holistic feeling respondents have about the destination. Results confirm that the French capital provides many tourist attractions, and that the city is a good place to do shopping. The third most positively rated attribute is the cultural attractiveness with an average of 4.2, which has always represented a major force as explained in the literature. If respondents attach great importance to the feeling of personal safety and the welcoming atmosphere of a destination, results show that these two attributes have been negatively rated when they relate to Paris with respective average scores of 2.6 and 2.4. The friendliness of Parisians is perceived as being low from both respondents who have been to Paris and those who have never visited the city; however, there are few differences in perception between the two samples that are relevant. Average scores show that students who have visited Paris assess the city as being unsafe compared to the ones who have never come, and this may be caused by negative personal experiences during their trip. The ability of local people to speak English is also more positively rated by students who came to Paris. Although French people have a reputation for having a low level in English, it seems that the Parisian language performance was slightly above students' expectations. If Bourcieu & Gallo (2013) consider that Parisians' inability to speak English is considered as a weakness, then the results show that it actually represents a force from Asian students' point of view and that Parisians' level of English is not so bad when compared to their expectations. The same reasoning is applicable for the notion of value for money. Prices are reputed to be very high, but the value offered remains above expectations. To understand if the Paris image has been affected by the recent politic turmoil, students were asked to express their opinion about the local political stability and it was quite positively rated (Lequesne, 2013). Finally, unlike the study made by Delom et al. (2012), the perception of respondents who have visited Paris is globally more positive than those who have not. The findings from the research support Stepchenkova & Mills's (2010) opinion, stating that people who have already visited a destination tend to have a better image than people who have not.

5 CONCLUSION

The aim of this paper was to measure the perceived image of Paris from the perspective of Asian students after publications in media sources picturing Paris negatively. The objectives were to analyze the characteristics that affect individuals' perception of a destination and to investigate the Paris destination image taking into account the holistic impressions of Asian students. The researcher found that people's perception of Paris remained quite similar as in previous years and that the City of Light is a cultural capital full of history and particularly attractive for its famous monuments. Socio-demographic and behavioral characteristics such as the respondents' age, gender and privileged social background influenced their motives and perception of Paris. The holistic components that emerged from this research confirm that the attributes of personal safety, cleanliness and welcoming atmosphere are below expectations. The Internet and word of mouth have been identified as the sources of information the most frequently used by the young generation when choosing a destination. Therefore, it revealed the importance for Paris to convey a more positive image using the Internet and by improving the service quality, and by enhancing the feeling of safety for both Asian tourists and the citizens of Paris.

It could have been even more interesting to understand the problem deeper by comparing the perception of Asian adults who travelled to Paris a long time ago with the new generation's ideas. In that case, socio-demographic factors such as age or gender would have provided a much more interesting insight. Moreover, future research should select a bigger sample and make sure that a sufficient number of people living in Asia are able to answer. The questionnaire could even be made more comprehensive, translated into Chinese, and transferred to local tourist agencies to broaden the sample .

REFERENCES

Alderman, L. (2013, August 20). A quest to make gruff service in France more gracious. *New York Times*. New York. Retrieved from http://www.nytimes.com/2013/08/21/world/europe/can-the-gruff-frenchman-become-the-gracious-frenchman.html?_r=3&

Amirou, R., Pauget, B., Lenglet, M., & Dammak, A. (2011). De l'image à l'imagerie en passant par l'imaginaire: une interprétation du tourisme à partir des représentations proposées par dix villes européennes. *Recherches En Sciences De Gestion*, *86*, 87–102. ISSN: 22596372

Anholt, S. (2005). *Brand new justice*. Oxford: Elsevier Ltd. doi:10:0-7506-6600-5

Aramberri, J., & Liang, C. (2012). The Chinese gaze: Imaging Europe in travel magazines. *Journal of China Tourism Research*, *8*(3), 284–301. doi:10.1080/19388160.2012.704248

Armstrong, G., & Kotler, P. (2013). *Marketing: an introduction* (Global ed.). Essex: Pearson Education Limited.

Avraham, E., & Ketter, E. (2008). Will we be safe there? Analysing strategies for altering unsafe place images. *Place Branding and Public Diplomacy*, *4*(3), 196–204. doi:10.1057/pb.2008.10

Balakrishnan, M. S., Nekhili, R., & Lewis, C. (2011). Destination brand components. *International Journal of Culture, Tourism and Hospitality Research*, *5*(1), 4–25. doi:10.1108/17506181111111726

Barnu, J., & Hamouche, A. (2013). Tourisme: Comment échapper au mythe du laquais. *La Gazette de La Société et Des Techniques*, (74), 1–4.

Becker, C. (2011). La marque France vue de Chine. *Revue Française de Gestion*, (218-219), 45–52. doi:10.3166/RFG.218-219.45-51

Beerli, A., & Martín, J. D. (2004). Factors influencing destination image. *Annals of Tourism Research*, *31*(3), 657–681. doi:10.1016/j.annals.2004.01.010

Berger, A. A. (2013). *Theorizing tourism: Analyzing iconic destinations* (p. 84). Walnut Creek: Left Coast Press.

Bilefsky, D. (2014, September 20). Chinese tourists find a movable feast best left behind. *New York Times*, p. 1. Paris. Retrieved from http://www.nytimes.com/2014/09/21/world/europe/chinese-tourists-are-disillusioned-after-visiting-paris.html?smid=tw-share&_r=0

Bonnal, F. (2011). Comprendre et gérer la marque France. *Revue Française de Gestion*, (218-219), 27–44. doi:10.3166/RFG.218-219.27-43

Borzyszkowski, J. (2013). Destination management organizations (DMO's) and crisis management. *Journal Of Tourism & Services*, *7*(2002), 6–18.

Bourcieu, S., & Gallo, J. (2013). La France doit restaurer son avantage comparatif à l'international. *Geoeconomie*, *67*. doi:10.3917/geoec.067.0169

Buhalis, D. (2012). The Formation of a tourist destination's image via information sources: the moderating effect of culture. *International Journal of Tourism Research*, *450*(8), 437–450. doi:10.1002/jtr

Chen, C.-F., & Tsai, D. (2007). How destination image and evaluative factors affect behavioral intentions? *Tourism Management*, *28*(4), 1115–1122. doi:10.1016/j.tourman.2006.07.007

Delom, C., Mazenk, F., Akar, F., Debray, G., Sardou, M., & Gao, B. (2012). *Analyse du potentiel touristique de la classe moyenne Chinoise pour l'Europe et la France* (pp. 1–109). Paris: Atout France.

Dinnie, K. (2011). *City branding: theory and cases* (p. 16). New-York: Palgrave Macmillan.

Echtner, C. M., & Ritchie, J. R. B. (2003). The meaning and measurement of destination image. *The Journal of Tourism Studies*, *14*, 37–48. doi:10037978

Fabius, L. (2014). Clôture des assises du tourisme (pp. 1–18). Paris: Assises du tourisme. Retrieved from http://www.diplomatie.gouv.fr/fr/IMG/pdf/DP-cloture-assises_cle88c13f.pdf

Fabry, P., & Lespinasse-Taraba, C. (2014). *Reseaux et medias sociaux dans le tourisme* (Second Edit., pp. 13–199). Paris: Atout France.

Fagan, C. (2011). Paris syndrome: A first-class problem for a first-class vacation. *The Altlantic*. Retrieved August 11, 2014, from http://www.theatlantic.com/health/archive/2011/10/paris-syndrome-a-first-class-problem-for-a-first-class-vacation/246743/2/#disqus_thread

Gunn, C. A. (1972). *Vacationscape: designing tourist regions*. Austin: University of Texas.

Hankinson, G. (2009). Managing destination brands: Establishing a theoretical foundation. *Journal of Marketing Management, 25*(1-2), 97–115. doi:10.1362/026725709X410052

Hankinson, G. (2012). The measurement of brand orientation, its performance impact, and the role of leadership in the context of destination branding: an exploratory study. *Journal of Marketing Management, 28*(7), 974–999. doi:10.1080/0267257X.2011.565727

Harrill, R. (2005). *Fundamentals of destination management and marketing*. Washington: International Association of convention & Visitor bureaux.

Herstein, R. A. M., Berger, R. O. N., & Jaffe, E. D. (2014). Five typical city branding mistakes: why cities tend to fail in implementation of rebranding strategies. *Journal of Brand Strategy, 2*(4). Retrieved from http://www.henrystewartpublications.com/jbs/v2

Hosany, S., Ekinci, Y., & Uysal, M. (2006). Destination image and destination personality: An application of branding theories to tourism places. *Journal of Business Research, 59*(5), 638–642. doi:10.1016/j.jbusres.2006.01.001

Hsu, C., Killion, L., Graham, B., Michael, G. J., & Huang, S. (2008). *Tourism marketing: An Asia-Pacific perspective*. Milton: John Wiley & Sons.

Irish, J. (2014, May 14). Chinese police to patrol Paris streets as France eyes tourism boost. *Reuters*. Paris. Retrieved from http://www.reuters.com/article/2014/05/14/us-france-china-tourists-idUSKBN0DU1A120140514

Jenkins, O. H. (1999). Understanding and measuring tourist destination images. *International Journal of Tourism Research, 1*(1), 1–15. doi:10.1002/(SICI)1522-1970(199901/02)1:1<1::AID-JTR143>3.3.CO;2-C

Kavaratzis, M. (2005). Place branding: A review of trends and conceptual models. *The Marketing Review, 5*(4), 329–342. doi:10.1362/146934705775186854

Kim, K., Hallab, Z., & Kim, J. N. (2012). The moderating effect of travel experience in a destination on the relationship between the destination image and the intention to revisit. *Journal of Hospitality Marketing & Management, 21*(5), 486–505. doi:10.1080/19368623.2012.626745

Lequesne, C. (2013). A new socialist president in the Elysée: Continuity and change in French EU politics. *Journal of Common Market Studies, 51*, 42–54. doi:10.1111/jcms.12040

Masson, M. (2014, August 9). Trois villes françaises dans le top 10 des villes les moins agréables au monde. *Le Figaro*. Paris. Retrieved from http://www.lefigaro.fr/conjoncture/2014/08/09/20002-20140809ARTFIG00076-trois-villes-francaises-dans-le-top-10-des-villes-les-moins-agreables-au-monde.php

Matthews, B., & Ross, L. (2010). *Research methods, a practical guide for the social sciences*. (Pearson Education limited, ed.). Essex. doi:10.1093/bjc/azs016

Martineau P. (1958) The personality of the retail store. Harvard Bus Rev; 36(January – February):47 – 55.

Margot-Duclot J.L., (2011), « Paris et la France », Revue Française de Gestion, 218-219, pp.67-89.

Morgan, N., Pritchard, A., & Pride, R. (2011). *Destination brands, managing place reputation* (3rd ed., pp. 5–5). Oxford: Elsevier Ltd.

Nyaupane, G. P., Paris, C. M., & Teye, V. (2011). Study abroad motivations, destination selection and pre-trip attitude. *International Journal of Tourism Research, 217*(10), 205–217. doi:10.1002/jtr.811

Park, Y., & Njite, D. (2010). Relationship between destination image and tourists' future behavior: Observations from Jeju island, Korea. *Asia Pacific Journal of Tourism Research, 15*(1), 1–20. doi:10.1080/10941660903510024

Poirier, A. (2013, July 12). Why tourists still have a passion for Paris. *The Guardian*. Bristol. Retrieved from http://www.theguardian.com/commentisfree/2013/jul/12/tourists-passion-paris-london

Reilly, M. D. (1990). Free elicitation of descriptive adjectives for tourism image assessment. *Journal of Travel Research.* doi:10.1177/004728759002800405

Ritchie, J. R. B., & Crouch, G. I. (2003). *The competitive destination.*

Oxfordshire: Cab international.

Saunders, M., Lewis, P., & Thornhill, A. (2012). *Research methods for business students* (6th ed., pp. 374–375). Essex: Pearson Education Limited.

Stepchenkova, S., & Mills, J. E. (2010). Destination Image: A meta-analysis of 2000–2007 research. *Journal of Hospitality Marketing & Management, 19*(6), 575–609. doi:10.1080/19368623.2010.493071

UNWTO. (2014). *Tourism in the world: key figures* (pp. 1–16). Madrid. Retrieved from http://dtxtq4w60xqpw.cloudfront.net/sites/all/files/pdf/unwto_highlights14_en_0.pdf

Vilchez, J. R., & Fabra, U. P. (2013). Valuing tourist destinations: An Oaxaca-, *429*(4), 417–429. doi:10.1002/jtr

World economic forum. (2013). *The travel & tourism competitiveness report 2013.* (J. Blanke & T. Chiesa, Eds.) (p. 166). Geneva: World Economic Forum. ISBN-13: 978-92-95044-40-1

Zilberstein, J. (2013, March 28). Les touristes chinois se sentent de plus en plus en insécurité à Paris. *Le Figaro*. Paris. Retrieved from http://www.lefigaro.fr/actualite-france/2013/03/28/01016-20130328ARTFIG00667-les-touristes-chinois-se-sentent-de-plus-en-plus-en-insecurite-a-paris.php

FHS - Salzburg University of Applied Sciences
Developing high potentials

In the four disciplines of engineering, business and social sciences, design, media & arts and health studies, the Salzburg University of Applied Sciences offers students a sound university education with international quality standards, supported by the principles of science, professional skills, diversity and sustainability.

Each single one of our employees ensures and develops the quality of the Salzburg University of Applied Sciences with their high technical and social skills, personal commitment and willingness to support and shape change. The Salzburg University of Applied Sciences ensures the required knowledge quality, knowledge diversity and depth of knowledge in its application of teaching, research & development / art-based research as well as organisation, and provides a current, high-quality infrastructure.

Innovation & Management in Tourism (IMT) is an exciting degree programme for future tourism experts who plan to be leading this rapidly growing sector in the areas of hospitality- and destination management. The programme, having a clear focus on Innovation, Imagineering and eTourism, is provided part time and taught in German and English for the Bachelor and part time and taught in English for the Master. IMT and its students were awarded several times during the last few years. Amongst others, the programme gained the Austrian Tourism Research Award, the TUI sustainability award, the Austrian Ministry´s sustainability award etc. The program runs its own research department and carries out a number of international research projects, especially in the field of Innovation and eTourism. This guarantees a state of the art know how transfer between scientists and students.

The Salzburg University of Applied Sciences develops potential
The teaching and research staff are interdisciplinary impulse-providers in the development of business, science and social spheres. The Salzburg University of Applied Sciences supports lifelong learning in its employees, students and graduates. Self-paced, self-directed learning and reflective action is required and promoted as a principle of the academic didactic.
The aim of the Salzburg University of Applied Sciences is to build up capacity and arouse curiosity, enthusiasm, passion and understanding for the different disciplines and cultures.
The cooperation network of the Salzburg University of Applied Sciences now comprises more than 100 partner institutions on almost all continents including Australia.

The Salzburg University of Applied Sciences designs futures
The Salzburg University of Applied Sciences competence center is aware of the dynamics of the future and responds by producing a well-educated workforce for companies and institutions. The University generates new knowledge and takes its responsibility within economy and society very seriously. Its commitment to innovation is reflected in the study programmes, the research topics and the selection of and participation in networks. The Salzburg University of Applied Sciences enables its graduates to participate in the solution of problems within human society.

Fachhochschule
Salzburg University
of Applied Sciences

FHS - Salzburg University of Applied Sciences

www.fh-salzburg.ac.at

IMC University of Applied Sciences Krems
Studying the international way

The IMC Krems is widely regarded as Austria's most international university of applied sciences, offering currently 26 innovative full-time and part-time degree programmes, in Business Studies, Health Studies and Life Sciences.

Tourism and Leisure Management degree programmes are provided for Bachelor full and part time and Master full time and are all taught entirely in English.

First-hand expertise

The highly practical, academic degree programmes offered at IMC Krems stand out for their strong focus on leadership qualities and soft skills. The curriculum also includes an extensive selection of language options, and project-based work in small groups, where direct access to teaching staff plays a key role. With students gaining exposure to first-hand knowledge and experience, the university is certainly not an 'education production line'.

A dedicated, international and highly qualified faculty motivates students to perform to the best of their ability, preparing them for international careers. Co-operations with research facilities and enterprises, as well as the extensive range of leisure activities on offer in the idyllic surroundings of Krems, round up the comprehensive offering for students.

Award-winning international environment

With 100 partner universities, many other partner programmes and students from 50 different countries the international environment defines day-to-day life at IMC Krems. Intercultural exchange, internships abroad, participation in international research projects and lectures given by internationally experienced full-time faculty and guest lecturers are all integral parts of this.

IMC University of Applied Sciences Krems was awarded the **quality seal for Innovation, Engagement and Quality** by the Sokrates Nationalagentur, for its proven commitment to an international environment and high student mobility.
Moreover, the **Foundation for International Business Administration Accreditation** (FIBAA), a leading international quality assurance agency, presented its quality seal to the IMC University of Applied Sciences Krems.

Practical experience for a successful career

The philosophy of IMC Krems is that learning, research and business should be closely interlinked. This plays a significant part in preparing students for the job market: 90% of all students are in permanent employment within three months of graduation.

IMC University of Applied Sciences Krems, Austria
www.fh-krems.ac.at

SPONSORS

On behalf of the Salzburg University of Applied Sciences, the IMC University of Applied Sciences Krems and all the participants of the Iscontour conference we would like to thank our sponsors for their support:

  Wirtschaftskammer Salzburg

  Salzburg Convention Bureau

 Prodinger / GFB Tourismusmarketing

  Tourismus Salzburg GmbH

  Stiegl Privatbrauerei

  TUI Austria

 SalzburgerLand Tourismus

  Springer

  European Travel Commission

  Red Bull

  International Federation for IT and Travel & Tourism